FRENCH REGIONAL COOKING

FRENCH REGIONAL COOKING

Anne Willan
& l'Ecole de Cuisine
La Varenne, Paris

William Morrow and Company, Inc.
New York   1981

ACKNOWLEDGEMENTS

Fitting together the pieces of this book has been a daunting task, a challenge I could never have faced on my own. It is with special pleasure, therefore, that I record my gratitude to my editorial associates at La Varenne. Above all I salute Faye Levy and Elisabeth Evans, on whose reading and research *French Regional Cooking* is founded. Nearer to the kitchen, La Varenne's chefs have provided masterly guidance with the recipes and I would like to express my appreciation to them, too. I have also been privileged in having the wise counsel of a true scholar of France and of French cooking, Jane Grigson.

In deciding what should go into this book and what should stay out, I have exercised my own judgement, sometimes against the considered opinion of my collaborators. The errors and eccentricities are therefore mine and should not be visited upon the many friends and colleagues who have helped me write this book.

A.W.

École de Cuisine La Varenne
34 rue St Dominique
Paris 75007 France

Editing and recipe research **Faye Levy**
Editing and text research **Elisabeth Evans**
Recipe testing **Linda Collister**
Recipe editing **Janet Jones**
Editorial, research and test kitchen assistants:
Robert Carmack, Alan Fine, Francesca George, Judith Hill, Jan Kuhl, Jane Parker, Margaret Ramsay, Caroline Schuck, Somchit Singchalee, Susan Stuck, Tina Ujlaki, Kathryn Welds

A Marshall Edition   Editor **Penny David**
Edited and designed by   Art Editor **Heather Garioch**
Marshall Editions Ltd   Picture Editor **Zilda Tandy**
71 Eccleston Square   Assistant Editor **Gwen Rigby**
London SW1V 1PJ   Production **Hugh Stancliffe**

Printed and bound in Belgium by Brepols SA

Library of Congress Catalog Card Number: 81-81996
ISBN 0-688-03670-8
First Edition
1 2 3 4 5 6 7 8 9 10

For Mark
sine quo non

Introduction

French regional cooking is a challenge. Unlike classical cuisine, there are no definitive recipes describing right and wrong; the country cook can play on a recipe theme, enjoying the liberty of a musician who improvises on a 19th-century Viennese waltz. Is such an interpretation any less genuine? Is a performance in Vienna more 'correct' than any other? Can a waltz be played as well in Cincinnati or Edinburgh?

The same goes for regional cooking. When is a cassoulet not a cassoulet? Like many a waltz, cassoulet is Traditional with a capital T. It originates from around Toulouse, but that is not to say that it cannot be executed well, and differently, by cooks from elsewhere in France and beyond. Yet there remains that sense of excitement about finding the best-ever cassoulet from the kitchen of a master near Toulouse itself. A dish does not happen by accident but is the product of the place and the people: of cooks who have had years of practice with an appreciative audience and with ingredients that are just right.

To pursue the musical analogy, learning all about waltzes is not only a matter of listening to the music and talking to musicians – and exercising one's own musical talents – but also of studying scores and consulting books. These are the principles I have followed. When travelling in different parts of France I have looked for artisan farmers, for markets and for food speciality shops, especially charcuteries and pâtisseries. Back home in Paris every recipe has been developed and tested at l'École de Cuisine La Varenne. Without the advice of our teaching chefs, not to mention research into the considerable literature on French regional cooking, I could not have written the book at all.

Regional recipes are usually simple, using few ingredients and straightforward techniques. Echoing this spirit, I have deliberately avoided complicated dishes like 'tripoux' (stuffed tripe from Auvergne) or luxuries like foie gras that in any case are rarely tackled at home but usually bought ready-prepared. I have also omitted some of the old-fashioned dumplings and puddings that reflect the former breadline diet of much of rural France, and which to modern tastes are disappointing – not to say inedible.

In many ways regional cooking can be said to have developed only in the last hundred years. Until then, cuisine was the privilege of the well-to-do; for the mass of the population living in rural areas, only festivals or some economic windfall offered promise of release from subsistence fare. But after World War I regional cooking began to prosper, encouraged by a new brigade of motorized cookery writers, led by Curnonsky, who seemed to track down a local speciality in every village inn. Their pioneering books have preserved a record which might otherwise have been lost, for today's visitor to the French provinces will find surprisingly little in the way of regional cooking in restaurants, whose chefs increasingly serve the same impersonal food everywhere. Yet rural France is tenacious: its population has barely diminished in the last 80 years, standing at 12·8 million today as against 14·4 million in 1901, and the affection for local culture and tradition remains strong, especially in the home kitchen.

This is an ambitious book – it takes a broad view of a large subject and therefore must be a personal view. I know that a specialist's perspective will be different from mine, and that many a generalist who, like myself, knows most of France a little rather than a little of France well, will demur at some points. Indeed, it might be asked why a foreigner should delve into the subject of French regional cooking at all. My response would be to borrow a supercilious quotation from Balzac's *Modeste Mignon*: 'Ce qu'il y a de plus étranger en France, pour les Français, c'est la France.' (What is most foreign in France, for the French, is France.) But in truth I have written this book because I love the French way of life and, it goes without saying, French cooking.

École de Cuisine La Varenne, Paris
May 1981

The regions and the recipes

Caesar divided France into three parts, and Napoleon, who established the modern system of 'départements', into 87. In cooking, I think a dozen divisions are appropriate, roughly based on the provincial boundaries found in France before the Revolution of 1789. These ancient boundaries reflected the country's history, climate and terrain and, therefore, still mirror its cooking traditions. Contrasts in style can be striking: sometimes the leadership has come from provincial cities like Lyon and Bordeaux. In other areas, it has been foreign cultures, notably from across the Pyrenees, the Alps and the Rhine, which have put their stamp on the region. North or south, east or west, all the regional cooking of France is dominated by the physical environment: the rivers, the mountains and the sea.

While most recipes are peculiar to a region, there are others which are found with minor variations, and perhaps under different names, in other parts of France. For instance, the addition or omission of a particular ingredient – some shallots, a few prunes, a little chopped ham – may suffice to change the name and the regional associations of a dish. In such cases I have sometimes positioned a recipe outside its native region, as a short variation on another recipe given in full.

The recipes in each chapter run from first courses through main dishes to desserts, breads and cakes, in a balance reflecting the cooking of the region concerned. Interspersed with the recipes are boxed features on important ingredients or culinary techniques. Each chapter closes with a discussion of the local cheeses and with a list of traditional specialities that travellers must look for in the region itself – like charcoal-baked fresh truffles or lamprey stew – that are hard to reproduce at home.

In the recipes, amounts are given first in metric measures and secondly in US standard equivalents. Amounts given in teaspoons and tablespoons should be measured level, not heaped. All the recipes have been tested for use with North American ingredients. Equivalent measures have been carefully calculated and have sometimes been adjusted to make proportions in a recipe just right. Follow one set of measures or the other to obtain the correct results.

A glossary of ingredients, cooking terms and methods on pages 312–314 discusses the few ingredients that differ significantly between France and other countries. The glossary also describes common procedures used in the recipes such as blanching bacon and making pastry; they are referred to in the text by an asterisk (*).

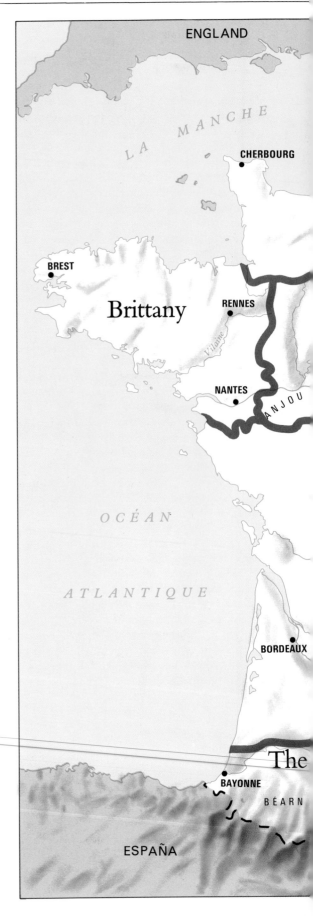

CALAIS

BOULOGNE

BELGIQUE

DEUTSCHLAND

ARTOIS

Somme

Champagne

PICARDIE

ARDENNES

LUXEMBOURG

LE HAVRE

ROUEN

Oise

Seine

Marne

and the

Alsace-
Lorraine

Normandy

ÎLE DE
FRANCE

PARIS

LORRAINE

NANCY

STRASBOURG

North

CHAMPAGNE

Meuse

VOSGES

ALSACE

The

Loire

ORLÉANAIS

Burgundy

and the

BERRY

Cher

DIJON

BOURGOGNE

Saône

Franche-Comté

FRANCHE-COMTÉ

JURA

SUISSE

TOURAINE

Loire

Lyonnais

and the Alps

POITOU

BOURBONNAIS

Allier

Loire

LYONNAIS

Mt Blanc

SAVOIE

Charente

The

Centre

CLERMONT-
FERRAND

LYON

Rhône

ALPES

LIMOUSIN

CANTAL

AUVERGNE

MASSIF

CENTRAL

DAUPHINÉ

GRENOBLE

ITALIA

The

PÉRIGORD

Dordogne

DAUPHINÉ

Southwest

Lot

QUERCY

Garonne

Tarn

CÉVENNES

Provence

Durance

Languedoc

MONTPELLIER

NICE

Pyrenees

GASCOGNE

TOULOUSE

LANGUEDOC

Rhône

and Gascony

Adour

PYRÉNÉES

MARSEILLE

MER

ANDORRA

ROUSSILLON

MÉDITERRANÉE

Brittany

I had read so much about Brittany, land of lace caps, oysters and salt cod, that when I finally saw for myself the patchwork of little fields and the cramped villages, huddling for shelter in valleys and inlets along the coast, they came as no surprise. Brittany is easy to enjoy, with its temperate climate and its doll's-house architecture. The cooking is no less pleasing, for crêpes, cider and superb seafood are bound to appeal. But these facile images are deceptive; of all the extremities of France, I feel that Brittany is the one most difficult to fathom.

Perhaps this is because it is a province of contrasts, where land and sea live in wary juxtaposition. The coastline is one of the most dangerous in the world, barbed with warning lighthouses, yet at the same time blessed with natural harbours. Some are great estuaries like Brest, home of the French navy, and Lorient, one of the largest fishing ports in France. Innumerable others shelter the fleets that are the mainstay of Brittany's oldest occupation: fishing.

Oysters are perhaps the most profitable local shellfish, bred on the sheltered southern coast, then shipped north to ports like Morlaix and Cancale to mature and take on character. They are rarely cooked, but served raw on the half shell with a vinegar sauce laced with chopped shallot or, for purists like me, merely a squeeze of lemon.

Alas, lobsters, the pride of Brittany, are now so expensive as to be almost beyond reach. Most are shipped directly to Paris, often after they have been fattened in seawater tanks on the rocks. (A commercial process for raising them from the egg has yet to be developed because lobsters, cannibal by nature, tend to eat each other the moment they are hatched.) Locally, mussels are much appreciated, cooked 'à la marinière' with onion, parsley and a splash of white wine, or deep fried, or stuffed with garlic butter, a method that also suits the indigenous clams ('palourdes'). Side by side in the market with sea urchins and sea scallops, I have also found 'pétoncles' (baby scallops) cheaply priced.

The same small boats that bring in the shellfish also yield a good supply of shallow-bottom fish like sole, turbot and sea bass. Humbler varieties such as whiting, eel and mackerel are often relegated to the stewpot for the local fish soup, 'cotriade', whose black and white colours, highlighted with orange mussels, evoke the northern Atlantic as clearly as the saffron-gold of bouillabaisse recalls the sunny Mediterranean. Tradition has it that cotriade began as a sailors' stew boiled up on board from any unwanted part of the catch. On land, a good cotriade contains a variety of fish, some plain like whiting, some rich like mackerel; it is flavoured with mussels and reinforced with potatoes. With this common base, cotriade can be rendered piquant with sorrel and enriched with cream.

Less picturesque than Brittany's coastal fleet but economically more important are the ocean-going ships that put to sea for months at a time. Much of the salt cod that was once a winter staple throughout France came from Breton ports. Boats plied the dangerous seas as far as Iceland and Newfoundland. Today, romance and risk are removed as most of the cod is located by radar and frozen at sea. On the south coast, however, industry remains more traditional and boats venture as far as Senegal in search of sardine, mackerel and tuna. This migrant tradition is echoed by the crêpe-makers to be found at fairs and by the grape-pickers who move from vineyard to vineyard in the autumn. In several towns throughout France there are still quarters known as 'La Bretonnerie' where transient workers used to take shelter.

The other face of Brittany is its interior, which the Gauls called 'Argoat' (the land of the woods), delineated by the limits of sea birds' flight from 'Armor', the land of the sea. Most of the woodlands have disappeared, but central Brittany, particularly to the west, remains less developed. This is the heart of 'Bretagne bretonnante' where Breton is still spoken – a Celtic tongue related to Cornish and Welsh. (1500 years ago writers were referring to Brittany as 'Britannia Minor' or Little Britain). Here the traditional foods have been those of subsistence agriculture: chestnuts, dried beans and buckwheat. As none of the three lends itself to making bread, the early Bretons substituted wafer-thin crêpes or 'galettes', served as main course, dessert, or snack at any time of day, just like a sandwich.

It was from this rocky unpropitious terrain of Argoat that Breton farmers developed their cunning system of 'bocage', tiny fields surrounded by earthen barriers, often planted with trees and impervious to the wind. (Wind, in Brittany, is ever-present. In the southwest corner in the Morbihan, not only are the coiffes designed with gaps to accommodate the breeze, but the church steeples are fretted with holes.) Within these plots flourish potatoes, cabbages, onions, carrots, garlic and all kinds of bean, with wild hydrangeas as hedges.

Some areas are less rugged; in the north around the Presqu'île de Ste Marguerite and the ancient ports of Roscoff, Tréguier and Paimpol, the land flattens to form part of the 'golden belt'. Here grow artichokes and cauliflowers, both chosen as emblems by the Breton 'coopérative agricole' and displayed on bumper stickers throughout France. The ranks of artichoke plants and luxuriant cauliflowers, stretching as far as the eye can see, are quite a sight. But there is chronic overproduction and roads barricaded with bristling artichokes in protest over low prices have become almost a ritual. Strawberries are more saleable and have a long pedigree in Brittany; the first Chilean plants (ancestors of our cultivated strawberry) were brought to Brest, next door to Plougastel, which is still in the centre of the Breton strawberry trade.

Moving southwards in the Breton peninsula, the land mellows to the 'pays nantais'. Nantes, at the mouth of the Loire, is the historical and spiritual capital of Brittany, for hundreds of years an unusual double port looking seawards to the East and West Indies and landwards to Paris and the heart of France. The area yields two of Brittany's riches: butter and white wine. Combined, they make the current darling of Paris restaurants, 'sauce beurre blanc', which is a reduction of dry white wine (preferably muscadet), vinegar and shallots, with butter whisked in to give a creamy consistency. Beurre blanc is good with 'Brittany' salmon (almost all of which now comes from Scandinavia) and it is the standard accompaniment to fresh pike from the Loire. (Up river, it is the cooks in the province of Anjou who claim credit for this sauce.) Much of Breton butter is 'demi-sel' (lightly salted) whereas in the rest of France butter without salt is preferred both in the kitchen and at table. 'Beurre salé' has even more salt, like the farmhouse butter of my childhood, which was buttercup-yellow and strong – almost cheesy – in taste. I have never liked it myself, but many regard it as a great treat.

The Bretons also put their butter to good use in cakes. 'Kouign-aman' is Breton for butter cake, but to describe it as a croissant dough layered with caramelized sugar gives only an inkling of this luscious, tricky pastry. 'Gâteau breton', a pound cake so

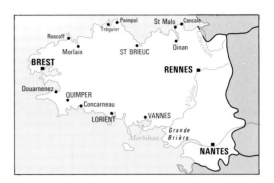

rich it resembles a butter biscuit, can include apples, raisins and candied cherries, while 'gâteau brestois' has ground almonds, lemon and curaçao. The dry, crusty breads from St Malo, called 'craquelins' are perhaps an acquired taste; not so the 'cornic' of Douarnenez (a type of croissant) and the raisin galettes of Vannes.

Brittany's meat is unremarkable but for the delicious 'pré-salé' lamb (sold so young I don't like to think about it) which is already flavoured with salt from the marshes on which it is raised. So meat is less popular than dishes based on fish or eggs; hens are kept wherever there is space for them and eggs are served in omelettes, in substantial 'fars' or puddings, and as a filling for crêpes. In Quimper, we were offered them 'brouillé', the egg scrambled directly on top of the crêpe while it cooked on the griddle, or 'miroir', where it was left unbroken so that the white set to a glassy shimmer. The rain beat on the window, the steam rose from the coats near the stove, as two dozen of us tucked into cider and assorted crêpes prepared by a little old lady and her daughter.

Crêpes and fars are foods from Brittany's past, in a province that is changing with startling speed. Not only as a vegetable garden, but also as a dairy, pork and poultry producer, Brittany now ranks at the top.

Without doubt, from being a troublesome backwater, notoriously bloody-minded from the Middle Ages to World War II, the region is heading helter-skelter for modernization, autoroutes and all. Already crêperies are franchised, squeezing out family businesses like that in Quimper, and the making of kouign-aman seems to be a dying art. Or is it? perhaps the legendary independence of every Breton will persist at least in the cooking, so that cotriade and home-made crêpes will remain a permanent part of the scene. Let's hope so.

SOUPE D'ÉTRILLES
Crab soup

Brittany has a strong dualist tradition. When God created sole, say the Bretons, the devil made skate, and when He made lobster, the devil responded with crab. Certainly there is little to be done with 'étrilles', jagged creatures with little meat, but to make delicious soups, although a large quantity is needed to make the concentrated broth for this one. If you have larger crabs, extract the meat and use it for something like the soufflé which follows, or recreate the gratin of crab made in St Malo, which is a mixture of crab-meat, white sauce and gruyère.

Serves 6

4 kg	live blue crabs or any small hard-shell crab	9 lb
	2 Tbsp vegetable oil	
	2 onions, sliced	
2·5 L	water	2½ qt
	pinch of saffron strands, steeped in 1–2 Tbsp boiling water	
	1 Tbsp coarse salt	
	2 large potatoes	
750 g	tomatoes, peeled	1½ lb
	1 Tbsp olive oil	
	2 cloves garlic, finely chopped	
	bouquet garni	
	salt and pepper	
	3 Tbsp heavy cream or crème fraîche*	
30 g	chopped parsley	¼ cup
	12 croûtes* fried in vegetable oil, then rubbed with garlic	
	grated gruyère cheese (for serving)	

Rinse the crabs thoroughly. To make a broth, heat 1 tablespoon vegetable oil in a very large pot and add a sliced onion. Sauté over a high fire for 2–3 minutes, then add half the crabs. (Cooking the crabs in two batches gives a stronger-flavoured broth.) Stir and add enough water to cover the crabs, some saffron and the coarse salt. Cover, bring to a boil and boil for 20 minutes. Remove the crabs, add the remaining crabs and boil them for 20 minutes. Crack the crabs, remove any meat and save it for another dish. Pound the leg and body shells in a heavy bowl with the end of a rolling pin until completely crushed. Return the crushed shells to the broth and simmer for 15 minutes or until reduced by half. Strain and measure 1·25 litres.

Halve the potatoes lengthwise, set each half flat on the cutting board and cut it in three lengthwise; then cut crosswise in thin slices. Cut the tomatoes in quarters, remove the seeds and dice the flesh. Strain the seeds and add the juice to the crab broth.

In another pot, heat the olive oil with a tablespoon of vegetable oil. Add the second sliced onion and the chopped garlic. Cook over a low fire, stirring often, for 3–4 minutes or until softened. Add the crab broth, more saffron, the bouquet garni, the sliced potatoes and the tomato squares; taste for seasoning. Simmer for 10 minutes or until the potatoes are just tender.

Just before serving the soup, add the cream; taste for seasoning, adding more saffron if necessary. Discard the bouquet garni and stir in the chopped parsley. Pour the soup into a tureen and serve the croûtes and grated cheese separately.

SOUPE AUX CRABES CUITS

If using cooked crabs, use half fish stock and half water. Cook the crushed shells in this mixture after extracting the meat; then proceed as above.

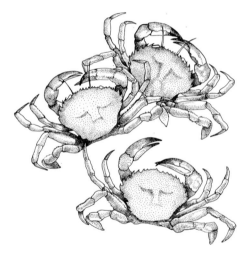

SOUFFLÉ AU CRABE
Crab soufflé

For this recipe, use the meat from large crabs in Britain, or from king, Dungeness or blue crabs in the USA; the shells can go towards crab soup. In the absence of fresh crabs, canned or frozen crab-meat makes a respectable soufflé.

Serves 6

250 ml	milk	1 cup
	1 slice onion	
	1 bay leaf	
	6 black peppercorns	
45 g	butter	3 Tbsp
	2 shallots, finely chopped	
15 g	flour	2 Tbsp
60 ml	heavy cream or crème fraîche*	$\frac{1}{4}$ cup
	salt and pepper	
	pinch of cayenne pepper	
	pinch of grated nutmeg	
	4 egg yolks	
250 g	cooked crab-meat, flaked	$\frac{1}{2}$ lb
	6 egg whites	
	1·5 L/1½ qt soufflé dish	

Heavily butter the soufflé dish. Bring the milk to a boil, add the onion, bay leaf and peppercorns, cover and leave in a warm place to infuse. In a saucepan melt the butter, add the shallots and cook over a low fire, stirring, until soft but not browned. Whisk in the flour and cook over a low fire, whisking, just until bubbling. Strain in the infused milk, whisking, and bring to a boil. Add the cream, season with salt, pepper, cayenne pepper and nutmeg and simmer for 2 minutes. Take from the heat and beat the egg yolks into the hot mixture so it thickens. Add the crab-meat and taste – the mixture should be highly seasoned.

Set the oven at very hot (220°C/425°F). Whip the egg whites until stiff, if possible in a copper bowl. Heat the crab mixture until it is hot to the touch. Add about a quarter of the egg whites and stir until well mixed. Add this to the remaining egg whites and fold together as lightly as possible. Pour the mixture into the prepared soufflé dish and bake in the heated oven for 12–15 minutes or until the soufflé is puffed and brown. Serve at once.

COTRIADE BRETONNE
Fish stew with sorrel and leek

The name 'cotriade' is linked to 'côte' (coast) where this hearty soup comes from. It is best made with a mixture of rich fish such as eel, monkfish and mackerel, and white fish like cod, haddock, hake and whiting. Alternatives in the USA are bluefish, red snapper and flounder.

Serves 6–8

750 g	rich fish	1½ lb
750 g	white fish	1½ lb
1 L	fish stock*	1 qt
750 ml	mussels	3 cups
500 g	raw sorrel OR	1 lb
250 ml	canned or cooked sorrel	1 cup
60 g	butter	4 Tbsp
500 g	potatoes	1 lb
	2 onions, chopped	
	2 leeks, chopped	
	2 cloves garlic, finely chopped	
	bouquet garni	
	salt and pepper	
250 ml	heavy cream or crème fraîche*	1 cup
	6–8 heart-shaped croûtes* fried in butter, then rubbed with garlic	

If using eel, skin and fillet it. Fillet the fish and use the heads, tails and bones of all the white fish to make the fish stock. Cut the fish fillets into 5 cm/2 in pieces, wash and dry them. Clean the mussels*. If using raw sorrel*, prepare it and cook it in half the butter, stirring often, for 15 minutes or until most of the liquid has evaporated.

Quarter the potatoes; then slice them thinly. In a large pot, heat the remaining butter and cook the onions, leeks and garlic for 2–3 minutes until soft but not brown. Add the fish stock, bouquet garni, salt, pepper and potatoes and simmer for 5 minutes or until the potatoes are slightly cooked. Add the rich fish, simmer for another 3–4 minutes and then add the remaining fish. Simmer for 5 more minutes until the fish are nearly tender. Add the cooked fresh or canned sorrel, the mussels in their shells and the cream. Continue simmering for 3 minutes or until the mussels open. Taste for seasoning; salt may not be needed since the mussels are salty. Discard the bouquet garni.

Serve the cotriade in the cooking pot or in a tureen, with the croûtes in a separate bowl.

SAUCE BRETONNE CHAUDE

This country sauce is made with hot broth for serving with eggs or white meats and with fish stock for serving with fish, especially cod.

Makes 600 ml/2½ cups of sauce

60 g	butter	4 Tbsp
	1 onion, thinly sliced	
	1 leek, white part only, split and thinly sliced	
	3 stalks of celery, thinly sliced	
	salt and pepper	
	1 tsp sugar	
60 g	mushrooms, cut in thin strips	2 oz
125 ml	white wine (preferably muscadet)	½ cup
30 g	flour	¼ cup
500 ml	broth or fish stock*	2 cups
	2 Tbsp heavy cream or crème fraîche*	

Melt half the butter in a pot and add the onion, leek, celery, a little salt and pepper and the sugar. Cover and cook over a low fire, stirring often, for 15–20 minutes or until the vegetables are very soft but not brown; be careful not to let them burn. Add the mushrooms and wine, bring to a boil and simmer for 5 more minutes or until the mushrooms are tender and the quantity of wine is reduced by about half.

Melt the remaining butter in another pan, whisk in the flour and cook over a low fire, whisking, until bubbling but not brown. Whisk in the broth and bring to a boil. Simmer for 2–3 minutes, whisking often; then add the vegetable mixture and the cream. Bring just to a boil and taste for seasoning. Serve hot.

BEURRE BLANC NANTAIS

White butter sauce

Many Breton cooks like to make beurre blanc with salted butter, declaring the flavour is less bland. To discourage the sauce from separating, one trick is to add a tablespoon of cream to the reduced wine and shallot mixture, then reduce again before whisking in the butter. Serve it with poached or grilled/broiled fish, or with cooked vegetables.

Makes 250 ml/1 cup of sauce

	3 Tbsp white wine vinegar	
	3 Tbsp dry white wine	
	2 shallots, very finely chopped	
250 g	very cold butter	1 cup
	salt and white pepper	

In a small saucepan (not aluminium) boil the vinegar, wine and shallots until reduced to 1 tablespoon. Cut butter in small pieces. Set the pan over a low fire and gradually whisk in the butter, a piece at a time, to make a smooth, creamy sauce. Work sometimes over a low fire and sometimes off the fire so that the butter softens and thickens the sauce without melting. Season to taste with salt and white pepper. Serve as soon as possible; if kept warm, the sauce will melt to become thin and oily.

SOLE AUX FONDS D'ARTICHAUTS FARCIS

Sole with stuffed artichoke bottoms

Artichokes are good for you, say many Bretons. One physician is said to have complained because his patients were not reimbursed for the cost of the artichokes that he prescribed.

The vegetables are so plentiful in Brittany that the bottoms are sometimes made into a purée for a variation of this recipe, with the sole fillets set on top and decorated with small mushrooms cooked slowly in butter instead of the shellfish. Dover sole is preferable for this dish, but any flat fish can be substituted. When mussels are not available, double the quantity of shrimps given in the recipe.

Serves 4

750 g each	2 sole	1½ lb each
	fish stock*	
750 ml	mussels	3 cups
100 g	cooked, peeled shrimps	3½ oz
	4 large artichokes	
	1 lemon	
30 g	butter	2 Tbsp
30 g	flour	¼ cup
	2 egg yolks	
	salt and pepper	

Skin and fillet the sole (if using any other flat fish, fillet it first, then skin the fillets). Use the bones and heads to make fish stock.

Clean the mussels*. Put them in a large pot, cover and cook over a high fire, tossing occasionally, for 5–7 minutes or until they open. Shell the mussels, discarding any that remain closed. Carefully pour the liquid into the fish stock, leaving any sand or grit behind. Combine the mussels and shrimps.

Prepare and cook the artichoke bottoms*. Heap some of the mussel and shrimp mixture on each artichoke bottom, put them on a buttered platter, cover and keep warm.

Wash and dry the sole fillets and fold in half, skin side inwards. Put them in a shallow pan and cover with fish stock. Cover with greaseproof/parchment paper, bring just to a boil and poach for 2–3 minutes or until the fish can be flaked easily with a fork. Drain well, reserving the stock. Arrange the fillets on the platter with the filled artichoke bottoms surrounding them, cover and keep warm.

Boil the fish stock until reduced to 500 ml. Melt the butter in a saucepan, whisk in the flour and cook for 1–2 minutes until foaming but not browned. Gradually whisk in the reduced stock and bring to a boil, whisking constantly. Simmer for a minute or two; if the sauce is thin, boil it until it coats a spoon lightly. Beat the yolks in a small bowl and gradually whisk in a few spoonsful of the hot sauce. Return the mixture to the saucepan and cook over low heat for 1–2 minutes until slightly thickened, but don't boil. Taste for seasoning; extra salt may not be needed since the mussels are salty. Spoon the sauce over the sole and the filled artichoke bottoms, brown quickly under the grill/broiler and serve.

COQUILLES ST JACQUES NANTAISE
Sautéed scallops with spices

Nantes was a centre for the 17th- and 18th-century French trade with the Orient, which accounts for the spices in this recipe.

Serves 6 as a first course or 4 as a main course

750 g	scallops	1½ lb
30 g	flour seasoned with salt and pepper	¼ cup
60 g	butter	4 Tbsp
	½ tsp curry powder or to taste	
	pinch of cayenne pepper	
	1 large onion, finely chopped	
	2 Tbsp cognac	
125 ml	white wine	½ cup
500 g	tomatoes, peeled, seeded and coarsely chopped	1 lb
	salt and pepper	
	3 Tbsp dry breadcrumbs	
30 g	melted butter	2 Tbsp
	DUCHESSE POTATO PURÉE	
500 g	potatoes	1 lb
	salt and white pepper	
30 g	butter	2 Tbsp
	1 egg yolk	
	pinch of grated nutmeg	
	1 egg, beaten with ½ tsp salt (for glaze)	

4–6 deep scallop shells; pastry bag; medium star tip

For the potato purée, cut the potatoes in equal pieces and put them in a pot of cold salted water. Cover, bring to a boil and simmer for 15–20 minutes or until very tender. Drain the potatoes thoroughly and work them back into the pan through a sieve or purée in a food mill. Add the butter with the egg yolk, salt, pepper and nutmeg to taste, and beat with a wooden spoon over a low fire until the purée is light; it should be stiff enough to pipe. Using the pastry bag, pipe a border of purée around each scallop shell.

Prepare the scallops*. Cut each into 2–3 diagonal slices and coat them lightly in the seasoned flour. Heat all but 1 tablespoon of the butter in a sauté pan until foaming. Add the scallops and sauté over a high fire, stirring occasionally, for 2–3 minutes or until golden brown; don't overcook the scallops or they will toughen. Half-way through cooking, sprinkle them with curry powder and cayenne pepper. When brown, remove the scallops to a plate.

Add the remaining tablespoon of butter and the onion to the pan and cook over a low fire until soft but not brown. Add the cognac, then the wine, and bring to a boil. Add the tomatoes and simmer for 4–5 minutes until the wine is well reduced and the tomatoes are pulpy. Taste and add more salt, pepper or curry powder if necessary. Combine the scallops with the sauce, spoon the mixture into the prepared shells and sprinkle with dry breadcrumbs, then the melted butter. Brush the potato border with egg glaze. Either bake the scallops in a very hot oven (220°C/425°F) for 7–10 minutes until browned, or grill/broil them until very hot and browned.

COQUILLES ST JACQUES AU CIDRE
Scallops with cider

Some of the largest scallop beds in Europe are off the coast of Brittany. A dry white wine such as muscadet can replace the cider in this recipe.

Serves 6 as a first course or 4 as a main course

750 g	scallops	1½ lb
45 g	butter	3 Tbsp
	3 shallots, chopped	
500 ml	dry cider	2 cups
	salt and pepper	
185 ml	heavy cream or crème fraîche*	¾ cup
	2 tsp arrowroot or potato starch, dissolved in 1–2 Tbsp water	
	juice of ¼ lemon	
	1 Tbsp chopped parsley	

Prepare the scallops* and cut each into 2–3 diagonal slices. Melt the butter in a shallow saucepan, add the shallots and cook over a low fire for 2–3 minutes or until softened. Add the cider, scallops, salt and pepper. Bring just to a boil and poach for 1–2 minutes over a low fire. Remove the scallops and drain on paper towels.

Boil the liquid for 5 minutes or until reduced to 5 or 6 tablespoons. Add the cream, bring back to a boil and gradually stir in enough of the dissolved arrowroot to thicken the sauce enough to coat a spoon; taste for seasoning. Just before serving, return the scallops to the sauce and reheat gently. Add lemon juice to taste. Spoon into scallop shells or a shallow serving bowl, sprinkle with parsley and serve hot.

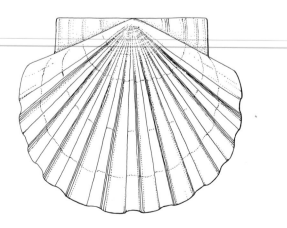

CRUSTACEANS

France, with its long sea coast and many rivers, is blessed with a generous supply of crustaceans – lobsters, crabs, prawns and shrimps – many of which come from Normandy and Brittany. Acknowledged king is the clawed lobster – the blue-black 'homard' which turns bright red when cooked and is at its best taken from cool northern waters, though some are also found in the Mediterranean. Female lobsters are valued for their coral (eggs) which is sometimes extruded under the body but more often appears as a thick black column when the body is cut open. (In a female, the two small feelers under the lobster at the junction of the body and tail are feathery, not stiff.) When cooked, the coral turns a vivid red, giving rich colour as well as taste to sauces.

'Langouste' (spiny lobster, rock lobster or crawfish) thrives in the waters of the Mediterranean, though it is found as far north as Brittany. Like a homard without claws, the langouste is less impressive in colour, being a reddish brown which darkens somewhat on cooking, and it has a less intense flavour. It must not be confused with its lightweight namesake, the 'langoustine', which is pale pink with long, spindly claws, and is found from Norway to the Adriatic. The Italian name for langoustine is scampi. Often referred to as Dublin Bay prawns, they are a valuable catch, though until the 1950s fishermen in the Irish Sea threw them away. Delicate, not to say bland, langoustines need careful cooking and are at their best served cold with mayonnaise; 6–12 make a serving.

Most so-called scampi are in fact 'crevettes', which the British would call prawns and the Americans shrimps. Common in France is the 9–10 cm/$3\frac{1}{2}$–4 in 'crevette rose' which is colourless when raw and a pretty pink when cooked. There are also larger deep-water varieties up to 20 cm/8 in long (here the British and Americans agree in calling them prawns) which are often cooked at sea and sold frozen. At the other end of the scale, there are baby shrimps or 'crevettes grises', which children equipped with nets and wading boots have fun collecting.

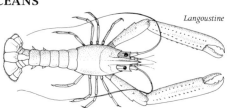

Langoustine

Shelling these tiny crustaceans is tedious, but has its rewards as crevettes grises have a spicy sea flavour quite unlike any other. They are used for bisque, as a garnish in sauces or, best of all, eaten on their own with brown bread and butter.

Generally the crab family can be divided into those valued for their meat and those good only for soup, with too little meat to be worth the picking. In France, 'tourteaux' are the main source of crab-meat; known simply as crabs in England, they closely resemble the US Dungeness crab. The 'araignée' or spider crab is full of flavour but less meaty, and the other common French crab, the 'étrille' (swimming crab), is good only for soup. Spider and swimming crabs are rarely sold in Britain and the USA, crab soup being made with one of the meatier, and more expensive, varieties.

Odd man out among these sea creatures is the freshwater crayfish or 'écrevisse', sometimes erroneously called a crawfish. Crayfish are about 15 cm/6 in long and look like miniature clawed lobsters; the best variety has deep red claws and body when cooked. Crayfish can still be caught in many French streams and lakes, but it takes patience, and most commercial supplies are farmed in ponds. They are sought after for gratins, for sauces in dishes like quenelles Nantua, and even for combining with chicken and veal. One of the ultimate luxuries is a dozen red-clawed crayfish, 'à la nage' (swimming) in hot court bouillon, with a herb-butter sauce into which to dip the tails.

Substantial though the French catch of crustaceans may be, it is not enough to satisfy the demand. Crayfish are imported from Central Europe, members of the larger shrimp and prawn family from the Caribbean and South America, and frozen lobster tails from West Africa. Fresh langoustes, inferior, say the French, to the native variety, are brought in from Morocco and in Paris high prices attract a large part of the Irish and British catch of homards, not to mention planeloads from North America. The attraction of crustaceans is not just their taste – they have a tantalizing allure which led to the courtesans of the Belle Époque being known as 'crevettes'.

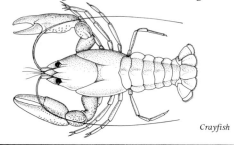

Crayfish

HOMARD À L'AMÉRICAINE

Lobster with garlic and tomatoes

Is it lobster 'à l'américaine' or should it be 'à l'armoricaine'? The debate has raged for decades. Some say the name comes from Armor, the ancient name for Brittany. Others claim the dish was invented by a Parisian restaurateur, Pierre Fraisse, for an American customer. This is the more likely explanation since lobster à l'américaine contains ingredients − olive oil, garlic and tomatoes − that are typical of Chef Fraisse's native Provence. Whatever the true story, this is a superb way to treat a lobster.

Serves 4

0·75−1 kg each	2 live lobsters	1½−2 lb each
	2 Tbsp olive oil	
	2 Tbsp vegetable oil	
	1 onion, chopped	
	3 shallots, finely chopped	
	1 clove garlic, crushed	
80 ml	cognac	⅓ cup
375 ml	white wine	1½ cups
250 ml	fish stock*, broth* or water	1 cup
500 g	tomatoes, coarsely chopped	1 lb
	bouquet garni	
	6 sprigs fresh tarragon OR	
	1 tsp dried tarragon	
	pinch of cayenne pepper	
	salt and pepper	
	2 Tbsp tomato paste	
30 g	butter, kneaded with	2 Tbsp
15 g	flour	2 Tbsp
	2 Tbsp heavy cream or crème fraîche*	
45 g	butter	3 Tbsp
	pinch of sugar (optional)	

Kill and cut up the lobsters*. Heat the two oils in a large skillet or sauté pan and add the pieces of lobster tail and claws, cut side down; sauté one minute over high heat. Turn the pieces over and continue cooking until the shells turn red. Take them out, put in the head pieces and feelers, and cook until they turn red also. Remove the lobster pieces and add the onion, shallots and garlic. Cook them gently until soft but not brown. Replace the lobster pieces and flame them with the cognac. Add the white wine, reserved lobster liquid, fish stock, tomatoes, bouquet garni, tarragon stems (reserve the leaves), cayenne pepper, salt and pepper. Cover and simmer for 12−15 minutes or until the meat is no longer transparent.

Take the lobster tails and claws from the cooking liquid, remove the meat and reserve it. Crush all the shells with a mortar and pestle or with a rolling pin and return them to the sauce.

Dilute the tomato paste in a few tablespoons of the sauce and add it to the remaining sauce. Simmer for 10 minutes and then strain, pressing on the lobster shells to extract all the liquid.

Mix the kneaded butter with the lobster coral and tomalley. Bring the sauce to a boil, take it from the heat and whisk in the kneaded lobster butter a little at a time. Heat the sauce gently until it thickens but don't boil it once this butter has been added. Put the lobster meat back into the sauce and add the cream. Leave the sauce on a low fire long enough to reheat the lobster pieces; then remove from the heat. Add the remaining butter in small pieces, shaking the pan so it is incorporated. Taste for seasoning. Add more cayenne pepper if necessary; a pinch of sugar may also be needed to compensate for the acidity of the tomatoes. When using fresh tarragon, chop the leaves and sprinkle them over the lobster just before serving.

Tarragon

20

LOTTE À L'AMÉRICAINE

Monkfish with garlic and tomatoes

Monkfish, known as the poor man's lobster because of its resilient texture, is excellent cooked à l'américaine. Any other firm-fleshed fish such as cod can be substituted, but it should be cooked for a shorter time.

Serves 4

1-kg	piece or steaks of monkfish, with bones	2-lb
250 ml	fish stock*	1 cup
30 g	flour, seasoned with salt and pepper	$\frac{1}{4}$ cup
	2 Tbsp olive oil	
125 g	butter	$\frac{1}{4}$ lb
	1 onion, chopped	
	1 carrot, chopped	
	1 clove garlic, crushed	
750 g	tomatoes, coarsely chopped	$1\frac{1}{2}$ lb
	bouquet garni	
125 ml	white wine	$\frac{1}{2}$ cup
	3 Tbsp cognac	
	2 sprigs fresh tarragon OR	
	1 tsp dried tarragon	
	pinch of cayenne pepper	
	salt and pepper	
	1–2 Tbsp tomato paste	
30 g	butter, kneaded with	2 Tbsp
15 g	flour	2 Tbsp
60 ml	heavy cream or crème fraîche*	$\frac{1}{4}$ cup
	pinch of sugar (optional)	

Remove the transparent second skin from the fish, fillet and use skin and bones to make the fish stock. Rinse and dry the fish and cut it into 4 cm/$1\frac{1}{2}$ in slices. Coat them with seasoned flour. In a large frying pan or sauté pan heat the oil with one quarter of the butter and sauté the fish, a few pieces at a time, until brown on all sides. Take them out, add the onion, carrot and garlic and cook until soft but not brown. Add the tomatoes, bouquet garni, white wine, cognac, tarragon stems (reserve the leaves), cayenne pepper, fish stock, salt and pepper. Bring to a boil, replace the fish and simmer for 15–20 minutes or until just tender. Transfer the fish to a platter, cover and keep warm.

Strain the sauce and boil for 5–10 minutes or until well reduced. Dilute the tomato paste in 2 tablespoons of water and add it to the sauce. If the sauce is too thin, whisk in the kneaded butter* a little at a time, checking the consistency of the sauce before adding more; it should coat a spoon. Add the cream and taste for seasoning; if necessary, add a pinch of sugar. Take from the heat and add the remaining butter in small pieces, shaking the pan until it is incorporated. Spoon enough sauce over the fish to coat it and serve the rest separately. If using fresh tarragon, chop the leaves and sprinkle them over the fish just before serving.

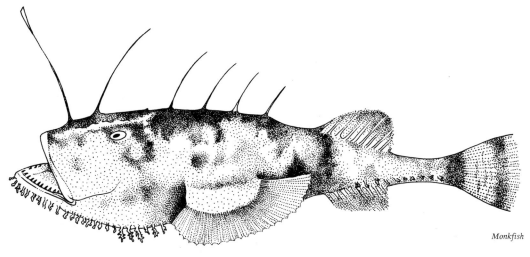

Monkfish

GRATIN DE THON AUX HARICOTS SECS

Tuna and white bean gratin

Fish and beans are characteristic ingredients in Breton cooking. Combining them in one recipe may seem unusual, but the Bretons eat beans with almost everything.

Serves 6

250 g	dried white beans	½ lb
	1 onion	
	salt and pepper	
	2 Tbsp heavy cream (optional)	
420 g	canned tuna in brine	14 oz
80 g	grated gruyère cheese	1 cup
15 g	dry white breadcrumbs	2 Tbsp
30 g	butter	2 Tbsp

Soak the beans overnight in cold water. Drain them, put them in a pot with the whole onion and cover generously with cold water. Bring to a boil and simmer for 1½ hours or until very soft, adding more hot water as it evaporates so that the beans remain covered with liquid. Add salt half-way through the cooking time. Drain the beans, discarding the onion. Set the oven at hot (200°C/400°F). Purée the beans, using a food mill or pushing them through a sieve, to remove the skins. Beat in the cream. Drain the tuna, shred it with a fork and mix into the bean purée. Stir in the cheese and add salt and pepper to taste. Spoon the mixture into a buttered baking dish, sprinkle with breadcrumbs and dot with butter. Bake in the oven for 15–20 minutes or until browned. Serve hot.

MORUE À LA MALOUINAISE

Salt cod with potatoes and cream

St Malo was once harbour to the notorious corsairs, but is now home to Brittany's cod fleet. Much of the cod is salted, but recipes abound for cooking it fresh as well. Just south of St Malo in Dinan, cod cheeks are deep fried and relished with a glass of cider.

Serves 4

500 g	salt cod	1 lb
500 g	potatoes	1 lb
	salt	
45 g	butter	3 Tbsp
	3 onions, sliced	
300 ml	heavy cream or crème fraîche*	1¼ cups

Soak the salt cod in a bowl of cold water for 1–2 days, changing the water and turning the cod several times. Drain the cod, put it in a pot, cover generously with cold water and bring just to a boil. Turn down the heat as low as possible and poach the cod for 15 minutes or until it flakes easily. Drain it thoroughly, flake the flesh, discarding any bones or dry pieces, and transfer it to a buttered baking dish.

Scrub the potatoes but don't peel them. Put them in a pot of cold salted water, bring to a boil and simmer for 15–20 minutes or until just tender. Peel the potatoes, cut them in rounds and arrange in the baking dish around the cod. Set the oven at hot (200°C/400°F).

Melt the butter in a frying pan, add the onions, cover and cook over a very low fire, stirring often, for 15–20 minutes or until soft but not brown. Spoon the onions over the cod, cover with the cream and bake, basting often, for 20 minutes or until cod and potatoes are golden. Serve hot.

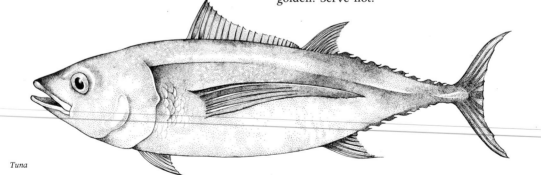

Tuna

MOULES OU PALOURDES FARCIES
Mussels or clams stuffed with herb butter
Large mussels or any small clams (little necks or cherrystones in the USA) can be used in this recipe. Be careful not to overcook them.

Serves 6

	1 shallot, finely chopped	
	1–2 cloves garlic, finely chopped	
250 g	butter, softened	½ lb
	3 Tbsp dry white wine, preferably muscadet	
	3 Tbsp chopped parsley	
	salt and pepper	
	6 dozen mussels or clams	

Pound the shallot and garlic in a mortar and put them in a bowl. Whisk in the butter, wine, parsley, and salt and pepper to taste. Alternatively, purée the butter with these ingredients in a food processor. The purée should be flavoured with more or less garlic to taste.

Wash the mussels* or clams* well. Use a sturdy knife with a flat, wide blade to open the shells. Holding a shell firmly in the hollow of your hand, force the knife blade inside, near the hinge, and turn the knife to cut the muscles holding the shell shut. Force the shell open and drain off any liquid. Leave the mussel or clam in the lower shell and discard the upper shell. Set the oven at very hot (220°C/425°F).

Spoon some of the butter mixture into each shell and set the shells in ovenproof platters or shallow baking dishes containing a layer of coarse salt to hold shells level. Bake for 3–5 minutes, or until the filling begins to boil. Serve very hot in the dishes.

ESCARGOTS À LA BOURGUIGNONNE
The well-known Burgundian recipe for snails uses the same butter recipe as above. Not surprisingly, this dish is also known in Brittany, where its name is 'escargots au beurre breton'. Cooked or canned snails can be used. Drain **24 large or 36 small snails.** Using the same number of snail shells, spoon a little of the butter mixture into each shell, place a snail on top, and spoon on more butter. Heat as above. Snails may be served in special escargot dishes instead of on a platter of coarse salt.

MERLAN DES MAREYEURS
Fishmonger's whiting
Whiting is caught off the coast of Lorient in southern Brittany where this simple dish is common. It is often made with herrings, known locally as 'gendarmes'. Fillets of plaice, flounder or haddock can be used, too.

Serves 4–6

	3 shallots, finely chopped	
125 ml	dry white wine, preferably muscadet or gros plant	½ cup
125 ml	water	½ cup
750 g	whiting fillets	1½ lb
	salt and pepper	
	3 Tbsp chopped parsley	
	1–2 Tbsp Dijon mustard	
125 g	cold butter	½ cup
	few drops lemon juice	

Set the oven at hot (200°C/400°F). Butter a shallow baking dish and put in the shallots, wine and water. Rinse and dry the fillets, fold them in half, skin side inwards, and lay them on top; season with salt and pepper and sprinkle with chopped parsley. Cover them with greaseproof/waxed paper and bake for 8–10 minutes or until the flesh is no longer transparent. Drain the cooking liquid into a saucepan or sauté pan. Arrange the fish on a platter, cover and keep it warm.

Boil the cooking liquid for 5 minutes or until reduced by half. Take from the heat and whisk in the mustard; then, with the pan sometimes over a low fire and sometimes off the heat, whisk in the butter in small pieces so that it thickens the sauce without melting and becoming oily. Add a few drops of lemon juice and taste for seasoning. Drain off any liquid that has escaped from the fish, coat the fish with sauce and serve immediately.

POULARDE À LA RENNAISE
Stuffed chicken with prunes

Although not a product of Brittany, prunes play an important role in Breton cuisine, thanks to water traffic down to Nantes from the Loire valley, where plum trees flourish. Muscadet would be the wine used in Brittany for this dish. The acidity of the muscadet in the sauce is balanced by the prunes, which also add special flavour to the stuffing.

Serves 4

300 g	prunes	10 oz
1·5 kg	chicken, including the liver	3-lb
150 g	ground pork, fat and lean mixed	5 oz
	1 shallot, chopped	
	2 Tbsp chopped parsley	
	salt and pepper	
	1 Tbsp oil	
15 g	butter	1 Tbsp
	1 carrot, sliced	
	1 onion OR the green top of 1 leek, sliced	
	1 stalk celery, sliced (optional)	
185 ml	white wine	¾ cup
SAUCE		
20 g	butter	1½ Tbsp
15 g	flour	2 Tbsp
500 ml	broth or water	2 cups
80 ml	white wine	⅓ cup
	1 egg yolk	
80 ml	heavy cream or crème fraîche*	⅓ cup
	trussing needle and string	

Soak the prunes in a bowl of hot water for 1 hour or until softened and plump. Remove the neck and wingtips from the chicken and reserve with the giblets, if available.

To make the stuffing: drain half of the prunes and chop them. Chop the chicken liver and mix it with the chopped prunes, pork, shallot, parsley, salt and pepper; fry a small piece of the stuffing until brown and taste for seasoning. Stuff the chicken with the mixture and truss it. Set the oven at moderately hot (190°C/375°F).

Heat the oil and butter in a heavy casserole and brown the chicken well on all sides. Add the chicken neck, wingtips, gizzard, carrot, onion and celery and cook them slowly with the chicken for 2–3 minutes or until they are slightly softened. Add the wine, salt and pepper. Bring to a boil, cover tightly and cook in the oven for 50–60 minutes or until the chicken is tender and a skewer inserted into the stuffing is hot to the touch when withdrawn. If necessary, uncover the casserole towards the end of the cooking so the chicken browns well.

While the chicken is cooking, make the sauce: melt the butter in a saucepan, whisk in the flour and cook, whisking constantly, until foaming. Gradually whisk in the broth and wine and bring to a boil. Drain the remaining prunes, add them to the sauce and simmer over a low fire, stirring occasionally, for 30 minutes or until the prunes are soft. (Stir carefully to avoid breaking up all the prunes, although a few broken ones will simply add flavour to the sauce.) Remove the prunes with a slotted spoon and set aside.

When the chicken is cooked, carve it, arrange the pieces on a platter and pile the stuffing in the centre. Keep it warm while finishing the sauce: add the sauce to the chicken juices and stir to dissolve the pan juices. Skim off the excess fat. Strain the sauce back into its pan, pressing hard on the vegetables to extract their flavour; reheat the sauce. Mix the egg yolk and cream in a small bowl and gradually whisk in some of the hot sauce. Return this mixture to the saucepan, add the prunes and cook over a low fire, stirring occasionally, until the sauce has thickened slightly; don't let it boil or it will curdle. Taste the sauce for seasoning. Spoon some of the sauce with the prunes over the chicken pieces. Serve remaining sauce separately.

CANARD AUX PETITS POIS

Roast duck with green peas

Nantes is famous for the delicate breed of duck raised in the Grande Brière, just to the west. In Brittany duck is often served with green peas, not only because nearly 25 per cent of French peas are grown there, but also because their sweet flavour is a good complement to the richness of the meat.

Serves 4

2–2·5-kg	duck	4–5-lb
	salt and pepper	
375 ml	broth	1½ cups
	2 Tbsp madeira	
	GARNISH	
1 L	shelled fresh green peas	1 qt
	salt and pepper	
	16–18 baby onions	
45 g	butter	3 Tbsp
	1 tsp sugar	
250-g	piece of lean bacon, cut in lardons	½-lb
	few sprigs of fresh savory OR 2 tsp dried savory	
	few Tbsp broth (optional)	
	trussing needle and string	

Set the oven at very hot (220°C/425°F). Season the duck inside and out with salt and pepper and prick the skin to release the fat during cooking. Truss the duck, place it on its side on a rack in a roasting pan with the neck and giblets (except for the liver), and roast in the heated oven for 15 minutes. Turn it on to the other leg and roast for another 15 minutes. Lower the oven heat to moderately hot (190°C/375°F). Lay the duck on its breast and roast for another 15 minutes. Finally set the duck on its back and roast for 15 minutes or until the juices from the centre of the duck run pink if it is lifted with a fork; the breast meat will be pink. If you prefer well-done meat, continue cooking the duck until the juices run clear.

Meanwhile, prepare the garnish: cook the peas in boiling salted water for 10–30 minutes (cooking time for peas varies enormously according to their size and age). Drain the peas, refresh with cold water and drain thoroughly. Put the onions in a heavy-based pan with two-thirds of the butter, sprinkle with sugar and cook gently, shaking the pan from time to time, for 12–15 minutes or until tender and caramelized. If the bacon is salty, blanch* it. Fry the bacon lardons in the remaining butter until lightly browned. Drain and combine them with the onions and peas. Season lightly.

Transfer the duck to a casserole and spoon the garnish around it, adding the savory and a few tablespoons of broth if the peas seem dry. Cover and keep warm so the flavours mellow while making the gravy: discard all the fat from the roasting pan, add the broth and heat, stirring to dissolve the pan juices. Pour the gravy, including the giblets, into a small pan; if necessary, boil to reduce until well flavoured. Add the madeira, bring to a boil and taste for seasoning. Strain the gravy into a sauce-boat. Serve the duck with the gravy separately.

SAUCISSES AU MUSCADET

Sausages in white wine

This dish is often served with chestnut purée. As in many traditionally poor areas, chestnuts are a Breton standby.

Serves 4

	4 very thick slices white bread, crusts removed	
125 ml	oil	½ cup
750 g	8 fresh country sausages	1½ lb
	2 shallots, finely chopped	
125 ml	dry white wine, preferably muscadet	½ cup
	1 tsp arrowroot or potato starch, dissolved in 1 Tbsp water	
45 g	butter	3 Tbsp
	2 Tbsp chopped parsley	
	salt and pepper	

Make notched bread cases: with a small serrated knife cut two parallel notches in each slice of bread (each notch will hold one sausage). Heat the oil in a heavy frying pan and brown the bread cases on both sides. Drain on paper towels and keep warm.

Discard all but 1 tablespoon of the oil in the pan. Prick the sausages with a fork and sauté in the oil for 10 minutes, turning them occasionally. Set 2 sausages on each slice of fried bread and keep warm.

Pour the excess grease from the pan. Add the shallots and wine, bring to a boil and simmer for 2–3 minutes or until the shallots are tender. Gradually whisk enough dissolved arrowroot into the simmering liquid to thicken it slightly. Off the fire, stir in the butter, a piece at a time, and the chopped parsley; taste for seasoning. Spoon the sauce over the sausages and serve immediately.

GIGOT D'AGNEAU À LA BRETONNE

Leg of lamb with white beans and tomatoes
Brittany is famous for the lambs which graze on marshes swept by sea winds. These 'pré-salé' (salt-meadow) sheep are found particularly near Mont St Michel and on the Crozon peninsula near Brest. Dried white beans flavoured with tomatoes are the standard accompaniment. In the USA, great northern, navy or pea beans can be used instead of French haricot beans.

Serves 6–8

2·7-kg	leg of lamb	6-lb
	2 Tbsp oil	
	1 onion, quartered	
	1 carrot, quartered	
	1 clove garlic, cut in 4–5 slivers (optional)	
	2 tsp rosemary (optional)	
	salt and pepper	
125 ml	broth or water (optional)	½ cup
	bunch of watercress	
BEAN AND TOMATO MIXTURE		
500 g	dried white beans	1 lb
	1 onion, studded with 4 cloves	
	1 carrot	
	bouquet garni, including a stalk of celery	
	salt and pepper	
30 g	butter	2 Tbsp
	2 onions, finely chopped	
	1 clove garlic, finely chopped	
750 g	tomatoes, peeled, seeded and chopped	1½ lb
80 ml	white wine	⅓ cup
	2–3 Tbsp chopped parsley	
GRAVY		
125 ml	white wine	½ cup
250 ml	broth* or water	1 cup
	salt and pepper	

To make the bean and tomato mixture: soak the beans overnight in cold water. Drain them and put them in a large pot with the clove-studded onion, carrot, bouquet garni and enough water to cover by at least 2·5 cm/1 in. Bring to a boil and simmer for 1½ hours or until the beans are very tender, adding salt and pepper half-way through cooking. Add more water as it evaporates to keep the beans covered with liquid. At the end of cooking, the beans should be moist but not soupy. Discard the onion, carrot and bouquet garni.

While the beans are simmering, cook the tomatoes: melt the butter in a sauté pan or shallow saucepan, add the chopped onions and garlic and cook slowly, stirring often, for 4–5 minutes or until soft but not browned. Add the tomatoes, white wine, salt and pepper. Cook over medium heat, stirring often, for 15–20 minutes or until nearly all the moisture has evaporated. Add the tomatoes to the cooked beans and taste for seasoning.

To roast the lamb: set the oven at very hot (230°C/450°F). Prepare the lamb by trimming away the skin and all but a thin layer of fat. Pour the oil into a roasting pan, add the quartered onion and carrot and put the lamb on top. Make several incisions in the lamb with the point of a knife and insert the slivers of garlic – the flavour will permeate the meat. Sprinkle the lamb with rosemary, salt and pepper. Sear the meat in the oven for 10–15 minutes or until browned; then lower the heat to hot (200°C/400°F) and continue roasting. Baste the lamb often during cooking and, if the pan juices start to brown too much, add a little broth or water. For rare meat, allow 20–24 minutes per kg/9–11 minutes per lb; for medium-done meat, allow 28–32 minutes per kg/13–15 minutes per lb. Transfer the lamb to a platter and let it stand in a warm place for 15–20 minutes before carving.

To make the gravy: discard the excess fat from the roasting pan but leave in the onion and carrot. Add the wine and stock to the roasting pan and boil, stirring to dissolve the pan juices. Simmer for 5–10 minutes or until well flavoured; strain the gravy into a small saucepan. Skim off the excess fat, bring the gravy to a boil and taste for seasoning. Keep hot until ready to serve. If necessary, reheat the bean and tomato mixture on top of the stove.

To serve; carve the lamb and replace it on the bone. Stir 2 tablespoons of chopped parsley into the beans, spoon them around the lamb and decorate the platter with watercress. Alternatively, place the uncarved leg of lamb on a platter decorated with the watercress; carve it at the table and serve the beans separately, sprinkled with more chopped parsley. In either case, spoon a little gravy over the meat to moisten it and serve the rest in a sauce-boat.

HARICOTS À LA BRETONNE

To serve the beans alone instead of as an accompaniment to meat, cook:

100 g	piece of bacon	3 oz

blanched*, if salty, in the pot with the beans. Then dice it and add it to the beans together with the tomato mixture. In this version, bean cooking liquid can replace the white wine.

KIG-HA-FARZ

Buckwheat pudding with meat and vegetables
'Kig-ha-farz' (meat in pudding) provides three courses in one pot: broth, meat and vegetables, and a sweet pudding. The pudding or 'farz' can vary from a simple combination of buckwheat flour and water to richer mixtures which include eggs, milk, butter, raisins or prunes. Any left-over pudding can be cut in small pieces and browned in a frying pan with sliced onions.

Serves 8–10

1-kg	piece of stew beef, such as round or rump	2-lb
750 g	fresh or salt-cured ham hock or shoulder	1½ lb
500 g	oxtail (optional)	1 lb
5 L	water	5 qt
	6 medium carrots	
	6 small turnips	
	3 leeks, trimmed and split	
	3 onions, studded with 2 cloves	
	1 stalk celery	
	bouquet garni	
	salt and pepper	
	1 medium cabbage	
60 g	butter	4 Tbsp
185 ml	broth, from cooking meat (for cooking cabbage)	¾ cup
	toast or buckwheat galettes (for serving)	
	PUDDING	
250 g	buckwheat flour	2 cups
125 ml	broth, from cooking meat	½ cup
250 ml	milk	1 cup
60 ml	heavy cream	¼ cup
	2 eggs, beaten	
60 g	butter, melted	4 Tbsp
	½ tsp salt	
	3 Tbsp sugar	
150 g	dark raisins	1¼ cups
trussing string; piece of strong cloth		

Tie each cut of beef and ham into a compact piece with string. Cut the oxtail at the joints. In a very large pot, heat the water with the carrots, turnips, leeks, onions, celery and bouquet garni. Add salt if using fresh pork, but not if using cured pork. Bring these ingredients to a boil, add the oxtail and poach over a low fire for 1 hour. Taste the broth for seasoning, add the beef and pork and continue poaching.

After the beef and pork have been cooking for 30 minutes, prepare the pudding mixture: in a bowl mix the flour with the broth, the milk, cream, eggs, melted butter, salt, sugar and raisins. Leave to rest for 1 hour; then set the cloth in a bowl, pour in the pudding mixture, and wrap it by tying with string on both ends.

Leave a little room for the pudding to swell during cooking. Add the pudding to the meat and vegetables and continue simmering for 1½ hours.

Forty-five minutes before the pudding is cooked, bring a pot of salted water to a boil. Cut the cabbage into 6–8 pieces and add them to the pot. Boil for 5–6 minutes; then drain. Heat the butter in the pot, add the drained cabbage and sauté briefly. Add broth, salt and pepper. Cover and simmer for 20 minutes. Keep warm.

Take the bag of pudding out of the simmering broth and leave it in a colander to drain. If the meat is not yet tender when pricked with a two-pronged fork, continue simmering it for 30 minutes more or until tender. Remove the beef and pork. Taste the broth for seasoning; if necessary, boil it quickly and reduce it until well flavoured. Cut beef and pork in medium-thick slices and arrange them on a large platter with the oxtail. Open the bag of pudding, slice it and arrange around the meats. Add the cabbage and other vegetables to the platter. Cover loosely and keep warm. Taste the broth and serve some of it first, either with toast or with buckwheat galettes cut in pieces. When serving the platter of meat, spoon broth over each portion to moisten it.

CANNING AND THE FOOD INDUSTRY

The flourishing food industry of Nantes and southern Brittany began with the sugar and spice trade with the West Indies in the 17th and 18th centuries, when Nantes was the first port of France. Starting with primitive sugar refineries and flour mills for ships' biscuits, modern biscuit factories have developed. Nantes is the home of the 'petit beurre'.

The canning industry came later and Brittany now supplies France with much of its canned fish. The season starts in March with mackerel, which is cooked in a spicy souse, filleted and then canned, usually with white wine and shallots. Next come sardines, which are salted, washed, hot-air dried and canned in oil. Tuna follows, most often cooked with spices and then canned in oil. When a lull comes in the fish catch, factories turn to canning local vegetables.

Women have always provided the labour for canning, while their menfolk have done the fishing. In the old days, before refrigeration, a bell would ring when the fleet came in, and the streets would resound to the clatter of women's clogs in the rush to work.

SALADE DE FONDS D'ARTICHAUTS AUX CHAMPIGNONS

Salad of artichoke bottoms and mushrooms

Artichokes, like cauliflowers, are emblems of Brittany and displayed on car bumper stickers throughout France. Breton artichokes are famous for their size — an artichoke bottom 10 cm/ 4 in wide is not uncommon — making them the ideal container for small vegetables like peas and onions, or for salads like this one of mushrooms.

Serves 4

125 g	mushrooms, very thinly sliced	¼ lb
	4 large artichokes	
	1½ lemons (for preparing artichokes)	
	1 Tbsp chopped chives or parsley	
	DRESSING	
	1 tsp lemon juice	
	1 Tbsp wine vinegar	
	salt and pepper	
60 ml	heavy cream or crème fraîche*	¼ cup
	1 clove garlic, finely chopped	

To make the dressing: whisk together the lemon juice, vinegar, salt and pepper. Gradually whisk in the cream; then add the garlic. Pour the dressing over the mushrooms and mix well. Cover tightly and leave to marinate for at least 2 hours.

Meanwhile, prepare and cook the artichoke bottoms* and leave to cool; arrange them on individual plates. Taste the mushroom mixture for seasoning and heap some in the middle of each artichoke bottom. Sprinkle with chopped chives or parsley just before serving.

SALADE ROSCOVITE

Cauliflower salad

Some versions of this salad from Roscoff on the north coast include cooked, quartered artichoke bottoms and white beans, and omit the mayonnaise and shrimps.

Serves 8

	1 cucumber	
	salt	
	1 medium cauliflower	
	2 potatoes	
250 ml	mayonnaise	1 cup
	2 tsp chopped tarragon	
	1 Tbsp chopped chervil	
60 g	cooked, peeled shrimps	2 oz
	2 hard-boiled eggs, quartered	
	VINAIGRETTE	
	1 Tbsp vinegar	
	salt and pepper	
	3 Tbsp oil	

Make the vinaigrette*. Slice the cucumber thinly, put into a colander and sprinkle with salt. Leave for 20–30 minutes to draw out the juices; then rinse and pat dry.

Meanwhile, separate the cauliflower into flowerets, discarding most of the stalk. Cook in a large pot of boiling salted water for 5–8 minutes; they should still be slightly crisp. Drain well and, while the cauliflower is still warm, mix it with about two-thirds of the vinaigrette. The cauliflower will absorb the flavour as it sits.

Put the potatoes in a pot of cold salted water, bring to a boil and simmer for 15–20 minutes or until just tender. Drain, peel while hot, slice and mix at once with the remaining vinaigrette.

Just before serving, gently mix the cauliflower, potato and cucumber with the mayonnaise; taste for seasoning. Sprinkle the salad with the chopped herbs and decorate with shrimps and hard-boiled eggs.

GALETTES AND CRÊPES

'The honour of a Breton cook rests not on her ragoûts or roasts, but on her ability to make galettes to perfection,' declares one Breton cookbook. Certainly, home-made Breton 'galettes', better known as 'crêpes', lacy and crisp, are very different from the ordinary version commonly sold in plastic bags by supermarkets.

Wrapped around a hot sausage or spread with butter or jam, galettes become the bread of Brittany. They used to form the whole meal: the first galette would be crushed into broth and eaten as a 'soupe', the second spread with lightly salted butter, and the third spread with butter and sugar, or a layer of jam. Even now crêperies may add a filling of egg or a slice of ham for lunch, but not much more. A common sight at Brittany's large markets and fairs are the heavy open-air 'galettières' or griddles with the 'galettier' skilfully spreading the thin batter with his special wooden rake and spatula. His expertise makes it seem deceptively easy, for a novice working at home requires practice to achieve the same results

even with all the right equipment. The consistency, the quantity of batter, or the heat of the griddle goes wrong. There may be no secret formula to Brittany crêpes, but there is certainly a 'tour de main'.

The term galette is used more widely in French-speaking eastern Brittany, while crêpe is often heard in the Breton-speaking west, where a galette is regarded as being thicker. In general, the richest batter is made with generous quantities of milk and eggs, and uses wheat flour. Buckwheat flour, the grain of the poor, is mixed only with water, salt and a minimum of milk. Buckwheat crêpes, with their more earthy flavour, are generally used with savoury filling and wheat-flour crêpes for desserts, but this rule is often broken. It is all a matter of individual taste, of where you come from and what language you speak.

GALETTES DE SARRASIN
Buckwheat galettes

At home it is very difficult to make galettes as thin as the ones that are cooked on the special griddles found in crêperies. However, galettes can be almost as lacy and thin if you use a crêpe pan or even a heavy frying pan.

Makes 12 galettes

250 g	buckwheat flour	2 cups
260 g	all-purpose flour	2 cups
10 g	salt	2 tsp
500 ml	milk	2 cups
375 ml	water, more if needed	1½ cups
125 g	butter, clarified*	¼ lb
	1 Tbsp oil (optional – for griddle)	

23 cm/9 in crêpe pan or frying pan
or a special crêpe griddle

Sift the two flours into a large bowl and add the salt. Make well in the centre, pour in half the milk and stir it into the flour with a wooden spoon to obtain a thick and very smooth paste. Beat it well for 1–2 minutes, then add the remaining milk in two batches, beating well after each addition. Let the batter rest for 30–40 minutes. Then add the water and beat well with a wooden spoon. Add more water, if necessary, to obtain a batter of the consistency of thick cream; beat well. Add half the clarified butter and stir until no trace of it is visible.

If you are using a crêpe pan or frying pan rather than a griddle, cook the galettes as for 'crêpes sucrées au froment' (see overleaf).

If using a griddle, preheat it over a medium fire for 5–10 minutes. Pour the oil on to the griddle and rub it with a wad of paper towel. Continue to heat the griddle for 10 minutes, then test its heat with a few drops of batter; they should set at once. Again wipe the griddle with a paper towel wad. Dip the wad into the remaining clarified butter and rub it on the griddle. Ladle batter on to the centre of the hot griddle and cover it completely by spreading the batter quickly to as thin a round as possible using a traditional wooden rake or the base of the ladle. Cook the galette quickly until lightly browned on the bottom, then turn it over and lightly brown the other side. Transfer to a plate. Continue to cook the galettes, wiping the griddle clean with paper towels and rubbing it with butter as necessary to prevent sticking. During cooking, pile galettes on top of one another to keep warm. If the batter becomes too thick, stir in another tablespoon of water.

Serve the galettes with salted butter, or with one of the following fillings. The galettes should not be overcooked in the first place, as they will be reheated with the filling.

GALETTES À L'OEUF

Put a cooked galette in a frying pan over a low fire and break an **egg** in the centre. Quickly spread the egg over the galette with a spatula, leaving a border at the edge, and sprinkle with salt and pepper. Leave over the fire just long enough to cook the egg slightly, then fold the galette in four to make a square. Turn over on to a plate, put a pat of butter on top and serve hot.

Alternatively, spread only the egg white on the galette and leave the yolk whole. When served the yolk should still be soft.

GALETTES AU FROMAGE

Put a cooked galette in the frying pan over a low fire and sprinkle with ½ **Tbsp butter** and **2 Tbsp grated gruyère cheese.** Leave over the fire for a few seconds to heat the galette and melt the cheese; then fold the galette in four to form a square. Serve hot.

GALETTES AU JAMBON

Put a cooked galette in a frying pan over a low fire, sprinkle with ½ **Tbsp melted butter** and cover with a thin slice of **cooked ham.** Leave over the fire for a few seconds to heat the galette and the ham, then fold the galette in half. Put a pat of butter on top and serve hot.

GALETTES AU JAMBON, AU FROMAGE ET À L'OEUF

Put a cooked galette in a frying pan over a low fire and break an **egg** in the centre. Quickly spread the egg with a spatula, sprinkle with salt and pepper and cover with a thin slice of cooked ham. Sprinkle with ½ **Tbsp melted butter** and **2 Tbsp grated gruyère cheese.** Heat the galette for a few seconds, then fold it in half and serve it hot

GALETTES AUX SARDINES

Wipe **2 fresh sardines** to remove the scales, sprinkle lightly with salt and pepper and grill/broil them for 2 minutes on each side, or sauté them in butter in a frying pan. Alternatively, use canned sardines but don't fry them. Split the sardines and remove the centre bone. Put a cooked galette in a frying pan over a low fire, then add 1 tablespoon melted butter and the sardine fillets. Heat the galette for a few seconds, roll it up and serve hot.

GALETTES AUX SAUCISSES

Grill/broil or sauté a medium-sized **sausage** until well browned. Put a cooked galette in a frying pan over a low fire and set the sausage in the middle. Heat the galette for a few seconds, roll it up and serve hot.

CRÊPES SUCRÉES AU FROMENT
Dessert crêpes

It requires skill and practice to make crêpes as they are made in Brittany. These crêpes 'au froment' are usually filled with butter and sugar. Other additions — for crêpes 'au miel' (with honey), 'aux fruits pochés' (with poached fruit) or 'à la confiture' (with jam) — are either spread on top of the crêpe or put inside with the butter.

Makes 16 crêpes

200 g	flour	1½ cups
65 g	sugar	⅓ cup
	pinch of salt	
500 ml	milk	2 cups
	1 large egg	
250 ml	water, or more as needed	1 cup
80 g	butter, melted	5 Tbsp
	½ tsp ground cinnamon OR 1 Tbsp cognac or rum as flavouring (optional)	
80 g	butter (for frying)	5 Tbsp
	butter and sugar (for serving)	

23 cm/9 in crêpe pan or frying pan or a special crêpe griddle

Sift the flour into a bowl, make a well in the centre, and add the sugar, the salt and three-quarters of the milk. Gradually whisk in the flour to make a smooth batter. Lightly whisk in the eggs, but don't beat the batter or it will become elastic and the crêpes will become tough. Stir in the melted butter with the remaining milk and half the water. Cover and let stand for 1–2 hours. Just before using, stir in enough water to give the batter the consistency of thick cream; add any flavourings.

If you are using a crêpe pan, brush or rub it with melted butter and heat it until a drop of batter sizzles at once. Add 2–3 tablespoons of batter to the hot pan, turning the pan quickly to coat the base evenly. Cook over a fairly high fire until light brown, and then toss the crêpe or turn it with a spatula. Brown the other side and turn it on to a plate. Rub the pan with more melted butter, as necessary, to prevent sticking.

If you have a special crêpe griddle, heat it over a medium fire until thoroughly hot and cook the crêpes as for galettes (see recipe).

Don't cook crêpes with a sugar content for too long, since they scorch easily. If the first finished crêpe is thick, add a little more water to the batter. Stack the crêpes on a plate as you make them to keep them moist and warm.

To serve, put a pat of butter on each crêpe, sprinkle with sugar and fold it in four. Leave it in the hot pan for a few seconds to melt the butter, and serve hot.

FARS AND PORRIDGES

As if to testify to its former isolation, Brittany has retained a taste for the outmoded puddings and porridges known in Breton as 'fars'. These include: 'far platt', a sweet batter with raisins, baked in the oven; and 'far en pochon', a pudding of flour, eggs, sugar and raisins that is simmered and eaten with vegetables, soup and bacon (very much like 'kig-ha-farz'). Most famous of all is 'far breton', which resembles a Yorkshire pudding flavoured with prunes or raisins, and is baked in a shallow dish so that the crust is crisp. All fars are substantial fare, calling for a hearty country appetite.

FAR BRETON
Prune flan

Dark raisins often replace the prunes in 'far breton', making 'far aux raisins'. Soak them in the rum for 30 minutes, drain them well and use the fruit and the rum as in this recipe.

Serves 6

125 g	prunes	4 oz
100 g	flour	¾ cup
500 ml	milk	2 cups
135 g	sugar	⅔ cup
	2 eggs	
	1–1½ Tbsp rum	

shallow baking dish (2 L/2 qt capacity)

Soak the prunes in a bowl of hot water for 2 hours or until soft; then drain them. Butter a baking dish thoroughly and spread the fruit in the baking dish. Set the oven at moderate (175°C/350°F).

Sift the flour into a bowl and make a well in the centre. Add the milk to the well and lightly whisk in the flour until just mixed. Strain if there are any lumps. Add the sugar, eggs and rum and stir to make a smooth batter. Pour the batter over the fruit and bake in the heated oven for 1½ hours or until well browned and dry when tested with a skewer. Cut the 'far' like a pie into wedges or into squares. Serve in the dish, lukewarm or at room temperature.

OMELETTE AUX POMMES
Apple omelette

This dessert is popular throughout Brittany and Normandy – both apple country. To serve six people, double the quantity of filling and make two omelettes, rather than trying to make a single large one which would be difficult to cook and fold. To make 'omelette aux pommes flambée' flame the filled omelette with calvados.

Serves 3

	2 dessert apples	
30 g	butter	2 Tbsp
40 g	sugar	3 Tbsp
	1½ Tbsp heavy cream (optional)	
	1 Tbsp calvados	
	4 eggs	
	pinch of salt	
	confectioners' sugar (for sprinkling)	
	25 cm/10 in omelette pan	

Peel and core the apples and cut them in thin slices. Heat half the butter in a frying pan, add the apple slices and sauté over a medium fire, stirring often, for 10 minutes or until tender but not falling apart. Sprinkle with sugar and continue to sauté the apples until lightly caramelized. Stir in the cream and calvados.

Beat the eggs, salt and remaining sugar until thoroughly mixed. Melt the remaining butter in an omelette pan over a medium fire, add the eggs and stir with a fork for a few seconds until they start to thicken. Stop stirring and let the omelette continue to cook, pulling the cooked egg from the sides of the pan to the centre with the flat of the fork and tipping the pan occasionally to pour uncooked egg to the sides. When the eggs are lightly set, spoon the apple filling on top, fold the omelette and slide it on to a buttered, flameproof platter. Sprinkle the omelette with sugar and glaze a few seconds under the grill/broiler.

TARTE AUX FIGUES FRAÎCHES
Fresh fig tart

Fig trees thrive in Brittany's temperate climate. Roscoff has a great fig tree planted in 1625 by Capuchin friars; it covers about 600 square metres and has been known to produce several hundred kilos of figs in a single year.

Serves 8

1 kg	fresh figs, peeled	2 lb
125 ml	red currant jelly (for glaze)	½ cup
	SWEET PIE PASTRY	
200 g	flour	1½ cups
2 g	salt	½ tsp
100 g	sugar	½ cup
	4 egg yolks	
	1 tsp vanilla extract	
125 g	butter	¼ lb
	POACHING SYRUP	
250 g	sugar	1¼ cups
1 L	red wine	1 qt
	pared rind of ½ lemon	
	28–30 cm/11–12 in tart pan	

Make the sweet pie pastry* and chill for 30 minutes. Set the oven at hot (200°C/400°F). Roll out the dough, line the tart pan* and blind bake* for 20–25 minutes or until completely cooked. (Don't let sweet pie pastry brown too much or it will be unpleasantly bitter.) Let the shell cool slightly in the pan before unmoulding, then transfer it to a rack to cool.

To make the poaching syrup: heat the sugar, wine and lemon rind in a medium pot until the sugar is dissolved. Bring the syrup to a boil and add the peeled figs. Bring the syrup back to a boil, lower the heat and poach the figs gently for 15–20 minutes or until they are slightly transparent and just tender, but still retain their shape. Let them cool in their syrup.

When the figs are cool, remove them carefully from the syrup and leave to drain. Make a glaze by boiling the syrup vigorously until it is reduced to about 250 ml. Discard the lemon rind. Stir in the red currant jelly and heat until the jelly is dissolved. Brush the bottom of the pie shell with glaze, arrange the whole figs on top and brush them with the remaining glaze. Serve at room temperature.

KOUIGN-AMAN
Yeast feuilleté with butter

Kouign-aman, a Breton version of puff pastry layered with sugar, is not easy to make. The gluten in the flour must not be developed, so the dough must be worked quickly and lightly, with generous rest between rollings, especially with US flour. But even if the dough is not perfect, kouign-aman always tastes good.

Serves 8

185 g	butter	6 oz
150 g	sugar	¾ cup
	sugar (for sprinkling)	
	YEAST DOUGH	
15 g	fresh yeast OR	1 cake
	1 pkg dry yeast	
200 g	all-purpose flour	1½ cups
60 g	cake flour	½ cup
185 ml	lukewarm water, or more	¾ cup
	as needed	
10 g	salt	2 tsp
	1 tsp sugar	
two 24 cm/9½ in layer pans or moules à manqué		

To make the yeast dough: dissolve the yeast in the water. In a large bowl mix the flour with the salt and teaspoon of sugar. Make a well in the centre, add the dissolved yeast and gradually mix in the flour, using one hand. If necessary, add more water to give a dough that is quite soft but does not stick to your hand. Continue to mix just until smooth, turning the dough over on to itself without kneading. Form a rough ball (as in making puff pastry*) and sprinkle with flour. Cover the dough and let rise in a warm place for 45 minutes. Then chill it in the refrigerator for 2 hours.

As in making puff pastry, pound on the butter to soften it. Roll out the yeast dough on a floured surface to a 30 cm/12 in square, set the butter in the middle and fold the dough around it. Chill for 1 hour. Do one 'turn' as in making puff pastry, then chill for another hour. Do a second turn and chill for an hour.

For the third turn, roll out the dough to a 30 × 45 cm/12 × 8 in rectangle and sprinkle about half the measured sugar down the centre. Fold the dough in three as in puff pastry. Chill for 1 hour. For the fourth turn, place the dough lengthwise and again roll it out to a rectangle. Sprinkle the remaining sugar down the centre, pressing it on to the dough with the rolling pin. Again, fold in three as for a business letter. Chill for 30 minutes. Thickly butter the pans.

Divide the dough into two squares and roll out each piece on a floured surface to a round the diameter of the pans. Set the rounds in the buttered pans, cover and let rise for 1 hour in a slightly warm place. If the butter appears to be leaking from the dough, move the pans to a slightly cooler place. Meanwhile set the oven at hot (200°C/400°F).

When the cakes have risen slightly in the pans, sprinkle them with a little sugar and bake for about 35 minutes or until golden brown and puffed. Unmould the cakes while hot and serve lukewarm.

GÂTEAU BRETON
Butter cake

The same recipe produces either a single round 'gâteau breton' or 18–20 individual 'petits gâteaux bretons'.

Serves 8

	6 egg yolks	
225 g	flour	1¾ cups
250 g	butter	½ lb
250 g	sugar	1¼ cups
23–25 cm/9–10 in springform pan or		
moule à manqué		

Set the oven at moderately hot (190°C/375°F). Thoroughly butter the cake pan. Set aside a teaspoon of the egg yolks for glazing.

Sift the flour on to a marble slab or board and make a large well in the centre. Cut the butter in small pieces and put it in the well with the sugar and egg yolks; work them together with your fingertips until the mixture is smooth. Gradually incorporate the flour using the fingers and heel of your hand, and then work the dough gently until smooth. It will be rather sticky at this point and must be mixed with the help of a metal spatula.

Transfer the dough to the buttered pan and smooth it to an even layer, flouring the back of your hand to prevent sticking. Brush the surface of the gâteau with the reserved egg yolk and mark a lattice design with a fork.

Bake in the heated oven for 20 minutes, then lower the heat to moderate (175°C/350°F) and continue baking for 30 more minutes or until the cake is golden and firm to the touch. Leave it to cool, then unmould carefully on to a rack.

PETITS GÂTEAUX BRETONS

To make the mixture into small round cakes about 5 cm/2 in across, divide the dough into 18–20 pieces, roll into balls on a floured board and flatten them into bun or cupcake pans, using the back of a fork. Brush with egg glaze, mark with a lattice design and bake in a moderately hot oven (190°C/375°F) for 20 minutes or until golden. Leave the cakes to cool in the pans before turning them out.

CHEESES

Breton independence of things French shows yet again in a local indifference, not to say scorn, for cheese. Old books quite often call it 'lait pourri' or rotten milk, and until the 1940s the Breton word 'formaj' did not even denote milk cheese, but suggested a kind of meat pâté.

Cheese-making never caught on here, partly because along the south coast salt pans yielded abundant salt to preserve the excellent Breton butter. From making butter, Bretons acquired a taste for buttermilk, and for farmers' cheeses and curd which are eaten very fresh, such as 'crémet nantais', an unsalted cheese with a creamy flavour, often served with whipped cream. 'Mingaux' from Rennes, are made of sweet and sour cream that is beaten thick, and served with fruit or crêpes and sugar. In fact 'fromage nantais', with its strong smell and pronounced flavour, is Brittany's only aged cheese; it is also called 'fromage du curé' because, like so many cheeses, it was developed by a priest

SPECIALITIES OF THE REGION
OTHER TRADITIONAL DISHES

Soupe aux moules St Brieuc
Mussel and sorrel soup

St Pierre brestoise
John Dory with shrimps, shallots and mussels

Soupe de sardines Douarnenez
Sardine and potato soup

Ragoût de mouton au kunpod
Mutton stew with raisin dumplings

Nominoë
Soup with chestnuts, egg yolks and cream

Porché de Dol
Stew of pig's ears and feet

Sole Rochebonne
Sole with mushrooms and artichoke purée

Bardatte nantaise
Cabbage stuffed with rabbit

Omelette de civelles
Baby-eel omelette

Ragoût bigoudin
Stew of sausages, cabbage, carrots and onions

Thon Concarneau
Tuna with carrots and peas

Biguénée
Slice of ham between two pancakes

Pain de maquereau Quiberon
Hot mackerel and potato loaf

Pommes bigoudin
Crusty potato cake

CHARCUTERIE

Andouilles de Guéméné-sur-Scorff
Smoked chitterling sausages

Pâté de haricots rouges
Sausage and red bean pâté

Jambon de Morlaix
Smoked cooked ham

Caillettes de Cornouaille
Sausage meatballs with a spicy sauce

PÂTISSERIE AND CONFISERIE

Sablés bretons
Butter biscuits

Crêpes dentelles
Wafer-thin rolled crêpes

La Pommée bretonne
Apples baked in crêpe batter sprinkled with crushed macaroons

Gelée de pommes
Apple jelly

The Southwest

Southwestern France is united more by its past than by its present. Its boundaries run close to those of the ancient dukedom of Aquitaine, brought to the English crown when Eleanor of Aquitaine was divorced from the French King Louis VII and married Henry II in 1152. The capital Bordeaux then ranked as the fourth city of England, after London, York and Winchester, lending it a cosmopolitan outlook and prosperity that have lasted to the present day. Its fine buildings still reflect the wealth and taste of its local merchants: 'Take Versailles, add Antwerp to it and you have Bordeaux,' quipped Victor Hugo.

Bordeaux maintains a lower profile than its close rival Lyon, but in many ways it is the equal of the so-called gastronomic capital of France. To both cities wine has brought the money and the appreciation needed to foster fine cooking. 'Entrecôte bordelaise', with its red wine sauce and garnish of bone marrow, can easily compete with the 'boeuf bourguignon' of Lyon and I, for one, would wish for a creamy 'mouclade' of Atlantic mussels rather than the 'matelote' fish stews of the Rhône. And Bordeaux has its St Émilion chocolate charlotte to match the celebrated chocolate gâteaux of Lyon.

Bordeaux, like Lyon, can draw upon a marvellous variety of fish, flesh and produce from the surrounding countryside. Visiting Bordeaux in 1953, writer Cyril Connolly was carried away: 'Pyramids of Dublin Bay prawns, lobsters, langoustes, sole and skate vie in the market with more unusual fish: lamprey, sturgeon, huge red chapons and enormous shad. Salt-marsh mutton, butter, cheese, ortolans and palombes from the Landes lead us on to the fruit and vegetable section, as fine as anywhere in the world.'

Ortolans, or bunting, were once the pride of the Landes, the area that lies, in a very literal sense, to the south of Bordeaux. On its flat and marshy ground the locals used to stand on stilts (the better to survey their flocks) while knitting woollen socks by the hour. Today ranks of pine trees block the view to the coastline fretted with lagoons which are natural nurseries for scallops, for Connolly's Dublin Bay prawns (also called scampi), for slippery little sole known locally as 'lawyer's tongues' and, most importantly, for oysters. Nestling in the immense, shallow bay of Arcachon, they take three years to grow to a saleable size.

Most of them are portugaises, valued more for their sturdy growth than for their flavour, which may be the reason why the Bordelais eat oysters with little sausages as well as the customary white wine.

Bordeaux does not lack for luxuries besides oysters. Early this century, Russian refugees taught local fishermen how to salt the roe of the Gironde sturgeon to make caviar comparable with the Russian 'sevruga'. Now the supply has dwindled, but at one time it was enough to supply the famous Restaurant Prunier in Paris. And a bare 80 kilometres to the east of Bordeaux is Périgord, source of most French truffles and of another great delicacy – foie gras.

River valleys apart, much of Périgord is a disappointment scenically. Bleak and stony, the uplands are covered with scrubby oaks, fosterparents to the truffle fungus. Of the foie gras geese there is little sign, for they are cosseted indoors, so no exercise can work off the effects of their copious meals. I am sure it is wishful thinking, but when I saw geese being force-fed they seemed to enjoy it, crowding around their master in an effort to be first in the queue.

One chilly day in Cahors – one of a dozen foie gras towns in Périgord and Quercy – I visited the Saturday market, where stallholders, wreathed in shawls and scarves, were keeping a sharp eye on rows of glistening goose livers ranging in colour from yellow ochre to baby pink (colour is no indication of quality). Less closely surveyed were the left-overs – the necks for stuffing and carcasses, giblets and feet for soup. 'The goose is a kind of hot-house, nurturing the ultimate in gastronomy,' said one admirer.

Certainly nothing is wasted. The meat of these force-fed birds goes into confit, a method of preserving that extracts much of the natural fat. This in turn is invaluable for making pastries and frying dishes like crisp potatoes sarladaise, perfumed with garlic or truffles and the ideal complement to goose confit. Just lately, foie gras of duck has become popular, with more and more of the boned breast meat being sold as 'magrets'. In effect duck steaks, magrets are fried or grilled just like beef, and served with the same red wine sauces. A Périgord speciality with magret is 'sauce aillade' of garlic, walnuts and walnut oil.

Périgord is also known for pâtés: pâtés of game and pâtés of poultry that in the old days were crammed with truffles. In all but the grandest of modern recipes these have disappeared, to be replaced by pistachios, hazelnuts and occasionally by walnuts, a local crop whose importance dates back at least to the 17th century. In Sarlat there is a charming 'Place aux Noix' where they used to be sold. Here and in Quercy to the south, walnuts are made into liqueur, preserved in armagnac or, most often, crushed for oil.

The name 'Quercy' is related to the word 'causses', the stony uplands so typical of Languedoc. In both regions, most activity is found in the river valleys that cut through the plateaux – the Dordogne in Périgord, the Lot in Quercy and the Garonne at the northern limit of Gascony. As the Garonne runs down to Bordeaux, the concentration of fruit trees in the 'vallée heureuse' is astonishing, many of them espaliered in military formation. Instead of the usual 'route des vins', signs point temptingly to a 'route des prunes'. Approaching Agen, the prune capital of France, the September air is sweet with the vanilla of drying plums.

The semicircle surrounding Bordeaux is completed by the splendid dairy country of Charente (also the home of the Charentais melon). Endowed with the sunniest coast on the Atlantic, Charente produces prime butter from pastures sown to replace vineyards destroyed by the phylloxera blight nearly a hundred years ago. The produce of the surviving vineyards has become a household word – cognac. At first sight I found the black buildings of Cognac forbidding – their colour comes from the fumes of evaporating brandy, but this morbid effect was quickly dissipated by the evident bustle of the famous houses which maintain ostentatious salerooms on the main roads. I preferred the dusty shop in the side street, crammed with cognacs of brands on their way to extinction where 'Pineau des Charentes', the cognac-based aperitif of the region, was proffered.

From the Landes, from Périgord, Quercy and Charente, all roads lead to Bordeaux. Not so with Poitou and the Vendée further north, which look more towards the Loire. Like Brittany, its peninsular neighbour, the Vendée is rural with a tradition of resistance to change. Its inhabitants share with the Charentais a taste for hearty food – 'ventrachous' (cabbage-eaters) they are disparagingly called. Besides good grazing, the Vendée and Poitou have an abundance of one much-appreciated product: goat's milk for making cheese.

Handy for Paris markets, Poitou is known for foods as varied as 'jaunes de Poitou' (leeks), game birds and hare. One Poitou curiosity is candied angelica, made from the sweet-smelling stalks of a medicinal plant and used in small quantities for decorating desserts. Much more to my, and most, tastes is the salt-marsh lamb of Poitou, celebrated for being the first of the season. It is raised in the Marais, the 'green Venice' area reclaimed from the sea where cows are perambulated in barges from pasture to pasture and frogs find a natural home among the fruits and vegetables of this fertile land. So mild flavoured is the baby lamb that it should be roasted only with butter and seasoning, then enjoyed with a bottle of fine red Bordeaux wine. Lamb needs to be a month or two old before it can be cooked with the favourite Poitou flavouring of garlic to which the locals are as addicted as the Marseillais.

The range of Bordeaux wines is enormous and a red or white can be found to accompany almost every dish. Equally broad-based is the cooking. Perhaps the greatest compliment to be paid to southwestern cuisine is that it means so many things. 'Bordelaise' is inseparable from red and white wine sauces, but it can also refer to wild mushrooms or a seasoning of garlic, shallot and parsley. Another half-dozen southwestern designations – Landaise, Périgourdine, Sarladaise, Charentaise, Vendéenne – are also part of the classical cook's repertoire. 'Great cooking and great wines,' declared King Henri IV, a celebrated gourmand who fought the English obstinately for Aquitaine, 'it is a paradise on earth.'

TERRINE DE BOEUF PAYSANNE

Beef terrine with herbs and ham

For this unusual terrine of beef, use a lean cut such as topside or silverside in Britain or top or bottom round roast in the USA. The meat is cut in strips rather than minced/ground, and the terrine is flavoured with ham and plenty of fresh herbs.

Serves 6–8

500 g	lean beef	1 lb
300 g	cooked ham	10 oz
300-g	piece of bacon	10-oz
	salt and pepper	
	1 tsp ground allspice	
125 ml	chopped parsley	½ cup
	2 Tbsp chopped herbs:	
	chives, chervil and tarragon	
	2 bay leaves, crumbled	
	2 cloves garlic, chopped	
	3 Tbsp armagnac or cognac	
	2 Tbsp water or broth	
	1 L/1 qt terrine with lid	

Set the oven at moderate (175°C/350°F). Cut the beef, ham and bacon in thin strips and put a layer of each in the terrine, beginning with the bacon and ending with the beef. Sprinkle the beef with very little salt (since the bacon is salty), and with some pepper, allspice, parsley, herbs, bay leaves, garlic and armagnac. Continue to fill the terrine by layering the meats in the above order and sprinkling them with the flavourings. Sprinkle any remaining flavourings on top and pour the water over them. Cover tightly. Bake the terrine in a water bath as for 'terrine de gibier' (right). Press and refrigerate the terrine at least 3 days before serving.

Serve from the mould, slicing the terrine carefully so it does not crumble.

TERRINE DE GIBIER

Game terrine

Game terrine is a speciality of Périgord and almost any kind of game can be used in this recipe – partridge, hare, venison, wild duck, rabbit, or the pheasant that is suggested.

Serves 12

1-kg	pheasant, with its liver	2-lb
150 g	veal escalope	5 oz
100 g	raw ham	4 oz
80 ml	cognac	⅓ cup
250 g	fatback or barding fat, thinly sliced	½ lb
250 g	lean pork	½ lb
250 g	pork fat	½ lb
250 g	lean veal	½ lb
	2 chicken livers	
	3 shallots, finely chopped	
	1 truffle, chopped, with liquid reserved (optional)	
	pinch of ground allspice	
	pinch of ground cloves	
	salt and pepper	
	1 bay leaf	
	1 sprig of thyme	
	luting paste*	
	1·5 L/1½ qt terrine with lid	

Cut the meat from the pheasant, discarding the skin and keeping the breast and leg meat in pieces as neat as possible; cut in thin strips. Cut the veal escalope and ham in thin strips also. Put the strips on a plate, add the cognac, cover and leave to marinate for at least 1 and up to 8 hours in the refrigerator.

Line the terrine with barding fat, reserving a few slices for the top. Set the oven at moderate (175°C/350°F). Work the bits of pheasant meat with the lean and fat pork, lean veal, chicken

---

SMALL BIRDS

It can be hard to share the French taste for little birds, whether they have been concealed in a pâté, like the larks of Pithiviers in the Orléanais, or are served unashamedly in full view on a croûte of bread. They are generally roasted with their innards, and a short time at a very high temperature is enough to sear them, leaving the meat still pink; tradition has it that they should 'fly through the oven'.

The French idea of fair game stretches a bit far for some tastes: sandpipers and oystercatchers are at risk on beaches, as well as sparrows, thrushes and blackbirds in the open country. More recherché are 'ortolans' (bunting), 'bécasses' (woodcock) or 'bec-figues' (fig-peckers), of which the Roman emperor Albinus was said to have

eaten a hundred at a sitting. Today a generous helping is two or three. Most small birds are netted, since shot damages their frail bodies and often they are specially fattened for the table, quadrupling their weight within a month. After this régime, a plump ortolan must be plucked over ice, otherwise it literally melts into fat.

In the Pyrenees, 'palombe' or 'ramier' (wood pigeon), caught during the spring or autumn migration, is popular. A wooden disc is spun high in the air so that the birds, mistaking it for a hawk, fly low for shelter into nets waiting to snare them. Wood pigeon is very different from bunting; dark and tough, it can need as long as five hours' simmering in a rich 'salmis' stew.

livers and the pheasant liver twice through the fine plate of a mincer/grinder. Beat in the shallots, truffle and its liquid, allspice, cloves, salt and pepper. Drain the meat strips and beat the cognac marinade into the minced/ground meat mixture. Sauté a small piece and taste it for seasoning – it should be quite highly seasoned, but remember that the ham will be salty.

Spread a quarter of the meat mixture in the lined terrine and top with a layer of pheasant and veal strips, pushing them down lightly into the minced/ground meat and making sure the strips do not touch the sides of the terrine. Spread them with another quarter of the meat mixture and top with a layer of ham strips. Spread half the remaining mixture on top, add another layer of pheasant and veal strips and cover with the remaining mixture, taking care that the terrine is tightly packed. Set the reserved slices of barding fat on top with the bay leaf and thyme. Cover with the lid. Use the luting paste to seal the gap between the mould and the lid.

Set the terrine in a water bath, bring the water to a boil and put it in the oven. Bake for $1\frac{1}{4}$–$1\frac{1}{2}$ hours or until a skewer inserted for 30 seconds into the mixture through the hole in the terrine is hot to the touch when withdrawn. While the terrine bakes, adjust the oven heat so the water keeps simmering; if too much water evaporates, add more. Let the terrine cool until tepid. Remove the luting paste and lid and press the terrine with a board or plate with a 1 kg/2 lb weight on top until cold.

Keep the terrine in the refrigerator for at least 3 days to allow the flavour to mellow before serving. Unmould the terrine, cut part of it in thick slices and arrange them overlapping on a platter. Alternatively, serve in the mould.

French cooking literature is full of horror stories about little birds. Lucien Tendret reported from the Dauphiné at the turn of the century, 'When sportsmen go out shooting in September, they are also provided with pepper and salt and if one of them kills a very fat bec-figue he plucks it, seasons it, carries it for some time outside his hat and eats it. I have been told that a bird, cooked in this way, tastes even better than if roasted.' In Gascony and the Landes it was the custom to feed ortolans on an ever more concentrated diet of armagnac to soften their bones; even more macabre, it was discovered that the birds could be fattened faster if they were blinded so that their attention did not wander from the matter in hand – eating.

SAUCE AILLADE
Garlic and walnut sauce

'Aillade' signals garlic, which here is used with walnuts and walnut oil to make an emulsified sauce on the lines of mayonnaise. Traditionally served with grilled/broiled breast of duck, sauce aillade is good with any of the same foods as 'sauce brique rose' of Languedoc.

Makes 300 ml/1¼ cups of sauce

80 g	walnut halves	⅔ cup
	4 cloves garlic	
	2 Tbsp cold water	
	salt and pepper	
250 ml	walnut oil	1 cup
	1 Tbsp chopped parsley	

Using a mortar and pestle, pound the walnut halves and garlic, adding the water gradually as you work to make a smooth paste. Season with a little salt and pepper. Add the oil a drop at a time, still pounding with the pestle. When the mixture begins to thicken, the oil can be added more quickly.

Alternatively, purée the walnut halves, garlic and water in a food processor or blender. With the blades still turning, gradually add the oil.

Taste the sauce for seasoning and stir in the chopped parsley.

SAUCE PÉRIGUEUX
Truffle sauce

This country cousin of the classic truffle sauce Périgueux is excellent with steak, roast beef or lamb. For extra flavour, dissolve the pan juices with a little broth, skim and add to the sauce.

Makes 500 ml/2 cups sauce

30 g	goose fat, lard or butter	2 Tbsp
	3 shallots, chopped	
	1 onion, sliced	
15 g	flour	2 Tbsp
750 ml	dry white wine, preferably graves	3 cups
1 L	well-flavoured broth	1 qt
	salt and pepper	
30–60 g	truffles (1–2 small cans)	1–2 oz

In a heavy pot heat the fat, stir in the shallots and onion and cook over a low fire until soft but not brown. Stir in the flour and cook over a low fire, stirring constantly until just beginning to brown. Stir in the wine, broth and a little salt and pepper. Bring to a boil and simmer uncovered, stirring occasionally, for 1 hour or until reduced by half. Strain into a clean pot. Stir in the truffle juice and cut the truffles in thin slices. Add the slices and simmer for 2–3 minutes. Taste for seasoning and serve hot.

LA CHAUDRÉE
Fish chowder

'Chaudrée' means the portion of fish which could be packed in a 'chaudière' (cauldron) allotted to the captain and crew of a fishing boat. One of the great specialities of Charente, this fish chowder is as important there as bouillabaisse in Provence. Like bouillabaisse, it is a whole meal and there are many versions, from a simple soup of fish boiled in white wine with garlic, to this chaudrée from the port of Fouras which should contain plenty of butter and a variety of fish such as sole, whiting, eel and hake. The Vendée version adds potatoes, cooked whole or cut in pieces, to the fish.

Serves 4–6

125 g	butter	¼ lb
	2 onions, quartered and studded with 2 cloves	
	5 cloves garlic, chopped	
	1 large bouquet garni	
1·5 kg	sea fish	3 lb
500 ml	dry white wine, preferably muscadet	2 cups
1 L	water, more if needed	1 qt
	8–12 round croûtes*, toasted in the oven or fried in butter, then rubbed with garlic	

Put half the butter in a heavy pot with the onions, garlic and bouquet garni. Scale and clean the fish, discarding fins, heads and tails and cut in large chunks (about 7·5 cm/3 in long). Wash the fish.

Add the fish to the pot; if using eel, put it at the bottom of the pot so it cooks more quickly than the other fish above it. Pour in the white wine and add enough water to come just to the top of the fish. Add salt and pepper, bring to a boil, skimming often. Simmer over a low fire for 10 minutes or until the fish are just tender. Discard the bouquet garni and the cloves, leaving the onion quarters.

Arrange the fish in a deep serving dish and keep warm. Taste the broth and boil it for 20–25 minutes to reduce until well flavoured. Add the remaining butter and cook over a low fire for 2–3 more minutes. Taste the broth for seasoning and pour it over the fish. Put the croûtes around the edge of the dish and serve immediately.

COLIN AUX CREVETTES ET AUX CÈPES
Hake with shrimps and wild mushrooms

Hake is popular all along the west coast. In the Basque country it is known as 'merlu' rather than 'colin', and is prepared more simply than in this recipe – which combines it with shrimps, cèpes and a rich butter sauce resembling béarnaise.

Serves 4

250 g	fresh cèpes OR	½ lb
25 g	dried cèpes	1 oz
1 kg	hake, cut in 4 steaks 2·5 cm/1 in thick	2 lb
30 g	butter	2 Tbsp
	1 Tbsp oil	
	½ clove garlic, chopped	
	1 shallot, chopped	
	1 tsp chopped parsley	
	1 tsp chopped tarragon	
	salt and pepper	
	20 medium shrimps	
50 g	grated gruyère cheese	½ cup
COURT BOUILLON		
250 ml	water	1 cup
250 ml	dry white wine	1 cup
	1 onion, sliced	
	½ bulb fennel, sliced	
	bouquet garni	
	pinch of saffron strands, steeped in 1–2 Tbsp boiling water	
	salt and pepper	
BUTTER SAUCE		
80 ml	dry white wine	⅓ cup
80 ml	vinegar	⅓ cup
	6 black peppercorns, crushed	
	½ clove garlic, crushed	
	2 shallots, chopped	
	4 egg yolks	
125 g	butter	¼ lb
	2 Tbsp tomato paste	
	2 tsp chopped tarragon	
	2 Tbsp chopped parsley	
	salt and pepper	

Prepare fresh or dried cèpes*. Wash and dry the hake.

Meanwhile, make the court bouillon by putting all the ingredients in a pot and simmering them for 20 minutes. Add the hake and poach for 10 minutes or until nearly tender. Transfer the fish and a little of the court bouillon to a shallow dish, cover and keep warm. Reserve the remaining court bouillon.

Cut fresh or dried cèpes in slices. Heat the butter and oil in a frying pan and add the garlic, shallot, parsley, tarragon and cèpes. Cook over a low fire for 10 minutes, stirring often. Raise the heat and cook over a high fire, tossing often, for another 10 minutes or until tender and the moisture has evaporated. Season with salt and pepper.

Cook the shrimps in boiling salted water for 2–3 minutes, drain and peel.

Make the butter sauce: put the wine, vinegar, peppercorns, garlic and shallots in a heavy saucepan and boil until about 2 tablespoons of liquid remain. Add 4 tablespoons of the reserved court bouillon and strain the mixture, pressing hard. Return the liquid to the saucepan and boil until about 2 tablespoons of liquid remain. Let cool slightly; then add the egg yolks and whisk constantly over low heat until the sauce thickens and the whisk leaves a visible trail on the base of the pan. With the pan still over low heat, vigorously whisk in the butter a piece at a time. Remove from the heat and whisk in the tomato paste. Stir in the shrimps, tarragon, parsley and salt and pepper to taste. Keep warm in a water bath while finishing the preparation of the fish.

Set the oven at very hot (220°C/425°F). Drain the fish and remove the skin. Put the cèpes in a buttered shallow baking dish and lay the fish steaks on top. Sprinkle them with grated cheese and bake in the oven for 10–12 minutes or until browned. Serve immediately, passing the sauce separately.

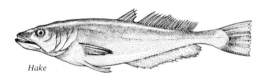

Hake

CABILLAUD À LA BORDELAISE
Baked cod with tomato and onion

Any white fish steaks can be baked with a tomato and onion purée like the cod here.

Serves 6

	6 cod steaks, 2·5 cm/1 in thick	
125 ml	oil	½ cup
	3 shallots, finely chopped	
65 g	flour	½ cup
50 g	grated gruyère cheese	½ cup
	3 Tbsp dried breadcrumbs	
	MARINADE	
	salt and pepper	
	1 onion, sliced	
	a few parsley stems	
	1 sprig of thyme	
	1 bay leaf	
250 ml	dry white wine, preferably bordeaux	1 cup
	2 Tbsp oil	
	TOMATO AND ONION PURÉE	
	3 Tbsp oil	
	2 onions, finely chopped	
500 g	tomatoes, peeled, seeded and finely chopped	1 lb
	1 clove garlic, chopped	
	salt and pepper	
	pinch of sugar	

Wash and dry the fish and marinate it: season the steaks with salt and pepper and put them in a shallow dish. Sprinkle with the sliced onion, parsley, thyme and bay leaf. Pour the wine over the fish, then the oil. Marinate for 45 minutes.

Meanwhile, prepare the tomato and onion purée: heat the oil in a frying pan, add the onions and cook over a low fire, stirring, until soft but not brown. Add the other purée ingredients and cook over a medium fire, stirring until the purée just falls from a spoon.

Drain the fish steaks, reserving the marinade, and dry them thoroughly on paper towels. Strain the marinade into the purée, boil to reduce by half and taste for seasoning. Set the oven at very hot (220°C/425°F).

Brush the fish steaks with 2 tablespoons of the oil and sprinkle both sides with chopped shallots. Coat them with flour on both sides, patting off the excess. Heat all but a tablespoon of the remaining oil in a frying pan until very hot. Brown the steaks on both sides over a high fire, but do not cook them completely.

Put the fish steaks in an oiled shallow baking dish and cover with the tomato and onion purée. Sprinkle with the grated cheese and the breadcrumbs, then with the remaining oil. Bake for 10 minutes or until the fish is tender and the cheese golden brown. Serve immediately from the dish.

OYSTERS

Oysters are curious creatures. There are two main kinds, flat and hollow, which will destroy each other if they live in the same bed. They also lead quite different sex lives. Flat oysters, regarded as the finest in flavour, are 'alternating hermaphrodites' which change sex to breed. The famous flat 'belons', originally from Rieuc-sur-Belon in southern Brittany, start life as spat, growing on tiles in the warm waters of the Gulf of Morbihan. Most hollow oysters, ('portugaises' and 'japonaises' are the common varieties) are bred in Japan or British Columbia. At six months both hollow and flat are transplanted, some to the bracing waters of northern Brittany, some to Bordeaux and some as far afield as Britain and Holland. Estuaries are ideal nurseries, for oysters flourish in sea water of low salinity, and after three or four years, first attached to tiles, then lying on frames in muddy 'parks', oysters are ready to eat.

Once removed from the water, an oyster is remarkably hardy, surviving a month or more if kept cool and moist. Louis XIV had convoys of oysters sent to Versailles, usually the giant 'pieds de cheval' (horse's feet), which are now uneconomic to exploit because of transport costs.

Advice on how to open oysters is varied, but it is wise to use a short stubby knife. Most authorities recommend tackling the hinge end first, wedging the knife between the shells. Surprise is the key to success – once the oyster tightens its muscle, it is doubly hard to prise open. A rotten oyster is easy to recognize from its appearance and smell, but the only protection against polluted oysters is to buy them from a reliable source.

Oysters acquire their taste from their habitat; the oysters of Marennes, north of Bordeaux, for instance, are greenish with an outstanding flavour due to algae in the water of the oyster beds. Today Arcachon oysters are exported all over Europe.

A platter of mixed oysters, 'claires' (the most delicate), portugaises (rough but with plenty of juice) and belons (the best of all), served with a fragrant glass of dry white wine, is a rare treat.

Oyster beds at Marennes

LA MOUCLADE VENDÉENNE
Mussel stew with saffron and cream

Tradition has it that the farming of mussels in the Vendée dates back to 1237, when an Irish skipper, Patrick Walton, was shipwrecked on the coast. He managed to swim ashore and began to hunt and fish. Soon the sticks supporting the nets of his bird-trap were covered with huge mussels, much larger than those growing on the rocks. Mussels are still cultivated in the same way. 'Moucle' is the local name for mussel, and mouclade draws on the best local ingredients: butter, cream, cognac and spices brought to La Rochelle from the Orient: saffron, cayenne pepper or curry powder. Recipes vary greatly: some use no cream, and one version based on onions and garlic has no spices at all.

Serves 4

4 L	mussels	4 qt
80 g	butter	5 Tbsp
500 g	onions, chopped	1 lb
	1 clove garlic, chopped	
125 ml	dry white wine, preferably gros plant	½ cup
	2 Tbsp cognac	
	pinch of saffron strands, steeped in 1–2 Tbsp boiling water	
	pinch of cayenne pepper	
	½ tsp curry powder	
	salt and pepper	
	1½ Tbsp flour	
125 ml	heavy cream or crème fraîche*	½ cup

Clean the mussels* and put them in a large pot. Cover and cook dry over a high fire, stirring occasionally, for 5–7 minutes or until they open. Discard the top shell of each and transfer the mussels to a deep serving dish, reserving the liquid. Cover the mussels and keep them warm.

Heat half the butter in a frying pan, add the onions and cook over a low fire, stirring, until soft but not brown. Then raise the heat and brown them lightly. Stir in the garlic and cook another 30 seconds; pour in the wine and cognac and flame them. Add the saffron with its liquid, the spices and pepper. Slowly pour in the mussel liquid, leaving behind any grit. Boil to reduce for 1 minute or until well flavoured.

Mix the remaining butter and the flour to a paste, forming a rich kneaded butter*.

Just before serving, heat the sauce and stir in the cream. Bring to a boil and whisk in the kneaded butter, a little at a time, until the sauce thickly coats a spoon. Simmer for 1–2 minutes and taste for seasoning: extra salt may not be needed, since the mussels are salty. Strain the sauce over the mussels and serve immediately.

COQUILLES ST JACQUES À LA BORDELAISE
Sautéed scallops with shallots and parsley

In Bordeaux scallops are cooked with the customary shallots and butter. In Mediterranean France the addition of one or two finely chopped cloves of garlic makes this dish 'coquilles St Jacques à la provençale'.

Serves 6 as a first course or 4 as a main course

750 g	sea scallops	1½ lb
	salt and pepper	
30 g	flour	¼ cup
60 g	butter	4 Tbsp
	4 shallots, chopped	
	6 Tbsp chopped parsley	

Prepare the scallops*, cut them in half horizontally and sprinkle them with salt and pepper. Roll them in the flour and shake off the excess.

Heat half the butter in a frying pan. Cook the scallops in batches so the pan is not crowded: add a layer of scallops and sauté over a medium fire for 2–3 minutes or until golden brown and just firm. Don't overcook, or the scallops will toughen. Return all the scallops to the frying pan with the remaining butter, the shallots and the parsley. Sauté together, tossing often, for 2 minutes; taste for seasoning. Transfer to a platter and serve immediately.

HOMARD À LA BORDELAISE

Lobster in red wine sauce

The Bordelaise habit of sautéing in butter with shallots and then simmering in wine is perfectly suited to lobster. Red or white wine may be used; cognac and cayenne pepper (a favourite spice with shellfish) help develop the flavour.

Serves 4

750 g each	2 live lobsters	1½ lb each
250 g	butter	½ lb
60 ml	oil	¼ cup
80 ml	cognac	⅓ cup
500 ml	red wine, preferably bordeaux	2 cups
	3 shallots, finely chopped	
	salt and pepper	
	pinch of cayenne pepper	
	juice of 1 lemon	
	1 Tbsp chopped parsley	

Kill and cut up the lobsters*. Mash the soft meat and the coral of the lobster with a tablespoon of the butter.

In a large frying pan, heat the oil and 2 tablespoons of the butter until very hot. Add the lobster pieces and cook over a high fire, turning them over occasionally, until they turn red. Add the cognac and flame; then add the red wine, shallots, salt, pepper and cayenne pepper. Cover and simmer for 12–15 minutes or until the meat is no longer transparent.

Remove the lobster pieces from the sauce. Extract the meat from the claws and snip the soft underside of the shell on each piece of tail meat so the flesh can be removed easily. Put the pieces in a deep serving dish, cover and keep them warm. Discard the body shells.

To finish the sauce: if necessary, boil to reduce the cooking liquid to 125 ml. Whisk in the mashed lobster meat and heat briefly over a low fire. Add the remaining butter a piece at a time, working sometimes over a low fire and sometimes off the heat so the butter softens and thickens the sauce without melting to oil. Don't let the sauce boil. Add the lemon juice and taste the sauce for seasoning.

To serve, spoon a little of the sauce over the lobster pieces and sprinkle them with chopped parsley. Serve the remaining sauce separately. Provide each person with a fingerbowl.

ÉCREVISSES BORDELAISE

Crayfish in white wine and vegetable sauce

Some people add a little raw ham to the vegetable sauce in which the crayfish are served; others add a chopped tomato. Substituting two cut up lobsters for the crayfish makes this recipe an alternative method of preparing 'homard à la bordelaise' (see recipe).

Serves 6 as a first course or 4 as a main course

1 kg	fresh crayfish	2 lb
90 g	butter	6 Tbsp
	2 onions, diced	
	2 shallots, chopped	
	2 carrots, diced	
	bouquet garni	
60 ml	cognac	¼ cup
185 ml	white wine, preferably a dry bordeaux	¾ cup
185 ml	fish stock*	¾ cup
	salt and pepper	
	4 egg yolks	
	pinch of cayenne pepper, or to taste	
	1 Tbsp chopped parsley	

Wash the crayfish and remove the intestinal vein of each one by twisting the central flange of the tail. In a large sauté pan melt a third of the butter, add the onions, shallots and carrots and cook gently until the vegetables are soft but not brown. Add the crayfish with the bouquet garni and cook for 1–2 minutes until the crayfish start to turn red. Add the cognac and flame. Add the white wine, fish stock, salt and pepper, cover and simmer for 8–12 minutes until the crayfish are cooked and bright red, shaking the pan often. Snip the underside of each crayfish with scissors to make removing the meat easier. Transfer the crayfish to a deep platter and keep warm.

Boil the cooking liquid if necessary until reduced to about 250 ml and transfer to a saucepan; skim off any fat. Just before serving, beat the egg yolks in a bowl and gradually beat in the hot cooking liquid. Return to the saucepan and heat gently, stirring until the sauce thickens slightly. Don't let it boil or it will curdle. Season it to taste with salt, pepper and a pinch of cayenne pepper: the sauce should be quite spicy. Take it from the heat and add the remaining butter in small pieces, shaking the pan so that it is incorporated. Pour the sauce over the crayfish, sprinkle with parsley and serve. Guests dismember the crayfish at table, so they will need fingerbowls and crab picks.

COGNAC, ARMAGNAC AND MARC

Cognac brandy has made the gastronomic fame of a part of Charente that is otherwise poorly endowed. Indeed, cognac was invented precisely because the local wines were so thin. In the 17th century, most wine from the Atlantic seaboard was exported to England or Holland and vintners experimented with boiling their wine in an effort to avoid tax and to reduce the volume for transport. To make this essence palatable, herbs were usually added, but the growers around Cognac discovered their product was even better on its own. It was called 'brandewijn', Dutch for burnt wine.

Brandy owes its characteristic flavour both to the grapes of the cognac region (the best comes from two small areas, Grande Champagne and Petite Champagne), and to the process of aging in casks of oak from the nearby Limousin. In cask brandy picks up colour and it also evaporates; in the town of Cognac the equivalent of 25,000 bottles is said to be lost each day. Most brandy is given only two or three years to mellow, but the best may be left up to 50 years in oak. Once in the bottle, brandy, unlike wine, does not change. Nowadays almost all well-aged brandy is mixed with younger vintages to make standard non-vintage blends which come in various qualities.

The same general principles are followed in Armagnac, part of Gascony to the southeast of Bordeaux. However, the local soil is different and armagnac is distilled only once, not twice like cognac, which gives it a harder, more earthy taste. Production of cognac is twelve times greater than that of armagnac and for many years the reputation of armagnac was eclipsed, but recently it has become more popular in France, helped by a series of advertisements showing a rustic Gascon in a beret downing his daily tot. Also emerging from obscurity is marc, a powerful spirit made in most wine areas, notably in Burgundy and Champagne. Unlike cognac and armagnac, marc is distilled not from wine but from the pulp or 'marc' left after grapes have been pressed.

Marc is used only occasionally in cooking, for charcuterie and some sauces, but cognac and armagnac play an important, if limited, role. (As with wine, it is a waste to use the more expensive labels.) In marinades they help tenderize meat, in pâtés and terrines they act as a preservative, and when added to sauces and ragoûts, they intensify the other flavours. With this in mind they are usually added towards the end of cooking, but sometimes cognac or armagnac is deliberately simmered for a long time to achieve a special concentration. Most spectacularly of all, cognac and armagnac are common in flamed dishes – an effect beloved by the maître d'hôtel but dismissed by most serious cooks as a piece of theatre, since boiling achieves the same effect of evaporating the alcohol.

CANARD SAUVAGE À LA BORDELAISE

Wild duck with cèpes

Cèpes are an excellent foil for the smoky flavour of game. In this recipe partridge, pigeon or pheasant can be used instead of wild duck.

Serves 2

250 g	fresh cèpes OR	8 oz
25 g	dried cèpes	1 oz
1-kg	wild duck	2-lb
60 ml	oil	¼ cup
	20 baby onions	
	1 clove garlic, chopped	
500 g	tomatoes, peeled, seeded and chopped	1 lb
375 ml	water	1½ cups
	2 Tbsp cognac or armagnac	
	bouquet garni	
	salt and pepper	
10 g	butter kneaded with	2 tsp
10 g	flour	1½ Tbsp
	4 heart-shaped or triangular croûtes*, fried in butter, then rubbed with garlic	
	trussing needle and string	

Prepare fresh or dried cèpes*. Clean and truss the duck. Heat three-quarters of the oil in a heavy casserole, add the duck and brown it on all sides. Remove it, add the baby onions and brown them also. Remove the onions and discard the fat from the pan.

Meanwhile, heat the remaining oil in a frying pan, add the garlic and tomatoes and cook over a high fire, stirring often, for about 15 minutes or until thick.

Return the duck to the casserole, add the cooked tomato mixture, water, cognac, bouquet garni, salt and pepper. Bring to a boil, cover and simmer over a low fire for 1 hour, or until nearly tender. The cooking time for wild duck varies enormously, depending on size and age. Add the baby onions and mushrooms and continue to simmer for 15 minutes or until the duck and onions are very tender. Transfer the duck to a platter with the onions and mushrooms and keep warm. Discard the bouquet garni.

Bring the sauce back to a boil and reduce, if necessary, until well flavoured. Whisk in kneaded butter*, a piece at a time, to thicken the sauce until it lightly coats a spoon. Spoon the reserved vegetables back into the sauce and reheat briefly. Taste for seasoning.

Discard the trussing strings from the duck and spoon the vegetables around it with a little sauce. Serve the remaining sauce separately. Arrange the croûtes around the duck and carve it at the table.

FRICASSÉE DE POULET AU COGNAC

Chicken fricassée with cognac

The flavour that the cognac imparts to the chicken in this dish is surprisingly subtle.

Serves 4

1·5-kg	chicken	3-lb
250 ml	cognac	1 cup
150 g	bacon, cut in lardons	5 oz
60 g	butter	4 Tbsp
	24 baby onions	
	salt and pepper	

Cut the chicken* in 8 pieces. Put it in a shallow dish and pour the cognac over it. Leave to marinate for 8–12 hours in the refrigerator, turning the pieces over occasionally.

The next day, drain the pieces, reserving the cognac, and pat them dry. Blanch* the bacon if it is salty.

Heat the butter in a frying pan or sauté pan and add the bacon and chicken pieces. Cook over a low fire, turning the pieces over occasionally, until the meat has stiffened but is not brown. Add the onions, the reserved cognac and a little pepper. Cover and cook over a low fire, turning the pieces over occasionally, for 25–30 minutes or until tender. Taste for seasoning, transfer to a platter and serve.

ENTRECÔTE À LA BORDELAISE

Entrecôte steak with beef marrow

Charente supplies Bordeaux not only with butter but with beef. There are two ways of serving this dish; in country districts cooks don't bother with the sauce bordelaise but simply top the steak with bone marrow and pour over it the pan juices dissolved in a little red wine. Any good cut of steak, cut 5 cm/2 in thick, can be used. If possible, ask the butcher to extract marrow from marrow bones; otherwise, use a sharp knife to remove it yourself.

Serves 4

1-kg	entrecôte steak	2-lb
	2 Tbsp oil	
	salt and pepper	
125 g	beef marrow, sliced	4 oz
	bunch of watercress	
	SAUCE BORDELAISE	
80 g	butter	5 Tbsp
	5 shallots, finely chopped	
250 ml	red wine, preferably bordeaux	1 cup
	salt	
	coarsely ground black pepper	
	pinch of thyme	
	pinch of grated nutmeg	
250 ml	broth	1 cup

Begin the sauce bordelaise: melt a tablespoon of the butter in a heavy saucepan, add the shallots and cook over a low fire for 3–4 minutes to soften. Add the wine, a pinch of salt and coarsely ground black pepper, the thyme and nutmeg. Boil until reduced by about half. Add the broth and boil again to reduce by about half.

Brush the steak with oil and sprinkle it with pepper. Leave to marinate for a few minutes while heating the grill/broiler to very hot. Put the marrow in a pot of simmering water and poach for 2–3 minutes or until just tender. Drain and dice the marrow, cover and keep warm.

Grill/broil the entrecôte for 8 minutes. Turn it over, sprinkle with salt and grill the other side for about 7 more minutes (for rare meat). While the steak is cooking, finish the sauce: reheat the sauce to boiling. Take it from the heat and stir in the remaining butter, a piece at a time. Stir in the diced marrow and taste the sauce for seasoning.

To serve, cut the steak in diagonal slices, arrange it on a platter and spoon over a little sauce. Decorate the platter with watercress and serve the remaining sauce separately.

ENTRECÔTE BORDELAISE II

Omit the sauce. Chop the poached marrow with 4 shallots, finely chopped and 3 Tbsp chopped parsley. After grilling/broiling the steak on one side, turn it over, sprinkle with salt and put the marrow mixture on top. Heat the blade of a knife or metal spatula and spread the marrow mixture very evenly over the steak; the heat will help to melt the marrow slightly.

Return the entrecôte to the grill and cook the other side. Transfer to a platter, being careful not to let the topping fall off.

ENCHAUD PÉRIGOURDIN
Roast pork loin with garlic

A cross between a roast and a pot roast, the 'enchaud' for every day is flavoured only with garlic and herbs. However, at Christmas, truffle replaces the garlic and the pork is spread with truffled meat stuffing before it is rolled. Either way, enchaud is excellent cold; the garlic version, spread with jellied cooking juices, topped with a gherkin pickle and put in bread makes a good sandwich.

Serves 6

1·5-kg	boned pork loin, bones reserved	3-lb
	salt and pepper	
	3 cloves garlic	
45 g	lard	3 Tbsp
250 ml	water	1 cup
	sprig of thyme	
250 ml	broth	1 cup
	trussing string	

One day ahead: sprinkle the pork with salt and pepper and use a knife to make evenly spaced incisions in the meat. Cut the garlic in thin slivers and put a sliver in each incision. Roll up the meat and tie in a neat cylinder with trussing string. Refrigerate overnight to allow the garlic flavour and seasonings to penetrate the meat.

The next day, set the oven at moderate (175°C/350°F). Melt the lard in a heavy casserole, add the pork and bones and roast the meat for 30 minutes, turning it over occasionally, until brown on all sides. Add the water, thyme, salt and pepper, cover and continue cooking for another 1½ hours or until very tender. Transfer to a cutting board, discard the trussing string and keep the meat warm.

Transfer the liquid from the casserole to a sauté pan, discarding the bones and thyme, and skim off the excess fat. Add the broth and bring to a boil. Taste and, if necessary, boil to reduce until well flavoured; taste for seasoning.

Cut the pork in medium-thick slices and arrange them overlapping on a platter. Serve the gravy separately.

LA DAUBE SANTONGEAISE
Beef stew with carrots

'Plus elle est demeurée sur le feu, meilleure elle est!' – the longer it stays on the fire, the better a daube is, say the cooks of Saintonge, an ancient province forming part of Charente.

Serves 6

200 g	bacon, cut in lardons	7 oz
30 g	butter	2 Tbsp
1 kg	beef shoulder, cut in 5 cm/2 in cubes	2 lb
1·5 kg	carrots, sliced	3 lb
	25 shallots	
1 L	red wine, preferably bordeaux	1 qt
	3 Tbsp cognac	
	1 calf's foot	
	bouquet garni	
	salt and pepper	

Blanch* the bacon if it is salty. Heat the butter in a heavy casserole and brown the beef in it on all sides over a medium-high fire. Remove the pieces and lightly sauté the carrots in the butter. Remove them and lightly sauté the whole shallots and bacon. Return the meat and carrots to the casserole and heat them; pour in the wine and cognac and flame them. Add the calf's foot, bouquet garni and a little salt and pepper and bring to a boil. Cover and simmer over a low fire for 4 hours, stirring occasionally, until the beef is very tender. There should be just enough sauce to moisten the meat; if necessary, remove the lid towards the end of cooking so that the sauce evaporates more rapidly. Discard the bouquet garni. Remove the meat from the calf's foot and return it to the stew, discarding the bone. Taste the sauce for seasoning. Serve hot.

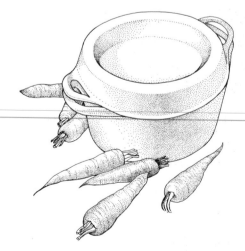

SHALLOTS AND ONIONS

Bordeaux is a centre for onions and shallots; they thrive in the river valleys and play a prominent part in the cooking. Classic steak bordelaise is based on a reduction of shallots and red wine, and dishes like cèpes, crayfish and scallops bordelaise would be lost without a chopped onion or a shallot or two.

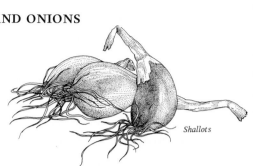

Shallots

Shallots and onions are by no means the same though they are closely related – the old name for shallot was 'onion of Ascalon', which was a prosperous port in Palestine at the time of the crusades. Surprisingly, both are members of the lily family which also includes leeks, garlic and chives. A shallot is less than a quarter of the size of the average onion; its flavour is pervasive, though it is less acrid than the onion's and provokes fewer tears. Shallots are good raw in salads and they are the basis of the delicate 'sauce beurre blanc' from the Loire. There are three kinds recognizable by the colour of their flesh: purple (called 'grey' by the French), red and greenish-white, which are the commonest. Purple shallots are reputedly the best, but all kinds are cooked alike.

Not so with onions. Their strength depends on the variety as well as their origin; the warmer the climate, the sweeter and fatter the onion. The mild Spanish or Bermuda onions used in salads are totally unsuited to Flemish carbonnade, which needs strong yellow onions to balance its flavour of beer and mustard. Like garlic, onions are stronger in winter, when they are dried. French radio recently advised listeners to count the skins on their onions, claiming that the more protective layers, the colder the winter weather outlook.

The flavour of onions is dramatically changed by the method of cooking. When sautéed gently in butter so they do not brown but dissolve gradually almost to a purée, they are sweet, even slightly sugary. This is the taste which should predominate in recipes like Alsatian 'zewelwai' (onion tart). If onions are browned, however, the flavour is sharper and more biting, the right touch for Lyonnais onion soup. By contrast, shallots are always lightly cooked; they will turn bitter if sautéed until brown. Chopped shallots are often used raw, almost like a herb, and around Bordeaux they are tucked under grilled steak in generous quantities.

Shallots are not to be confused with baby onions, much used in France for garnishes. When fresh, baby onions taste very like spring onions (sometimes called scallions in the USA), but the flavour intensifies when they are dried. To peel onions easily, blanch them for a minute or two in boiling water to soften the skins.

Onions have a long history as household remedies: a roast onion was a cure for earache and one 19th-century English cookbook recommends a raw onion, taken an hour before bedtime, as a cure for insomnia. Clearly it paid to know one's bedfellow as well as one's onions.

Spanish, yellow and red onions

ROGNONS DE VEAU À LA BORDELAISE
Veal kidneys with cèpes

'Bordeaux likes cèpes as cèpes love oil', runs a local catch-phrase; wild mushrooms certainly appear in a remarkable number of Bordelais recipes. They are usually fried in oil with a touch of garlic as here, but some cooks prefer olive oil or butter. Excess liquid is always a problem with cèpes, so be sure to use a high heat to sauté them. Use vegetable oil when making the coulis and omit the sugar and basil. In this recipe the cèpes are served apart from the kidneys, so steak or another meat can be substituted.

Serves 4

150 g	bacon, cut in lardons	5 oz
500 g	veal kidneys	1 lb
250 ml	tomato coulis (see recipe)	1 cup
	2 Tbsp oil	
30 g	butter	2 Tbsp
	CÈPES À LA BORDELAISE	
500 g	fresh cèpes OR	1 lb
50 g	dried cèpes	2 oz
80 ml	oil	⅓ cup
	2 shallots, finely chopped	
	salt and pepper	
	a few drops of lemon juice	
	2 Tbsp chopped parsley	

Prepare fresh or dried cèpes*, reserving the soaking water from dried cèpes. Slice the caps off the cèpes and chop the stems.

If the bacon is salty, blanch* it. Skin the kidneys if necessary and cut them in half lengthwise. Use scissors to cut out the cores.

To cook the cèpes: heat the oil in a frying pan until very hot. Add the cèpes and sauté over a high fire for 5 minutes or until they begin to brown; then cook over a medium fire for another 10 minutes or until tender. Add the shallots and continue to cook over a medium fire for 2–3 more minutes, tossing occasionally. Season with salt and pepper to taste and add a little lemon juice and the chopped parsley. Add the mixture to the tomato coulis and reheat.

Heat the oil and butter in a frying pan, add the bacon and sauté until lightly browned but not crisp. Stir the bacon and 125 ml of the cèpe soaking liquid (or water if using fresh mushrooms) into the tomato mixture; taste for seasoning and keep warm. Add the kidneys to the hot fat and cook over a high fire for 4–5 minutes on each side or until well browned on the outside but rare in the centre. Season each side after it has cooked. Transfer the cèpe and tomato mixture to a platter, set the kidneys on top and serve immediately.

RIS DE VEAU AUX TRUFFES
Sweetbreads with truffles

Sweetbreads are also braised, less expensively than in this recipe, with two or three tomatoes instead of the truffles.

Serves 4

750 g total	2 pairs veal sweetbreads	1½ lb total
	salt and pepper	
60 g	butter	4 Tbsp
	1 onion, sliced	
	2 Tbsp cognac	
250 ml	dry white wine, preferably bordeaux	1 cup
125 ml	broth	½ cup
125 g	mushrooms, thinly sliced	¼ lb
	juice of ½ lemon	
	1–2 whole canned truffles, with their liquid	
15 g	flour	2 Tbsp
250 ml	heavy cream or crème fraîche*	1 cup

Soak the sweetbreads in cold water for 1–2 hours, changing the water once or twice; drain and rinse. Put them in a pot of cold salted water, bring to a boil and simmer for 5 minutes. Drain, rinse and trim the sweetbreads, discarding ducts and skin. Press them between two plates with a weight on top and leave until cold.

Melt half the butter in a sauté pan, add the onion and cook over a low fire until soft but not brown. Add the sweetbreads and brown them lightly over a medium fire. Add the cognac and flame. Pour in the wine, bring to a boil and add the broth, salt and pepper. Cover and simmer over a low fire for 40 minutes or until the sweetbreads are very tender. Transfer them to a platter and keep warm. Reserve the liquid.

Meanwhile, put the mushrooms in a saucepan with the lemon juice, salt, pepper and a few tablespoons of water. Cover tightly and cook over a high fire until the liquid boils to the top of the pan. Cut the truffles in thin strips, reserving their liquid.

Melt the remaining butter in a heavy saucepan, whisk in the flour and cook over a low fire, whisking, until bubbling but not brown. Strain in the cooking liquid from the sweetbreads and bring to a boil, whisking. Stir in the mushrooms with their cooking liquid and the truffles with their liquid. Simmer for 5–10 minutes or until the sauce is well flavoured and thick enough to coat a spoon. Stir in the cream and bring to a boil. Cut the sweetbreads into thick diagonal slices and add them to the sauce. Heat briefly before serving and taste for seasoning. Serve from a deep dish.

TRUFFLES

'Here we supped and lay, having amongst other dainties, a dish of truffles, which is a certain earth-nut, and found out by a hog trained to it, and for which these animals are sold at a great price. It is in truth an incomparable meat.' John Evelyn came to this conclusion at Vienne in 1644.

For centuries truffles have maintained an aura of mystery which modern science has not yet been able to dispel. The strangeness of the rough, lumpy appearance is heightened by the jet-black interior, a colour matched by no other food – even a black olive looks pale beside a slice of truffle. As for flavour, one small fresh truffle is enough for a whole dish, while its aroma is extraordinarily pervasive, penetrating eggshells to the raw egg and forcing its way through wrappings of paper or plastic. A whiff of truffle is heavenly but close proximity to the heavy, fungoid smell is enough to turn the stomach.

The greatest truffle puzzle of all is how they are propagated. Truffles grow underground on the roots of oak trees but the places where truffles choose to grow seem arbitrary – they will appear in one field (called a 'truffière') but not in another, under one tree but not the next. In general they cannot be cultivated, though clearing the ground of other plants seems to help them spread, and spores sown under controlled conditions sometimes produce truffles; recent experiments in California are encouraging.

Given the presence of truffles, the final problem is how to find them. According to some experts there is a fly which is a tell-tale sign of truffles underfoot. Truffle hunting remains surprisingly primitive, a matter of a man with his dog or pig, trained to smell the treasure hidden a few centimetres underground. A pig is said to be more sensitive, but less obedient, than a dog. When the animal starts to rootle, his master quickly intervenes, dropping a tempting titbit or handful of corn as distraction while the truffle is dug up.

Most are about the size of a walnut, but giant truffles of 10 cm/4 in or more in diameter are sometimes found – a prize to be sealed in a glass jar, so earning its owner a fortune. The fresh truffle season lasts from November to March and restaurants often serve fresh truffles 'sous la cendre' (baked in charcoal) or in a puff pastry case. Untreated fresh truffles lose their aroma and taste after a week or so. At home they are brushed clean and then preserved in fat or in cognac or madeira. However, most truffles are commercially canned, a process which shrinks them to half their original size. Second-best though the taste is, canned truffles are all that most cooks can get and their stark black outline is still valued for the touch it adds to delicate pâtés and to the eye-catching aspics of a grand buffet.

The truffles of Périgord and Quercy are outstanding for colour and taste and, as far as the French are concerned, no other region can compete. However, Italians would maintain that the white truffles of Piedmont, uninspiring though they look, being a grubby beige, outdo black truffles in intensity of flavour. Provence produces second-grade black truffles on a commercial scale and in several other regions, notably Alsace, Savoy and Burgundy, truffles can be found, though their quality is unreliable. In Périgord and Provence, for instance, white truffles exist as well as black ones, but they are greatly inferior to those of Italy, hardly worth the gathering.

In recent years, the supply of truffles has steadily diminished and a considerable proportion of canned truffles bearing a French label are, in fact, unearthed in Italy and Spain. Whether fewer truffles are growing in France or whether there are simply fewer Frenchmen looking for them, even at today's enormous prices, is an enigma. Even in the 1800s, Brillat-Savarin considered truffles to be 'a luxury of grands seigneurs and of kept women', for truffles are supposed to be an aphrodisiac. Times have not changed and, as far as country cooks are concerned, the truffle is a bauble for millionaires and three-star restaurants.

MARCASSIN À LA GIRONDINE
Marinated wild boar with chestnuts

In this recipe the meat can be marinated in a cooked mixture, as for 'marcassin ardennaise', or simply soaked in a good red wine as described. The Gironde river is bordered by many of the most famous Bordeaux vineyards.

Serves 6–8

1·5–2-kg	boned loin or haunch of young wild boar, including the bones	3–4½-lb
100 g	pork fat or fatback, cut in thin strips	4 oz
750 ml	red wine, preferably bordeaux	3 cups
750 g	fresh chestnuts	1½ lb
500 ml	broth or water	2 cups
	salt and pepper	
30 g	butter	2 Tbsp
	1 onion, chopped	
	3 Tbsp oil	
	SAUCE	
125 g	butter	¼ lb
	2 carrots, chopped	
	1 onion, chopped	
	1 clove garlic, chopped	
30 g	flour	¼ cup
250 ml	broth	1 cup
	bouquet garni	
	salt and pepper	
	2 Tbsp armagnac or cognac	
	1 shallot, finely chopped	
	1 Tbsp raspberry or blackberry jelly	
	larding needle	

Trim any fat and gristle from the boar and lard* it with the pork fat. Put the boar in a deep bowl (not aluminium), pour the wine over it and add the trimmings and any bones. Marinate for 2 days in the refrigerator, turning the meat occasionally. Drain the meat, reserving the marinade ingredients.

Begin the sauce: heat half the butter in a heavy pot and add the reserved boar bones and trimmings, the carrots and onion. Cook over a medium fire, stirring often, until light brown. Stir in the garlic and the flour and cook over a low fire, stirring constantly, until bubbling and golden brown; be careful not to let the flour burn. Stir in the broth and two-thirds of the marinade liquid, add the bouquet garni and a little salt and pepper and bring to a boil. Simmer the sauce, uncovered, stirring often, for 1 hour or until well flavoured and thick enough to coat a spoon.

While the sauce is simmering, peel the fresh chestnuts*. Put them in a pot with the broth, salt and pepper and simmer them for 20–25 minutes or until just tender. Drain the chestnuts thoroughly. Melt the butter in the pan, add the onion and cook over a low fire until soft; then cook over a medium fire until lightly browned. Add the chestnuts and a pinch of salt and pepper and heat over a low fire, tossing occasionally, until coated with the butter. Cover and keep warm.

Set the oven at very hot (220°C/425°F). Pat the meat dry with paper towels and sprinkle it with salt and pepper. Put the meat in a roasting pan with the oil and roast in the oven, basting often, for 30–40 minutes; allow 20 minutes per kg/10 minutes per lb for rare meat. Transfer to a platter, arrange the chestnuts around it and keep warm.

Finish the sauce: discard the fat from the roasting pan and add the armagnac, remaining marinade liquid and shallot. Bring to a boil, stirring to dissolve the pan juices, and boil until reduced by half. Add to the sauce and, if necessary, simmer the sauce a little more until it coats a spoon. Strain the sauce, pressing hard on the vegetables, and reheat it. Whisk in the raspberry jelly, take from the heat and whisk in the remaining butter. Taste for seasoning.

Carve the meat and replace on the bone, or carve it at the table. Serve the sauce separately.

LAPIN AUX PRUNEAUX
Rabbit with prunes

The French are not averse to nibbling a simple prune, particularly if it comes from Agen, though more often the prunes are stuffed with prune purée or almond paste. Prunes are baked in pies and cakes, and sweet-sour combinations such as pork, rabbit and even veal with prunes are common throughout France.

Serves 4

	1 rabbit	
180 g	prunes	6 oz
	1 Tbsp oil	
15 g	butter	1 Tbsp
15 g	flour	2 Tbsp
250 ml	red wine	1 cup
250 ml	broth	1 cup
	1 clove garlic, crushed	
	bouquet garni	
	salt and pepper	
	1 Tbsp chopped parsley	
	MARINADE	
125 ml	red wine	½ cup
	1 large bouquet garni	
	1 onion, coarsely chopped	
	1 carrot, coarsely chopped	
	6 black peppercorns, slightly crushed	
	1 Tbsp oil	

Cut the rabbit* in 6 or 7 pieces. Marinate the rabbit: put the pieces in a bowl (not aluminium) and add the marinade ingredients: wine, bouquet garni, onion, carrot and peppercorns. Pour the oil on top. Cover and leave at room temperature, turning occasionally, for 4–12 hours. Alternatively, the rabbit can be marinated in the refrigerator for 1–2 days. Pour boiling water over the prunes, cover and leave to soak for about 3 hours.

Drain the rabbit and pat dry with paper towels. In a sauté pan or shallow casserole heat the oil and butter and brown the rabbit pieces on all sides. Remove from the pan, add the onion and carrot from the marinade and sauté lightly until soft. Sprinkle the flour over the vegetables and cook, stirring, until the flour browns. Stir in the marinade and red wine and bring to a boil. Add the broth, garlic, bouquet garni, salt and pepper. Replace the rabbit pieces, cover and simmer for 25 minutes. Transfer them to another shallow casserole and strain the sauce over the rabbit, pressing hard on the vegetables. Drain the prunes, add them to the rabbit, cover and simmer for 10–15 minutes or until rabbit and prunes are tender.

Transfer the rabbit to a serving dish and spoon the prunes on top. If necessary, boil to reduce the sauce until it just coats a spoon; taste for seasoning and spoon it over the rabbit. Sprinkle with parsley just before serving.

LAPIN À LA FLAMANDE

As well as the prunes, add:

125 g	bacon, cut in lardons	4 oz
55 g	raisins	6 Tbsp

Blanch* the bacon if it is salty, and sauté lightly in butter before adding these ingredients to the rabbit for the last 10–15 minutes of cooking.

POMMES DE TERRE SARLADAISE
Potato cake with goose fat

Sautéed potatoes sarladaise, from the heart of the truffle country, can be flavoured with truffle or, more economically, with garlic. They are the ideal match for confit of goose or duck.

Serves 4		
1 kg	potatoes	2 lb
125 g	goose or duck fat	$\frac{1}{4}$ lb
	salt and pepper	
	1 medium truffle OR	
	1 clove garlic, chopped	
	3 Tbsp chopped parsley	
	28 cm/11 in heavy frying pan	

Slice the potatoes in medium-thick rounds. Heat three-quarters of the goose fat in the frying pan, add the potatoes with a little salt and pepper and sauté them over a medium fire, tossing them often, for 15 minutes or until nearly tender. Sprinkle with the truffle and parsley, add the remaining fat and taste for seasoning. Press the potatoes flat in the pan and continue to cook them without stirring for about 5 minutes, pressing them together and slightly crushing them so they form a cake. Turn the potato cake out on to a platter; it should be golden brown. Serve immediately.

HARICOTS VERTS À LA LANDAISE
Green beans with ham

By no means all green beans in France are baby 'haricots verts'. This recipe is designed for sturdy big beans which are cooked until very tender, not crisp as is the current fashion. For 'haricots verts poitevine', you omit the ham and sauté the vegetables in butter instead of goose fat.

Serves 6 as an accompaniment		
1 kg	green beans	2 lb
	salt and pepper	
45 g	goose fat	3 Tbsp
	2 onions, chopped	
	the white part of 2 split leeks, chopped	
	2 shallots, chopped	
200 g	raw ham, cut in fine dice	7 oz
	1 Tbsp flour	
	1 clove garlic, chopped	
	1 egg yolk	
	1 Tbsp vinegar	
	2 Tbsp chopped parsley	

Cook the beans in a large pot of boiling salted water for 5–6 minutes or until just tender. Drain, reserving 250 ml of the liquid.

Meanwhile, heat the goose fat in a saucepan, add the onions, leeks, shallots and ham and cook over a low fire, stirring often, until soft but not browned. Stir in the flour and cook over a low fire, stirring constantly, until bubbling. Add the garlic, reserved bean liquid and a pinch of pepper and bring to a boil, stirring. Simmer over a low fire, stirring often, for 10 minutes. Stir in the beans and simmer for 2–3 more minutes.

Just before serving, beat the egg yolk with the vinegar and beat in a few spoonsful of the hot sauce. Return the mixture to the saucepan and heat over a low fire, stirring constantly, until slightly thickened. Don't boil or the sauce will curdle. Taste for seasoning; extra salt may not be needed since the ham is salty. Sprinkle with chopped parsley and serve immediately.

GOATS

Goats will thrive almost anywhere on almost any food, but in France over a quarter of them are found in Poitou and the Vendée, where the best goat cheese comes from. In back lanes in France it is still common to see a goat or two munching on the grass verge for free pasture is not to be despised, particularly when it yields milk for making cheese.

Goats also flourish in Corsica and parts of Provence where there is a taste for their meat and the climate does not favour cattle. 'Chevreau' (kid) makes much better eating than mature goat, though the meat of a young female 'chèvre' is palatable cooked in a stew. Billy goats ('bouc' in French, a word with the same root as 'boucher' or butcher) are useless except for breeding; not only are they belligerent, but as soon as they mature they develop a peculiarly unpleasant smell and taste. Male kids are, therefore, usually killed in the spring, before they are four months old; their meat is delicate and suitable for the same recipes as baby lamb; it tastes like veal, for which it may be an unacknowledged substitute.

In medieval times, kid was a speciality at the Feast of Kings on January 6, when it would be prepared with sage, sweet white wine and allspice, for plenty of seasoning is needed if the meat is not to be insipid. Along the Loire and in Poitou it is a feature of 'pot de biquet' spring festivals when herds are culled of male kids; blanquette of kid is cooked with carrots and onions in a cream sauce, while joints of roast kid are flavoured with aromatic herbs and charred by an open fire.

FROMAGE DE CHÈVRE MARINÉ
Marinated goat cheese

For this recipe the goat cheese should be firm but not dry.

Serves 4–8

75 g each	4 small round goat cheeses	2½ oz each
	2 bay leaves	
	2 tsp black peppercorns	
	2 sprigs of thyme	
	a few tiny dried red hot peppers (optional)	
500 ml	olive oil, more if needed	2 cups

Put the cheeses in a large jar with the bay leaves, peppercorns, thyme and hot peppers. Add enough olive oil to cover generously. Cover with the lid and leave at least 2 weeks before using. The cheeses are good for 6–8 weeks, but will soften if kept too long.

To serve, drain the cheeses and accompany them with French bread. As you use them, more cheeses can be added. The olive oil left over is excellent for salads.

SALADE DE FROMAGE DE CHÈVRE MARINÉ
Marinated goat cheese salad

Use strong-flavoured salad greens which can stand up to the pungent cheese.

Serves 4–8

1 head chicory
1 head romaine lettuce
3 stalks celery
4 marinated goat cheeses (see above)
4–8 slices wholewheat bread, crusts discarded
VINAIGRETTE
6 Tbsp olive oil from marinating cheese
2 Tbsp vinegar
salt and pepper

Make the vinaigrette*. Wash the greens and dry thoroughly. Use a vegetable peeler to remove the strings from the celery and cut it into thin sticks. Either leave the cheeses whole or cut each in half horizontally. Cut each slice of bread into a circle slightly larger in diameter than the cheese. Set the bread rounds on a baking sheet and put the cheeses on them.

Top the greens and the celery with enough vinaigrette to moisten them and taste for seasoning. Arrange around the edges of plates.

Grill/broil the cheeses until bubbling and brown. Transfer each, still on its bread round, to the centre of a plate and serve immediately.

PIGNOLA
Pine nut cake

Among the pine forests of the Landes grow the stone pines which produce 'pignons' (pine nuts). The method of making 'pain de Gênes', rich in ground almonds instead of pine nuts, follows that for 'pignola' very closely, and is therefore given here to avoid repetition.

Serves 6–8

	SWEET PIE PASTRY	
200 g	flour	1½ cups
	4 egg yolks	
	½ tsp salt	
100 g	sugar	½ cup
	1 tsp vanilla extract	
125 g	butter	¼ lb
	FILLING	
125 g	butter	¼ lb
150 g	pine nuts	1 cup
110 g	whole blanched almonds, ground	¾ cup
135 g	sugar	⅔ cup
	3 eggs	
35 g	potato starch or cornstarch	¼ cup
	½ tsp baking powder	
	pinch of salt	
	27–30 cm/11–12 in pie or tart pan with removable base	

Make the sweet pie pastry* and chill for 30 minutes or until firm. Roll out the pastry and line the pan*. Prick the base and chill for 15–20 minutes. Set the oven at moderately hot (190°C/375°F).

Meanwhile, prepare the filling: heat a third of the butter in a frying pan, add the pine nuts and sauté, stirring, over a medium fire until lightly but evenly browned. Leave to cool. Melt the remaining butter in a small saucepan and leave to cool.

Mix the ground almonds and sugar in a bowl and add the eggs one by one, beating after each addition until the mixture is very light and thick. Sift the potato starch with the baking powder and salt over the mixture and fold them in as lightly as possible. Just before they are completely mixed in, carefully fold in the melted butter.

Pour the mixture into the lined pan and bake for 10–12 minutes or until the batter begins to set. Working quickly, scatter the pine nuts over the top in one even layer. Return the pan to the oven and continue baking for another 17–20 minutes or until the pastry is brown and the filling is firm; turn down the heat to low (150°C/300°F) if the cake browns too quickly. Unmould the cake and transfer to a rack to cool. Serve the cake at room temperature.

PAIN DE GÊNES

Strictly speaking, its origins are Italian, but nowadays this rich cake is found throughout France.

Butter a 20–23 cm/8–9 in round cake pan, line with a circle of greaseproof/parchment paper, and butter the paper. Prepare only the cake filling, omitting the pine nuts and using only

80 g	butter	5 Tbsp

Add 1 Tbsp kirsch after mixing in the eggs. Pour the mixture into the pan and bake in a moderately hot oven (190°C/375°F) for 30–35 minutes or until the cake springs back when lightly pressed with a fingertip. Turn out on to a rack to cool. Sprinkle with confectioners'/icing sugar just before serving.

MERVEILLES CHARENTAISES
Cognac fritters

These 'merveilles' (sweet fritters) are flavoured with the most famous Charentais product, cognac.

Serves 4–6

200 g	flour	1½ cups
	1 egg	
	pinch of salt	
100 g	sugar	½ cup
	½ tsp baking powder	
	½ tsp orange flower water	
	2 tsp cognac	
	2 Tbsp water	
45 g	butter	3 Tbsp
	deep fat (for frying)	
	confectioners' sugar (for sprinkling)	

Prepare the dough as for sweet pie pastry*, adding the baking powder, orange flower water, cognac and water to the well. If the dough is very soft and sticky, roll it in a little flour. Wrap and chill for at least 2 hours or until firm.

Heat the deep fat to 180°C/355°F on a fat thermometer. Roll out the dough about 3 mm/⅛ in thick and cut it in thin strips about 5 cm/2 in long. Twist 3 strips together for each merveille. Plunge a few merveilles at a time into the deep fat and fry for 2–3 minutes or until golden brown.

Transfer to paper towels to absorb the excess fat. Sprinkle the merveilles with the sugar and serve hot or at room temperature.

ST ÉMILION AU CHOCOLAT
Chocolate and macaroon charlotte

The wine town of St Émilion is as famous for its macaroons as the city of Nancy. In this recipe they are used instead of the usual sponge fingers for lining the charlotte mould.

Serves 6

	25 medium macaroons (see recipe)	
	4 Tbsp cognac	
	4 Tbsp water	
	FILLING	
95 g	butter	6 Tbsp
100 g	sugar	$\frac{1}{2}$ cup
100 g	semi-sweet chocolate, chopped	$3\frac{1}{2}$ oz
80 ml	milk	$\frac{1}{3}$ cup
	1 egg yolk	
	CHOCOLATE ROYAL ICING	
100 g	semi-sweet chocolate, chopped	$3\frac{1}{2}$ oz
100 g	confectioners' sugar, sifted	$\frac{3}{4}$ cup
	1 egg white	
	1 Tbsp warm water	
	1 L/1 qt charlotte mould	

The day before serving, make macaroons that are soft in the centre.

For the filling: thoroughly cream the butter and the sugar. Melt the chocolate in a water bath. In a small saucepan bring the milk to a boil, pour it over the chocolate and mix well. Cool slightly, beat in the egg yolk and leave to cool completely. Beat the chocolate-yolk mixture into the creamed butter and sugar at high speed until lightened in colour.

Butter the charlotte mould. In a small bowl mix the cognac and the water. Dip each macaroon briefly in the cognac mixture and place a layer of macaroons in the base of the charlotte mould, flat side down. Arrange two rows of macaroons up the sides of the mould, flat side out. Spoon half the chocolate filling into the mould and top with another layer of soaked macaroons. Pour on the remaining filling and cover with the remaining soaked macaroons, flat side up. Cover with a plate with a weight on top and chill overnight.

A short time before serving, turn out the charlotte on to a platter. Make the chocolate royal icing: melt the chocolate in a water bath and let cool slightly. With a wooden spoon beat the sugar with the egg white. Beat this mixture into the chocolate. Lastly beat in the water. Pour the icing on the charlotte and spread it quickly with a metal spatula, letting it run down the sides if you like. Serve chilled.

TOURTEAU FROMAGER
Cream cheese cake in pastry

The name of this cheesecake comes from 'tourte' or tart, but a tourteau rises so much in the oven it is almost spherical, with a characteristic thick black crust. In Poitou tourteau is made with fresh goat cheese, which gives an extra bite to the flavour.

Serves 6

15 g	melted butter	1 Tbsp
100 g	cottage cheese	$3\frac{1}{2}$ oz
	2 eggs, beaten to mix	
50 g	sugar	$\frac{1}{4}$ cup
65 g	flour	$\frac{1}{2}$ cup
	$\frac{1}{2}$ tsp baking powder	
	PIE PASTRY	
95 g	flour	$\frac{3}{4}$ cup
45 g	butter	3 Tbsp
	1 egg yolk	
	2–3 Tbsp water	
15 cm/6 in heatproof soup bowl, 5–8 cm/2–3 in deep		

Thoroughly butter the bowl. Make the pastry* and chill 30 minutes. Roll out the dough and line the bowl, trimming off the excess. Chill it. Set the oven at hot (200°C/400°F).

Make the filling: mix the butter and cheese and purée in a blender or food processor until very smooth. Put the eggs and the sugar in a bowl over a pan of hot water and whisk until very light and the mixture forms a ribbon when the whisk is lifted; if using an electric beater, no heat is necessary. Fold in the sifted flour and baking powder followed by the melted butter and cheese mixture. Pour into the pastry-lined bowl – it should be full. Bake in the heated oven for 35–45 minutes or until well browned and a skewer inserted in the centre comes out clean. Traditionally the top should be very dark, almost black; if the tourteau is cooked but not yet dark enough, put it under a hot grill/broiler for a few seconds.

CHEESES

Red wine and cheese are hailed as a great combination, yet neither Burgundy nor Bordeaux produces a cheese to match its wines. Near Bordeaux, in fact, scarcely any cheese is produced at all, and locals eat edam from Holland, a taste dating from the 18th century when the Dutch traded their cheese for Bordeaux wine. The dairy country of Charente devotes its milk to producing butter, and only in Poitou is cheese production important.

This is the territory of the goat, once called the 'poor man's cow'. Nowadays, however, goat cheese is expensive; a goat in good form produces only about 4 litres of milk a day, compared with up to 20 litres from a cow, and goats are notoriously capricious – the weather, a strange face, a stray rock in her path will all make the supply from a goat run dry; the very adjective 'capricious' comes from the Latin word for goat. All types of goat cheese are made in Poitou: some round, some cylindrical, and even some wrapped in chestnut leaves like 'couhé-vérac'. Typical is 'la-mothe-St-Héraye', a soft white disc about 10 cm/4 in across, which develops a full-bodied flavour. Its life, together with that of half a dozen others, has been saved by dairies which now produce it on a commercial scale, but many more obscure farm cheeses like 'St-Maixent', uneconomic to make and to market, are almost extinct.

One Poitou goat cheese, however, is thriving. 'Chabichou' is a truncated cone about 7 cm/3 in high which, though soft and mild when fresh, sharpens with age. The name is a diminutive of the Arabic 'chebli' meaning cheese. Left behind after their defeat at Poitiers in 732, Arab soldiers took to raising goats and selling cheese. Two types survive today: fresh 'chabichou laitier' which is served usually with fruit for dessert, and aged chabichou which has a fine coral-yellow rind; too many grey or black spots on this are a bad sign.

The character of all goat cheeses changes on keeping as, unlike many cow cheeses, they are always made with unpasteurized milk and contain bacteria and enzymes which develop flavour. As a result they change taste almost from day to day, and are sold as 'one week old', 'two weeks old', and so forth. Almost all of them are eaten, like chabichou, at every stage from mild to tingling piquancy. Goat cheeses also vary much more with the seasons than cow's milk cheeses, being fragrant in spring and summer and then turning more acid as the herbage dries in winter.

OTHER SPECIALITIES OF THE REGION
TRADITIONAL DISHES

Purée vendéenne
Cream of broad bean soup

Soupe aux huîtres
Oyster soup

Oeufs en cocotte périgourdine
Baked eggs with truffle sauce

Escargots en omelette
Omelette with chopped snails

Truite farcie du Périgord
Trout stuffed with ham and cèpes

Pain de brochet d'Angoulême
Pike loaf

Lamproie au sang
Lamprey and leeks in red wine and blood sauce

Anguilles aux pruneaux
Eel and prune stew with shallots and red wine

Moules bordelaise
Mussels with white wine and tomato

Poulet sauté à la bordelaise
Chicken with artichokes, potatoes and fried onion rings

Poulet aux huîtres
Sautéed chicken with oysters

Dinde truffée
Roast turkey larded with truffles and stuffed with truffled meat

Cou d'oie farci
Goose neck stuffed with pork and foie gras

Confit d'oie à l'oseille
Confit of goose with sorrel

Pigeons aux petits pois
Baked pigeon with green peas, baby onions and bacon

Perdreau farci au foie gras
Roast partridge stuffed with foie gras and truffles

Bécasse rôtie landaise
Roast woodcock with cognac and foie gras sauce

Pluvier en salmis
Plover stew

Le pirot
Sautéed goat with green garlic and sorrel

Cuissot de chevreau à la poitevine
Roast leg of goat with herbs and vinegar

Entrecôte aux huîtres
Entrecôte steak with grilled oysters and shallot purée

Brezolles de veau à la quercynoise
Moulded sliced veal, layered with ham and herb stuffing

Veau à l'oseille à la mode de Niort
Braised veal with vegetables and cognac, served with sorrel

Cochon de lait farci
Stuffed roast sucking pig

La mique
Giant dumpling with salt pork and vegetables

Cassoulet quercynois
Cassoulet of beans, confit and fresh sausages

Tripes à la mode d'Angoulême
Tripe simmered with white wine, tomatoes and garlic

Truffes sous la cendre
Charcoal-baked truffles

Truffes en pâte
Truffles in puff pastry

Cèpes farcis poitevine
Cèpes stuffed with ham

Mojettes à la crème
Fresh white beans with garlic and cream

Pommes de terre confites aux cèpes
Potatoes and cèpes baked in goose fat

CHARCUTERIE

Pâté de perdrix rouge
Truffled red partridge pâté

Pâté de foie gras truffé
Pâté of foie gras with truffles

PÂTISSERIE AND CONFISERIE

Bottereaux
Liqueur-flavoured pastry fritters

Soufflé à l'angélique de Niort
Soufflé of candied angelica

Tourtisseaux
Yeast fritters, flavoured with orange flower water

Chocolats à l'angélique de Thouars
Chocolate with candied angelica

The Pyrenees and Gascony

The Pyrenees are a neglected part of France, but they have not always been so. The Romans stopped there to enjoy the natural resources, establishing thermal stations in the foothills. In medieval times a brisk traffic in pilgrims crossed the Pyrenees on their way to Santiago de Compostela in Spain, a shrine which today is outdone by Lourdes in the French foothills. Some travellers took the easy coastal route around the Pyrenees, but many climbed the mountain pass at St Jean Pied de Port, which is still a gateway to the Iberian peninsula. So remote from Paris, local lords like the kings of Navarre, the dukes of Gascony and counts of Foix enjoyed an enviable independence, maintaining armies and sizeable courts. Their influence on the region remains, for the territorial and cultural divisions their courts established still stand.

On the western coast lies the Basque country which, until the end of the 16th century, was part of Navarre. 'Peppery as the Welsh, proud as Lucifer, and combustible as his matches,' was Richard Ford's pithy assessment of the Basque people in his 19th-century *Handbook for Spain*, and certainly they are fiercely independent in politics and speech. Flaming red is the Basque colour, from their tiled roofs to their scarlet berets and red is also the theme of Basque cooking, which is dominated by peppers, both the common sweet pepper and a more piquant variety, the 'piment d'Espelette', named after a little village in the hills behind Biarritz.

In October Espelette holds a festival when the houses are festooned with peppers hanging up to dry. The menu at a local inn, tourist trap though it is, neatly sums up the Basque repertoire: 'elzekaria' (vegetable soup); 'merluza, salsa verde' (hake with a green sauce quite unlike any other, made with peas and asparagus); and 'tripoxa' (tripe sausages) served with the local hot sauce which comes in a bottle, like tabasco. 'Axoa' proves to be the ubiquitous Basque stew flavoured with green and red peppers, in this instance made with veal, but more familiar in the form of 'poulet basquaise'. Equally representative is 'pipérade', a tricky mixture of sautéed green and red peppers, onions and tomatoes thickened with eggs to form a purée. Good pipérade is delicious, but bad pipérade can separate so much as to become almost inedible.

For dessert a choice was offered of sheep's milk yogurt – a reminder of the importance of wool to the mountain economy – or 'gâteau basque', made of sweet pie pastry sandwiched with a light rum-scented pastry cream. Even better is the home-made version I found one summer Sunday at a roadside stall. The cream had been replaced by a layer of fresh plums and apricots (cherries are popular, too), which had been baked inside the sweet dough to give a moist, tart filling.

The Basques are great fishermen, former champion hunters of the whales that used to be found in the Bay of Biscay. Now the main catch is tuna, swordfish, sardines and as much as 400 tonnes of anchovies a day. The sardines are usually fried and the tuna is baked, perhaps with tomato, peppers and white wine as at St Jean de Luz, or with onions, olive oil, garlic and parsley as in Bayonne. Assorted small fish go into 'ttoro', the Basque fish stew that can be flavoured mild or hot with Espelette pepper. Such spicing is relative, however, and Basque dishes never approach the searing intensity of Texan cooking or a hot Indian curry.

If the Basques are partial to pepper, they are also great users of salt for preserving anchovies, cod and pork. The name of Bayonne, largest city in the area, is synonymous with succulent ham that is dry-cured to eat raw or to use as a flavouring in dishes like eggs basquaise. Hanging with the hams in Pyrenean charcuteries are strings of dry mountain sausages, some spiced with chili like Spanish 'chorizo', the skins of others encrusted with peppercorns or grey with wood ash.

Surviving from the meagre days when any meat was a luxury are dishes based on white cornmeal. Maize was introduced to France from the New World in the early 16th century and rapidly replaced millet in dishes like 'millas', although the old millet-related names were kept. Found in both the Pyrenees and Languedoc, millas is a stiff porridge like polenta which can be sliced for frying and there is even a sweet version called 'millassou' which is flavoured with orange flower water.

The Basque country spills over into Béarn, birthplace of Henri IV, who was King of Navarre until he assumed the more prestigious title of King of France in 1589. It was Henri who hoped, with some optimism, to put a chicken in every family pot on Sunday and 'poule au pot' is indeed a speciality of Béarn. Equally homely are

Béarnais soups which range from 'tourrin', an onion soup redolent of garlic and thick with egg yolk (in the mountains tourrin is called 'ouliat', meaning unctuous) to 'cousinat' made with leeks, beans, carrots and any other vegetables in season.

The pride of them all is 'garbure', which can contain almost any vegetable, simmered in broth; and with which it is mandatory to serve croûtes of bread plainly baked or topped, as I like them, with cheese. With the addition of ham, salt pork and goose 'confit', garbure transcends a mere soup — the vegetables cooked in the broth are made into a gratin, to serve as a main course with the meat, while the broth is brought separately to the table at the beginning of the meal. In a variant from Gascony, the cooked meat and some of the vegetables are layered together in a casserole, while the broth and remaining vegetables are served first. Everyone likes plenty of garlic in the pot, and gherkin pickles or peppers in vinegar are passed round with the meat.

In gastronomic circles Gascony has long been a famous name. The first so-called regional cookbook, which appeared in 1740, was called *Le Cuisinier Gascon*, though in fact the recipes had little to do with the province. Gascony is skirted on the north by the rich valley of the Garonne which produces all the fruit and vegetables a cook could desire. 'Gascony is rich, by virtue of its splendid food products known throughout the world, yet few are the people who come to taste them on the spot,' remarks chef André Daguin from Auch. He is referring to armagnac and the local foie gras from fattened geese and ducks whose meat is made into confit.

The canning of foie gras, confit and bottled fruits macerated in armagnac is a Gascon cottage industry, with the shops and roads lined with signs for 'produits régionaux', each with a different brand name. Jams are another local speciality, often using fruits like bilberries or quince that are otherwise ignored: a pity, because their flavour when cooked is excellent. For no one can say Gascons do not make the most of what they have in the kitchen. Their ingenuity, not to say tightfistedness, is celebrated by 'Gascon whites', an ironic reference to chefs who simply switch the buttoning of their double-breasted white jackets to expose the clean underside.

For meat, Gascony can turn south to the flat land around Tarbes, the most fertile

pocket lying along the Pyrenees. Although Tarbes itself is nondescript as towns go, I happened to arrive on market day and was instantly taken back 30 years to my rural childhood, when the weekly market was the centre of commercial, not to mention social, life. That day in Tarbes the streets were jammed with vehicles, by no means all motor-propelled. A wooden cart contained a small calf, blindfolded against fright with a grubby sweater; bicycles were laden like packhorses and the publicity for a small van read 'pulls like a mule'. Every imaginable object was changing hands, from ploughs to seeds to squawking chickens and rabbits for the pot. Here and there mountain poverty showed in the modest items offered for sale: half a dozen cheeses, bundles of leeks and onions, a pile of butter yeast cakes 'made specially for market day'. There was no sign of the cornucopian display to be found in richer areas like Normandy or the Rhône valley.

The eastern segment of the Pyrenees, before they run down to the Mediterranean plains of Languedoc and Roussillon, is the Ariège — bleak, untraversed ground, stony even in the river valleys. This was the last stronghold of the Albigensian heretics who caused so much trouble in the 12th century; and no wonder. The forbidding grey castle of Foix, the capital, still looks impregnable. It is only one of half a dozen similar fortresses scattered across the landscape.

From the scarlet of the Basque country to the grey of Ariège is less than 300 kilometres west to east as the crow flies, which is certainly not the way the roads go. Much of the cooking — vegetable soups, confit, Bayonne ham, the old-fashioned millas — is common to the whole region. But a surprising number of dishes, like ttoro, cousinat and particularly cakes and pastries, are found only in specific areas. Local dishes have remained local, tribute to the power of geography over greed.

TTORO
Peppery fish soup

Like all fish soups, ttoro was originally designed to use inexpensive fish with a poor texture or too many bones, such as conger eel, gurnard or scorpion fish. Now hake and monkfish are usually added, with mussels and possibly even some scampi. At its simplest, ttoro is cooked only with sautéed onions, garlic, herbs and water and is spiced with hot pepper, but tomatoes and white wine are often included. Fish like monkfish which cook more slowly than the rest should be cut in smaller pieces.

Serves 6

1 kg	mixed fish	2 lb
80 ml	olive oil	$\frac{1}{3}$ cup
	2 onions, sliced	
	5 cloves garlic, chopped	
	bouquet garni	
375 ml	dry white wine	$1\frac{1}{2}$ cups
1·5 L	water	$1\frac{1}{2}$ qt
	1 tomato, peeled, seeded and chopped	
	1 tsp paprika	
	salt	
	$\frac{1}{4}$ tsp hot red pepper or cayenne pepper, more to taste	
750 ml	mussels	3 cups
30 g	flour	$\frac{1}{4}$ cup
	6 large scampi (optional)	
	2 Tbsp chopped parsley	
	12–14 round croûtes*, fried in oil, then rubbed with garlic	

Cut off and discard the fins from the fish. Scale the fish and cut in pieces, reserving the heads and tails. Wash the fish pieces, heads and tails.

Heat 1 tablespoon of the oil in a large pot and add the onions, garlic and bouquet garni. Cook over a low fire for 5 minutes or until soft but not brown; then add the white wine and boil until reduced by half. Stir in the water, fish heads and tails, tomato, paprika, salt and a pinch of the hot pepper. Bring to a boil, cover and simmer over a low fire for about 1 hour. Clean the mussels*.

Dry the fish, sprinkle with salt and hot pepper and coat lightly with flour, patting off the excess. Heat the remaining oil in a shallow flameproof casserole and quickly brown the pieces of fish on both sides. Discard any excess oil. Strain the broth over the fish, add the scampi and simmer for 5 minutes. Add the mussels and simmer for 5 more minutes or until the mussels open and the fish are tender. Taste the broth for seasoning; it should be quite hot but extra salt may not be needed since mussels are salty. Sprinkle with parsley, arrange a few croûtes around the edge of the casserole and serve immediately. Pass the remaining croûtes separately.

BROYE or MILLAS
Cornmeal porridge

Broye is half soup, half porridge, made with white cornmeal and vegetable broth. When cooked until thick and left to cool, the mixture is stiff enough to slice and toast or fry like Italian polenta. Also called 'millas', broye is often made with the broth from garbure, then served with the vegetables, or it is good with a daube of beef or with tripe. The white cornmeal used in the Pyrenees is very fine, though not a powder like cornflour/cornstarch. Coarser cornmeal should be worked in a blender to the right consistency.

Serves 6–8

100 g	white cornmeal, more if needed	$\frac{3}{4}$ cup
1 L	vegetable cooking liquid or milk	1 qt
	salt and pepper	
	milk (optional: for serving)	
	goose fat from confit (optional: for serving)	

Whirl the cornmeal in a blender until fine. Bring the liquid to a boil in a heavy casserole. Sprinkle the cornmeal into the boiling liquid, stirring constantly to prevent lumps. Bring back to a boil and simmer over a low fire, stirring constantly, for 10 minutes or until the mixture is thick but still falls easily from a spoon. Taste for seasoning. If you prefer it thicker, continue simmering. Spoon into bowls and serve at once; if the broye is left, it gets much thicker. To enrich the soup (if it was made with milk), add a little milk or goose fat to each bowl.

BROYE or MILLAS II

Continue cooking the broye for 10 minutes until it is so stiff that it no longer sticks to the sides of the pan. Use a long-handled wooden spoon to stir because the mixture splutters.

Spread the millas in a greased cake pan to form a 5 cm/2 in layer and leave to cool. To serve, cut the millas in 1 cm/$\frac{3}{8}$ in slices and either fry them in lard until golden or bake them in a hot oven until brown.

PIPÉRADE BASQUAISE

Pepper and tomato purée with eggs

The name 'pipérade' comes from 'piper' (hot red pepper). This dish can be made in three ways: as a rolled omelette filled with the vegetable mixture, as a flat omelette, or as a vegetable purée thickened with eggs as in this recipe. The mixture must cook slowly, because the eggs will form lumps if the heat is too high. This tendency is accentuated by moisture in the vegetables, so the purée must be thick before the eggs are added. For pipérade au jambon, top with a thin slice of Bayonne or similar ham per person.

Serves 4

	½ dried red chili pepper OR a pinch of hot red pepper or cayenne pepper	
	4 Tbsp oil	
	2 onions, chopped	
	3 red or green peppers, cored and chopped	
	2 cloves garlic, chopped	
1 kg	tomatoes, peeled, seeded and chopped	2 lb
	salt	
	8 eggs, beaten to mix	

If using a chili pepper*, prepare and chop it. Heat the oil in a frying pan, add the onions and cook over a low fire until soft but not brown. Stir in the peppers, chili pepper (if using) and garlic and cook over a low fire, stirring often, for 5 minutes. Add the tomatoes and a little salt and cook over a medium fire, stirring often, for 20 minutes or until the mixture is very thick and most of the liquid has evaporated. Season to taste, adding the hot red pepper or cayenne pepper at this stage.

Add the beaten eggs to the vegetable purée and stir over a very low fire for 3 minutes or until the mixture has thickened but remains soft and moist. Taste for seasoning. Transfer to a serving dish and serve immediately.

'Piments d'Espelette'

PLACE-NAMES IN COOKING

Classical cookbooks often refer to regions or places in France, using them as shorthand for certain combinations of ingredients. 'Basquaise', for instance, usually means that the dish is flavoured with peppers or ham; anything 'périgourdine' should contain truffles, and 'lyonnaise' suggests a lot of onions. The same term can be applied to all manner of main ingredients, for instance, eggs, chicken, veal and beef, are all prepared with mushrooms in a white wine sauce 'à la chasseur' (hunter's style).

Often a method of cooking is also implied, as in 'provençale', which means that olive oil is used for frying and the dish is flavoured with garlic. Many of these names date back to the 18th century, when particular places became celebrated for the excellence of their products, like the cheese of Savoy in 'savoyarde', or for the way in which the ingredients were combined, as with the mushrooms, baby onions, lardons of bacon and red wine sauce which add up to 'bourguignonne'.

The French language is rich in adjectival forms of place-names. 'Lyonnais' obviously means 'from Lyon', but who would know that 'poniot' means from Le Puy, 'manceau' from Le Mans and 'moussipontin' from Pont à Mousson?

When used in cooking, these expressions are in the feminine singular: 'pommes sarladaise' is really shorthand for 'pommes à la façon sarladaise' (literally, potatoes in the Sarlat fashion). But there is a catch to these handy geographical descriptions. They are not an infallible guide to the cooking of a particular region.

Not only is the cooking of Burgundy infinitely more varied than is denoted by 'à la bourguignonne', but often classical cookbooks refine and elaborate on a regional theme until it would be scarcely recognizable on home ground. 'Sole dieppoise', for instance, with its garnish of mussels and mushrooms in a white wine and cream sauce, is very much a restaurant creation; in Dieppe itself the fish is much more likely to be simmered with the other ingredients as a soup.

And, just occasionally, regional descriptions are wildly misleading since it is often the chef of a smart city restaurant who originally bestowed them on a particular dish. 'Sauce béarnaise' has nothing to do with Béarn; it was a 19th-century creation of the restaurant Henri IV at St Germain-en-Laye outside Paris. As Henri de Navarre, the king had ruled over Béarn – hence sauce béarnaise.

HAM

Most mountain regions of France make ham, but the most celebrated type, which has been renowned since the Middle Ages, is the 'jambon de Bayonne' from the Pyrenees. Bayonne ham's distinction is due to its firm fat and its aromatic flavour. As with all hams, the name refers not just to the place of origin (nowadays most Bayonne hams come from nearby towns in the Basque country), but also to the method of curing. Bayonne ham, for instance, is salted and often rubbed with red Espelette pepper; Ardennes ham is smoked as well as salted; Auvergne, Alsace, Savoy and central Brittany each has its own type of ham, cured by various combinations of salting, smoking and drying.

Traditionally hams are cured to keep for at least three months and up to a year; the method used for classic Bayonne ham is typical. First the quality of the pork is vital: the pig should be plump but not fatty, fed on a diet of maize, household swill and acorns picked up in the woods. Secondly the skill with which the ham is salted is all-important. Bayonne hams are rubbed with salt every day for three days, using local salt from Salies-de-Béarn; then they are left to pickle in a special brine containing red wine and herbs for 20–30 days. Finally they may be hung for a week or two in the fireplace to smoke, or they may be kept in sifted cinders. They are sometimes rubbed with coarse pepper, particularly around the bone, which is the first place to be attacked by flies.

The hams hanging from a farmhouse ceiling, wrapped tightly in their protective butter-muslin, are a form of rural wealth whose value can be appreciated by looking at today's ham prices. In Bayonne charcuteries, the different parts of a ham are sold at different prices, the most expensive being the lean, moist slices from the centre. Less costly, because less weight is lost during curing, are mild hams such as 'jambon de Paris' and 'jambon d'York', which are always sold cooked. Again, Paris and York refer to the cure, rather than the place of production. The first is lightly salted boned ham sold in block shapes and the second unboned smoked ham.

Most mountain hams are cut in thin slices to be eaten raw as a first course or in a sandwich – without butter, say Bayonne ham connoisseurs, because the fat is so delicious – but 'lou jamboû pertout que hé boû' runs a Basque saying (ham is good in everything). Certainly ham is a recurrent theme in the local cooking, in the same way that anchovies are in Provence. Ham is the dominant flavour in the vegetable stew 'cousinat à la bayonnaise', adds interest to rice baked with eggs à la bayonnaise and is indispensable to a good chicken basquaise. As with all strong ingredients, seasoning must be carefully handled if the finished dish is not to be too salty. If raw ham is to be cooked it is important to remember that sautéing it for a long time intensifies its saltiness.

RIZ À LA BAYONNAISE
Rice with ham and baked eggs

This simple dish is good served with a tomato coulis (see recipe) as accompaniment.

Serves 6

30 g	butter	2 Tbsp
	1 onion, chopped	
60 g	slice of Bayonne ham or other raw ham, diced	2 oz
200 g	rice	1 cup
375 ml	broth	1½ cups
	salt and pepper	
	1 bay leaf	
50 g	grated gruyère cheese	½ cup
	6 eggs	
	1 L/1 qt baking dish	

Heat the butter in a sauté pan, add the onion and cook over a low fire until soft but not brown. Stir in the ham and the rice and sauté over a low fire, stirring constantly, until the rice is transparent but not brown. Stir in the broth, salt and pepper, and add the bay leaf. Bring to a boil, cover tightly and cook over a low fire for 20 minutes or until the rice is just tender and the liquid has been absorbed. Meanwhile, set the oven at very hot (220°C/425°F).

Leave the cooked rice in the covered pan for 10 minutes without stirring. Discard the bay leaf and stir in three-quarters of the cheese. Taste for seasoning: extra salt may not be needed since ham is salty.

Spoon the rice mixture into the buttered baking dish. Make 6 hollows in the mixture and break an egg into each. Sprinkle with the remaining cheese. Bake in the hot oven for 10 minutes or until the egg whites are just set but the yolks are still soft. Serve at once.

MORUE BASQUAISE
Salt cod with peppers and tomatoes

Salt cod is a Basque favourite dating back to the time when cod fishing was an important industry. Its pungent flavour is ideally suited to the 'basquaise' garnish of onions, garlic, tomatoes and a mixture of green and red peppers.

Serves 6

1 kg	salt cod	2 lb
	2 Tbsp olive oil	
	2 large onions, chopped	
	white part of 2 leeks, split and thinly sliced	
	6 cloves garlic, chopped	
600 g	peppers, cored and cut in strips	1¼ lb
750 g	tomatoes, peeled, seeded and chopped	1½ lb
	bouquet garni	
185 ml	white wine	¾ cup
	salt and pepper	

Soak the salt cod in water for 1–2 days, changing the water occasionally.

When ready to cook, put the cod in a pot, cover generously with water and bring just to a boil. Leave to cool in the liquid.

Heat the olive oil in a saucepan, add the onions, leeks and garlic and cook until soft but not brown. Add the peppers and cook over a low fire, stirring until slightly softened. Add the tomatoes and bouquet garni, bring to a boil and simmer for 10 minutes. Add the wine, an equal volume of cooking liquid from the cod and a pinch of pepper. Simmer uncovered for 20 minutes or until quite thick. Discard the bouquet garni. Set the oven at moderate (175°C/350°F).

Drain the cod and flake the meat, discarding the skin and bones. Mix with the sauce and taste for seasoning; salt may not be needed since the cod is salty. Transfer the mixture to a baking dish and bake for 20 minutes or until bubbling. Serve hot from the dish.

TRUITES AU LARD
Trout with bacon

The villages of the Pyrenees are among the few places where trout still come from mountain streams and are not just bred in ponds. In this recipe they are flavoured with bacon.

Serves 4

250 g each	4 trout	8 oz each
200 g	bacon, cut in small lardons	7 oz
30 g	butter or lard (optional)	2 Tbsp
	salt and pepper	
30 g	flour	$\frac{1}{4}$ cup
	2 cloves garlic, chopped	
	2 Tbsp wine vinegar	
	2 Tbsp chopped parsley	

Cut the fins off the trout and trim the tails to a 'V'. If they are not already cleaned, clean them through the gills without slitting the stomach. Wash the fish thoroughly and pat dry.

If the bacon is very salty, blanch* it. Heat it in a large frying pan until the fat runs; if the frying pan remains rather dry, add the butter. Sprinkle the trout with salt and pepper and coat with flour, patting off the excess. Sauté them in the pan with the bacon for 4–5 minutes on each side, or until tender and golden brown. Transfer the trout to a platter, sprinkle with the bacon, cover and keep warm.

Add the garlic to the hot pan and sauté briefly until soft but not brown. Remove the pan from the heat and add the vinegar; stand back as it will splutter. While still foaming, pour the vinegar over the fish, sprinkle with chopped parsley and serve immediately.

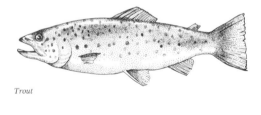

Trout

MERLUZA, SALSA VERDE
Hake in green sauce

Basque green sauce is not a sauce at all, but a garnish of green peas, asparagus and chopped parsley. Often baby potatoes are included and fish and vegetables are baked together with plenty of garlic and hot red pepper.

Serves 4

350 g	little new potatoes (optional)	$\frac{3}{4}$ lb
	salt	
250–375 ml	shelled fresh or frozen peas	1–1$\frac{1}{2}$ cups
500 g	asparagus	1 lb
150 g each	4 slices hake	5 oz each
30 g	flour	$\frac{1}{4}$ cup
	3 Tbsp olive oil	
	3 cloves garlic, finely chopped	
	pinch of hot red pepper or cayenne pepper	
	3 Tbsp chopped parsley	
125 ml	water	$\frac{1}{2}$ cup

Put the potatoes in a pot of water, add salt and bring to a boil. Simmer for 15 minutes or until just tender and drain.

Cook the peas in boiling salted water until just tender: 15 minutes for fresh or 5 minutes for frozen peas. Rinse under cold water and drain thoroughly. Peel the asparagus and trim off the stalks; they can be used for soup. Cook the tips in boiling salted water for 3–5 minutes or until just tender. Rinse under cold water and drain thoroughly.

Set the oven at moderately hot (190°C/375°F). Wash and dry the hake. Season the slices of hake with salt and coat them in flour, patting off the excess. Heat 2 tablespoons of the oil in a frying pan, add the hake slices and brown lightly on both sides. Transfer to a shallow baking dish. Sprinkle with the garlic and hot pepper. Add the potatoes around the edges of the baking dish and top with the asparagus tips and the peas. Sprinkle with a little salt and with the parsley, then with the remaining oil. Pour in the water, cover and bake in the oven for 15–20 minutes or until the fish is tender. Serve hot from the dish.

Canigou

HORSEMEAT

The Pyrenees are one of the last refuges of the traditional workhorse, but the horse population of France has plummeted from two and a half million 30 years ago to 370,000 today, a figure which includes the pedigree bloodstock of Normandy. To most Anglo-Saxons the idea of selling horses for human consumption is disgusting. Not so in France, where horsemeat is surprisingly in demand, particularly on Mondays, when all other butchers are closed.

Even small French towns have their horse butcher, denoted by a golden horse's head above the shop. Cuts of horsemeat bear the same names as beef and look very similar, though the meat is less fatty and much darker in colour. Each muscle is enveloped in whitish tissue, normally removed by the butcher. Nutritionally speaking, horsemeat closely resembles beef except that it contains a much higher proportion of glycogen – a sugar-related compound which can give horsemeat a slight tell-tale sweetness. As well as selling raw meat, butchers do a brisk trade in horsemeat pâtés and assorted sausages. However, horsemeat rarely appears in recipe books for the simple reason that it is a direct – and often clandestine – substitute for beef.

In the 19th century, horsemeat enjoyed a vogue at banquets, such as that given by the city of Paris in 1865 which included horsemeat à la mode, horsemeat filet with mushrooms, and salad dressed with horsemeat oil. Roasts were particularly well regarded and Joseph Favre, a well-known food authority of the time, even claimed that horse filet was superior to beef. Doctors recommended it for cases of tuberculosis since horses, unlike cattle, rarely carry the tuberculin bacillus. Today, chopped horsemeat is advised for children and convalescents.

Until very recently, the great advantage of horsemeat was its low price. Unlike cattle, worn-out old horses still made acceptable eating and before machines took over on the farm the supply was plentiful. But now, much of the 100,000 tonnes of horsemeat consumed in France annually is imported from Central Europe and the Americas, provoking periodic scandals about the conditions under which old nags are shipped to the slaughterhouse. Prices have risen so much that today horsemeat costs almost as much as beef, and one would have thought that its chief attraction had disappeared. But habits die hard and there will always be eccentric gourmets who maintain that horse filet cannot be equalled.

SALMIS DE PALOMBES
Wood pigeon stew

This salmis, traditionally served on All Saints' Day (the meat of the pigeon is appropriately dark) is very different from the classic recipe in which the carcass of a roast bird is crushed in a mortar, then used to flavour the sauce. Here the bird is cut in pieces and simmered in red wine with onions and ham for as long as five hours, since wood pigeon is notoriously tough. Domestic pigeon (squab in the USA) can be substituted, and will take only an hour or so to cook.

Serves 4

300 g each	2 squab	10 oz each
	3 Tbsp oil	
	20–24 baby onions	
150 g	Bayonne ham or raw ham, cut in small dice	5 oz
15 g	flour	2 Tbsp
250 ml	red wine, preferably bordeaux	1 cup
500 ml	broth or water	2 cups
	bouquet garni	
	salt and pepper	
	8 croûtes*, fried in butter	

Quarter each bird. Heat 2 tablespoons of the oil in a heavy casserole and brown the pieces of bird well on all sides. Remove them and set them aside. Add the baby onions and the diced ham to the casserole and brown them as well. Remove them and set aside. Add the remaining oil and heat it.

Whisk in the flour and cook over a low fire, whisking constantly, until just beginning to brown. Whisk in the wine and broth and bring to a boil. Add the bouquet garni and a little pepper and return the birds to the casserole. Simmer partly covered over a low fire for 4–5 hours for wild pigeons or 1 hour for domestic pigeons/squabs or until nearly tender. Return the onions and ham to the casserole and continue simmering uncovered until the birds and onions are tender.

If the sauce is not thick enough to coat a spoon, lift out the birds, onions and ham. Simmer the sauce, stirring often, until thick and rich. Reheat the birds and garnish in the sauce. Discard the bouquet garni and taste the sauce for seasoning; extra salt may not be needed since the ham is salty. Serve the salmis in a shallow dish surrounded by the croûtes.

POULET BASQUAISE
Chicken with peppers

This recipe from the Basque country is very different from the bland 'poulet basquaise' of classic cuisine. Here hot red pepper is added to taste and recipe books warn that too much can burn the tongue. There should be plenty of sauce to moisten the boiled rice which is the standard accompaniment.

Serves 4

	$\frac{1}{2}$ small fresh or dried red chili pepper OR a large pinch of hot red pepper or cayenne pepper	
1·5-kg	chicken	3-lb
	salt and pepper	
30 g	flour	$\frac{1}{4}$ cup
	1 clove garlic, halved	
60 ml	olive oil	$\frac{1}{4}$ cup
750 g	tomatoes, peeled, seeded and coarsely chopped	$1\frac{1}{2}$ lb
500 g	green peppers, each cored and cut in 8 strips	1 lb
125 g	mushrooms, sliced (optional)	4 oz
125 g	Bayonne ham or other raw ham, diced	4 oz
	1 Tbsp chopped parsley	

If using a chili pepper*, prepare and chop it.

Cut the chicken* in 4 pieces. Sprinkle the pieces with salt and pepper and lightly flour them, patting off the excess. Rub a heavy casserole with the garlic halves and discard them. Heat the oil in the casserole over a medium-high fire, add the chicken pieces and brown them on all sides. Stir in the tomatoes, green peppers, mushrooms, ham and hot pepper. Cover and cook over a low fire for 25 minutes. Uncover the casserole so the sauce reduces gradually as the chicken cooks and continue to simmer over a low fire for 30 minutes or until the chicken is tender. Taste for seasoning, adding hot red pepper at this stage if no chili pepper was used; extra salt may not be needed since the ham is salty. Sprinkle with parsley and serve from the casserole.

FOIES DE VOLAILLE AUX RAISINS
Chicken livers with grapes

This Gascon dish combines two regional products: poultry and grapes. Locally it would probably be made with foie gras (fattened fresh goose or duck liver), but chicken livers are suggested here as a good alternative. Black or green grapes may be used; both types should be seeded (or use seedless grapes) and the thick skins of black grapes should be removed by blanching the grapes in boiling water for 30 seconds, then draining and peeling them.

Serves 2–3 as a main course

250 g	large chicken livers	$\frac{1}{2}$ lb
30 g	flour	$\frac{1}{4}$ cup
30 g	butter	2 Tbsp
	salt and pepper	
	1 Tbsp armagnac or cognac	
125 ml	broth	$\frac{1}{2}$ cup
	8 mushroom caps	
	2 Tbsp milk	
	pinch of grated nutmeg	
125 g	grapes, pitted	$\frac{1}{4}$ lb
	$\frac{1}{2}$ tsp sugar (optional)	
	8 round croûtes*, fried in oil and butter	

Remove any green spots or veins from the livers. If the livers are large, cut them in diagonal slices; otherwise, cut them in half. Coat them in flour, patting off the excess.

Heat the butter in a frying pan, add the livers with salt and pepper and sauté them, tossing occasionally, over a medium-high fire for 2–3 minutes until they are well browned on the outside but still pink inside. Transfer to a dish and keep warm.

Add the armagnac to the pan and flame it. Add the broth and the mushrooms, cover and simmer for 5 minutes or until tender. Using a slotted spoon, transfer the mushrooms to the serving dish.

Add the milk to the pan, season with salt, pepper and nutmeg and bring to a boil. Add the grapes and simmer for 1–2 minutes or until just heated through. Taste again, adding a little sugar if the grapes are tart.

Spoon the livers on to the croûtes and spoon the sauce and grapes over and around them. Top each with a mushroom and serve immediately.

POULE AU POT
Boiled stuffed chicken with vegetables

There is no standard recipe for poule au pot. In the country, the chicken is often cooked simply with vegetables, leaving out the meat. Some of the broth may be used to cook rice as an accompaniment, or the broth may be thickened as a sauce, with olives and baby onions added as a garnish for the chicken. To make the bird go further, extra stuffing wrapped in blanched cabbage leaves can be added to the pot. Left-over chicken is never a problem; it is excellent cold with mayonnaise, or it may be reheated in a tomato sauce.

Serves 8

1·5-kg	beef or veal shank	3-lb
5 L	water	5 qt
	1 onion, studded with 2 cloves	
	large bouquet garni	
	salt	
	10 black peppercorns	
	1 stalk celery	
	1 cinnamon stick (optional)	
about	large chicken or boiling	about
2-kg	fowl	4½-lb
750 g	medium carrots	1½ lb
1 kg	leeks, trimmed and split	2 lb
500 g	medium turnips	1 lb
125 g	very fine noodles OR	¼ lb
	1 small loaf French bread,	
	sliced diagonally	
	coarse salt, for serving	
	STUFFING	
35 g	fresh breadcrumbs	¼ cup
125 ml	milk	½ cup
200 g	Bayonne ham or other raw	
	ham, ground	
	1 clove garlic, finely chopped	
	4 Tbsp chopped parsley	
	the chicken liver and heart, chopped	
	1 egg, beaten	
	salt and pepper	
	½ tsp ground allspice OR	
	pinch of grated nutmeg	
	trussing needle and string	

Put the shank in a large kettle. Add the water and bring slowly to a boil, skimming often. Add the onion, bouquet garni, salt, peppercorns, celery and cinnamon stick and simmer un-covered, skimming occasionally, for 2 hours.

Meanwhile, prepare the stuffing: soak the breadcrumbs in the milk and squeeze dry. Mix them with the ham, garlic, parsley, chicken liver and heart and beaten egg, and season with pepper and allspice or nutmeg. Salt may not be needed since the ham is salty. Beat very well until thoroughly mixed. Sauté a small piece of

stuffing and taste for seasoning. Stuff the bird and truss it.

Add the bird to the pot and continue to simmer, uncovered, for 1 hour. Add the carrots, leeks and turnips with more salt if needed and continue to simmer for another hour or until the meat, chicken and vegetables are very tender. Be sure there is always enough liquid to cover the meats and vegetables.

If serving the broth with noodles: a short time before serving, spoon about 1 litre of broth into a separate pan and simmer the noodles for 5 minutes or until tender. If serving with bread, toast the slices in a moderate oven (175°C/350°F) for 10–15 minutes or until golden brown.

Transfer the beef and chicken to a board and discard the trussing string. Boil the broth to reduce it by one-third or until well flavoured. Cut the beef in medium-thick slices and arrange them on a large platter. Carve the chicken, pile the stuffing on the platter and arrange the pieces of chicken on top. Arrange the carrots, leeks and turnips around the meat and chicken. Cover the platter with foil and keep hot.

Strain the broth, taste for seasoning and skim off as much fat as possible, first with a metal spoon and then with strips of paper towel. If serving with bread, put the slices in soup bowls and pour the broth over them. Otherwise serve the noodles in the broth. Serve the meat platter as a main course, accompanied by coarse salt.

POT-AU-FEU

Omit the chicken and stuffing from the above recipe, and add to the pot with the shank:

1-kg	blade portion of beef chuck	2-lb
1-kg	beef short ribs	2-lb
After 1½ hours of cooking add:		
1 kg	beef marrow bones	2 lb

(wrapped in cheesecloth so that the marrow does not fall out during cooking). Add the vegetables 30 minutes after the marrow bones.

When serving the broth, if you prefer, scoop the beef marrow out of the bones and spread it on the browned bread. Put a few slices in each soup bowl and pour the broth over them. Alternatively, add the marrow bones to the meat platter and use spoons to scoop out the marrow. Serve the meat platter with coarse salt, gherkin pickles and mustard.

THE POT-AU-FEU FAMILY

If any dish can be regarded as fundamental, it must be 'pot-au-feu': 'In the common pot-au-feu lies the foundation of empires,' said Mirabeau. Since its beginnings in the days of the cauldron, when all available ingredients were simmered together in a pot over the open fire, pot-au-feu has acquired its own dos and don'ts. Variations on the classic recipe include 'potée', associated with the more austere parts of France like Auvergne and Lorraine, the 'hochepot' of Flanders and the 'poule au pot' of Béarn.

Today's pot-au-feu is based on beef – partly lean meat such as top rump (rump pot roast in the USA), partly leg of beef (US heel of round) or some other tough cut with plenty of bone and gelatine to add richness to the broth. A few marrow bones should be included, wrapped in cheesecloth so that the marrow does not dissolve during long cooking. To add colour to the broth, an onion may be singed over the fire, but the meat itself is never browned as this prevents the juices flavouring the broth. In hochepot, however, the meats (as many as four may be used: beef, veal, lamb and pork) are deliberately browned to seal in their flavour before the water is added. For poule au pot the key ingredient is a large boiling fowl, often stuffed with a dressing of pork, Bayonne ham and herbs.

Root vegetables – carrots, turnips, leeks, parsnips, onions, celery – are the other important elements of pot-au-feu and its variants, added, one by one, during the course of cooking so they emerge butter-tender but unbroken. The meat, too, should be very tender, soft enough to be pierced easily with a two-pronged fork. Flavour is added with salt (not too much as the broth may be boiled down to concentrate it for serving), peppercorns, a few whole cloves, bay leaf, thyme and garlic to taste.

Finally, pot-au-feu must be served in style. A great platter is obligatory, with room for all the vegetables to be set in neat piles around the edge, with the sliced meats overlapping down the centre. Accompaniments may include two kinds of mustard, tomato or horse-radish sauce, and gherkin pickles; for poule au pot, these are replaced by coarse salt. The broth of pot-au-feu is served first, if possible in a traditional tureen, and it may be reinforced with a handful of vermicelli noodles, or with toasted croûtes of bread spread with marrow from the marrow bones. Any left-over broth is invaluable for soups and sauces. Poule au pot follows the same pattern, with the chicken cut up and piled, with the stuffing, in the centre of the dish.

Potée is a pot-au-feu made with pork rather than beef, heavier and less refined. Given the versatility of the pig, potée varies much more than pot-au-feu, containing the cook's choice of salt or fresh pork, bacon, ham hocks and a wide range of sausages. Potée also includes cabbage, that mundane vegetable which grows almost anywhere and which gives such excellent flavour to soup. Dumplings can be added, to cook while floating on top of the broth, or wrapped in cabbage leaves and packed tightly to simmer in a separate pot. The potée of Auvergne is firmly loyal to cabbage, but that of Berry is based on dried red kidney beans. In Lorraine, potatoes or beans also play an important part, with fresh white kidney beans for a spring potée and dried beans in a winter one. The ingredients of potée are often presented all together, the meats, vegetables and broth being served in one bowl as a hearty soup.

The making of any dishes in the pot-au-feu family is quite an art. The flavours of the different ingredients must be nicely balanced and they should be poached, not simmered, to just the right stage. The broth must be skimmed often so that at the end of cooking it does not need to be clarified with egg white. The best pot for a pot-au-feu, say purists, is made of earthenware.

CONFIT

'Confit' is an almost exclusively French method of salting meats and poultry, then preserving them in fat. It is hard to understand why it is not universal, since making confit is simplicity itself, requiring only three or four ingredients and little time or skill. Although usually associated with duck and goose, in fact any meat with a fairly high fat content can be preserved this way; all over south-western France and throughout the length of the Pyrenees to Languedoc, the charcuteries are full of confit of pork, tongue, sausages, even pig's feet, as well as of poultry. In the mountains, where storing food for the winter is still an important activity, the autumn, when the pigs are killed, is the high season for confit. Confit is perfectly good made with the fatty breed of duck found in the USA.

Whatever the meat or bird, it is normally preserved in large pieces. These are thickly coated in coarse salt, with thyme and bay leaf added, and left to pickle for between 6 and 36 hours. Pickling time depends on the flavour wanted and the thickness of the meat; the longer it is left, the stronger the flavour will be, although eventually the confit can become inedibly salty. The confit is then cooked in large quantities of fat; goose is normally cooked in goose fat, which can be bought in tins, duck in duck fat and pork in lard. However, lard can be used for everything, or fat left from previous confits can be reused after straining, although after three or four cycles it becomes too salty. The fat must be sufficient to cover the meat, which is cooked extremely slowly on top of the stove or in the oven, until it is almost falling apart – so soft, say country cooks, that a straw can be inserted right through the meat.

When cool enough to handle, the meat is packed in a crock and completely covered with melted fat to seal it. A tight seal is vital, for all air must be excluded from the meat and the crock should be banged on the table to extract air bubbles. When the fat has set, any air pockets must be filled with more melted fat. Then a cloth is laid on the fat, topped with a thick layer of coarse salt right to the edges of the crock, and the whole pot is covered with stout paper tied with string. In a cool place, the paper lid is sufficient covering for a month; in a refrigerator, the confit will keep much longer. If left in a warm place, confit goes rancid and acquires a musty taste.

In any case, confit should be left at least a week to mature before being eaten. It has a flavour all its own, though it can be compared to ham. Drained of the preserving fat, it is used to enrich soups and stews, particularly those based on vegetables, but most often confit is served alone, cooked gently in a little of its fat until it is hot and brown; the crisp brown skin on confit of goose and duck is a particular treat.

As accompaniment, potatoes fried in fat from the confit are a must – the best are wafer-thin, and crisp with a hint of garlic. Vegetable accompaniments may be added to balance the richness of confit. Lentils or dried beans are popular, or a stew of green peas and onions, or a purée of sorrel, spinach or chestnuts, while confit of goose deserves the luxury of a few wild mushrooms. Confit is also good cold, particularly in a salad dressed with tarragon vinegar and walnut oil, another southwestern speciality.

CONFIT DE CANARD
Confit of duck

Often only the legs and thighs of the duck are used for confit, and the breast, called a 'magret', is cooked like a steak. If you intend to serve the duck alone instead of using it to flavour other dishes such as cassoulet, reduce the amount of salt in this recipe by one-third.

Serves 3–4

1·8-kg	large duck	4-lb
50 g	coarse salt	3 Tbsp
	1 tsp ground black pepper	
	2–3 sprigs of thyme	
	2–3 bay leaves, crumbled	
1·5 kg	lard or goose fat, more if needed	3 lb

Cut the duck* in 8 pieces, trimming the neck and wings and removing the backbone; these bones can be used for soup. Rub each piece of duck with some of the coarse salt and put it in a crock or terrine. Sprinkle with pepper and the remaining salt and add the thyme and bay leaves. Cover and leave in a cool place for 6–12 hours, depending on how strong a flavour you want, turning the pieces occasionally.

When ready to cook, wipe the excess salt from the duck pieces. Set the oven at low (150°C/300°F). Lay the duck pieces skin side down in a flameproof casserole and cook over a low fire for 15–20 minutes or until the fat runs and the duck browns lightly. Add enough lard or goose fat to cover the browned duck, cover and cook in the oven for 2 hours or until the duck is very tender and has rendered all its fat.

To preserve the duck: pour a layer of rendered duck fat in the base of a small terrine and leave until set. Pack the pieces of duck on top and pour over enough fat to cover them completely, adding melted lard if necessary. Cover the crock and keep in a cool place at least a week for the flavour to mellow. If sealed with a cloth sprinkled with salt and then covered with paper, confit will keep for several months in a cool place.

To serve the confit by itself: leave it in a warm place until the fat runs. Drain it, then fry it in a little fat until it is very hot and the skin is crisp and brown. Transfer to a platter and serve very hot. Keep the left-over fat for frying.

CONFIT D'OIE

To substitute **goose** for the duck in the above recipe, double the quantities of all the seasonings, including the salt.

CONFIT DE PORC
Confit of pork

When sealed with a cloth topped with a layer of salt, then covered in sturdy paper, confit de porc will keep several months in an earthenware crock.

Serves 6

1·5 kg	pork shoulder, cut in six pieces	3 lb
	2–3 Tbsp coarse salt	
750 g	lard, more if needed	1½ lb
	ground black pepper	
	large pinch of thyme	
	3 bay leaves, crumbled	
	trussing string	

Tie each piece of pork in a compact bundle. Put them in a shallow dish, sprinkle with the coarse salt and leave in the refrigerator overnight or for 2 nights, depending on the strength of flavour you want.

When ready to cook the pork, wipe it to remove excess salt. Melt the lard in a heavy pot and leave until cool but not set. If using the oven, set it at low (150°C/300°F). Add the pork to the melted lard with pepper, thyme and bay leaves; the lard should completely cover the pork. Cover and cook in the heated oven or over a very low fire, stirring occasionally, for 3 hours or until the meat is almost falling apart. Remove the pieces of pork, let cool slightly and discard the strings. Pack the pork in an earthenware crock and cover with the cooking fat. If there is not enough fat to cover, melt more lard and add it. Let cool completely. Cover the confit and keep it in a cool place for at least a week before serving.

To serve the confit, put the crock in a warm place so that the fat gradually melts sufficiently for you to remove the meat. Heat 2–3 tablespoons of the fat in a frying pan over a medium fire, and cook the pieces of pork for 10–12 minutes until they are very hot and brown. Lift out the confit with a slotted spoon and serve hot, or at room temperature. The left-over fat can be used for frying.

ÉPAULE DE MOUTON À LA BÉARNAISE
Braised stuffed lamb with peppers

This shoulder of lamb is stuffed with bread-crumbs flavoured with garlic and parsley, rather than with the usual French meat stuffing.

Serves 6

1·8-kg	shoulder of lamb, boned, with the bones	4-lb
	salt and pepper	
30 g	lard	2 Tbsp
	1 green and 1 red pepper, each cored and cut in strips	
250 ml	broth	1 cup
250 ml	white wine	1 cup
	STUFFING	
	6 slices white bread, crusts discarded	
125 ml	white wine	$\frac{1}{2}$ cup
30 g	lard	2 Tbsp
	4 cloves garlic, chopped	
	2 shallots, chopped	
	3 Tbsp parsley	
	1 egg yolk	
	salt and pepper	
	trussing string	

Prepare the stuffing: soak the bread in the wine until softened. Meanwhile, heat the lard in a frying pan, add the garlic, shallots and parsley and sauté gently until soft but not brown. Squeeze out the excess liquid from the bread. Stir in the garlic mixture, egg yolk and plenty of salt and pepper. Leave to cool. Set the oven at hot (200°C/400°F).

Trim the skin and all but a thin layer of fat from the lamb. If necessary, cut to enlarge the pocket left when the bones were removed. Lay the lamb on a board, skin side down; spread it with stuffing. Roll up and tie in a cylinder.

Heat the lard in a heavy casserole, add the lamb and brown it on all sides. Add the wine, broth, salt and pepper and bring to a boil. Cover and braise in the oven for $1\frac{1}{4}$ hours or until nearly tender.

Put the peppers in boiling salted water and boil for 2 minutes. Drain, rinse with cold water and drain well. Add the peppers to the casserole and braise 10–15 minutes more or until hot when tested with a skewer inserted into the centre of the meat for 30 seconds. Transfer the lamb and peppers to a platter, cover and keep them warm. Taste the cooking liquid and boil if necessary until concentrated. Season the gravy, skim off fat and strain into a sauce-boat.

To serve, discard the trussing strings and cut the lamb in medium-thick slices. Arrange them on the platter with the peppers. Alternatively carve the lamb at table. Pass gravy separately.

GIGOT DE SEPT HEURES
Braised leg of lamb with garlic

Versions of gigot de sept heures turn up wherever tough mutton made the recipe appropriate. The leg is cooked for literally six or seven hours, at the end of which it is meltingly tender and full of flavour from the vegetables. Despite the large amount used, at the end of cooking the garlic flavour is scarcely perceptible.

Serves 8

2-kg	leg mutton or mature lamb	4–5-lb
	2 cloves garlic	
	large bouquet garni	
	salt and pepper	
4 L	water, more if needed	4 qt
	GARNISH	
	3 carrots, sliced	
	3 small turnips, halved and sliced	
	3 medium leeks, trimmed, split and sliced	
	$\frac{1}{2}$ small celery root, halved and sliced	
	3 medium onions, thinly sliced	
	10 cloves garlic or to taste, chopped	
	trussing string	

Set the oven at very low (120°C/250°F). Trim the mutton of all excess fat. (Mutton fat has a very strong flavour.) Cut the 2 garlic cloves in slivers and stud the meat with them. Tie the meat tightly with string and put it in a very large ovenproof pot with the bouquet garni, a small pinch of salt, and enough water to cover it by three-quarters. Bring the water to a boil on top of the stove and skim well. Cover the pot and put it in the preheated oven.

After an hour, turn the meat over, and continue to cook it very slowly, uncovered, for another 4 hours, turning occasionally. The water should scarcely bubble; if it simmers, turn down the heat. If the meat gets dry during cooking, add more water. After 4 hours, add the sliced garnish vegetables and a little salt and pepper. After another hour, remove the meat from the pot and leave it still tied with string in a warm place while finishing the vegetables.

Cook the vegetables and the cooking broth on top of the stove over high heat until the vegetables are soft and the broth has reduced to about a quarter of the original volume. Strain the vegetables and keep them warm. Taste the broth, reduce it again if necessary and season it. Remove the strings from the lamb and carve it in thick slices. Serve with the vegetables and with the unthickened broth as gravy.

GARBURE BÉARNAISE

Pork stew with vegetables and confit

Three dishes, all cooked in one pot, emerge when making garbure béarnaise. The meats should include ham and lean salt pork (shoulder is a good cut), sliced and served on a separate platter. As accompaniment, the vegetables are layered with goose confit and fat salt pork in a shallow gratin dish, then baked to form a brown crust. The broth is left to be served as a first course, or it may be passed with the meat and vegetables.

Serves 10–12

500-g	pork shoulder, salt-cured if possible	1-lb
250-g	piece of salt pork belly	$\frac{1}{2}$-lb
500-g	fresh or salt-cured ham hock	1-lb
250 g	dried white beans	$\frac{1}{2}$ lb
	large bouquet garni	
3·5 L	water	$3\frac{1}{2}$ qt
	1 small head cabbage	
500 g	potatoes	1 lb
500 g	carrots	1 lb
	2 onions, each studded with a clove	
	2 turnips	
	2 leeks, trimmed and split	
	3 cloves garlic	
250 g	green beans	$\frac{1}{2}$ lb
	pinch of hot red or cayenne pepper	
	10–12 slices of country bread	
	4 pieces goose or duck confit, halved (see recipe)	
100 g	grated gruyère cheese	1 cup
80 g	goose fat, melted	5 Tbsp
	salt and pepper	
25 × 13 cm/10 × 5 in shallow baking dish		

Soak the salt pork, ham and dried beans overnight in separate bowls of cold water. Drain and put the meats in a pot. Cover with fresh water and bring to a boil. Simmer for 10 minutes. Taste the water; if it is very salty, drain the meats and repeat the simmering process in fresh water. Drain thoroughly. Drain the beans.

Put the pork in a pot with the beans and bouquet garni. Add the water and bring to a boil. Simmer for 1 hour. Discard the cabbage ribs and cut the leaves in strips. Add the cabbage, potatoes, carrots, onions, turnips, leeks, garlic and green beans, season with a pinch of hot pepper and bring to a boil. Skim thoroughly, cover and simmer for 2 hours or until the meats are tender and the vegetables are so soft that they are falling apart. If any meat is tender before the end of cooking, remove it.

Meanwhile, heat the oven until hot (200°C/400°F). Bake the bread slices until crisp.

To make the gratin: lift out the salt pork and vegetables with a slotted spoon, leaving the pork shoulder and ham hock to keep warm in the broth. Cut the salt pork belly in slices and the vegetables in rough pieces. In the baking dish arrange a layer of vegetables, top with salt pork slices, add another layer of vegetables and top with the pieces of confit. Set the bread on top and sprinkle with half the cheese. Spoon three-quarters of the goose fat over the bread. Taste the broth for seasoning and pour in enough to come nearly to the level of the bread. Bake in the hot oven for about 30 minutes or until brown. Stir the browned crust into the meat and vegetables and sprinkle with the remaining cheese. Top with the remaining goose fat. Return to the oven for another 15 minutes or until well browned. The gratin should now be very thick.

To serve: drain and carve the pork shoulder in medium-thick slices. Cut the ham hock in pieces and put both meats on a platter. The broth may be a first course, or can be served together with the gratin and the platter of meat.

RAGOÛT DE MOUTON
AUX OLIVES VERTES
Mutton stew with green olives

Pyrenean mutton is at its best after the sheep have been feeding all summer in the mountains. The high pastures grow aromatic herbs which give a special flavour to the meat in stews like this one.

Serves 6

250 g	green olives, pitted	1¼ cups
	1 Tbsp olive oil	
15 g	butter	1 Tbsp
1 kg	boned shoulder of lamb or	2 lb
	mutton, cut in 5 cm/2 in cubes	
	2 tsp flour	
1 kg	tomatoes, peeled, seeded	2 lb
	and chopped	
	3 cloves garlic, chopped	
	salt and pepper	

Blanch the olives* if they are very salty. Heat the oil and butter in a pot, add the lamb cubes and brown them on all sides over a high fire.

Sprinkle with the flour, stir well and cook over a low fire until lightly browned. Stir in the tomatoes, garlic and olives and add a pinch of pepper. Cover and simmer over a low fire, stirring occasionally, for 1 hour, or until the meat is tender. Taste for seasoning. Transfer the meat and garnish to a shallow dish and serve hot.

COUSINAT À LA BAYONNAISE
Vegetable stew with ham

Bayonne has given its name to the bayonet, manufactured in the city since 1703, but here 'bayonnaise' means nothing more menacing than a garnish of ham. In this stew, almost any vegetables can be used, particularly if they are tough and need long cooking, so the selection given here is only a start.

Serves 4–6

	6 tiny artichokes OR 3 medium ones	
30 g	lard	2 Tbsp
125 g total	2 thick slices Bayonne ham or raw ham, diced	4 oz total
500 g	fresh broad beans OR	1 lb
375 g	lima beans, shelled	¾ lb
500 g	whole baby carrots or sliced medium carrots	1 lb
	white part of 12 spring onions	
500 g	green beans	1 lb
	2 green peppers, cored and quartered	
250 ml	broth or water	1 cup
125 ml	white wine	½ cup
375 g	tomatoes, peeled, seeded and coarsely chopped	¾ lb
	salt and pepper	

Remove the tough bottom leaves and cut about 2·5 cm/1 in from the top of the baby artichokes. If using medium artichokes, shape artichoke bottoms* by removing all the leaves.

Heat the lard in a heavy casserole, add the ham and brown it lightly. Stir in the artichokes, broad beans, carrots, onions, green beans and peppers. Add the broth and bring to a boil. Cover and simmer for 30 minutes, stir in the wine and continue to simmer for another 15 minutes. Stir in the tomatoes and simmer for 15 minutes more. Finally, remove the cover and simmer for another 30 minutes or until the vegetables are very tender and the mixture is thick. Add pepper and taste; salt may not be needed since the ham is salty. Serve hot from the casserole.

POIS CHICHES AU GRAS
Chick-pea and sausage casserole

Like all dried vegetables, chick-peas are a
standby in the Pyrenees. Here they are combined with salt pork and two kinds of sausage in
a casserole rather like cassoulet. The chick-peas
should be thoroughly soaked, though they will
never cook to a purée like dried beans.

Serves 6

500 g	chick-peas	2¼ cups
	bouquet garni	
	1 onion, studded with a clove	
	3 cloves garlic, unpeeled	
	pinch of baking soda	
200 g	pork rind	7 oz
250 g	salt pork belly	½ lb
250-g	garlic sausage for poaching	½-lb
	2 carrots, quartered	
	salt and pepper	
	3 Toulouse or other fresh sausages (see recipe)	

Soak the chick-peas overnight in cold water.
Drain and rinse them and put them in a large pot
with the bouquet garni, whole onion, garlic,
baking soda and water to cover. Bring to a boil,
cover and simmer for 1 hour.

Meanwhile, put the pork rind and salt pork in
a pot of cold water, bring to a boil and simmer
for 10 minutes. Rinse under cold running water
and drain thoroughly.

Add the pork rind and salt pork to the chick-
peas and simmer for 1 hour more. Add the
poaching sausage and carrots and simmer for
another 30 minutes or until the meats, chick-
peas and carrots are tender. Taste for seasoning
and add pepper; salt may not be necessary. Slice
the poaching sausage and salt pork. Discard the
bouquet garni, onion, garlic and pork rind.

Just before serving, grill/broil the Toulouse
sausages for 10–15 minutes or until golden
brown. With a slotted spoon, transfer the chick-
peas to a shallow bowl and arrange the meats
and carrots around them. Moisten with a little of
the broth. Serve hot.

POIS CHICHES À L'OCCITANE

Serve left-over chick-peas and meats as a lukewarm or cold salad: dice the meats and put
them in a bowl with the chick-peas and strips of
red peppers preserved in oil. Moisten with olive
oil and lemon juice and flavour with salt,
pepper, chopped parsley and chopped garlic.

HARICOTS SECS EN SALADE
White bean salad with tomato and egg

White beans are often used for this salad as a
colour contrast to the tomatoes and peppers, but
chick-peas or any cooked dried beans can be
substituted.

Serves 4

250 g	dried white beans	½ lb
	salt and pepper	
	1 onion, finely chopped	
	1 green pepper, cored and diced	
	2 cloves garlic, finely chopped	
	2 tomatoes, diced	
	2 hard-boiled eggs, sliced	
	VINAIGRETTE	
	2 Tbsp vinegar	
	salt and pepper	
	6 Tbsp oil	

Soak the dried beans overnight in cold water
and drain. Put them in a pot with enough water
to cover generously. Simmer over a low fire for
30 minutes, add salt and pepper and continue
cooking for another 30 minutes or until just
tender. Drain thoroughly; the cooking liquid
can be saved for making soup.

Make the vinaigrette*. Mix the warm beans
with the vinaigrette, onion, pepper and garlic
and taste for seasoning. Leave at room temperature for a few hours so the flavours blend. A
short time before serving, stir in the tomatoes
and taste again for seasoning. Decorate with the
sliced eggs and serve.

CAKES AND PASTRIES OF THE PYRENEES

The cakes and pastries of the Pyrenees are as diverse as the areas they come from. The classic gâteau from the Basque area, 'feuilleté béarnaise', is a flat, flaky pastry made not with the usual puff pastry but with a dough resembling that for Austrian strudel. It is pulled into a very thin sheet which is then brushed with fat, sprinkled with armagnac or rum and piled in layers that are sometimes interleaved with fruit.

More conventional is the feuilleté of Bayonne, a round or square puff pastry case filled with almond pastry cream and topped with browned almonds and sugar. Also from Bayonne comes 'touron', a solid cake of almond paste that slices to reveal multicoloured stripes of strawberry,

pistachio, coffee and chocolate with hazelnuts. More like a candy than a cake, touron tends to be correspondingly expensive.

In Béarn and Gascony, prunes are popular made into a rich purée and spread between sweet crumbling dough as 'galette aux pruneaux'. Gascons also layer puff pastry with sliced apples that have been macerated overnight in sugar and armagnac to make a wonderful crisp pie they call a 'croustade'. Much seen locally is 'pastis', which simply means pastry, not the anis-flavoured drink. Most often pastis turns out to be a yeast cake that is half brioche, half pound cake. It has a chewy, sustaining texture and sells well on market stalls.

GÂTEAU BASQUE

Gâteau with pastry cream

In effect, a double-crust tart with a pastry cream filling, gâteau basque is easily recognized by the lattice which is always traced with a fork on the top crust.

Serves 6–8

SWEET PIE PASTRY		
225 g	flour	1¾ cups
	1 egg	
	1 egg yolk	
	½ tsp salt	
150 g	sugar	¾ cup
	1 Tbsp rum	
150 g	butter	5 oz
	1 egg, beaten with ½ tsp salt (for glaze)	
RUM PASTRY CREAM FILLING		
250 ml	milk	1 cup
	pinch of salt	
	2 egg yolks	
65 g	sugar	⅓ cup
25 g	flour	3 Tbsp
	2 Tbsp rum	

20–23 cm/8–9 in round cake pan or moule à manqué

Make the sweet pie pastry*. Wrap and chill for 30 minutes or until firm. Make the pastry cream* filling. Set the oven at moderately hot (190°C/375°F) and lightly butter the pan.

Roll out two-thirds of the pastry and line the pan* with it, leaving the pastry slightly over-hanging at the edges. Spread with the cool pastry cream. Roll out the remaining pastry and cut it to an even round the same diameter as the pan. Lay it over the pastry cream and press firmly to join it to the bottom layer of dough. Fold both layers together to seal and to prevent

the filling from escaping. Brush the top with egg glaze and use a fork to score it in the charac-teristic lattice design. Bake in the oven for 1 hour or until golden brown. Unmould on to a rack, turn right side up and leave to cool. Serve at room temperature.

GÂTEAU BASQUE AUX CERISES

Instead of the pastry cream filling, melt 3–4 Tbsp cherry jelly and let cool slightly. Fill the lined pan with:

500 g	pitted dark cherries	1 lb

and pour the jelly over them. Cover with the remaining pastry and bake as above.

GÂTEAU BASQUE AUX PRUNEAUX

Substitute a prune filling for the pastry cream. Soak:

500 g	prunes	1 lb

overnight if they are dry. Pit them and put them in a pot with:

250 ml	water	1 cup

Simmer for 10–15 minutes or until very soft. Mash them or purée them in a food processor. Return them to the saucepan, add:

25 g	sugar	2 Tbsp

and cook over a low fire, stirring constantly, until thick. Leave to cool.

HONEY

Much like sheep, the honey bees of southern France are migrant. In the Pyrenees the bees' journey takes place in three stages: the hives travel to the flowering colza fields in April, to the lime and acacia trees in June, and end up in September on heather-clad mountain slopes. In Languedoc the bees are nourished on rosemary, which gives white, large-grained honey. In Provence, after wintering on the plains, the hives are taken to the barren northern hills where the bees feed first on wild thyme in June and then on the lavender that blooms in July and August.

The diet of bees affects the flavour of their honey; the piquancy of heather or the bouquet of lavender does not suit every taste. The finest honey is made when the bees first swarm after hibernation. As an old English rhyme runs, 'A swarm of bees in May is worth a load of hay.'

Virgin honey flows from the combs under the heat of the sun. Anonymous 'table honey' is extracted using high heat and a centrifuge, which destroys any individuality. Pressing gives an even higher yield of lower-quality honey.

Until sugar became cheap in the 16th century, honey was the principal sweetening agent, so it appears in many traditional recipes. Its flavour has an affinity with spices such as ginger and nutmeg, and any bread or cake containing honey mellows if it is tightly wrapped and kept for a week or two.

GALETTE AUX PRUNEAUX

Prune galette

This unusual galette is not flat but has sweet fruit filling spread between the pastry layers.

Serves 6–8

1 L	water	1 qt
200 g	sugar	1 cup
500 g	prunes	1 lb
30 g	butter, cut in small pieces	2 Tbsp
	PIE PASTRY	
345 g	flour	2⅔ cups
180 g	butter	6 oz
	1 egg	
	1 egg yolk	
	2 tsp brandy	
8 g	salt	1½ tsp
	1–2 Tbsp water (optional)	
	23–25 cm/9–10 in springform pan	

Make the pie pastry: sift the flour on to a work surface and make a large well. Pound the butter to soften. Put the butter, egg, egg yolk, brandy and salt in the well and work with the fingertips of one hand until partly mixed. Gradually draw in the flour, pulling the dough into large crumbs with the fingertips of both hands. If the crumbs are dry, sprinkle with just enough water to moisten. Press the dough together; it should be soft but not sticky. Work small portions of dough, pushing it away from you, then gathering it up with a spatula, until it is smooth and pliable. Press the dough into a ball, wrap and chill for 30 minutes or until firm.

Meanwhile, combine the water and three-quarters of the sugar in a saucepan, add the prunes and bring slowly to a boil. Simmer for 20–25 minutes or until the prunes are very tender. Drain the prunes, halve them and remove the stones. Leave to cool. Set the oven at moderately hot (190°C/375°F). Butter the pan.

Roll out about one-third of the pastry to a very thin round and use it to line the base and sides of the pan. Arrange one-third of the prune halves on the dough in an even layer. Roll out the remaining dough to a thin layer and cut three more rounds the same diameter as the pan. Place one round on the first prune layer and arrange another third of the prunes on top. Cover with the second round and top with the remaining prunes. Add the last round of dough using a little water to seal it to the pastry on the side of the pan. Trim the sides to make a neat border.

Sprinkle the galette with the remaining sugar, dot with the pieces of butter and bake for 1 hour or until a skewer inserted in the centre for 30 seconds is hot to the touch when withdrawn. If the top browns too quickly, lower the heat to moderate (175°C/350°C) after 45 minutes. Cool on a rack; serve at room temperature.

GALETTE BÉARNAISE AUX POMMES

Peel and core:

1 kg	apples	2 lb

and slice them in thin rings. Heat:

60 g	butter	2 oz

in a frying pan, add half the apple slices and sauté over a medium fire for 3 minutes or until lightly browned. Sprinkle them with:

80 g	sugar	6 Tbsp

turn the slices over and contine to cook for another minute or two until lightly caramelized. Repeat with the remaining slices, adding equal quantities of butter and sugar. Reserve an apple slice and layer the rest with pastry, as in the prune version; put the single apple slice on top. Sprinkle with sugar, dot with butter and bake.

FEUILLETÉ BÉARNAISE

Feuilleté with goose fat and armagnac

'Feuilleté béarnaise' is unlike any other French pastry. Made by pulling pliable dough to a huge, wafer-thin square, it should be so thin, runs the tale, that you can read your love-letters through it. Then the dough is brushed with goose fat and layered with sugar, armagnac and apples before baking; melted butter can be used instead of goose fat.

Serves 6

	PASTRY DOUGH	
200 g	all-purpose flour	1½ cups
90 g	cake flour	¾ cup
	1 egg	
125 ml	lukewarm water, more if necessary	½ cup
	½ tsp lemon juice	
	pinch of salt	
	FILLING	
125 g	goose fat, melted	¼ lb
50 g	sugar	4 Tbsp
	4 Tbsp armagnac	
	1 apple, peeled and finely sliced	
28 cm/11 in pie pan		

For the pastry dough: sift the flour on to a work surface and make a well in the centre. Beat the egg with the water, lemon juice and salt, and add to the well. Quickly mix in the flour with your fingers – the dough should be pliable but not dry; if necessary, add more water.

Flour the work surface and knead the dough, picking it up and throwing it down on the board for 5–7 minutes until it is shiny and very smooth. Cover it with an upturned bowl and leave for 25–30 minutes. Set the oven at moderately hot (190°C/375°C), and brush the pie pan with goose fat.

Flour the work surface and roll out the dough to as large a square as possible. Cover it with a damp towel and leave for 15 minutes. Using both hands, and starting from the centre, pull the dough out to a paper-thin sheet, with as few holes as possible. It helps to have two people working and it should be possible to make a 2-metre/6-ft square; trim any thick edges from the dough. Cut the dough in 25 cm/10 in squares.

Set a layer of pastry dough in the pie pan, brush it with goose fat, sprinkle with sugar and armagnac and add a slice or two of apple. Continue adding layers until all the dough and filling is used, finishing with a layer of dough brushed generously with fat. Bake the feuilleté in the preheated oven for 30–40 minutes or until brown and crisp. Serve it lukewarm.

TRUFFES AU CHOCOLAT

Chocolate truffles

Bayonne is famous for chocolates as well as ham. The taste dates from the 16th century, and was brought there by the Jews who were chased over the border from Spain by the Inquisition. At first, chocolate was lightly spiced with cinnamon and cloves and drunk without sugar, and until quite recently it remained a luxury, served in the afternoon with bread, quince jam and a slice of hard mountain cheese.

Makes 40 truffles

	GANACHE	
250 ml	heavy cream	1 cup
375 g	semi-sweet chocolate, chopped	12 oz
	COATING	
	confectioners' sugar	
300 g	semi-sweet chocolate, chopped	10 oz
150 g	cocoa	1 cup
piping bag and medium plain tip		

Bring the cream to a boil. Take from the heat, add the chopped chocolate and beat until smooth. Pour the ganache into a metal bowl and beat it with a wooden spoon over ice until it is completely cool and thick. Pipe the ganache in walnut-sized mounds on greaseproof/parchment paper. Chill thoroughly for about ½ hour or until firm. Dip your hands in sugar and roll each chocolate mound to a ball. Replace them on the paper and chill again until very firm.

For the coating: melt the chocolate carefully in a water bath, taking care not to heat the chocolate above body temperature. Spread the cocoa in a tray. Using a fork, take each ball of ganache and dip it in the melted chocolate. Put it immediately in the tray of cocoa and spoon a little cocoa over it. Continue until the tray is nearly filled with truffles but leave enough space for them to move around easily without sticking. Shake the tray gently to be sure the truffles are coated with cocoa. Transfer the truffles to a clean piece of paper.

Sift the cocoa and continue coating the remaining truffles. Chill the truffles thoroughly; the flavour improves if they are layered with paper and stored in a container for 1–2 weeks.

CHEESES

Traditional cheese-making survives in the Pyrenees as nowhere else. In the rugged mountain economy, where sheep come first and cattle a close second, shepherds still make their cheeses in remote huts known as 'cujulas'. The task of herding the flocks is taken in hand by the intelligent little 'farou' or 'labrit' dogs of the Pyrenees, so the herdsmen need do little more than milk their animals and count them at nightfall. The cheese they make is called 'fromage des Pyrénées' and comes black-skinned when made with cow's milk and red-skinned when made with sheep's milk. (As in all cheese-making districts, the whey left after pressing the curds often goes to feed a pig — one reason why cheese country is often ham and sausage country too.) The texture of both types of fromage des Pyrénées is slightly resilient and permeated with tiny holes; the cow's milk cheese is mellow, while the sheep's milk version has a hint of salty-sour. A new creamy variant of fromage des Pyrénées sold under the brand name 'St-Albray' is also becoming popular; it is made in a characteristic scalloped round, easy to cut in wedges.

A few Basque sheep cheeses, such as 'ardi-gasna' and 'esbareich', are made and sold locally; both are shaped like a flat loaf and taste pleasantly nutty. Any extra sheep's milk production tends to end in the caves of Roquefort in Languedoc.

OTHER SPECIALITIES OF THE REGION
TRADITIONAL DISHES

Purée de Ciboure
Potato, dried bean and olive soup

Pâté de saumon de la Nive
Salmon pâté

Soupe de poissons biarrotte
Fish soup with carrots, sorrel and lettuce

Morue à l'ail
Salt cod with garlic

Gasconnade
Roast leg of lamb with garlic and anchovies

Le hachau de veau
Veal stew with ham, garlic and peppers

Porc frais à la basquaise
Pork loin braised in milk

Tripes à la paloise
Tripe with Bayonne ham and armagnac

La méture
Cooked cornmeal with eggs and Bayonne ham

Ragoût de cèpes
Cèpes stew

CHARCUTERIE

Tripotcha
Mutton blood sausage with red pepper and nutmeg

Louquenkas
Pork sausage with red pepper and garlic

PÂTISSERIE AND CONFISERIE

Pain à l'anis
Anise-flavoured white bread

Pâte de cédrat
Citron fruit jellies

Gâteau à la broche
Batter cake cooked on a turning spit

Cruchades
Fried cornmeal cakes

Millassou
Cornmeal pudding with raisins

Bistorto
Yeast ring with saffron and anise

Normandy

To go to Normandy for me is to go home, not just because we happen to have a house there, but because Normandy reminds me irresistibly of my native Yorkshire. Illogical, say historians; a romantic illusion, declares my husband; but why should the Viking marauders who, in the 9th and 10th centuries, invaded the plains of eastern England and the rich valleys of Normandy, not have left their mark on both? The well-built, rubicund people, countrymen to the toes of their boots, look alike and there are striking similarities in the cooking.

Normans and Yorkshiremen love pork and all the products of the pig – sausages, tripe, black pudding (the French 'boudin noir'), brawn (often called head cheese) and ham. Both are partial to potatoes and view greens and salads as 'a waste of good space,' in my Yorkshire father's words. They are great eaters of cheese and buttery, slightly solid cakes, and their delight is apple pie.

The best apple pies in the world surely come from Normandy, far outstripping their Yorkshire counterparts with top and bottom crust. Three or four kinds are standard in local pastry shops. One has thinly sliced apples arranged cartwheel-fashion in a sweet dough, then sprinkled with sugar and baked so the edges of the apples brown in a flower design. Another embeds apples, or sometimes pears, in an almond cream, which browns to a crisp crust. Farmhouse apple pies may have a crisp caramel topping, or the apple slices may be caramelized in butter and sugar. But the Normans do not stop there. They consume their crab apples, biting little fruits that cannot be eaten raw, though they are good for jelly, as cider and calvados, and regularly add apples to fish, poultry, meat and even to their boudin sausages.

The archetypal Norman image of flowering apple trees, lazy cows and thatched black and white timbered farmhouses is borne out by dry statistics. Acre for acre, Normandy has twice the pasture of any other French province. In the Auge valley, home of the finest calvados, the grass is said to grow so fast that a stick left lying out at night is covered by morning. Here flourishes the Norman version of bocage, with its imposing ranks of beech trees which serve as both windbreak and fuel (and incidentally caused the invasion tanks considerable trouble in World War II). Norman farms are often arranged in 'masures', with grassy courtyards loosely enclosed by timbered cowsheds, a thatched farmhouse and sometimes a dovecote.

The traditional wealth of the province lies in its black and white cattle with their characteristic sunglass markings – a prize beast can produce a dozen gallons of milk a day. Small wonder, then, that the Normans are great consumers of cream. They add cream to pork normande, which is braised with apples and calvados, to pheasant vallée d'Auge, baked with mushrooms, and to sole normande, which is garnished with mussels, shrimps and mushrooms. Cream also appears in various soups, vegetable dishes and desserts. In the words of the *Guide Michelin*, 'cream dresses everything.' Dare one say overdresses? Partial though I am to cream, particularly to the unpasteurized Norman cream with its splendid nutty sweetness, a little goes a long way.

As well as cream, the name of Normandy is synonymous with the finest cheese and butter. The cathedral at Rouen boasts a late 15th-century 'butter tower' financed by dispensations sold to those faithful who wished to consume cream and butter during Lent. And butter leads naturally to pastries. Each village boulanger makes his own butter biscuits, called 'sablés' (sandy) because of their crumbly texture; they are easily identified by the lattice decoration marked on the top with a fork. 'Douillons' are pear dumplings wrapped in butter pastry, and 'bourdelots', the apple version, are equally rich.

Side by side with the cow on a Norman farm lives the pig. Raised on household scraps and windfalls from the orchard, the family pig fattens at half the speed of an animal reared for the commercial market and, say the Normans, the meat has twice the flavour. In my childhood the dismemberment of the pig was a highlight of the year. The fire roared in the range, the fat old cook turned pinker and more strident as the kitchen filled with bowls of unmentionable meats. We enjoyed the results of this activity for the next six months, and so it still is in Normandy. During autumn the local charcutier, who is the only one licensed to perform the actual killing, is booked for months in advance on his only free day, Sunday. The dispatch and division of the pig take several hours and the carcass may be hung from a handy tree in the orchard.

In the old days, most of the fresh meat, particularly the legs, shoulders and loin, was salted, then hung high in the open fireplace and left to smoke well away from the heat. Today, the choice cuts of fresh meat are more often frozen. Tougher parts like the neck may be made into several kinds of pâté The innards, however, are the base for creative dishes which differ from region to region.

In the Pays de Caux, north of the Seine, the pig's intestines become casings for boudin noir – blood sausage that includes diced fat, onions simmered to a pulp and cream. Mortagne, on the southern border of Normandy, holds an annual competition occasionally won by butchers from Bury and Rochdale in the north of England – another Viking link? Around Vire smoked sausages called 'andouilles' are made from and stuffed with the large intestines of the pig; these are eaten cold and, when sliced, reveal dizzy circles of dark and light meat. The Vire 'andouillettes', sausages that are grilled until slightly charred, use pork for the casings, and are stuffed with veal.

After the rustic but limited charms of apple, pork and cream, the other great Norman speciality – seafood – comes as a breath of fresh air. The vast bulk of the catch is made within the English Channel. The variety of fish that comes into our local port of Dieppe is extraordinary: turbot, halibut, hake, bream, dab, monkfish, mullet, not to speak of lesser types like wrasse, gurnard, trigger fish, shad and flounder. The fishmonger always has on display at least two dozen kinds, often so fresh that it requires resolution and a strong hand to trap their flapping fins.

Reigning supreme is the incomparable Dover sole. This is a different species from lemon sole, grey sole, flounder and their kin and there is, unfortunately, no substitute for the genuine article. Restaurateurs value Dover sole for its resilient texture which enables them to reheat it with impunity. In classical cooking, Dover sole is served in countless ways; like the Normans, I prefer it 'à la meunière' in brown butter.

The unity of Normandy's gastronomic image is deceptive, as its geography allows for a good deal of variety. The rolling pastures of Bray in the east, the 'little Switzerland' where 'petit suisse' cheese originated, are quite unlike the Lilliputian layout of the Cotentin peninsula running up to Cherbourg, which shares with the Channel Islands, just off the coast, specialities like 'gâche', an egg bread often flavoured with dried fruit. To the south,

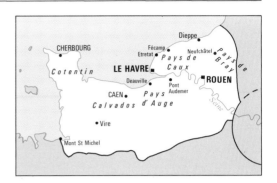

Vire is the heart of cattle country and of Norman butter, so it seems natural that the town square should be occupied, not by the usual 'mairie' but by a commodious auction mart and that the main restaurant should offer two kinds of butter, salted and sweet, at its tables. The local butter vies with that of Charente in southwestern France for richness and fresh flavour. The best French butter remains firm, almost waxy, in the warmest kitchen, thus simplifying tricky preparations like puff pastry and its low whey content means it scarcely needs to be clarified for frying.

Due west of Vire is Mont St Michel, whose specialities of lamb raised on the adjacent salt marshes and omelettes belong at least as much to Brittany. Almost as famous as the island itself is Mère Poulard, who installed her restaurant there towards the end of the last century. From the eye-catching copper bowl and long-handled frying pan to the apparently casual approach to cooking the omelette itself, even to her choice of pseudonym ('poularde' is a plump chicken), Mère Poulard made a theatrical performance of frying omelette after omelette over an open fire.

'Le Havre, Rouen and Paris are but a single town and the Seine its main street,' remarked Napoleon. This rings particularly true of the produce; for generations the river made Normandy the natural supplier to the metropolis. The renown of many a Parisian restaurant has been built on the best food from Normandy farmers and fishermen (Dieppe is the nearest port to Paris) and the region still yields some of the finest ingredients in France. Unlike Burgundy, however, it does not consume them and Norman cooking can be a disappointment. The Rouennais are reputed to be so cautious they consume only the income on their incomes; simple country fare is the Norman forte and in this they have a long and happy experience.

CRÈME DE CREVETTES
Cream of shrimp soup

Shrimp shells and heads, as well as the meat, are important in giving flavour to this cream soup. In Normandy 'grey' baby shrimps are often used, but larger pink shrimps or prawns are good too.

Serves 4

80 g	butter	5 Tbsp
	1 carrot, diced	
	1 onion, diced	
	1 stalk celery, diced	
500 g	medium, raw, unpeeled shrimps	1 lb
250 ml	white wine	1 cup
	sprig of thyme	
	1 bay leaf	
	salt and pepper	
250 ml	water	1 cup
125 ml	heavy cream or crème fraîche*	$\frac{1}{2}$ cup
	MEDIUM WHITE SAUCE	
45 g	butter	3 Tbsp
45 g	flour	5 Tbsp
750 ml	milk	3 cups
	salt and pepper	

Make the white sauce*. In another pot, melt half the butter and add the carrot, onion, celery and shrimps or prawns. Sauté over a medium fire, stirring often, for 10 minutes. Add the wine, thyme, bay leaf and a little salt and pepper and simmer for 10 more minutes. Strain the cooking liquid into the white sauce, reserving the shrimps.

Peel about a third of the largest shrimps and set aside. Using a mortar and pestle, rolling pin or food processor, crush the shells with the remaining unpeeled shrimps. Add them to the soup and simmer for 5 minutes. Pour the soup through a fine strainer, pressing hard on the shrimps and pouring the water over them to extract all the liquid. Reheat the soup, stir in the cream and bring just to a boil. Take from the heat and stir in the remaining butter, piece by piece. Add the whole shrimps and taste for seasoning. Pour the soup into a tureen or ladle it into bowls; each serving should contain a few shrimps.

SOUPE NORMANDE
Potato and cabbage soup

In contrast to the soups of classical French cooking, whose fat must be skimmed off, this vegetable soup has fat added to give it 'eyes'. Tradition has it that a 'blind' soup must go back in the pot. Even a small amount of Norman cooking fat transforms what would otherwise be an ordinary vegetable soup. If one type of bean is not available, omit it and use more of the other. Lima beans or green peas may also be included, but peas should not be added until the last 20–25 minutes of cooking.

Serves 6–8

100 g	dried white beans	$\frac{1}{2}$ cup
1·75 L	water	$1\frac{3}{4}$ qt
	salt and pepper	
750 g	potatoes, cut in large cubes	$1\frac{1}{2}$ lb
	1 stalk celery, thickly sliced	
	2 leeks, trimmed, split and cut in chunks	
	1 small cabbage	
125 g	green beans, cut in 2–3 pieces	$\frac{1}{4}$ lb
45 g	seasoned cooking fat (see opposite)	3 Tbsp

Soak the dried beans overnight in cold water and drain.

Bring the water to a boil in a large pot, salt lightly and add the white beans. Cover and simmer for 30 minutes; then add the potatoes, celery and leeks. Continue simmering for half an hour while you prepare the cabbage.

Bring a second pot of salted water to a boil. Wash the cabbage, boil it for 7–8 minutes, drain and shred. Add the cabbage, green beans and fat to the soup with a pinch of salt and pepper. Cover and cook over a low fire for another half hour or until all the vegetables are tender; taste for seasoning. Ladle the soup into a tureen or individual bowls and serve.

LA GRAISSE NORMANDE
Seasoned cooking fat

This cooking fat is used in Normandy as lard is in other regions. It is a mixture of chopped animal fat, usually beef and pork but sometimes even mutton, that is rendered in the same way as lard, but with vegetables and herbs added for flavour. It can be used instead of oil or butter in many vegetable dishes and roasts, such as 'canard à la rouennaise'.

Makes 1 kg/2 lb cooking fat

1 kg	beef kidney fat, coarsely chopped	2 lb
500 g	pork fat, coarsely chopped	1 lb
	1 medium onion, studded with a clove	
	2 leeks, trimmed, split and cut in chunks	
	2–3 carrots, quartered	
	1–2 turnips, quartered (optional)	
	1 small parsnip, quartered	
	bouquet garni	
	pinch of marjoram or rosemary	
	salt and pepper	
	cheesecloth	

Melt the beef and pork fat in a heavy pot over a low fire, stirring often, for 30 minutes. Add the onion, leeks, carrots, turnips, parsnip, bouquet garni, marjoram and a pinch of salt and pepper. Cover and simmer over a low fire or in a very low oven (95°C/200°F) for 5 hours, stirring occasionally to prevent the vegetables from sticking. When all the fat has been rendered, strain it through cheesecloth into a bowl and pour into stoneware crocks. Cool until set; then cover with greaseproof/waxed paper for storage.

PÂTÉ DE FOIE DE PORC
Pork liver pâté

Pork liver is the mainstay of many an unassuming 'pâté maison' such as this. Not only is pork liver inexpensive, but its flavour (which can be strong) is agreeably muted by being baked in a terrine.

Serves 10–12

250 g	barding fat or mild bacon, thinly sliced	½ lb
600 g	pork, at least half of it fat	1¼ lb
600 g	pork liver	1¼ lb
	2 onions, quartered	
	2 Tbsp parsley leaves	
	2 tsp tarragon leaves	
	2 eggs, beaten to mix	
	3 Tbsp cognac	
	salt and pepper	
	2 bay leaves	
	2 sprigs of thyme	
	luting paste*	
terrine with tight-fitting lid (2 L/2 qt capacity)		

Line the terrine with barding fat or bacon, reserving a slice for the top. Set the oven at moderate (175°C/350°F).

Using the fine plate, mince/grind together the pork, liver, onions, parsley and tarragon; then put it through a second time. Mix in the eggs, cognac, salt and pepper and beat with a wooden spoon to distribute the seasoning thoroughly. Sauté a small piece of the mixture and taste for seasoning; it should be quite spicy.

Pack the mixture into the lined terrine. Cut the reserved slice of barding fat into thin strips and set them on top in a lattice pattern. Lay the bay leaves and sprigs of thyme on top of the fat and cover with the lid. Use the luting paste to seal the gap between the terrine and the lid. Set the terrine in a water bath, bring the water to a boil on top of the stove; then cook in the heated oven for 2–2½ hours or until a skewer inserted into the mixture through the hole in the terrine lid is hot to the touch when withdrawn after 30 seconds. Adjust the heat so the water keeps simmering; if too much water evaporates add more.

Remove the terrine from the water bath and let cool until tepid. Take off the luting paste and the lid and press a board or plate with a 1 kg/2 lb weight on top until the pâté is cold.

Keep the pâté in the refrigerator for at least 3 days or up to a week to allow the flavour to mellow before serving it. Serve the pâté in the terrine mould.

CROQUETTES DE CAMEMBERT
Camembert fritters

The camembert chosen for these fritters should not be overripe.

Serves 4

30 g	flour, seasoned with salt and pepper	$\frac{1}{4}$ cup
	1 egg, beaten to mix with 1 Tbsp water and 1 Tbsp oil	
100 g	dry white breadcrumbs	1 cup
	fat for deep frying	
	bunch of parsley	
	FRITTER MIXTURE	
250 g	camembert cheese	$\frac{1}{2}$ lb
60 g	butter	4 Tbsp
45 g	flour	$\frac{1}{3}$ cup
375 ml	milk	$1\frac{1}{2}$ cups
	3 egg yolks	
	1 tsp Dijon mustard	
	salt and white pepper	
	pinch of grated nutmeg	
4 cm/1$\frac{1}{2}$ in diameter cookie cutter		

Make the fritter mixture: discard the rind from the camembert and chop the cheese. Melt the butter in a medium pot over a low fire, whisk in the flour and cook until foaming. Whisk in the milk, bring to a boil and simmer for 2–3 minutes, whisking. Add the cheese and egg yolks to the white sauce and simmer, stirring constantly, for 2 minutes or until smooth and thick but still soft enough to fall from the spoon (unlike many cheeses, camembert does not cook into strings). Take from the heat and add the mustard; season to taste with salt, pepper and nutmeg. Pour the mixture into a buttered flameproof tray or cake pan large enough to make a 1·25 cm/$\frac{1}{2}$ in layer and chill overnight.

To cut out the fritters, warm the tray a moment or two over the heat to melt the butter and loosen the mixture. Use the cutter to stamp out rounds of the cheese mixture. Coat them with seasoned flour; brush them with the beaten egg and coat with breadcrumbs.

Heat the deep fat to 180°C/355°F on a fat thermometer. Fry the fritters, a few at a time, until golden brown. Drain them thoroughly on paper towels and keep warm in a moderate oven (175°C/350°F) with the door slightly open while frying the rest of the fritters.

Discard the parsley stems and thoroughly dry the sprigs. Let the fat cool slightly, then toss in the parsley; stand back as the fat will splutter. After 30 seconds, or when the spluttering stops, lift out the parsley with a slotted spoon and drain it on paper towels. Arrange the fritters, overlapping, on a platter, sprinkle them with fried parsley sprigs and serve at once.

OEUFS AU PLAT À LA CRÈME
Baked eggs with cream

When baked eggs are cooked perfectly, the whites are set and the yolks are still soft.

Serves 4

45 g	butter	3 Tbsp
	salt and pepper	
	8 eggs	
125 ml	heavy cream (preferably crème fraîche*)	$\frac{1}{2}$ cup
	pinch of grated nutmeg	
a shallow, flameproof baking dish or 4 individual gratin dishes		

Set the oven at hot (200°C/400°F). Melt the butter in the baking dish, sprinkle with salt and pepper and break in the eggs, being careful not to break the yolks. Cook over a low fire for 3 minutes or until the whites are just beginning to set. Spoon a tablespoon of cream over each egg and sprinkle with nutmeg. Bake in the oven for another 5–7 minutes for a large dish or 4–5 minutes for individual dishes, or until the whites are set but the yolks are still soft. Halfway through cooking time, baste the eggs with the cream. (Don't worry if the butter rises to the top and seems to have separated. This will not affect the flavour.) Serve the eggs immediately; if you wait they will overcook in the heat of the dish.

OEUFS AU PLAT À LA CIBOULETTE
Before spooning on the cream, sprinkle the eggs with chives.

OEUFS AU PLAT AUX CROÛTONS
Before spooning on the cream, sprinkle the eggs with tiny croûtons*.

OEUFS EN COCOTTE À LA CRÈME
Instead of cooking the eggs in a shallow dish, put them in ramekins and bake in a water bath in a moderately hot oven (190°C/375°F) for 7–10 minutes, or until the egg whites are just set. This is the classic 'oeufs en cocotte' with a double dose of cream.

OMELETTE DE LA MÈRE POULARD

Mère Poulard was always reticent about her 'secret' recipe. 'As for my adding cream,' she is said to have declared, 'that suggestion is pure invention. We do, however, have the best butter in France, and we don't skimp on it. We do not let the butter brown in the pan and, above all, we are careful not to overcook the omelette.' The perfect omelette, say French cooks, should be 'baveuse' (literally, dribbling).

This gave no clue to the tantalizing question of why Mère Poulard's omelettes were so light. Was it because the eggs were beaten very thoroughly before cooking, or were the eggs separated and the whites whipped separately? There has never been an answer.

Serves 2		
	4 very fresh eggs	
	salt and pepper	
30 g	butter	2 Tbsp
	23 cm/9 in omelette pan	

Whisk the eggs vigorously with salt and pepper for about 5 minutes; their volume should more than double. Heat the butter in the omelette pan over a moderately high fire. When it is foaming, add the eggs and stir briskly with the flat of a fork for 8–10 seconds until they start to thicken. Stop stirring and let the omelette continue to cook, pulling cooked egg to the centre of the pan and tipping it occasionally to pour uncooked egg to the sides. Be careful not to overcook; the omelette should be soft and creamy at the centre.

To fold the omelette, hold the pan handle in your left hand with the pan facing towards you. Tip the pan towards you and give the handle a sharp tap with the right hand to flip the edge of the omelette. Tip the omelette on to a plate so that it rolls into a neat shape. Serve at once.

OMELETTE SOUFFLÉE

Separate the eggs instead of leaving them whole. Whisk the yolks in a bowl with salt, pepper and 2 Tbsp heavy cream until the mixture is light and very thick. In another bowl beat the egg whites until stiff. Fold a little of the egg whites into the yolk mixture; then pour this mixture back into the remaining whites, folding them together as lightly as possible. When cooking, the omelette should be stirred, but there is no need to tip the pan because the mixture is thicker than in the previous version.

MARMITE DIEPPOISE

Fish stew with spices

Dieppois chefs, like their Breton colleagues in Nantes, have traditionally been partial to the spices brought back by merchant ships. But one chef has given a timely warning about over-seasoning fish: 'Do not kill them a second time.' Instead of expensive sole and turbot, grey/striped mullet, monkfish or whiting may be used. If shrimps, scampi or scallops are not available, omit them and add more vegetables. The mussels, however, give vital character to the stew.

Serves 8–10

500 g each	4 sole or flounder	1 lb each
2 kg	turbot or halibut, cut in 8 steaks	4½ lb
1 L	mussels	1 qt
250 ml	white wine	1 cup
500 g	cooked, peeled baby shrimps (optional)	1 lb
80 g	butter	5 Tbsp
	2 leeks, trimmed, split and chopped	
	2 stalks celery, chopped (optional)	
	2 large onions, chopped	
	3 dried fennel twigs, tied with string, OR 1 tsp fennel seed	
	2 tomatoes, peeled, seeded and chopped	
	salt and pepper	
	8 scampi (optional)	
	8 scallops (optional)	
45 g	flour	⅓ cup
250 ml	heavy cream or crème fraîche*	1 cup
	pinch of cayenne pepper	
	1 tsp curry powder, or to taste	
	pinch of paprika	
	1 Tbsp chopped parsley	

Fillet the sole and cut each fillet in half cross-wise. Cut each turbot steak in 4 pieces, removing the bone. Use the heads, tails and bones of the fish to make a simple stock: wash them, just cover with water, bring to a boil and simmer for 20 minutes. Strain; then add enough water to make 1·25 L fish stock. Wash the pieces of fish and pat dry. Clean the mussels*. Put them in a pot with the wine, cover and cook over a high fire, tossing occasionally, for 5–7 minutes or until the mussels open. Drain, reserving the liquid. Discard the top shells, leaving the mussels in their bottom shells. Put them in a bowl with the shrimps, cover and keep warm.

Heat 2 tablespoons of the butter in a large stew pot. Add the chopped leeks, celery, onions and fennel twigs and cook over a low fire, stirring, until soft but not brown. Add the tomatoes and simmer, stirring occasionally, for 10 minutes. Stir in the fish stock and a little salt and pepper. Add the turbot, bring to a simmer and cook for 2 minutes. Add the scampi, the prepared scallops* and sole and simmer for 5 more minutes or until all are just tender. Transfer the fish to a serving bowl, cover and keep warm; reserve the liquid and discard the fennel twigs.

In another pot heat the remaining butter, add the flour and cook over a low fire, whisking, until foaming but not brown. Whisk in the reserved fish cooking liquid; then carefully pour in the reserved mussel liquid, leaving any sand or grit behind. Bring to a boil, whisking, and simmer for 2 minutes; the sauce should be lightly thickened, like a rich soup. Stir in the cream, cayenne and curry powder and taste for seasoning; salt may not be needed since the mussel liquid is salty. Pour the sauce over the fish in the serving bowl and sprinkle with paprika and chopped parsley. Top with the mussels and shrimps and serve.

Honfleur

TURBOT VALLÉE D'AUGE
Turbot with apple and cider sauce

Around Etretat, a whole 'turbot vallée d'Auge', cooked in cider, is traditional at first communion celebrations. However, any large flat fish can be baked as in this recipe.

Serves 4–6

1·5 kg	turbot	3-lb
	1 leek, trimmed, split and sliced	
	2 apples, peeled and sliced	
	salt and pepper	
375 ml	dry cider	1½ cups
375 ml	fish stock* or water	1½ cups
250 g	mushrooms	½ lb
	a few drops of lemon juice	
250 ml	heavy cream or crème fraîche*	1 cup
125 g	butter	¼ lb

Set the oven at hot (200°C/400°F). Clean the turbot, remove the fins and trim the tail to a 'V'. Wash and dry the fish.

Butter a very large baking dish or roasting pan and sprinkle it with the sliced leek and apples. Lay the turbot on top with its white side up, season with salt and pepper and pour the cider and fish stock over it. Bring to a boil on top of the stove; then bake in the oven, basting often, for 35–45 minutes or until a skewer inserted into the thickest part of the fish is hot when withdrawn after 30 seconds. Carefully transfer the turbot to a platter, cover and keep warm. Strain the liquid into a shallow pan, pressing hard on the leek and apples to extract the juice.

While the fish is cooking, put the mushrooms in a small pot with a few tablespoons of water, salt, pepper and a little lemon juice. Cover and cook over a high fire for 5 minutes until the liquid bubbles up to the top of the pot and the mushrooms are tender. Drain, reserving the liquid; sprinkle the mushrooms over the turbot and keep it warm.

For the sauce: add the mushroom liquid to the liquid from the turbot and boil until reduced to about 125 ml. In another small pot boil the cream until reduced by half; then add it to the fish-mushroom reduction and continue to boil until the mixture has reduced by about one quarter; it should be thick enough to coat a spoon lightly. Whisk in the butter a piece at a time, keeping the pan sometimes over low heat and sometimes off the heat so the butter softens and thickens the sauce without melting. Don't let the sauce get too hot or it will separate. Taste for seasoning, then spoon some of the sauce over the turbot. Serve the remaining sauce separately.

LES DEMOISELLES DE CHERBOURG
Baby lobsters with calvados

These 'maiden' baby lobsters, poached in court bouillon and served simply with their calvados-flavoured bouillon, are one of the finest Norman delicacies. Instead of serving the lobsters with bowls of melted butter, add a little fresh butter to the reduced liquid off the heat. Also, the calvados may be replaced by cognac.

Serves 4

500 g each	4 small live lobsters	1 lb each
	2 Tbsp calvados	
	2 Tbsp chopped parsley	
	salt and pepper	
	1 large bunch of parsley	
125 g	butter, melted	¼ lb
	COURT BOUILLON	
	3 carrots, sliced	
	3 onions, sliced	
	bouquet garni	
	pinch of salt and pepper	
	pinch of cayenne pepper	
750 ml	white wine	3 cups
750 ml	water	3 cups

Put all the ingredients for the court bouillon into a large pot, bring to a boil and simmer for 20 minutes. Add the lobsters, cover and simmer another 12–15 minutes. Remove them and reserve the liquid. With a sharp, sturdy knife, halve the lobsters lengthwise. Crack the claws. Discard the tough head sac but not the green tomalley or any coral, which will be scarlet. Keep the lobsters hot, moistened with a little of their liquid.

Boil the reserved liquid for 5–10 minutes or until reduced by about one-third. Discard the bouquet garni. Stir in the calvados and chopped parsley; taste for seasoning. Serve the lobsters on a bed of parsley, with the sauce and the melted butter in separate bowls. Provide finger-bowls, nutcrackers for cracking the shells and lobster forks, if you have them.

THE SHELLFISH PLATTER

The standard opening to a good meal all along the northern coast of France is a seafood platter. This can range from a modest handful of winkles and baby shrimps to a gala display of eight or ten different shellfish, their subtle colours offset by a background of crushed ice and dark seaweed. Eaten raw on the half shell, oysters, clams, mussels and baby scallops are all scrupulously fresh. A couple of sea snail varieties – winkles and whelks – are so common that they are always included, after boiling in a concentrated court bouillon to make them edible. Better platters include some large pink shrimps as well as the baby grey ones. The best of all have a few frail, pale pink langoustines draped over the edge. A favourite addition is a crab or two split down the middle and with the claws cracked so the meat is easy to remove.

The work involved in extracting recalcitrant titbits from the shells can be considerable, but that is part of the fun, as is the paraphernalia involved – a wire stand so everyone can see and reach the fish, crab pickers, nutcrackers, pins for the winkles, and fingerbowls. The hard-earned morsels are then eaten with mayonnaise, onion- or shallot-flavoured vinaigrette, thinly sliced brown bread, butter and plenty of chilled white wine.

MOULES MARINIÈRE

Small piquant mussels are a speciality of Dieppe. As early as the 16th century a rapid system for transporting seafood to Paris had been developed. Caravans of packhorses called 'chasse-marées' (tide chasers), with a barrel of fish and water slung on each side, travelled from the coast at a trot with a bellman clearing the way, entering the city on what is still called the Boulevard Poissonnière (Fish Boulevard).

The variation of mussels in a simple cream sauce is a speciality both of northern France and of Normandy, where cider is sometimes used instead of wine.

Serves 4

3 L	mussels	3 qt
250 ml	white wine	1 cup
	3 shallots OR 1 onion, very finely chopped	
	bouquet garni	
	salt and pepper	
	2 Tbsp coarsely chopped parsley	
	cheesecloth (optional)	

Clean the mussels*. In a large pot (not aluminium) combine the wine, shallots, bouquet garni and plenty of pepper. Bring to a boil and simmer for 2 minutes. Add the mussels, cover and cook over a high fire, stirring occasionally, for 5–7 minutes or until the mussels open. Sprinkle the mussels with chopped parsley, stir and taste the liquid for seasoning; extra salt may not be needed since the mussels are salty.

Serve the mussels in soup bowls and spoon the cooking liquid over them, leaving behind any sand or grit that has fallen to the bottom of the pot, and discarding the bouquet garni. Alternatively, the liquid can be strained through cheesecloth before the parsley is added.

MOULES À LA CRÈME

Cook the mussels (see left). Discard their top shells, leaving the mussels in their bottom shells. Keep them warm in a shallow serving bowl or tureen. Discard the bouquet garni and carefully pour the cooking liquid into a pan, leaving any sand or grit behind. Bring to a boil and add to the liquid:

125 ml	heavy cream or crème fraîche*	$\frac{1}{2}$ cup

Make kneaded butter* for thickening from:

30 g	butter kneaded with	2 Tbsp
15 g	flour	2 Tbsp

Bring the cream mixture just to a boil and whisk in enough of the kneaded butter, a piece at a time, to thicken the sauce slightly. Simmer for 2 minutes, taste for seasoning and add the chopped parsley. Spoon the sauce over the mussels and serve at once.

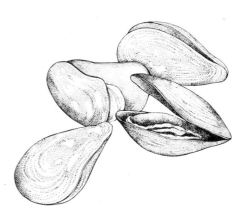

FILETS DE SOLE NORMANDE
Sole with shrimps and mussels

To Parisians Normandy means the sea: they spend their vacations on the beaches from Dieppe to Deauville (a chilly pastime as depicted by Boudin); and a good deal of the seafood sold in Paris comes from Normandy. This recipe combines three of the best – Dover sole, mussels and baby shrimps – with a classic creamy velouté sauce. Any other fish fillets, or even small whole fish, can be used. Traditionally, the edge of the dish is decorated with crescents of puff pastry or fried croûtons.

Serves 4 as a main course or 6–8 as a first course

500 g each	4 sole	1 lb each
500 ml	fish stock*	2 cups
1 L	mussels	1 qt
60 ml	dry cider or white wine	$\frac{1}{4}$ cup
	2 shallots, finely chopped	
250 g	mushrooms, thinly sliced	$\frac{1}{2}$ lb
	salt and white pepper	
250 g	cooked, peeled baby shrimps	$\frac{1}{2}$ lb
	VELOUTÉ SAUCE	
80 g	butter	5 Tbsp
30 g	flour	$\frac{1}{4}$ cup
500 ml	liquid from cooking fish	2 cups
	2 egg yolks	
60 ml	heavy cream or crème fraîche*	$\frac{1}{4}$ cup

Fillet the sole and use the heads, tails and bones to make fish stock.

Clean the mussels*. Put them in a large pot with the cider, cover and cook over a high fire, shaking occasionally, for 5–7 minutes or until the mussels open. Drain, reserving the liquid. Shell the mussels and set them aside.

Wash and dry the sole fillets and fold the ends neatly underneath, skinned side inwards. Thoroughly butter a flameproof baking dish, sprinkle it with the shallots and mushrooms and lay the fillets on top; season with salt and white pepper. Pour the fish stock over the sole; then add the mussel liquid, being careful to leave any sediment behind. Cover with buttered paper and bring to a boil; poach on top of the stove or in a moderate oven (175°C/350°F) for 7–8 minutes or until the fish just flakes easily.

Carefully remove the fillets from the liquid and drain them well on paper towels. Arrange them on a heatproof platter, cover and keep warm. If necessary, reduce the cooking liquid, including the shallots and mushrooms, to 500 ml.

Make the velouté sauce: in a heavy-based pan melt half the butter, whisk in the flour and cook for 1–2 minutes until foaming but not brown. Let cool slightly; then gradually whisk in the reduced liquid with the shallots and mushrooms. Bring the sauce to a boil, whisking constantly, and simmer for 2 minutes or until reduced to a coating consistency; remove from the heat. Whisk the egg yolks and cream in a bowl; then whisk in a few spoonsful of the hot sauce. Pour this mixture back into the pan of sauce, whisking rapidly. Put the sauce back on the fire and heat gently until it thickens slightly. Don't boil or it will curdle. Take the sauce from the heat and add the remaining butter in small pieces, shaking the pan until it is incorporated. Add the shrimps and mussels. Taste the sauce for seasoning and spoon it over the sole. Brown the dish under a very hot grill/broiler and serve at once.

CANARD À LA ROUENNAISE
Stuffed duck with liver

To cooks, 'rouennaise duck' means a bird that has been dispatched by smothering so that its blood does not escape, but gives richness and flavour to the meat. The custom began with ducks reared in the Seine Valley, where, tethered to apple trees, they thrived in the mild climate. In the 19th century, a clever restaurateur, Père Mechenet, invented (or rather revived) the duck press for his 'canard à la rouennaise'. To make it, the bird is quickly roasted, then the legs are removed and cooked further, while the bones are pressed to give juices that are mixed with red wine and cognac to make a rich sauce.

The dish is rare, even in Rouen (the Tour d'Argent in Paris is one of the few restaurants to offer it) as smothered ducks can be kept only a few hours. Other Normandy recipes for preparing duck are, however, less problematic, such as this one for a roast bird with a liver-thickened sauce. The same sauce is also good with grilled/broiled lamb chops.

Because the stuffing is very concentrated, the duck is not filled completely. Don't worry if the sauce is slightly grainy. The liver, which is a substitute for duck blood, adds the same richness but the sauce is not completely smooth.

Serves 4

1·8-kg	duck, with liver and giblets	4-lb
	salt and pepper	
	1 onion, quartered	
	1 carrot, quartered	
500 ml	red wine	2 cups
	1 Tbsp chopped parsley	
	STUFFING	
180 g	bacon, diced	6 oz
	1 large onion, chopped	
	3 chicken or duck livers, plus the liver of the duck	
	2 Tbsp chopped parsley	
	salt and pepper	
	pinch of ground allspice	
	ROUENNAISE SAUCE	
125 g	butter	¼ lb
	1 onion, chopped	
	1 shallot, chopped	
250 ml	red wine	1 cup
185 ml	broth	¾ cup
	salt and pepper	
	a few drops of lemon juice	
	3 chicken livers, chopped	
	trussing needle and string	

To make the stuffing: if the bacon is salty, blanch* it. In a frying pan, sauté the onion gently with the bacon until the onion is soft but not brown. Drain off the excess fat. Cut each liver in 3 pieces, add to the mixture and sauté about 30 seconds. Remove from the heat and add the parsley, a little salt, pepper and allspice. Chop the mixture with a knife. Set the oven at very hot (220°C/425°F).

Stuff the duck with the liver mixture and truss it. Lay it on its side on a rack in a roasting pan, sprinkle with salt and pepper and prick the skin to release fat during cooking. Chop the duck giblets and put them in the roasting pan with the onion and carrot. Roast the duck for 15 minutes; then turn the bird on to its other side for 15 minutes.

Discard excess fat as it gathers in the bottom of the pan. Lower the oven heat to moderately hot (190°C/375°F). Lay the duck on its breast and roast for 15 minutes more. Finally set the duck on its back and roast another 15 minutes. A short time before the end of cooking, add the red wine to the pan and continue roasting the duck until the juices from the centre of the duck run pink when pricked with a skewer. If you prefer well done meat, continue cooking the duck until the juices run clear. Transfer the duck to a platter, cover and keep warm. Reserve the roasting liquid.

Meanwhile, start the rouennaise sauce: in a saucepan, melt about a quarter of the butter, add the onion and shallot and brown them lightly. Add the wine and broth and boil, uncovered, for 5 minutes or until reduced by half. Strain in the wine from the roasting pan, add a little salt and pepper, and boil until only about 250 ml liquid remains. Skim thoroughly of fat, add lemon juice and set aside. Work the chicken livers through a fine sieve (this prevents the livers from becoming grainy when added to the sauce).

Just before serving, heat the sauce to lukewarm. Remove from the heat and whisk in the liver purée. Put the sauce back on a very low fire, stirring, for 2–3 minutes or until hot and slightly thickened; don't let the sauce boil or it will become too grainy. Remove from the heat, whisk well and stir in the remaining butter, a piece at a time. Taste for seasoning.

Carve the duck and spoon the stuffing into the centre of the platter. Spoon some sauce over the duck and sprinkle with chopped parsley. Serve the remaining sauce separately.

CIDER AND CALVADOS

A cider-apple tree is easily recognized by its heavy tangle of branches and mass of little, wizened fruit. In Brittany and Normandy, the trees are everywhere: scattered in hedgerows, grouped in orchards, or dotted about the fields. In autumn the countryside is littered with piles of orange and red apples awaiting the cider presses that go from farm to farm.

After pressing – the usual mix is two-thirds cider apples (which are inedibly bitter) to one-third sweet – the pure apple juice may be bottled at once to make the esteemed 'cidre bouché', which is left to ferment naturally in the bottle; the French word 'cidre' refers only to alcoholic cider, not to apple juice, as it does in the USA. Alternatively, the juice may be diluted with half as much water, then passed again through the apple pulp to make an everyday drink. In bad years even more water may be added, producing what is known as 'petit bère'.

The best cider of all comes from the Auge valley in southern Normandy and, like wine, it requires care in the making. Conventional wisdom has it that the winds must be in the right direction and the moon in the right quarter before the cider is bottled. Windfalls must not be used, only apples picked from the tree; the best flavoured cider comes from late-ripening fruit which has been touched by the first frost of the season.

Although it is still made in the country, today cider is a comparatively neglected drink. In 1913 the French downed three times as much cider as beer, and even more surprisingly, the consumption of wine was only 50 per cent more than that of cider. A few Norman growers have invested in the trees needed to make vintage cider distinctive, on the lines of vintage wines, but the vast bulk of commercial cider is nondescript in name and flavour.

Calvados (the name comes from the Calvados area of Normandy) is distilled from cider, bearing the same relation to it as brandy to wine. The best calvados is aged twelve to fifteen years in oak, but this is rare. The smoother calvados bears an 'appellation contrôlée' label, but most is fiery stuff, particularly appropriate to the custom of the 'trou normand' – a generous glass downed in the middle of a meal to clear the palate for the final course. The average brew certainly speeds the digestion as well.

In cooking, cider and calvados each blends well with a surprising number of ingredients, but it is important to use a dry cider and a mature calvados.

St Aubin

FILET MIGNON DE PORC NORMANDE
Pork tenderloin with apples

When fillet of pork is not available, use a boned, rolled loin of pork for this dish. It should be cooked in a moderate oven, allowing $1\frac{1}{2}$–2 hours for a 1 kg/2 lb loin.

Serves 4

	1 Tbsp oil	
15 g	butter	1 Tbsp
375 g each	2 pork tenderloins	$\frac{3}{4}$ lb each
	2 medium onions, sliced	
	2 tart apples, peeled, cored and sliced	
	3 Tbsp calvados	
	1 Tbsp flour	
375 ml	broth	$1\frac{1}{2}$ cups
	salt and pepper	
80 ml	heavy cream or crème fraîche*	$\frac{1}{3}$ cup
	CARAMELIZED APPLE SLICES	
	2 tart apples, unpeeled	
30 g	butter	2 Tbsp
25 g	sugar	2 Tbsp

Heat the oil and butter in a shallow casserole and brown the tenderloins on all sides over medium heat. Remove them, add the onions and cook until soft but not brown. Add the apples and continue cooking over fairly high heat until the apples and onions are golden brown. Replace the tenderloins, pour the calvados over them and flame. Stir the flour into the juices, add the broth, salt and pepper and bring to a boil. Cover and simmer, stirring occasionally, for 40–50 minutes or until the meat is tender when pierced with a skewer.

When the meat is nearly tender, prepare the apple garnish: core and thickly slice the apples, leaving the skin. Heat the butter in a frying pan. Dip one side of each apple slice in the sugar and place them sugared side down in the hot butter. Cook over high heat for 4–5 minutes or until caramelized. Sprinkle the rest of the sugar on the apples, turn them over and brown on the other side. Cover and keep warm.

When the pork is tender, remove it from the pan and carve it diagonally in medium slices. Arrange the slices overlapping on a platter, cover and keep warm while finishing the sauce. Strain the cooking juices into a small pot, pressing to purée the apples. Bring to a boil and, if necessary, reduce to a coating consistency. Add the cream, bring just back to a boil and taste for seasoning. Spoon some of the sauce over the pork and garnish the dish with the caramelized apple slices. Serve the remaining sauce separately.

TRIPES À LA MODE DE CAEN
Tripe with calvados

The reputation of Normandy tripe is probably due as much to the excellence of the local cattle as to the method of cooking, which is really very simple. The tripe is baked with onions, carrots and calf's feet, with cider and calvados giving the 'Norman flavour'. When the tripe is tender, the cooking liquid should be glossy and concentrated, so that when it is cold it sets to a stiff aspic. Most French charcuteries sell it in wedges. Tripe used to be the standard pick-me-up at the end of market day in Normandy, when it was consumed with dry cider or white wine to balance the richness, then followed by a glass of calvados. With such sustenance, the homeward path must have seemed short indeed.

Serves 8–10

2 kg	fresh tripe	$4\frac{1}{2}$ lb
	4 calf's feet	
	3 Tbsp oil	
1 kg	onions, sliced	2 lb
750 g	carrots, sliced	$1\frac{1}{2}$ lb
	bouquet garni	
	salt and pepper	
250 ml	dry cider or white wine	1 cup
60 ml	calvados	$\frac{1}{4}$ cup

Thoroughly wash the tripe under cold running water and cut it in 5 cm/2 in squares. Blanch the tripe and calf's feet by putting them in a large pot of cold water, bringing it to a boil and boiling 5 minutes. Drain and rinse them. Set the oven at moderate (175°C/350°F).

Heat the oil in a large flameproof casserole, add the onions and carrots and cook slowly, stirring occasionally, until soft but not brown. Add the tripe, calf's feet, bouquet garni, salt and water to cover; the casserole should be filled to the top. Bring to a boil, cover and cook slowly in the oven, stirring occasionally, for 5 hours or until very tender.

A short time before serving, stir in the cider, calvados and a pinch of pepper, bring back to a boil and simmer uncovered for 15 minutes or until the gravy is glossy. Taste for seasoning and remove the bouquet garni. Serve the hot tripe and vegetables in deep bowls, with liquid.

BOUDIN BLANC
White chicken and veal sausages

White boudin sausages are often served with caramelized slices of apple, called 'pommes en l'air' because they are tossed in the pan to brown evenly. A more common accompaniment is potato purée or sautéed potatoes.

Serves 4–6

	large sausage casings (for stuffing)	
60 ml	milk	¼ cup
60 ml	heavy cream or crème fraîche*	¼ cup
	1 onion, finely chopped	
100 g	fresh breadcrumbs	¾ cup
250 g	lean veal	½ lb
250 g	fat pork	½ lb
250 g	boned chicken, veal or turkey	½ lb
	2 egg whites	
	1 truffle, drained and chopped (optional)	
	1 tsp ground allspice	
	salt and white pepper	
30 g	butter	2 Tbsp
	COOKING LIQUID	
1·5 L	water	1½ qt
750 ml	milk	3 cups
	1 carrot, diced	
	1 onion, diced	
	1 leek, trimmed, split and diced	
	1 stalk of celery, diced	
	salt and pepper	
	sausage-stuffing tube or large funnel; string	

Soak the sausage casings in cold water for several hours until pliable. Scald the milk and the cream with the chopped onion and leave to infuse for 15 minutes. Strain the milk mixture over the breadcrumbs and leave to cool.

Work the veal, fat pork and chicken twice through the fine plate of a mincer/grinder; then work it in two batches to a fine paste in a food processor. Put the mixture in a bowl and stir in the egg whites, soaked breadcrumbs, truffle and liquid, allspice and plenty of salt and white pepper. Sauté a small piece of the mixture and taste for seasoning; it should be quite spicy. Beat with a wooden spoon until very smooth.

To fill the sausages: drain the casings. Very carefully insert the sausage stuffer or funnel at one end of one casing and spoon in the filling, pushing it down into the casing. Be careful, as casings tear easily. Don't fill them too tightly or they will burst during cooking. Prick the sausages with a pin to remove air holes and tie them at 15 cm/6 in intervals with string.

To cook the sausages: bring the water and milk to a boil in a large pot with the carrot, onion, leek, celery, salt and pepper. Lower the sausages into the pot, cover and poach for 18–20 minutes at about 90°C/195°F; don't boil or the sausages will burst. Let the sausages cool overnight in the liquid.

To finish, drain the sausages, heat the butter in a skillet and fry them for 4–5 minutes or until very hot and golden. Alternatively, brush them with melted butter and grill/broil. Serve hot.

BLANQUETTE DE POMMES DE TERRE AUX POIREAUX

White potato and leek stew

This stew looks more attractive if it is browned under the grill before serving, though strictly speaking a 'blanquette' should remain white.

Serves 4–6

60 g	butter	4 Tbsp
500 g	leeks, trimmed, split and sliced	1 lb
	1 Tbsp flour	
625 ml	milk	2½ cups
1 kg	potatoes, thinly sliced	2 lb
	salt and pepper	
	pinch of ground nutmeg	
	bouquet garni	

In a heavy, medium-sized pot melt 3 table-spoons of the butter, add the leeks and cook slowly, stirring for 5 minutes or until soft but not brown. Sprinkle the flour over them and cook over low heat, stirring, for about 1 minute. Add the milk and bring to a boil, stirring to prevent lumps. Add the potatoes, salt, pepper, nutmeg and bouquet garni. Cover and cook over a very low fire, stirring often to prevent burning, for 45 minutes or until the potatoes are tender but not falling apart. Discard the bouquet garni and taste the stew for seasoning. Pour it into a shallow buttered baking dish. If you like, dot the top with the remaining butter and brown under the grill/broiler.

SALADE CAUCHOISE

Potato salad with ham

The Pays de Caux, the 'land of chalk', is also a land of potatoes, which are served with most main dishes. This salad, flavoured with ham and celery, could accompany cold meats or be served as a first course.

Serves 4

	1 bunch celery	
750 g	firm potatoes, unpeeled	1½ lb
	2 Tbsp white wine vinegar	
	salt and pepper	
125 ml	heavy cream or crème fraîche*	½ cup
	juice of ½ lemon	
125 g	cooked ham, cut in thin strips	4 oz

Cut the celery in very thin strips, reserving the leaves, and soak in iced water for 1–2 hours.

Scrub the potatoes and put them in cold salted water; cover, bring to a boil and simmer for 15–20 minutes or until just tender. Drain, peel and, while still warm, cut in thick slices.

Immediately spoon the vinegar over the warm potatoes; sprinkle with salt and pepper (warm potatoes absorb the seasonings better).

Not more than 1–2 hours before serving, whip the cream and beat in the lemon juice, a little at a time, so the mixture thickens slightly.

Drain the celery and dry it on paper towels. Combine the celery, potatoes and ham; then carefully stir in the cream. Taste the salad for seasoning, pile it in a glass bowl and decorate the edge with celery leaves. Serve at room temperature.

SAUCE NORMANDE

Cider and cream sauce

Serve this sauce with meats and with typical Norman vegetables like cauliflower, salsify, leeks, carrots and celeriac/celery root. Sauce Normande is also made to serve with fish, using the liquid (wine, cider or fish stock) in which the fish was cooked.

Makes 750 ml/3 cups of sauce

100 g	butter	7 Tbsp
	1 onion, thinly sliced	
30 g	flour	¼ cup
500 ml	dry cider or white wine	2 cups
	salt and pepper	
	pinch of grated nutmeg	
250 ml	heavy cream or crème fraîche*	1 cup
	a few drops of lemon juice	

Melt a tablespoon of the butter in a pot, add the onion and brown lightly over a low fire. Add half the remaining butter and mix well. Stir in the flour and continue to cook over a low fire, stirring, until the mixture foams. Whisk in the cider and bring to a boil. Season with salt, pepper and nutmeg and simmer for 7–8 minutes or until the sauce lightly coats a spoon. Stir in the cream and bring the sauce back almost to a boil. Remove the pan from the heat and whisk in the remaining butter, a piece at a time. Add a few drops of lemon juice and taste for seasoning. Don't reheat the sauce or the butter will separate.

BRIOCHE

There are many theories as to the origin of brioche. The inhabitants of St Brieuc in Brittany, the 'briochains', claim to have invented it, though they appear to have convinced only other Bretons. Another theory ascribes this butter bread to Brie; that region is famous for its cheese, not butter, but proponents of this theory claim that Brie cheese used to be one of the ingredients in brioche. Most likely, brioche comes from the old Norman word 'brier', which describes the kneading technique still used in mixing the dough. Bearing this out, the brioches of Gournay in the butter country of Normandy are among the most famous. For extra-rich brioches, use 50 per cent as much butter again.

Makes 15 small or 2 large brioches

15 g	fresh yeast OR	1 cake
	1 pkg dry yeast	
	2 Tbsp lukewarm water	
460 g	flour, more if needed	3½ cups
	7 eggs	
12 g	salt	2½ tsp
30 g	sugar	2½ Tbsp
250 g	unsalted butter	½ lb
	1 egg, beaten with ½ tsp salt (for glaze)	
15 small or 2 medium (15 cm/6 in) brioche pans		

In a small bowl crumble the yeast over the water. Mix in enough of the flour to make a soft, sticky dough and let this starter rise in a warm place for 15–20 minutes. Then sift the remaining flour on to a board or marble slab and make a large well in the centre. Add the yeast starter, eggs, salt and sugar. Briefly mix the central ingredients; then sprinkle some of the flour over the wet mixture so it is no longer visible. Draw in the remaining flour with both hands, pulling the dough into large crumbs with the fingertips. Knead the dough into a ball; it should now be soft and rather sticky. If very soft, add more flour.

Knead the dough by lifting it up and slapping it down on the work surface for 5–10 minutes until it is very smooth and elastic. Pound the butter to soften it thoroughly; then work it into the dough. Knead the dough again by slapping it lightly on the work surface only until the butter is thoroughly incorporated. Transfer the dough to a lightly floured bowl and sprinkle it with a little more flour. Cover the bowl with a damp cloth and let the dough rise at room temperature for 2 hours or until nearly doubled in bulk.

Transfer the risen dough to a floured board or marble and fold it in thirds, patting it to knock out the air. Return the dough to the bowl and cover with a damp cloth. Let rise at room temperature until doubled in bulk, or overnight in the refrigerator.

Butter the pans. Divide the dough into 15 pieces for individual brioches or in half for large brioches. Pinch off a third of each piece of dough and shape both the large and small pieces into balls. Set a large ball in the base of each pan, press the centre down to form a hollow and set a smaller ball or 'head' of dough inside it. Let rise in a warm place for 15 minutes for small brioches and 40–45 minutes for large brioches, or until the pans are almost full. Meanwhile, set the oven at very hot (220°C/425°F).

When the brioches have risen, brush them with egg glaze. Bake small brioches 15–20 minutes or until well browned and hollow-sounding when tapped on the bottom. Bake large brioches for 15 minutes; then reduce the temperature of the oven to moderately hot (190°C/375°F) and bake for another 30–40 minutes, or until the brioches start to pull away from the sides of the pan and sound hollow when tapped on the bottom. Turn out on to a rack to cool.

LA TERRINÉE
Baked rice pudding

This pudding is also called 'bourregoule', meaning 'gob-stopper' in old French. It can be baked overnight so it has a golden crust or it can be done in the coals of the hearth. Instead of cinnamon, orange flower water, vanilla, nutmeg or bay leaves can be added for flavour, and brown sugar can replace the white.

Serves 4–6

130 g	round-grain rice	⅔ cup
85 g	sugar	7 Tbsp
2 L	milk, more if needed	2 qt
	1 tsp ground cinnamon	
	a pinch of salt	
2·5 L/2½ qt deep baking dish		

Set the oven at low (150°C/300°F). Mix all the ingredients together in the baking dish and bake for 1 hour. If all the milk has already been absorbed, stir in more to make the rice soupy. Continue cooking for 1 hour longer, or until the rice is very tender. At the end of cooking all the milk should be absorbed, so the rice holds its shape and a golden crust forms. Serve hot or cold from the dish.

LA GÂCHE
Flat yeast bread

Gâche from the Cotentin becomes 'gosh' in the Channel Isles and 'falue' in other parts of Normandy. All mean an oval yeast bread sometimes incorporating raisins. 'Cookeboodram' is from Dunkerque, near the Belgian border.

Makes 4 loaves

7 g	fresh yeast OR	$\frac{1}{2}$ cake
	$\frac{1}{2}$ pkg dry yeast	
125 ml	lukewarm milk	$\frac{1}{2}$ cup
290 g	flour, more as needed	$2\frac{1}{4}$ cups
	2 eggs	
5 g	salt	1 tsp
8 g	sugar	2 tsp
75 g	butter	5 Tbsp
	1 egg, beaten with $\frac{1}{2}$ tsp salt	
	(for glaze)	

In a small bowl crumble the yeast over 3–4 tablespoons of the milk. Mix in enough of the flour to make a soft, sticky dough and let this starter rise in a warm place for 15–20 minutes. Sift the remaining flour on a board or marble slab and make a large well in the centre. Add the yeast starter, eggs, salt, sugar and remaining milk. Briefly mix the centre ingredients. Draw in the flour with both hands, pulling the dough into large crumbs with your fingertips. Knead the dough into a ball; it should be soft but not sticky, so add more flour if necessary.

Knead the dough by lifting it up and slapping it on the work surface for 5–10 minutes until very smooth and elastic. Pound the butter to soften it, then work it into the dough. Knead the dough again to incorporate the butter thoroughly. Transfer the dough to a lightly floured bowl and sprinkle it with a little more flour. Cover with a damp cloth and let rise at room temperature for 2 hours or until nearly doubled.

Transfer the risen dough to a floured board or marble slab and fold in thirds, patting to knock out the air. Divide the dough into 4 parts. Pat out each into an oval about 1 cm/$\frac{3}{8}$ in thick and 20 cm/8 in long; set on a buttered baking sheet. Let rise for 30 minutes or until nearly doubled. Set the oven at very hot (220°C/425°F).

When the loaves have risen, brush them with egg glaze. Press a fingertip into the dough 6–8 times to form a pattern. Bake in the oven for 15–20 minutes or until firm and golden brown.

COOKEBOODRAM
After adding the butter to the dough, knead in:

50 g	raisins	$\frac{1}{3}$ cup

Bake in a 20 × 7·5 × 6 cm/8 × 3 × 2$\frac{1}{2}$ in buttered loaf pan for 50–60 minutes or until browned and hollow-sounding when tapped underneath.

MIRLITONS
Almond and cream tartlets

There are several versions of these tartlets, which are familiar in Parisian bakeries. In Cherbourg mirlitons have whipped egg whites folded into the filling, as well as a few crushed macaroons for flavour. However, the mirlitons of Rouen, filled simply with eggs, almonds, sugar and cream, are the most famous.

Makes 10 tartlets

	30 whole blanched almonds	
	confectioners' sugar (for sprinkling)	
	PIE PASTRY	
260 g	flour	2 cups
125 g	butter	$\frac{1}{4}$ lb
	2 egg yolks	
	2 Tbsp sugar	
	$\frac{3}{4}$ tsp salt	
	5–6 Tbsp cold water	
	FILLING	
	4 eggs	
200 g	sugar	1 cup
100 g	ground almonds	$\frac{3}{4}$ cup
	2 Tbsp heavy cream	
	10 tartlet pans (9 cm/3$\frac{1}{2}$ in diameter)	

Make the pie pastry*, adding the sugar to the well with the egg yolks; chill for 30 minutes. Roll out the pastry very thinly and line the tartlet pans*; chill another 30 minutes. Set the oven at moderately hot (190°C/375°F) and put a baking sheet in the oven to heat.

Meanwhile, make the filling: beat the eggs with the sugar until thick and light. Stir in the ground almonds and the cream. Spoon some of the mixture into each tartlet shell to fill it by three-quarters and set the shells on the hot baking sheet in the oven; after 15 minutes, take the tartlets from the oven and put 3 almonds on each, pointing them towards the centre. Return the tartlets to the oven and continue baking for another 12–18 minutes or until lightly browned and the filling is set. Transfer them to a rack to cool slightly before unmoulding. Sprinkle them heavily with the sugar before serving warm or at room temperature.

CRÈME FRAÎCHE

'Crème fraîche' is a key French ingredient; its outstanding characteristics are a high butterfat content and a slightly fermented taste, which becomes stronger as the cream matures. This flavour is vital in certain dishes, notably soups, and fish and poultry sauces. Sweet cream, however thick and rich, simply does not add the same piquancy. When used with desserts, crème fraîche is less crucial, and it should be less than a week old so the taste is still delicate. Many cooks are happy to substitute sweet cream here.

The high butterfat content of French crème fraîche (it can run up to 60 per cent) is almost as important as its flavour, particularly in sauces. Crème fraîche is often described as unctuous, that is, it has a smoothness and body that thickens rather than thins mixtures. It can also be boiled to half or a quarter its original volume without danger of curdling, making it indispensable to the reduced, concentrated sauces of French cooking.

The reason crème fraîche has such special qualities is that it contains lactic acid and other ferments. All raw cream contains these ferments, but pasteurization kills them. Most countries leave it at that, so their cream remains sweet, but the French put the ferments back. At first crème fraîche is sweet and almost pourable, but after two or three weeks it acquires a tart, almost cheesy flavour, and is stiff enough to support a spoon.

Crème fraîche is easy to make at home*.

TARTE AUX POIRES NORMANDE
Pear and almond cream tart

In this delicious pie, the pear halves are thinly sliced, then slightly flattened in a layer of almond cream, so they fan out like petals. The almond cream browns during baking so the pie looks like an opened flower when done. For 'tarte aux pommes normande', use three or four dessert apples instead of the pears.

Serves 8–10

	3–4 ripe pears	
	sugar (for sprinkling)	
125 ml	apricot jam glaze*	½ cup
	PIE PASTRY	
200 g	flour	1½ cups
95 g	butter	6 Tbsp
	1 egg yolk	
	½ tsp salt	
	4–5 Tbsp cold water	
	ALMOND CREAM	
100 g	butter	6 Tbsp
100 g	sugar	½ cup
	1 egg, beaten to mix	
	1 egg yolk	
	2 tsp kirsch	
100 g	whole blanched almonds, ground	½ cup
15 g	flour	2 Tbsp
	23–25 cm/9–10 in pie or tart pan	

Make the pie pastry* and chill it for 30 minutes or until firm. Roll out the dough, line the pan* and flute the edges. Chill again until firm. Set the oven at hot (200°C/400°F) and place a baking sheet in the oven to heat.

Make the almond cream: cream the butter, gradually beat in the sugar and continue beating until the mixture is light and soft. Gradually add the egg and yolk, beating well after each addition. Add the kirsch; then stir in the ground almonds and the flour. Pour two-thirds of the almond cream into the chilled pastry, spreading it evenly.

Peel the pears, halve them and scoop out the cores and stem fibre. Cut the pear halves crosswise in very thin slices and arrange them on the almond cream in a wheel pattern, keeping the slices of each half pear together; then press them gently to flatten the slices a little. Spoon the remaining almond cream into the spaces between the pear halves.

Bake the pie on the hot baking sheet near the bottom of the heated oven for 10–15 minutes or until the pastry dough begins to brown. Lower the oven heat to moderate (175°C/350°F) and continue baking for another 5–10 minutes or until the pears are tender and the almond cream is set; then sprinkle the pie with sugar and bake for 20 minutes more or until the sugar melts and caramelizes slightly. Cool the pie on a rack.

A short time before serving, brush the surface of the pie with melted apricot jam glaze. Serve at room temperature.

TARTE AUX POMMES GRILLAGÉE

Latticed apple tart

This pie owes its excellence to the concentrated apple and butter marmalade which is so thick that it does not soak into the pastry.

Serves 4

	1 egg, beaten with $\frac{1}{2}$ tsp salt (for glaze)	
125 ml	apricot jam glaze*	$\frac{1}{2}$ cup
	PUFF PASTRY	
375 g	unsalted butter	$\frac{3}{4}$ lb
260 g	all-purpose flour	2 cups
120 g	cake flour	1 cup
8 g	salt	$1\frac{1}{2}$ tsp
	$1\frac{1}{2}$ tsp lemon juice	
185 ml	iced water, more as needed	$\frac{3}{4}$ cup
	APPLE MARMALADE	
1·5 kg	tart apples	3 lb
90 g	butter	6 Tbsp
	1 vanilla bean	
	pared rind of 1 lemon	
	squeeze of lemon juice	
100 g	sugar, or to taste	$\frac{1}{2}$ cup
	23–25 cm/9–10 in pie or tart pan	

Make the puff pastry* and chill it for 1 hour or until firm.

Make the apple marmalade: peel, core and thinly slice the apples. Spread a heavy-based pan with two-thirds of the butter and put in the apples, vanilla bean, lemon rind and juice. Spread the remaining butter on a piece of foil and lay it over the apples. Cover and cook gently, stirring occasionally, for 20–25 minutes or until the apples are very soft. Remove the vanilla bean and pieces of lemon rind; then add the sugar. Cook over a high fire, stirring constantly, until the purée is so thick that it just falls from the spoon; let it cool.

Roll out two-thirds of the dough and line the pie pan*, being sure to form a rather high rim; prick the base lightly with a fork. Spread the apple mixture in the pie shell. Roll the remaining dough in a long strip and cut into strips 6 mm/ $\frac{1}{4}$ in wide. Brush the pie rim with egg glaze; then arrange the dough strips in a lattice on the apple purée, pressing the ends to seal the strips to the rim without stretching them. Brush the lattice with egg glaze and chill the pie for 15 minutes. Set the oven at very hot (220°C/425°F); put a baking sheet in the oven to heat.

Glaze the chilled pie again; then bake on the heated baking sheet for 20–25 minutes or until the pastry is puffed and brown and the apple mixture starts to bubble. Cool the pie on a rack.

Before serving, brush the pie with melted apricot jam glaze. Serve warm or at room temperature.

SABLÉS DE BOURG-DUN

Butter biscuits

Sablés in Normandy come large or small, crumbly or crisp. This is one village version.

Makes 12 cookies

200 g	flour	$1\frac{1}{2}$ cups
	4 egg yolks	
	$\frac{1}{2}$ tsp salt	
100 g	confectioners' sugar	$\frac{3}{4}$ cup
	grated rind of 1 orange or 1 lemon	
	juice of $\frac{1}{2}$ orange OR 1 lemon	
125 g	butter	$\frac{1}{4}$ lb
	1 egg, beaten with $\frac{1}{2}$ tsp salt (for glaze)	
	10 cm/4 in diameter cookie cutter	

Sift the flour on to a marble slab or board and make a large well in the centre. Put the egg yolks, salt, sugar and orange or lemon rind and juice in the well. Pound the butter to soften it slightly; then add it to the well and use the fingertips of one hand to work it quickly with the other ingredients until partly mixed. Gradually incorporate the flour, using the whole hand. Knead the dough with the heel of the hand until it is smooth and peels easily from the board in one piece. Press the dough into a ball, wrap it and chill for 30 minutes or until firm.

Set the oven at moderately hot (190°C/375°F) and butter two baking sheets. Roll out the dough to a 6 mm/$\frac{1}{4}$ in thickness, cut out rounds with the cutter and set them on a baking sheet. Press the pastry trimmings into a ball, roll it out and cut more sablés. Brush the sablés with beaten egg and mark a triangle on each with the prongs of a fork. Chill the sablés for 15 minutes; then bake in the heated oven for 10–15 minutes or until lightly browned. Sablés burn easily and will be bitter if overcooked. Transfer them to a rack to cool.

CHEESES

'Qui dit "fromage" dit "Normandie",' (when one talks of cheese one talks of Normandy) said an expert on regional gastronomy. Indeed, most people immediately associate Normandy with cheese, especially soft creamy cheeses based on the rich milk of the region's black and white cows. Normal cheeses, however, like Norman cooking, have a limited repertoire. Four names in particular are worth mentioning, and each of them is outstanding: pont-l'évêque, livarot, neufchâtel, and the much-imitated, capricious camembert.

Pont-l'évêque, a square golden cheese, was regarded as ancient even in the medieval *Roman de la Rose*. At its best, it is slightly runny, rich and assertive without being pungent. Generally, quality is good as much of the supply is still farm-produced, but pont-l'évêque ages rapidly and can become unpleasantly strong. Chilled dry cider is its traditional companion.

Livarot, another ancient cheese, is considered by many to be the finest pungent cheese in France. About 12·5 cm/ 5 in across, it is a more tangy version of pont-l'évêque that owes at least some of its flavour to being aged in airtight cellars, the walls plastered with hay and mortar. To retain the creamy interior, livarot is wrapped in bands of sedge, enclosing the reddish brown crust. A similar cheese, also with a long history, is 'petit lisieux'.

Neufchâtel, from eastern Normandy, is a fresher cheese usually sold within three weeks of making, though if kept a week or two longer it takes on an attractive piquancy. It is made in rounds, logs and heart shapes. Other very rich creamy cheeses appropriately called 'triple crèmes' are Brillat-Savarin and Chateaubriand. Mildest of all is the square, foil-wrapped 'demi-sel' (half-salted), a soft cream cheese produced by the big commercial dairies, which also attempt to reproduce Normandy's most famous cheese – camembert.

Camembert comes from the archetypally Norman pays d'Auge. A farmer's wife, Marie Harel, is credited with inventing the cheese in the 18th century, but the contribution of a Monsieur Ridel is at least as important. He made the first characteristic thin wooden containers that allow the cheese to travel without spoiling, thus assuring its nationwide distribution.

A perfect camembert is soft and pale throughout; it bulges from the rind when cut, but does not run. Napoleon is said to have kissed the Norman waitress who first served him such a treasure.

Camembert is imitated as far afield as the USA and Russia, and even in France quality can be poor. It is a cheese which does not take kindly to pasteurization, a process required for any cheese traded within the Common Market of Europe. And French farmhouse camemberts, made from the raw milk of individual herds, are unfortunately few and far between today. Less than perfect camembert does, however, make delicious croquettes.

Choosing the ideal camembert is not easy. The rind should be white and the cheese should feel supple throughout, which shows that it is uniformly ripe. A cheese that is firm will have a white, chalky middle when cut, while a dark and wrinkled rind denotes a cheese that is overripe. Smell is a good test: camembert should have a heady aroma with no trace of ammonia. It should, says one lyrical gourmet, smell like the feet of a god.

OTHER SPECIALITIES OF THE REGION
TRADITIONAL DISHES

Maquereaux à la mode du Cotentin
Mackerel with fennel and gooseberries

Cailles en douillons à la normande
Apples stuffed with quail and baked in pastry

Pâté chaud de sole fécampoise
Hot pâté of sole with oysters in pastry

Râble de lièvre à la cauchoise
Saddle of hare with cream sauce

Pain de poisson dieppoise
Fish loaf with mussel sauce

Jambon au cidre
Ham baked with cider

Côtes de veau Vallée d'Auge
Veal chops with baby onions, mushrooms, calvados and cream

Gigot d'agneau de pré-salé de Mont St Michel
Roast leg of salt-marsh lamb

Caneton rôti de Duclair
Roast pressed duck with liver sauce

Salade normande
Salad of apples, shellfish and fresh cheese with herbs

CHARCUTERIE

Saucisse en gelée de Pont Audemer
Pork sausage in aspic

Tripes à la crème de l'Avranchin
Tripe in cream sauce

PÂTISSERIE AND CONFISERIE

Beignets de pommes à la normande
Apple fritters

Roulettes
Rolls of croissant-type dough

Sucre de pommes de Rouen
Apple sugar sticks

Couronne de pommes à la normande
Calvados custard ring with poached apples in centre

The Loire

The Loire

The Loire is the longest river in France. During its 1000-kilometre passage to the Atlantic, it changes character radically from the bleak mountain gorges of the Massif Central to the blooming sun-lit Val de Loire that meanders west from Orléans. On a first enthusiastic visit to this valley in 1847, Gustave Flaubert described it thus: 'The whole landscape is pretty, varied without monotony, light, graceful, but it is a beauty which caresses without captivating, which charms without seducing and which, in a word, has more good sense than grandeur, and more wit than poetry. C'est la France!'

The Loire valley has been a cradle of French culture to many a Frenchman and foreigner. It was here that I explored my first French castle, the massive fortress of Angers, capital of Anjou. And it was near the Loire that, aged thirteen, I ate my first memorable French meal. The simple menu of sole meunière with little mushrooms, followed by wild strawberries marinated in Cointreau, epitomized the 'good sense' instanced by Flaubert. Blessed with fish, fruit and vegetables that are second to none, the cooks of the Loire valley let them stand on their own merits. Fish are poached, then served with a herb butter or a beurre blanc, a sauce as 'native' to the Loire as to Brittany; fresh fruits are served alone or with 'crémets', a type of fresh cheese.

In fact, to talk of the food of the Loire amounts to talking more of ingredients than of cooking. The fine vegetables go back to the time of King Charles VIII at the end of the 15th century. After a visit to Italy, where the Renaissance was at its height, Charles brought back to his favourite château of Amboise artists, builders and, most importantly for French eating, gardeners. In the hospitable climate of the Loire valley, where winter temperatures at Angers match those of Valence on the edge of Provence, new vegetables like lettuce, artichokes and green peas flourished. The poet Ronsard rhapsodized: 'Artichokes and salad greens, asparagus, parsnips and the melons of Touraine, all are more tempting than great mounds of royal meats.'

Growing asparagus is an art which provides a good example of the care that is needed, even with today's technology, to produce the best vegetables. Late one spring, at the height of the asparagus season, I looked in vain for beds sprouting the healthy green fronds that I remembered in my mother's garden. The mystery was solved only when I tracked down some asparagus pickers at work, bent double inspecting an immaculate brown field with not a suspicion of growth. It turned out that to obtain the white asparagus so prized in France, each bed must be stripped every day, the stems of asparagus cut deep under the earth with a special knife so only a thumb's breadth of head ever sees daylight.

The Loire valley has also long been a home for new fruit trees. François I's queen was a keen gardener and gave her name 'reine-claude' to greengage plums, while 'reinette' (little queen) apples come from Orléans and Le Mans. Apricots, melons, peaches and particularly pears have all been the subjects of horticultural experiment, starting with the pear tree planted near Tours in the 15th century by St François de Paule and called, appropriately, 'bon chrétien'. The fruits 'give an idea of the bounty of paradise', declared a contemporary observer and, as proof, the bon chrétien pear is still cultivated.

In season, fruit tarts and cakes adorn the windows of Loire valley pastry shops like so many flowers — greengage, red strawberry and cherry, golden apricot and mirabelle plum. In my favourites, the fruit is baked in a 'quatre quarts' (pound cake) dough, or in custard like a quiche. In winter the Loire fruits can be enjoyed as 'pâte de fruits', hard fruit jellies which are somewhat sweet for my taste, though they look so tempting, often shaped like the fruit from which they are made. And Loire valley cooks, crazy about prunes, put them in pies, add them to fish stews, rabbit or chicken, stuff them with dried apricot purée and, best of all, poach them in wine. This taste for prunes dates from the first crusades when plums were apparently brought from Damascus. So well did the trees acclimatize in the Loire valley that a local expression grew up: 'pour les prunes' meaning 'for nothing'.

Away from the Loire itself, the land rises only slightly, so that the orchards and market gardens continue with little break, particularly around Tours. The Touraine is known as the garden of France. The espaliered lines of fruit trees, the meticulous rows of lettuce and spinach flanked by protective poplars give the impression of a giant market garden.

The meandering curves of the Loire have long been famous for their fish, and it is a rare stretch of bank that lacks a patient fisherman, even on weekdays. Pike are still abundant and 'sandre' (pickerel), introduced only recently, are becoming more and more common; being predators and not bottom feeders, both are excellent eating, though pike has too many bones for comfort and is best in a fish pâté. A few salmon are still netted for sale but the once-famous 'alose' (shad) have almost disappeared. With both, the traditional accompaniment is sorrel in a purée or shredded in a butter sauce, where its acidity is the ideal foil for the richness of the fish. Loire eel, on the other hand, seem to be indestructible. Eel is the principal ingredient in 'matelote de la Loire', a fish stew flavoured with mushrooms, cream and local vouvray wine.

Away from the river, fishing is even more competitive in the ponds and lakes of Sologne, a wooded low-lying area south of Orléans and an easy weekend drive from Paris. Carp and perch are raised for sport, and hunting is serious business, with 160,000 shooting licenses issued each year. The roads are lined with 'propriété privée' signs and my husband and I were turned back in very short order from a Sunday stroll in the woods by two large guard dogs and an alert gamekeeper. Sologne is rich in game, with wildfowl on the lakes and pheasant, deer and a few wild boar in the woods. Game dishes are traditional, with rich sauces based on wine marinades, and sweet accompaniments like tart baked apples or a compote of red currants.

One excellent way to make a little game go a long way is to put it in a pâté, a speciality of both Sologne and the Orléanais to the north. Outside Pithiviers the town sign reads 'land of larks and honey', an idyllic image that is rapidly shattered when one realizes that the larks are not there to sing, but to be netted for the local pâté. More to the popular taste is the famous gâteau Pithiviers, a puff pastry round filled with almond frangipane and now found throughout France.

The most legendary pâté of all comes from Chartres, whose inhabitants, relates chronicler Gregory of Tours, attempted to distract Attila the Hun by offering him an outsize hare pâté. History does not relate if they succeeded, but since the time of Louis XIV, the game pâtés of Chartres have been gastronomically renowned.

Chartres lies at the centre of the Beauce, the granary of France created by monks who cleared the surrounding countryside

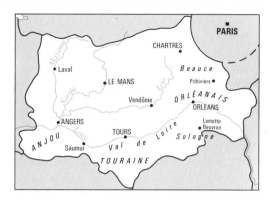

while building Chartres cathedral. Bakers are depicted at work in several of the windows; indeed, they themselves financed some of these outstanding medieval works of art. Today the farmers of the Beauce are so rich that envious observers allege their preoccupations to be 'wheat, maize and Côte d'Azur'. Local dishes show similarities to those of the Loire valley: pâtés, rillettes and 'omelette beauceronne' with bacon, potatoes and sorrel. In nearby Gâtinais, walnuts and honey used to be the trademark, though nowadays when a walnut tree is felled, it is rarely replaced. The honey is more evident, appearing in a quantity of rather sticky sweets, endearingly wrapped to look like bees. Less fanciful and much more appetizing is 'pain d'épices' (spice bread) and its little cousins, 'nonnettes', which are spice cakes topped with icing.

Lying at the other end of the Loire valley, towards the river mouth, Anjou is also something of an outsider. Less sheltered than Touraine and with thinner soil, Anjou is turning more and more to cattle, for both beef and milk production. Here the cooking resembles that of Brittany, with crêpes and butter cakes much in evidence.

If anything sums up the Loire for me it is a visit to friends who live on le Loir, a tributary of its more famous sister. The sun shone and time slid by as I sipped a chilled muscadet on the terrace overlooking the lush, smug valley. Lunch was 'tarte tourangelle', a kind of quiche containing rillettes, with a salad dressed with walnut oil. A short walk, a somewhat longer nap and the day had waned. I was a victim of indolence, a recognized failing even among German troops stationed in the Loire in World War II. 'Anjou is the paradise of dining in tranquillity,' declared Curnonsky, founder of the Académie des Gastronomes and the Loire's most famous epicure. His large girth would certainly seem to prove it.

FEUILLETÉ SOLOGNOTE
Feuilleté of game

One day when Charles IX was out hunting in Sologne, it is said, he was captured by some brigands. At dinner he was regaled with such a splendid example of the local speciality of game pâté that, when returned to freedom, he granted its creator the title of 'pâtissier du roi'. This feuilleté can be made with any game by substituting the same weight of meat for the birds used here.

Serves 6–8 as a first course

	PUFF PASTRY	
250 g	unsalted butter	½ lb
175 g	all-purpose flour	1⅓ cups
80 g	cake flour	⅔ cup
5 g	salt	1 tsp
	1 tsp lemon juice	
125 ml	iced water, more as needed	½ cup
	1 egg, beaten with ½ tsp salt (for glaze)	
	FILLING	
1·8 kg total	1–2 wild ducks, pheasants or partridges including the livers	4 lb total
125 g	lean pork, ground	4 oz
60 g	pork fat, ground	2 oz
	1 egg	
	2 Tbsp cognac	
	1 small can chopped truffles (optional)	
	pinch of ground allspice	
	pinch of ground nutmeg	
	salt and pepper	

Make the puff pastry* and chill it for 1 hour or until firm.

Prepare the filling: remove the skin from the birds. With a sharp knife cut all the meat from the bones; it should weigh about 400 g/13 oz. Finely mince/grind the meat with the lean pork, the pork fat and the livers. Add the egg, cognac, truffles with their liquid, allspice, nutmeg, salt and pepper, beating well to mix all the flavourings. Sauté a small piece of the mixture and taste for seasoning.

Roll out the dough to a 38 cm/15 in square and trim the edges neatly. Cut out one rectangle 15 × 33 cm/6 × 13 in and another slightly larger. Transfer the smaller rectangle to a moistened baking sheet. Spoon the meat mixture down the centre, leaving a 2·5 cm/1 in border. Brush the border with cold water. Cover with the second rectangle of pastry, pressing the edges together firmly. Scallop the edges all round with a knife and chill for 15–20 minutes. Set the oven at very hot (220°C/425°F).

Brush the pastry with egg glaze and score a simple design on top. Bake for 15 minutes or until the pastry puffs and it begins to turn brown. Lower the oven temperature to hot (200°C/400°F) and continue baking for 20–30 minutes or until a skewer inserted into the filling for 30 seconds is hot to the touch when withdrawn. Serve hot.

NOUZILLARDS AU LAIT
Cream of chestnut soup

In the most rudimentary form of this peasant recipe, cooked chestnuts were simply spooned into bowls and covered with boiling milk. This more sophisticated soup is surprisingly rich, though it contains no eggs or cream.

Serves 4

750 g	chestnuts	1½ lb
30 g	butter	2 Tbsp
	1 onion chopped	
	3 stalks celery, chopped	
1 L	broth	1 qt
	salt and pepper	
500 ml	milk	2 cups
	1 tsp chopped parsley (optional)	

Peel the chestnuts*. Melt the butter in a large pot, add the onion and celery and cook over a low fire, stirring often, for 10 minutes or until softened. Add the chestnuts, broth, salt and pepper. Cover, bring to a boil and simmer over a low fire, shaking the pot occasionally, for 20 minutes or until the chestnuts are nearly tender.

Bring the milk to a boil, add it to the chestnuts and simmer for 15 minutes more or until the nuts are completely tender. Taste for seasoning and add the parsley. Spoon the soup into bowls and serve hot.

NOUZILLARDS EN PURÉE

When the chestnuts are tender, purée the soup in a food mill or blender and reheat it with:

125 ml	heavy cream or crème fraîche*	½ cup

CRÈME DE CRESSON

Cream of watercress soup

Since the acid in watercress will curdle milk, the watercress leaves in this soup are blanched and then thoroughly simmered in broth before any milk is added.

Serves 4

400 g	1 medium bunch watercress	13 oz
90 g	butter	6 Tbsp
	1 medium potato, thinly sliced	
375 ml	broth or water	1½ cups
	salt and pepper	
375 ml	milk, more if needed	1½ cups
60 ml	heavy cream	¼ cup
	pinch of grated nutmeg	

Wash the watercress, discard the stems and reserve the sprigs; keep 12 leaves for decoration. Put the bunch of watercress in a large pot of boiling water. When the water comes to a boil, drain the watercress, rinse it under cold running water and squeeze it dry. Put the 12 leaves in a small pan of boiling water, bring back to a boil, drain and rinse them.

In a heavy saucepan melt 2 tablespoons of the butter, add the watercress sprigs and cook over a low fire, stirring, for 2–3 minutes until dry. Add the potato, broth and a little salt and pepper and bring to a boil. Cover and simmer, stirring occasionally, for 15–20 minutes or until the potatoes are tender. Purée the soup in a blender and strain it to remove strings, or work it through a vegetable mill. Return it to the pan, add the milk and reheat it. The soup should be thick and rich, particularly if it is to be served hot; if serving it cold, thin it with a little more milk.

Add the cream and bring just to a boil. Season the soup to taste with salt, pepper and nutmeg. Remove from the heat and stir in the remaining butter. Serve the soup hot or chilled in bowls, each one decorated with 3 watercress leaves.

CRÈME D'ÉPINARDS

Substitute:

500 g	spinach	1 lb

for the watercress and decorate the bowls of soup with a spoonful of cream instead of the watercress leaves.

SOUPE SOLOGNOTE AU LAPIN

Rabbit and mushroom soup

One old poacher's trick to hide illicit game is to immerse the pieces in a vegetable soup; here the rabbit is reduced after long cooking to a discreetly anonymous purée. To make 'soupe solognote au poulet', substitute a medium-sized chicken for the rabbit.

Serves 4

	1 rabbit	
30 g	butter	2 Tbsp
250 ml	white wine	1 cup
1 L	broth or water	1 qt
500 g	onions, sliced	1 lb
	bouquet garni, including a few stems fresh tarragon	
	salt and pepper	
250 g	mushrooms	8 oz
	juice of ½ lemon	
	3 egg yolks	
185 ml	heavy cream or crème fraîche*	¾ cup
	2 Tbsp chopped parsley	
	rye bread croûtons* fried in oil and butter	

Cut the rabbit* in 6 or 7 pieces. Heat the butter in a large pot, add the rabbit pieces and brown them lightly over a low fire. Add the wine, broth, onions, bouquet garni and a little salt and pepper. Bring to a boil and simmer over a low fire, skimming often, for 45 minutes or until the rabbit is tender.

Meanwhile, purée the mushrooms in a food mill or processor. Sprinkle with lemon juice to prevent them from discolouring.

When the rabbit is tender, remove the pieces and strain the broth; if necessary, boil to reduce it until well flavoured. Discard the bones and any cartilage from the rabbit and either purée the flesh in a food processor or work it twice through the fine plate of a mincer/grinder. Alternatively, the rabbit meat can be puréed with the broth in a blender. Add the mushrooms to the rabbit broth and simmer for 5 minutes. Add the puréed rabbit meat and simmer, stirring, for another 5 minutes.

Just before serving, heat a soup tureen. Beat the egg yolks and cream in a bowl and gradually whisk about 250 ml of the hot soup into them. Return this mixture to the pot and heat over a low fire, whisking constantly, for 2–3 minutes or until the soup is slightly thickened; don't boil or it will curdle. Add the parsley and taste for seasoning. Pour the soup into the warm tureen and serve, passing the croûtons separately.

TARTE TOURANGELLE AUX RILLETTES

Egg custard tart with rillettes

To ensure a crisp crust for this version of quiche, which has a rich filling of pork rillettes, the tart shell must be baked first without the filling.

Serves 6–8

PIE PASTRY		
200 g	flour	1½ cups
95 g	butter	6 Tbsp
	1 egg yolk	
	½ tsp salt	
	4–5 Tbsp cold water	
RILLETTES FILLING		
150 g	rillettes (see recipe)	5 oz
	a few small rillons, quartered if large (optional – see recipe)	
	2 Tbsp chopped parsley	
	1 Tbsp chopped mixed fresh herbs	
	4 eggs	
160 ml	milk	⅔ cup
80 ml	heavy cream or crème fraîche*	⅓ cup
	salt and pepper	
	pinch of grated nutmeg	
	23–25 cm/9–10 in tart or pie pan	

Make the pie pastry* and chill for 30 minutes or until firm. Line the pan* with the pastry and chill for a further 30 minutes. Set the oven at moderately hot (190°C/375°F) and put a baking sheet in the oven to heat. Blind bake* the pastry shell on the hot baking sheet and let cool slightly, leaving the baking sheet in the oven. Lower the oven to moderate (175°C/350°F).

For the filling: spread the rillettes in the cooled pastry shell and scatter the rillons on top. Sprinkle with parsley and herbs. Beat the eggs, milk and cream together and add salt, pepper and nutmeg to taste.

Set the pie shell on the hot baking sheet and pour the egg mixture over the rillettes. Bake in the heated oven for 30–35 minutes or until the filling is set and golden brown; don't overcook or the filling will curdle. Serve warm or at room temperature.

OEUFS À LA TRIPE

Hard-boiled eggs with onions

This dish has nothing to do with tripe, but earns its name from strips of hard-boiled egg white which, by a stretch of the imagination, can be thought to resemble real tripe. Originally from Laval in Mayenne, oeufs à la tripe should really be left white, though often they are topped with breadcrumbs and cheese and browned under a grill/broiler.

Serves 8 as a first course or 4 as a main course

60 g	butter	4 Tbsp
750 g	onions, thinly sliced	1½ lb
30 g	flour	¼ cup
500 ml	milk	2 cups
	salt and pepper	
	pinch of grated nutmeg	
	8 hard-boiled eggs	
	2 Tbsp dry breadcrumbs or grated parmesan cheese OR	
	1 Tbsp chopped parsley	

Melt the butter in a saucepan, add the onions and cook over a low fire, stirring often, for 15–20 minutes or until soft but not brown. Mix in the flour and continue to cook for 2–3 minutes or until bubbling. Add the milk, salt, pepper and nutmeg and bring to a boil, stirring constantly; then lower the heat and simmer, stirring, for 2–3 minutes.

Slice the hard-boiled eggs, carefully stir them into the hot sauce and heat thoroughly. Taste for seasoning. Pour the mixture into a deep ovenproof serving dish and, if you like, sprinkle with breadcrumbs or cheese and brown under the grill/broiler. Otherwise, sprinkle it with parsley. Serve very hot.

RILLONS, RILLAUDS or RILLOTS

'Rillons d'oie' are a variation of the classic pork rillons, made by substituting boned goose meat for the pork in this recipe.

Serves 10 as a first course

2 kg	fresh breast or belly of pork, without bones	4½ lb
30 g	lard or oil	2 Tbsp
125 ml	water	½ cup
15 g	salt	1 Tbsp
	pepper	
	pinch of ground allspice (optional)	
	1 bay leaf	
	pinch of thyme	

Cut the meat into 7 cm/3 in cubes. Heat the lard in a large, shallow, heavy-based pot, add the pork and brown on all sides over medium heat. Add the water, salt, pepper, allspice, bay leaf and thyme. Cover tightly and cook over a low fire, stirring often (but being careful not to break up the pieces of meat), for 2 hours or until the meat is just tender but not falling apart. Taste for seasoning.

If the rillons are to be served hot, remove the meat from the fat, drain briefly on paper towels and serve. Reserve the fat for other uses.

If the rillons are to be eaten cold, put the meat in jars or stone crocks and pour over enough of the fat to cover it. If well sealed with fat, rillons can be kept in a cool place for up to 2 weeks. Scrape or melt off excess fat before serving.

RILLETTES DE TOURS

Different cities have different versions of this dish. In Tours they are made of pure pork; half of the lean pork in this recipe is replaced with an equal quantity of goose to make 'rillettes du Mans', or with an equal quantity of rabbit for 'rillettes d'Orléans'. Serve rillettes at room temperature as a spread for fresh bread or toast; gherkin pickles and black olives are the traditional accompaniments.

Serves 12 as a first course

1·6 kg	lean pork, including a few bones	3½ lb
900 g	fat pork	2 lb
25 g	salt	5 tsp
10 g	ground pepper	2 tsp
	pinch of ground nutmeg	
	½ tsp ground allspice	
	pinch of thyme	
	2 bay leaves	
500 ml	water, more if needed	2 cups

Set the oven at low (160°C/320°F). Cut the lean and fat pork in 5 cm/2 in cubes and put them in a large heavy pot. Add the salt, pepper, nutmeg, allspice, thyme, bay leaves and three-quarters of the water and slowly bring to a boil, stirring constantly. Cover tightly and cook in the oven, stirring occasionally, for 4–5 hours or until all the fat has melted and is clear. As the liquid evaporates, add more water gradually to prevent the meat from sticking. Rillettes should cook slowly; never let them boil in the oven.

Drain the pork, discarding the bay leaves. Reserve the fat and leave it to cool. Shred the meat with two forks, discarding the bones. When the fat is nearly cold, mix it with the meat; taste for seasoning. Pack the rillettes into glass jars or stone crocks, cover with waxed paper and tie the paper in place with string. Store in a cool, dry place for at least 2 days before serving. If sealed with a layer of melted lard, rillettes can be kept for up to 2 weeks.

RILLETTES AND RILLONS

'Rillettes' and 'rillons' are very much a Loire speciality, though rillettes, often of indifferent quality, are found in charcuteries throughout France. They date back at least to the 15th century and are simplicity itself to make. Half pâté, half purée, rillettes are usually made from fat pork. The proportions of fat to lean vary from half to almost equal. The meat is baked very slowly in a closed pot until it falls apart, in much the same manner as English potted meat. It is then shredded with a fork, mixed back into the melted fat and left to set. Very little seasoning is added – salt, pepper and perhaps a little spice. The rillettes of Tours are leaner than those of Le Mans, which have quite big and delicious chunks of fat in them. The best rillettes have an attractive rough texture with none of the glutinous consistency which results from using poor-quality scraps instead of prime meat.

Any fatty cut of meat will do for rillettes, providing it is of good quality; for many years rillettes have been made with rabbit, duck and, best of all, with goose as well as with pork. Nowadays some restaurants offer so-called rillettes of salmon and mackerel. These are usually mixtures of flaked fish with butter but, delicious though they may be, their only resemblance to true rillettes is their slightly rough texture.

Rillons, also called rillauds or rillots, are cubes of pork measuring 5–6 cm/ 2–2½ in after cooking, that are baked very slowly, like rillettes, in a closed pot. Sometimes the meat is salted and left for a few hours to pickle lightly before cooking, and often bones are left in the meat to add flavour. However, rillons are cooked only until tender, not soft. Like rillettes, rillons need the best pork, and the 'blanc de l'ouest' pigs raised north of Angers are considered particularly fine for the purpose. Rillons made with ham are a speciality of Vendôme, on the northern edge of the Loire valley.

In a menu rillettes and rillons occupy the same place as a terrine and are served in the same way, with crusty bread. Rillons are often preferred hot with fried apple rings or mustard and with mashed potato; one excellent way of reheating them is to flame them in brandy, which balances their richness. In some areas of the Loire, rillons taken with a glass of white wine still form a hearty farmers' breakfast.

Essonne

SANDRE À L'OSEILLE
Pickerel with sorrel

There are several ways of preparing pickerel with sorrel: the sorrel can be cooked with the fish, added to a separate sauce, or stuffed inside the fish, as here. Half herb, half vegetable, sorrel tastes like a sharp spinach. The nearest substitute is spinach mixed with a few leaves of watercress, and if used in this recipe both should be blanched for a minute in boiling water and then well drained before being cooked in butter.

Serves 4

1·5-kg	pickerel	3-lb
250 g	fresh sorrel OR	½ lb
125 ml	canned sorrel	½ cup
60 g	butter	4 Tbsp
	2 onions, thinly sliced	
	pinch of thyme	
	1 bay leaf, crumbled	
375 ml	dry white wine, preferably saumur or vouvray	1½ cups
	salt and pepper	
250 ml	heavy cream or crème fraîche*	1 cup

Set the oven at moderate (175°C/350°F). Cut the fins from the fish and trim the tail to a 'V'. Scale and clean the fish; wash it and dry thoroughly.

Prepare the sorrel*. Heat half the butter in a frying pan or shallow pot, add the fresh sorrel and cook over a low fire, stirring often, for 10 minutes or until most of the liquid has evaporated. Leave to cool. (If using canned sorrel, drain it well and cook quickly in butter until dry.) Stuff the stomach cavity of the fish with the sorrel.

Spread the onions in a buttered shallow flameproof dish and lay the fish on top; score the fish lightly a few times with a knife. Add the thyme, bay leaf, wine, salt and pepper. Cover with buttered foil and bake in the oven, basting often, for 45 minutes or until a skewer inserted in the centre of the fish for 15–20 seconds is hot to the touch when withdrawn. Carefully transfer the fish to a platter, cover and keep warm while making the sauce.

Add the cream to the cooking liquid and boil until reduced to 250 ml; taste for seasoning. Strain into a small pot and whisk in the remaining butter in small pieces; don't boil or the sauce will separate. Pour the sauce over the fish and serve immediately.

MATELOTE DE LA LOIRE
Eel stew with mushrooms and onions

The high flames of the wood fire over which a matelote was traditionally cooked would set alight the wine and cognac and flame the sauce.

Serves 4–6

0·75–1 kg	eel, skinned	1½–2 lb
	1 Tbsp oil	
60 g	butter	4 Tbsp
	1 onion, chopped	
	2 shallots, chopped	
	1 clove garlic, chopped	
500 ml	dry white wine, preferably vouvray	2 cups
	3 Tbsp cognac	
	2–3 sprigs parsley	
	sprig of fresh thyme	
	1 bay leaf	
	salt and pepper	
30 g	butter, kneaded with	2 Tbsp
15 g	flour	2 Tbsp
	GARNISH	
	16–18 baby onions	
	salt and pepper	
250 g	small mushrooms, stems trimmed level with caps	½ lb
15 g	butter	1 Tbsp
	juice of ½ lemon	
	8–12 heart-shaped croûtes*, fried in oil and butter	

Cut the eel in 5 cm/2 in pieces, wash and dry them. Heat the oil and half the butter in a large, shallow saucepan, add the onions and shallots and cook over a low fire, stirring, for 5 minutes or until softened. Stir in the garlic and add the eel. Pour in the wine and cognac and add the parsley, thyme, bay leaf and a little salt and pepper. Bring just to a boil and poach uncovered for 15 minutes or until the fish flakes easily.

Meanwhile, prepare the garnish: simmer the onions in boiling salted water for 12–15 minutes or until tender; drain. Put the mushrooms in a pot with the butter, lemon juice, salt, pepper and 3–4 tablespoons of water. Cover and simmer for 5 minutes or until tender.

Transfer the fish to a deep platter, piling it up, and keep warm. Strain the cooking liquid into a small pot, and boil for 5 minutes or until well flavoured. Whisk in the kneaded butter*, a piece at a time, until the sauce thickens to the consistency of thin cream. Stir in the onions and mushrooms with their cooking liquid, heat thoroughly and taste for seasoning. Take the sauce from the heat and stir in the remaining butter, piece by piece. Spoon the sauce and garnish over the fish, arrange the croûtes around the edge of the platter and serve at once.

MATELOTES

The word 'matelot' means boatman. Those of the Loire, in a natty blue uniform slashed in red, used to be highly organized to cope with the dangerous river in the days when it was the chief highway into France. A chain of ports and inns along the banks must have stimulated local cooking, and helped create the rich tradition of 'matelotes'.

These fish stews are found throughout France, wherever there is water to fish in. Far more versatile than 'potée', their meat equivalent, matelotes vary enormously from region to region. Most use freshwater fish, like 'matelote alsacienne', cooked in riesling wine and cream, or 'matelote bourguignonne', made with red wine. The most famous sea-fish version is 'matelote normande' which can include mussels and shrimps as well as fish, and is

flavoured with cider and crème fraîche.

The Loire stew is most commonly made with eel simmered in white wine with baby onions and mushrooms, and sometimes enriched with cream. Pike, carp and trout may be added. An eel matelote with white wine and mushrooms is named after Rabelais, while the matelote from Chinon, known for its château and its flowery red wine, is cooked with the local vintage, flavoured with bacon and garnished with croûtons traditionally cut in the shape of fishes' teeth.

A good matelote should be a stew, not a soup; the cooking liquid should be concentrated and thickened, though lightly, so as to form a sauce. Some matelotes use only one fish; others mix eel with lighter fish such as perch, pike, carp and trout. Many recipes advise adding the firmer fish and leaving the more delicate ones to have a minimum of cooking at the end; above all, matelote must not be overcooked, or the fish will fall into rags. Heads can be added to the pot for flavour, but before serving they must be discarded; the cooked fish may also be trimmed for a tidier presentation.

Matelote is served in a shallow bowl with fried croûtons. The vegetables in the stew itself form the accompaniment, so all that is needed to complete the dish is a sprinkling of chopped parsley.

PETITE FRITURE
Deep-fried little fish

Petite friture has always been a great speciality of Loire mariners and it is still served in little cafés all along the river. To make the perfect friture the fish must be fresh and small – not exceeding 10 cm/4 in long; they abound in the Loire and its tributaries. Fillets of larger white fish can also be cut in thin strips and fried in the same way; they are called 'goujonnettes' after 'goujon', the most common little fish in the Loire. In Britain, whitebait is the nearest equivalent to goujon, and in the USA, smelts can be used in this recipe.

Serves 6–8 as a first course or
4 as a main course

1 kg	very fresh smelts	2 lb
	fat for deep frying	
250 ml	milk	1 cup
200 g	flour, seasoned with salt and pepper	1½ cups
	salt	
	1 bunch of parsley, washed and thoroughly dried	
	2 lemons, cut in wedges	

Wash the fish and dry thoroughly. Dip the fish in the milk and shake off the excess, then toss them lightly with your fingers in seasoned flour so that they are completely coated. Spread out the fish after coating to prevent them from sticking to each other. Heat the deep fat to very hot (180°C/360°F) on a fat thermometer. Coat and fry a few fish at a time, stirring occasionally, until golden brown. Drain them on paper towels and keep hot in a moderate oven (175°C/350°F) with the door slightly open while frying the rest. Sprinkle lightly with salt.

Remove the fat from the fire and cool for about 30 seconds. Tie the dry parsley with a long string and toss it into the fat; stand back as it will splutter. After 10 seconds or when the spluttering stops, lift out the parsley by the string, drain it and detach the sprigs. Pile the fish on a platter, sprinkle with parsley sprigs and decorate with lemon wedges. Serve at once, very hot.

SAUTÉ DE POULET À L'ANGEVINE
Sauté of chicken with mushrooms and onions

In the 17th century the Sarthe, to the north of the Loire, was famous for its chickens fed on aniseed and musk. Today Loué in the same district produces chickens with a special red label ('label rouge') which, it is claimed, rival those of Bresse. Each bird is numbered and its quality is controlled by a committee of producers and consumers. To merit the name 'angevine', this recipe should be made with Anjou wine.

Serves 4

1·5 kg	roasting chicken	$3\frac{1}{2}$ lb
	salt and pepper	
30 g	flour	$\frac{1}{4}$ cup
	1 Tbsp oil	
45 g	butter	3 Tbsp
	18–20 baby onions	
	2 shallots, chopped	
185 ml	white wine, preferably muscadet	$\frac{3}{4}$ cup
250 g	mushrooms, quartered	$\frac{1}{2}$ lb
125 ml	heavy cream or crème fraîche*	$\frac{1}{2}$ cup
	1 Tbsp chopped parsley	

Cut the chicken* in 8 pieces. Season the pieces with salt and pepper and roll them in the flour, patting off the excess. Heat the oil and butter in a sauté pan over a medium fire. Starting with the legs and thighs (which need the longest cooking), add the chicken pieces to the pan, skin side down. When they are beginning to brown, add the wing pieces and finally the breast; when all the pieces are brown, turn them over, brown the other side for 1–2 minutes, and remove.

Add the onions to the pan and sauté them over a fairly high fire, shaking the pan so that they brown evenly. Replace the chicken, making sure it is in contact with the bottom of the pan, and add the shallots. Pour in the wine, cover tightly and cook over a low fire for 25 minutes. Add the mushrooms and continue to cook for another 10–15 minutes or until the chicken is very tender. Transfer the chicken pieces to a platter with the onions and mushrooms. Cover and keep warm while finishing the sauce.

Skim any fat from the cooking liquid, add the cream and boil, stirring, for 2–3 minutes or until the sauce thickens enough to coat a spoon; taste it for seasoning. Spoon the sauce over the chicken, sprinkle it with parsley and serve.

CUL DE VEAU À L'ANGEVINE
Veal with herbs and sorrel

The traditional accompaniments to this braised veal are sautéed mushrooms, braised celery (see recipe), or creamed morels (see recipe). Often pieces of pork rind or a pig's foot are added to the veal in the casserole to give a rich, syrupy braising liquid.

Serves 6

1·4-kg	boned veal roast	3-lb
125 g	butter	$\frac{1}{4}$ lb
	salt and pepper	
	4 Tbsp chopped herbs: chives, chervil, tarragon, parsley	
	2 onions, sliced	
	2 carrots, sliced	
185 ml	white wine, preferably muscadet	$\frac{3}{4}$ cup
185 ml	broth	$\frac{3}{4}$ cup
	bouquet garni	
	24 baby onions	
	1 tsp sugar	
500 g	fresh sorrel OR	1 lb
250 ml	canned sorrel	1 cup
80 ml	heavy cream or crème fraîche*	$\frac{1}{3}$ cup
	1 egg yolk	
	trussing string	

Cut the roast almost in half lengthwise, so it can open up like a book and lie flat. Spread the meat with half the butter and sprinkle it with a little salt and pepper and the chopped herbs. Roll it up and tie it in a neat cylinder. Set the oven at hot (200°C/400°F).

Heat another 2 tablespoons of the butter in a heavy flameproof casserole. Add the meat with the sliced onions and carrots and cook over a medium fire, turning the meat often, until it browns on all sides. Add the wine, broth and bouquet garni. Cover and braise the veal in the oven, basting occasionally, for $1\frac{1}{2}$ hours or until very tender.

While the veal is cooking, glaze the baby onions: put them in a frying pan with another tablespoon of butter, the sugar, a pinch of salt and pepper and water just to cover. Bring to a boil and simmer over a medium fire for 20 minutes or until the water has evaporated and the onions are tender and shiny.

Prepare the fresh sorrel*. Heat the remaining butter in a heavy-based pot, add the fresh sorrel and cook over a low fire, stirring often, for 10–15 minutes or until most of the liquid has evaporated. If using canned sorrel, drain it well, then cook it quickly in butter until dry.

When the veal is cooked, transfer it to a platter, discard the trussing strings, cover and keep warm. Strain the cooking liquid into a small pot, skim off any fat and bring to a boil; reduce, if necessary, until well flavoured. Stir in half the cream, bring back to a boil and taste for seasoning. Reheat the onions and toss over a high fire until lightly caramelized. Add them to the veal sauce.

Beat the remaining cream with the egg yolk. Reheat the sorrel, remove from the heat and beat in the yolk mixture. Return the pot to a low fire, stirring constantly, for 2 minutes or just until the sorrel has slightly thickened. Don't let the mixture boil. Taste for seasoning, spoon into a shallow serving dish and keep warm.

Cut the veal in thick slices and arrange them, overlapping, on a platter. Spoon the sauce and onions over the meat and serve immediately, passing the dish of sorrel separately.

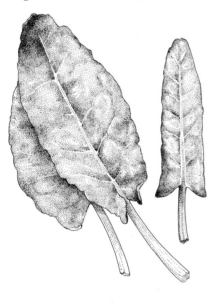

NOISETTES DE PORC AUX PRUNEAUX

Pork noisettes with prunes

'Prunes de Tours' are famous. The name is ambiguous, for it could refer to the city, or to the 'tours' (towers) in which fresh plums used to be dried for the winter.

	Serves 4	
	8–12 prunes	
250 ml	dry white wine, preferably vouvray	1 cup
	pinch of ground cinnamon	
750 g	boned pork loin	1½ lb
	salt and pepper	
25 g	flour	3 Tbsp
45 g	butter	3 Tbsp
80 ml	heavy cream or crème fraîche*	⅓ cup
	1 Tbsp red currant jelly	
	squeeze of lemon juice (optional)	
	trussing string	

Soak the prunes in the wine for a few hours or overnight; then drain them, reserving the liquid. Pit the prunes and put them in a pot with the reserved liquid and a pinch of cinnamon. Simmer, covered, for 30 minutes, or until tender.

Meanwhile, roll and tie the pork at intervals of 2·5 cm/1 in. Slice the meat between the strings to make 'noisettes' and sprinkle with salt and pepper. Flour each slice, patting off the excess. Heat the butter in a large frying pan, add the pork noisettes and sauté over a medium fire for 5 minutes on each side or until no longer pink in the centre. Transfer the pork to a platter and discard the strings. Drain the prunes, reserving the liquid, and arrange them on the platter around the pork. Cover and keep warm while finishing the sauce.

Add the prune liquid to the frying pan and boil, stirring, until the liquid is reduced to about 125 ml. Stir in the cream and jelly, bring just to a boil and taste for seasoning; add a squeeze of lemon juice if the sauce is too sweet. Spoon the sauce over the pork and serve immediately.

CIVET DE LIÈVRE
Hare stew

The name 'civet' comes from 'cive', the Latin for onion. Nowadays civet refers to a ragoût of game, made with red wine, baby onions, mushrooms, lardons and with the blood from the animal used as liaison. In places where hare is available, the blood is often sold in a little pot with the carcass. Without blood, the dish becomes a simple ragoût – good, but lacking the richness of a true civet. The following recipe can also be made with rabbit*, which should be cut in 7–8 pieces instead of 12–13.

Serves 6

2–2·3-kg	hare, with the blood	4–5-lb
250-g	piece lean bacon, cut in lardons	½-lb
	1 Tbsp oil	
	2 onions, quartered	
45 g	flour	⅓ cup
750 ml	red wine, preferably bourgueil	3 cups
500 ml	broth*	2 cups
	1 clove garlic, crushed	
	bouquet garni	
	salt and pepper	
	½ tsp ground allspice	
45 g	butter	3 Tbsp
	24 baby onions	
250 g	mushrooms, quartered (optional)	½ lb
80 ml	blood from the hare	⅓ cup
	1 Tbsp chopped parsley	
	12 triangular croûtes*, fried in oil and butter or toasted	

Cut the hare in 12–13 pieces: separate the legs from the loin part and cut each leg diagonally in two. Cut the loin in 4 or 5 pieces. Cut the rib section in 2 pieces and the shoulder section in half with one foreleg in each section.

If the bacon is very salty, blanch* it. If you prefer to cook the hare in the oven rather than on top of the stove, set the temperature at moderately low (160°C/320°F).

Heat the oil in a large sauté pan and fry the bacon until the fat runs. Add the onion quarters and cook over a low fire until they begin to brown. Remove the bacon and onions and drain off all but 2 tablespoons of the fat. Add the pieces of hare to the pan and cook over a high fire to brown them lightly on all sides. (If necessary, brown them in two batches.) Sprinkle the flour over the hare, stir to mix and cook until brown. Add the wine and boil for 2–3 minutes, stirring; then add the broth, garlic, bouquet garni, salt, pepper and allspice. Replace the bacon and onions. Cover, bring to a boil and simmer very gently on top of the stove or cook in the oven for 1 hour or until the hare is very tender.

Meanwhile heat the butter in a frying pan, add the baby onions, season them and sauté for 5–10 minutes or until brown and just tender. Remove them, add the mushrooms and sauté also until tender. Combine the mushrooms and onions and reserve.

When the hare is tender, transfer it with the bacon to another pan, add the reserved onions and mushrooms and keep warm while finishing the sauce.

Strain the sauce into a pot and skim off any fat from the surface. To thicken it with blood, bring the sauce to a boil, remove from the heat and whisk it into the blood. Strain the sauce over the hare pieces and heat very gently, shaking the pan constantly, until the sauce just thickens slightly; don't let it boil or the sauce will separate. If not using blood, boil the sauce, stirring often, until thick enough to coat a spoon, and strain it over the hare. Taste the sauce for seasoning. Transfer the hare to a deep serving dish, sprinkle with parsley and arrange the croûtes around the edge.

CHAMPIGNONS DE PARIS

The familiar white button mushrooms called 'champignons de Paris' really deserve the name, having been grown commercially in limestone caves along the Seine as early as the 17th century. However, they were not intensively cultivated until sterilized mushroom spawn was developed at the Pasteur Institute in Paris in the 1890s. For mushrooms have one weakness: they are prone to disease, and their growth must, therefore, be carefully controlled.

An ideal climate is offered by the caves along the Loire river, which are not natural but were quarried in the 15th and 16th centuries by the builders of the great châteaux. Galleries stretch for many kilometres into the cliffs, making it easy to provide a constant temperature with plenty of humidity. And mushrooms require no light.

Now cultivation takes place on a large scale, with even modest enterprises producing a tonne of mushrooms a day. The spawn is planted in bags or trays containing a mixture of pasteurized horse dung and straw – the stables of the École de Cavalerie at Saumur are strategically located near by. After 60 days or so the first growth comes and from then on it is a question of stripping the beds each day. In the long, dark galleries, the workers wear miners' lamps and so great is the risk of transmitting bacteria that they change their shoes and wash in disinfectant when moving from gallery to gallery.

Although the principal crop from the caves along the Loire is the white champignons de Paris, locals prefer the flavour of a brown mushroom. Brown or white, two-thirds of the crop goes straight to the cannery.

PETITS POIS À LA CRÈME

Green peas with cream

While the peas are cooking, some cooks cover the pot with a soup plate of cold water, which condenses the steam and keeps the peas moist.

	Serves 4	
1·5 kg	fresh green peas OR	3 lb
500 g	shelled peas	1 lb
	1 head lettuce	
30 g	butter	2 Tbsp
	6 baby onions or spring onions, sliced	
80 ml	boiling water	⅓ cup
10 g	sugar	2 tsp
	salt and pepper	
	bouquet garni	
185 ml	heavy cream or crème fraîche*	¾ cup

Shell the fresh peas. Wash the lettuce and cut it in strips, discarding the stem. Melt the butter in a pot and add the onions, lettuce and peas; stir until all are coated with butter. Add the boiling water, sugar, salt, pepper and bouquet garni. Cover and cook over a low fire for 15–20 minutes or until the peas are tender. Remove the lid and boil any liquid rapidly for 2–3 minutes or until the moisture has evaporated. Discard the bouquet garni and stir in the cream. Bring just to a boil and taste for seasoning. Transfer to a serving dish or serve from the pot.

SALADE À L'HUILE DE NOIX

Salad with walnut oil

Salad is not always a separate course in the Loire, unlike other regions. Often a salad accompanies roast chicken, or is served with a cheese like the local Ste-Maure. Walnut oil with cider vinegar is a favourite dressing and in the old days the walnuts would be crushed between two millstones, then heated to extract the oil. Often a bit of bread would be dipped into the newly pressed oil as a quick snack.

Serves 4
1 head lettuce
salt and pepper
20 walnut halves, coarsely chopped
8 small croûtes*, toasted and, if you like, rubbed with garlic
VINAIGRETTE
2 Tbsp cider vinegar or wine vinegar
salt and pepper
2 tsp Dijon mustard (optional)
6 Tbsp walnut oil

Make the vinaigrette* and set aside. Separate the lettuce leaves, remove large ribs, wash the leaves and dry thoroughly.

To serve, put the lettuce leaves in a salad bowl and add the vinaigrette. Toss well and taste for seasoning. Sprinkle the walnuts and croûtes over the salad and serve immediately.

Villandry

CELERIS BRAISÉS

Braised celery

If celery is to be served with roast meat or poultry, it can be partly braised, then placed around the roast to finish cooking in the meat juices, thus absorbing their flavour.

Serves 4

	1 bunch of celery	
125 g	bacon, diced (optional)	4 oz
30 g	butter	2 Tbsp
	12 baby onions	
250 ml	broth, more if needed	1 cup
	bouquet garni	
	salt and pepper	

Wash the celery and use a vegetable peeler to remove the large strings from the outer stalks. Cut it in 7·5 cm/3 in lengths, discarding the leaves. Blanch the celery by putting it in a pot of boiling water for 5 minutes, then drain it. If you prefer to braise the celery in the oven, set the temperature at moderate (175°C/350°F).

If the bacon is very salty, blanch* it. Heat the butter in a sauté pan or flameproof casserole, add the bacon and fry it until the fat runs. Add the onions, brown them lightly over a medium fire and remove them. Add the celery and sauté lightly for 2 minutes. Pour in the broth and add the bouquet garni, salt and pepper. Cover and braise over a low fire or in the heated oven for about 30 minutes. Add the onions and continue to braise for another 20–30 minutes or until the celery and onions are tender. Add more broth

during cooking if the pan begins to get dry.

When the vegetables are tender, transfer them with the bacon to a shallow serving dish and keep warm. Discard the bouquet garni and, if necessary, boil the cooking liquid until reduced to about 125 ml. Taste for seasoning and pour the liquid over the celery. Serve hot.

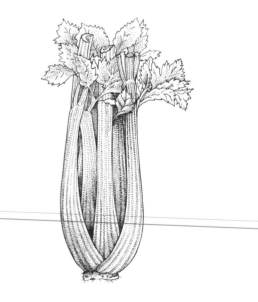

126

ASPERGES AU BEURRE D'ESTRAGON

Asparagus with tarragon butter

In France asparagus is picked white, while still hidden underground, though it will turn into the green stems familiar in Britain and North America if left to sprout in the open air. While white asparagus is the most prized in France, green asparagus can be prepared and cooked in the same way. Dried tarragon, however, cannot take the place of fresh and if it is not available use fresh parsley and chives instead.

Serves 4

1 kg	asparagus	2 lb
	salt	
	TARRAGON BUTTER SAUCE	
	5 sprigs of fresh tarragon	
	3 Tbsp white wine vinegar	
	3 Tbsp dry white wine	
	2 shallots, very finely chopped	
	2 Tbsp heavy cream or crème fraîche*	
250 g	butter, very cold	½ lb
	salt and white pepper	
	trussing string	

Choose asparagus spears of the same thickness so that they cook evenly. Snap the stems to remove the fibrous ends and peel the lower part of the stem with a vegetable peeler. With large asparagus, particularly white asparagus, it is important to cut deeply enough to remove the tough outer fibres as well as the skin. Wash the asparagus and tie it with string in 4 bundles.

Bring a large shallow pan of salted water to a boil. Lay the asparagus bundles horizontally in the pan; they should be covered with water and not overlap too much. Cover and boil for 8–10 minutes for green asparagus or 12–15 minutes for white asparagus, or until the stems are almost tender when pierced with a knife. Lift out the bundles and drain; cover and keep warm.

Meanwhile, make the sauce: chop the tarragon leaves and reserve the stems. In a small saucepan (not aluminium) boil the vinegar, wine, shallots and tarragon stems until about 2 tablespoons of liquid remain. Add the cream and boil until the mixture is again reduced to about 2 tablespoons. Discard the tarragon stems.

Set the pan over low heat and whisk in the butter gradually, in small pieces, to make a smooth, creamy sauce. Work sometimes over low fire and sometimes off the heat, so that the butter softens and thickens the sauce without melting. Season to taste with salt and white pepper and stir in the chopped tarragon.

Transfer the asparagus to individual plates or to a platter and remove the strings. Serve at once, passing the sauce separately.

FÈVES À LA TOURANGELLE

Beans with ham

'Fèves' – fava or broad beans – have thick skins which should be peeled off after the beans have been boiled and before they are added to the sauce. North American lima beans can also be used in this recipe, but they do not need peeling.

Serves 4

2 kg	unshelled beans OR	4½ lb
250 g	shelled beans	8 oz
	salt and pepper	
80 g	butter	5 Tbsp
	24 baby onions	
200 g	cooked ham, diced	7 oz
	2 egg yolks	
	1 Tbsp chopped fresh herbs: parsley, chervil or chives	

Shell the beans and cook them in a large pot of boiling salted water for 20 minutes or until tender. Drain thoroughly, reserving the cooking liquid. Peel the thick skins from the beans and keep warm.

While the beans are cooking, make the sauce: heat the butter in a frying pan, add the onions and cook over a low fire for 15 minutes or until lightly browned and nearly tender. Add the ham and 60 ml of the reserved cooking liquid and simmer over a low fire for 5 more minutes.

Just before serving, beat the yolks with another 60 ml of the reserved cooking liquid and stir the mixture into the onions and ham. Heat over a very low fire, stirring constantly, until slightly thickened; don't boil or it will curdle. Taste the sauce for seasoning, mix it with the beans and taste again for seasoning. Pile in a serving dish, sprinkle with chopped herbs and serve immediately.

CRÊPES BELLE ANGEVINE
Pear crêpes with Cointreau

These crêpes are filled with pears – the 'belle angevine' is a stewing pear – and flavoured with Cointreau, a liqueur which originated in Angers. Any other orange-flavoured liqueur can be used instead. The Norman version of these crêpes, with apples and calvados, is perhaps even better known.

Serves 6, makes 12–14 crêpes

	CRÊPES	
130 g	flour	1 cup
	pinch of salt	
250 ml	milk	1 cup
	3 eggs	
	1 Tbsp Cointreau (optional)	
30 g	melted butter or oil	2 Tbsp
60 g	clarified butter* or oil (for frying)	4 Tbsp
	FILLING	
90 g	butter	6 Tbsp
1 kg	pears, peeled, cored and sliced	2 lb
100 g	sugar, or to taste	½ cup
	4–8 Tbsp Cointreau	
	15–18 cm/6–7 in crêpe pan or frying pan	

Make the crêpe batter and cook the crêpes (see page 32), piling them on a plate to keep warm.

Make the pear filling: heat the butter in a shallow pan, add the sliced pears and cook over a low fire, stirring often, for 20 minutes or until softened to a thick purée. Add the sugar and continue to cook over a low fire, stirring constantly, for 5 more minutes or until the mixture begins to stick to the pan. Remove from the heat, and add 4 tablespoons of the Cointreau. Taste and add more sugar if necessary. Keep the filling warm. Set the oven at very hot (230°C/450°F). Butter a baking dish.

Fill the crêpes with the warm pear mixture and either roll them like cigars or fold them in half. Arrange the filled crêpes in a single layer in the baking dish. Bake in the heated oven for 4–5 minutes or until very hot.

If you prefer to flame the crêpes, heat the remaining Cointreau in a small pan. Light the liqueur, pour it flaming over the crêpes and serve at once.

POIRES BELLE ANGEVINE
Pears in red wine

The horticultural gardens of Angers, the 'Doyenné du Comice', were, until their closure in 1925, renowned for the development of new pears. Among their offerings are 'comice', the finest dessert pear of all, and 'belle angevine' which is good for poaching. In this recipe, the red wine turns the pears a pretty pink.

Serves 6

1·5 kg	6 firm pears	3 lb
100 g	sugar, more if needed	½ cup
1 L	red wine	1 qt
	strip of lemon rind	
	5 cm/2 in piece of cinnamon stick	
	lemon juice (optional)	
	2 Tbsp pear brandy (optional)	

Choose a saucepan that will just hold the pears standing upright. Put the sugar, wine, lemon rind and cinnamon stick in the pan and heat until the sugar is dissolved; boil for 5 minutes. Let cool slightly.

Peel the pears and core them carefully from the base, leaving the stem. Cut a thin slice off the bottom of each pear so it stands upright. Immerse the pears in syrup, adding water, if necessary, to cover them. Cover with the lid and poach over low heat for 20–45 minutes or until the pears are tender. (Cooking time depends on the variety and ripeness of the pears.)

Let the pears cool to tepid in the syrup; drain them and arrange in a shallow serving dish. Strain the syrup and reduce over high heat for 5–10 minutes or until thick enough to coat a spoon; don't allow it to caramelize. Adjust the flavouring, adding sugar or lemon juice to taste. Let the syrup cool slightly, and spoon it over the pears. Chill thoroughly and add the pear brandy just before serving.

CHICOLLE
Peaches in red wine
These marinated peaches are delicious by them-selves, but the true chicolle, with toast soaked in the wine, is well worth trying. The recipe is ancient, deriving from sweet soups like 'la rôtie' in which small pieces of bread were simmered in red wine sweetened with honey. In this recipe, strawberries can be used instead of peaches and sponge fingers can take the place of toast.

Serves 4

	4 ripe peaches	
100 g	sugar	½ cup
125 ml	water	½ cup
500 ml	dry red wine	2 cups
	4 slices toast	

Peel the peaches 1–2 days ahead: if they are very ripe, simply scrape them with a small knife to peel. Usually, however, peaches must be scal-ded: put them in a pot of boiling water, boil for 10 seconds, then transfer them to a bowl of cold water and peel them. Halve or quarter the peaches, discarding the pits.

Put the peaches in a bowl and sprinkle them with sugar. Add the water and enough red wine to cover them. To prevent the peaches from floating, cover them with an overturned plate which just fits the bowl. Refrigerate overnight or for up to 2 days.

Serve the peaches cold, in individual bowls, accompanied by toast, either dipped in the wine or crumbled in it to make a sort of soup.

PRUNEAUX AU VOUVRAY
Prunes in white wine
Instead of being cooked, the prunes in this recipe can be loosely packed in a jar, covered with wine and left to soak for a week or more. Be sure to keep them constantly immersed. Red wine can be substituted for the vouvray.

Serves 6

500 g	prunes	1 lb
750 ml	dry white wine, preferably vouvray	3 cups
100 g	sugar	½ cup
	CHANTILLY CREAM	
250 ml	heavy cream	1 cup
	2 tsp sugar	
	1 tsp vanilla extract	

Three to four days ahead, wash the prunes and put them in a large bowl. Pour the wine over them, cover and leave to soak overnight at room temperature.

The next day, transfer the prunes and wine to a large pot, add the sugar and bring to a boil.

Simmer over a low fire for 20–25 minutes or until the prunes are just tender; leave to cool. Refrigerate for 2–3 days; the prunes will absorb some of the wine.

Just before serving, make the chantilly cream: in a chilled bowl beat the cream until it starts to thicken. Add the sugar and vanilla and continue beating until the cream is stiff enough to stick to the whisk.

Put the prunes with their liquid in small dessert dishes. Serve cold and pass chantilly cream separately.

CRÉMETS D'ANGERS
Moulded fresh cheese
Crémets is a very light fresh cheese which stiffens on standing, so it can be unmoulded. It is often set in heart shapes, called 'coeurs à la crème', and special white porcelain moulds with draining holes are made for it. These can be hard to find outside France and a heart-shaped cake mould, with holes punched for drainage, does just as well. Crémets can be served simply with cream and sugar, but it is at its best with fresh strawberries or raspberries.

Serves 6

750 ml	crème fraîche*	3 cups
	4 egg whites	
	sugar or vanilla sugar (for serving)	
coeur à la crème mould (1 L/1 qt capacity)		
or several small moulds; cheesecloth		

Make the crémets 1 to 2 days before serving: line the mould with cheesecloth. In a large bowl, whip two-thirds of the crème fraîche until it holds soft peaks. In another bowl, whip the egg whites into the crème fraîche and continue beating until stiff. Spoon the mixture into the mould, and set it on a dish. Leave to drain in the refrigerator for at least 8, and up to 36 hours.

An hour or two before serving, turn the mould out on to a platter. Serve the crémets with separate bowls of sugar or vanilla sugar, and the remaining crème fraîche.

CRÉMETS D'ANGERS II
If you don't have crème fraîche, use the same quantity of **heavy cream** but add:

250 g	cream cheese	8 oz

Gradually beat the cream into the cheese then beat the whipped egg whites into this mixture. Serve as above, replacing the crème fraîche with lightly whipped cream.

FRUIT TARTS AND PIES

Every region of France has its own fruit tarts, but for sheer ingenuity the bakers of the Loire must surely beat the band. The classic pastry shell, packed with fruit and topped with glaze, is only the beginning of the story. The shell may be made of biscuit like 'pâte sucrée'; a layer of pastry cream, flavoured with some suitable liqueur, may support the fruit; the fruit itself can be all of one kind or a mixture of different ones arranged in concentric circles; and the tarts may be decorated with a design of halved almonds under the glaze.

Fruits such as strawberries, cherries, raspberries, grapes and oranges can simply be peeled, pitted, washed and sliced as appropriate, but fruits such as pears and peaches which discolour easily must first be poached in syrup. It is astonishing how the appearance of an open tart is transformed by a generous coating of glaze. For red fruits, a coating of red currant jelly is the rule, although occasionally jelly with the same flavour as the fruit filling is substituted. Green, white and yellow fruits are coated with apricot glaze.

The most common shape for a fruit tart is circular; the bigger the diameter the more spectacular the tart, but the more difficult to serve. Restaurants favour 'bandes', narrow tarts of 50 cm/20 in or more in length that are easy to cut crosswise in neat servings. A bande is made of puff pastry rolled in a rectangle with thin strips of dough laid along the sides to contain the fruit. Puff pastry lends itself to rectangular shapes, an attractive one being a square with a twisted knot of dough at each corner.

In most fruit tarts the fruit is added after baking, but sometimes the fruit is cooked in the pastry with a filling like the custard in Alsatian fruit quiches or the almond frangipane in the pear tart of Normandy.

There are closed fruit pies, too, like 'pompe', made in Auvergne with an apple filling. Such pies often have a hole punched in the middle so that cream can be poured into the warm pie just before serving, as with the 'piquenchagne' pear pie of the Bourbonnais. In another version, the dough is simply slashed and the corners turned back to expose the fruit before baking. There is even the apple 'tarte des demoiselles Tatin' (opposite), named after two impoverished gentlewomen from Lamotte Beuvron in Sologne, who were forced to earn their living by baking their father's favourite apple pie with caramel topping. This tart is turned upside-down – an anomaly which has made it the pride of such legendary restaurants as Maxim's.

TARTE AUX FRUITS
Fruit tart with pastry cream

Apricots, peaches, strawberries, raspberries, cherries, grapes or tangerines – or a mixture of different fruits – are all suitable for this tart. An alternative is to omit the pastry cream and brush a thin layer of glaze in the shell before adding the fruit and glazing it.

Serves 6

500 g	fresh fruit	1 lb
185 ml	apricot jam glaze or red currant jelly glaze*	¾ cup
	SWEET PIE PASTRY	
130 g	flour	1 cup
	3 egg yolks	
	pinch of salt	
65 g	sugar	⅓ cup
	¾ tsp vanilla extract	
80 g	butter	⅓ cup
	POACHING SYRUP (optional)	
100 g	sugar	½ cup
500 ml	water	2 cups
	1 vanilla bean	
	pared rind and juice of 1 lemon	
	PASTRY CREAM	
375 ml	milk	1½ cups
	pinch of salt	
	1 vanilla bean OR 2 Tbsp kirsch	
	5 egg yolks	
90 g	sugar	7 Tbsp
30 g	flour	¼ cup
	23–25 cm/9–10 in pie or tart pan	

Make the sweet pie pastry* and chill for 30 minutes or until firm. Set the oven at hot (200°C/400°F).

If using apricots or peaches, first prepare the poaching syrup: in a saucepan heat the syrup ingredients until the sugar dissolves. Bring to a boil. Pit the fruit, halve it, and put it in the syrup. Poach apricots 5–8 minutes and peaches 8–12 minutes. Leave to cool in the syrup; drain. Peel the peaches.

Line* the pie pan and blind bake* the pastry until the shell is light golden. Watch it carefully because sweet pie pastry burns easily. Transfer the shell to a rack to cool.

Make the pastry cream* and let cool to tepid.

Wash strawberries only if they are sandy, then hull them. Pick over raspberries; pit cherries and grapes if necessary. Peel the tangerines and divide into segments, discarding any seeds.

Not more than 4 hours before serving, spread the cream in the pastry shell. Arrange the fruit on top. Melt the glaze over low heat and brush it over the fruit. Serve at room temperature.

TARTE DES DEMOISELLES TATIN
Caramelized apple tart

The secret of this upside-down apple pie is to cook the butter and sugar with the apples so the juice caramelizes and flavours deep inside the fruit. The tart should be served warm, with a bowl of whipped cream or crème fraîche* if you like.

Serves 8–10

185 g	butter	6 oz
400 g	sugar	2 cups
2·8 kg	golden delicious apples	6 lb
	PUFF PASTRY	
250 g	unsalted butter	½ lb
175 g	all-purpose flour	1⅓ cups
80 g	cake flour	⅔ cup
5 g	salt	1 tsp
	1 tsp lemon juice	
125 ml	iced water, more as needed	½ cup
	1 egg, beaten with ½ tsp salt (for glaze)	
	heavy-based round mould or frying pan (30–35 cm/12–14 in diameter)	

Make the puff pastry* and chill it for 1 hour or until firm. Set the oven at moderately hot (190°C/375°F).

Cut the butter in thin slices and arrange them evenly in the base of the mould; sprinkle with the sugar. Peel, halve and core the apples. Arrange the apple halves upright in tightly packed concentric circles on top of the sugar. They should fill the mould and be tightly packed. Heat on top of the stove for 15–20 minutes or until a golden caramel is formed. At first this caramel will be pale and liquid from the juice of the apples. Keep cooking so that it evaporates and darkens and is absorbed by the apples. If the apples are still uncooked, transfer the mould to the bottom shelf of the heated oven and bake for 5–10 minutes or until they are tender. Let the apples cool a little until the steam disappears. Raise the oven temperature to very hot (220°C/425°F).

Roll out the dough to 6 mm/¼ in thick and cut out a circle slightly larger than the diameter of the mould. Transfer the circle to a tray and chill for 15 minutes. Set the circle of dough on the apples so that they are completely covered. Bake for another 10 minutes or until the crust is puffed and golden brown. Lower the oven temperature to moderate (175°C/350°F) and continue baking for 10–15 minutes or until the pastry is crisp. Let the tart cool slightly in the mould; then turn it out on to a heat-proof platter. If any apple sticks to the bottom of the pan, remove it with a metal spatula and replace on the tart. Serve warm.

GÂTEAU DE PITHIVIERS
Feuilleté with almond filling

A gâteau de Pithiviers is instantly recognizable by its scalloped edges and domed centre, marked with curved slashes to resemble the petals of a flower. The top should be thinly glazed with melted sugar, but this is difficult to do without a professional salamander grill.

Serves 6–8

PUFF PASTRY		
375 g	unsalted butter	$\frac{3}{4}$ lb
260 g	all-purpose flour	2 cups
120 g	cake flour	1 cup
8 g	salt	$1\frac{1}{2}$ tsp
	$1\frac{1}{2}$ tsp lemon juice	
215 ml	iced water, more as needed	$\frac{7}{8}$ cup
	1 egg beaten with $\frac{1}{2}$ tsp salt (for glaze)	
	granulated or confectioners' sugar (for sprinkling)	
ALMOND FILLING		
125 g	butter	$\frac{1}{4}$ lb
125 g	sugar	10 Tbsp
	1 egg	
	1 egg yolk	
120 g	whole blanched almonds, ground	$\frac{2}{3}$ cup
15 g	flour	2 Tbsp
	2 Tbsp rum	

Make the puff pastry* and chill for 1 hour or until firm.

Prepare the filling: cream the butter in a bowl. Add the sugar and beat until soft and light. Beat in the egg and egg yolk. Stir in the almonds, flour and rum; don't beat the mixture at this point or the oil will be drawn out of the almonds.

Roll out half the pastry to a circle. Using a pan lid as a guide, cut out a 25 cm/10 in round with a sharp knife. Roll the remaining dough slightly thicker than the first circle; cut another round the same size. Set the thinner round on a baking sheet and mound the filling in the centre, leaving a 2·5 cm/1 in border. Brush the border with egg glaze. Lay the remaining round on top and press the edges together firmly. Scallop the edge of the gâteau by pulling it in at regular intervals with the back of a knife. Brush the gâteau with egg glaze and, working from the centre, score the top in curves like the petals of a flower; don't cut through to the filling. Chill for 15–20 minutes. Set the oven at very hot (220°C/425°F).

Pierce a few holes in the centre of the gâteau to allow steam to escape. Sprinkle it with sugar and bake in the heated oven for 20–25 minutes or until puffed and brown on the top. Lower the oven temperature to hot (200°C/400°F) and continue baking for 15–20 minutes or until firm, lightly browned on the sides and glazed with melted sugar on top. If the sugar has not melted by the time the pastry is cooked, grill/broil it quickly until shiny. Cool the gâteau on a rack. Serve slightly warm or at room temperature.

QUATRE QUARTS
Pound cake

'Quatre quarts' means literally four quarters and is the French version of pound cake, which uses approximately equal weights of flour, butter, sugar and eggs. A delicious Loire variation has fresh fruit – cherries, strawberries or raspberries – baked in the batter.

Serves 6–8

160 g	flour	$1\frac{1}{4}$ cups
	2 tsp baking powder	
	pinch of salt	
185 g	butter	6 oz
175 g	sugar	$\frac{7}{8}$ cup
	3 eggs	
	$\frac{1}{2}$ tsp vanilla extract OR grated rind of 1 lemon or 1 orange	
	confectioners' sugar (for sprinkling)	
	20–23 cm/8–9 in round cake pan	

Brush the cake pan with melted butter, line the base with a circle of greaseproof/parchment paper and butter it also. Lightly sprinkle the pan with sugar, discarding the excess. Set the oven at moderate (175°C/350°F).

Sift the flour with the baking powder and the salt. Cream the butter in a bowl, add the sugar and beat for 5 minutes or until light and fluffy. Add the eggs one by one, beating well after each addition. Beat in the flavouring. Fold the flour into the mixture in three batches. Spoon the batter into the prepared pan; tap the pan to knock out any air bubbles. Bake in the heated oven for 35–40 minutes or until the cake shrinks slightly from the sides of the pan and the top springs back when lightly pressed with a fingertip. Turn out on to a rack to cool.

Just before serving, sprinkle the top of the cake with the icing/confectioners' sugar.

QUATRE QUARTS AUX FRUITS

For the fruit version, pit:

250 g	fresh cherries	8 oz
or clean:		
200 g	fresh raspberries	7 oz

Spoon half the batter into a 23–25 cm/9–10 in pan and arrange the fruit over it. Top with the remaining batter. Bake for 45–50 minutes or until the cake shrinks from the sides of the pan. Turn on to a rack to cool.

CHEESES

Mention of the Loire valley does not bring cheese to the mind of the average Frenchman, but in fact several popular cheeses come from this general area. On the spot, a fresh cheese called 'crémets' is eaten with sugar and cream or with fruit.

Touraine is a centre for goat cheese, with 'Ste-Maure' the favourite among half a dozen others. The tangy Ste-Maure is shaped in a long cylinder with a straw running through the centre and the best is farm produced, or 'fermier'. 'Olivet', a cow cheese, is traditional to the Orléanais. There are two types: 'olivet bleu', which is not a blue cheese at all but has a bluish rind from aging in chalk caverns, and 'olivet cendré', sooty-black from maturing in ashes.

Most famous of all cheeses from the Loire area is 'port-salut', created by Trappist monks at the monastery of Port-du-Salut near Le Mans. The monastic contributions to the cheeses of France are many, spurred on, at least in part, by the search for additions to the table on meatless days of religious fast, and port-salut is best known both in and out of France. When the monks sent their first delivery of this cheese to Paris in 1873, abbey records state that it was sold out within the hour. The name was bought by a French firm and today port-salut, with its orange rind and creamy, innocuous centre, is a household word, as are its facsimiles 'St-Paulin' and 'Bonbel', both of them brand names for port-salut.

OTHER SPECIALITIES OF THE REGION
TRADITIONAL DISHES

Omelette beauceronne
Bacon, potato and sorrel omelette

Pâté angevine d'anguilles et de lamproie
Eel and lamprey pâté

Perches grillées au fenouil
Grilled perch with fennel

Ris de veau aux champignons langeaise
Sweetbreads with mushrooms

Gigot de mouton de Sologne à l'eau
Poached leg of mutton

Canard sauvage orléanaise aux beignets de pommes
Wild duck with apple fritters

Cuissot de chevreuil ou de marcassin à la tourangelle
Leg of venison or wild boar with prunes and red wine

La chouée
Green cabbage with butter and vinegar

Coulemelle au vinaigre d'Orléans
Grilled wild mushrooms with wine vinegar

Artichauts d'Anjou farcis
Artichokes stuffed with meat, mushrooms and herbs

CHARCUTERIE

Terrine orléanaise de lièvre
Hare terrine

Pâté de Chartres
Stuffed partridges in pastry

Andouille et andouillette de Tours
Chitterling sausages

Langue de boeuf angevine en gelée
Beef tongue in aspic

Boudin de sanglier orléanaise
Wild boar sausage

Pieds de porc St Antoine
Boned pig's feet with truffle stuffing

Charbonnée de Touraine
Liver and lungs in red wine and blood sauce

Boudins aux raisins
Little blood sausages with white raisins

PÂTISSERIE AND CONFISERIE

Cotignac d'Orléans
Apple and quince jelly

Pâtes de fruits de Beaugency
Hard fruit jellies

Pain d'épices de Pithiviers
Spiced honey bread

Pâtés aux prunes d'Angers
Plum turnovers

Les croquants orléanais
Crisp nut cakes

Pruneaux fourrés de Tours
Stuffed prunes

The Centre

My first encounter with the Massif Central, the volcanic plateau that dominates the centre of France, was symbolic. After days of searing sun in Languedoc, the weather broke one night in a fierce storm. The following morning when I climbed the road into Cantal, the clouds were down on the hilltops and the cattle huddled dismally in the fields. The standard dress was no longer a sunhat but a woolly sweater, and the shops were selling hearty mountain foods – cabbage, potatoes, pork pâtés and a huge variety of breads. Looking at a contour map, the reason is clear: the mountains of central France are a formidable obstacle, dividing east from west and north from south, with the isolation of the region itself making it one of the most rural in France. And also one of the most scenically bizarre: 'The face of the country everywhere exhibits the origin in subterranean fire,' wrote Arthur Young.

The highest peaks of the Massif Central are to be found in Auvergne, famous for its lace, its folk music and its cows. During summer the herds are taken up to grassy plateaux formed on the rich soil of long-extinct volcanoes known as 'puys', where their milk is made into cheese. In the old days, the herdsmen moved with the cows and lived in curious stone houses called 'burons' in which the most important chamber was a large dairy lined with stone shelves for the curing of cheese.

In winter Auvergne is bleak; snow comes before Christmas, and in early September in St Flour I shivered in the open market, as I sampled the wild bilberries which are scooped from the mountainside with a shovel-like comb, a 'peigne à myrtilles', rather like that used for carding wool. The warmest place was a church, converted to the sale of a marvellous array of local cheeses – piquant, aged cantal which resembles cheddar, creamy St-Nectaire, the cylindrical blue 'fourme-d'Ambert', and 'bleu-d'Auvergne', which was made originally in imitation of roquefort, using cow's rather than sheep's milk.

Like the Pyrenees, Auvergne is noted for its salted hams and dried sausages, which festoon the ceilings of charcuteries. In St Flour I saw some good-looking pâtés clad in a rich crust, plus a substantial bread called 'pompe aux grattons', which proved to be a brioche dough enriched not with butter but with cracklings, the crisp bits of fat left when rendering lard. Grattons (also known

as 'fritons') may be pressed into a block to form a kind of pâté like rillettes, particularly good when bits of goose or duck are included with the pork. 'Le pounti' is a savoury cake, based on eggs, chopped bacon and Swiss chard, the traditional lunch taken by labourers to the fields. Many shops specialize in 'tripoux', tripe wrapped in pretty little bundles, flavoured with garlic and cooked with white wine, broth and herbs. When I investigated the recipe I realized why tripoux are one of those regional specialities that home cooks are only too happy to leave to professionals – they require such esoterica as veal mesentery, sheep's feet and rumen tripe, not to mention several hours of preparation and 8–10 hours' simmering on the stove.

Given the climate, the cooks of the Massif Central go for calories rather than finesse so perhaps it is no coincidence that the mother of that renowned trencherwoman, Catherine de Medicis, belonged to the powerful family of the Counts of Auvergne. Surprisingly, this homely cuisine has had a great success in Paris, where many cafés and restaurants were traditionally run by Auvergnats who fled the grinding poverty of the mountains to seek their fortune in the capital in the last century.

Cabbage is the symbol of Auvergne and the basis of its most famous dish, 'potée'. But the potato is even more important to mountain cooking. 'Aligot' consists of mashed potatoes that are beaten over the heat with cheese and cream to make a kind of fondue. Like fondue, aligot demands a robust appetite and plenty of wine to chase it down. A lighter, though less well-known version, called 'patranque' is based on bread. Potatoes are also fried with bacon and cheese to form a cake known somewhat optimistically as 'truffade' (potatoes have been called the truffles of the poor) or, most popular of all, they are baked as a pie in puff pastry, then doused with cream. Potato pies are also found well to the north of Auvergne, in the rolling countryside of Berry and the Bourbonnais, where they are known as 'tartouffes' or 'truffats' and are often flavoured with onion.

However, Auvergne is no longer on the bread- or potato-line. During the last century railways and the automobile have brought a certain prosperity epitomized by Clermont-Ferrand, home of the Michelin tyre company, whose restaurant guides have sealed the fate, for better or worse, of many a French chef. North from Clermont runs the valley of the Grande Limagne, once marshy and the homeland of frogs and now a rich valley of farms and gardens. From the hills north and south of Clermont spring two of the most famous of French mineral waters, Perrier and Vichy. To visit the once-fashionable spa of Vichy is to step into another, more secluded, age of bandstand concerts and afternoon teas at the pâtisserie, punctuated at regular intervals by doses of the mellifluous-sounding waters – Célestins, Chomel, Lucas and Parc.

North from Vichy, the Grande Limagne flattens towards Moulins, the prosperous market centre of the Bourbonnais. The arable land of the Bourbonnais has none of the fertility of the north, so farmers divide their attention between the raising of cattle and the growing of maize and cereals to feed them. In its preoccupation with the soil and the seasons, the bucolic life of the Bourbonnais depicted in 1904 in *La Vie d'un Simple* is not so very different today. The author, a peasant by birth, moved from farm to farm at harvest. In one place he was regaled with buttery galettes and pastries unknown in his usual diet of onion soup and rye bread; their richness quickly sickened him. He talks of rabbit and hare, caught as the fields were mown and cooked 'en civet' in a blood-thickened sauce, but in general meat was rare and eggs were kept for visitors – 'food for Parisians.'

In the Limousin, to the southwest of the Bourbonnais, beef and veal still predominate and outside the town of Limoges, still famous for its porcelain, the population density is one of the lowest in France, the ideal environment for exiling unwanted personalities ('limoger' means to be forcibly retired). Local cooking tends to be substantial, with puddings like the famous 'clafoutis' made of tart black cherries and 'farcidure', a kind of dumpling found as far afield as the Landes and Auvergne. Farcidure means 'firm stuffing' and texture is almost the only common denominator of the many different types. Farcidures can be poached like dumplings or sautéed in a frying pan, a reminder of the many pancakes found throughout central France like 'farinette', made with buckwheat flour and filled with meat and vegetables, or 'sanciau' from the Bourbonnais, which can be thick or thin, sweet or savoury.

The Bourbonnais is inseparable from Berry, just to the north, where flocks of

sheep are a reminder of the medieval wool fortune made by Jacques Coeur, lover of King Charles VII's favourite, Agnès Sorel, and by the 14th-century Duc de Berry who commissioned the *Très Riches Heures*, an illuminated manuscript which shows each activity of the agricultural year. The Berrichons were considered to have skulls as thick as those of their sheep. One wily shepherd bringing his flock to Paris knew that taxes levied at the gates started with a hundred sheep. So he brought 99; the customs man counted them, then pushed in the shepherd: 'There's the hundredth!'

Nowadays most sheep are destined for the table, perhaps to be cooked with potatoes and garlic 'en cassette', as in Auvergne, in a black earthenware casserole with high sides which retain moisture. Beef is served with a Berrichonne red wine sauce deliberately left unreduced and more acid than similar sauces in Burgundy.

The Bourbonnais and Berrichons are lucky not only with beef but with game. Pheasants and partridge abound in the open fields and the heaths and ponds of La Brenne have long supplied wildfowl. Agnès Sorel hunted in the forest of Tronçais, the finest oak forest in France, which still harbours deer and wild boar. Driving through it one day I came upon a deer hunt in French style, the riders clad in green frock coats with great horns slung around their shoulders. The master of hounds waved us down, the better to hear the baying of his pack, and in the silence I was reminded of another moment in Auvergne. As I wandered beside a lake, across the still water came a sound rarely heard amid the modern clamour: the triumphant clucking of a hen which has just laid an egg.

BRIOCHE DE GANNAT
Cheese brioche

Gannat is a small town on the northern edge of Auvergne cheese country. For authenticity, this brioche should be made with cantal cheese, but a well-aged gruyère can be used instead.

Makes 1 large loaf

125 ml	milk	$\frac{1}{2}$ cup
60 g	butter	4 Tbsp
	1 tsp sugar	
260 g	flour, more if needed	2 cups
5 g	salt	1 tsp
	pinch of pepper	
15 g	fresh yeast OR	1 cake
	1 pkg dry yeast	
	2 eggs	
125 g	grated cantal or gruyère cheese	$1\frac{1}{4}$ cups
	1 egg, beaten with $\frac{1}{2}$ tsp salt (for glaze)	
	$23 \times 10 \times 7\cdot5$ cm/$9 \times 4 \times 3$ in loaf pan	

Heat the milk, butter and sugar until the butter melts; let cool to lukewarm. Sift the flour into a bowl with the salt and pepper and make a well in the centre. Add the lukewarm milk mixture to the well. Crumble the yeast over the liquid and leave for 5 minutes or until dissolved. Add the eggs and mix the centre ingredients with your fingertips, gradually drawing in the flour to make a soft dough. Knead it on a floured work surface for 10 minutes or until smooth and elastic, adding more flour if necessary to prevent sticking. Put the dough in an oiled bowl and turn the dough over so the top is oiled. Cover with a damp cloth and let rise in a warm place for 45–60 minutes or until doubled in bulk.

Butter the loaf pan. Knead the dough lightly and work in the cheese, reserving 2 tablespoons for the top. Shape the dough into a loaf, set it in the pan, cover and let rise in a warm place for 45–60 minutes or until the dough reaches the top of the pan. Set the oven at hot (200°C/400°F).

Brush the loaf with egg glaze and sprinkle with the reserved cheese. Bake in the heated oven for 35–45 minutes or until brown and the loaf sounds hollow when tapped on the bottom. Transfer to a rack to cool.

RISSOLES D'AUVERGNE
Fried pork turnovers

Since they are deep fried, these little pork turnovers should be served at once.

Makes 22 turnovers

PIE PASTRY		
260 g	flour	2 cups
125 g	butter	$\frac{1}{4}$ lb
	2 egg yolks	
5 g	salt	1 tsp
	5–6 Tbsp cold water	
FILLING		
250 g	ground pork, equal parts fat and lean	$\frac{1}{2}$ lb
	4 Tbsp chopped herbs: parsley, chives, chervil, tarragon	
	2 Tbsp fresh breadcrumbs	
	salt and pepper	
	$7\cdot5$ cm/3 in plain or fluted round cutter	

Make the pie pastry* and chill for 30 minutes or until firm.

Prepare the filling: mix the pork with the herbs, breadcrumbs, salt and pepper. Knead until smooth. Sauté a small piece of the mixture and taste for seasoning.

Roll out the dough about 6 mm/$\frac{1}{4}$ in thick and cut circles with the cutter. Put a small ball of filling in the centre of each circle, brush the edges with water and fold in half to enclose the filling. Press the edges firmly to seal. Chill for 30 minutes or until firm.

Heat the deep fat to 175°C/350°F on a fat thermometer. Fry a few turnovers at a time for 6–7 minutes or until golden brown. Drain them on paper towels and keep warm in a moderate oven (175°C/350°F) with the door open while frying the rest. Serve immediately.

RISSOLES DE ST FLOUR

Instead of the pork filling, make a cheese one by mixing together:

125 g	cream cheese	4 oz
75 g	diced cantal or gruyère cheese	$2\frac{1}{2}$ oz
	2 egg yolks	
	2 tsp chopped chives	
	1 tsp chopped chervil	
	salt and pepper to taste	

Fry these turnovers for only 5–6 minutes.

PATRANQUE or ALIGOT AU PAIN
Bread and cheese purée

Aligot made with mashed potatoes flavoured with cheese is one of the most famous of all Auvergnat dishes. In this recipe breadcrumbs take the place of potatoes to make a light version of cheese fondue. Served in bowls it makes a hearty first course; for a main course, try it with grilled sausages.

Serves 6

750 ml	milk, more if needed	3 cups
300 g	12 slices stale wholewheat or white bread, crusts discarded	10 oz
90 g	butter	6 Tbsp
300 g	cantal or gruyère cheese, thinly sliced	10 oz
	salt and pepper	

Bring the milk to a boil in a medium pan, crumble the sliced bread into it and simmer over a low fire, stirring constantly, until the milk is absorbed and the mixture is smooth. Add a little more milk if the bread can absorb it; the amount varies enormously with the type of bread. Add the butter and cheese and continue stirring until the mixture is smooth and the cheese melts like fondue. Season to taste with a little salt and plenty of pepper. Ladle the aligot into individual bowls and serve hot.

St Germain Lembron, Basse Auvergne

PÂTÉ DE POMMES DE TERRE
Potato feuilleté

This is the richest version of potato pie, where the potatoes are baked inside rounds of puff pastry, then moistened with cream poured through a hole in the pastry. The pie can be served as a first course, or as an accompaniment to meats.

Serves 6–8

	PUFF PASTRY	
250 g	unsalted butter	$\frac{1}{2}$ lb
175 g	all-purpose flour	$1\frac{1}{3}$ cups
80 g	cake flour	$\frac{2}{3}$ cup
5 g	salt	1 tsp
	1 tsp lemon juice	
125 ml	iced water, more if needed	$\frac{1}{2}$ cup
	1 egg, beaten with $\frac{1}{2}$ tsp salt (for glaze)	
	FILLING	
500 g	potatoes	1 lb
	salt and pepper	
	pinch of grated nutmeg	
80 ml	heavy cream or crème fraîche*	$\frac{1}{3}$ cup

Make the puff pastry* and chill for 1 hour or until firm.

Meanwhile, prepare the filling: peel the potatoes and cut in thin slices. Plunge them into boiling salted water and simmer for 5 minutes or until partly cooked but still firm. Rinse under cold running water and drain thoroughly. Season well with salt, pepper and nutmeg. Leave to cool completely.

Lightly sprinkle a baking sheet with water. Roll out a little less than half the pastry to a thin round. Using a pan lid as a guide, cut a 25 cm/ 10 in circle with a sharp knife. Roll out the remaining dough slightly thicker than the first round and cut a slightly larger circle. Set the smaller circle on the baking sheet and arrange the potato slices overlapping in the centre, leaving a border. Brush the border with egg glaze. Set the larger circle on top and press the edges together firmly to seal. Scallop the edge by pulling in the pastry at intervals with the back of a knife. Brush with egg glaze. With a knife, score a 12 cm/5 in circle on top of the pie to form a 'hat'. Chill the pie for 15 minutes. Set the oven at very hot (220°C/425°F).

Bake the pie in the heated oven for 20–25 minutes or until puffed and brown. Warm the cream. Cut the 'hat' from the pie and carefully pour in enough cream to fill it. Replace the hat and serve immediately.

FROGS

Cookbooks often link frogs' legs with the town of Riom in the Grande Limagne valley, where nowadays scarcely a frog is to be found. Grimod de la Reynière, writing in the *Almanach des Gourmands* in 1806, extolled the merits of the frogs of Riom. 'Frogs are a delicate dish, But they are not to everyone's taste,' he remarked. 'A gourmand has no such false reluctance; his first duty is to taste everything with an open mind.'

To overcome such prejudices, Escoffier disguised frogs' legs in a pink chaudfroid sauce coated with champagne aspic, entitling the creation 'nymphes à l'aurore'. In fact the meat on a frog's leg could offend no one; white and delicate, it tastes very like chicken. Recipes compensate for lack of flavour by adding white wine, garlic, herbs and cream, as in frogs' legs 'poulette' with a sauce of white stock, lemon juice and parsley. In the Lyonnais and the Massif Central, frogs' legs are often deep fried. In the Jura they turn up in soup (the carcasses, which are mostly bone, make excellent broth), and most popular of all, they are sautéed in butter or oil 'en persillade', with garlic and fresh parsley. This used to be a favourite dish in Languedoc, where frogs were once cheaper than butchers' meat and the frog-man walked the streets of Béziers crying 'la gragnota, la gragnota'.

A frog may live for 20 years, but is ideal for eating at 4–5 years old. Then the legs of a plump young frog will weigh 25 g/1 oz, about a third of the total weight. Frogs abound wherever there is shallow fresh water – in the marshes of Poitou, in the streams of Haute Auvergne and the ponds of the Dombes east of Lyon. As with so many delicacies, however, there are not enough wild frogs to supply French kitchens, or perhaps not enough sure-footed frog-catchers. Nowadays they are raised in artificial ponds, and many are imported from Yugoslavia.

The association of the frog with France goes back a long way – the Roman name for Paris was Lutetia (mud-land) and, later on, the heraldic device of the French kings was 'three toads erect, saltant' (jumping). The English have called the French 'frogs' for centuries and even today the joke about the Englishman settling to his first meal in France, at Calais, can raise a laugh. 'Do you have frogs' legs?' he enquires aggressively. 'Mais oui, monsieur,' is the waiter's anxious reply. 'Well then, hop it, and get me a ham sandwich.'

GRENOUILLES À LA MODE DE RIOM
Deep-fried frogs' legs

Like the asparagus of Argenteuil, now a Paris suburb, the frogs of Riom have been swept away by civilization: in this case the draining of the Grande Limagne marshes in the last century.

Serves 4–6

	24 pairs of frogs' legs	
	3 Tbsp cognac	
	salt and pepper	
	fat for deep frying	
	3 egg whites	
45 g	flour	$\frac{1}{3}$ cup
	1 bunch of parsley, divided in sprigs	
	2 lemons, quartered	

If necessary, prepare the frogs' legs by trimming the spines and the tips of the feet. Wash and dry the legs. Put them in a shallow dish with the cognac and plenty of salt and pepper; marinate for 30 minutes.

Heat the deep fat to 175°C/350°F on a fat thermometer. Whip the egg whites until stiff. Drain the frogs' legs, roll them in flour and dip them in the egg whites until coated. Fry them in the hot fat, a few at a time, for 8–10 minutes or until tender and golden brown. Drain thoroughly on paper towels and keep warm in a moderate oven (175°C/350°F) with the door open while frying the rest.

Be sure the parsley is dry. Let the fat cool slightly and toss in the parsley sprigs; stand back as they will splutter. After 30 seconds, or when the spluttering stops, lift out the parsley with a slotted spoon and drain on paper towels.

Arrange the frogs' legs on a platter, sprinkle them with fried parsley sprigs, and decorate with lemon quarters. Serve at once.

TOURTE DE SAUMON
Salmon feuilleté

In the good old days the river Allier was famous for its salmon. In this recipe slices of the fish are layered with a filling of puréed salmon and wild mushrooms in a puff pastry case. A herb and butter sauce can be served as accompaniment. Pie pastry is an alternative to puff pastry, and other wild or cultivated mushrooms may be substituted for the cèpes.

Serves 8

PUFF PASTRY		
250 g	unsalted butter	½ lb
175 g	all-purpose flour	1⅓ cups
80 g	cake flour	⅔ cup
5 g	salt	1 tsp
	1 tsp lemon juice	
125 ml	iced water, more if needed	½ cup
	1 egg, beaten with ½ tsp salt (for glaze)	
SALMON FILLING		
300 g	fresh cèpes OR	10 oz
30 g	dried cèpes	1 oz
2 kg	salmon OR	4½ lb
1 kg	salmon fillets, free of skin and bone	2 lb
	2 egg yolks	
80 g	butter	5 Tbsp
	salt and pepper	
	pinch of grated nutmeg	
	1 egg white	
250 ml	heavy cream or crème fraîche*	1 cup
HERB SAUCE (optional)		
250 g	butter, cold	1 cup
	2 Tbsp water	
	juice of ½ lemon, more if needed	
	salt and pepper	
	1 Tbsp chopped chervil	
	2 tsp chopped tarragon	

Make the puff pastry* and chill for 1 hour or until firm.

Meanwhile, prepare the filling: prepare fresh or dried cèpes*. Clean and fillet the whole salmon; wash the fillets and pat dry. Cut half the salmon in thin diagonal slices (escalopes) and purée the rest in a food processor. Add the egg yolks and all but 1 tablespoon of the butter and purée again. Alternatively, work the fish twice through the fine plate of a mincer/grinder; then purée it with the butter and yolks in a blender or beat them into the fish with a wooden spoon. If possible, also work the mixture through a drum sieve. Put the fish mixture into a metal bowl set in a pan of iced water. Stir in salt, pepper and nutmeg. With a wooden spoon, beat in the egg white. Gradually beat in the cream and taste again for seasoning. Keep in the refrigerator while rolling out the pastry. Finely chop mushrooms and squeeze in a cloth to extract all moisture.

Sprinkle a baking sheet with a little water. Roll out half the pastry to a thin round and, using a pan lid as a guide, cut out a 25 cm/10 in circle with a sharp knife. Roll out the remaining dough slightly thicker than the first and cut a slightly larger circle. Set the smaller circle on the baking sheet and spread the chilled salmon mixture in the centre, leaving a border. Put a layer of chopped mushrooms on top. Arrange the salmon slices slightly overlapping on top of the mixture, season them lightly and dot with the remaining butter. Brush the border with egg glaze. Set the second circle on top and press the edges together firmly. Decorate the edges by pressing with the prongs of a fork. Brush the pie with egg glaze and chill for 15–20 minutes. Set the oven at hot (200°C/400°F).

Bake the pie in the heated oven for 30–40 minutes or until puffed and brown. Keep it warm while making the herb sauce.

For the herb sauce: cut the butter into small cubes. In a small saucepan (not aluminium) put the water, lemon juice, salt and pepper. Bring to a boil. With the pan over a low fire, whisk in the butter gradually, one piece at a time, to make a smooth creamy sauce. Work sometimes over low heat and sometimes off the heat, so that the butter softens and thickens the sauce without melting. Stir in the chervil and tarragon and taste for seasoning, adding more lemon juice if necessary. Serve at once. Serve the pie hot, with the herb sauce separate.

POULET FARCI À LA LIMOUSINE
Chicken with chestnut stuffing

Chicken with chestnut stuffing is a dish for family Sunday luncheon, while the turkey version has become the standard French Christmas dinner, served early in the morning after Midnight Mass. Instead of acting as garnish, the chestnuts may be roasted, peeled and added to the stuffing.

Serves 4

750 g	fresh chestnuts	1½ lb
	1 stalk celery	
500 ml	broth, more if needed	2 cups
	salt and pepper	
	pinch of sugar	
1·5-kg	chicken	3-lb
45 g	butter	3 Tbsp
	STUFFING	
	1 Tbsp lard or butter	
	1 onion, chopped	
125 g	ground pork, fat and lean mixed	¼ lb
	1 Tbsp chopped parsley	
	1 Tbsp cognac	
	pinch of ground allspice (optional)	
	salt and pepper	
	trussing needle and string	

Peel the chestnuts*. Put them in a pot with the celery, broth, salt, pepper and a pinch of sugar. Simmer for 20–25 minutes, or until the chestnuts are nearly tender, adding more broth to keep them covered. Set the oven at moderately hot (190°C/375°F).

Make the stuffing: heat the lard in a frying pan, add the onion and cook over a low fire until soft but not brown. Leave to cool. Thoroughly mix the onion with the pork, parsley, cognac, allspice, salt and pepper. Drain a quarter of the chestnuts and stir them into the stuffing. Sauté a small piece of the mixture in the frying pan and taste for seasoning. Stuff the chicken with the mixture and truss it.

Sprinkle the chicken with salt and pepper. Heat the butter in a heavy casserole, add the chicken and brown it on all sides over a medium fire. Roast uncovered in the oven for 25 minutes or until very brown. Add the remaining chestnuts with their liquid, cover and continue to cook in the oven for 25 minutes longer or until the chicken is tender and a skewer inserted in the stuffing for 30 seconds is hot to the touch when withdrawn. If the pan becomes dry during cooking, add more broth or water.

When the chicken is cooked, discard the piece of celery and taste the gravy. If it is thin, remove the chicken and chestnuts and keep them warm. Boil the gravy until well flavoured, and taste for seasoning. Replace the chicken and chestnuts and serve them in the casserole.

DINDE AUX MARRONS

To substitute a turkey for the chicken in the previous recipe, double the amount of stuffing. Instead of browning the turkey in a casserole, roast it in the oven, allowing 2½–3 hours for a 3–4-kg/6–8-lb turkey. During cooking, add broth if the pan gets dry. Put in the chestnuts only for the last 20 minutes of cooking, and at that point cover the turkey with foil.

OMELETTE BRAYAUDE
Potato, ham and cheese omelette

The farmers around Riom and Châtelguyon in the Grande Limagne valley are known as 'brayauds' and are famous for their gourmandise. They have given their name to several recipes including 'gigot brayaude', a leg of lamb simmered with vegetables and quantities of garlic in the manner of 'gigot de sept heures' (see recipe), as well as to this potato omelette flavoured with ham and cantal cheese.

Serves 2

100 g	raw ham, thinly sliced	3½ oz
30 g	lard or oil	2 Tbsp
	2 potatoes, diced	
	5 eggs, beaten	
	salt and pepper	
50 g	grated cantal or gruyère cheese	½ cup
	2 Tbsp heavy cream or crème fraîche*	
	23 cm/9 in omelette pan	

Cut the ham in fine dice. Heat the lard in the omelette pan, add the ham and cook over a medium fire until slightly stiffened; remove. Add the potatoes to the pan and sauté over a medium fire, tossing often, for 8–10 minutes or until just tender and lightly browned.

Season the eggs with pepper and very little or no salt (if the ham is salty). Return the ham to the pan, heat it and add the eggs. Cook the mixture over medium heat, stirring briskly with the flat of a fork, until the omelette is almost as thick as scrambled eggs. Leave it to cook a few seconds; it should be well browned on the bottom and almost firm on top. Take the pan from the heat, set a heatproof plate over the top and turn out the omelette. Slide it back into the pan, sprinkle with the cheese and spoon the cream over it. Quickly brown the bottom over a medium fire. Slide the omelette on to a platter and serve hot.

TOURTE DE POULET

Chicken pie

Tourte de poulet is a kind of 'coq au vin' baked in pastry. Just before serving, a sauce made from the white wine marinade is poured into the pie to moisten it.

Serves 4–6

1·5-kg	chicken, with its liver	3-lb
200 g	bacon, cut in lardons	7 oz
30 g	butter	2 Tbsp
	20 baby onions	
	salt and pepper	
	1 tsp tomato paste	
125 ml	broth	$\frac{1}{2}$ cup
	1 tsp potato starch or arrowroot	
	dissolved in 2 tsp cold water	
	MARINADE	
125 ml	white wine	$\frac{1}{2}$ cup
	1 onion, sliced	
	2–3 bay leaves, crumbled	
	2–3 sprigs thyme	
	salt and pepper	
	2 Tbsp oil	
	PÂTÉ PASTRY DOUGH	
485 g	flour	$3\frac{3}{4}$ cups
250 g	butter, or mixture of two parts butter and one lard	1 cup
	2 eggs	
	2 Tbsp oil	
10 g	salt	2 tsp
	2–3 Tbsp cold water	
	1 egg, beaten with $\frac{1}{2}$ tsp salt (for glaze)	

2·5 L/2½ qt shallow oval baking dish or 25 cm/10 in pie pan with removable base

Marinate the chicken: cut it into 8 pieces*, discarding the skin. Put the chicken pieces and the liver into a dish and pour the white wine over them. Scatter the slices of onion, the bay leaf and the thyme over the chicken and sprinkle with a little salt and pepper. Sprinkle the oil on top and leave to marinate for 1–2 hours.

Meanwhile, make the pâté pastry dough* and chill for 30 minutes or until firm.

If the bacon is very salty, blanch* it. Sauté the lardons in 1 tablespoon of the butter. Butter the baking dish. Set the oven at very hot (220°C/425°F). Roll out three-quarters of the dough and use it to line the dish. Trim the edge neatly with a knife or scissors, leaving about 5 cm/2 in of dough overhanging.

Drain the chicken pieces, reserving the marinade, and put them with the liver into the lined pan. Sprinkle with the baby onions and the lardons. Spoon in 2 tablespoons of the reserved marinade and sprinkle with a little salt and pepper. Fold the overhanging dough over the chicken and press it firmly so that it sticks; the centre section of the filling will not yet be covered. Brush the folded dough with egg glaze.

Roll out the remaining pastry and cut an oval or circle about 2·5 cm/1 in larger than the uncovered area of filling. Reserve any pastry trimmings. Set the dough on the pie, pressing to seal it to the glazed pastry. Brush the whole pie with glaze. Cut strips, leaves, diamonds or other shapes from the dough trimmings, set them on the pie and glaze them also. Stick a rolled piece of foil through the centre of the pie to make a 'chimney' for steam to escape.

Bake the pie in the hot oven for 30 minutes or until it begins to brown. Lower the heat to moderate (175°C/350°F), cover the pie with foil and bake for another 45–55 minutes or until the chicken pieces are tender when tested with a skewer; the skewer should be hot when withdrawn from the pie. Remove the 'chimney'.

Strain the remaining marinade into a small saucepan, whisk it with the tomato paste and the broth and bring to a boil. Pour in the potato starch mixture, whisking constantly, and bring back to a boil. Taste for seasoning. Slowly pour the mixture into the hole of the baked pie. Brush the top crust of the pie with the remaining butter.

Serve the pie hot from the baking dish, cutting out the central 'hat' to reach the pieces of chicken. After the chicken has been served, cut and serve the pastry case.

TOURTIÈRE DE POULET AUX SALSIFIS

In this variation, salsify is substituted for the bacon.

Omit the bacon. Peel:

500 g	salsify	1 lb

putting them immediately in a bowl of water with a few tablespoons of vinegar. Simmer in salted water with the juice of 1 lemon for 20 minutes or until partly tender, and drain thoroughly. Cut each in 4 pieces. Add to the pie with the chicken.

CANARD À L'AIGRE-DOUX
Sweet-sour duck with cherries

In the Limousin where this dish is a speciality, tart cherries grow wild in the hedgerows. Canned tart cherries can be used instead of fresh ones (they need less cooking), but the dish tastes quite different if sweet cherries are substituted.

Serves 2–3

1·5-kg	duck	3-lb
	salt and pepper	
	1 Tbsp butter	
500 g	tart cherries, unpitted	1 lb
250 ml	broth	1 cup
	trussing needle and string	

Set the oven at very hot (220°C/425°F). Season the duck inside and out with salt and pepper and truss it. Heat the butter in a heavy casserole. Lay the duck in the butter on one side and roast in the oven for 15 minutes. Turn it on to the other leg and roast for another 15 minutes. Discard the excess fat from the casserole. Lower the oven heat to moderately hot (190°C/375°F).

Lay the duck on its breast, add a third of the cherries to the casserole and roast the duck for 15 more minutes. Finally set the duck on its back and roast another 15 minutes or until the juices from the centre of the duck run pink if it is lifted with a fork; the breast meat will be pink. If you prefer meat well done, continue cooking the duck until the juices run clear. Transfer the duck to a platter and keep warm.

Add the broth to the casserole and bring to a boil, stirring. If necessary, boil to reduce until well flavoured. Strain the broth, pressing hard on the cherries from the pan. Skim off excess fat.

Discard the trussing strings from the duck and return it with the gravy to the casserole. Add the remaining cherries and simmer over a low fire for 10 minutes or until the cherries are just tender. Taste the broth for seasoning and, if necessary, skim off any fat that has dissolved from the duck into the sauce. Transfer the duck to a platter and spoon the cherries around it. Pass the gravy separately.

PERDRIX AUX LENTILLES
Braised partridge with lentils

The centre of France is great lentil country; those of Le Puy are renowned for their colour, a deep green marbled with turquoise – a result of the local volcanic soil. This particular recipe is good for tough old partridges and pheasants that need long cooking; rabbit can be used instead.

Serves 4

250 g	bacon, cut in lardons	½ lb
500 g each	2 partridges	1 lb each
30 g	lard	2 Tbsp
	1 onion, chopped	
	1 carrot, diced	
	2 bouquets garnis	
185 ml	white wine	¾ cup
185 ml	broth	¾ cup
	salt and pepper	
175 g	lentils	1 cup
	1 onion, studded with a clove	
	1 clove garlic	
	trussing needle and string	

If the bacon is very salty, blanch* it.

Truss the partridges. Heat the lard in a heavy casserole, add the bacon and fry briefly until lightly browned; remove it. Add the partridges and brown them well on all sides. Add the chopped onion and carrot and cook over a medium fire until they soften. Return the bacon to the casserole and add 1 bouquet garni, the wine, broth and a pinch of pepper. Cover and simmer, turning the partridges over occasionally, for 1–1½ hours or until the birds are tender.

While the meat is cooking, pick over the lentils, discarding any stones, and wash them well. Put in a pot with enough water to cover generously; bring to a boil and skim. Add the whole onion, a bouquet garni and the garlic. Cook over a low fire for 50–60 minutes or until the lentils are tender and most liquid is absorbed. Discard the onion, garlic and bouquet garni.

When the partridges are cooked, take them from the casserole, discard the trussing strings and cut the birds in half; reserve the cooking liquid but discard the bouquet garni. Add the birds, bacon and vegetables to the lentils, cover and heat over a low fire for 10 minutes to blend the flavours.

Boil the reserved cooking liquid until well flavoured to make gravy. Taste for seasoning.

Strain the gravy, add a little to the lentils and taste them for seasoning. Either serve from the casserole or set the partridge halves on top of the mounded lentils on a platter; serve the remaining gravy separately.

PIGEONNEAUX À LA CRÈME
Pigeons with cream

The cooking time in this recipe varies greatly with the age of the pigeons. Young birds, called squabs in the USA, take an hour or so, but tough old pigeons take much longer to become tender. The pigeons will look their best surrounded by piles of baby vegetables, a speciality of the town of Bourges where they are grown in irrigated gardens like the hortillonnages of Amiens.

Serves 4

	4 squabs	
	salt and pepper	
	4 thin slices of barding fat	
	or mild bacon	
15 g	lard or oil	1 Tbsp
30 g	butter	2 Tbsp
250 ml	white wine	1 cup
250 ml	broth	1 cup
30 g	butter kneaded with	2 Tbsp
15 g	flour	2 Tbsp
250 ml	heavy cream or crème fraîche*	1 cup
	trussing needle and string	

Lightly season the pigeons or squabs with salt and pepper. Wrap each bird in a slice of barding fat and truss it.

Heat the lard and butter in a heavy casserole and brown the birds well on all sides. Discard the fat from the casserole and add the wine and broth. Bring to a boil, cover and simmer for 1 hour or until the birds are tender. Lift them out and cut them in half, discarding the trussing strings. Arrange the birds overlapping on a platter and keep them warm.

Bring the broth back to a boil and whisk in the kneaded butter*, a little at a time, until the sauce is thick enough to coat a spoon. Stir in the cream and bring back to a boil; taste for seasoning.

Coat the birds with a little of the sauce and serve, passing the rest of the sauce separately.

BOEUF DE LA ST JEAN
Beef stew with summer vegetables

A century or so ago they chose a sacrificial cow at Massiac in Auvergne during the fair in early June. Her horns garlanded, she grazed for weeks in the pasture of her choice. She was slaughtered on the feast of St Jean and the meat was distributed to the inhabitants of the town.

Serves 4–6

125 g	mild bacon, cut in thin slices	4 oz
1·2 kg	beef brisket, cut in 5 cm/2 in cubes	2½ lb
375 ml	dry white wine	1½ cups
375 ml	water	1½ cups
	bouquet garni	
200 g	fresh pork sausages	7 oz
	3 heads of lettuce	
	1 large onion	
250 ml	shelled peas	1 cup
	2 carrots, quartered OR	
	8 baby carrots	
	1 turnip, cut into 4–6 pieces	
	salt and pepper	
	pinch of fresh basil leaves	
	pinch of savory (optional)	
	1 stick celery, chopped	
	1 Tbsp prepared mustard	
	2 Tbsp capers, drained	
	4 gherkin pickles, sliced	
30 g	dry breadcrumbs	⅓ cup
30 g	butter	2 Tbsp

Heat the bacon in a heavy-based casserole until the fat runs, add the beef and brown it on all sides over a high fire. Add the wine, water and bouquet garni and bring to a boil. Cover and simmer over a low fire for 2 hours.

Prick the sausages, put them in a pot, cover with water and bring to a boil. Drain, halve and add to the casserole. Simmer uncovered for 30 minutes. Put the vegetables in a pot of boiling salted water; simmer 5 minutes. Drain thoroughly, halve the lettuces and cut the onion in 4–6 pieces. Add the vegetables to the meat with a little salt, pepper, basil, savory and celery. Cover and simmer 20–30 minutes or until very tender.

Set the oven at very hot (220°C/425°F). Put the bacon in a buttered shallow baking dish; top with the beef cubes. Put the sausages in the centre and the vegetables between the beef cubes. Strain the meat cooking liquid into a saucepan and boil to thicken slightly. Whisk in the mustard; taste for seasoning. Coat the meats and vegetables generously with sauce. Top with the capers and pickles, sprinkle with breadcrumbs and dot with butter. Bake 15 minutes or until brown. Serve hot from the dish.

VEAU À LA BOURBONNAISE

Roast veal with olives and mushrooms

Despite the distance from the south, olives are a popular ingredient in the Bourbonnais. Here they combine with mushrooms as a garnish for veal cooked en cocotte. If possible, wrap the veal in barding fat and tie it.

Serves 4

	2 Tbsp oil	
15 g	butter	1 Tbsp
1-kg	rolled veal shoulder	2-lb
	salt and pepper	
	1 onion, sliced	
	1 carrot, sliced	
	bouquet garni	
250 ml	broth	1 cup
	SAUCE	
75 g	butter	5 Tbsp
	1 onion, sliced	
	1 carrot, sliced	
750 ml	broth	3 cups
	pinch of thyme	
	1 bay leaf	
	salt and pepper	
30 g	flour	$\frac{1}{4}$ cup
125 ml	heavy cream or crème fraîche*	$\frac{1}{2}$ cup
	GARNISH	
300 g	mushrooms, quartered	10 oz
	salt and pepper	
80 g	black olives, pitted	$\frac{1}{2}$ cup
80 g	green olives, pitted	$\frac{1}{2}$ cup

Set the oven at moderate (175°C/350°F). Heat the oil and butter in a heavy casserole, add the veal and brown it on all sides. Sprinkle with salt and pepper. Reduce the heat, add the onion and carrot and cook slowly for 2–3 minutes or until slightly softened but not brown. Add the bouquet garni, cover the pan and cook in the oven for $1\frac{1}{4}$–$1\frac{1}{2}$ hours or until the meat is tender when pricked with a two-pronged fork. If necessary, occasionally add a little of the broth to prevent burning.

While the meat is cooking, begin the sauce: melt 1 tablespoon of the butter in a saucepan, add the onion and carrot and cook over a low fire, stirring occasionally, until soft but not brown. Add the broth, thyme, bay leaf and a pinch of salt and pepper. Bring to a boil and simmer uncovered over a low fire for 1 hour.

Meanwhile, prepare the garnish: put the mushrooms in a saucepan with a pinch of salt, pepper and 3–4 tablespoons water. Cover and cook over a high fire for 5 minutes or until tender. Drain the mushrooms, reserving the liquid. Blanch the olives* if they are very salty.

Finish the sauce: melt the remaining butter in a heavy-based saucepan, whisk in the flour and cook for 1–2 minutes or until foaming but not brown. Let cool slightly; then strain in the simmering broth and mushroom liquid, whisking. Bring to a boil, whisking constantly, and simmer for 5–10 minutes. Stir in the cream and bring back to a boil. Add the mushrooms and olives and simmer, stirring occasionally, for 15 minutes. Taste the sauce for seasoning.

When the veal is tender, transfer it to a board and discard the strings and barding fat if used. Add the remaining broth to the pan and bring to a boil, stirring to dissolve the pan juices. Strain the gravy, skim off as much fat as possible, and, if necessary, reduce until concentrated in flavour. Taste for seasoning.

Slice the veal and arrange the slices overlapping on a lightly buttered platter. Spoon a little gravy over the slices and spoon the sauce with garnish around the edge. Reheat briefly in the oven until the veal is hot and lightly glazed. Serve the remaining gravy separately.

LANGUE DE BOEUF AUX CORNICHONS
Beef tongue with gherkins

Beef tongue is regarded as a luxury in France, worth cooking with a rich meat sauce (the meat is discarded, so use cheap cuts such as neck or shin). This recipe with gherkin pickles comes from the Bourbonnais; in the sheep country of Berry the same recipe is made with sheep's tongues (they need a much shorter cooking time) and served with turnips.

Serves 6

1·5-kg	fresh beef tongue	3-lb
50 g	firm pork fat or mild bacon, cut in small lardons	2 oz
	2 Tbsp chopped parsley	
	1 tsp chopped chives	
	salt and pepper	
	pinch of ground allspice	
	3 gherkin pickles, thinly sliced	
	COOKING LIQUID AND SAUCE	
75 g	firm pork fat or mild bacon, thinly sliced	3 oz
	2 onions, each studded with 2 cloves	
	2 carrots	
125-g	piece stewing beef	$\frac{1}{4}$-lb
125-g	piece stewing veal	$\frac{1}{4}$-lb
	1 bay leaf	
	2 sprigs thyme	
1·25 L	broth, more if needed	5 cups
	salt and pepper	
30 g	butter	2 Tbsp
15 g	flour	2 Tbsp
	larding needle (optional)	

Soak the tongue in cold water for 1 hour and drain it. Blanch it: put it in a pan of cold water, bring it slowly to a boil and simmer it for 10 minutes. Drain the tongue, rinse with cold water and drain thoroughly. Peel the tongue, removing the bones and gristle from the roots and reserving them.

Roll the lardons of pork fat in a mixture of half the parsley, with the chives, salt, pepper and allspice. Use them to lard* the tongue.

Put the tongue in a heavy casserole with the reserved trimmings, the sliced pork fat, onions, carrots, piece of beef, piece of veal, bay leaf, thyme and enough broth to cover. Add salt and pepper and bring to a boil. Cover and simmer over a low fire for $3\frac{1}{2}$-4 hours or until the tongue is tender when pricked with a two-pronged fork. Transfer the tongue to a platter and keep it warm. Boil the broth until reduced to about 500 ml and skim off the excess fat.

In a heavy-based pan, melt the butter, whisk in the flour and cook over a low fire, whisking constantly; bring to a boil and simmer for 5–10 minutes or until the sauce lightly coats a spoon.

Meanwhile, carve the tongue in thin diagonal slices, starting at the tip and slanting the knife so the slices are of even size. Arrange them overlapping on a platter. Add the gherkin pickles to the sauce, taste for seasoning and spoon them over the tongue with a little of the sauce. Sprinkle with the remaining chopped parsley and serve, passing the remaining sauce separately.

CASSETTE D'AUVERGNE
Roast leg of lamb with potatoes

The juices from a leg of lamb give a delicious flavour to potatoes baked at the bottom of this casserole. The traditional accompaniments are colourful – green lentils, braised cabbage and baked red kidney beans.

Serves 8

250 g	bacon, cut in lardons	$\frac{1}{2}$ lb
2 kg	potatoes	$4\frac{1}{2}$ lb
	salt and pepper	
1 L	broth, more if needed	1 qt
2-kg	leg of lamb	$4\frac{1}{2}$-lb
	3 cloves garlic, cut in slivers	
60 g	butter	4 Tbsp

If the bacon is very salty, blanch* it. Generously butter a large shallow baking dish or casserole. Thinly slice the potatoes and mix with the lardons. Spread them in layers in the baking dish, sprinkling each layer lightly with pepper. Add enough broth just to cover the potatoes. Set the oven at very hot (230°C/450°F).

Trim off the skin and all but a thin layer of fat from the lamb. Make a few incisions in the meat and insert the garlic slivers. Spread the butter over the lamb, sprinkle with salt and pepper and set it on top of the potatoes. Sear the meat in the oven for 10–15 minutes or until browned; then lower the heat to hot (200°C/400°F) and continue roasting. Baste the lamb often while cooking and, if the pan juices start to brown too much or the potatoes to dry out, add a little broth or water. For rare meat, allow 20–24 minutes per kg/9–11 minutes per lb; for medium meat, 28–32 minutes per kg/13–15 minutes per lb. Lower the heat if the lamb or the potatoes brown too quickly. Serve the lamb from the baking dish; it may be carved either in the kitchen or at the table.

PETIT SALÉ AUX LENTILLES
Salt pork with lentils

'Petit salé', 'lightly salted', refers to the salt pork cooked with lentils in this bistro standby. The best cuts are shoulder, blade roast or spare ribs.

Serves 4

300 g	lentils	$1\frac{3}{4}$ cups
	1 onion, studded with 2 cloves	
	1 clove garlic, crushed	
	bouquet garni	
	salt and pepper	
	2 Tbsp chopped parsley	
	SALT-CURED PORK	
2 L	water	2 qt
	pinch of thyme	
	$\frac{1}{2}$ bay leaf	
	1 clove garlic, sliced	
	12 juniper berries	
	10 black peppercorns	
	1 clove	
400 g	coarse salt	$1\frac{3}{4}$ cups
25 g	saltpetre	4 tsp
50 g	sugar	$\frac{1}{4}$ cup
1-kg	piece of pork OR	2-lb
2-kg	spare ribs	$4\frac{1}{2}$-lb

At least one day before cooking, prepare the pork: bring a quarter of the water to a boil in a small pot and add the herbs, garlic and spices. Cover and simmer for 10 minutes. Meanwhile, heat the salt, saltpetre and sugar in the remaining water, stirring until dissolved. Strain the herb-flavoured boiling water into this mixture and cool completely. Put the meat in a large container (not metal) and pour the salt water over it to cover the meat completely. Cover and refrigerate for at least 12 hours or up to 2 weeks.

If the meat has been in the brine for up to 3 days, rinse it before cooking. If it has been in the brine longer, soak it in water for 1 hour.

Put the pork in a pot and add enough cold water to cover. Bring to a boil and poach for 5 minutes over a low fire. Taste the water and if it is very salty, discard it and start again with fresh water. Poach the pork for 30 minutes more.

Meanwhile, pick over the lentils, discarding any stones, and wash thoroughly. Add them to the pork with the onion, garlic and bouquet garni. Poach uncovered for $1\frac{1}{2}$ hours or until the pork is tender. Remove the pork and discard the onion and bouquet garni. If a large amount of liquid remains, drain the lentils. Taste them for seasoning and add pepper; they may already have enough salt from the cured pork. Put the lentils in a serving dish. Cut the pork in slices or the ribs in pieces and arrange them overlapping around the edge of the lentils. Sprinkle the lentils with chopped parsley and serve.

BACON AND SALT PORK

The little Auvergnat boy was asked: 'Whom do you like best, maman or papa?' 'I like bacon best,' he replied.

Before the advent of canning, bacon and salt pork were often the only meats available in winter. Curing is done either by covering the pieces of meat with dry coarse salt or with a mixture of salt, saltpetre, sugar and seasonings, or by immersing them in brine. Results vary enormously, depending on the breed of pig (there are 'baconers' and 'porkers'), on the curing method and seasonings and, in the case of bacon, on whether the side of pork is smoked after it has been salted.

Most bacon is made from the chest meat, thickly layered with fat, which runs under the belly of the pig. This is called 'lard fumé' or 'lard salé' in France, depending on whether it is smoked or salted, 'streaky bacon' in Britain (where it can be smoked or green, i.e. unsalted) and simply 'bacon' in North America (where it is always smoked). Confusingly, what the French call 'bacon' the British identify as 'back bacon' and the Americans as 'Canadian bacon'; this is generally taken from the lean meat running along the backbone.

In France lard fumé and lard salé come with the rind on; this is often used to give flavour and gelatine to broth and stews. Usually sold by the piece, lard fumé and lard salé are cut into 'lardons' (dice) for ragoûts like boeuf bourguignon and to flavour dishes like 'salade au lard', but can also be sliced to enrich

sauerkraut, or left whole and cooked in cassoulet or potée. Lard fumé and lard salé render comparatively little fat and should be cooked only until tender; if fried too long, they go tough rather than crisp. In Britain, both kinds of streaky bacon can be cooked until fairly crisp, and American bacon cooks crispest of all. No matter where it comes from, bacon that has been strongly salted or smoked may need blanching* for many recipes.

The French also salt inexpensive, meaty cuts of pork such as spare ribs, hocks and belly to make 'petit salé', which is a favourite addition to dried beans or lentils. Petit salé is easy to make at home (see opposite). It resembles British salt pork, but it is not the same as the fatty salt pork sold in the USA. This contains few or no streaks of lean meat and often comes from the 3–4 cm/$1\frac{1}{2}$ in layer of fat which runs around the outside of a pig. In France this layer is cut off to make sheets of fresh barding fat or strips for larding.

SANGLIER À L'AUVERGNATE
Braised wild boar with red wine

In this recipe the meat is braised slowly for a long time, so mature wild boar ('sanglier') can be used rather than baby boar ('marcassin'), which is usually roasted. Pork can be substituted when boar is not available. In Auvergne, the meat is served with braised chestnuts, lentils or red kidney beans, and in one recipe a glass of cognac is sprinkled with loving care over the wild boar just before serving.

Serves 6

1·5-kg	piece of wild boar – leg or loin, with bones if possible	3-lb
200-g	piece barding fat (optional)	7-oz
	2 Tbsp oil	
30 g	lard	2 Tbsp
	2 Tbsp marc or cognac	
	2 onions, sliced	
	2 carrots, sliced	
	salt and pepper	
	1 Tbsp flour	
	3 cloves garlic	
750 ml	red wine	3 cups
	bouquet garni	
	2 slices rye bread, crusts discarded	
	2 Tbsp wine vinegar	
	trussing string	

Bone the piece of boar. Wrap the meat in barding fat (if used) and tie in a neat roll with string. Set the oven at moderately low (160°C/325°F).

In a large heavy casserole, heat the oil and lard, add the boar and brown it well on all sides over a high fire. Add the marc, onions, carrots, salt and pepper and cook over a low fire, stirring the vegetables often, until soft but not browned. Stir the flour into the vegetables and continue to cook over a low fire, stirring, until lightly browned. Stir in the garlic; then pour in enough red wine nearly to cover the meat. Add the boar bones and bouquet garni. Bring to a boil, cover and cook in the oven until almost tender.

While the meat is cooking, soak the bread in the vinegar. After 2–2¼ hours, when the meat is nearly tender, squeeze the bread dry so that it forms crumbs and stir them into the liquid – the sauce should coat a spoon but should not be thick. Continue to cook in the low oven for 30 minutes or until the meat is tender. Transfer the meat to a platter, carve it in medium-thick slices and keep warm.

Skim excess fat off the sauce and strain it, pressing hard on the vegetables. Taste the sauce for seasoning, spoon a little over the meat and serve the rest separately.

POTÉE AUVERGNATE
Boiled pork with stuffed cabbage

The cabbage which is a vital ingredient in any potée is here used to wrap pork filling; these cabbage rolls are cooked separately but served with the broth as a first course.

Serves 6

500-g	piece salt bacon	1-lb
1-kg	rolled pork shoulder, preferably salt-cured	2-lb
4 L	water	4 qt
	10 black peppercorns	
	bouquet garni	
	1 onion, studded with 1 clove	
350 g	carrots, halved and cut in even lengths	¾ lb
	3 stalks celery, cut in even lengths	
	2 medium turnips, quartered	
500 g	leeks, trimmed, split and cut in even lengths	1 lb
	1 loaf rye bread, sliced	
	salt and pepper	
	CABBAGE ROLLS	
	12 outer leaves of 1 large green cabbage	
250 g	ground pork, lean and fat mixed	½ lb
	1 clove garlic, chopped	
70 g	fresh white breadcrumbs	½ cup
	1 egg, beaten to mix	
	pinch of grated nutmeg	
	salt and pepper	
	2 pieces cheesecloth	

Put the salt bacon in a large pot. If using salt-cured pork shoulder, add it to the pot as well. Pour in enough cold water to cover and bring to a boil. Poach for 5 minutes over a low fire and taste the water; if it is very salty, discard it and repeat with fresh water. Drain the meats thoroughly.

Return the bacon to the pot and add the fresh or cured pork shoulder, water, peppercorns and bouquet garni. Bring slowly to a boil, skimming often. Cut the onion in half, char it over a gas flame or directly on an electric burner, and add it to the pot; it will give colour to the broth. Partly cover the pot, leaving a small gap for evaporation, and simmer over a low fire for about 2 hours.

While the meat is simmering, prepare the cabbage rolls: blanch the cabbage leaves in a large pot of boiling water for 5 minutes. Drain the leaves, refresh them under cold running water and drain thoroughly. Mix together the minced/ground pork, garlic, breadcrumbs, egg, nutmeg and plenty of salt and pepper. Sauté a small piece of the mixture; taste for seasoning.

Put a tablespoon of the stuffing on each cabbage leaf and roll up, turning in the sides to enclose the stuffing. Pack the cabbage leaves tightly in a shallow pan so they do not unroll. After the pork has cooked for about 1 hour, spoon enough broth over the cabbage rolls to cover them. Cover with a lid and simmer for 45–60 minutes or until firm.

Tie the carrots in a piece of cheesecloth. After the pork has simmered for about 2 hours, add the carrots to the pot of soup and simmer another 20 minutes. Tie the celery, turnips and leeks in another piece of cheesecloth, add them to the pot and simmer for 15 more minutes or until all the meats and vegetables are tender.

Meanwhile, set the oven at low (150°C/300°F). Bake the bread slices in the oven until they are crisp.

Lift the meat and vegetables from the broth. Carve the pork shoulder in medium-thick slices and arrange them down the centre of a large platter. Slice the bacon and pile it at either end. Arrange the vegetables around the meat, cover the platter with foil and keep hot.

Strain the broth with the liquid from the cabbage rolls. Reheat the broth and add pepper to taste; salt may not be needed. Skim as much fat as possible from the broth. Put 2 cabbage rolls and 2 bread slices in each soup bowl, pour the broth over them and serve, passing the remaining bread separately. Serve the meat and vegetable platter as the main course.

LE POUNTI
Ham and Swiss chard flan

Half meat loaf, half vegetable soufflé, pounti comes from the mountains of Auvergne. Some recipes include a good deal of meat, while others emphasize the vegetables. Pounti can also be flavoured with whole prunes or with raisins.

Serves 6–8

150 g	bacon, chopped	5 oz
90 g	cooked ham, chopped	3 oz
	1 onion, finely chopped	
	1 clove garlic, finely chopped	
	7 Tbsp chopped parsley	
	2 large leaves Swiss chard OR	
150 g	spinach, chopped	5 oz
85 g	flour	$\frac{2}{3}$ cup
500 ml	milk	2 cups
	4 eggs	
	pepper	
	1·5 L/1$\frac{1}{2}$ qt shallow baking dish	

If the bacon is salty, blanch* it. Chop together the bacon, ham, onion, garlic, parsley and Swiss chard or spinach. Set the oven at moderate (175°C/350°F).

Sift the flour into a bowl, make a well and gradually stir in the milk. Whisk in the eggs to make a batter and add a pinch of pepper. Stir the batter into the bacon mixture. Pour into the buttered baking dish and bake for 50–60 minutes or until set. Serve it hot or at room temperature, cut in wedges like a cake.

FARCIDURE
Wholewheat pancakes with bacon

'Farcidure', literally, 'firm stuffing', is a typical peasant supper dish. It can be based on potatoes, bread dough or even crêpe batter, and flavoured with whatever meats or vegetables happen to be available. This particular version is a speciality of Limousin.

Serves 4

500 g	wholewheat bread, crusts discarded, cut in cubes	1 lb
500 ml	milk	2 cups
200 g	bacon	7 oz
	3 eggs	
	3 Tbsp chopped parsley	
	2 cloves garlic, finely chopped	
	2 Tbsp flour	
125 ml	heavy cream or crème fraîche*	½ cup
	salt and pepper	
	4 Tbsp oil (for frying)	
	20 cm/8 in frying pan	

In a bowl, soak the bread in the milk until it is soft and the milk is absorbed. Cut half the bacon in lardons and blanch* them if salty. Finely chop the remaining bacon.

Add the eggs, parsley, chopped bacon and garlic to the soaked bread and mix well. Stir in the flour, followed by the cream and season with a little salt and pepper.

Heat a tablespoon of the oil in the frying pan, add a few of the lardons and cover them with enough batter to cover the base of the pan, as if making a thick pancake. Fry until brown, turn over and brown the other side. Continue frying the remaining mixture, adding oil as necessary. Serve hot.

CÈPES À LA LIMOUSINE
Cèpes with cream

The volcanic soil of the Massif Central is excellent for mushrooms. In this recipe any kind of wild mushroom, fresh or dried, can be used and it is also a good way to enliven cultivated mushrooms for serving on toast as a first course, or as an accompaniment to meat or chicken.

Serves 4–6

500 g	fresh cèpes OR	1 lb
50 g	dried cèpes	2 oz
	2 Tbsp oil	
30 g	butter	2 Tbsp
	salt and pepper	
	1 onion, finely chopped	
	1 clove garlic or 1 shallot, finely chopped	
250 ml	heavy cream or crème fraîche*	1 cup
	1 Tbsp chopped parsley (optional)	

Prepare the fresh or dried cèpes*. Heat the oil and butter in a frying pan. Add the cèpes with salt and pepper and sauté over a high fire for 2–3 minutes. Add the onion and garlic and cook over a low fire, stirring occasionally, for 15–20 minutes or until the cèpes are tender. Stir in the cream, bring to a boil and simmer for 2–3 minutes; taste for seasoning.

Spoon into a serving dish, sprinkle with chopped parsley and serve hot.

MORILLES À LA CRÈME

Replace the cèpes with fresh or dried **morels**. Prepare the mushrooms*; rinse them thoroughly to get rid of any sand and cut off the ends of the stalks. Put the morels in a heavy pot, cover and cook for 2–3 minutes over a medium fire. Drain and discard the liquid. Continue cooking as if using cèpes (above).

ALIGOT

Potato and cheese purée

In contrast to cheese fondue, which is cooked only until the cheese melts, the cheese and potato mixture for aligot should be beaten over the heat so the cheese cooks to form long ribbons which are cut ('aligoter' in the local dialect) for serving. Dry gruyère or sharp cheddar cheese can be used instead of cantal.

Serves 4

1 kg	potatoes	2 lb
	salt	
60 g	butter	4 Tbsp
250 ml	heavy cream or crème fraîche*	1 cup
350 g	grated cantal cheese	3½ cups
	pepper	

Peel the potatoes and cut each in 2 or 3 even chunks. Put them in a pot, cover with cold water and add a pinch of salt. Bring to a boil and simmer for 15–20 minutes or until the potatoes are tender when pierced with a knife or skewer; they should be quite soft.

Drain the potatoes thoroughly and, while still hot, push them through a sieve or purée in a hand food mill. Put the purée in a heavy saucepan, add the butter and beat the potatoes with a wooden spoon over a low fire until light and fluffy. Without removing the mixture from the low fire beat in the cream, then the cheese and continue beating constantly with a wooden spoon until the aligot forms long ribbons when it falls from the spoon. Add pepper, taste for seasoning and serve very hot.

LA TRUFFADE

Cheese and potato cake

Truffade is often served with small poached sausages which resemble baby Lyon sausages.

Serves 4

150 g	bacon, cut in lardons	5 oz
1 kg	potatoes	2 lb
30 g	lard or oil	2 Tbsp
	salt and pepper	
250 g	cantal or gruyère cheese, diced or cut in thin strips	8 oz
	25 cm/10 in non-stick frying pan	

If the bacon is very salty, blanch* it. Thinly slice the potatoes. Heat the bacon in the frying pan until the fat runs but do not brown it. Remove it, add the lard to the frying pan and heat it. Add the potatoes, sprinkle them lightly with salt and pepper, cover and cook over a low fire for 5 minutes. Return the bacon to the pan and continue to cook uncovered over a low fire, tossing or stirring often, for 25 minutes or until tender. Don't worry if some of the potatoes are crushed; this will help hold the mixture in a cake. Stir in the cheese and taste for seasoning.

Turn the fire to high and let the mixture cook without stirring, to brown the bottom. Press on it occasionally to hold it together. When the potato cake is brown, run a knife around the edge of the pan and turn the cake out on to a platter. Serve hot.

MINERAL WATER

The centre of France is notable for producing two of life's staples – bread and water. The French drink more bottled water than anyone else, and a third of it comes from the Massif Central, whose annual output is 300 million litres. The waters of Badoit (slightly fizzy) and Volvic (still, with a low mineral content) are distributed throughout France. Half a dozen others, such as Royat and Mizérieux, enjoy local renown, and are credited with miraculous powers over the digestion. Although Perrier, the sparkling water from the hills north of Nîmes, has a 2000-year history, it has only recently made a hit in the United States and Britain, where it is much drunk as an aperitif with ice and lemon.

The most famous water of all is that of Vichy, a still-fashionable spa and the site of half a dozen springs, each with different mineral properties and each emerging from the ground at a different temperature. One Vichy source reaches 66°C and the little-known water of Chaudes Aigues, heated by volcanic pressure within the Auvergne mountains, almost simmers at 82°C. Part of the cure at most resorts is to drink quantities of different waters at the appropriate temperature; 'curistes' carry graded glasses in little raffia bags, to measure their daily ration. 'The water has been not inappropriately compared to heated soda-water,' was the laconic comment from Murray's *Guide* a century ago, 'the principal ingredient being carbonate of soda and carbonic acid in excess.' 'A good imitation of purgatory,' shuddered Madame de Sévigné.

By no means all of France's bottled water comes from the Massif Central. Évian enjoys a prime tourist site on Lake Geneva, while Vittel in the Vosges, like many spas, specializes in treatments consisting of bubbling baths. Most potent of all is Contrexéville, its pronounced taste betraying the presence of minerals said to be good for the liver and kidneys and to combat gout, high cholesterol, obesity and rheumatism. Fact or fiction, extravagant claims used to be made on behalf of bottled waters, their labels covered with recommendations from doctors and gold medals granted at public exhibitions. Now advertising is strictly controlled by the French government, as is the purity of the waters themselves which are bottled as they bubble from the ground.

Why do the French shun tap water? Who knows? Contamination is a thing of the past. Town supplies taste as good as the contents of any bottle; the flavour of Paris water is tested daily. Yet French housewives continue to lug home crates of mineral water. Life starts with Évian, a neutral water used for both batteries and babies; for many citizens, it draws to a close with state-supported visits to spas whose waters do battle with the infirmities of old age.

CAROTTES À LA VICHY
Glazed carrots

Carottes à la Vichy are supposedly cooked in mineral water from Vichy. If small, the carrots are usually left whole and trimmed to leave a stub of green leaves for colour; if large, they may be sliced or cut in sticks.

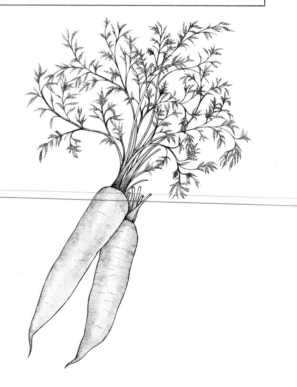

Serves 4		
500 g	carrots, cut in even pieces	1 lb
	salt	
30 g	butter	2 Tbsp
	2 tsp sugar	

Put the carrots in a large pot of cold water, bring to a boil and simmer for 2–3 minutes. Drain and rinse under cold running water.

Return the carrots to the pot with enough water to cover them. Add a pinch of salt and cook over a medium fire for 10–15 minutes or until nearly all the water has evaporated. Add the butter and sugar and continue to cook, tossing often, until the carrots are coated with a shiny glaze. Taste for seasoning and serve.

CLAFOUTIS LIMOUSIN
Cherry flan

In the Limousin, tiny fresh black cherries are used for this pudding, but canned tart cherries can be substituted if they are well drained. Clafoutis is also good, if less traditional, made with halved apricots or plums in summer, or with prunes in winter.

Serves 6

500 g	tart cherries	1 lb
25 g	flour	3 Tbsp
	pinch of salt	
50 g	sugar	$\frac{1}{4}$ cup
	4 eggs	
500 ml	milk	2 cups
	2 egg yolks	
	4 Tbsp cognac OR 3 Tbsp kirsch	
	confectioners' sugar (for sprinkling)	
	shallow baking dish (2 L/2 qt capacity)	

Set the oven at moderately hot (190°C/375°F). Spread the cherries in the buttered baking dish.

Sift the flour into a bowl with the salt, and stir in the sugar. Gradually beat in the eggs, two at a time, alternating with the milk, and continue beating until just mixed. Beat in the yolks. Strain the batter over the cherries, and spoon the cognac on top. Bake for 45 minutes or until the clafoutis is puffed and brown. Let cool until warm: it will sink slightly. Sprinkle with the sugar and serve warm.

PIQUENCHAGNE or LE POIRAT
Walnut pear pie

Pear pie is a speciality of both the Bourbonnais, where it is called 'piquenchagne', and of Berry where the same pie becomes 'le poirat'. However, le poirat is always made with pears, whereas piquenchagne may contain quinces or apples in a yeast dough. The pastry in this particular recipe is based on walnuts, but ground toasted hazelnuts or ground almonds can be used instead.

Serves 8

750 g	pears	1$\frac{1}{2}$ lb
	1 Tbsp sugar	
125 ml	heavy cream, lightly whipped	$\frac{1}{2}$ cup
	SWEET WALNUT PIE PASTRY	
225 g	flour	1$\frac{3}{4}$ cups
60 g	walnuts, finely ground	$\frac{1}{2}$ cup
	1 tsp cinnamon	
	1 egg	
135 g	sugar	$\frac{2}{3}$ cup
150 g	butter	5 oz
	23–25 cm/9–10 in pie pan; 6 cm/2$\frac{1}{2}$ in cutter	

Make the sweet walnut pie pastry as for sweet pie pastry*, working the ground walnuts and cinnamon in with the flour. Chill for 30 minutes or until firm.

Roll out two-thirds of the dough and line the pan* with it. Peel, core and quarter the pears and arrange them in a cartwheel pattern in the pan. Cover the centre with slices of the remaining pears. Roll out the remaining dough to a round the same diameter as the top of the pan. Using the cutter, cut a circle out of the centre of the round, leaving a ring. Brush the edge of the bottom pastry layer lightly with water. Lay the ring on the pears and press the edges firmly on to the bottom layer of dough. Brush the ring with water and sprinkle with the sugar. Chill for 10–15 minutes so the pastry is firm. Set the oven at moderately hot (190°C/375°F).

Bake for 30–40 minutes or until the pastry is well browned and the pears are tender. Unmould the pie and serve warm. Just before serving, pour the whipped cream into the centre.

TARTE AU FROMAGE BLANC
Cream cheese tart

Tarte au fromage blanc is as popular in Alsace as it is in Auvergne.

Serves 6–8

PIE PASTRY		
200 g	flour	1½ cups
95 g	butter	6 Tbsp
	1 egg yolk	
	½ tsp salt	
	4–5 Tbsp water	
CHEESE FILLING		
425 g	cream cheese	14 oz
	2 Tbsp heavy cream	
135 g	sugar	⅔ cup
	2 eggs	
	1 egg yolk	
	2 Tbsp flour	
	grated rind of 1½ lemons	
	1 tsp vanilla extract	
	30 cm/12 in pie or tart pan	

Make the pie pastry* and chill for 30 minutes or until firm. Line the pie pan* with the pastry and chill for 30 minutes. Set the oven at very hot (220°C/425°F) and put a baking sheet into the oven to heat. Blind bake* the pastry shell on the hot baking sheet. Let the pie shell cool, leaving the baking sheet in the oven.

Make the filling: beat the cream cheese with the cream. Beat the sugar into the cheese mixture, a little at a time. Beat in the eggs, one at a time, and then the yolk. Stir in the flour, lemon rind and vanilla. Set the pie shell in the pan on the hot baking sheet. Pour the filling into the shell and bake for 10 minutes. Turn down the heat to moderately low (160°C/325°F) and continue baking for 20–25 minutes or until the filling is firm and lightly browned on top. Turn off the oven, leave the door slightly open and let the pie cool in the oven; this helps to prevent it sinking. Serve cold.

CORNETS DE MURAT
Rolled wafer biscuits

These 'cornets' from the town of Murat, deep in Auvergne, are crisp rolled biscuits quite unlike the usual cream horns made of puff pastry. They are said to imitate the shape of the local alpenhorn. Pastry shops sell the cornets empty, to be filled at home with chantilly cream.

Makes 30 cornets

80 g	butter	5 Tbsp
135 g	confectioners' sugar	1 cup
	3 egg whites	
65 g	flour	½ cup
	1 tsp heavy cream	
	1 Tbsp rum OR	
	1 tsp orange flower water	
CHANTILLY CREAM		
500 ml	heavy cream	2 cups
25 g	sugar	2 Tbsp
	1 tsp vanilla extract	
pastry bag with small star tip; several pastry tips with small openings		

Set the oven at hot (200°C/400°F). Butter 2 or 3 baking sheets.

Cream the butter and sugar. Gradually beat in half of the egg whites, beating very well after each addition. Add 1 heaped teaspoon of the flour and mix thoroughly. Gradually beat in the remaining egg whites. Stir in the remaining flour, followed by the cream and rum; mix well.

Drop teaspoons of the mixture on to a baking sheet, spacing them well apart, and tap the baking sheet sharply on the table to flatten the mounds. Refrigerate the rest of the mixture until ready to use it. Bake the cornets in the heated oven for 4–5 minutes or until brown around the edges. Use a metal spatula to loosen them from the baking sheet, but leave them on it to keep warm. Roll each cornet slightly and press it firmly inside a pastry tip to form a pointed cone shape with one end completely closed. Let cool slightly in the pastry tip until set; then remove from the tip and transfer to a rack to cool. Shape the cornets as quickly as possible; once they cool, they become brittle and are impossible to roll. If they do become brittle, return them to the oven for 1 minute to soften. Follow this procedure with the rest of the mixture, working with only one baking sheet of cornets at a time.

Make the chantilly cream: in a chilled bowl, beat the cream until it starts to thicken. Add the sugar and vanilla and continue beating until the cream is stiff enough to stick to the whisk. Just before serving, use the star tip to pipe the cream into the cornets. Serve at once.

BOURRIOLS
Buckwheat yeast pancakes

Bourriols are quite thick, more like a Scotch drop scone or an American breakfast pancake than the lacy galettes of Brittany, which are also made with buckwheat flour. Spread with butter, bourriols take the place of bread, and they may be served with sugar, honey or jam as a dessert. The batter is made the day before baking and rises enormously despite the tiny quantity of yeast used in it. Indeed, bourriols are surprisingly light in spite of their name: 'bourrer' means to stuff.

Makes 10 large bourriols, to serve 5

125 g	potatoes, unpeeled	$\frac{1}{4}$ lb
	salt	
375 ml	milk, more if needed	$1\frac{1}{2}$ cups
250 ml	water	1 cup
4 g	fresh yeast OR	$\frac{1}{4}$ cake
	$\frac{1}{4}$ pkg dry yeast	
95 g	all-purpose flour	$\frac{3}{4}$ cup
95 g	buckwheat flour	$\frac{3}{4}$ cup
	lard or butter (for frying)	
	25 cm/10 in frying pan	

Cook the potatoes in salted water for 20–25 minutes or until tender. Drain, peel and crush them, using a potato masher or fork.

Put the potatoes in a very large bowl and stir in the milk and water. Crumble the yeast over the mixture and let stand for 5 minutes or until dissolved. Stir in both types of flour and add a pinch of salt. Beat the batter thoroughly until smooth. It should resemble crêpe batter; add a little more milk if it is too thick. Cover and leave to rise overnight in the refrigerator. It will increase greatly in volume.

The next day, beat the dough briefly to knock out the air. Stir in a little more milk, if necessary, to give the batter the consistency of thick cream.

Heat the frying pan and brush it with lard. Cook the pancakes like crêpes (see recipe), browning them on both sides. Serve them hot.

CROQUANTS
Hazelnut biscuit cakes

Many kinds of 'croquants', crusty cakes designed for dipping in wine, are made in France. Most, like these, are flavoured with nuts and baked in a long bar which is sold by weight in pastry shops for cutting in slices.

Makes 6 croquants

130 g	hazelnuts	1 cup
200 g	flour	$1\frac{1}{2}$ cups
	$\frac{1}{2}$ tsp baking powder	
	$\frac{1}{2}$ tsp salt	
65g	sugar	$\frac{1}{3}$ cup
	1 egg yolk	
150 g	butter	5 oz
	1 egg, beaten with $\frac{1}{2}$ tsp salt	
	(for glaze)	

Set the oven at hot (200°C/400°F). Toast the hazelnuts in the oven for 8–10 minutes or until lightly browned. Transfer them immediately to a sieve or a cloth and rub off their skins while hot. Coarsely chop the nuts.

Sift the flour and baking powder on to a work surface and make a large well in the centre. Add the salt, sugar and egg yolk to the well and mix them with your fingers until the sugar dissolves. Pound the butter to soften it slightly and add it to the well. Quickly work it with the other ingredients in the well until partly mixed. Gradually draw in the flour, pulling the dough into large crumbs, and mix gently without kneading. If the dough is worked too much, the croquants will be tough. Mix in the hazelnuts and press the dough into a ball. Wrap the dough and chill for 30 minutes or until firm. Lower the oven temperature to moderately hot (190°C/375°F).

On a baking sheet, pat out the dough 2 cm/$\frac{3}{4}$ in thick to a rectangle about 7·5 cm/3 in by 33 cm/13 in.

Brush the dough with the egg glaze and score a simple design on top. Bake for 15 minutes or until lightly browned and firm. Transfer to a rack to cool; then cut into slices 5 cm/2 in wide.

PAIN AUX NOIX
Walnut bread

The basic dough for this 'pain aux noix' can be varied to make different types of bread. For 'pain aux raisins', substitute raisins for the nuts, but use a slightly smaller quantity. When neither nuts nor raisins are included, the recipe becomes pain de campagne'; this can be baked in the same way, as cakes, or shaped into oval loaves and baked on a buttered baking sheet.

Makes 2 loaves

400 g	wholewheat flour	$3\frac{3}{4}$ cups
130 g	all-purpose flour	1 cup
500 ml	lukewarm water	2 cups
	1 Tbsp honey	
15 g	fresh yeast OR	1 cake
	1 pkg dry yeast	
12 g	salt	$2\frac{1}{2}$ tsp
150 g	walnut halves, broken in half	$1\frac{1}{4}$ cups
	1 egg, beaten with $\frac{1}{2}$ tsp salt (for glaze)	
	two 18 cm/7 in round cake pans	

Put both types of flour in a bowl, make a well in the centre and pour in a quarter of the water. Add the honey; then crumble the yeast over the ingredients in the well and stir to dissolve. Add the remaining water and the salt and stir gently, gradually drawing in the flour to make a smooth dough. Add more flour if necessary to make a dough that is soft and slightly sticky. Turn the dough out on to a floured board and knead it for 5–10 minutes or until smooth and elastic, adding more flour if it sticks to the board. Put the dough in a lightly oiled bowl, turn it over so the top is oiled and cover with a damp cloth. Leave to rise in a warm place for $1–1\frac{1}{2}$ hours or until doubled in bulk. Butter the pans.

Knead the risen dough lightly to knock out the air, then knead in the walnuts. Shape the dough into 2 round loaves on a floured board. Set them in the pans, cover with a damp cloth and leave to rise again in a warm place for 30 minutes or until the dough has doubled in size. Meanwhile set the oven at very hot (220°C/425°F).

Before baking, slash the top of each loaf 3 or 4 times with a knife and brush with egg glaze. Bake for 15 minutes or until the loaves begin to brown. Lower the heat to moderately hot (190°C/375°F) and continue baking for another 30–40 minutes, or until the loaves sound hollow when tapped on the bottom. Turn out on to a rack to cool.

BREAD

In the French diet, bread is indispensable; it appears on the table at every meal. A common snack after school is a stick of bread stuffed with a bar of chocolate. Breakfast often consists of toasted crusts left from the night before; expensive croissants are kept for special occasions.

However, the Frenchman's hearty consumption of bread is not just habit; many French dishes like pâtés and terrines, rich sauces and stews are specifically designed to be served with bread. The traditional 'souper' (supper) implies the taking of bread, since by definition a 'soupe' must contain croûtons or toast. Without them, soupe changes its name to 'potage'. And in France to clean one's plate with a hunk of bread is no solecism, as in Anglo-Saxon countries.

Most French villages have a resident 'boulanger' who produces the straight and narrow 'baguette' – the 65 cm/25 in loaf which means 'French bread' to every foreigner – twice and sometimes thrice daily. Delicious though it is, French bread, made only with soft wheat flour, water, salt and yeast, has the drawback of becoming almost inedibly stale within a day. The life of the country baker is not easy: most take off only one day a week (never Sunday) and many make a daily round, delivering bread to the door and impaling it on a nail or dropping it into a special canvas sack.

France has been self-sufficient in cereals

for a thousand years. There have been hard times; crop failures preceded the Revolution of 1789 and many people in the mobs who attacked Versailles were starving. 'Let them eat brioche,' cried Marie-Antoinette, possibly unaware that brioche, too, is based on wheat flour. In general, however, wheat breads have been universal except in the most backward areas like Brittany, the Pyrenees and Auvergne, where peasants had to resort to buckwheat or rye flour. As Thomas Jefferson wrote when travelling in France in 1787, 'Their bread is half wheat, half rye, made once in three or four weeks to prevent too great a consumption.'

In those days selling bread short-weight or adding impurities like sand was a heinous, but not uncommon, offence: a corrupt baker would be dragged in shame through the streets with the offending loaf hung around his neck. In addition there was always a danger of ergot-induced hallucinations (known as St Anthony's Fire) resulting from baking with diseased flour. St Anthony's Fire is not necessarily a thing of the past; it was almost certainly at the root of terrifying occurrences at Pont St Esprit, near Avignon, in the summer of 1951 when there were dramatic outbreaks of animal and human madness in which half a dozen people died and scores suffered severe nervous disorders.

Bread should be baked until the crust is crisp and the crumb chewy, with plenty of body. Leaven, the starter used by bakers and made from a previous batch of bread, gives a more nutty loaf than fresh yeast. Bread dough should be allowed to rise at a slow but steady pace so as to develop flavour. Because it takes longer to rise, a larger loaf tastes better than a small one, and a round loaf better than a long one.

In the old days, the shaped dough was left to rise in special loaf-shaped wicker baskets lined with canvas. Knowing when to start and finish rising the dough in hot, cold, dry or humid conditions required considerable skill. At the strategic moment, the risen dough was tipped upside-down onto long-handled peels (from the French 'pelle', meaning spade). It was then put to bake in an oven heated by burning faggots of wood which were raked out once the oven was glowing hot. 'Wood-fired' ovens are now heated from below, the flues carrying smoke from the wood to flavour the bread. The peel remains standard equipment, but in most bakeries modern technology is now substituted for the five senses: 2,000 baguettes an hour is the rule in large establishments and the result, needless to say, is depressingly mediocre.

Given the declining quality of the baguette, more rustic breads are making a comeback. 'Pain de campagne', together with wholewheat 'pain complet', can be found almost anywhere. 'Pain de seigle' (rye bread), a lighter version of the black bread of Eastern and Central Europe, is popular in Alsace and Brittany, while Auvergnat and Bourbonnais bakers experiment with cheese, herb and even onion breads. The 'pain flamand' of the north is a semi-white loaf, marked with a characteristic deep cross. Equally popular there are the local round 'pistolet' rolls, golden with malt extract, their tops slashed with a brisk karate chop of the hand before baking.

Richer and with a whiter dough are the various breads known by their regional names such as 'gâche' or 'faluche' from Normandy and Brittany, and 'fouace' from the south. Some are savoury and baked flat, ready-made for sandwiches, while others are sweetened with candied peel or rock sugar. The 'pogne' of the Rhône valley is a larger loaf, so rich as to be almost a brioche. By contrast, mountain breads are often baked in 'couronne' circles, rugged and slightly charred, with a central hole which fits nicely round a bicycle handlebar.

To imitate the baker's baguette at home requires almost superhuman effort and a good deal of practice. The home cook in France may run up the occasional batch of brioche, or perhaps a kugelhopf or some babas, but the making of the daily bread is left, with gratitude, to the boulangerie down the road.

CHEESES

None of the cheeses of central France would make the top ten famous names. Yet the volume and variety produced there is impressive: hard cantal, resembling mature English cheddar; the blues 'fourme-d'Ambert' and 'bleu-d'Auvergne'; the creamy 'St-Nectaire'; not to mention a clutch of goat cheeses. Quality, too, is high, for with a long tradition of cheese-making behind them, local producers know what a good cheese should taste like, even if each cheese no longer receives individual attention as 'fromage fermier'.

The labour which used to go into a single massive cantal cheese was considerable, and was echoed on a smaller scale with fourme-d'Ambert and St-Nectaire, the only local cheeses still made regularly on the farm. A single wheel of cantal, which weighs up to 45 kg/100 lb, required a day's milk from 30 cows and was made in much the same way as any other hard cheese. After mixing with rennet in a deep bucket, the milk formed curds, which were drained and left for three days to settle. The curd was then salted and packed into wooden moulds, a procedure called 'fourmage', hence the name 'fromage'. To ensure close texture, sitting on the fresh cantal for an hour was suggested, before the cheese was transferred to the dairy and left to mature from three to six months.

Now cantal is made in cooperative dairies, but cheese authority Pierre Androuet still calls it 'a very good buy'. Like all mountain cheeses, the best cantal is made when the cows are out to grass in the summer; allowing time for aging, it is thus at its peak when bought in the late autumn and early winter months. Aged cantal is an excellent, nutty table cheese and, having a fat content similar to gruyère, it can be grated for cooking. Immature cantal, sold as 'tomme', is used in dishes like aligot and truffade, where it adds a creamy texture without too strong a taste.

St-Nectaire, made in the Mont Dore mountains to the northeast of Cantal, is an ancient cheese which was known to the Romans. Made in a 20 cm/8 in disc, it is a fairly soft cheese that is matured by aging on mats of rye straw. The blue fourme-d'Ambert is a tall narrow cylinder about 15 cm/6 in across. Always sliced in horizontal rounds for serving, fourme-d'Ambert has a pronounced flavour and a creamy texture which easily becomes dry. Bleu-d'Auvergne, made with pasteurized cow's milk, is reliable but it does not approach the fineness of its sheep's milk

counterpart, roquefort, from farther south, in Languedoc.

The most famous goat cheese in France, crottin de Chavignol, comes from Sancerre, sufficiently upstream on the river Loire (which rises in the heart of the Massif Central) to be considered a cheese of the Centre. The fragrant dry white wine of Sancerre makes an unexpectedly good marriage with crottin, whose graphic name adds to its renown: 'crottin' means dung, a realistic if coarse description of the appearance of these little cheeses when they darken with age to hard dry balls.

Other goat cheeses with the less picturesque name of 'chevrotins' are made on farms in Berry and the neighbouring Bourbonnais. To distinguish them from one another they are often named after the nearest town, such as 'chevrotin de Moulins', 'chevrotin de Souvigny' and 'chevrotin de Valençay'. The last was originally shaped in a distinctive Egyptian pyramid. The story goes that Talleyrand, who had been given the splendid Château de Valençay by Napoleon, offered his patron some of the local cheese. The pyramid reminded the Emperor all too vividly of his disastrous campaign on the Nile, so Talleyrand, a diplomat in all things, slashed off the top of the Valençay cheese; it retains the truncated shape to this day.

OTHER SPECIALITIES OF THE REGION
TRADITIONAL DISHES

Soupe aux choux et au fromage de Cantal
Cabbage, potato and bacon soup with layers of rye bread slices and strips of cantal cheese

Potage aux marrons du Limousin
Cream of chestnut and vegetable soup

Oulade
Bacon, vegetable and dried bean soup

Oeufs pochés à l'auvergnate
Poached eggs with cabbage and sliced sausage

Oeufs à la cantalienne
Fluffy baked eggs with cheese

Écrevisses à la menthe de Haute Auvergne
Crayfish with mint

Pâté de truites d'Auvergne
Trout pâté

Truites aux épinards limousine
Trout baked with spinach, garlic and parsley

Carpe farcie d'Auvergne
Baked carp with a bread, mushroom and garlic stuffing

Écrevisses à la limousine
Crayfish in a creamy tomato and tarragon sauce

Poitrine de veau farci à la limousine
Braised breast of veal with chestnut stuffing, cabbage and lardons

Anguilles en gelée
Eels in aspic

Poulet au fromage gannatoise
Roast chicken in cheese sauce

Poulet en barbouille du Berry
Chicken with bacon in red wine and blood sauce

Perdrix en estouffade
Partridge stew

Oyonnade du Bourbonnais
Goose in red wine and blood sauce with bacon and baby onions

Mouton en salmis
Mutton stew with red wine and potatoes

Jambon clermontoise
Roast ham with chestnuts

Côtes de porc à l'auvergnate
Pork chops with cabbage, cream and cheese

Pommes de terre au lard à l'auvergnate
Potatoes baked with lardons and garlic

CHARCUTERIE

Gâteaux de foie de cochon
Patties of pork liver with mushrooms

Pâté de pâques berrichonne
Easter pork pâté with hard-boiled eggs

Pâté du Limousin
Pork pie baked in brioche

Galantine de cochon de lait
Galantine of sucking pig

Jambon cru d'Auvergne
Auvergne raw ham

Tourte auvergnate
Pork, veal, ham and onion pie baked in lard pie pastry

PÂTISSERIE AND CONFISERIE

Gâteau de citrouille
Puréed pumpkin cake

Gargouillau
Pears baked in batter

Pompe aux pommes
Apple pie or a large apple turnover

Tarte aux pruneaux ou gouerre au cirage
Latticed prune pie

Gâteau de noix et de marrons
Walnut and chestnut cake

Flaugnard limousine
Baked custard flan

Mias bourbonnais
Cherry and custard tart

Pralines d'Aigueperse
Praline candies

Champagne and the North

Most travellers setting foot in the north of France speed south at once, their first stop Paris or the vineyards of Champagne. What a pity! They miss all sorts of unexpected pleasures, like a steaming bowl of Boulogne mussels or dish of baby vegetables from the market gardens of Amiens. They fly past the wooded hills of the Ardennes, home of brook trout, wild mushrooms and a few highly prized wild boar. They pass up Laon cathedral, where horned oxen usurp the place of saints on the façade, a tribute to the worth of cattle in medieval economies.

My own particular favourite is Arras, where I had the good luck to encounter the Saturday market held in that astonishing square, custom built by the Flemish 500 years ago for exactly the same purpose of trade. A glance at the jostling crowd bore witness to one local favourite – plump, crisp waffles, sold at many a roadside stand in the region. Fresh and topped with cream, plain and dry, or coated with royal icing, they are traditional at festivals like Mardi Gras. At the vegetable stalls as it was winter at the time, chicory was number one: fat white heads of the top quality, spindly second graders, and the rejects with curly green tops. The cultivation of chicory is almost exclusively Flemish, hence its North American name of Belgian endive.

Closer inspection of the merchandise disclosed the second great northern speciality – roots. Root vegetables dominate northern cooking, in stews like 'hochepot', a generous pot-au-feu flavoured with juniper berries, or 'carbonnade', a beef stew flavoured for sweetness with beer, mustard and onions. To the east of Paris, the little town of Crécy-en-Brie has given its name to carrot soup, while leeks have become a regional trademark, appearing in soups, gratins and the well-known 'flamiche'. This is a kind of quiche, often made with yeast dough rather than shortcrust pastry, and flavoured with onion, leek or pumpkin. Best of all, perhaps, is cheese flamiche, in which the malodorous local 'maroilles' cheese is tamed to a pleasant tang.

The north is also cabbage country, as soldiers who train on the lower lying areas of Champagne, the 'Champagne humide', know all too well: for many years the local cabbages have been a staple in their diet. In imaginative hands, however, cabbage can take on many guises. It can be stuffed, boiled for soup, braised (red cabbage goes with red wine, and white or green cabbage with white) or it may be blanched for salad. At a more elevated level, it comes as a surprise that the wine that has made the province of Champagne a household word scarcely features in the cooking. Cost has little to do with it: once heated, champagne loses the bubbles fermented with so much effort and reverts, in effect, to the original still wine base from which it was made – dry but undistinguished. Classical dishes cooked 'au champagne' benefit not a whit from all those sparkling bubbles.

The North's finest baby vegetables are grown in 'hortillonnages', picturesque market gardens that are crisscrossed by canals, notably at Amiens, the capital of Picardy, which Louis XIII called his 'little Venice'. Each small plot is hand-tilled. The punt is the only sensible means of locomotion, as I discovered one day the hard way. Attracted by willow-shaded gardens stretching into the distance, my husband and I plunged intrepidly in our station wagon in the wake of a Citroën 'deux chevaux'. The road degenerated into a track, then into a path with water crumbling the banks so we had a few centimetres' clearance on each side. The deux chevaux had vanished. Impossible to turn; unthinkable to reverse. After thankfully climbing a 1 in 4 cobbled exit to the street, we appreciated at least one of the reasons why baby vegetables are so expensive.

Vegetables are all well and good, but to the northern way of thinking, meat, and plenty of it, is a must, and a liking for lamb dates back to the Middle Ages. (The Flemish trade in wool made Arras a synonym for fine wall tapestries.) The pork andouillettes of Troyes in Champagne stand second to none and pig's feet cooked for 48 hours until the bones are edible, in the style of Ste Menehould, were enjoyed at the court of Louis XV and are still a speciality of this market town. Another speciality, particularly around Amiens, is pâtés, wrapped in a pastry crust and served hot or cold. The finest are based on duck or game, be it hare or partridge, which thrive in the flat terrain, or just the humble rabbit.

There is no avoiding the fact that vast areas of northern France, stretching down to the southern border of Champagne, are monotonously flat, though the observation of Arthur Young in 1787 that 'Picardy is uninteresting. Champagne in general, where I saw it, ugly,' seems peremptory. The unbroken terrain of northern France has for a thousand years and more been an open invitation to battle, its map as densely packed with famous sites of war — Agincourt, Malplaquet, the Marne and Somme — as it is with modern industrial cities. In agricultural terms, the spreading fields of potatoes, grain and sugar beet mean wealth. Paul Verlaine, whose mother came from Arras, described his holidays which he used to spend 'among vast fields of sugar beet and colza, relieved only by clumps of trees and ponds stretching towards the flat horizon with the occasional glow of a factory chimney.'

Flour milling and sugar refining are the natural complement to such large-scale cultivation, so it is not surprising that northern pastries are good. The Flemish 'tarte au sucre' could hardly be simpler — bread dough topped with brown sugar and the local version of the universal French 'flan' (egg custard) is baked in bread dough with a lattice finish. Both here and in Champagne, I noticed the popularity of 'pain d'épices', the honey-flavoured bread with a mixture of spices. For the feasts of St Rémi and St Nicolas it is baked, like gingerbread men, in carved wooden moulds handed down from generation to generation.

It was in a café at Dunkerque, contemplating the pleasant prospect of lunch to come, that I was served a crisp ginger wafer with my coffee, a Flemish custom that is particularly appealing to one brought up on a daily ginger biscuit with morning tea. And lunch more than lived up to expectations: the menu offered mussels in cream and eel 'au vert' (in a green herb sauce), so typical of Flanders, but I settled for herring marinated in white wine and 'waterzooi', the stew that can be based on fish or chicken served in a sauce of root vegetables enriched with cream.

Much of the local catch of herring is handled at Boulogne, which lands a third of France's fish. For salting, the herrings are filleted, then layered in salt for eight to ten days so a brine is formed. They can also be smoked, a tricky process demanding the expertise of a 'maître saureur' (master curer). The best 'harengs saurs' are very lightly cured, wonderful with a vinaigrette dressing and the hot potato salad served also in Alsace and Lyon with hot sausage. The exact mixture of oak and beech used for smoking is reputed to be a Boulogne secret, passed from father to son, while in Dunkerque just along the coast walnut is

preferred, producing a smoked herring called a 'craquelot'. In the herring season there is always a little group on the quay awaiting the arrival of the little 'canots', rowboats with their cargo of baby herring, spanking fresh for deep frying, baking in wine, or grilling with mustard sauce.

The Boulonnais, the region encircling Boulogne, is unexpectedly fertile for it is an exception to the prevailing northern rule of thin soil. In much of the north, the natural riches of Normandy or Burgundy are missing, and good husbandry is a requirement for success. It is no coincidence that Artois is the home of the Artesian well; the first one in Europe was sunk there in 1126. The prosperity that made northern France a crossroads of trade in the Middle Ages was always based on struggle and the Boulonnais is the former breeding ground of the massive Flemish horses that proved such doughty chargers in the days of mailed combat. One legacy of this hard-won security and prosperity is the bevy of Gothic churches scattered across its plains; another is the solid worth of the cooking, a throwback to the days of corpulent burghers and obedient, hardworking citizenry.

FLAMICHE AUX POIREAUX
Leek tart

There are many versions of 'flamiche', which means gâteau in Flemish. For 'flamiche aux oignons', replace the leeks with sliced onions.

Serves 6

	PIE PASTRY	
260 g	flour	2 cups
125 g	butter	$\frac{1}{4}$ lb
	2 egg yolks	
5 g	salt	1 tsp
	5–6 Tbsp cold water	
	1 egg, beaten with $\frac{1}{2}$ tsp salt (for glaze)	
	FILLING	
1 kg	leeks, trimmed and split	2 lb
30 g	butter	2 Tbsp
	salt and pepper	
	3 egg yolks	
60 ml	heavy cream or crème fraîche*	$\frac{1}{4}$ cup
	23 cm/9 in pie or tart pan	

Make the pie pastry* and chill for 30 minutes. Roll out two-thirds of the dough and line the pan*. Chill for another 30 minutes or until firm.

Meanwhile, prepare the filling: slice the leeks. Melt the butter in a frying pan and add the leeks with salt and pepper. Cover with a piece of buttered foil and the lid and cook over a low fire, stirring often, for 20–25 minutes or until very soft; don't allow them to brown. Let cool; then beat in the yolks and cream. Taste for seasoning. Pour the filling into the lined pan. Set the oven at hot (200°C/400°F).

Roll out the remaining dough to a 25 cm/10 in circle. Brush the edges of the bottom layer of dough with egg glaze and lay the circle on top, pressing the edges of both circles together; glaze the top. Make a hole in the centre to allow steam to escape. Bake for 30–35 minutes or until golden brown. Unmould the flamiche and serve warm or at room temperature.

FLAMICHE AU MAROILLES
Cheese yeast tart

If maroilles cheese is not available, use any strong soft cheese such as munster or vacherin (in Europe) or liederkranz (in North America). Or, at a pinch, try a well-aged camembert.

Serves 8–10

	YEAST DOUGH	
200 g	flour	1$\frac{1}{2}$ cups
15 g	fresh yeast OR	1 cake
	1 pkg dried yeast	
125 ml	lukewarm milk	$\frac{1}{2}$ cup
	2 eggs	
5 g	salt	1 tsp
110 g	butter, softened	7 Tbsp
	FILLING	
180 g	maroilles cheese, without rind, finely sliced	6 oz
30 g	butter	2 Tbsp
	1 egg	
	1 egg yolk	
125 ml	heavy cream or crème fraîche*	$\frac{1}{2}$ cup
	salt and pepper	
	pinch of grated nutmeg	
	23 cm/9 in pie pan or layer pan	

Sift the flour into a bowl, make a well in the centre and crumble in the yeast. Pour half the milk over the yeast and let stand for 5 minutes or until dissolved. Add the rest of the milk, the eggs and the salt. Mix them together with your fingers, gradually drawing in the flour to make a dough that is soft and slightly sticky. Knead the dough by slapping it against the sides of the bowl or on a marble slab for 5 minutes or until very elastic. Beat in the softened butter. Transfer the dough to an oiled bowl, cover with a damp cloth and leave to rise in a warm place for 1–1$\frac{1}{2}$ hours or until doubled in bulk.

Knead the dough lightly to knock out the air. Put it in a buttered pan and use the oiled back of a spoon or your knuckles to flatten the dough so it lines the pan.

For the filling: cover the dough with the sliced cheese and dot with the butter. Beat the egg and yolk with the cream, season with a little salt, pepper and nutmeg and pour the mixture over the cheese. Leave the flamiche in a warm place to rise for 15 minutes. Set the oven at hot (200°C/400°F).

Bake the flamiche in the heated oven for 45–55 minutes or until the filling is browned and the pastry is crisp. Serve at once.

ANDOUILLES AND ANDOUILLETTES

'Andouillettes' are the object of what must be one of the most exclusive gastronomic societies in the world: the 'Association Amicale d'Amateurs d'Authentiques Andouillettes' (AAAAA) whose membership is limited to five. They divide into two camps – those who prefer the dry, vigorous andouillettes from Vire (in Normandy), and the lovers of the unctuous, moist sausages from Troyes in Champagne and towns like Aire-sur-la-Lys and Cambrai further north.

By no means everyone shares the enthusiasm of the AAAAA and, reading the list of ingredients, it is easy to understand why. Andouillettes consist of the small intestines of the pig mixed with parts of pig, calf or beef stomach, and stuffed into themselves. Even when freshly made, the flavour of a good andouillette is often called earthy, and it is an acquired taste. Unfortunately, when badly prepared or stale, andouillettes taste fetid. As they are sold already cooked or smoked, they need only to be grilled/broiled before being served. Favourite accompaniments are mashed potatoes, fried onions and lentils, split peas or red kidney beans, with an obligatory topping of mustard.

Andouilles are similar to andouillettes, but are made with the large intestine. They are cooked and smoked, and served cold and thinly sliced as a first course. In the north they are often accompanied by leeks in a mustardy vinaigrette. Their dark skin and the undulations of pink and white meat inside the sausage itself are unmistakable.

POTAGE PICARD AUX POIS
Pea soup

'Potage picard' is equally good made with dried or fresh peas, though the taste is quite different. With fresh peas the soup is also known as 'potage St Germain', after a town near Paris where peas were grown once upon a time. Now it is a fashionable suburb.

Serves 4

500 g	split peas OR	1 lb
1·5 kg	fresh green peas, shelled OR	3 lb
500 g	frozen peas	1 lb
150-g	piece of bacon	5-oz
1 L	water, more if needed	1 qt
	sprig of thyme	
	salt and pepper	
	pinch of sugar (optional)	
75 g	butter	5 Tbsp
	croûtons* fried in butter	

If using split peas soak them for 1 hour in cold water to cover; then drain. Blanch* the bacon. Put split, fresh or frozen peas in another pot with the water. Add the bacon and thyme. Bring to a boil, cover and simmer for 20 minutes for frozen peas, 30 minutes for fresh peas, or $1\frac{1}{4}$ hours for split peas, or until very tender.

Dice the bacon and set aside. Discard the sprig of thyme; then purée the soup in a blender or food processor, or work it through a food mill or sieve. Return the diced bacon to the soup. If the soup is very thick, add enough water so that it pours easily from the spoon, but is still rich; soup made with fresh or frozen peas should be slightly thinner than split pea soup.

Just before serving, bring the soup back to a boil, add a little pepper and taste for seasoning.

A pinch of sugar often brings out the flavour of fresh peas. Add the butter to the soup in small pieces, stir until almost melted, and pour the soup into a tureen or individual bowls. Serve the croûtons separately.

SAUCE PICARDE
Onion sauce

This 'sauce' is in fact sliced onions cooked in butter until they become a coarse purée. Traditionally served with roast pork, veal or grilled sausages, 'sauce picarde' is also good with hard-boiled eggs and can be thinned with broth or milk to make soup.

Serves 4

45 g	butter	3 Tbsp
20 g	flour	$2\frac{1}{2}$ Tbsp
250 ml	water	1 cup
420 g	onions, thinly sliced	14 oz
	2 Tbsp vinegar	
	salt and pepper	
250 ml	broth	1 cup
	2–3 Tbsp pan juices from roast pork or veal (optional)	

Melt the butter in a pot, add the flour and cook over a low fire, whisking constantly, for 2–3 minutes or until very lightly browned. Whisk in the water and bring to a boil. Add the onions, vinegar, salt and pepper, cover and simmer over a low fire, stirring often, for 1 hour or until the onions have softened to a purée. Stir in the broth and pan juices, if available, bring back to a boil and, if necessary, boil to reduce the sauce until it has become quite thick. Taste it for seasoning and serve the sauce very hot.

PETITS PÂTÉS CHAUDS
Hot pork pâtés in pastry

Little hot pâtés are made throughout France. This recipe comes from Champagne. A variation in the ingredients of the meat filling gives a pâté characteristic of the Cévennes: 'pâté de foie de volaille à la languedocienne'.

Makes 20 small pâtés

125 g	bacon, diced	4 oz
125 g	veal escalope, diced	4 oz
125 g	cooked ham, diced	4 oz
	1 egg, beaten with $\frac{1}{2}$ tsp salt (for glaze)	
	MARINADE	
	2 Tbsp white wine	
	2 Tbsp cognac	
	2 Tbsp madeira	
	pinch of thyme	
	1 bay leaf	
	$\frac{1}{2}$ onion, chopped	
	2 tsp oil	
	PÂTÉ PASTRY DOUGH	
600 g	flour	$4\frac{2}{3}$ cups
350 g	butter, or 1 part lard and 2 parts butter	$\frac{3}{4}$ lb
	2 eggs	
	2 Tbsp oil	
12 g	salt	$2\frac{1}{2}$ tsp
	4–8 Tbsp cold water	
	MEAT MIXTURE	
125 g	lean pork	4 oz
125 g	fat pork	4 oz
125 g	veal	4 oz
90 g	chicken livers	3 oz
	2 Tbsp white wine	
	1 Tbsp cognac	
	1 egg	
	1 tsp ground allspice	
	salt and pepper	

If the bacon is very salty, blanch* it. Place the bacon, diced veal and ham in a shallow dish. Add the marinade ingredients, mix well and leave to marinate for 30–45 minutes. Make the pâté pastry dough as for pie pastry* and chill for 30 minutes or until firm.

For the meat mixture: work the lean and fat pork with the veal and chicken livers twice through the fine plate of a mincer/grinder. Mix with the wine, cognac, egg, allspice, salt and pepper; then work the mixture with your fingers until it holds together. Drain the diced bacon, veal and ham and mix them with the minced/ground meat. Sauté a small piece of the mixture and taste for seasoning.

Roll out the pastry dough 6 mm/$\frac{1}{4}$ in thick on a floured board and cut it into 12·5 cm/5 in squares. In the centre of each square spread a

PÂTÉS EN CROÛTE

Correctly, when talking of pâtés, the words 'en croûte' are redundant, for the literal meaning of 'pâté' is 'pastried', i.e. with pastry. When closed ovens were developed, however, the protective coating of pastry became unnecessary and more and more pâtés were baked in terrine moulds. Gradually the word assumed its present meaning of a meat or fish mixture, usually of fine texture,

Quai de Troyes

layer of filling in a 4 × 7·5 cm/1$\frac{1}{2}$ × 3 in rectangle, mounding it well. Cut 1·25 cm/$\frac{1}{2}$ in squares from each corner of the dough. Brush the edges of the dough with egg glaze and wrap up the pâtés like parcels. Turn them over and set them, seam side down, on a baking sheet. Brush with glaze.

Roll out the dough trimmings and decorate the tops of the pâtés with leaves or with shells, made by marking small fluted rounds of dough in a rayed pattern with the back of a knife. Brush the decorations with glaze. Make a small hole in the top of each pâté with the point of a knife and insert a 'chimney' made of a strip of foil or greaseproof/waxed paper rolled around a baked in a terrine; 'terrine' mixtures tend to be coarser and more robust. However, the agreeable custom of wrapping things in pastry has not entirely disappeared, particularly in northern France. Amiens pâtés en croûte – a mixture of duck, foie gras and rabbit – have been famous since the 17th century. Reims goes in for pigeon pâté en croûte and when thrushes can be found in the Ardennes, they are clapped inside a crust. In Champagne pâté contains large pieces of goose.

The crust itself can be a pie crust, but the French like to make it into pâte à pâté by adding whole eggs so that the dough is more pliable and holds its shape better during cooking. Lard is often used instead of butter, particularly when the filling contains pork. Puff pastry is another alternative, but this rich dough is wasted around a moist filling, as it goes soggy instead of rising.

spoon handle; this allows steam to escape. Chill the pâtés for 15 minutes. Set the oven at hot (200°C/400°F).

Bake the pâtés in the hot oven for 12–15 minutes or until they begin to brown. Lower the heat to moderate (175°C/350°F) and continue baking 25–30 minutes or until a skewer inserted in the centre of a pâté is hot to the touch when withdrawn after 30 seconds. If the pâtés brown too quickly, cover them loosely with foil during cooking. Discard the paper chimneys and serve the pâtés hot.

PÂTES DE FOIE DE VOLAILLE À LA LANGUEDOCIENNE

Prepare the pastry as above. Omit the diced meats and substitute the following for the minced/ground meat mixture:

250 g	ground lean pork	8 oz
250 g	ground veal	8 oz
250 g	chopped raw chicken livers	8 oz

Work the mixture twice through the fine plate of the mincer/grinder or in a food processor, transfer it to a metal bowl set over a pan of ice and beat well with a wooden spoon. Add 1 egg with plenty of salt and pepper; beat until the mixture holds together. Continue as above.

HARENGS MARINÉS
Marinated herring

Given the amount of white wine and vinegar,
the flavour of these herrings will mellow and
they can be kept for at least 3–4 days in the
refrigerator. For a stronger flavour, increase the
amount of vinegar. In the North a tablespoon of
juniper berries is often added to the wine with
the vegetables to make 'Harengs marinés aux
baies de genièvre'. The Normans often replace
half the wine with dry cider, for 'Harengs
marinés au cidre'.

Serves 4–6

500 ml	white wine	2 cups
	2 carrots, sliced	
	2 onions, sliced	
	large bouquet garni	
	10 black peppercorns	
	1 clove	
	salt	
750 g total	4–6 small fresh herrings	1½ lb total
125 ml	vinegar	½ cup
	2 Tbsp olive oil	

In a medium pot bring the wine to a boil with
the carrots, onions, bouquet garni, peppercorns, clove and a pinch of salt. Simmer over a
low fire for 30 minutes or until the vegetables
are tender.

While the mixture is simmering, prepare the
herrings: cut off the fins and trim the tails to a
'V'. Clean, scale and wash the fish and pat dry
on paper towels. Put them in a deep flameproof
serving dish or gratin dish.

When the vegetables are tender, add the
vinegar and bring back to a boil; pour the
mixture over the herrings. Simmer only 2
minutes; then take from the heat and taste the
liquid for seasoning. Pour the olive oil on top
and leave to cool; the fish will continue to cook
in the heat of the liquid. When cool, store the
fish in the refrigerator overnight or up to 4 days.
Serve at room temperature with the vegetables
in the marinade.

GRATIN DE QUEUES DE CREVETTES
Gratin of shrimps

This recipe is best made with prawns or large
shrimps, called in France 'bouquets roses'. In
Savoie and the Dauphiné the dish is made with
crayfish.

Serves 4

2 L	water	2 qt
	sprig of thyme	
	1 bay leaf	
	salt and pepper	
1 kg	raw shrimps, in their shells	2 lb
50 g	grated gruyère cheese	½ cup
	RICH CREAM SAUCE	
250 ml	milk	1 cup
	1 slice of onion	
	1 bay leaf	
	6 peppercorns	
45 g	butter	3 Tbsp
15 g	flour	2 Tbsp
	salt and pepper	
	pinch of cayenne pepper	
	pinch of grated nutmeg	
80 ml	shrimp cooking liquid	⅓ cup
	2 egg yolks	
125 ml	heavy cream or crème fraîche*	½ cup

Bring the water to a boil with the thyme, bay
leaf, salt and pepper. Add the shellfish and
poach for 2–3 minutes. Drain, reserving the
liquid, and peel.

Make the rich cream sauce: prepare a medium
béchamel sauce* from the milk, onion, bay leaf,
peppercorns, 2 tablespoons of the butter and the
flour. Season with salt, pepper, cayenne pepper
and nutmeg. Strain the measured prawn or
shrimp cooking liquid into the sauce and bring
to a boil. Beat the yolks and cream in a bowl.
Whisk a little of the hot sauce into the yolk
mixture; then whisk this mixture back into the
sauce. Heat gently, whisking constantly, until
slightly thickened; don't boil the sauce or it will
curdle. Remove from the heat and stir in the
remaining butter and the prawns/shrimps.
Taste for seasoning.

Spoon the prawn/shrimp mixture into a
buttered shallow baking dish. Sprinkle with the
grated cheese and brown under the grill/broiler.
Serve immediately from the baking dish.

COQ EN PÂTE

Chicken in pastry

A bird with a handsome head is an asset for this dish, since custom dictates that the head peep out from the blanket of pastry.

Serves 6

1·8-kg	chicken, cleaned but preferably with head attached	4-lb
	SOUR CREAM PIE PASTRY	
450 g	flour, more if needed	3½ cups
210 g	butter	7 oz
	2 eggs	
10 g	salt	2 tsp
	6 Tbsp sour cream or crème fraîche*	
	1 egg, beaten with ½ tsp salt (for glaze)	
	STUFFING	
30 g	white bread, crusts removed	1 oz
125 ml	milk	½ cup
250 g	veal	½ lb
250 g	fat pork	½ lb
150 g	calf, pork or chicken livers	5 oz
	1 egg	
	pinch of thyme	
	salt and pepper	

Make the pie pastry*, substituting sour cream for water, and chill for 30 minutes or until firm.

Slit the skin on the neck of the chicken and remove the neck, leaving the head attached to the skin. Pull any pinfeathers from the head and skin. Using a sharp knife, remove the wishbone from the chicken to make carving easier.

Prepare the stuffing: soak the bread in the milk; then squeeze it dry. Mince/grind together the veal, fat pork, soaked bread and livers. Beat in the egg, thyme, salt and pepper. Sauté a small piece of stuffing and taste for seasoning. Fill the chicken with the stuffing. Make a hole in the centre of the neck skin and push the head through it. Slit the tendons in each chicken leg just above the knuckle (so the knee bends) and make a slit in the skin on each side of the chicken near the tail. Bend the legs and insert them in the slits. Chill the chicken until ready to wrap it in the pastry. Butter a baking sheet.

Roll out three-quarters of the dough to a 45 cm/18 in square. Set the chicken diagonally on top, breast side down. Fold the two smaller corners of pastry over the chicken and brush them with egg glaze; then fold over the other two corners and stick them to the glazed pastry. Trim off any excess pastry. The chicken should now be totally enclosed. Make a hole in the pastry so that the head emerges. Turn the chicken over on to the baking sheet with the breast facing upwards and the head resting on the baking sheet. Brush lightly with egg glaze.

Roll out most of the remaining dough to an oval about the same size as the top surface of the wrapped chicken. Press it on top of the chicken and brush lightly with glaze. Roll out the remaining dough and cut out crescent or leaf decorations. Stick them on the oval and glaze them also. Chill the wrapped chicken for 15–20 minutes. Set the oven at very hot (220°C/425°F).

Cover the chicken's head with foil. Bake the chicken 15–20 minutes or until it begins to brown; turn down the oven to moderately hot (190°C/375°F), cover the chicken with foil and bake another 1½–1¾ hours or until a skewer inserted into the stuffing is hot to the touch when withdrawn after 30 seconds.

Transfer the chicken to a platter. Cut off the top oval of pastry and remove the chicken, leaving the head. Spoon the stuffing back into the pastry base. Carve the chicken and arrange the pieces on top of the stuffing. Set the pastry oval on top at an angle and serve.

COQ À LA BIÈRE

Chicken with beer

Laced with beer and juniper eau-de-vie, this northern treatment of chicken is an interesting contrast to the more delicate 'coq en pâte' from Champagne. Gin with a few crushed juniper berries can be used instead of genièvre.

Serves 4

1·8–2 kg	chicken or young cock	4–4½ lb
	2 Tbsp oil	
30 g	butter	2 Tbsp
	2 shallots, chopped	
60 ml	genièvre	¼ cup
15 g	flour	2 Tbsp
250 ml	dark beer	1 cup
250 g	mushrooms, halved if large	½ lb
	bouquet garni	
	salt and pepper	
60 ml	heavy cream or crème fraîche*	¼ cup
	1 Tbsp chopped parsley	

Cut the chicken* in 8. Heat the oil and butter in a heavy, shallow casserole. Add the chicken pieces and brown them well. Lower the heat, add the shallots and cook 2 minutes until soft. Flame with the genièvre. Sprinkle the chicken pieces with flour; turn them over and cook 1 minute. Add the beer, mushrooms, bouquet garni, salt and pepper. Bring to a boil, cover and simmer 45 minutes until the chicken is tender.

Discard the bouquet garni, skim off excess fat and add the cream. Bring to a boil and taste for seasoning. Serve the chicken in the casserole, sprinkled with chopped parsley.

LE HOCHEPOT
Oxtail, meat and vegetable stew

Traditionally made in a tall pot of glazed earthenware, the name 'hochepot' comes from 'hocher', to stir or shake the pot. Almost any meat can be used, with oxtail and a pig's head or ears added for richness. The main difference between hochepot and pot-au-feu is that for hochepot the meat is browned in fat before the liquid is added.

Serves 8–10

750 g	beef short ribs, chopped into 2 pieces	1½ lb
500 g	pork loin or breast	1 lb
500 g	shoulder or breast of veal (optional)	1 lb
500 g	lamb or mutton shoulder, breast or neck	1 lb
750 g	oxtail, cut in sections	1½ lb
60 g	lard or oil	¼ cup
	salt and pepper	
	12 black peppercorns	
	1 Tbsp juniper berries	
	2 cloves of garlic	
	bouquet garni	
	1 onion, studded with 2 cloves	
	1 pig's foot (optional)	
	6 medium leeks, trimmed and split	
	6 stalks celery	
	6 medium carrots	
	3 medium turnips	
	1 parsnip (optional)	
	1 small celery root, quartered (optional)	
	1 small loaf French bread	
	8–10 small fresh sausages	
	coarse salt and Dijon mustard (for serving)	

Tie each cut of meat (except the oxtail) into a compact piece. Put the beef in a very large tall pot and add enough water to cover generously. Bring to a boil, skimming often. Drain, rinse the meat with cold water and return it to the pot.

Meanwhile, heat the lard in a large, heavy frying pan and brown the pork well on all sides; transfer it to the pot. Brown the oxtail, veal and lamb in the same way; then transfer them to the pot. Dissolve the pan juices with a little water and add to the pot with enough water to cover all the meats generously. Bring to a boil, skimming often. Add the salt, peppercorns, juniper berries, garlic, bouquet garni, onion and pig's foot. Simmer for 1½ hours; then check the veal and mutton with a two-pronged fork: if they are tender, remove and keep warm. Simmer the beef and pork for another 30 minutes while preparing the vegetables.

Tie the leeks and celery stalks in separate bunches and set aside. If you like, tie the carrots, turnips, parsnip and celeriac/celery root individually in pieces of cheesecloth so they are easy to lift out; add them to the pot of meat with more water to cover, if necessary. After they have simmered for 15 minutes, add the leeks and celery and continue to simmer another 15 minutes or until all the meats and vegetables are very tender. If the vegetables finish cooking before the meat, remove them and set aside.

Cut the bread in 1 cm/⅜ in slices and toast in a moderate oven (175°C/350°F) for 10–15 minutes or until golden brown. Fry the sausages in a hot frying pan for 5–7 minutes or until cooked and brown.

To finish, return the veal and mutton to the pot and heat for 5–10 minutes. Then lift out the meat and vegetables. Carve the meats in thick slices, but leave the oxtail in sections. Arrange the meat on a large platter surrounded by piles of the vegetables; reserve a few carrots and leeks for the broth. Cover the platter with foil and keep hot.

Strain the broth and, if necessary, boil to reduce until well flavoured. Reheat and taste for seasoning; skim off the fat. Cut the reserved carrots and leeks in small pieces and add them to the broth. Serve the broth first, accompanied by the toast, and then the platter of meat and vegetables, accompanied by coarse salt and mustard.

CARBONNADE DE BOEUF À LA FLAMANDE

Beef stew with beer

This was once a dish of grilled meat, flavoured with mustard – the name 'carbonnade' comes from 'charbon' meaning coals. Nowadays the beef is cooked in the oven as a stew, with beer. In the North, a hot white mustard is used for the croûtes rather than the milder mustard from Dijon.

Serves 4

80 ml	oil	$\frac{1}{3}$ cup
30 g	butter	2 Tbsp
1 kg	beef chuck eye roast, cut in 4 thick slices	2 lb
750 g	onions, thinly sliced	1½ lb
45 g	flour	5 Tbsp
1 L	beer	1 qt
250 ml	broth	1 cup
	salt and pepper	
	pinch of grated nutmeg	
	bouquet garni	
	CROÛTES	
	2–3 crusty rolls	
	1–2 Tbsp mustard	

Set the oven at hot (200°C/400°F). Heat half the oil with the butter in a frying pan, add the beef slices and brown them well over high heat; if necessary, brown them in two batches.

Heat the remaining oil in a flameproof casserole. Add the onions and cook over a low fire, stirring often, for 15 minutes or until soft. Raise the heat and brown the onions slightly; then stir in the flour. Bake in the oven, stirring often, for 10 minutes to brown the flour. Stir in the beer, broth, salt, pepper, nutmeg and bouquet garni, add the meat and bring to a boil on top of the stove, skimming occasionally. Return the casserole to the oven and simmer uncovered, stirring often, for 2½ hours or until the meat is very tender when pricked with a two-pronged fork.

For croûtes: cut rolls in thick slices and set them on a baking sheet. Bake in the oven until crisp and brown. Spread with a thick layer of mustard and reserve.

When the beef is cooked, discard the bouquet garni and taste the sauce for seasoning. Arrange the croûtes on top of the beef and baste them lightly with sauce. Grill/broil for 5–10 minutes until the top is browned. Serve in the casserole.

VEAU FLAMANDE

Braised veal with dried fruit

Northerners like pronounced flavours. They cook their meat not only with vinegar or beer but also with fruit.

Serves 6

120 g	prunes	$\frac{3}{4}$ cup
100 g	dried apricots	$\frac{1}{2}$ cup
45 g	butter	3 Tbsp
750 g	veal leg, centre roast	1½ lb
500 ml	broth	2 cups
	pinch of thyme	
	salt and pepper	
45 g	raisins	$\frac{1}{3}$ cup

Soak the prunes and apricots for about 1 hour in enough hot water to cover generously; drain.

Meanwhile, heat the butter in a heavy casserole over a medium fire, add the veal and brown it on all sides. Add the broth, thyme, salt and pepper. Cover tightly and cook over a low fire for 45 minutes, turning the meat occasionally so it does not dry out. Add the prunes, apricots and raisins and continue to cook for another 45–55 minutes or until the meat is tender when pierced with a two-pronged fork. Remove the meat, transfer it to a platter and carve in medium-thick slices; cover and keep it warm.

Simmer the cooking liquid and fruit, uncovered, until the liquid is reduced by half and is slightly thickened; taste for seasoning. Arrange the fruit around the meat and spoon over some of the gravy. Serve the remaining gravy separately.

PIEDS DE PORC PANÉS
Grilled pig's feet

Pig's feet as cooked by the charcutiers of Ste Menehould – for 48 hours so that the bones are soft enough to be eaten – are a curiosity. Their recipe is secret, possibly involving some type of pressure cooking. Grilled pig's feet, as in this recipe, certainly have much more flavour since the meat is not overdone.

Serves 4

	4 pig's feet	
250 ml	dry white wine	1 cup
2 L	well-flavoured broth, more if necessary	2 qt
	2 onions, each studded with 4–5 cloves	
	2 carrots	
	sprig of thyme	
	2 bay leaves	
	15 black peppercorns	
	a few sprigs of parsley	
	salt and pepper	
125 g	butter, melted	$\frac{1}{4}$ lb
100 g	fresh breadcrumbs	$\frac{3}{4}$ cup
	Dijon mustard (for serving)	
	cheesecloth	

Put the pig's feet into a large pot of cold water, bring to a boil and simmer for 5 minutes. Refresh the pig's feet with running water, scrape them clean, rinse and drain well. Split the feet lengthwise without completely separating the two halves. Bind each foot tightly with a cloth to hold it in its original shape.

In a large pot bring the wine and broth to a boil with the onions, carrots, thyme, bay leaves, peppercorns, parsley and salt. Add the pig's feet and more broth to cover, if necessary. Cover and simmer over a very low fire for 6 hours or until the meat is very soft and falling from the bones (unwrap the cloth to check). Add water if necessary during cooking to keep the pig's feet covered. Leave to cool in the liquid.

When the pig's feet have cooled, carefully remove them from the cooking liquid. Remove the cloth and drain thoroughly on paper towels. Heat the grill/broiler or the oven to very hot (220°C/425°F).

Roll the pig's feet in the melted butter, then in the breadcrumbs. Grill/broil until golden brown or heat in a roasting pan for 20–30 minutes in the oven. Sprinkle with pepper and serve immediately, with mustard.

LAPIN EN GELÉE
Rabbit in aspic

This simplest of rabbit recipes can be served hot or, even better, cold, when the cooking juices set to form a light herb-flavoured aspic.

Serves 4

	1 rabbit, with its liver	
360 g	bacon, cut in thin slices	12 oz
	2 large onions, cut in thick rounds	
	pinch of thyme	
	2 bay leaves, crumbled	
	salt and pepper	
310 ml	white wine	$1\frac{1}{4}$ cups
500 ml	broth, more if needed	2 cups
	3 L/3 qt terrine	

Set the oven at hot (200°C/400°F). Cut the rabbit* into 8 or 9 pieces.

Put half the bacon slices in the base of the terrine. Separate the onion into rings and cover the bacon with a layer of about a third of the onions, a pinch of thyme and a little bay leaf. Top with half the rabbit pieces and sprinkle them with salt and pepper. Add another layer of onions and sprinkle with thyme and bay leaf. Add the remaining pieces of rabbit and its liver and sprinkle with salt and pepper. Top with the remaining onion slices and remaining bacon. Pour in the white wine and enough broth barely to cover. Press the ingredients down well and cover the terrine tightly.

Put the terrine in the hot oven until the liquid comes to a boil. Turn down the heat to moderately hot (190°C/375°F) and cook for $2\frac{1}{2}$–3 hours or until the rabbit is very tender. Taste the cooking liquid for seasoning. Leave to cool; then chill several hours or until set.

Serve cool or at room temperature from the terrine.

MARCASSIN ARDENNAISE

Marinated wild boar with celery root

Fresh baby wild boar is a delicacy rarely found outside hunting areas like the Ardennes, though baby boar is now being bred in some parts of France. A leg of venison or even a loin of pork can be substituted in this recipe.

Serves 12

3·5-kg	a leg of young wild boar	7½-lb
	5 Tbsp oil	
75 g	butter	5 Tbsp
65 g	flour	½ cup
1 L	broth	1 qt
	salt and pepper	
2 kg total	2 celery roots	4½ lb total
	1 lemon	
300 g	lean bacon, cut in lardons	10 oz
	MARINADE	
	bouquet garni	
	12 black peppercorns	
	1 Tbsp juniper berries	
	2 cloves	
60 ml	oil	¼ cup
	2 carrots, sliced	
	2 onions, sliced	
	2 stalks celery, sliced	
	3 shallots, sliced	
	2 cloves garlic, sliced	
1·5 L	red wine	1½ qt
	small pinch salt	
	cheesecloth	

Trim off any dark parts of meat or excess fat from the boar, coarsely chop and reserve them.

Make the marinade: tie the bouquet garni, peppercorns, juniper berries and cloves in cheesecloth. Heat half the oil in a large pot and add the carrots, onions, celery, shallots and garlic. Cook over a low fire, stirring often, for 5 minutes or until softened. Add the wine, reserved meat trimmings and a small pinch of salt. Bring to a boil, cover and simmer over a low fire for 1 hour or until all the vegetables are tender; let cool completely. Put the meat in a deep bowl or casserole (not aluminium), pour the marinade over it and sprinkle with the remaining oil. Leave in the refrigerator for 2–3 days or at room temperature for 1 day, turning the meat from time to time.

Drain the meat and pat it dry with paper towels. Strain the marinade and reserve it separate from the vegetables, meat trimmings and seasonings. Set the oven at very hot (220°C/425°F).

Begin preparing the sauce: in a heavy-based pot heat 3 tablespoons of the oil and 2 tablespoons of the butter until the butter foams. Add the vegetables and meat trimmings from the marinade and cook over a low fire, stirring, for 3–4 minutes. Add the flour and cook, stirring constantly, for 5 minutes or until light brown. Pour in the strained marinade and the broth, add the cheesecloth bag of seasonings and bring to a boil, stirring; season with a little salt and pepper. Simmer over a very low fire, stirring often to prevent sticking, for 1–1½ hours or until the sauce is reduced to about 750 ml.

Meanwhile, roast the meat: put the remaining oil in a large roasting pan, set the boar on top and roast in the heated oven for 45 minutes.

While the sauce is simmering and the boar is roasting, peel the celeriac/celery roots and rub them with a cut lemon. Cut the roots into 2·5 cm/ 1 in dice and sprinkle with the juice of the lemon to prevent browning. If the bacon is very salty, blanch* it. After the boar has roasted for 45 minutes, discard the grease in the roasting pan and add 1 tablespoon butter, then the celery and bacon; sprinkle with salt and pepper. Lower the heat to moderate (175°C/350°F) and continue roasting, stirring the celery and bacon occasionally, for another 45 minutes or until the boar is tender. Transfer the meat to a carving board. If the celery root is not yet tender, roast it a few more minutes. Transfer the bacon and celery root to a platter and keep warm.

Strain the sauce and taste for seasoning. Add the remaining butter a piece at a time, shaking the pot to incorporate it. Carve the meat, replace the pieces on the bone, and set it on the platter with the celery and bacon. Spoon a little sauce over the meat and serve the rest separately.

Celeriac/celery root

THE CHICORY FAMILY

The chicory family is confusing. For one thing, the curly-headed members such as 'escarole' and 'frisée' look quite unlike their plump-headed white cousin, which the English call chicory, the Americans Belgian endive and the French 'endive'. Conversely, what the French call 'chicorée' and the Americans call chicory – a curly-leaved green plant – is endive in England. To add to the confusion, the name also appears on many packets of coffee, for the inexpensive root of one variety of chicory is roasted and ground, then added to coffee to reduce its cost.

Names apart, plump-headed white chicory (endive in North America) is quite different from the green members of the family, although they are all winter vegetables. Its cultivation requires constant attention. Grown under the ground in 'forceries' (forcing beds) through which hot pipes run, chicory plants are covered with straw and a roof of corrugated iron. Darkness as well as heat is essential; as soon as the leaves are allowed to peep into the light, they start to curl and turn green instead of forming the tight, closely packed white bulb that is the ideal. They are even sold wrapped in purple paper to exclude the light. In France chicory is grown in a small area near the Belgian border, which is responsible for virtually all French output. Even more chicory, however, is grown in Belgium, hence its American name. Chicory tends to be bitter when grown elsewhere, due either to unsuitable soil or to poor care. Bitterness is undetectable by eye and cannot be eradicated in cooking. A slight and pleasant bite, however, is characteristic.

Chicory (UK)/Belgian endive (US)

Endive (UK)/chicory (US)

ENDIVES À L'ARDENNAISE
Belgian endive with ham

Braised chicory/endive ('endives braisés') is a popular winter accompaniment to meats and is particularly good when thoroughly cooked so that it becomes lightly caramelized. When wrapped in ham and coated with white sauce and cheese as here, it becomes either a first course or a light main course. Without the ham, this dish is known simply as 'endives au gratin'.

Serves 8 as a first course or 4 as a main course

1 kg	8–10 heads Belgian endive	2 lb
	1 tsp sugar	
	salt and pepper	
350 g	8–10 thin slices cooked ham	$\frac{3}{4}$ lb
50 g	grated gruyère cheese	$\frac{1}{2}$ cup
	MEDIUM WHITE SAUCE	
500 ml	milk	2 cups
60 g	butter	4 Tbsp
30 g	flour	$\frac{1}{4}$ cup
	salt and pepper	
	pinch of grated nutmeg	

Set the oven at moderate (175°C/350°F). Wipe the chicory/endive, discard any wilted leaves and trim the stems. With the point of a knife, hollow each stem so the chicory cooks more evenly. Lay the chicory in a buttered casserole and sprinkle with the sugar, salt and pepper. Cover and bake in the heated oven for 45–55 minutes or until the chicory is tender.

Let the chicory cool slightly; then roll each head in a slice of ham and arrange them diagonally in a buttered, shallow baking dish. Raise the oven heat to hot (200°C/400°F).

Make the white sauce* and spoon it over the chicory; sprinkle with the grated cheese. Bake in the hot oven for 15–20 minutes or grill/broil until very hot and browned. Serve hot from the baking dish.

TOURTE DE POTIRON PICARDE
Pumpkin and onion feuilleté

Two kinds of pumpkin are generally grown in France. One variety, 'citrouille' gets its name from its light yellow, citrus colour; the other, 'potiron', is darker, juicier, with a more delicate taste. They are interchangeable in recipes.

Serves 8

	PUFF PASTRY	
250 g	unsalted butter	$\frac{1}{2}$ lb
175 g	all-purpose flour	$1\frac{1}{3}$ cups
80 g	cake flour	$\frac{2}{3}$ cup
5 g	salt	1 tsp
	1 tsp lemon juice	
125 ml	iced water, more as needed	$\frac{1}{2}$ cup
	1 egg, beaten with $\frac{1}{2}$ tsp salt (for glaze)	
	FILLING	
1 kg	pumpkin	2 lb
125 ml	water	$\frac{1}{2}$ cup
	30 baby onions	
	salt and pepper	
	pinch of nutmeg	
125 g	butter	$\frac{1}{4}$ lb
	25–28 cm/10–11 in tart or pie pan	

Make the puff pastry* and chill for 1 hour or until firm.

Meanwhile, make the filling: peel the pumpkin, discard any seeds and fibres, and cut the flesh in small cubes. Put them in a shallow pot with the water, onions, salt, pepper and nutmeg. Cover, bring to a boil and simmer over a low fire for 20 minutes or until tender; drain thoroughly. While the mixture is still warm, add the butter and taste for seasoning. Let cool.

Butter the tart pan. Roll out half the puff pastry to about 3 mm/$\frac{1}{8}$ in thickness. Using a pan lid as a guide, cut a circle about 5 cm/2 in larger in diameter than the tart pan. Gather up the dough on the rolling pin and slide it carefully into the pan. Press the dough lightly into the corners of the pan without stretching it. Roll out the remaining pastry to the same thickness and cut another circle about 2·5 cm/1 in larger in diameter than the pan. Fill the lined pan with the pumpkin mixture and cover with the second circle, pressing to seal the edges. Flute the edges to decorate. Chill for 15–20 minutes. Set the oven at very hot (220°C/425°F).

Brush the chilled pie with egg glaze and cut a few slits in the top to let steam escape. Bake in the heated oven for 20 minutes or until the pastry begins to brown; then lower the heat to moderate (175°C/350°F) and bake for another 15 minutes or until the pastry is puffed, well browned and firm. Serve hot or at room temperature.

CHOU À L'ARDENNAISE
Cabbage with apples and juniper berries

Juniper berries add a northern bite to white cabbage braised with white wine. Red cabbage can receive similar treatment, but with red wine, plus a sweet and sour touch of vinegar and red currant jelly. Both types of cabbage are good with sausages, ham, roast pork and braised beef.

Serves 6

	1 medium head cabbage, quartered and cored	
	salt and pepper	
	2 Tbsp oil or lard	
350 g	tart apples, peeled, cored and diced	$\frac{3}{4}$ lb
250 ml	white wine	1 cup
	15 juniper berries (optional)	

Set the oven at medium (175°C/350°F). Put the cabbage in a large pot of salted water, bring to a boil and blanch for 5 minutes. Drain thoroughly and shred.

Heat the oil in a casserole and stir in the cabbage and apples. Add the wine, salt, pepper and juniper berries. Bring to a boil, cover and braise in the heated oven for 35–45 minutes or until very tender. Check occasionally and, if the cabbage starts to stick, add a few tablespoons of water; if, towards the end of cooking, the cabbage seems watery, remove the lid and bake uncovered to evaporate liquid. Taste the cabbage for seasoning and serve it from the casserole.

CHOU ROUGE À L'ARDENNAISE

Prepare as above but with red cabbage and red wine, and cook the cabbage for about 1 hour. Before serving, stir 1 Tbsp beaten red currant jelly and 1 tsp vinegar into the cabbage. Taste for seasoning and serve.

SALADE DE BETTERAVES AUX NOIX

Beet salad with walnuts

Beetroot/beet has always been popular in the North, and at one time wine was made from it.

Serves 4

250 g	2 plump heads Belgian endive	½ lb
125 g	a few bunches lamb's lettuce or other greens	¼ lb
	2 large beets, cooked and peeled	
	salt and pepper	
50 g	walnuts, coarsely chopped	½ cup
VINAIGRETTE		
	1 Tbsp vinegar or lemon juice	
	salt and pepper	
	1 tsp Dijon mustard	
	3 Tbsp salad oil	

Make the vinaigrette* and set aside.

Wipe the chicory/endive, discard any wilted leaves and trim the stems. Cut each head of chicory into 2 cm/¾ in diagonal slices. Wash the lamb's lettuce very thoroughly to remove all sand; drain it well. Mix the chicory and the lamb's lettuce in a large salad bowl.

Just before serving, cut the beetroot/beets in medium dice and add them to the greens. Toss with the vinaigrette and taste for seasoning. Sprinkle with chopped walnuts and serve.

POTATOES

Almost 40 per cent of all French potatoes are grown in Champagne and northern France, so it is appropriate that their pioneer Antoine-Auguste Parmentier should have been born in Montdidier, in Picardy. It was not until the middle of the 18th century, more than 200 years after potatoes had been brought back from the New World, that the French began to cultivate them seriously. Louis XVI was interested in any food that might relieve the famine plaguing rural France in the 1760s and '70s, and Parmentier, an eccentric scientist with a gift for publicity, caught the King's attention. He planted fields of potatoes in the Bois de Boulogne just outside Paris and had them ostentatiously guarded by soldiers to encourage people to steal such an apparently precious vegetable, and so become acquainted with it. To demonstrate their versatility, Parmentier gave a dinner at which all the dishes were based on potatoes, served with 20 sauces. He even persuaded Marie-Antoinette to wear potato flowers in her hair. From here it was a short step to the French table.

No other vegetable is used so often in French country cooking. Potatoes appear most often on the tables of northern and

central France, not only as accompaniments but also as an important ingredient in most mixed vegetable soups and meat potées. Most common is the boiled potato, the favourite both with fish and many pork dishes such as choucroute. Running it a close second is potato purée, a smooth complement to strong-flavoured dishes such as andouillettes. Sliced potatoes are used often in regional cooking, whether sautéed as potato cakes or baked either as rich gratins or under main course ingredients such as fresh herrings in the North or a whole leg of lamb in the Centre. In northern France potatoes often are added to salads, not only of dandelion greens, but also with chicory/Belgian endive. Brittany even has a sweetened potato fritter for dessert.

As with so many fruits and vegetables, varieties of potato differ from country to country. However, they all fall into two categories: firm, waxy potatoes that are good for boiling and hold their shape during cooking, and mealy types that purée easily. New potatoes tend to be waxy, but some soften as they grow larger. Both types are used to make 'frites', the pride of Flanders and a treat distributed free at Montdidier once a year, in honour of its famous son.

SALADE DE PISSENLITS AU LARD CHAMPENOISE

Hot dandelion and bacon salad

Marc adds character to the champenois version of this popular salad. Any robust greens such as endive/chicory or escarole can be used instead of dandelions.

Serves 8

300 g	dandelion greens	10 oz
300 g	small new potatoes, unpeeled	10 oz
	salt and pepper	
180 g	piece of lean bacon, cut in lardons	6 oz
30 g	lard or oil	2 Tbsp
60 ml	wine vinegar	$\frac{1}{4}$ cup
60 ml	marc or calvados	$\frac{1}{4}$ cup

Thoroughly wash the greens, drain and dry on paper towels. Put the potatoes in cold salted water, bring to a boil and simmer for 15–20 minutes or until almost tender; they should be slightly undercooked.

Meanwhile, if the bacon is salty, blanch* it. Set a pottery bowl in a water bath and heat until hot but not scalding to the touch. When the potatoes are cooked, drain them, peel and slice them thinly into the warm bowl. Add the greens, cover and keep warm while frying the lardons.

Heat the lard in a frying pan, add the bacon and fry until lightly browned but still tender. Discard excess fat, leaving about 6 tablespoons; pour the bacon and fat over the greens and potatoes and toss until well mixed. Add the vinegar to the hot pan, standing back from the fumes, and cook until reduced by half. Add the marc, simmer for another 30 seconds and pour it over the salad. Sprinkle with pepper, toss well, taste for seasoning and serve at once.

PARIS AND THE ÎLE DE FRANCE

Paris and its environs can conveniently be defined by drawing a circle with a 50-kilometre radius centred on Notre Dame. This nucleus, which accounts for less than 1·5 per cent of the French land area, contains some 18 per cent of the population of France. It falls within the historic Île de France whose boundaries extend further outwards, notably to the north and east towards Champagne. The Île de France includes such cities as Soissons, Fontainebleau, Rambouillet and Beauvais, peaceful even today – though no longer, alas, with the 'sixteen hundred botanical varieties, six thousand species of insect, and one hundred and four different kinds of fungus' which Mercier noted around Paris in the 1780s.

In the days before railways could bring fresh fruits and vegetables from afar, Paris depended on its village outskirts for immediate food supplies. Argenteuil was famous for asparagus, Montreuil for peaches, Montmorency for cherries, Vaugirard for strawberries, St Germain for peas and Clamart for peas, artichokes and butter. Now swallowed up by urban expansion, these communities of the Île de France are immortalized in the names of classic dishes like 'potage St Germain' and 'canard Montmorency'. Mushroom caves along the Seine, home of 'champignons de Paris', have now moved to the Loire. A little further afield, to the north of Paris, lies Chantilly, of cream fame, and, to the east, the great cheese area of Brie: the Île de France has been the dairy as well as the garden of the French capital.

Typical of Île de France cooking are vegetable dishes like 'potage cultivateur' and 'navarin printanier', a ragoût of lamb with baby carrots, onions, potatoes, turnips, peas and green beans. There are also a few specifically Parisian dishes which are the big-city counterpart of regional cooking. 'Pâtés Pantins', for example, named after one of the gates of Paris, are filled with sausagemeat and strips of pork and wrapped in a characteristic cylinder of pastry; 'petits pâtés parisiens' are round, also with a pork stuffing. Left-over cold beef seems to be a Parisian preoccupation: in 'miroton' the beef is reheated in broth, then pepped up with gherkin pickles and a sprinkling of vinegar, while in 'salade parisienne' it is dressed with onion, flavoured with vinaigrette and garnished with potatoes, carrots and hard-boiled eggs. The onion soup and grilled pig's feet of the brasseries of Les Halles (former wholesale markets) have become an institution.

Because of its wealth and dense population, Paris has always been a magnet to provincial emigrants seeking their fortunes in food, whether as chefs, charcutiers, pâtissiers, 'traiteurs' (caterers) or more humble employees in cafés, brasseries and markets. Many brought the cooking traditions of their native province with them, but with few exceptions they could offer little resistance to the blandishments of Parisian restaurant culture, its soups velvety with cream and butter, its boned meats, and its sauces strained to remove bits of offending vegetable (the classic 'mother' sauces – béchamel, espagnole and hollandaise – all originated here). Appropriately, the very word 'restaurant' was coined in Paris over 200 years ago, when an innkeeper began to offer bowls of bouillon as a 'restauratif'. Since then, the food business in Paris has never looked back.

LES GALOPINS
Bread pancakes

In a well-run household, nothing is wasted; in Picardy, stale bread is used for these pancakes.

Makes 14–16 pancakes

250 g	dry white bread, with the crusts	$\frac{1}{2}$ lb
500 ml	milk	2 cups
	5 eggs	
	pinch of salt	
60 g	butter	4 Tbsp
	sugar (for sprinkling)	
	23 cm/9 in frying pan	

Cut the bread in very thin slices and put them in a bowl. Bring the milk to a boil and pour three-quarters of it over the bread. Stir in more milk, little by little, as it is absorbed; don't add so much that the mixture becomes soupy. Mash the bread with a fork until quite smooth. Beat the eggs with a pinch of salt and whisk them into the bread. Add more milk, if necessary, so the batter is just pourable.

Heat a tablespoon of the butter in the frying pan until foaming. Pour in enough batter to cover the base of the pan, tipping it to spread the batter in an even layer. Cook over a medium fire for 2–3 minutes or until browned on the bottom. Slide the pancake on to a plate; then turn it over into the frying pan and brown the other side. The pancakes should be fluffy inside and thicker than crêpes. Keep them warm while you continue with the rest of the batter, buttering the pan as necessary to prevent sticking.

Serve the pancakes hot, sprinkled generously with sugar.

GAUFRES À LA FLAMANDE
Yeast waffles

In northern France, outdoor stands selling fresh waffles are almost as common as the vendors of 'frites' and date back at least to medieval times. In France waffles are usually topped with sugar or whipped cream, rather than with melted butter, and they are often shaped as hearts instead of in the usual grid pattern.

Makes 4–5 waffles

8 g	fresh yeast OR $\frac{1}{2}$ pkg dry yeast	$\frac{1}{2}$ cake
60 ml	lukewarm water	$\frac{1}{4}$ cup
200 g	flour	$1\frac{1}{2}$ cups
310 ml	milk, more if needed	$1\frac{1}{4}$ cups
	2 eggs	
5 g	salt	1 tsp
25 g	sugar	2 Tbsp
60 g	butter, melted	4 Tbsp
	$\frac{1}{2}$ tsp vanilla extract OR 1 tsp rum (optional)	
	brown or white sugar (for serving)	
	waffle iron	

In a small bowl crumble the yeast over the water, stir and leave for 5 minutes. Sift the flour into a bowl, make a well in the centre and add the yeast mixture, two-thirds of the milk, the eggs, salt, sugar, melted butter and vanilla. Briefly mix the centre ingredients, then gradually whisk in the flour to obtain a thick batter; don't beat or the waffles will be tough. Cover and let rise for $1\frac{1}{2}$–2 hours or until the batter has doubled in volume.

Heat the waffle iron until hot and brush it lightly with oil. Stir the remaining milk into the batter, adding more milk, if necessary, to obtain a batter which is very thick but just pourable. Transfer the batter to a pitcher or measuring cup with a spout. Pour enough batter on to the waffle iron just to fill the holes. Close the lid and cook over a fairly high fire for 4–5 minutes on each side. Carefully lift the lid; if it resists, cook another 30 seconds and try again. Brush the iron with a little more oil before cooking more waffles. Sprinkle the waffles with sugar and serve as soon as possible.

TARTE AU SUCRE
Sugar yeast cake

This yeast cake with a sugar topping is popular in the North, which is sugar beet country. You can double the quantity of dough and use half for 'pain brioché', a rich bread that the French like to toast for breakfast (see below).

Serves 6–8

60 g	butter, softened	4 Tbsp
110 g	light or dark brown sugar	½ cup
	YEAST DOUGH	
80 ml	lukewarm milk	⅓ cup
	1 Tbsp sugar	
8 g	fresh yeast OR	½ cake
	½ pkg dried yeast	
200 g	flour, more if needed	1½ cups
	2 eggs	
	¾ tsp salt	
100 g	butter	6 Tbsp
	25–27 cm/10–11 in pie or tart pan	

Make the yeast dough: put the lukewarm milk in a small bowl, add the sugar and crumble in the yeast. Leave for 5–10 minutes. Sift the flour on to a marble slab or board and make a well in the centre. Add the eggs, salt and dissolved yeast mixture. Briefly mix the central ingredients; then draw in the flour with both hands, pulling the dough into large crumbs with the fingertips. Knead the dough for 5–10 minutes or until very smooth and elastic, adding more flour if necessary so that the dough is not too sticky. Pound the butter to soften it thoroughly; then work it into the dough, slapping the dough on the work surface, just until the butter is thoroughly incorporated. Transfer the dough to a lightly oiled bowl, cover with a damp cloth and let rise in a warm place for 2 hours or until nearly doubled in bulk. Thoroughly butter the pie pan.

Transfer the risen dough to a floured work surface and fold it in thirds, patting it to knock out the air. Flour your hands and flatten the dough into the base (not the sides) of the pan. Let rise for 15 minutes; then spread with soft butter and sprinkle with the brown sugar. Let rise for another 15 minutes. Set the oven at hot (200°C/400°F).

Bake the sugar yeast cake in the hot oven for 15–20 minutes or until the dough is brown and firm. Serve at room temperature, either in the pan or unmoulded.

PAIN BRIOCHÉ

After folding the risen dough in thirds on the floured work surface, shape it into a rectangle and set in a buttered 20 × 10 × 6 cm/8 × 4 × 2½ in loaf pan and leave to rise for about 30 minutes. Brush with egg glaze and bake in a hot oven (200°C/400°F) for 30 minutes or until golden brown and hollow-sounding when tapped on the bottom.

FLAN
Latticed custard tart

'Flan' or custard tarts are made everywhere in France, often with pie pastry. The Picard yeast dough version, topped with a pastry lattice and sometimes containing prunes, is exceptionally good. In other regions the yeast dough is shaped in small rings or figures of eight, with the custard baked in the holes.

Serves 6–8

	BRIOCHE DOUGH	
8 g	fresh yeast OR	$\frac{1}{2}$ cake
	$\frac{1}{2}$ pkg dry yeast	
	1 Tbsp lukewarm water	
260 g	flour	2 cups
	4 eggs	
6 g	salt	$1\frac{1}{4}$ tsp
15 g	sugar	$1\frac{1}{4}$ Tbsp
125 g	unsalted butter	$\frac{1}{4}$ lb
	1 egg, beaten with $\frac{1}{2}$ tsp salt	
	(for glaze)	
	FILLING	
250 ml	milk	1 cup
100 g	sugar	$\frac{1}{2}$ cup
	3 eggs	
55 g	flour	6 Tbsp
160 ml	heavy cream	$\frac{2}{3}$ cup
	1 tsp vanilla extract	
	pinch of salt	
23–25 cm/9–10 in shallow cake pan or deep pie pan		

Make the brioche dough (see recipe), cover with a damp cloth and let rise at room temperature until doubled in bulk. Pat the dough to knock out the air; then cover and chill until firm enough to roll out.

Make the filling: heat the milk until lukewarm. In a bowl, whisk the sugar with the eggs until light and thick; then gently stir in the flour. Gradually whisk in the lukewarm milk, the cream, vanilla and salt. Butter the cake pan.

Roll out one quarter of the dough and cut in thin strips; set aside. Pat out the remaining dough and line the pan with it. Pour in the filling and leave in a warm place for 20 minutes so that the dough rises. Set the oven at hot (200°C/400°F).

Bake the flan in the heated oven for 15 minutes or until the custard begins to set. Arrange the reserved strips of dough on the flan to form a lattice and brush the ends with egg glaze, pressing them firmly on to the edges of the dough. Carefully brush the edge of the flan and the lattice with glaze. Lower the oven heat to moderately low (165°C/325°F) and bake for another 45–50 minutes or until the dough is well browned and the filling is set. Leave to cool before unmoulding. Serve at room temperature.

DARTOIS
Feuilleté with pastry cream

Some think this puff pastry was created in Artois; others that it was made up by a vaudeville artist named Dartois, who was born in Artois in 1788. In any case, the earliest mention of puff pastry, 'gâteau feuilleté', comes from the North in a charter granted by Bishop Robert of Amiens in 1311.

Serves 6–8

	1 egg white, beaten until frothy	
	sugar (for sprinkling)	
	PUFF PASTRY	
250 g	unsalted butter	$\frac{1}{2}$ lb
175 g	all-purpose flour	$1\frac{1}{3}$ cups
80 g	cake flour	$\frac{2}{3}$ cup
5 g	salt	1 tsp
	1 tsp lemon juice	
125 ml	iced water, more as needed	$\frac{1}{2}$ cup
	PASTRY CREAM	
375 ml	milk	$1\frac{1}{2}$ cups
	pinch of salt	
	5 egg yolks	
90 g	sugar	7 Tbsp
40 g	flour	$\frac{1}{3}$ cup
	1 Tbsp rum	

Make the puff pastry* and chill for 1 hour or until firm. Make the pastry cream*, let it cool, and flavour it with rum.

Roll out the dough to a 25 × 35 cm/10 × 14 in rectangle. Trim the edges neatly and cut the rectangle in half lengthwise. Transfer one half to a moistened baking sheet and spoon the pastry cream down the centre to within 2·5 cm/1 in of the edges. Brush the edges with cold water and cover with the second rectangle of pastry, pressing the edges together. Scallop the edges all round with a knife and chill for 15–20 minutes. Set the oven at very hot (220°C/425°F).

Prick the top of the dartois 2–3 times and bake in the heated oven for 20–25 minutes or until puffed and browned; then brush it with beaten egg white, sprinkle generously with sugar and continue baking for another 5–10 minutes or until the sugar becomes a shiny glaze and the pastry is crisp. Transfer to a rack to cool.

PAINS AUX AMANDES
Almond biscuits

In Flanders these biscuits accompany coffee, which is invariably sharp with chicory. The best cafés offer a free second cup from a tall brass coffee-pot.

Makes 50 biscuits

160 g	flour	1¼ cups
	½ tsp ground ginger	
	pinch of ground cinnamon	
	½ tsp ground allspice	
125 g	butter	¼ lb
110 g	light brown sugar	½ cup
	½ tsp baking powder	
20 g	sliced almonds	3 Tbsp

Sift the flour, ginger, cinnamon and allspice on to a marble slab and make a well in the centre. Pound the butter to soften it; then add it to the well along with the brown sugar and baking powder. Using the fingertips, quickly work the ingredients in the well until partly mixed. Gradually draw in the flour, pulling the dough into large crumbs. Knead the dough in three or four portions on the work surface, pushing it away with the heel of your hand and gathering it up with a dough scraper or rubber spatula until it is pliable and peels away easily in one piece. Press the dough into a rectangular block measuring 15 × 7·5 × 2·5 cm/6 × 3 × 1 in, wrap and chill for 30 minutes or until firm enough to slice. Heat the oven to hot (200°C/400°F).

Cut the dough into wafer-thin slices and transfer them to a baking sheet lined with foil. Sprinkle each biscuit with two or three almond slices, pressing them in lightly. Bake in the oven for 5–7 minutes or until golden brown. Transfer the biscuits to a rack to cool.

CHEESES

The North is the land of strong cheeses. Many resemble the most famous, 'maroilles', which is rinsed with beer as it matures and acquires a reddish-brown rind. When ripe it is aptly named 'vieux puant' (the old stinker) and has an odour so strong that people refuse to share the same room with it. But maroilles is addictive and its devotees have included a handful of kings, among them Philippe-Auguste, Charles VI and François I. The people in the town of Maroilles are so proud of their cheese that they have built a monument in its honour.

'Dauphin', named for the dauphin son of Louis IX, and sometimes shaped like a crescent or a fish, is a variant of maroilles flavoured with tarragon and pepper and aged in the same way. An even stronger smelling cheese, the cone-shaped 'boulette d'Avesnes', is made from imperfect maroilles cheeses which are mashed and flavoured with parsley, tarragon and pepper before being left to mature. 'Mimolette', bright orange and hard with a rough rind, looks like a Dutch cheese, as indeed it is. However, a good deal of mimolette is also made and consumed in France; it is a reliable cheese with an agreeably piquant flavour.

Further south the cheeses are milder: 'chaource', 'caprice des dieux' and 'Pierre Robert' are among several mild, high-fat cheeses from Champagne. 'Carré de l'est', a square cheese resembling a mild camembert, is made both here and in Lorraine. Champagne also produces many 'cendré' (cinder) cheeses – 'barbery', 'cendré d'Argonne' and 'cendré de Champagne' to name a few – relatively low-fat cheeses cured in cases filled with wood ashes, and which have a sharp flavour. Their modest fame is quite eclipsed by their neighbour to the west, 'brie'.

Brie is the most famous of all French cheeses: Charlemagne is reported to have tasted brie in 774, and, more than a thousand years later, as the official ambassador of Louis XVIII, Talleyrand took some to the negotiations at the Congress of Vienna, declaring King Brie was the only monarch to whom he could be faithful.

A pale, shallow wheel about 36 cm/14 in across, brie at its best is deep cream inside, soft but not runny, and with nuances of flavour that have been compared to hazelnuts and to vintage wine. Like all soft cheese, good brie is hard to find. It varies with the seasons – it is at its best from November to May – and it must be made with unpasteurized milk and stored at the proper temperature so that the ripening process is not interrupted. More reliable in quality, but less subtle than brie, is 'coulommiers', a smaller cheese made down the road from Meaux, the centre of brie production.

This area just south and west of Paris is also known for cream cheeses which are delivered fresh to the capital. 'Boursin' flavoured with garlic and herbs is best known, but it is also sold plain or rolled in crushed peppercorns. Best of all, perhaps, is 'fromage de Fontainebleau', a whipped cream cheese like the 'crémets' of the Loire, served as dessert with crème fraîche and a sprinkling of sugar.

OTHER SPECIALITIES OF THE REGION
TRADITIONAL DISHES

Anguille au vert
Eel in green herb sauce

Ramequin douaisien
Bread rolls with kidney and herb stuffing

Courquignoise
Spicy fish and shellfish stew

Ficelle picarde
Crêpe with ham and mushrooms

Craquelot
Grilled smoked herring

Potée champenoise
Pot-au-feu of pork, ham, sausages and vegetables

Truite ardennaise
Sautéed trout with ham and cream sauce

La menouille
Bacon stew with beans, onions and potatoes

Hareng boulonnaise
Herring and potato salad in a mustard vinaigrette

Boudins de lapin
Rabbit dumplings

Waterzooi de poissons
Freshwater fish stew in butter sauce

Canard en croûte
Stuffed duck in pastry

Moules à la bière
Mussels in beer

Poularde en gelée champenoise
Chicken in aspic of still champagne

Maquereaux flamands en papillotes
Mackerel in paper cases with herb butter

Jets de houblon à la crème
Hop shoots in cream

CHARCUTERIE

Pâté de foie aux pruneaux
Liver pâté with prunes

Boudin à la flamande
Blood sausage served with semolina, almonds and raisins

Pot Je Vleese, terrine flamande
Rabbit, veal and pork terrine

Jambon d'Ardennes
Raw smoked Ardennes ham

Langue fumée de Lille
Smoked tongue

PÂTISSERIE AND CONFISERIE

Taliburs
Pear dumplings

Nonnettes
Little honey cakes with royal icing

Anglois
Plum tart

Gâteaux St Nicolas
Spiced Christmas biscuits

Pains picards à la noix
Little nut cakes

Sucre d'orge
Barley sugar

Gâteau battu
Rich yeast cake

Bêtises de Cambrai
Mint humbugs

Burgundy and the Lyonnais

Burgundy can justly claim to be the place where good French eating began. Starting in the 14th century, when Philip the Bold extended his Duchy by marrying Marguerite of Flanders, the Burgundian court at Dijon became a centre for all the arts. A century later the reigning duke added a stupendous kitchen to his palace, the better to serve his guests. Its ample construction, featuring an octagonal chamber with four stone fireplaces leading to a single chimney, prompted the gastronome Curnonsky to exclaim, 'Some have built a hearth in their kitchen, but the dukes of Burgundy, they made a kitchen from their hearth.'

The political power of the Duchy waned, but Burgundy remained a cultural force, straddling the main highway from the Mediterranean to the north. The Renaissance was eagerly welcomed and the lead in hospitality taken by the dukes was followed up by the inns of Burgundy, particularly those on the road north to Paris. When, in August 1677, Madame de Sévigné stopped at Saulieu (to this day an outstanding 'étape'), she was given a great welcome at the Auberge Dauphin. She recorded fish in meurette sauce, and mustard made with verjuice, and she drank so much good wine that she got tipsy for the first time in her life. Contrite, she donated a statue to the local church.

Today Burgundy retains its reputation for good cooking, so that many authorities claim that the true gastronomic heart of France lies not in Paris but in the old Duchy and the neighbouring province of Lyonnais. At least part of the credit goes to the local produce. For the cook the region contains just about everything. The finest chickens in France come from Bresse, south of Dijon, and the Charolais country next door has given its name to a breed of beef cattle that is exported throughout the world. The Morvan hills are famous for their ham, and the curious marshes of the Dombes shelter a few harried wildfowl and an abundance of frogs. Fruits and vegetables thrive in the soft climate, particularly south of Lyon, which is but 300 kilometres from the Mediterranean by way of the Rhône. Not that Burgundy need look to the sea for its fish. The Saône and the Rhône both flow through here, and the region is laced with their many tributaries and lakes.

A few years ago I was given a guided tour of this largesse by Léa, one of the surviving 'mères', the women cooks of Lyon. Léa began her career as a café waitress, sleeping under the bar counter at night. When one day the cook was sick, Léa took over the stove, and has never left it since. We set off from her bistro, strategically placed in Lyon opposite the open market along the banks of the Saône. Shopping cart in one hand, vintage car horn in the other to clear the path, we worked our way from merchant to merchant, buying a crate of dandelion greens here and some pots of fresh cheese there, poking the pears and looking the fish directly in the eye. Like all expert shoppers, Léa played one seller against another, never buying from the same stall every day. When we reached the end of the 600-metre long line, the little cart was piled high with merchandise. We crossed the road to her tiny kitchen and Léa set to work, instinctively faithful to at least two of the golden rules: use the freshest of ingredients, and prepare them at the last possible moment.

Léa belongs to a cooking tradition which began with the development of restaurants at the time of the Revolution, when service in noble houses went into decline. Starting around 1760 with Mère Guy, who was known for her matelote of river fish, by the turn of the last century cooking in Lyon was dominated by women. Few remain, but 'les mères' have passed on a robust, homely cuisine that provides a refreshing counterpoint to the studied sophistication of the great male chefs, such as Dumaine, Point, Bocuse and Troisgros, who have clustered in Burgundy and the Lyonnais. From Mère Guy on, the women have kept closer to home with dishes like 'quenelles au gratin' or 'poularde de Bresse rôtie'.

If Bresse is synonymous with the finest in French chickens, Charolais says the same for beef. Large, buff and uninspiring in appearance, the Charolais answers the modern demand for a high yield of lean meat. Mature beasts can weigh up to a tonne – 'meat mills' they are called. By English and American standards, the Charolais steak can be a disappointment: mild and chewy, even verging on the tough. The meat is much more appropriate to old-fashioned slow cooking, as in the classic 'boeuf bourguignon' simmered with bacon, mushrooms and red wine, or 'boeuf à la mode' braised with vegetables.

North of Bresse and the Charolais lies the heart of Burgundy, a soothing landscape replete with turreted châteaux and Romanesque abbeys. Luckily for laymen, the good works of the church have often extended to food and wine, and nowhere more successfully than here. The Hospice, the charity hospital founded in Beaune in 1443, today owns parcels of the finest vineyards of the Côte d'Or, not to mention Chablis, the Mâconnais and Beaujolais. At its annual wine auction, three banquets are customary which, like the vineyard celebrations at the end of harvest, are called 'paulées'. Traditional paulée fare includes potée made with beef, chicken and vegetables; civet of hare; brioches; fruit tarts and one of the great Burgundian creations, 'pochouse'. Pochouse is a freshwater fish stew, usually including perch, pike, carp and trout, with eel for richness and bacon and white wine for flavour; the sharp Burgundian aligoté is particularly suitable.

The use of white wine in cooking is not, however, so very typical of Burgundy. To cook red meats with red wine is hardly remarkable, but the local red wine 'sauce meurette' is designed to go with eggs and brains, and there is even a red wine soup. Around Mâcon, pochouse becomes matelote, the fish cooked in red instead of white wine, and the Nivernais stew of chicken en matelote includes eel in a red wine sauce. In Dijon I have eaten some memorable snails that were cooked, not in the usual overwhelming garlic butter, but in sauce meurette flavoured with tarragon and served in a little copper casserole.

In Lyon itself the art of eating is taken just as seriously at home as in restaurants. The delicacies provided by the rôtisseurs, incorporated in the city in 1688, and the charcutiers, founded in 1543, are still in great demand. Gastronomic societies flourish such as the Francs-Mâchons (Free-Munchers) and The Académie du Lapin whose seven members represent the feet, ears and tail of the rabbit. Burgundian groups such as the Commanderie des Cordons bleus and the Chevaliers du Tastevin have spread worldwide from Dijon.

On home ground both the Lyonnais and Burgundians are adventurous about their food. As well as stocking a dozen kinds of sausage of more or less attributable origin, charcuteries sell a huge range of pâtés, terrines and quenelles (a great Lyon favourite) as well as the hams and bacon which flavour so many regional dishes. Fish markets routinely offer baby eels and fresh crayfish, and it is a poor greengrocer who does not display salad greens such as

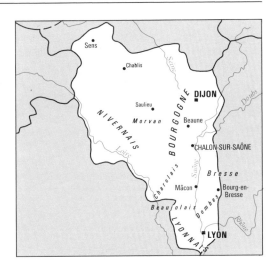

'mâche' (lamb's lettuce) and 'roquette', with its bitter purple leaves, as well as root artichokes, 'cardoons' or 'crosnes', curly little roots also known as Chinese artichokes. Cheese shops appear equally versatile, if somewhat dominated by goat cheese, a taste which goes hand in hand with the kid meat sold in many markets. Even in Burgundy, however, a certain audacity is required to tackle kid's sweetbreads or a 'fireman's apron', a piece of deep-fried tripe in breadcrumbs.

More understandable is the Lyonnais love of chocolate, first developed by confiseurs from Italy in the 18th century. Little cakes vary from cups of nougat filled with chocolate cream to chocolate meringues and chocolate-coated petits fours. Every pâtissier has his special gâteau in which the chocolate is often combined with almonds, or chestnuts from the nearby Nivernais. The finest are crowned with chocolate curls that pâtissiers need years to perfect.

As well as its cooks, Burgundy has had its gastronomic chroniclers, many of whom have designated Lyon the 'capital of French gastronomy'. As one chauvinist puts it, 'Parisians taste everything without tasting anything; the Lyonnais eat.' The novelist Colette pays touching tribute to Burgundy's traditions: 'I was born in the country, in a region where people still treasured recipes, which I have never found in any cooking guide, as they would the secret of a perfume or some miraculous balm. They were passed on by word of mouth alone, on the occasion of some christening of a first-born, or a confirmation. They escaped, during lengthy wedding feasts, from lips unlocked by vintage wines.' Is there a more succinct account of French country cooking?

GRATINÉE LYONNAISE
Onion soup with cheese

Onion soup, a bistro favourite throughout France, epitomizes the hearty cooking of Lyon. A 19th-century traveller exclaimed, 'After a meal of onion soup, sausage, a good St-Marcellin cheese and a bottle of Juliénas, nothing more is needed but a good night's sleep.'

Serves 4–6

90 g	butter	6 Tbsp
750 g	onions, thinly sliced	1½ lb
	salt and pepper	
	1 whole onion, peeled	
	1–2 tsp sugar	
1·5 L	broth	1½ qt
	1 loaf French bread OR 2–3 long crisp rolls, cut in thick slices	
200 g	grated gruyère cheese	2 cups
	4–6 eggs (optional)	
	4–6 Tbsp port wine (optional)	
4–6 individual ovenproof soup bowls (marmites)		

Melt half the butter in a shallow, heavy-based pan. Add the sliced onions, salt and pepper and press a piece of buttered paper or foil on top. Cover and cook gently, stirring occasionally, for 20–30 minutes or until the onions are very soft. Remove the lid and paper and continue cooking until golden; don't allow them to burn. This browning gives flavour to the soup.

In a separate pan melt another tablespoon of butter, add the whole onion and toss it until coated in butter. Sprinkle with the sugar and cook gently until very dark brown all over. Add the whole onion to the sliced onions and continue to cook together for 1–2 minutes. Add the broth with a little salt and pepper and simmer for 20–30 minutes; taste for seasoning. Discard the whole onion. Set the oven at low (150°C/300°F).

While the onions are simmering, bake the sliced bread until dry and lightly browned. Melt the remaining butter. Set 2–3 slices of bread in individual marmites and pour the soup over them. Sprinkle generously with grated cheese, moisten each bread slice with melted butter and grill/broil until browned. Mix each egg yolk with a tablespoon of port, lift the side of the browned topping and pour in the mixture. Serve at once; onion soup must be scalding hot.

SOUPE AU POTIRON ET AUX POIREAUX
Pumpkin and leek soup

'In passing through the Maconnois,' wrote Tobias Smollett in 1766, 'I observed a vast quantity of very large pompions [pumpkins] with the contents of which they thicken their soup and ragoûts.' And so they still do, two centuries later.

Serves 6

350 g	potatoes	¾ lb
750 g	pumpkin	1½ lb
	white part of 4 leeks, split	
1 L	water, more if needed	1 qt
	salt and pepper	
75 g	butter	5 Tbsp
	a few sprigs chervil OR	
	1 tsp chopped chives	
	½ tsp sugar (optional)	

Halve the potatoes, or quarter them if large. Peel the pumpkin and remove any seeds and fibres: you should have about 625 g/1¼ lb peeled flesh. Cut it into pieces about the same size as the potatoes. Cut the leeks into 2–3 pieces. Put all the vegetables into a large pot with the water and some salt. Cover, bring to a boil and simmer for 30 minutes or until the vegetables are very tender. Purée the vegetables and liquid in a food mill or blender.

Return the puréed soup to the pot and bring it back to a boil; add more water if it is too thick. Remove from the heat and stir in the butter, a piece at a time. Add the chervil and taste for seasoning; if the soup lacks flavour, add the sugar. Serve very hot.

SOUPE AUX COURGES
Substitute the same quantity of winter squash for the pumpkin.

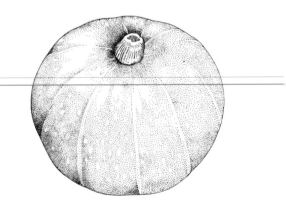

Potiron

LA CERVELLE DE CANUT
Fresh cheese with herbs

The 'Canuts' are the silk weavers of Lyon, though why they call this cheese spread their 'cervelle' (brains) is undisclosed. Its original name of 'claqueret' is more explanatory: 'claquer' means to slap, an action, said the men of Lyon, that kept their cheese and their wives in good order.

Serves 6–8

400 g	cream cheese*	13 oz
80 ml	heavy cream or crème fraîche*	$\frac{1}{3}$ cup
	2 Tbsp white wine	
	1 Tbsp oil	
	1 tsp wine vinegar (optional)	
	2 cloves garlic, finely chopped	
	2 Tbsp chopped parsley	
	2 Tbsp chopped chives	
	salt and pepper	
	boiled or steamed potatoes, fresh bread or toast (for serving)	

Beat the cheese until very smooth; then whisk in the cream, wine, oil and vinegar, if using. Stir in the garlic, parsley and chives with salt and pepper to taste. Spoon the mixture into a small bowl and serve with hot boiled or steamed potatoes or as a spread for bread or toast.

CORNIOTTES BOURGUIGNONNES
Cheese feuilletés

Corniottes, in the shape of cocked hats, are triangles made of puff pastry with a savoury or sweet filling based on the fresh cheese that is so popular in Burgundy.

Makes 9 corniottes

50 g	grated gruyère cheese (for topping)	$\frac{1}{2}$ cup
	PUFF PASTRY	
250 g	unsalted butter	$\frac{1}{2}$ lb
175 g	all-purpose flour	$1\frac{1}{4}$ cups
80 g	cake flour	$\frac{2}{3}$ cup
5 g	salt	1 tsp
	1 tsp lemon juice	
125 ml	iced water, more as needed	$\frac{1}{2}$ cup
	1 egg yolk, beaten with 1 tsp water (for glaze)	
	CHEESE FILLING	
250 g	cream cheese*	8 oz
	2 eggs	
180 g	gruyère cheese, diced	6 oz
	salt and pepper	
	12 cm/5 in pastry cutter	

Make the puff pastry* and chill for 1 hour or until firm.

For the filling: beat the cream cheese with the eggs and stir in the diced gruyère cheese. Add salt and pepper to taste. Set the oven at hot (200°C/400°F). Sprinkle a baking sheet with water.

Roll out the pastry about 6 mm/$\frac{1}{4}$ in thick and cut it in rounds with the pastry cutter. Put a spoonful of filling in the centre of each round and brush the edges of the pastry with egg glaze. Fold up the round from three directions to form a triangle that nearly encloses the filling, pinching the angles to seal. Set the pastries on the prepared baking sheet and chill for 15 minutes or until firm.

Brush the pastries with the glaze and bake them in the hot oven for 15 minutes; then sprinkle them with the grated cheese and bake for another 10–15 minutes or until golden brown. Serve hot or at room temperature.

CORNIOTTES SUCRÉES

Sweet cheese triangles are also made in Burgundy. Replace the gruyère with sugar and flavour the cheese filling mixture with vanilla or orange flower water in place of the salt and pepper.

LES GOUGÈRES
Cheese choux puffs

The cathedral town of Sens, lying on the old road from Paris to Burgundy, likes to claim credit for the original 'gougère'. But farther south, Burgundians proper have long been serving this cheese pastry as their traditional accompaniment to a glass of beaujolais. As one wine connoisseur put it, 'Gougère is not a cheese, though it has that savour, nor a pastry, though it has that appearance. It is the ideal bridge between main course and dessert, allowing the last glass of wine to be enjoyed with delight.' Gougère can be made as separate puffs or in a large ring. The individual puffs can be served with or without filling.

Serves 4 or makes 20 puffs

CHEESE CHOUX PASTRY		
185 ml	water	¾ cup
	½ tsp salt	
80 g	butter	5 Tbsp
95 g	flour	¾ cup
	3–4 eggs	
60 g	gruyère cheese, diced	2 oz
	pinch of ground pepper	
	pinch of grated nutmeg	
	2 Tbsp grated gruyère cheese (for sprinkling)	
CHEESE FILLING		
500 ml	milk	2 cups
	1 slice of onion	
	bay leaf	
	6 black peppercorns	
30 g	butter	2 Tbsp
20 g	flour	2½ Tbsp
	salt and pepper	
	pinch of grated nutmeg	
	2 Tbsp heavy cream or crème fraîche*	
65 g	grated gruyère cheese	⅔ cup

Make the choux pastry*, stirring in the diced cheese after the last egg has been added. Season the dough to taste with pepper and nutmeg. Set the oven at very hot (220°C/425°F).

Thoroughly butter a baking sheet. Use two spoons to pile the dough in 2·5 cm/1 in mounds, leaving plenty of room for them to puff out to about 7·5 cm/3 in. Sprinkle the mounds with the 2 tablespoons of grated cheese and bake for 25–30 minutes or until golden brown and crisp.

Meanwhile, make a thin béchamel sauce* for the cheese filling. When the puffs are baked, slit each one and let cool slightly so steam can escape. Reheat the sauce, stir in the cream and grated cheese and taste for seasoning. Spoon some of the hot filling into each puff. Serve hot or lukewarm.

LA GOUGÈRE

Butter a 23 cm/9 in pie pan or baking dish and, using two spoons, arrange the dough in puffs around the sides, not quite touching each other; leave the centre of the pan empty. Sprinkle the puffs with grated cheese and bake for 30–35 minutes or until golden brown; they will expand to touch each other and form a ring. Spoon the filling into the centre of the ring and return the pan to the oven for 3–4 minutes to reheat the filling. Cut gougère in slices and serve a spoonful of filling with each.

RIGODON BOURGUIGNON
Ham flan

In the days when every 'maison bourgeoise' in lower Burgundy had its bread oven, 'rigodon' was cooked after the bread on baking day. Half pudding, half omelette, it needs gentle heat and can be flavoured with cooked meat or poultry as an alternative to ham.

Serves 4

200 g	cooked ham or bacon, thinly sliced	7 oz
625 ml	milk	2½ cups
	5 eggs, beaten	
45 g	flour	⅓ cup
	salt and pepper	
	pinch of ground allspice	
	pinch of thyme	
30 g	butter	2 Tbsp
	1·5 L/1½ qt shallow baking dish	

Cut the ham or bacon in tiny dice. If using bacon, blanch* it if it is salty and sauté it for 2–3 minutes in a frying pan until the fat runs but the bacon is not yet crisp. Butter the baking dish and sprinkle the ham or bacon over the bottom. Set the oven at moderate (175°C/350°F).

Bring the milk to a boil in a medium pot. In a bowl whisk the eggs and flour until smooth; gradually add the hot milk, whisking vigorously so the milk does not cook the eggs. Season with salt, pepper, allspice and thyme.

Pour the mixture into the baking dish, dot with the butter and bake in the heated oven for 35–40 minutes or until set and golden brown; a knife inserted into the mixture should be dry when withdrawn. Serve rigodon from the dish, either warm or at room temperature.

JAMBON PERSILLÉ
Ham aspic with parsley

The quality of this dish depends on the ham used to make it. In Burgundy the ham is lightly cured so the meat in the aspic is rosy pink and the flavour not too salty. If possible, use similar unsmoked raw ham or gammon in Britain. Good cooked ham, or US processed ham, can also be substituted; if so, the ham should not be blanched, and it should be added to the calf's feet and bones half-way through cooking as it will need only about an hour of simmering. The preferred white wine is a Burgundian chablis or aligoté. Some cooks, however, sprinkle the ham cubes with a little wine vinegar instead of with the wine, and substitute a little chopped garlic for the shallots.

Serves 10–12 as a first course

about 3 kg	shank half of a country-cured ham or 2 hocks	about 7 lb
	2 calf's or pig's feet, split	
500 g	veal bones	1 lb
	2 onions	
	large bouquet garni	
	12 black peppercorns	
	1 leek, trimmed and split	
	3 stalks celery	
	2 carrots	
580 ml	white wine	2⅓ cups
	6 shallots, very finely chopped (optional)	
	3 Tbsp chopped parsley	
	salt and pepper	
cheesecloth; 3–4 L/3–4 qt deep bowl or terrine		

If the ham is very salty, soak it overnight in cold water, changing the water once or twice. Blanch the ham, calf's feet and veal bones by putting them in cold water, bringing it to a boil and simmering for 5 minutes. Drain them and rinse under cold running water. Halve the onions and singe them over an electric plate or gas burner until very dark to give colour to the aspic.

In a large, heavy-based pot (not aluminium) put the ham, calf's feet, veal bones, bouquet garni, peppercorns, onions, leek, celery, carrots, 500 ml white wine and enough water to cover. Bring slowly to a boil, skim well and simmer for 2½–3½ hours or until the ham is tender enough to be pulled apart with a fork. Skim the mixture often during cooking to remove the fat that rises to the surface and to keep the mixture clear. Add more water if necessary, to keep the meat covered.

Let the mixture cool slightly; then lift out all the meat with a slotted spoon. Discard the skin, remove the meat from the bones and calf's feet, and set aside. Boil the cooking liquid to reduce to about 1·5 litres and well flavoured. Pull the meat into large chunks with two forks and mix it with the remaining white wine, shallots and parsley. Discard the bouquet garni, peppercorns and vegetables. Strain the cooking liquid through cheesecloth and taste for seasoning. Place a layer of meat loosely in a deep bowl or terrine and spoon over enough liquid barely to cover. Let cool. Continue to make similar layers until all the meat is used. Pour over enough liquid to cover.

Cover and chill the ham aspic for 3–4 hours or until firmly set. It can be refrigerated for 7–10 days; the flavour mellows with standing.

To serve: run the point of a knife around the bowl and unmould the aspic on to a platter. Serve the aspic at room temperature, cutting it in wedges like a cake. If using a terrine, slice the aspic in the terrine.

JAMBON DE PÂQUES

Layer the ham with 5–6 whole hard-boiled eggs, placed at approximately equal intervals in the bowl or terrine. Pour the reduced liquid over the top. Traditionally, this dish is served on Easter Monday.

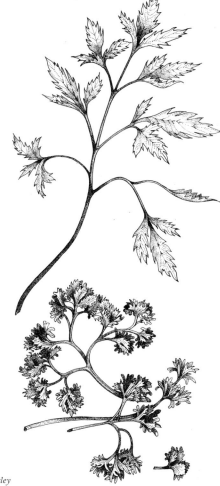

Parsley

SAUCISSON AUX TRUFFES ET AUX PISTACHES

Sausage with truffles and pistachio nuts

Although sausages like this one are nowadays found in all parts of France, the Lyonnais claim to have invented the recipe.

Makes a 1 kg/2 lb sausage

	large sausage casing (30–40 cm/12–16 in)	
	30 g/1 oz can of truffles	
750 g	lean pork	1½ lb
250 g	pork fat	½ lb
12 g	salt	2¼ tsp
	large pinch of white pepper	
	pinch of grated nutmeg	
	2 Tbsp cognac, port or madeira	
	2 Tbsp pistachios, peeled	
	sausage-stuffing tube or large funnel; string	

Soak the casing in cold running water; then attach it to the tap and run water through to rinse it. Chop the truffles, reserving their liquid.

Work the lean and fat pork through the fine plate of a mincer/grinder. Put in a bowl with the salt, pepper, nutmeg and cognac and beat well to mix in the seasonings. Beat in the pistachios and then the truffles, with their liquid. Sauté a small piece of the mixture and taste it for seasoning; the mixture should be highly seasoned.

Attach one end of the casing to a sausage stuffer or wide-based funnel and tie the other end with string. Push the meat mixture through the sausage stuffer into the casing, easing it down towards the tied end. Shape it into a compact sausage 25–30 cm/10–12 in long, but be careful not to pack the casing too tightly or the sausage will burst. If there are many air pockets in the sausage, prick them with a pin. Tie the other end of the sausage with string. Refrigerate overnight.

To cook the sausage, bring a large pan of water to a boil, add the sausage and poach over a low fire for 1 hour or until hot in the centre when tested with a skewer; to avoid bursting the sausage don't let the water temperature rise above 90°C/195°F. Cut in fairly thin slices, discarding the casing. Serve warm or at room temperature.

SAUCISSON EN BRIOCHE

Either buy French garlic sausage for this or make 'saucisson aux truffes et aux pistaches' (left).

Serves 8

1-kg	whole sausage	2-lb
	1 egg, beaten with ½ tsp salt (for glaze)	
	BRIOCHE DOUGH	
15 g	fresh yeast OR	1 cake
	1 pkg dry yeast	
	2 Tbsp lukewarm water	
460 g	flour, more if needed	3½ cups
	7 eggs	
12 g	salt	2¼ tsp
30 g	sugar	2½ Tbsp
250 g	unsalted butter	½ lb
	two 23 × 12 × 10 cm/9 × 5 × 4 in loaf pans	

Prepare the brioche dough (see recipe), cover and let rise at room temperature until doubled in bulk. Pat to knock out the air, cover and chill until firm enough to roll out.

If the truffle sausage is already poached, remove the skin; if it is raw, poach it according to the recipe. Poach French garlic sausage for 45 minutes–1 hour or until hot in the centre when tested with a skewer; don't let the water temperature rise above 90°C/195°F. Cool the sausage and remove the skin. Cut the sausage in half crosswise. Butter the loaf pans.

Roll out the dough to a 45 × 18 cm/18 × 7 in rectangle and cut in half crosswise. Brush the dough with egg glaze. Brush the sausage halves with egg glaze also and roll them lightly in flour. Set each sausage lengthwise on a piece of dough and wrap the dough around it. Pinch the edges to seal well and turn the dough over so that the seam is underneath. Pinch the ends of each roll to seal and put in the pans. Cover with a damp cloth and let rise at room temperature for 25–30 minutes or until the pans are almost full. Set the oven at hot (200°C/400°F).

Brush the loaves with egg glaze and bake them for 40–45 minutes or until the brioche is well browned and starts to pull away from the sides of the pan. Turn out on to a rack to cool. Serve warm or at room temperature, cutting each loaf into thick slices and discarding the ends so each person has a serving of sausage.

SAUCISSON EN BRIOCHE II

Reserve a little dough for decoration. Set the wrapped sausages on a buttered baking sheet, seam side down, and brush with glaze. Decorate with bands of the reserved dough and glaze again. Let rise for 15 minutes. To prevent the brioche from spreading too much in the oven, chill for 30 minutes before baking.

LYON CHARCUTERIE

The term charcuterie (from 'chair cuite', meaning cold meat) covers two general categories: prepared foods such as salads and quiche lorraine, and any product of the pig. The charcutiers of Lyon, long recognized as the finest in France, excel at the latter. 'Among the Lyonnais,' wrote the 17th-century poet Dulaurier, 'none think of making a good meal without bacon or ham.'

Half a dozen sausages are special to the region. The most famous, 'rosette de Lyon', is a salami-type sausage which is dried in the Monts du Lyonnais around St Symphorien, a town that has so many meat factories it has earned the name 'little Chicago'. 'Cervelas lyonnais', so called because it once contained 'cervelle' (brains), is now made of pure pork. It may be smoked for everyday use or flavoured with truffles or pistachios for festive occasions, and it is eaten cold, with no further preparation. Similar in texture, but served hot, is 'saucisson à l'ail' (garlic sausage), which can be bought cooked or uncooked. Bistros serve it with hot potato vinaigrette and grander restaurants like to wrap it in brioche. Lyon also has its own andouillettes, tripe sausages based on veal, not to mention black and white 'boudins' and 'andouilles'. 'Judru' is more esoteric; it is flavoured with marc and made from the intestines of pigs which in the old days would have fed on acorns in the woods under the ancient privilege of 'pannage'.

Pig's trotters, 'grattons' (cracklings), head cheese, and sow's ears – the Lyonnais love them all. 'Ferchusse', a dish of heart, lungs and spleen cooked with red wine and garlic, used to be made when a pig was killed. Nowadays the locals regale themselves on succulent hams from the Morvan, some raw and smoked, others cooked. Ham goes into dishes like 'saupiquet', flavoured with vinegar and juniper, and 'jambon persillé', where the ham is cooked with white wine, then layered in a bowl with chopped parsley until it sets to a stiff hemisphere. The contrast of pink ham and green parsley makes this one of the prettiest of all presentations.

POCHOUSE

Fish stew with white wine

Pochouse or pauchouse – both spellings are common – fish stew has its origin in the variety of fish native to Burgundy's many rivers. The pochouse made in the 16th century by an inn-keeper at Chalon-sur-Saône included 'salmon, pike, trout, perch, eel in fine condition', all still standard ingredients. Traditionally two of the fish should be rich like salmon and eel, and two should be white fish such as pike, trout, perch, carp and catfish.

Serves 8–10

2 kg	mixed freshwater fish	$4\frac{1}{2}$ lb
1 L	fish stock*	1 qt
	2 Tbsp marc or cognac	
	bouquet garni	
	salt and pepper	
125 g	lean bacon, cut in lardons (optional)	4 oz
60 g	butter	4 Tbsp
	1 onion, finely chopped	
	2 cloves garlic, finely chopped	
250 ml	dry white wine (preferably burgundy)	1 cup
45 g	butter, kneaded with	3 Tbsp
30 g	flour	$\frac{1}{4}$ cup
125 ml	heavy cream or crème fraîche*	$\frac{1}{2}$ cup
	a few drops of lemon juice	
	2 Tbsp chopped parsley	
	8–10 triangular croûtes*, fried in oil and butter, then rubbed with garlic	

Discard the fins and scale and clean the fish, leaving the skin on all but the eel. Cut eel into 5 cm/2 in slices and other fish into 2 cm/$\frac{3}{4}$ in pieces. Use the heads and tails to make the fish stock. Wash the fish pieces and pat dry. Put them in a large bowl with the marc, bouquet garni, salt and pepper and leave to marinate for 30 minutes–1 hour.

If the bacon is salty, blanch* it. Fry the bacon in a tablespoon of the butter until lightly browned; drain on paper towels.

Heat the remaining butter in a large pot, add the onion and garlic and cook gently until soft but not brown. Add the wine, fish stock, salt and pepper. Bring to a boil, add the fish and its marinade, cover and simmer for 10 minutes or until the fish just flake easily. Remove the pieces of fish, cover and keep them warm in a little of the liquid; discard the bouquet garni. If necessary, boil the cooking liquid until reduced to about 500 ml. Whisk enough of the kneaded butter*, a piece at a time, into the boiling liquid until the sauce thickens to the consistency of thin cream. Stir in the cream, add the bacon and fish and taste the sauce for seasoning; leave the pochouse in a warm place for 5 minutes for flavours to blend. Add a few drops of lemon juice and the parsley and taste again.

Serve the pochouse in deep plates and pass the croûtes separately.

SUPRÊMES DE BROCHET DIJONNAISE

Larded pike fillets in white wine and cream sauce

This is one of the few dijonnaise recipes that does not invariably incorporate mustard, though some versions omit the step of larding the fish and do include some mustard instead.

Serves 4

600 g	pike fillets	$1\frac{1}{4}$ lb
45 g	firm pork fat, cut in thin strips	$1\frac{1}{2}$ oz
	3 shallots, finely chopped	
	bouquet garni	
250 ml	dry white wine, preferably chablis	1 cup
	2–3 tsp marc or brandy	
	salt and pepper	
250 g	mushrooms, sliced (optional)	$\frac{1}{2}$ lb
185 ml	heavy cream or crème fraîche*	$\frac{3}{4}$ cup
	larding needle	

With the point of a knife, make small incisions in the pike fillets. Use the larding needle to insert the strips of pork fat. Put the fillets in a dish with the shallots, bouquet garni, wine and marc. Sprinkle with salt and pepper and leave to marinate overnight.

The next day, set the oven at very hot (220°C/ 425°F). Transfer the fish with the marinade ingredients and mushrooms to a heavily but-tered baking dish. Bake the fish, basting often, for about 15 minutes or until it can be easily flaked with a fork. Transfer the fish to a platter, reserving the cooking liquid, and keep the fish warm.

Put the cooking liquid with the shallots and mushrooms in a heavy-based saucepan and boil for 3–4 minutes to reduce. Add the cream and boil together until the sauce is thick enough to coat a spoon. Discard the bouquet garni and taste for seasoning. Spoon the sauce over the fillets and serve.

GÂTEAU DE FOIES DE VOLAILLE
Hot chicken liver mould

The chickens of Bresse are famous for the whiteness of their livers as well as of their meat. This liver mousse, its richness balanced by a tomato sauce, is a great local speciality.

Serves 6–8

	16 green olives, pitted	
250 g	chicken livers, cut in pieces	$\frac{1}{2}$ lb
	$\frac{1}{2}$ clove garlic, crushed	
30 g	flour	$\frac{1}{4}$ cup
	4 eggs, beaten to mix	
	4 egg yolks	
60 ml	heavy cream or crème fraîche*	$\frac{1}{4}$ cup
375 ml	milk	$1\frac{1}{2}$ cups
	pinch of grated nutmeg	
	salt and pepper	
500–625 ml	tomato coulis (see recipe)	$2–2\frac{1}{2}$ cups
1·5 L/1$\frac{1}{2}$ qt charlotte mould or soufflé dish		

If the olives* are very salty, blanch them.

Oil the mould, line the base with a round of greaseproof/parchment paper and oil the paper. Set the oven at moderately low (160°C/325°F).

Purée the chicken livers with the garlic in a food processor or blender; then pour into a bowl. Beat in the flour, then the eggs, egg yolks, cream, milk, nutmeg, salt and pepper to taste; the mixture should be delicately seasoned without being bland. Work it through a sieve. Pour the mixture into the mould, but don't fill it more than three-quarters full as the gâteau will rise.

Set the mould in a water bath and bring the water almost to a boil. Transfer to the heated oven and cook for 30 minutes or until the mixture has partly thickened. Drop in the olives; if they are added at the beginning of cooking they float. Continue cooking for 30–35 minutes or until a skewer inserted in the centre of the gâteau comes out clean; the mixture will shrink a little from the sides of the pan.

To serve, run a knife around the sides of the mould, set a platter on top, turn both upside down and give a quick shake so the gâteau falls on to the platter. Pour some of the tomato sauce over the gâteau and serve the rest separately.

GÂTEAU DE FOIES DE VOLAILLE À LA NANTUA

Serve the gâteau with a Nantua sauce (see 'quenelles Nantua') instead of tomato sauce and garnish the dish with crayfish, prawns or shrimps.

POULARDE EN DEMI-DEUIL
Chicken with truffles

Plumper and more tasty than a mere 'poulet', a 'poularde' is a mature bird, a worthy match for the rarity of truffles. An interesting version of this recipe can be made by substituting dried morels or cèpes for the truffles. The dried mushrooms are soaked and then inserted under the skin as the truffles are.

Serves 6

	1 medium can whole truffles, with their liquid	
2-kg	large chicken or capon	$4\frac{1}{2}$-lb
	1 onion, quartered	
	1 carrot, quartered	
	1 stalk celery, cut in pieces	
	6 black peppercorns	
	bouquet garni	
	salt	
1–1·5 L	broth	1–1$\frac{1}{2}$ qt
VELOUTÉ SAUCE		
	reduced broth, from cooking chicken	
75 g	butter	5 Tbsp
30 g	flour	$\frac{1}{4}$ cup
125 ml	heavy cream or crème fraîche*	$\frac{1}{2}$ cup
	squeeze of lemon juice	
trussing needle and string		

Drain the truffles, reserving the liquid, and cut 8–10 thick slices; chop the remainder.

Lay the chicken on its back on a board and insert the truffle slices between the breast and the skin of the chicken, lifting the skin gently from the meat so it does not break. The truffle slices should show through the skin in a neat pattern. Truss the bird.

Put the chicken in a large pot with the onion, carrot, celery, peppercorns, bouquet garni, salt and broth to cover. Cover, bring to a boil, and poach for 1$\frac{1}{4}$–1$\frac{1}{2}$ hours or until the bird is tender when pierced in the thigh with a skewer. Transfer to a platter, cover and keep warm. Boil the broth until reduced to 625 ml.

For the sauce: heat 2 tablespoons of the butter in a medium pot, whisk in the flour and cook until foaming but not browned. Let cool slightly, then stir in the reduced broth and bring to a boil, stirring constantly. Simmer for 2 minutes or until the sauce is thick enough to coat a spoon lightly. Add the cream and bring just to a boil. Add the lemon juice and remaining truffles and liquid; taste for seasoning. Take from the heat and stir in the remaining butter, a piece at a time. Spoon a little of the sauce over the chicken and the base of the dish; the truffles should still show through the skin of the bird. Serve the remaining sauce separately.

CHICKENS

For centuries fine French chickens have come from Bresse, where the climate suits not only the birds, but also the maize and buckwheat grown to fatten them. Bresse chickens are a special breed, noted for their large size and their plump breast meat, and recognizable by their blue feet. To be sold as a Bresse chicken (and thus command a higher price), a bird must belong to the Bressane breed and be raised near Bresse, although not necessarily hatched there. The bird must also range freely in the open air and be fattened in accordance with certain rules. Recently other areas have started to impose similar standards, listing the age, weight and way the bird was fed on a label attached to each one.

In these days of battery-raised chickens, the distinctions between different ages and sizes of chicken are often blurred. However, most traditional recipes were evolved to cook a particular type of bird, so that a 'coq' for example would receive quite different treatment from a 'poulet'. Most Bresse chickens are fattened to be 'poulardes', plump young hens of at least 1·5 kg/3 lb and up to double that weight; their excellent flavour makes them ideal for roasting. Smaller poulets or spring chickens, though nowadays they are available all year round, weigh about 1–1·5 kg/2–3 lb. The best of these are grain-fed ('poulet de grain') and are usually cut up to grill or to sauté. Most delicate of all are 'poussins', baby chickens just large enough for one or two people, but, even in France, single-portion poussins are hard to find, and are reserved for the most careful roasting en cocotte with butter and herbs.

The cock may be king of the farmyard, but not of the kitchen. Tough, sinewy and weighing up to 4 kg/9 lb, an old cock bird needs long simmering and is often first marinated, as in 'coq au vin'. Females are preferable; an elderly 'poule', long past laying eggs, makes excellent eating when simmered as poule au riz or poule au pot, having far more flavour than her junior in age, the poularde. Both of these older birds give a richer broth than younger chickens do.

Given the desirability of females for their eggs and for the pot, the vast majority of male chickens face one of two fates: to be fattened and killed young as a coquelet (a little bird which lacks the delicacy of a poussin), or to be neutered and grow to immense size as a 'capon'. The capon is a noble bird, kept for wedding feasts and festivals such as Christmas.

COQ AU VIN

The mature 'coq' that would give this dish its characteristic flavour would need longer to cook than an average bird: allow at least twice the length of time given in this recipe.

Serves 4–6

2-kg	chicken	4½-lb
125 g	bacon, cut in lardons	¼ lb
	1 Tbsp oil	
15 g	butter	1 Tbsp
	18–20 baby onions	
250 g	mushrooms, quartered	½ lb
20 g	flour	2½ Tbsp
375 ml	broth	1½ cups
	1 clove garlic, crushed	
	2 shallots, finely chopped	
	bouquet garni	
	salt and pepper	
	1 Tbsp chopped parsley	
	MARINADE	
375 ml	red wine	1½ cups
	1 onion, thinly sliced	
	1 carrot, thinly sliced	
	1 stick celery, thinly sliced	
	bouquet garni	
	1 clove garlic, sliced	
	6 black peppercorns	
	2 Tbsp olive oil	

For the marinade: in a saucepan (not aluminium) combine the wine, onion, carrot, celery, bouquet garni, garlic, peppercorns and olive oil. Bring to a boil, simmer 5 minutes and let cool completely.

Cut the chicken* into eight pieces. Pour the marinade over the bird, cover and leave at room temperature for 6 hours or in the refrigerator for 10–12 hours, turning the pieces occasionally.

Drain the pieces of chicken and pat dry with paper towels. Strain the marinade and reserve both the liquid and the vegetables. If the bacon is very salty, blanch* it. If you want to simmer the chicken in the oven, set the oven at moderate (175°C/350°F).

In a sauté pan or shallow casserole heat the oil and butter and fry the bacon until well browned and the fat is extracted. Take out the bacon and set on one side; add the pieces of chicken, skin side down to the pan. Cook over a medium fire until brown; turn and brown the other side. Remove the pieces of chicken, add the onions and sauté until lightly browned. Take them out, add the mushrooms, sauté until tender and remove them also.

Discard all but 2 tablespoons of the fat, add the onion, carrot and celery from the marinade and cook over a low fire until soft but not browned. Sprinkle with the flour and cook until foaming. Stir in the reserved marinade and the broth, and add the pieces of chicken, garlic, shallots, bouquet garni, salt and pepper. Simmer over a low fire or in the oven for 45–60 minutes or until the bird is just tender. Take out the chicken pieces, set aside with the bacon and keep warm.

Put the baby onions in a large casserole. Strain the sauce over them, pressing well on the vegetables, and simmer for 10 minutes or until the onions are nearly tender. Add the mushrooms and simmer 2–3 minutes or until the sauce is reduced to a thin, coating consistency. Return chicken and bacon to the sauce and taste for seasoning. Serve the coq au vin from the casserole, sprinkling it with the chopped parsley just before serving.

POULARDE AUX ÉCREVISSES
Chicken with crayfish

Poultry with crayfish, on the face of it an odd combination, has long been popular in Burgundy and now is a 'nouvelle cuisine' favourite. If you cannot get crayfish, substitute prawns or large shrimps.

Serves 5–6

1·8-kg	chicken	4-lb
	2 Tbsp oil	
60 g	butter	4 Tbsp
	12 crayfish	
	2 Tbsp marc or cognac	
	1 small onion, chopped	
	2 shallots, chopped	
	1 clove garlic, chopped	
	1 Tbsp tomato paste	
50 g	flour	$\frac{1}{4}$ cup
500 ml	dry white wine	2 cups
500 ml	broth	2 cups
	salt and pepper	
	bouquet garni	
60 ml	heavy cream or crème fraîche*	$\frac{1}{4}$ cup

Cut the chicken* into eight pieces. Heat the oil and the butter in a large sauté pan or a shallow flameproof casserole. Add the crayfish and sauté over a high fire until they turn red. Remove them and add the chicken pieces. Brown them on all sides over a medium fire. Return the crayfish to the pan and flame with the marc. Set the oven at hot (200°C/400°F).

Stir in the chopped onion, shallots, garlic, tomato paste and flour and cook over a low fire, stirring constantly, for 5 minutes. Pour in the wine and add enough broth to cover the chicken. Add salt, pepper and bouquet garni; bring to a boil and simmer uncovered over a low fire for 10 minutes. Remove the crayfish and reserve.

Transfer the pan of chicken to the oven and bake uncovered for 20 more minutes or until the chicken is tender. Transfer the chicken pieces to a platter and keep warm.

Taste the cooking liquid and skim off the excess fat. If necessary, boil to reduce until well flavoured and of coating consistency, stirring occasionally to prevent the flour from sticking.

Strain the sauce into a shallow pan, bring to a boil and stir in the cream. Return the chicken pieces to the sauce and simmer for 2 minutes. Add the crayfish and simmer for another minute to reheat them. Taste for seasoning. Arrange the chicken pieces on the platter, coat them with some of the sauce and set the crayfish around them; serve the rest of the sauce separately. Provide your guests with fingerbowls.

CAILLES MORVANDELLES AUX RAISINS
Quail with grapes

Wild quail were once abundant in the Morvan, the heart of Burgundy, so it was natural to cook them with vine leaves, which add a bitter touch, and grapes, for sweetness. Nowadays most quail are farmed like chickens. Two quail per person are the usual serving. The same recipe can be made with young pigeons or, in North America, squab or rock cornish hens.

Serves 4

	8 quail (including livers)	
	16–20 fresh vine leaves OR	
	a small can vine leaves, drained	
	and rinsed with cold water	
	thin sheet barding fat, OR	
	8 thin slices mild bacon	
	2 Tbsp oil	
60 g	butter	4 Tbsp
	salt and pepper	
500 g	green grapes	1 lb
	(preferably seedless)	
	2 Tbsp cognac	
125 ml	broth	½ cup
	8 rectangular croûtes*,	
	fried in butter	
	STUFFING	
	3 slices white bread, crusts removed	
80 ml	milk	⅓ cup
60 g	fat bacon	2 oz
	2 chicken livers	
	the 8 quail livers	
	1 Tbsp cognac	
	pinch of ground allspice	
	salt and pepper	
	trussing string	

If necessary, clean the quail; discard the heads and necks and reserve the livers and giblets.

Make the stuffing: soak the bread in the milk and squeeze it dry. If the bacon is very salty, blanch* it. Work the bacon, chicken livers, quail livers and bread through the fine plate of a mincer/grinder or purée them in a food processor. Add the cognac, allspice and salt and pepper to taste. Stuff the quail and wrap each bird in 2 vine leaves and then in a piece of barding fat; tie neatly with string. Set the oven at hot (200°C/400°F).

Heat the oil and butter in a large sauté pan or ovenproof casserole, add the quail and giblets and season with salt and pepper. Brown the birds on all sides for 8–10 minutes over a medium fire; then transfer them to the oven and roast for 15–20 minutes or until a skewer inserted into the stuffing for 30 seconds is warm to the touch when withdrawn. Meanwhile, prepare the grape garnish: using a paperclip, remove any seeds from the grapes and, if the skins are thick, blanch and peel them.

When the quail are done, transfer them to a platter, discard the barding fat, vine leaves and strings, cover and keep warm. Discard the grease from the pan, add the cognac and broth and stir to dissolve the pan juices. Strain into a saucepan, add the grapes and heat over a low fire for 2–3 minutes; be careful not to overcook them. Taste the gravy for seasoning. Set the quail on the croûtes and spoon the grapes and pan juices over and around them. Serve at once.

PINTADE AUX CHOUX

Guinea hen with cabbage and sausages

Cabbage and guinea hen are popular together in northern France as well as in Burgundy. Pheasant can be braised in the same way and, in the USA, rock cornish hen is an alternative.

Serves 4

1·5-kg	guinea hen	3–3½-lb
125-g	piece of bacon	4-oz
1-kg	cabbage	2-lb
	salt and pepper	
	1½ Tbsp lard or oil	
60 g	fat bacon, cut in 4 slices	2 oz
	6–8 small carrots OR	
	2 large carrots, quartered	
375 ml	broth	1½ cups
250 ml	white wine	1 cup
	1 onion, studded with a clove	
	bouquet garni	
150 g total	16 small sausages	5 oz total
	2 Tbsp chopped parsley	
	trussing needle and string	

Truss the hen. Blanch* the piece of bacon. Cut the cabbage in 6–8 wedges, discarding the core, and cook in boiling salted water for 8–10 minutes or until almost tender. Drain it thoroughly; then separate the leaves. Set the oven at moderate (175°C/350°F).

Heat the lard in a large casserole and brown the guinea hen on all sides. Take it out, let the pan cool slightly, and lay the fat bacon slices on the bottom. Add half the cabbage and sprinkle with a little salt and pepper. Put the hen on top, surrounded by the carrots, and cover with the remaining cabbage. Season with salt and pepper. Pour in the broth and wine. Add the onion and bouquet garni, pushed well down into the cabbage, and top with the piece of bacon. Cover and simmer in the heated oven for 1–1¼ hours or until the hen and the carrots are tender. Add the sausages to the casserole during the last 10 minutes of cooking, pushing them down into the cabbage.

When the hen is tender, transfer the cabbage to a colander, using a slotted spoon. Discard the onion and bouquet garni. Pile the drained cabbage in the centre of a large platter. Either set the hen on top or cut it into quarters, discarding the backbone, and set the pieces on top. Arrange the sausages and carrots around the edge of the cabbage. Cut the piece of bacon in slices and arrange them on the cabbage also. Cover the dish and keep it hot in a low oven while finishing the sauce. Discard the fat bacon from the casserole and strain the juices into a small pan. Boil until well flavoured and reduced to about 375 ml. Taste for seasoning. Spoon a little sauce around the cabbage platter and serve the rest separately. Sprinkle the platter with parsley just before serving.

BOEUF BOURGUIGNON

Few dishes are better known, yet more often maltreated, than boeuf bourguignon. It requires well-aged beef (Burgundians would specify Charolais) with plenty of connective tissue to dissolve during cooking to enrich the sauce. Suggested cuts are US rump or chuck and British chuck or round steak. A hearty red wine like a beaujolais or a young burgundy will add substance. Above all, boeuf bourguignon must be cooked slowly, never at more than a simmer, for 3–4 hours if need be, until the meat is tender but not falling apart. In the old days, the beef was cooked in one piece, rather than in the chunky pieces which are now customary. Often the croûtes are omitted and the beef is served with boiled potatoes. The flavour of this dish mellows if it is made at least a day ahead.

Serves 4

0·75–1 kg	beef stewing meat, cut in 5 cm/2 in cubes	1½–2 lb
60 ml	oil	¼ cup
125 ml	red wine, preferably burgundy	½ cup
25 g	flour	3 Tbsp
250 ml	broth	1 cup
	salt and pepper	
	pinch of sugar (optional)	
	4 heart-shaped or triangular croûtes*, fried in oil and butter	
	1 Tbsp chopped parsley (for sprinkling)	
	MARINADE	
750 ml	red wine, preferably burgundy	3 cups
	1 onion, sliced	
	1 carrot, sliced	
	bouquet garni	
	1 clove garlic, crushed	
	6 black peppercorns	
	2 cloves	
	pinch of salt	
	2 Tbsp oil	
	GARNISH	
250-g	piece of bacon, cut in lardons	½-lb
	16–20 baby onions	
250 g	mushrooms	½ lb

It is not necessary to marinate the beef, but you will still need the marinade ingredients. If you wish to marinate the meat, place it in a bowl (not aluminium), cover with the wine and add the marinade ingredients, pouring the oil over the meat last. Leave at room temperature for one day, stirring it 3 or 4 times; alternatively, marinate the meat in the refrigerator for 2 days. Drain the meat, reserving the marinade; keep the onion and carrot separate. Dry the pieces of meat thoroughly with paper towels.

If the bacon is very salt, blanch* it. Heat half the oil in a heavy-based frying pan and brown the pieces of beef on all sides, a few at a time. Set them aside and continue with the garnish: add the bacon to the frying pan and cook over fairly high heat until brown but not crisp. Remove the bacon, add the onions and brown them also. Remove the onions, add the mushrooms and cook over moderate heat until tender and lightly browned. Reserve the garnish ingredients. Discard excess fat from the frying pan and add the wine. Bring to a boil, stirring to dissolve the pan juices.

In a heavy-based dutch oven or flameproof casserole, heat the remaining oil, add the reserved onion and carrot from the marinade and cook slowly, stirring occasionally, until soft but not brown. Add the flour and cook, stirring, until the mixture is a rich brown; don't allow it to burn. Stir in the remaining marinade ingredients, the wine from the frying pan, the broth and a little salt and pepper. Return the meat to the pan and bring the stew to a boil. Cover tightly and simmer on top of the stove or in a low oven (150°C/300°F), stirring occasionally, for 3–4 hours, or until the meat is tender.

When the meat is tender, transfer it to another casserole and strain the sauce over the beef. Stir in the garnish of bacon, onion and mushrooms and simmer gently for 15 minutes or until the onions are tender and the flavours are blended. Taste for seasoning; if necessary, add a pinch of sugar to counteract the acidity of the wine. Serve the stew in the casserole or in a shallow bowl, with the croûtes around the edge. Sprinkle the beef with chopped parsley.

APPELLATION CONTRÔLÉE

Trust the French to be first into the business of controlling the quality of what they eat and drink. The original and most famous accord was that of 1855 which classified the best Médoc wines into five growths, establishing standards which were far in advance of their time and which still hold today. From these beginnings has evolved the far-reaching system of 'appellation contrôlée', a phrase familiar on most bottles of wine and which is now also applied to certain foods, especially French cheeses. 'Nobody can unite a country which has 265 kinds of cheese,' said a despondent General de Gaulle in 1951. Not only is every step in the making of an appellation product regulated and inspected, but the French have also tackled a more elusive subject: what makes a certain product special?

The first and overriding consideration is geographical location. To earn appellation status, a product must have a specific place or area of origin and distinguishing characteristics reflecting 'local, faithful and constant methods' of production. Among the cheeses, roquefort has been subject to an appellation law since 1925 and now about two dozen others are on the list. Brie from two production zones, Meaux and Melun, is eligible for an appellation, as are beaufort from the Alps and maroilles from Flanders. Despite its fame, camembert is absent – so many people make it in so many different places that the courts held the name to be in the public domain. The appellation label has also been acquired by a few fruits and vegetables, such as walnuts from Grenoble, olives from Nyons and green lentils from Le Puy; by honeys from Lorraine and the Vosges; by some poultry, notably chickens from Bresse, and in 1979, by butter from Poitou and Charente.

Appellation status, other than for wine, is, however, still a rarity and few products or producers can meet all the tests. The possession of an appellation label is a matter of pride and of commercial good sense – a Bresse chicken, for instance, commands at least double the price of an anonymous supermarket bird. Surprisingly, canned foie gras and canned truffles do not carry an appellation label, a reflection of the quantity of foie gras and truffles acquired outside the traditional processing areas, often from abroad.

To protect other foods with more flexible legislation, two new designations have recently been developed: 'label rouge' and 'label régional'. Label rouge, indicated by a distinctive red label, will soon cover 200 products, notably poultry breeds from many areas, but also certain fruits, vegetables and even seeds, wheat varieties and meat. Producers' organizations jealously guard their rights: woe betide anybody who abuses the certifying authority of the 'Association for the defence of traditional breeding of Charolais beef from the Bourbonnais'!

Commercial self-interest is certainly involved, but underlying the cobweb of legislation are the strong regional instincts of the average French farmer and, for that matter, of the average French consumer. In no other country is there quite the same conviction. Roquefort cheese must be aged in the caves at Roquefort-sur-Soulzon, and no other caverns will do. The finest French gruyère comes from the Franche-Comté, the fattest prunes from Agen and the most select guinea fowl from the Drôme. It all goes back to the 'terroir', that little bit of mother earth in some corner of France – Auvergne, Provence, Normandy – that means home to each Frenchman. His terroir is like no other and so, therefore, are its products.

BOEUF À LA MODE
Braised beef with vegetables

'Boeuf à la mode' is good either hot or cold, and many cooks serve it both ways, hot one day and cold the next, when the beef and vegetables are layered in a terrine and chilled before being unmoulded. In Britain, top rump or topside are good cuts to use; eye of round or bottom round are good in the USA. The pork fat that lards the meat adds richness. The gelatine that sets the cooking liquid should come from the calf's feet and veal bones and the aspic is never clarified, say connoisseurs, since the egg white used to clarify it detracts from the flavour. This first recipe is for hot beef, the second for cold.

Serves 6–8

2-kg	beef roast	4½-lb
60 g	firm pork fat or mild bacon, cut in small lardons	2 oz
	2 calf's or pig's feet, split	
1 kg	veal bones, cracked	2 lb
250-g	piece lean bacon, diced	½-lb
750 ml	broth, more if needed	3 cups
	salt and pepper	
	4 Tbsp madeira (optional)	
	MARINADE	
	1 clove garlic, peeled	
	1 large bouquet garni	
	6 black peppercorns	
	3 cloves	
500 g	onions, quartered	1 lb
350 g	carrots, quartered	¾ lb
	2 stalks celery, cut in short sticks	
500 ml	red wine, preferably burgundy	2 cups
	1 Tbsp oil	
	GARNISH	
1 kg	baby or medium carrots	2 lb
	salt	
1 kg	baby onions	2 lb
1 kg	turnips	2 lb
750 g	green beans, trimmed and cut in 2–3 pieces	1½ lb

larding needle; trussing string; cheesecloth

One or two days before serving, lard* the meat with the pork fat, tie it in a neat cylinder and marinate it: put the beef in a deep bowl (not aluminium). Tie the garlic, bouquet garni, peppercorns and cloves in cheesecloth and add them to the bowl with the onions, carrots and celery. Pour the wine over these ingredients, then pour the oil on top. Cover and refrigerate for 12–24 hours, turning the meat occasionally.

Braise the beef: first blanch the calf's feet and veal bones by putting them in cold water, bringing to a boil, simmering for 5 minutes and draining. Blanch* the bacon. Drain the beef and pat it dry with paper towels. Strain the marinade: reserve it, with the vegetables and the cheesecloth bag of flavourings. Set the oven at moderately low (160°C/320°F).

In a large flameproof casserole, fry the bacon until browned and remove it. Add the beef, brown it well on all sides and remove. Add the reserved marinade vegetables to the casserole and cook gently until they begin to brown. Replace the browned beef and bacon, then add the reserved marinade, seasonings in cheesecloth, the broth and a little salt. Tuck the bones and the calf's feet down beside the meat, cover the pan and bring to a boil. Braise in the heated oven for 2½–3 hours or until the meat is very tender when pierced with a skewer. Baste the meat occasionally and add more broth if the pan is dry. Let the meat cool to tepid; then remove it and strain the cooking liquid, reserving the calf's feet. There should be about 1 litre of liquid. Add more broth if necessary or, if there is too much liquid, boil it until reduced. Chill it, if you like, to make skimming the fat easier.

Skim all the fat from the cooking liquid, bring

it to a boil, add the madeira and taste for seasoning. If you like, finely chop the skin and meat from the calf's feet and add to the liquid.

For the garnish: shape the carrots in 5 cm/ 2 in ovals, cook in boiling salted water for 15–20 minutes or until tender, and drain. Cook the onions in boiling salted water for 12–15 minutes or until tender, and drain. Peel the turnips, shape them into ovals the same size as the carrots, and cook in boiling salted water for 10–15 minutes or until tender; drain. Cook the beans in boiling salted water for 8–20 minutes (depending on size) until just tender, drain, rinse with cold water, and drain again. If you prefer, to add flavour to the vegetables they can be cooked in strained cooking liquid from the beef. Combine the beef, vegetables and cooking liquid in a casserole.

Half an hour before serving, heat the beef in its casserole gently until very hot. Serve the beef, vegetables and gravy in the casserole, or slice the beef, discarding the strings, and arrange it on a platter with the vegetables piled around it and the gravy spooned over the top.

BOEUF À LA MODE EN GELÉE

Cook the beef and vegetables as for hot boeuf à la mode. Let them all cool, keeping them separate. Discard the strings from the beef and carve it in thick slices. Spoon a thin layer of cooking liquid into a 2 L/2 qt rectangular terrine and chill until set. Arrange the slices of meat overlapping down the centre of the terrine. Using about a third of the vegetables, arrange lengthwise rows of beans, baby onions, carrots and turnips down each side of the beef. Spoon over enough cooking liquid to cover them completely and almost cover the meat. Chill until set. Add a second layer of vegetables, cover them with cooking liquid and chill again until set. Finally fill the terrine with the remaining vegetables, pour the rest of the cooking liquid over them and chill for at least 4 hours, or overnight.

To serve, run a knife around the edge of the mould and turn the aspic out on to a platter. Cut a few slices so the layered pattern of vegetables can be seen and, if you like, decorate the platter with watercress.

LE SAUPIQUET
Sautéed ham in cream sauce

The name 'saupiquet' probably comes from 'piqué de sel' meaning 'spiced with salt'. The dish dates back at least to the 16th century. Burgundian saupiquet recipes are based on sliced ham in a cream sauce spiced with vinegar, pepper and often with juniper berries, a dish which has little in common with the saupiquet of Languedoc, made with the blood and chopped liver of a rabbit.

Serves 4

100 g	butter	7 Tbsp
30 g	flour	$\frac{1}{4}$ cup
185 ml	dry white wine	$\frac{3}{4}$ cup
375 ml	broth	$1\frac{1}{2}$ cups
	salt and pepper	
	5 juniper berries	
	5 shallots, finely chopped	
	5 black peppercorns, crushed	
80 ml	wine vinegar	$\frac{1}{3}$ cup
about	4 thick slices cooked	about
500 g	York or country ham	1 lb
60 ml	heavy cream or crème fraîche*	$\frac{1}{4}$ cup
	2 tsp chopped mixed parsley and tarragon	

Melt 2 tablespoons of the butter in a small pot. Add the flour and cook over a low fire, whisking, for 3–4 minutes or until foaming and straw-coloured; be careful not to let the flour brown. Whisk in the wine and broth. Add salt, pepper, juniper berries and half the shallots. Bring to a boil, whisking, and simmer over a low fire for 10 minutes.

Meanwhile, put the peppercorns in a medium pot with the remaining shallots. Add the vinegar and boil until the liquid has almost completely evaporated. Add the wine sauce and simmer for 15 minutes or until well flavoured.

Heat another 2 tablespoons of the butter in a frying pan and brown the ham slices lightly on each side. Transfer them to a platter and keep warm.

Stir the cream into the sauce, bring to a boil and taste for seasoning. Take from the heat and whisk in the remaining butter, a piece at a time. Strain some of the sauce over the ham slices and sprinkle with the chopped herbs. Strain the rest of the sauce into a sauce-boat and serve it separately.

ROGNONS À LA MOUTARDE
Sautéed kidneys with mustard

Either veal kidneys or lamb's kidneys are suitable for this recipe.

Serves 4

about 500 g	kidneys	about 1 lb
45 g	butter	3 Tbsp
	salt and pepper	
	2 shallots, finely chopped	
	3 Tbsp cognac	
250 ml	red wine, preferably burgundy	1 cup
125 ml	broth	$\frac{1}{2}$ cup
250 ml	heavy cream or crème fraîche* (optional)	1 cup
	1 Tbsp Dijon mustard, or to taste	
	1 Tbsp chopped parsley	

Skin the kidneys if necessary, halve them and cut out the core with scissors; cut veal kidneys in chunks or lamb's kidneys in half to form crescents. Heat the butter in a frying pan and add the kidneys with salt and pepper. Sauté over a very high fire for 2–3 minutes for veal or 1–2 minutes for lamb's kidneys, or until brown on all sides but still pink inside. Don't overcook or they will become tough. Transfer the kidneys to a strainer, draining off and discarding any juice that escapes.

Add the shallots to the pan and stir over a low fire for 1 minute. Add the kidneys, pour in the cognac and flame. Remove the kidneys, pour the red wine into the pan and boil until reduced by half. Add the broth and boil again until reduced by half. Stir in the cream and bring just to a boil; take from the fire, stir in the mustard and taste for seasoning. Replace the kidneys and heat gently for 1–2 minutes to blend the flavours and heat the kidneys. Don't boil the mustard or the flavour will be bitter.

Transfer the kidneys and sauce to a serving dish, sprinkle them with parsley and serve immediately.

THE MUSTARD OF DIJON

There is no town like Dijon.

There is no mustard like that at Dijon. Well before this 15th-century couplet was written, the Dukes of Burgundy, ensconced in their capital city of Dijon, were in the habit of giving barrels of mustard to departing guests. Mustard was used in Roman times, but if one is to believe French legend, it was not until the 14th century that mustard received its present name. In 1382 the Duke of Burgundy granted a coat of arms to Dijon bearing the motto 'Moult Me Tarde' (Much awaits me), a trademark adopted by the makers of mustard. Today any dish 'à la dijonnaise' is flavoured with mustard.

In cooking, mustard should be added just before serving, as boiling makes it bitter. The amount needed varies, since mustard may be mild, coarse-grained or smooth, herbal or plain; one 17th-century

mustard maker produced 90 different kinds. Like almost all French mustard, that of Dijon is ready-prepared, the grains having been ground and mixed with wine, 'verjus' (the juice of sour grapes), and a variety of herbs and flavourings. It is the high-quality mustard plants grown in abundance in the region, combined with verjus made from Burgundy grapes rather than with vinegar, that gives Dijon mustard its well-rounded flavour.

Besides its ability to make bland dishes more interesting by adding a piquant taste, mustard is supposed to stimulate the appetite; it is a remedy for ailments ranging from headaches, fevers, whooping-cough and asthma to liver and stomach complaints. Traditionally mustard footbaths are a cure for colds and mustard plasters for bronchitis.

CÔTES DE VEAU DIJONNAISE

Veal chops with mustard

Instead of being sautéed in a frying pan, these veal chops can be cooked and served in a shallow casserole.

Serves 4

	3–4 Tbsp oil	
	4 large veal chops	
	1 Tbsp flour	
185 ml	white wine	$\frac{3}{4}$ cup
185 ml	broth	$\frac{3}{4}$ cup
	bouquet garni	
	salt and pepper	
60 ml	heavy cream or crème fraîche*	$\frac{1}{4}$ cup
	2 Tbsp Dijon mustard, or to taste	
	1 Tbsp chopped parsley	

Heat half the oil in a large frying pan, add the chops and brown them on both sides. Take them out and add enough of the remaining oil to make 2 tablespoons. Stir in the flour and cook until bubbling. Add the wine, broth, bouquet garni, salt and pepper and bring to a boil, stirring.

Replace the chops, cover and simmer on top of the stove, or in a moderate oven (175°C/350°F) for 40–45 minutes or until tender.

Arrange the chops overlapping on a platter, cover and keep warm. If necessary, boil the sauce to reduce it until well flavoured. Add the cream and bring just to a boil; take from the heat and stir in the mustard. Don't boil the mustard or the flavour will be bitter. Discard the bouquet garni and taste for seasoning. Spoon some of the sauce over the chops and serve the remaining sauce separately. Sprinkle with chopped parsley and serve.

CÔTES DE VEAU DIJONNAISE II

Baby onions and lardons of lean bacon can be added as a garnish. Before browning the chops, blanch*:

150 g	lardons of bacon	5 oz

and then brown them in the oil. Remove them and brown 18 baby onions. Remove the onions and discard all but 2 tablespoons of fat; then continue as above, adding the bacon and onions after the chops have cooked for 25 minutes.

CERVELLES EN MEURETTE

Brains poached in red wine

'Meurette' combines four of the most typical Burgundian ingredients – bacon, onions, mushrooms and red wine. As well as accompanying brains or eggs as in these two recipes, sauce meurette is excellent with fish: the fish is poached in wine, which is then used to make the sauce. Folklore has it that the fish must be alive when they go into the pot.

Serves 4

about 750 g	2 sets calf's OR 4 sets sheep's brains	about 1½ lb
	2–3 Tbsp vinegar	
60 g	butter	4 Tbsp
	1 onion, thinly sliced	
	1 carrot, thinly sliced	
	1 stalk celery, thinly sliced	
	1 clove garlic, crushed	
1 L	red wine, preferably burgundy	1 qt
500 ml	broth	2 cups
	bouquet garni	
	6 black peppercorns	
	salt and pepper	
45 g	butter, kneaded with	3 Tbsp
25 g	flour	3 Tbsp
	pinch of sugar (optional)	
	4 oval croûtes*, fried in oil and butter	

Soak the brains for 2–3 hours in a bowl of water with the vinegar, changing the water once or twice. Pull off or trim any skin or membrane from calf's brains, but not from sheep's brains. Wash them well to remove all traces of blood.

Heat 1 tablespoon of the butter in a pot, add the onion, carrot, celery and garlic and cook over a low fire, stirring, for 3–4 minutes or until softened. Add the wine, broth, bouquet garni, peppercorns and a small pinch of salt; bring to a boil and simmer for 15 minutes or until the vegetables are tender. Add the brains, cover and poach for 15–20 minutes or until they are quite firm to the touch. Don't boil or the brains will fall apart. Transfer them to a platter, cover and keep warm while making the sauce.

Boil the wine mixture until reduced by half. Whisk enough of the kneaded butter*, piece by piece, into the boiling wine mixture to thicken the sauce to a light coating consistency. Simmer for 2–3 minutes, strain and taste for seasoning. If the sauce is too acidic, add a pinch of sugar. Take from the heat and stir in the remaining butter, a piece at a time.

Put one sheep's brain or half a calf's brain on each croûte, and coat with some sauce; serve at once, with the remaining sauce separately.

OEUFS POCHÉS EN MEURETTE

Bring the wine and broth to a boil in a sauté pan. In two batches, poach **8 very fresh eggs** in the mixture for 3–4 minutes or until the yolk is fairly firm but still soft to the touch. Transfer the eggs to paper towels to drain and trim any strings of white. Cook the vegetables in the butter, add the poaching liquid with the herbs and seasoning and make the sauce as above. Prepare a garnish of:

150 g	lardons of bacon, blanched*	5 oz
125 g	mushrooms, quartered	¼ lb

and 16–20 baby onions, all sautéed in a little butter until brown. Simmer the garnish for 2–3 minutes in the thickened sauce. Meanwhile, reheat the eggs by putting them in a bowl of hot water for about 30 seconds. Drain on paper towels, set the eggs on croûtes and spoon the sauce and garnish over them.

LA RAPÉE MORVANDELLE

Grated potato and cheese gratin

This baked potato cake is a winter dish, which used to be cooked in a 'tourtière' with three legs so it stood firmly in hot coals. Hollow, like a saucer, the lid held more coals so the contents of the pot were cooked from above and below.

Serves 4

45 g	butter or walnut oil	3 Tbsp
1 kg	potatoes	2 lb
125 g	cream cheese	4 oz
125 ml	heavy cream or crème fraîche*	½ cup
	3 eggs, beaten to mix	
120 g	grated comté or gruyère cheese	1¼ cups
	1 Tbsp cognac	
	salt and pepper	
	2 L/2 qt shallow baking dish	

Set the oven at hot (200°C/400°F). Spread the butter in the baking dish. Grate the potatoes and drain thoroughly; to rid them of all excess moisture, squeeze them gently and pat dry with a cloth. Working quickly so that the potatoes don't discolour, mix them with the other ingredients. Season to taste.

Spread the potato mixture in the baking dish. Bake in the hot oven for 45 minutes or until golden brown and crisp on top (some of the fat will bubble up to the top and keep the mixture from drying out). Serve hot.

TOPINAMBOURS AUX NOIX
Jerusalem artichokes with walnuts

The arrival of Jerusalem, or root, artichokes in France from the New World coincided with the visit of Indians of the Brazilian Tupinamba tribe to the court of Louis XIV. The vegetable is now a good deal more popular around Lyon than in its native USA.

Serves 4

750 g	Jerusalem artichokes	1½ lb
	salt and pepper	
	1 Tbsp walnut or vegetable oil	
30 g	butter	2 Tbsp
	pinch of sugar	
60 g	walnut pieces	½ cup

Peel the artichokes and cut each into 2 to 3 equal pieces. Put them in a pot with cold water to cover, add salt and boil over a high fire for 5 minutes; drain thoroughly.

Heat the oil and butter in a frying pan and add the artichokes, salt, pepper and sugar. Sauté over fairly high heat for 10 minutes; then add the walnuts and sauté for another 5 minutes or until the artichokes are tender and golden brown. Taste for seasoning. Transfer to a dish for serving.

SALADE DE CHOU AU LARD
Hot cabbage salad with bacon

Traditional salads with a hot dressing such as this one, and the dandelion and bacon salad of Champagne (see recipe for 'salade de pissenlits'), are popular with the chefs of 'nouvelle cuisine'.

Serves 6

750 g	1 medium cabbage	1½ lb
150 g	bacon, diced	5 oz
	3 Tbsp wine vinegar	
	salt and pepper	

Wash the cabbage leaves, drain them and shred with a knife. If the bacon is very salty, blanch* it. Fry the bacon in a large frying pan for 3–4 minutes or until the fat runs and the bacon is slightly crisp. Take the pan from the heat and add the wine vinegar; stand back as the vinegar will splutter. Add the cabbage and salt and pepper and toss over a high fire for 2–3 minutes or until the cabbage is slightly wilted and well coated with bacon fat and vinegar. Turn it into a bowl and taste for seasoning. Serve immediately, while the bacon fat is still hot.

CARDONS À LA CRÈME
Cardoons with cream

Cardoons have a pleasantly sharp flavour reminiscent of Jerusalem artichokes and fennel, all of which are good cooked 'à la crème', as in this recipe. The leaves and prickly outer stalks are not used; only the inner stalks are eaten.

Serves 4

15 g	flour	2 Tbsp
2 L	water	2 qt
	salt and pepper	
	2 lemons	
1 kg	cardoons	2 lb
45 g	butter	3 Tbsp
185 ml	heavy cream or crème fraîche*	¾ cup

To prevent the cardoons from discolouring, prepare a 'blanc' for cooking them: mix the flour with 3–4 tablespoons of the water. Bring the remaining water to a boil in a large pot; then add salt and the juice of 1 lemon. Whisk in the flour mixture and bring back to a boil, stirring occasionally.

Meanwhile, prepare the cardoons: discard any brown or soft stalk and peel the remaining stalks with a vegetable peeler to remove the strings. Halve the second lemon, rub the stalks with it, and cut them into 7·5 cm/3 in pieces. Add the stalks to the boiling blanc and simmer over a low fire for 1 hour or until tender; drain thoroughly.

Heat the butter in a pan, add the cardoons and cook over low heat, stirring occasionally, for 5 minutes. Add the cream and heat thoroughly; season to taste with salt and pepper. Transfer to a shallow dish and serve.

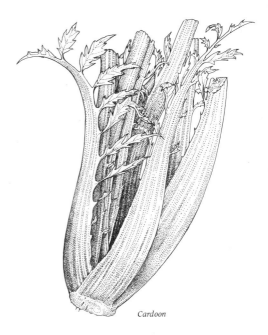

Cardoon

OEUFS BRESSANE
Chocolate and praline eggs

The eggs of Bresse deserve notice as well as the chickens. Visiting Bourg-en-Bresse in 1882, Henry James sat down to bread and butter and boiled eggs that were 'so good I am ashamed to say how many of them I consumed. It might seem that an egg which has succeeded in being fresh has done all that can reasonably be expected of it. But there was a bloom of punctuality, so to speak, about those eggs of Bourg, as if it had been the intention of the very hens themselves that they should be promptly served.' The following 'eggs' are an inspiration of the local chocolate shops.

Makes 6 filled eggs

	6 eggs	
	PRALINE	
90 g	whole, unblanched almonds	$\frac{1}{2}$ cup
100 g	sugar	$\frac{1}{2}$ cup
	GANACHE	
150 g	semi-sweet chocolate, chopped	5 oz
80 ml	heavy cream	$\frac{1}{3}$ cup
	1–2 Tbsp Grand Marnier	

With a small sharp knife, carefully pierce the pointed end of an egg. Use scissors to cut a round from the top, leaving a hole with a diameter of about 2·5 cm/1 in. Hold the shell upside down and shake it gently to remove the contents; the egg white and yolk can be used for another dish. Repeat with the other eggs. Wash the shells thoroughly; then heat them in a low oven (150°C/300°F) for 10 minutes or until dry. Let the shells cool.

Make the praline*.

Make the ganache: melt the chocolate in a small pan set in a water bath of hot water; stir until smooth. In another pan bring the cream to a boil and stir it into the melted chocolate. Let cool slightly; then stir in the Grand Marnier. Beat the praline into the ganache; the mixture will be thick, but pourable. Transfer it to a measuring cup and pour the mixture into the eggs, filling them level with the top of the shell. Chill for 3–4 hours or until firm. The eggs are best if kept several days for the flavour to mellow.

Decorate the eggs as you like. They can be topped with a browned almond, or encircled with a bow of ribbon. For Easter, pattern the shells using oil or poster paints, in the manner of Russian Easter eggs.

Serve the eggs at room temperature, presented in an egg carton. Use egg cups for serving.

GÂTEAU LYONNAIS
Chocolate and chestnut cake

Olivier de Serres, often called the father of French agriculture, wrote in 1599 of the chestnuts of Lyon, 'which is known throughout France for its trade in this fruit.' If using fresh chestnuts instead of canned chestnut purée for this recipe, peel the chestnuts* and simmer them until soft in a mixture of milk and water. Then drain and purée in a food processor or blender.

Serves 8

	CAKE	
90 g	semi-sweet chocolate, chopped	3 oz
	4 eggs, separated	
200 g	sugar	1 cup
200 g	canned unsweetened chestnut purée	7 oz
	FROSTING	
150 g	semi-sweet chocolate, chopped	5 oz
	2 Tbsp water	
	2 egg yolks	
125 ml	heavy cream	$\frac{1}{2}$ cup
	1 Tbsp sugar	
	$\frac{1}{2}$ Tbsp rum, or to taste	

20–23 cm/8–9 in springform pan or round cake pan

Butter the pan and line the bottom with a buttered round of greaseproof/parchment paper. Set the oven at moderate (175°C/350°F).

Make the cake: melt the chocolate in a small bowl over a pan of hot water and set aside until cool but not set. Beat the egg yolks with three-quarters of the sugar and the chestnut purée until thick and light. Whip the egg whites until stiff, add the remaining sugar and continue to whip for another 30 seconds or until glossy. Stir the chocolate into the chestnut mixture, then fold in a quarter of the egg whites. Add this mixture to the rest of the whites and fold them together gently. Pour the mixture into the lined pan. Bake in the heated oven for 30–35 minutes or until a skewer inserted in the cake comes out dry. Let the cake cool in the pan; then carefully unmould it and set aside on a rack.

Make the frosting: melt the chocolate with the water in a small pan set in a water bath; whisk until smooth. Remove from the heat and beat the yolks one at a time into the hot mixture. Return the pan to the water bath and whisk for 1–2 minutes until slightly thickened. Remove from the water bath and set aside until cool but not set. Whip the cream until it holds a shape; then fold it into the cooled chocolate mixture (if warm it will melt the cream). Add the sugar and rum to taste. Spread the frosting on the top and sides of the cake and transfer it to a platter.

PAIN D'ÉPICES
Spice bread

'Pain d'épices' originated in Flanders with the spice trade, but has long been a speciality of Dijon, where as 'gâteau ducal' it was served at all Burgundian feasts. The original recipe is an odd one, containing only honey, spices, rye flour and a raising agent. The bread easily forms a hard crust, and in the last century was baked in special wooden moulds to keep it moist. Nowadays a lining of newspaper in the pan serves the same purpose. Without the spices and honey, this recipe gives 'pain de seigle' – simple rye bread.

Serves 8

250 g	rye flour	2¼ cups
225 g	all-purpose flour, more if needed	1¾ cups
5 g	salt	1 tsp
	2 tsp aniseed	
410 ml	lukewarm water	1⅔ cups
25 g	fresh yeast OR 1½ packages dry yeast	1½ cakes
	1 tsp brown sugar	
350 g	honey	1 cup
	1½ tsp ground ginger	
	1½ tsp ground allspice	
23 × 12 × 10 cm/9 × 5 × 4 in loaf pan		

Put both the flours, the salt and aniseed into a bowl. Make a well in the centre and pour in the lukewarm water. Crumble the yeast over the water, add the brown sugar and let stand for 5 minutes or until dissolved. Gradually draw in the flour to make a smooth dough; add more flour if necessary to obtain a dough that is soft and slightly sticky. Turn the dough out on to a floured board and knead it for 5–10 minutes or until smooth and elastic, working in more flour as necessary to prevent the dough from sticking to the board. Put the dough in a lightly oiled bowl and turn the dough over so the top is oiled. Cover with a damp cloth and leave to rise in a warm place for 1–1½ hours or until doubled in bulk. Line the pan with several thicknesses of newspaper and finally with a layer of greaseproof/parchment paper or foil. Set the oven at low (160°C/320°F).

Knead the risen dough lightly to knock out the air; then work in the honey, ground ginger and allspice. Beat the dough for 5 minutes – it will be very sticky. Spoon it into the loaf pan, cover and leave to rise in a warm place for 45 minutes–1 hour or until almost doubled in bulk. The dough should reach the top of the pan.

Bake in the heated oven for 3–3½ hours or until a skewer inserted into the bread comes out clean. If the top of the bread browns too quickly, cover it with foil. Let cool in the pan before turning out. Wrap the bread tightly in foil or plastic wrap and keep a few days so it becomes moist before serving.

PAIN DE SEIGLE

Make rye flour dough and let rise as for pain d'épices. Omit honey, aniseed, ground ginger and ground allspice. Knead the plain rye dough, then shape it into a loaf. Put it into a pan and let rise as above. Set the oven at moderately hot (190°C/375°F). Brush the loaf with egg glaze and bake for 40–50 minutes or until it sounds hollow when tapped on the bottom. Pain de seigle is best eaten the day it is baked.

GALETTES FLAMANDES

Hazelnut and candied orange tartlets

The name of these popular Burgundian tartlets is a reminder that for 150 years Flanders belonged to the Duchy of Burgundy.

Makes 12–14 tartlets

120-g	piece of candied	4-oz
	orange peel	
	SWEET PASTRY	
345 g	flour	2⅔ cup
	1 egg	
	1 egg yolk	
150 g	sugar	¾ cup
185 g	butter	6 oz
	1 tsp rum	
	TOPPING	
65 g	hazelnuts	½ cup
75 g	almonds	½ cup
200 g	sugar	1 cup
	6 egg whites	
60 g	candied orange peel,	2 oz
	chopped	
45 g	sliced almonds	½ cup
	confectioners' sugar (for sprinkling)	
12–14 tartlet moulds (9 cm/3½ in diameter)		

Make the pastry as for sweet pie pastry* and chill for 30 minutes or until firm. Butter the tartlet moulds and line* them. Cut the piece of candied peel in 12 or 14 small circles, ovals or other decorative shapes; set aside. Cut the peel trimmings in thin strips and scatter them in the lined moulds. Chill 30 minutes more. Set the oven at moderate (175°C/350°F).

Meanwhile, make the topping: toast the hazelnuts in the oven for 8–10 minutes or until lightly browned. Transfer them immediately to a sieve or a cloth and rub off their skins while hot. Lower the oven heat to low (150°C/300°F) and put a baking sheet in the oven to heat. Mince/grind the almonds and hazelnuts with half the sugar. Beat the egg whites until stiff; then add the remaining sugar and beat for another 30 seconds to make a stiff, glossy meringue. Fold the nut mixture and chopped candied peel into the meringue.

Spoon in enough topping to fill the tartlets. Sprinkle with sliced almonds, then with the sugar. Decorate each tartlet with a piece of the cut-out candied peel and set on the hot baking sheet. Bake in the oven for 30 minutes or until the pastry is browned and the topping is set. Let the tartlets cool slightly before unmoulding.

CASSIS

The association of Dijon with cassis (the word refers both to black currants and to the liqueur made from them) dates from the turn of the century. When phylloxera blight killed many grape vines, it was found that currant bushes grew well in abandoned vineyards. The fruit was cultivated both for jam and for 'crème de cassis', a liqueur which dates back to the Middle Ages. Now the grapes are back, but black currants have remained, appearing in local confections like 'cassinines' or 'pâte de cassis'. Many think the best use of all is in a glass of 'kir', which consists of a teaspoon or two of crème de cassis topped up with white wine, preferably the flinty local aligoté. The excellent marriage of white wine and cassis took its modern name from Canon Kir, mayor of Dijon and Resistance hero, who converted both Premier Khrushchev and the future Pope John XXIII to it.

PÂTE DE CASSIS

Black currant jellies

'Pâte de framboises' is made in the same way as 'pâte de cassis', by substituting raspberries for the black currants.

Makes 750 g/1½ lb fruit jellies

1 kg	black currants	2 lb
550 g	sugar	2¾ cups
	sugar (for rolling)	
20 cm/8 in square cake pan		

Lightly oil the pan. Put the black currants in a pan, cover and simmer until the fruit can be easily mashed to a pulp. Remove from the heat and push through a drum sieve. Return to the pan, stir in the sugar and heat gently until dissolved. Boil for 20–25 minutes, stirring constantly with a wooden spoon and skimming occasionally, until the mixture comes away from the sides of the pan and reaches 110°C/230°F on a sugar thermometer. Pour into the oiled pan. Leave in a cool place for several days. Cut in 2·5 cm/1 in cubes and roll in sugar.

CHEESES

Burgundians make many good cheeses, but unfortunately for the rest of France, they eat most of them – only about half of the cheeses produced there and in the Lyonnais are ever sold outside the region. One reason is the preponderance of fresh cheeses, which do not travel well. In local restaurants, creamy fresh cheese is always offered as an alternative to the standard cheese board, to be eaten like a dessert with a topping of crème fraîche and sugar. Other fresh cheeses are flavoured with garlic and herbs, like 'cervelle de canut' of Lyon made with cow's milk, and 'claquebitou', a soft goat cheese from the uplands around Beaune.

Most powerful of all is the local 'fromage fort', a generic name for the fermented mixtures of cheese, herbs and spirits that are concocted in other areas of France too. In Burgundy fromage fort is made with grated cow or goat cheese combined with marc or wine, tarragon, thyme, bay leaf and often the water in which leeks have been cooked. After it has been sealed in a crock for an indefinite period, the name – strong cheese – can be taken literally. Most aged cheeses of the region are less aggressive.

Those made with cow's milk like 'St-Florentin', 'soumaintrain', 'cîteaux' and 'les laumes' are soft, spicy and go beautifully with the local wine. 'Époîsses', Napoleon's favourite, is slightly stronger as, during the last month of curing, it is washed with marc.

Burgundy and the Lyonnais also have their share of goat cheeses. The average size here is about 2 cm/$\frac{3}{4}$ in thick and 10 cm/4 in in diameter and varies from soft to dry, depending how long it has been aged. There are hundreds of variations and as many different names. The 'petit bressan' comes as a truncated cone, the 'charolais' is a tall cylinder, while the 'montrachet', appropriately wrapped in grape leaves, is good with the wine of the same name. All have their own characteristic flavour – piquant, nutty or dry. The smallest is the 'bouton de culotte' (trouser button) which amounts only to a pungent mouthful.

Burgundians, do, however, share one cheese with the rest of France – 'bleu de Bresse'. Created after World War II, with the flavour of a blue cheese and the creamy texture of a brie, bleu de Bresse has proved a bestseller, becoming a standard item on the shelves of grocery shops.

OTHER SPECIALITIES OF THE REGION
TRADITIONAL DISHES

Écrevisses à la chablisienne
Crayfish with white wine sauce

Truites à la montbardoise
Trout stuffed with spinach and shallots

Grenouilles à la crème de Dombes
Frogs' legs in cream sauce

Fonds d'artichauts au foie gras Mère Fillioux
Artichoke bottoms with foie gras

Le saladier lyonnais
Cold platter of sheep's feet, chicken livers, hard-boiled eggs and herring

Lapin rôti à la moutarde
Roast rabbit with mustard

Jau au sang
Chicken in blood-thickened sauce

Poulet au vinaigre de Roanne
Chicken in vinegar sauce

Poulet en matelote nivernaise
Chicken with eel in red wine sauce

Poularde en vessie
Chicken in pig's bladder

Marcassin farci au saucisson
Young wild boar stuffed with sausage

Galimafrée à la Vauban
Shoulder of lamb stuffed with chopped lamb, mushrooms, garlic and herbs

CHARCUTERIE

Pâté de pigeonneau
Pigeon pâté

Lièvre en terrine
Hare terrine

PÂTISSERIE AND CONFISERIE

Tarte à la lyonnaise
Almond, kirsch and breadcrumb tart

Galette pérougienne
Flat yeast cake with buttery sugar topping

Escargots en chocolat
Chocolate snails

Les anis de Flavigny
Anise candy

Languedoc

I think of Languedoc as a land of smells: the soothing perfume of lime, mint, camomile and verbena on a market stall, destined for herb teas; the acrid odour of maturing cheese in the caves of Roquefort; the lingering whiff of fish soup in the narrow street of a fishing port – an aroma so heavily tinged with garlic that it sends my husband hastily in search of fresher air. For Languedoc is a very Mediterranean province, sunburned, parched and colourful, especially in its southern extension, the Roussillon, the 'red land' bordering Spain.

Unlike its well-trodden neighbour Provence, Languedoc has been a latecomer to the twentieth century. Not for nothing did Robert Louis Stevenson choose a sure-footed donkey for travel in the Cévennes mountains, then as now one of the wildest parts of France. None the less, with its varied terrain and long history of civilization (the first Roman settlement in Gaul was on the coast at Narbonne), Languedoc has always contained many of the elements essential to good living. It was Racine who, when staying in Uzès in 1661, remarked that twenty caterers could make a living there, but a bookseller would starve to death.

Languedoc's coastline is placid and flat, bordered by immense lagoons which harbour a proliferation of fish. In the old days they were so plentiful that the nets were simply dragged on to the beach between two boats, but now the search extends to deeper waters for sardine, lemon sole, red mullet, skate, octopus, scampi and all the makings of a good 'bourride', the rich fish soup which rivals bouillabaisse. Bourride is pale, flavoured only with garlic, onion, herbs and olive oil, with none of the distracting tomato and saffron found in bouillabaisse. Aïoli sauce is its indispensable accompaniment – a thick, pungent garlic mayonnaise which is served with anything from snails to vegetables to hard-boiled eggs.

In the still coastal waters, plump mussels grow to a huge size, ideal for stuffing or for making soup. A wide range of clams is available such as 'palourdes' and the little 'clovisses' that are so good with rice and pasta, or simmered with garlic, herbs and white wine. Many fish are barbecued outdoors, as befits the warm climate, and in the Roussillon a Catalan tone is added with peppers and green olives. This abundance of local fish makes for good eating since most of it is dispatched directly to the table,

but the industry is on a small scale, the whole of Languedoc producing a mere twelfth of the tonnage of the herring port of Boulogne on the English Channel.

Far more important than fish commercially are the region's fruit and vegetables, almost all grown under irrigation. Many of France's first peaches, apricots, cherries, plums and melons come from the sheltered corner of the Roussillon, with the sun-drenched areas of Languedoc not far behind. By growing produce in greenhouses or under plastic wraps, there can be three crops a year beginning with beans, parsley and early potatoes, then tomatoes and cucumbers, and ending with winter lettuce and greens. These techniques are so recent, however, that the fruit and vegetables to be found in traditional recipes tend to be hot-climate staples like figs, tomatoes and aubergines.

One fruit is more important to Languedoc than any other: the grape. One department alone, the Hérault, produces a fifth of all the wine in France and to most Frenchmen the regions of Roussillon, Corbières and Minervois denote the most basic of red 'vins de table'. I had never thought vines could be boring until I drove from the Camargue to the Pyrenees – or was I subconsciously affected by the knowledge that so much of the wine produced there is what the British call 'plonk'? One exception is the unique sweet muscat of Frontignan, so rich, golden and heavy that it runs completely against current tastes. Now scarcely known outside France, frontignan was once popular in England, where home-made gooseberry wine was sometimes called English frontignan.

Admittedly, copious draughts of red wine are the appropriate accompaniment to many of the local recipes, which often depend on dried legumes. The most famous of all Languedoc specialities, 'cassoulet', with its white kidney beans, is only the start of the story. In Béziers, heart of the wine country, I noticed several grocery shops, with huge 100-kilo sacks of split peas, chick-peas, green and orange lentils and at least four different kinds of bean. Propped against them were sacks of cornmeal and a grain I could not immediately identify but which turned out to be semolina for North African couscous, evidence of the sizeable Arab population.

Arabs have been lured back to the French labour force four hundred years after their expulsion by Henri of Navarre. While their medieval presence lingers in names like Castelsarrasin and the narrow streets and tall, blank-walled houses of old Languedoc, the proliferation of Arab pastry shops and the busy trade in African spices attest to their return. Couscous itself has spread throughout France and is becoming almost as naturalized as sauerkraut. Paella, too, has infiltrated most coastal parts of France, a mark of the Catalan traditions which link the Roussillon with Spain over the border. Bullfighting thrives as far east as the Rhône and Nîmes, where 'cuadillas' (bull's testicles) are supposedly served after a big fight, no doubt as a restorative for the toreadors.

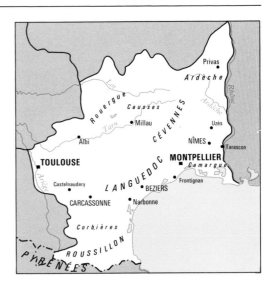

Inland from the Mediterranean, Arab and Spanish spices are replaced by more traditional French seasonings – garlic and the herbs of the 'garrigues', the aromatic scrub which covers much of the uplands. Sheep are the only animals which adapt to this harsh terrain and for a thousand years and more life in the mountains has revolved around them. In summer flocks graze on the Cévennes and on the causses, the grey limestone plateaux to the west, moving slowly across common pasture lands. Then in the autumn the sheep make their way down to the more sheltered valleys, accompanied by their shepherd and his dogs. The flocks yield wool, milk for roquefort and mutton which is redolent of the herb-strewn ground. Now that the lonely life of the herder has less and less appeal, I was astonished how often, when crossing the Cévennes, I saw a nursery-rhyme shepherd in a smock and black shovel hat, crook in hand, surrounded by his sheep. The continuing poverty of the Cévennes and the depopulation of its villages is a reminder of the old, hard life of rural France.

Economy is therefore a habit in Languedoc, and a little is made to go a long way in dishes like 'alycuit', a stew of chicken giblets and trimmings whose name comes from 'aile' (wing) and 'cou' (neck). All the innards like tripe, both calf's and sheep's, are popular and there is even a dish called 'cabassol' made of lamb's head and feet cooked as a pot-au-feu. Pliny reported the local sausages as the best in Gaul and to this day pork is a mainstay, particularly in the Rouergue, where roquefort cheese is made. After seeing the number of feet, tails and other odds and bobs on sale in the market, I was reassured to find that 'oreillettes de Toulouse' were sweet fritters, owing nothing to the ear but their shape.

Toulouse is known for candied violets, though most are now imported. From the north-eastern extremity of Languedoc, the Ardèche, come fresh and canned chestnuts and the entire French supply of candied marrons glacés. Moving south towards the sea, the land flattens to the plains around Nîmes, once the granary of the lower Languedoc, but now turned over to fruit and vegetables. Finally comes the Camargue, the huge marshy area formed by the Rhône delta. Here and there the waving green reeds which line the canals are marked by the acid green of paddy fields, for this is the only place in France that is wet and warm enough to grow rice. The strain is similar to that grown in Indo-China, small and firm when cooked.

From rice to roquefort cheese, the food of Languedoc covers a good deal of ground, but much of the land is still occupied by grapes. What could be more appropriate than this delightful account of a wine harvest feast: 'A fire of vine stocks is kindled. Kilometres of sausages are grilled, or at any rate a great many, for the sausages are supplied by the vigneron or his manager and pride plays a role in their supply. . . . Each picker brings only his bread; as to the rest: pork pâté, cold boudin sausage and fritons as charcuterie, fresh tomatoes with salt and potato salad in oil for vegetables also form part of the tradition. Red, rosé and white wines, the bottle of pastis as apéritif for the men and muscat for the women and young people, roquefort and cantal cheese with dry biscuits form an equally important part of the accessories.'

217

SOUPE AUX POIS CHICHES
Chick-pea soup

Chick-peas used to be simmered with a pinch or two of wood ashes (a primitive form of baking soda) to make them tender. The chick-peas left over from this soup make a good salad (see 'pois chiches en salade'), or they can be mixed with some shredded raw spinach leaves, then heated in oil and served as a vegetable.

Serves 4–6

500 g	chick-peas	1 lb
3 L	cold water, more if needed	3 qt
	pinch of baking soda	
3 L	boiling water	3 qt
	salt and pepper	
	2 Tbsp olive oil	
	1 onion, sliced	
	2 leeks, trimmed, split and sliced	
	1 tomato, peeled and cut in 6 pieces	
	croûtons* fried in oil	

Soak the chick-peas overnight in cold water. Drain, discarding the soaking water, and rinse them well. Put them in a large pot with the cold water and baking soda. Bring to a boil and simmer uncovered over a low fire for 1 hour. Drain, discarding the water.

Return the chick-peas to the pot with the boiling water. Add a pinch of salt and simmer uncovered over a low fire for 1 more hour or until the chick-peas are very tender; test by trying to remove the skin from a few chick-peas – it should come off easily. Drain the vegetables and return the cooking liquid to the pot.

While the chick-peas are simmering, heat the oil in a frying pan and add the onion and leeks. Cook over a low fire for 10 minutes or until softened. Add the tomato and cook over a medium fire, stirring, for 5 more minutes or until the vegetables are lightly browned. Add a few spoonsful of the chick-pea liquid and bring to a boil.

When the chick-peas are tender, add the contents of the frying pan to the pot of reserved cooking liquid with a pinch of pepper. Add half the chick-peas and continue to simmer for another 30–45 minutes or until they are so soft that they can easily be crushed. (Keep the remaining chick-peas for another recipe.) Purée the soup in a food mill or a blender. For a rougher texture, simply crush the peas with a spoon or a potato masher. Return the soup to the pot, reheat it and taste for seasoning.

Serve the soup hot, with the croûtons in a separate bowl.

POIVRONS ROUGES À LA CATALANE
Red peppers stuffed with rice salad

The cooking of Catalonia has spilled over the Pyrenees and across into Roussillon.

Serves 4

150 g	rice	¾ cup
	salt	
	4 red peppers	
60 ml	oil	¼ cup
200 g	tomatoes, diced	7 oz
	½ small sweet onion, finely chopped	
	1 Tbsp capers, drained	
50 g	green olives	¼ cup
	2 hard-boiled eggs, quartered	
	VINAIGRETTE	
	1 Tbsp vinegar	
	salt and pepper	
	3 Tbsp oil	

Set the oven at very hot (220°C/425°F).

Cook the rice in a large quantity of boiling salted water over a high fire for 12–15 minutes or until just tender. Drain and leave to cool.

Meanwhile, put the peppers in a baking dish with the oil and bake for 10 minutes or until tender. Discard the cores and seeds, halve the peppers lengthwise and put in a serving dish.

Make the vinaigrette* and mix enough of it into the rice to moisten it. Stir in the tomatoes, onion and capers; taste for seasoning.

Spoon the rice salad into the peppers and decorate with the olives and hard-boiled eggs. Serve at room temperature.

Today virtually all of France's salt comes from the Salins du Midi, great salt-water lakes which occupy 8,000 hectares (nearly 20,000 acres) behind Aigues Mortes, capital of the Camargue. Evaporation takes place in several stages. First the brine is concentrated sufficiently for sand and other impurities to be filtered off. Then the clear brine is run into pans where, as the water evaporates, salt crystallizes and falls to the bottom. This is the purest salt, usually containing 96 per cent sodium chloride, though its exact composition depends on the rate of evaporation and so on the weather and the time of year.

A certain mystique attaches to salt from special sources, which may have a particular chemical composition or an attractive appearance. One of the most famous French salins was at Arc-et-Senans in Franche-Comté; there the water from nearby springs was heated in great halls that formed part of a futuristic model town designed in the 18th century by the architect Nicolas Ledoux. Less refined, but cheaper, was 'bay salt' from Bourgneuf in southern Brittany. From medieval times to the present day a mixture of soil, seaweed and seawater has been evaporated in the sun to produce salt in large quantities there. Bourgneuf was a major salt port for three centuries, and the easy availability of salt contributed to the growth of the Breton trade in salt cod. Many cooks still use it today in dishes like pot-au-feu, and at least one Paris bakery attributes the flavour of its bread to Bourgneuf salt.

Salt is still an invaluable preservative for meat and fish where refrigeration facilities are limited. Man needs salt in his diet to survive, although a normal intake of meats and vegetables usually contains sufficient natural salt; however, without salt most food – particularly bread – is so bland as to be unpalatable.

Fine table salt is used most often in the kitchen, but the cheaper coarse or rock salt is useful in pickling and for salt water for boiling. 'Coarse salt is for salting and fine salt for seasoning,' say chefs.

SAUCE BRIQUE ROSE
Tomato and meat sauce

The name and the colour of this sauce evoke the dazzling rose-red brick used to build medieval cathedrals like those of Toulouse and Albi. The sauce goes well with poached meats and grilled/broiled duck breasts; sometimes chopped 'confit' of duck or 'boudin' blood sausages are added, particularly when the sauce is to be served with pasta, gnocchi, 'millas' (see recipe), or poached or hard-boiled eggs.

Makes about 500 ml/2 cups of sauce

60 g	goose fat	$\frac{1}{4}$ cup
500 g	ground pork, fat and lean mixed	1 lb
	2 onions, chopped	
	10 cloves garlic, chopped	
1 kg	tomatoes, peeled, seeded and chopped	2 lb
	bouquet garni	
	salt and pepper	
	2 Tbsp chopped herbs: tarragon, parsley and chervil	

Melt the goose fat in a heavy pot, add the pork and cook over a low fire, stirring, for a few minutes or until lightly browned. Stir in the onions, garlic, tomatoes, bouquet garni, salt and pepper. Bring to a boil and simmer uncovered over a low fire, stirring occasionally, for 30 minutes or until very thick. Discard the bouquet garni, taste for seasoning and stir in the chopped herbs. Serve hot.

AÏOLI
Garlic mayonnaise

'Aïoli' refers not only to the sauce made with garlic, egg yolks and olive oil, but also to a complete dish where the sauce is served with boned salt cod, hard-boiled eggs, squid or snails and vegetables such as carrots, potatoes, artichokes and green beans.

Makes 500 ml/2 cups of sauce

	12–16 cloves garlic, coarsely chopped	
	salt	
	white pepper (optional)	
	2 egg yolks	
500 ml	olive oil, at room temperature	2 cups
	juice of 2 lemons, more if needed	
	2 tsp lukewarm water	

Using a mortar and pestle, work the garlic with a little salt and pepper until smooth; then work in the egg yolks. Add the olive oil drop by drop, stirring constantly with the pestle. Once the sauce has started to thicken, the oil can be added more quickly. When half the oil has been added, stir in the lemon juice and water and then continue to add the remaining oil.

Alternatively, purée the garlic, egg yolks and seasoning in a food processor or blender. With the blades still turning, add the oil in a thin stream. Add lemon juice and water at the end.

Taste the aïoli and add more lemon juice, salt and pepper if necessary.

GARLIC

The French have long been convinced that garlic, like wine, is good for you. Garlic was the principal ingredient in 'four thieves' vinegar', sold in Marseille in 1722 as a preventative against the plague. In the adventures of Tartarin de Tarascon, Alphonse Daudet reports that the local doctor dosed his patients with garlic soup. The medicinal properties of garlic do not detract from its popularity. Garlic stalls are prominent in every market-place, and from Narbonne on the coast to Uzès in the hills, garlic fairs are held throughout Languedoc each year.

The three main kinds of garlic are easily distinguished. White garlic is the mildest and keeps for about six months; violet garlic is of medium strength and keeping time, and rose or red garlic, the strongest of all, is reputed to be good for a year or more. When cooked, garlic mellows agreeably, so that recipes like garlic soup, calling for 24 cloves per litre, or 'pistache de mouton', a shoulder of lamb cooked not with pistachios but with up to 50 whole garlic cloves, are not the devilish threat that might be expected. The flavour of raw garlic is a good deal stronger, but some cooks still use two cloves per person in aïoli.

The fresher the garlic, the milder the taste. In winter, or when only dry garlic is available, less may be needed in a recipe.

To judge the age, pinch the whole bulb. If fresh it will be plump and firm. As it dries it will acquire more wrinkles and papery skin until finally the cloves disintegrate to dust and are unusable. Commercial garlic powder is no substitute for the real thing.

LA BOURRIDE
Garlic fish stew

Bourride is popular all along the Mediterranean coast and so important is the distinction between it and bouillabaisse (see recipe) that markets sell different mixtures of fish to make the two soups. Favourites for bourride are sea bass, sea-bream, John Dory, whiting and, among firmer fish, monkfish and conger eel.

Serves 6

1·5 kg	salt-water fish	3 lb
1·5 L	fish stock*	1½ qt
	1 onion, sliced	
	sprig of thyme	
	1 bay leaf	
	1 stalk of fennel OR a pinch of fennel seed	
	pared strip of orange rind	
	1 sprig of parsley	
	2 cloves garlic, crushed	
	salt and pepper	
	1 Tbsp olive oil	
	1 small loaf French bread	
250 ml	aïoli (see recipe)	1 cup
	5 egg yolks	

Discard the fins and scale and clean the fish. Cut the fish in thin slices; if using monkfish, fillet it and cut the fillets in chunks. Wash and dry the fish; use the heads and tails to make fish stock. In a large pot put the onion, thyme, bay leaf, fennel, orange rind, parsley and garlic. Add the fish stock, salt, pepper and olive oil and bring to a boil. Add the firm fish and simmer for 5 minutes; then add the remaining fish and simmer over a low fire for 15 minutes or until just tender. Transfer the fish to a platter, cover and keep warm. Strain the broth and keep hot.

Set the oven at low (150°C/300°F), cut the bread in thin slices and toast until crisp.

Just before serving, whisk the aïoli with the egg yolks in a heavy-based saucepan. Gradually whisk in the hot broth. Heat over a low fire, stirring constantly, until the soup thickens to the consistency of thin cream; don't let the soup boil or it will curdle. Taste for seasoning.

Ladle some soup into each bowl, add a few pieces of fish and set a piece of toast on top. Serve immediately, passing more toast separately with a platter of the remaining fish.

CLOVISSES OU PALOURDES À LA BITTEROISE

Clams with garlic and parsley

In Languedoc all sorts of clams, soft- and hard-shelled, are prepared in this way and may be served hot or cold.

Serves 3–4 as a first course

1·5 kg	small clams	3 lb
30 g	butter	2 Tbsp
	1 onion, chopped	
	2 cloves garlic, chopped	
250 ml	dry white wine	1 cup
	a few stems of parsley	
	pinch of thyme	
	1 bay leaf	
	5 black peppercorns	
	GARLIC AND PARSLEY SAUCE	
125 ml	milk, more if needed	½ cup
30 g	butter	2 Tbsp
25 g	flour	3 Tbsp
	3 cloves garlic, finely chopped	
	3 Tbsp chopped parsley	
	pinch of ground allspice	
	salt and pepper (optional)	

Clean the clams*.

Heat the butter in a pot, stir in the onion and garlic and cook over a low fire until soft but not brown. Add the wine, parsley, thyme, bay leaf and peppercorns and bring to a boil. Simmer for 1 minute.

Add the clams to the pot, cover and cook over a high fire, stirring occasionally, for 4–5 minutes or until open. Remove the clams with a slotted spoon. Discard the loose half of each shell, leaving the clam in the half to which it has adhered. Strain the cooking liquid into a bowl and leave for a few minutes so any sand settles in the bottom. Pour the liquid into another bowl, leaving the sandy part of the liquid behind.

Measure the cooking liquid and make it up to 500 ml with milk. Make a thin white sauce*, using the butter, flour and measured liquid but don't add salt. Add the chopped garlic, parsley and allspice. Add the clams to the sauce and simmer for 5 minutes, stirring occasionally. Taste for seasoning; salt may not be needed since the clams are salty. Serve in shallow bowls with fingerbowls for rinsing.

CLOVISSES OU PALOURDES À LA BANYULAISE

Fry 2 tomatoes, peeled, seeded and finely chopped, and 1 green pepper, cored, seeded and finely chopped, with the onion and garlic until soft. Remove them, cook the clams as above, then return the tomato and pepper to the finished sauce with the clams.

TRUITES AU COURT BOUILLON

Poached trout

A Languedoc touch is added to these trout by the garlic in the court bouillon.

Serves 6

250 g each	6 trout	½ lb each
	COURT BOUILLON	
1·5 L	water	1½ qt
500 ml	dry white wine preferably gaillac	2 cups
	1 onion, sliced	
	1 carrot, sliced	
	2 shallots, sliced	
	3 cloves garlic	
	bouquet garni	
	salt	
	10 black peppercorns	
	MUSHROOM GARNISH AND SAUCE	
60 g	butter	4 Tbsp
	1 onion, finely chopped	
150 g	mushrooms, thinly sliced	5 oz
15 g	flour	2 Tbsp
500 ml	court bouillon (above)	2 cups
	salt and pepper	
	3 egg yolks	
	a few drops of lemon juice	
	pinch of cayenne pepper	
	2 Tbsp chopped parsley	

Simmer all the court bouillon ingredients for 20 minutes in a wide pan. Let cool. Discard the fins of the trout and trim the tails. Clean them through the gills and wash thoroughly. Put them into the cool court bouillon, cover with foil, bring just to a boil and poach 12–15 minutes or until just tender. With a small knife, gently remove the skin. Drain and carefully transfer the fish to a platter, cover and keep warm. Strain the court bouillon.

Prepare the sauce: melt the butter in a saucepan, add the onion and cook over a low fire until soft but not brown. Add the mushrooms and cook over a medium fire 3–4 minutes. Stir in the flour and cook over a low fire, stirring, until foaming. Stir in the court bouillon and a little salt and pepper, bring to a boil and simmer over a low fire, stirring occasionally, for 10 minutes.

Just before serving, beat the egg yolks with a little lemon juice. Beat in a few tablespoons sauce; return this mixture to the sauce, off the heat. Heat gently for 1–2 minutes, stirring constantly, until slightly thickened; don't let the sauce boil or cook too long or it will curdle. Add cayenne pepper and parsley and taste for seasoning. With a slotted spoon scatter the mushrooms over the trout. Coat the trout with some of the sauce and serve the rest separately.

LOUP AU BEURRE DE MONTPELLIER
Bass with herb butter

The aromatic butter, served here with sea bass, is good with almost any poached fish, such as salmon, snapper, pompano and trout. Don't hesitate to substitute other herbs like basil, chives or oregano, provided they are fresh.

Serves 6

1·5-kg	1 medium sea bass	3-lb
	1 large bunch of parsley (for serving)	
	HERB BUTTER	
90 g	watercress	3 oz
90 g	spinach leaves	3 oz
60 g	parsley sprigs	2 oz
60 g	fresh chervil	2 oz
	1 sprig fresh tarragon, stem removed	
	6 anchovy fillets, soaked in water or milk	
	2 small gherkin pickles	
	15 capers, drained	
	1 clove garlic	
500 g	butter	1 lb
	1 tsp Dijon mustard	
	a few drops of lemon juice	
	salt and pepper	
	COURT BOUILLON	
	1 onion, studded with 1 clove	
	1 carrot, sliced	
	bouquet garni	
250 ml	white wine	1 cup
3 L	water, more if needed	3 qt
	salt and pepper	

Prepare the herb butter: remove the stems from the watercress and spinach and the large stalks from the parsley. Add the watercress, spinach, parsley, chervil and tarragon to a pot of boiling water and boil for 1–2 minutes. Drain them thoroughly, then squeeze them dry in a cloth. Drain the anchovies and purée them in a food processor or blender with the pickles, capers and garlic until very smooth; remove. Soften the butter and purée it with the herbs. Beat in the anchovy mixture, mustard, lemon juice and salt and pepper to taste. Alternatively, chop the blanched herbs and greens, anchovies, pickles, capers and garlic as finely as possible; beat them into the butter and add the mustard, lemon juice, salt and pepper.

Put all the ingredients for the court bouillon in a fish poacher or roasting pan large enough to contain the fish and bring to a boil. Simmer for 20 minutes and let cool.

Meanwhile, cut off and discard the fins from the fish and trim the tail to a 'V'. Scale the fish, clean and wash it. Put the fish in the cooled court bouillon, adding more water to cover if necessary, and bring just to a boil. Cover and poach for 25–30 minutes or until a skewer inserted into the thickest part of the fish is hot to the touch when withdrawn. While the fish is poaching, make a bed of parsley on an oval serving platter.

Carefully transfer the fish to paper towels to drain; then set it on the bed of parsley. Serve the herb butter separately in a sauceboat.

DARNES DE SAUMON OU DE LOUP AU BEURRE DE MONTPELLIER

Poach steaks of salmon or sea bass in the court bouillon for 7–10 minutes or until just tender. Drain and serve on a bed of parsley, with a pat of herb butter on each steak.

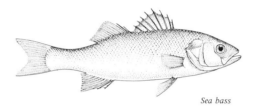

Sea bass

BRANDADE DE MORUE
Purée of salt cod

Salt cod, not hard, dried stockfish, should be used for brandade. The cod must be gently poached, never boiled, otherwise it turns stringy. Oil and hot milk are beaten in slowly to form a light smooth emulsion. The controversial ingredient is garlic; poet Frédéric Mistral said that crushed garlic is permissible, but most cooks prefer just to rub the bowl with the cut clove. In the opinion of some gastronomes of Nîmes, to add any garlic at all is sacrilege.

Serves 6

750 g	salt cod	1½ lb
310 ml	olive oil	1¼ cups
250 ml	milk	1 cup
	1 clove garlic, chopped (optional)	
	pinch of grated nutmeg	
	a few drops of lemon juice	
	pinch of white pepper	
	12 triangular croûtes*, fried in olive oil, then rubbed with garlic	

Soak the cod in cold water for 1–2 days, changing the water several times. Drain it, put it in a large pan of cold water, cover and bring just to a boil. Poach over a low fire for 8–10 minutes or until barely tender, drain and cool slightly. Flake with a fork, discarding all skin and bone.

Heat two-thirds of the oil in a saucepan until very hot. Scald the milk in another saucepan. Add the flaked cod to the oil and beat vigorously with a wooden spoon over a low fire, crushing and separating the fibres; to prevent the cod from browning move the pan on and off the fire as you beat. Stir in the garlic.

For a very fine brandade, transfer the cod mixture to a mortar and using a pestle gradually beat in the remaining olive oil and the hot milk. Otherwise, leave the cod in its pan over low heat and use a wooden spoon to beat in a tablespoon of the remaining oil alternately with a tablespoon of the milk. After the oil is used up, continue adding the remaining milk by tablespoons, beating well after each addition; don't add the milk too quickly or the purée will thin and no longer be emulsified. The finished purée should be white, smooth and stiff enough to hold its shape. If it is very stiff, beat in a little more milk. Season the brandade to taste with grated nutmeg, lemon juice and pepper.

Brandade can also be made in an electric food processor. Add the hot oil and milk to the cod a little at a time. Don't overwork or the purée may become too soft, lacking texture.

Pile the brandade in a shallow bowl and surround it with the croûtes.

BRANDADE DU VENDREDI
Make a firm purée of:

500 g	potatoes, peeled	1 lb

by simmering them in lightly salted water until tender; drain. Return them to a low fire for a few seconds to dry; then immediately push them through a sieve. For the brandade, use only:

250 ml	olive oil	1 cup

Heat two-thirds of the oil and add the cod as above. Beat in the potato purée by tablespoonsful, alternating with the remaining olive oil and the milk. Don't use an electric food processor for this version. The croûtes may be omitted.

BRANDADE AUX TRUFFES
Add a chopped truffle to the finished brandade. This is traditional for Christmas Eve supper, a fasting meal before Midnight Mass.

is cured more slowly. 'Merluche' or 'stockfish', often confused with salt cod, is the strongest tasting of all; it is made from hake which is so thoroughly dried that it will keep a year or more.

The stronger the cure, the more important it is to soak salt cod in water to remove the salt and soften the flesh. As long as 48 hours may be needed and the water must be changed several times. Before the days of the diesel engine, bargees who carried salt cod inland were in the habit of towing it under water. Perhaps the most ingenious method of desalting was devised by a Monsieur Ramadier, who had a flush toilet installed in his house at Decazeville in the Rouergue. He simply placed his salt cod in the cistern, where the water was changed regularly without any effort.

Salt cod calls for strongly flavoured partners. The Basques add peppers, tomatoes and plenty of garlic. The Bretons combine it with beans, onions and potatoes. In Languedoc salt cod is served with chick-peas as a penitential dish and during Lent in Auvergne it is cooked with walnut oil, garlic, parsley and cream. By far the most famous salt-cod recipe, however, is 'brandade', popular throughout southern France. A tricky purée made with olive oil and milk, good brandade is light and creamy, but made by a heavy hand or with inferior cod, it can be appallingly strong and chewy. Brandade is addictive; in the last century, President Thiers, a native of Marseille, ate so much that his doctors banned it from his table, whereupon he hid pots of it in his library for consumption on the sly.

ESCARGOTS À LA LANGUEDOCIENNE

Snails with anchovy and walnut sauce

Snails gathered in the 'garrigues' are preferred for this dish because they feed on the aromatic plants, such as thyme, rosemary and fennel, that grow there.

Serves 4–6

	36 large snails or 48 'petits gris' snails, fresh or canned	
	a few basil leaves (optional, for fresh snails)	
	pinch of ground cloves (optional, for fresh snails)	
	ANCHOVY AND NUT SAUCE	
	6 anchovy fillets, soaked in milk	
80 g	walnuts, finely chopped	$\frac{2}{3}$ cup
	OR	
80 g	almonds, finely chopped	$\frac{1}{2}$ cup
	1 clove garlic, finely chopped	
	2 Tbsp finely chopped parsley	
	3 Tbsp olive oil	
60 g	bacon, diced	2 oz
60 g	cooked ham, diced	2 oz
	2 Tbsp cognac	
	1 Tbsp tomato paste	
250 ml	broth	1 cup
	pepper	
	2 Tbsp fresh breadcrumbs	

If using fresh snails, prepare, clean and cook them (see below), adding a few leaves of basil and a pinch of ground cloves to the cooking liquid. Alternatively, if using canned snails, drain and rinse them.

For the sauce: drain the anchovies, finely chop them and mix with the chopped walnuts, garlic and parsley. Briefly chop all these ingredients together; then mix them with a tablespoon of the olive oil. If the bacon is very salty, blanch* it. Heat the remaining oil in a heavy-based pan, add the ham and bacon and brown well. Add the anchovy and walnut mixture and simmer over a low fire, stirring, for 2 minutes. Stir in the cognac, tomato paste and broth and bring to a boil.

Add the snails to the sauce. Simmer over a low fire for about 10 minutes. Add pepper to taste; salt will probably not be needed. Stir in the breadcrumbs to thicken the sauce. Transfer to a hot serving bowl and serve at once.

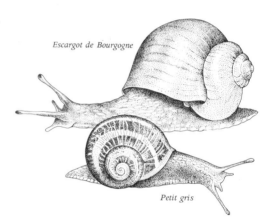

Escargot de Bourgogne

Petit gris

SNAILS

In France, snail-hunting is a national sport, calling for little more than a plastic bucket and a back that bends easily. 'Défense de ramasser les escargots' (snail-gathering forbidden) is to be taken as seriously as the routine prohibitions against hunting and fishing, especially in wine-growing regions. Where there are vines, there are snails. In summer they feed on the leaves and in winter they hibernate under the roots to escape the frost which would split their shells.

Snails are known as the 'oysters of Burgundy', the region which has given its name to the finest variety, the large beige 'escargot de Bourgogne'. The best moment to pick them, say the connoisseurs, is while they are 'dormeurs', or sleeping, when the vines are dug in the late fall. After two or three weeks' hibernation they are still fat, but need no cleaning, a great boon to the cook. More common than Burgundy snails, but less tasty, are 'petits gris', smaller grey snails that appear after rain even in the gardens of central Paris. The vineyards of Languedoc harbour a couple of other kinds, too small to be worth exploiting commercially, but consumed with relish there.

Snails are easy enough to raise, having the inherent advantage that they can only escape at a crawl. One way to pen them in is to surround them with a big ring of wood ash. Snail parks date back to Roman times; modern ones can pack a million snails into 200 square metres. Here the voracious eaters are fed on cabbage, and wheat or oats to make them plump. However, as with foie gras and a dozen other delicacies, there are no longer enough producers in France, and about three-quarters of all escargots de Bourgogne are actually imported from Eastern Europe. The reason is simple: snails are easy to raise or to gather but the devil to clean on a large scale.

When freshly gathered snails are to be prepared at home, they must first be

ENCORNETS FARCIS
Baked squid with tomato stuffing

'Encornet' resembles its near relation, the 'calamar' (flying squid). Either can be used in this dish, as can the American squid found all down the Atlantic coast to the Gulf. For 'encornets farcis aux épinards à la provençale', add the chopped tentacles to the spinach stuffing of 'sardines farcies aux épinards' (see recipe) and stuff the squid with this mixture.

Serves 4

250 g each	4 medium squid	½ lb each
	STUFFING	
150 g	white bread, crusts removed	5 oz
185 ml	milk	¾ cup
	3 Tbsp olive oil	
	1 small onion, chopped	
500 g	tomatoes, peeled, seeded and chopped	1 lb
	salt and pepper	
	2 cloves garlic, chopped	
	2 Tbsp chopped parsley	
	2 egg yolks	
	SAUCE	
	2 Tbsp olive oil	
	1 onion, chopped	
	1 clove garlic, chopped	
	1 bay leaf	
15 g	flour	2 Tbsp
250 ml	white wine	1 cup
250 ml	water	1 cup
	salt and pepper	
	pastry bag and large plain tip (optional)	

Carefully clean the squid and discard the spine, the eyes and any black skin. Cut the tentacles from the body and wash all parts under cold running water; dry well. Chop the tentacles. Set the oven at moderate (175°C/350°F).

Prepare the stuffing: soak the bread in the milk; then squeeze out as much liquid as possible. Heat the oil in a frying pan, add the onion and cook over a low fire for 5 minutes or until softened. Add the chopped tentacles and sauté them with the onions over a medium fire for 5 more minutes. Add the tomatoes, salt and pepper and continue to cook for another 15 minutes or until the excess liquid has evaporated. Remove from the heat and stir in the garlic, bread and parsley. Beat in the egg yolks and taste for seasoning.

Fill the squid two-thirds full of stuffing, using a pastry bag with a large plain tip, if you like; be careful not to overfill the squid or they will burst during baking. Lay the squid in an oiled baking dish and bake for 20 minutes.

Meanwhile, make the sauce: heat the oil in a saucepan, add the onion and cook over a low fire, stirring often, until soft but not brown. Add the garlic, bay leaf and flour and continue to cook, stirring constantly, for 1–2 minutes or until foaming. Stir in the wine and water, add salt and pepper, bring to a boil and simmer for 10 minutes.

Strain the sauce over the squid and bake for 30 minutes or until they turn white and are tender when pricked with a skewer. Taste the sauce for seasoning and serve hot from the dish.

purged of any poisonous herbs by being left without food for a week in a ventilated box outdoors. They are sprinkled with water to keep them moist; finally, in the last two days, they are fattened on a few spoonsful of flour. To find live snails on sale is rare, but when they are, they will usually be 'à jeun', starved and fattened in this manner.

Before cooking, the snails are soaked in water for 10 minutes, then drained and left to emerge from their shells. Immobile snails may be dead and are discarded. Next the snails are tossed in a container with a cup of coarse salt to draw out their sticky juice. Finally, after a last thorough rinse, they are simmered for 2 hours in a pot of boiling water flavoured with thyme, bay leaf, salt, peppercorns and white wine. After draining, the snails are extracted from their shells and the soft stomach at the extremity discarded. Some cooks remove the snails from their shells after a brief blanching, then continue to simmer them without their shells.

Few town cooks bother with this rigmarole; most buy the snails ready cooked or in cans. Most often snails are put back in their shells and doused with the time-honoured garlic and herb 'bourguignonne' butter. Sometimes they are coated in garlic-flavoured batter and fried in oil, or served in tarragon-flavoured brown sauce in the manner of the old Chapeau Rouge restaurant in Dijon. In Languedoc snails are served 'à la languedocienne' in a piquant sauce of anchovy, ham and cognac, with walnuts to add texture. Much touted on tourist postcards is 'cargolade' – snails which are roasted in their shells over a fire of vine stocks – but picturesque though it sounds, this method of cooking is far less reliable than the usual simmering in court bouillon. Sometimes a huge pot of hot snails is set on the table and guests are left to help themselves, spearing the snails from their shells and dipping them in aïoli sauce. Hearty eaters, it is said, can manage a hundred or more.

OMELETTE AUX COURGETTES
Zucchini omelette

For this flat omelette there should be a thicker layer of egg mixture in the pan than for an ordinary folded omelette, to prevent it from drying out while it is being cooked on both sides.

Serves 3–4

300 g	small zucchini	10 oz
	3 Tbsp olive oil	
	salt and pepper	
	8 eggs	
	28 cm/11 in omelette pan	

Wipe the courgettes/zucchini but don't peel. Cut them in small dice. Heat the oil in the omelette pan, add the courgettes, salt and pepper and sauté over a medium fire for 8 minutes or until just tender and light brown; don't overcook or they will be soft.

Meanwhile, in a bowl beat the eggs with a little salt and pepper until thoroughly mixed. Add the eggs to the courgettes in the warm pan and stir briskly with a fork over a medium fire. Continue stirring until the mixture is almost as thick as scrambled eggs. Leave the omelette to cook until well browned on the bottom and almost firm on top. Take from the fire, set a heatproof plate over the top of the pan and turn out the omelette. Slide it back into the pan and brown the other side. Serve hot or cold.

OMELETTE AUX ARTICHAUTS

Use **4 tiny artichokes** instead of the courgettes/zucchini. Discard the stalks and the bottom leaves, cut the tips off the remaining leaves, quarter the artichokes and discard the chokes. Cook the artichokes in the oil for 10 minutes or until just tender; drain and slice.

Alternatively, use **4 large artichoke bottoms***. Simmer them in boiling salted water for 10 minutes or until nearly tender. Drain and dice them; then sauté in the olive oil until just tender and light brown.

Add the beaten eggs to the artichokes and continue as above.

POULET BRAISÉ TARNAISE
Braised chicken with pork and olive stuffing

This recipe from the Tarn area of western Languedoc can also be made with guinea fowl. The stuffing should be coarse, with its ingredients cut to the size of small olives so that they do not bind together during cooking.

Serves 4

1·5-kg	chicken with the giblets	3-lb
	salt and pepper	
	3 Tbsp oil	
60 ml	hot water	$\frac{1}{4}$ cup
250 ml	broth	1 cup
	STUFFING	
100 g	green olives	$\frac{1}{2}$ cup
	1 Tbsp oil or goose fat	
	1 chicken gizzard, diced	
	1 chicken heart, diced	
30 g	thinly sliced raw ham, diced	1 oz
75 g	dried salami-type sausage, cut in thin slices and diced	2$\frac{1}{2}$ oz
75 g	fresh breast of pork, diced	2$\frac{1}{2}$ oz
	1 chicken liver, diced	
	2–3 cloves garlic	
	pepper	
	trussing needle and string	

Make the stuffing: soak the olives in water for 1 hour; drain and pit them. Heat the oil in a frying pan and add the chicken gizzard and heart, with the ham, sausage and pork. Sauté over a medium fire for 5 minutes; then add the liver and sauté for another minute. Remove from the heat and mix with the garlic, olives and some pepper.

Stuff the chicken with the mixture, truss it and sprinkle it with salt and pepper. In a heavy casserole, heat the oil, add the chicken and brown it on all sides over a medium fire. Lay the chicken on its side and add a tablespoon of the hot water; stand back as it will splutter. Cover and cook over a low fire for 15 minutes. Turn the chicken on to its other side, add another tablespoon of hot water, cover and cook another 15 minutes. Continue this procedure, turning the chicken next on its breast and finally on its back, gradually adding the remaining water. Cook for a total of 1 hour or until the chicken is tender when pricked with a skewer. Transfer the chicken to a platter, discard the trussing strings, cover and keep warm.

Discard the excess fat from the casserole and stir in the broth. Bring to a boil and taste; boil the gravy to reduce, if necessary, until well flavoured. Taste for seasoning.

Carve the chicken at the table, serving each person a few spoonsful of stuffing, and pass the gravy separately.

POULE AU RIZ AU SAFRAN
Poached chicken with saffron rice

In the middle ages, saffron for dying wool was grown around Albi, but now the finest saffron, distinguished by its long dark-coloured strands, comes from southern Spain. If you use a chicken rather than a boiling fowl in this recipe, the cooking time should be reduced to about 1 hour.

Serves 4

1·7-kg	boiling fowl	4-lb
	1 onion, stuffed with 2 cloves	
	2 carrots, quartered	
	2 cloves garlic	
	bouquet garni, including a celery stalk and a stem of tarragon	
250 ml	white wine	1 cup
1 L	broth or water, more if necessary	1 qt
	salt and pepper	
	1 Tbsp lard or oil	
	1 onion, chopped	
250 g	rice	1¼ cups
	pinch of saffron strands, steeped in 1–2 Tbsp boiling water	
	grated parmesan or gruyère cheese (optional – for serving)	
	trussing needle and string	

Truss the fowl and put it in a large pot with the whole onion, the carrots, garlic and bouquet garni. Pour in the white wine and enough broth just to cover, add salt and pepper and bring to a boil. Cover and simmer over a low fire, skimming occasionally, for 1¼–1½ hours or until tender when the thigh is pierced with a two-pronged fork. Remove the fowl, discard the trussing strings and cut the bird in 6 to 8 pieces, discarding the skin; cover and keep warm. Skim the excess fat from the cooking liquid, strain and boil until it is reduced to 750 ml. Taste it for seasoning.

Heat the lard in a heavy-based casserole, add the chopped onion and cook over a low fire, stirring often, until soft but not brown. Add the rice and continue to stir over a low fire until the rice becomes transparent and absorbs the fat. Add the reduced cooking liquid, salt, pepper and saffron and its liquid. Cover and simmer over a low fire for 20 minutes or until the rice is tender and has absorbed all the broth. Let the rice stand for 10 minutes off the heat to firm up the grains; then stir lightly with a fork and taste for seasoning. Add the chicken pieces to the rice, cover and reheat briefly. If you like, sprinkle with grated cheese and serve hot from the casserole.

CANARD AUX NAVETS DE BÉZIERS
Duck with turnips and wine

Béziers is famous for the long black-skinned turnips grown near by, which are at their best with duck.

Serves 3–4

2–2·5-kg	duck	5-lb
	1 Tbsp oil	
	1 Tbsp butter	
15 g	flour	2 Tbsp
185 ml	white wine	¾ cup
375 ml	broth	1½ cups
	bouquet garni	
	salt and pepper	
	12–16 baby onions	
500 g	turnips, quartered and shaped in ovals	1 lb
	1 tsp sugar	
60 ml	madeira	¼ cup
	1 Tbsp chopped parsley	
	trussing needle and string	

Set the oven at hot (200°C/400°F). Truss the duck. Heat the oil and butter in a casserole over a low fire and brown the duck on all sides for 20–30 minutes or until the fat beneath the skin of the duck has melted. (If the duck is very fatty, browning may take even longer.)

Remove the duck and drain all but 2 table-spoons of the fat from the pan; reserve 2–3 more tablespoons of the fat for later use. Add the flour to the pan and cook, stirring, until browned; don't allow it to burn. Add the wine, two-thirds of the broth, bouquet garni, salt and pepper and bring to a boil. Replace the duck, cover and cook in the oven for 20–25 minutes.

Meanwhile, heat the reserved duck fat in a large frying pan and sauté the onions until browned on all sides but still firm; remove them and set aside. Add the turnips to the duck fat, sprinkle them with sugar and sauté until brown on all sides; the sugar caramelizes and helps browning. Remove the turnips and add them to the onions.

Arrange the onions and turnips around the duck in the casserole and baste them with cooking liquid. Continue cooking, uncovered, for 20–25 minutes or until the vegetables and the duck are tender; if the sauce gets too thick during cooking, add more broth.

Transfer the duck to a platter, spoon the vegetables around it, cover and keep warm while finishing the sauce; skim any fat from the surface of the sauce. Add the madeira, bring to a boil and taste for seasoning. Spoon a little of the sauce over the duck and sprinkle the vegetables with chopped parsley. Serve the remaining sauce separately.

CASSOULET DE TOULOUSE

The white kidney beans on which cassoulet is based (in cassoulet territory several kinds are sold) have evoked pages of comment: they should be 'long-grained, plump, fresh, creamy and with a thin skin so as to soak up the aroma of the other ingredients,' specifies one cookbook. The 'other ingredients' are a tale in themselves, as cassoulet varies from town to town as well as from cook to cook. The cassoulet of Castelnaudary is supposed to contain sausages with fresh and salt pork to flavour the basic white beans, while in Carcassonne a leg of mutton may be added, with a partridge when in season. The cassoulet of Toulouse is richest of all, with confit of goose or duck included with the mutton and pork. Onions, garlic and herbs are standard ingredients. Some cooks like to add a few tomatoes, others bake cassoulet with a topping of breadcrumbs to be stirred into the beans as a thickening, while in yet another variation the beans are baked until they dissolve almost to a purée. In any case they should always be done until soft and melting. At its most basic, cassoulet can consist simply of sausage and beans, but there is no denying that the complete Toulouse recipe makes quite a feast.

Serves 8

1 kg	dried white beans	2 lb
	salt and pepper	
2·5-kg	duck, OR	5½-lb
	4 pieces of duck or goose confit	
300 g	garlic poaching sausage	10 oz
200 g	pork rind (optional)	7 oz
500 g	bacon or salt pork,	1 lb
	cut in lardons	
750-g	lamb breast	1½-lb
1·5-kg	lamb shoulder, boned	3-lb
60 g	goose or duck fat or lard	¼ cup
300 g	baby onions	10 oz
750 g	pork loin, cut in	1½ lb
	5 cm/2 in cubes	
300 g	saucisses de Toulouse	10 oz
	(see opposite)	
1 kg	tomatoes, peeled, seeded	2 lb
	and coarsely chopped	
185 ml	white wine	¾ cup
1·5 L	broth, bean liquid or	1½ qt
	water, more if needed	
	large bouquet garni	
	pinch of basil or savory (optional)	
	3–4 cloves garlic, chopped	
	1 Tbsp tomato paste	
60 g	dry breadcrumbs	⅔ cup
	trussing needle and string (optional)	

Soak the dried beans overnight in cold water and drain. Put them in a pot with enough water to cover generously and bring to a boil. Simmer for 25 minutes; add salt and continue to cook for another 25–30 minutes or until nearly tender. Set the oven at very hot (220°C/425°F).

Meanwhile, if using fresh duck, truss it and lay it on one side in a roasting pan; roast in the oven for 10 minutes. Turn the duck on to its other side and roast another 10 minutes. Discard the excess fat from the roasting pan. Turn the duck on its breast and roast 10 more minutes. Finally set the duck on its back and roast another 10 minutes. Lower the oven temperature to moderately hot (190°C/375°F).

Poach the garlic sausage in a pan of water for 30 minutes; drain and slice it. Blanch the pork rind by putting it in cold water and simmering for 10 minutes. Rinse it under cold running water, drain thoroughly and mince/grind it. If the bacon is very salty, blanch* it also.

Remove the skin and trim the excess fat from the lamb breast and shoulder. Cut both into 5 cm/2 in cubes. Heat half of the goose fat in a large, heavy casserole and lightly brown the bacon and baby onions; remove them and add the remaining fat to the casserole. Heat it, brown the lamb cubes on all sides and remove them. Add the cubes of pork, brown them also and remove. Lightly brown the Toulouse sausages in the fat, remove and cut them in chunks.

Put the chopped tomatoes in the large casserole with the minced/ground pork rind, the browned bacon, onions, lamb and pork. Add the wine, broth, bouquet garni, basil, garlic, tomato paste and a little salt and pepper. Bring to a boil, skimming occasionally. Cover and bake in the oven for 50–60 minutes or until nearly tender, adding more broth or water if the pan becomes dry.

Cut the roast duck* in 8 pieces, discarding the trussing strings. If using confit, melt the fat slightly to remove the pieces and cut each piece in two. Add the fresh duck or confit, Toulouse sausages and sliced garlic sausage to the casserole. Cover and continue to bake for 30 minutes. Raise the oven temperature to hot (200°C/400°F).

Drain the beans and put in large or medium baking dishes with all the meats and the onions. The dishes should be almost full, with the meats half-covered by the beans. Taste the meat cooking liquid for seasoning and discard the bouquet garni. Ladle enough of the cooking liquid into the dishes to moisten the cassoulet well but don't let it become too soupy. Sprinkle with the breadcrumbs and bake for 30 minutes–1 hour, depending on the size of the dishes, or until a golden-brown crust has formed. Serve hot from the baking dish.

SAUCISSES DE TOULOUSE

Fresh pork sausages

Toulouse sausages are very simple, made of pure pork seasoned only with salt and pepper and, on occasion, with garlic. Their character comes from the special back fat which is used, and the way the meat is coarsely chopped to give extra texture to the sausage. For 'saucisses à l'ail', add 1–2 cloves of crushed and chopped garlic to the mixture.

Serves 5, or makes 10 sausages

750 g	lean pork	1½ lb
250 g	pork fat	½ lb
	1 tsp peppercorns, coarsely crushed	
	salt and pepper	
	pinch of grated nutmeg	
50 g	small sausage casings, about 2 m/2 yd total	2 oz
sausage-stuffing tube or large funnel; string		

Work the lean and fat pork through the coarse plate of a mincer/grinder. Add the peppercorns, salt, pepper and nutmeg and mix well. Chill overnight so the spices blend. Sauté a small piece of the mixture and taste for seasoning.

Soak the casings in cold water for several hours; rinse them with cold water, letting the water run through them.

Tie one end of one casing closed and attach the open end to the base of a funnel or sausage stuffer. Push the casing up the funnel until the closed end is reached. Work the sausage filling through the funnel into the casing, letting the casing fall as the stuffing fills it. If using a sausage stuffer attached to a mincer/grinder, work the stuffing through the mincer into the casing. Don't pack casings too tightly, or they will burst during cooking. When a length of casing is stuffed, tie the end closed with string.

Prick any air pockets in the sausages with a small pin. Tie at about 20 cm/8 in intervals.

To serve, brush with melted butter and grill/broil; alternatively poach in water for 10 minutes and drain thoroughly.

CAILLETTES DE LANGUEDOC

Sausage cakes with liver and chard

'Caillettes' made of sausagemeat wrapped in lacy caul fat and fried are a popular version of sausages. This version is from the Nîmes area.

Serves 6

about 125 g	1 large piece of caul fat	about ¼ lb
250 g	leaves of Swiss chard or spinach, without stems	½ lb
	salt and pepper	
60 g	lard	4 Tbsp
	1 onion, chopped	
	2 cloves garlic, chopped	
125 g	bacon	¼ lb
250 g	lean pork	½ lb
250 g	pork liver	½ lb
	3 Tbsp chopped parsley	
	pinch of thyme	
	½ bay leaf, crumbled	
	6 sage leaves (optional)	

Soak the caul fat in cold water for about 30 minutes to make it pliable. Set the oven at moderately hot (190°C/375°F).

Plunge the chard or spinach leaves into a large pot of boiling salted water and cook over a high fire for 5 minutes. Drain, refresh under cold running water and drain well. Squeeze to remove excess moisture. Chop the leaves.

Heat 1 tablespoon lard in a frying pan, add the onion and cook over a low fire until soft but not brown. Add the garlic and cook 1 minute.

If the bacon is very salty, blanch* it. Mince/grind the pork, bacon and pork liver. Put the meats in a bowl and stir in the chard, onion, garlic, parsley, thyme, bay leaf, salt and pepper. Sauté a small piece and taste for seasoning.

Drain the caul fat and spread it on a working surface. Shape the meat mixture into 6 balls, each about the size of a medium potato, and put them on the fat. Cut around each ball, leaving enough fat to fold over it. Wrap the balls and set a sage leaf on each. Put them in a greased baking dish. Melt the remaining lard and spoon it over them. Bake, basting frequently, 30–35 minutes or until browned and a skewer inserted in the meat for 30 seconds is hot to the touch when withdrawn. Serve hot or cold.

CAILLETTES PROVENÇALES AUX TOMATES

Halve and seed **3 large tomatoes**. Sprinkle them with a mixture of **1 chopped garlic clove** and **2 Tbsp chopped parsley** and season with salt and pepper. Oil a baking dish with olive oil, add the tomatoes and caillettes and baste both with more olive oil. Bake as above.

FARCI DU LAURAGAIS À LA POÊLE
Pork pancake

This 'farci' from the Lauragais hills near Toulouse is little more than a giant hamburger made of pork. The mixture is fried in a frying pan to make a cake that is cut in wedges for serving hot or cold. Farci can also be crumbled into soup instead of the usual bread.

Serves 4–6

100 g	lean bacon, diced	4 oz
500 g	ground pork, equal parts fat and lean	1 lb
100 g	dry breadcrumbs	1 cup
	1 onion, finely chopped	
	2 cloves garlic, finely chopped	
	pinch of thyme	
	1 Tbsp chopped chives	
	salt and pepper	.
80 g	goose fat	5 Tbsp
	23–25 cm/9–10 in frying pan	

If the bacon is very salty, blanch* it.

Beat together the minced/ground pork, breadcrumbs, bacon, onion, garlic, thyme, chives, salt and pepper.

Sauté a small piece of the mixture and taste for seasoning. Shape the mixture into a flat cake the same diameter as your frying pan. Chill for about 1 hour to soften the breadcrumbs.

Heat the goose fat in the frying pan, add the meat cake and cook over a medium fire for 10–12 minutes on each side or until firm and golden brown. Serve hot or cold.

AUBERGINES ET TOMATES À LA NÎMOISE
Stuffed eggplant with tomato and ham

These two recipes from Nîmes illustrate the versatility of this useful vegetable. In the first, tomatoes baked beside the aubergines/eggplants prevent them from becoming too dry. In the second, the aubergine is stuffed with 'fenouil' (fennel), which grows wild in Roussillon; it is so abundant that one chain of hills is called La Fenouillède.

Serves 4

about 500 g	2 small eggplants, unpeeled	about 1 lb
	salt and pepper	
	juice of ½ lemon	
about 500 g	4 firm, ripe tomatoes	about 1 lb
80 ml	olive oil, more if needed	⅓ cup
	TOPPING	
50 g	fresh breadcrumbs	1 cup
150 g	raw ham	5 oz
	2 cloves garlic	
	3 Tbsp parsley leaves	
	3 Tbsp olive oil	
	pepper	
	dry breadcrumbs (for sprinkling)	

Cut off and discard the stems and halve the aubergines/eggplants lengthwise. With a knife, deeply score the cut side of the flesh in a border near the skin and slash the centre; be careful not to puncture the skin. Sprinkle with salt and lemon juice and leave for 20–30 minutes to draw out the bitter juices. Halve the tomatoes crosswise and squeeze gently to remove the seeds. Turn the halves upside down on a rack to drain. Set the oven at moderately hot (190°C/375°F).

Wipe the aubergines dry with paper towels. Heat the oil in a frying pan and fry them, cut side down, for 8–10 minutes or until well browned, adding more oil if necessary to prevent them from burning.

Meanwhile, prepare the topping: mince/grind together the breadcrumbs, ham, garlic and parsley. Stir the olive oil into the mixture and add pepper to taste; salt will probably not be needed because the ham is salty.

Put the aubergines and tomatoes cut side up in an oiled baking dish and sprinkle them with salt and pepper. Spread a thin layer of topping mixture on each aubergine and put a teaspoonful in each tomato; this is more a topping than a stuffing, so don't pack it tightly. Sprinkle with dry breadcrumbs and bake for 20–25 minutes or until the vegetables are tender. Serve hot or at room temperature from the baking dish.

AUBERGINES À LA NÎMOISE II

Omit the topping. After frying the aubergines/eggplants, carefully scoop out their flesh and chop it, reserving the shells. Prepare a stuffing by soaking:

55 g	fresh breadcrumbs	6 Tbsp
in:		
60 ml	milk	$\frac{1}{4}$ cup

and squeezing them dry; mix them with the chopped aubergine, **2 cloves chopped garlic, 4 Tbsp chopped fresh fennel root OR 2 tsp dried fennel leaves, 2 Tbsp chopped parsley, 1 Tbsp chopped chives** and salt and pepper to taste. Season the aubergine shells and tomatoes with salt and pepper and fill them with the mixture. Sprinkle with:

60 ml	olive oil	$\frac{1}{4}$ cup

and bake as above.

PETITES COURGETTES FARCIES
Stuffed baby zucchini

This stuffing can be used for other vegetables such as tomatoes, aubergines/eggplants and peppers; a platter of mixed stuffed vegetables is a meal in itself.

Serves 4

625 g	4 small zucchini	$1\frac{1}{4}$ lb
	2 Tbsp oil	
250 ml	tomato coulis (see recipe)	1 cup
30 g	grated parmesan cheese	$\frac{1}{4}$ cup
	STUFFING	
	salt and pepper	
65 g	rice	$\frac{1}{3}$ cup
200 g	ground meat – veal, pork, beef, chicken or a mixture	7 oz
	2 cloves garlic, finely chopped	
	2 eggs	

Prepare the stuffing: bring a large pot of salted water to a boil, add the rice and cook over a high fire for 12–15 minutes or until just tender. Drain, rinse under cold running water and thoroughly drain again. Mix the rice with the minced/ground meat, garlic, eggs, salt and pepper. Sauté a small piece of the mixture and taste; it should be quite highly seasoned. Set the oven at hot (200°C/400°F).

Halve the courgettes/zucchini lengthwise and carefully scoop out the centre with the seeds. Put the courgettes in an oiled baking dish and fill them with the stuffing, mounding it well. Sprinkle with the oil and bake for 15 minutes. Lower the oven temperature to moderate (175°C/350°F). Spoon the tomato coulis over the courgettes and continue baking for another 15 minutes or until tender. Sprinkle with the parmesan cheese and serve hot from the dish.

ALYCUIT À L'OCCITANE
Giblet stew

In Languedoc all the chicken trimmings are put in this stew – wing bones, necks, hearts, gizzards, livers and even the feet – but wings or necks only can be used if you prefer. In winter, peas and artichokes are replaced by partly precooked wild mushrooms and chestnuts.

Serves 4–6

1·5 kg	goose, turkey, duck or chicken giblets	3 lb
125 g	goose fat or lard	½ cup
	salt and pepper	
	1 large onion, diced	
	2 carrots, diced	
	4 cloves garlic, crushed	
750 g	tomatoes, peeled, seeded and coarsely chopped	1½ lb
	bouquet garni	
250 ml	white wine	1 cup
250 ml	broth or water, more if needed	1 cup
	2 large artichokes	
	1 lemon	
250 g	shelled green peas	1½ cups
	2 Tbsp chopped parsley	

Trim off the upper part of the hearts and cut the necks in pieces. Cut the gizzards in half and the wings in half through the joint. Cut the livers in pieces or, if large, in diagonal slices and keep them separately.

Heat all but 2 tablespoons of the goose fat in a heavy pot. Add the giblets (except for the livers) with salt and pepper and cook over a high fire until well browned. Remove the wings and hearts; reserve. Stir in the onion, carrots, garlic, tomatoes and bouquet garni and sauté for a minute; then stir in the wine and enough broth to cover by half. Bring to a boil, cover and simmer over a low fire for 30 minutes, stirring occasionally. Return the wings and hearts to the pot and continue to simmer for 45 minutes, stirring occasionally. Prepare the artichoke bottoms*; quarter them, add them to the stew with the peas and simmer for 45 minutes longer or until the giblets and vegetables are tender. If the sauce becomes too thick during cooking, add more hot broth or water; if it is too watery at the end of cooking, remove the giblets and vegetables and boil the sauce to reduce it. Taste for seasoning and discard the bouquet garni.

Heat the remaining fat in a frying pan. Season the pieces of liver and sauté over a high fire until well browned all over but still pink inside.

Serve the giblets and vegetables with their sauce in a deep serving dish, arranging the livers on top. Sprinkle with parsley and serve at once.

GIGOT AU GENIÈVRE
Roast leg of lamb with juniper

Juniper, a common bush in the 'garrigues' of Languedoc, is usually associated with game, but it makes an excellent seasoning for this leg of lamb garnished with wild mushrooms.

Serves 6–8

2–2·5-kg	small leg of lamb	5-lb
	4 cloves garlic	
30 g	juniper berries	¼ cup
750 g	cèpes or other mushrooms	1½ lb
75 g	OR dried cèpes	2½ oz
125 g	butter	¼ lb
	salt and pepper	
	pinch of thyme	
	pinch of crushed bay leaf	
	pinch of rosemary	
	pinch of crushed sage leaves	
500 ml	broth	2 cups
	2 Tbsp chopped parsley	

Two days before serving, trim the skin and all but a thin layer of fat from the lamb. Cut the garlic cloves in thin slivers. With the point of a knife, make several incisions in the meaty part of the lamb and insert the garlic slivers and some juniper berries into each. Cover and refrigerate for 2 days so the flavours of the garlic and juniper permeate the meat.

Prepare fresh or dried mushrooms or cèpes*.

Set the oven at very hot (230°C/450°F). Spread half the butter on the lamb and sprinkle it with salt, pepper, thyme, bay leaf, rosemary and sage. Put the meat in a roasting pan and sear it in the hot oven for 10 minutes or until it starts to brown. Lower the oven temperature to hot (200°C/400°F), add the broth and remaining juniper berries to the pan and continue roasting. For rare meat, allow a total of 20–24 minutes per kg/9–11 minutes per lb; for medium meat, allow 28–32 minutes per kg/13–15 minutes per lb. Baste the meat often during cooking. Transfer the lamb to a platter or board and let it stand in a warm place for about 15–20 minutes before carving it.

Strain the gravy into a shallow pan, add the mushrooms (including liquid from dried mushrooms), taste and simmer, covered, over a low fire for 10 minutes or until the mushrooms are tender and the gravy is well flavoured. Remove from the heat and stir in the remaining butter and the parsley; taste for seasoning.

The lamb may be carved in the kitchen, with the slices of meat replaced on the bone and the leg put on a platter, or it may be carved at the table. With a slotted spoon, arrange the mushrooms around the lamb. Serve the gravy separately.

POIS CHICHES EN SALADE
Chick-pea salad

This is a good way of serving cooked chick-peas or, for that matter, cooked dried beans or lentils. In Provence a type of dried fish roe called 'poutarge' is sometimes grated on top.

Serves 4

250 g	chick-peas	½ lb
	2 green or yellow peppers, cored, seeded and cut in thin strips	
	1 tsp chopped tarragon	
	1 tsp chopped parsley	
	TUNA VINAIGRETTE	
	3 Tbsp canned tuna in oil, drained	
	1 onion, very finely chopped	
	1 tsp Dijon mustard	
	2 Tbsp vinegar	
	1 clove garlic, finely chopped	
	pinch of thyme	
	salt and pepper	
100 ml	olive oil	7 Tbsp

Soak the chick-peas and cook until just tender (see 'soupe au pois chiches'). Keep them warm.

Make the tuna vinaigrette: mash the tuna as finely as possible and beat in the onion, mustard, vinegar, garlic, thyme and a little salt and pepper. Gradually beat in the oil so that the dressing emulsifies. Taste for seasoning.

Put the warm chick-peas with the peppers in a bowl. Toss with the dressing, taste for seasoning and pile in a salad bowl. Sprinkle the salad with the tarragon and parsley. Serve lukewarm or at room temperature.

GALETTE DE POMMES DE TERRE ARDÈCHOISE
Potato cake with garlic

Use a well-seasoned omelette pan for frying these potatoes, otherwise they will stick. They are good with any grilled or roast meat.

Serves 4

500 g	potatoes	1 lb
	3–4 cloves garlic, chopped	
	1 Tbsp chopped parsley	
	salt and pepper	
80 g	goose fat or olive oil	⅓ cup
	23–25 cm/9–10 in frying pan	

Peel the potatoes and put them in a bowl of cold water. Drain and dry well with paper towels. Cut the potatoes first in thin slices, then in very thin strips; if possible, cut them on a mandoline. Mix the potatoes with the garlic, parsley, salt and pepper. Work fast so that the potatoes don't discolour.

Heat the goose fat in the frying pan and add the potatoes. Press them down firmly with a lid or heatproof plate that is slightly smaller than the diameter of the pan. Cook the potatoes for 5 minutes over a medium fire, remove the lid and continue cooking for 15–20 minutes or until the potatoes are brown on the bottom. Set a large heatproof plate over the frying pan and turn both over so that the potato cake falls into the plate; slide the cake back into the frying pan. Cook for another 10–15 minutes or until the second side is browned; the potatoes should hold together like a cake. Serve immediately.

PETITS PÂTÉS DE PÉZÉNAS
Sweet mutton pies

These little pastries, which contain mutton sweetened with sugar, resemble mince pies and date back to medieval times when sugar, like salt, was added to meat as a seasoning. Traditionally the pâtés are served as a dessert and are fashioned like fat-stemmed mushrooms with the filling inside the stem, as in this recipe. However, this shape is tiresome to make and more and more of these pâtés are simply rounds of dough sandwiched with the filling.

Makes about 16 pâtés

	PIE PASTRY	
390 g	flour	3 cups
180 g	butter	6 oz
	3 egg yolks	
7 g	salt	1½ tsp
	7–9 Tbsp cold water	
	1 egg, beaten with ½ tsp salt (for glaze)	
	MUTTON FILLING	
180 g	lean mutton	6 oz
150 g	kidney fat or suet	5 oz
	1 Tbsp flour	
145 g	brown sugar	⅔ cup
	grated rind of 1 lemon	
	10 cm/4 in and 4 cm/1½ in cutters	

Make the pie pastry* and chill for 30 minutes or until firm.

Meanwhile, make the filling: mince/grind the mutton and fat with the flour. Beat in the brown sugar and grated lemon rind.

Butter a baking sheet. Roll out the pastry about 6 mm/¼ in thick. Use the large cutter to cut rounds and set them on the baking sheet. Put a spoonful of filling on each round, leaving a wide border, and brush the edges of the pastry with egg glaze. Use both hands to bring the pastry together from the sides and pinch it to seal at the top; you will have a four-sided pastry with the filling almost enclosed. Brush the pastries with egg glaze. Roll out the pastry trimmings and cut small rounds. Lightly press a round on top of each pâté to cover the filling and brush with glaze. Prick the top once or twice with a skewer. Chill the pâtés for 15 minutes. Set the oven at hot (200°C/400°F).

Bake the pâtés for 25–30 minutes or until golden brown and a skewer inserted in the filling for 30 seconds is hot to the touch when withdrawn. Serve hot or cold.

FLAN AUX MARRONS
Baked custard with chestnuts

French flans are based either on custard mixtures or on pastry cream. They can be baked in pastry, like the 'flan' of Champagne; in a caramelized dish, as here, or in a plain buttered dish, like 'far breton', whose alternative name is 'flan breton'.

Serves 6

250 g	fresh or canned chestnuts	½ lb
	pinch of salt	
	4 eggs	
100 g	sugar	½ cup
500 ml	milk	2 cups
	1 Tbsp rum	
	CARAMEL	
90 g	sugar	7 Tbsp
60 ml	water	¼ cup
	1·25 L/5 cup round cake pan or shallow baking dish	

Make the caramel: in a heavy-based pot, heat the sugar in the water until dissolved; then boil steadily to a deep brown caramel. Immediately pour it into the cake pan, tilting the pan to coat the base and sides with a thin, even layer of caramel. Leave to cool and set.

Meanwhile, peel fresh chestnuts* and simmer them in lightly salted water for 20–25 minutes or until tender. Drain fresh or canned chestnuts thoroughly. Lightly crush the chestnuts but leave some pieces; the mixture should not be a purée. Set the oven at moderate (175°C/350°F).

Beat the eggs with the sugar and stir in the milk and rum. Pour the mixture into the caramel-coated pan and set the pan in a water bath. Bring the water just to a boil on top of the stove and bake in the heated oven for 10–15 minutes or until thickened but not set. Drop the chestnuts by tablespoonsful on to the flan mixture at approximately equal intervals. Continue to bake for another 25 minutes or until set. Remove from the water bath.

Unmould just before serving. Serve the flan either lukewarm or cold.

CHESTNUTS

The chestnut tree, with its prickly green edible fruits, is a common sight growing wild in French forests and along lanes and the borders of fields. At one time it provided staple food in poorer areas like the Cévennes, Périgord, Brittany and Corsica, and was nicknamed the 'bread tree'. When the chestnuts fell and were gathered, people would stamp on them with spiked boots to break off the outer husk. The nuts were then spread on slatted shelves and smoked dry in special barns, a process which took about ten days. Shrunk from their skins, the chestnuts were easy to peel and would keep almost indefinitely. They were ground to make flour for bread, could be boiled or grilled to eat with soup and used for stuffing.

Nowadays, dried chestnuts are rare in France, for most are sold fresh or in cans. Commercial production centres in the Ardèche in northern Languedoc, where trees are planted in neat groves so the nuts can be gathered easily. The large fat 'marron' is the cultivated version of the wild 'châtaigne'. In each husk there is one marron or two or three châtaignes, which are smaller with flat sides. For the cook, the extra work in peeling little châtignes is worth the effort, since they have a less cloying texture than marrons, and a more delicate, perfumed flavour.

Four firms in Privas, capital of the Ardèche, specialize in canning chestnuts, either whole in water, or as sweetened or unsweetened purée. The finest nuts, however, are reserved to make marrons glacés, a 16-step operation requiring infinite time and patience, hence their lofty price. The skin of the shelled chestnut is removed by hand, since machines destroy some of the flavour, and for two days the chestnuts are basted day and night in vanilla syrup. Then, little by little, the vanilla bath is heated and more and more sugar is added until the chestnuts are preserved to the melting consistency so much appreciated by people with a sweet tooth. A thin coating of sugar glaze completes this expensive luxury for the market.

OREILLETTES DE TOULOUSE

Feuilleté fritters

The dough for these fritters is layered like puff pastry so that when fried it curls to look like little pig's ears ('oreillettes'). They are traditional at the Feast of Kings on Twelfth Night, and on Shrove Tuesday.

Serves 8

200 g	flour	1½ cups
	2 eggs, beaten to mix	
	1 Tbsp rum or armagnac	
	pinch of salt	
	1 Tbsp water (optional)	
125 g	butter	¼ lb
	deep fat (for frying)	
	confectioners' sugar (for sprinkling)	

Sift the flour on to a work surface and make a well in the centre. Add the eggs, rum and salt to the well. Using your fingertips, gradually draw in the flour and pull the dough into large crumbs. If the crumbs are dry, sprinkle them with water. Mix the dough gently without kneading it, just until smooth. Wrap and chill it for 2–3 hours or until firm.

Pound the butter until softened. On a cold work surface, roll out the dough to a rectangle, set the butter in the centre and fold the dough to enclose the butter, as in making puff pastry*. Do two turns, chill for 30 minutes, do two more turns and chill for another 30 minutes.

Roll out the dough 6 mm/¼ in thick and cut it in 7.5 cm/3 in diamonds. Meanwhile, heat the deep fat to 185°C/365°F on a fat thermometer. Fry the fritters, a few at a time, for 4–5 minutes or until golden brown. Drain them on paper towels and keep warm in a low oven with the door open while frying the rest. Sprinkle with sugar and serve immediately.

CHEESES

In the northern hills of Languedoc lies a little town that has become a household word: Roquefort. Folklore has it that roquefort cheese was discovered by a shepherd who found some mouldy bread and cheese abandoned in a cave. For once, folklore may be right, since the pronounced, yet creamy flavour of good roquefort, so different from other blue cheeses, is due specifically to the *penicillium glaucum roqueforti* mould which grows only in the special climatic conditions found in the local limestone caves. Attempts to recreate these conditions elsewhere have failed. To make the cheese, curd from sheep's milk is 'seeded' with mouldy breadcrumbs and rubbed with salt. It is pierced so that the air can penetrate and permit the mould to develop in the cheese, then left in the chilly, damp atmosphere of the caves to age for three months.

The name of roquefort has been protected since 1411, when Charles VI gave the villagers of Roquefort-sur-Soulzon exclusive right to cure cheeses in their caves. This monopoly was reaffirmed in 1925 with a ruling that roquefort cheese must be made of sheep's milk, must be produced by traditional methods and aged in the caves of Roquefort-sur-Soulzon. The source of the milk, however, was left deliberately vague. Sheep are even meaner with their milk than goats – they cannot be counted on for even a full litre a day – and the local sheep population is not up to producing roquefort on the present scale of 12 million kilos a year. Sheep's milk, already moulded into cheese, is therefore sent to Roquefort from as far afield as Corsica and the Pyrenees, as well as from the rest of Languedoc, where the commercial success of the cheese has revived sheep farming. Few sheep are now raised primarily for wool but rather for their lambs and for their milk. A few sheep cheeses are made on an artisan scale in Languedoc but the vast bulk of the sheep's milk goes towards cylinders of roquefort.

There are many imitations of roquefort – 'bleu des causses', for example, a cow cheese made in Languedoc around Millau and also aged in natural caves, started as a copy of roquefort but now has its own 'appellation contrôlée'. Genuine roquefort is labelled with a little red sheep in an oval frame. Each cylinder is about 25 cm/10 in across and weighs 2·5 kg/5½ lb. The cheese continues to ripen inside its foil wrapping after leaving the caves, reaching maturity two to three weeks later. A perfectly ripe roquefort has a yellowish colour and a smooth, buttery texture, with the mould evenly distributed. White crumbly roquefort with all the veining at the centre has been cut before its prime.

Thousands have extolled the merits of roquefort, but Casanova surely had the last word: 'Lithe as a doe she spread the tablecloth, set two places and then served some Roquefort cheese with a wonderful glazed ham. Oh, what an excellent pair are Roquefort and Chambertin for stimulating romance and bringing a budding love affair to quick fruition!'

OTHER SPECIALITIES OF THE REGION
TRADITIONAL DISHES

Soupe à l'ail
Garlic soup

Omelette aux pignons
Pine nut omelette

Oeufs sur plat albigeoise
Eggs baked with goose confit

Pâtés aux anchois de Collioure
Anchovy pâtés

Thon aux olives
Fresh tuna with olives

Civet de langouste au banyuls
Spiny lobster stew with banyuls wine

Poulpe au riz
Octopus with saffron rice

Soupe de poissons à la catalane
Fish soup with garlic and mussels

Escargots de mer
Sea snails with aïoli

Canard ou pigeon en salmis
Duck or pigeon in red wine sauce

Oie en daube
Braised goose

Cou d'oie farci à la façon de Limoux
Goose neck stuffed with sausagemeat, currants and pistachios

Dindonneau farci toulousaine
Turkey stuffed with sausagemeat, chestnuts and cèpes

Blanquette d'agneau
White stew of lamb

Rôti de veau cévenole
Roast veal with chestnuts

Pistache
Mutton stew with beans, tomatoes and garlic

Mesturet languedocien
Cornmeal mush mixed with puréed steamed pumpkin

Salade de fruits au banyuls
Fruit salad with sweet banyuls wine

CHARCUTERIE

Foie salé aux radis
Salted pork liver with radishes

Jambon salé de la Montagne Noire
Dried mountain ham

Terrine d'oie
Goose terrine

Melsat
Pork sausage with milk, bread and eggs

PÂTISSERIE AND CONFISERIE

Tarte aux raisins
Grape tart

Amenlous
Almonds baked in pastry

Confiture de figues
Fig jam

Gimblettes d'Albi
Hard ring-shaped biscuits flavoured with candied citrus fruit

Caladons
Crisp orange biscuits

Pain de Modane
Brioche with candied fruit, topped with coarse sugar

Navettes d'Albi
Pastry boats with raisins and whole almonds

Petits jeannots
Triangular biscuits with anise

Alsace-Lorraine

When, a decade ago, we lived in Luxembourg, Alsace and the Vosges were our escape route to French cooking. The first glass of chilled riesling, the first slice of quiche lorraine, always tasted better than anything further north. We regaled ourselves on wild mushrooms and game, on trout and kugelhopf. Their excellence was not just in our imagination, for a glance at the map in restaurant guidebooks shows that this corner of France offers some of the finest cooking. It has done so for a long time. Even in the Middle Ages, Alsace was known as the 'wine cellar, the granary and the larder of the surrounding countryside'. The same orchards and fields of grain still flourish on the rich alluvial plain of the Rhine, sheltered by the Vosges mountains whose eastern foothills are the home of some of the finest white wines in France.

At first glance, Alsace might be a part of Germany. The escarpment of the Vosges is dotted with picturesque castles straight out of a teutonic fairy tale: Franckenbourg, Haut-Koenigsbourg, Kientzheim and Ramstein. The houses with their steepled medieval roofs echo German domestic architecture. The people have the same stocky, buxom build and speak Alsatian, a German dialect also found across the river in the Black Forest. But a closer look reveals the influence of France. At midday, every bicycle sports a slender, crisp-crusted baguette rather than a stubby German loaf, and despite the local patois, the dominant language is French.

The same dichotomy shows in the cooking. Sauerkraut, dumplings and sweet yeast breads might appear solidly German, but tasting proves the difference. Alsatian sauerkraut is flavoured with local riesling wine and the meats are more varied than across the border: German-style dumplings are popular in Alsace, but so are more sophisticated French pâtés and mousselines, including the sublime foie gras. Seasonings range from French herbs to German caraway, aniseed and juniper. Horse-radish rivals French mustard as the condiment for boiled beef.

Predictably, portions are copious in Alsace and any meat is accompanied either by potatoes or by 'spaetzli', a twisted type of noodle whose trail I followed into a local kitchen. The cook was using a potato masher with coarse holes to force the dough into a large pan of boiling water, where it buckled into its characteristic tortured shapes. I have discovered that at home a colander will do the same trick.

Pork is an overwhelming favourite in both Alsace and Lorraine, whether freshly roasted with plums and cabbage, salted or smoked for ham or bacon, or made into one of the innumerable kinds of sausage. Strasbourg sausage is indispensable to a classic Alsatian sauerkraut and fresh pork sausage is always added to 'potée lorraine', a hearty stew of pork, root vegetables, dried beans and cabbage. It is no accident that two of the region's staple dishes are based on cabbage. The winter climate is damp and cold (the Vosges have just enough snow for skiing) so that local vegetables are limited to cabbage, Brussels sprouts and roots. Luckily, the autumn also brings with it one of the treasures of Alsace and Lorraine: plump Michaelmas goose, which is roasted with an apple or chestnut stuffing. Alsace adds sauerkraut as an accompaniment and in Lorraine there is an old recipe with swedes/rutabagas and beer.

What Alsatians value most about the goose, however, is not its meat, but its liver when this has been specially fattened to make foie gras. According to locals, their foie gras is superior to that of Périgord because of its smoother texture and more winy flavour. My initiation into the versatility of foie gras took place in an Alsatian auberge, where I ordered the dish of the day, chicken with noodles. But what noodles! Freshly made and chewy, they were loaded with large morels and dice of foie gras, a treat that more than compensated for the mosquitoes which pursued me relentlessly all night in my attic under the eaves.

Despite the long distance from the sea, Alsatians have been spoiled when it comes to fish. The Rhine and its tributary, the Ill (in the local dialect, Alsace becomes 'Illsass', the country of the Ill), used to abound in salmon, shad, lamprey, eel, pike and quantities of the more humble perch and carp. Unfortunately, supplies are no longer as abundant as they were in 1647, when 143 salmon were sold in a single day at the Strasbourg market, and monster carp of nearly 20 kilos were commonly caught in the Rhine. Lakes in the Vosges still shelter trout which, at their freshest, are served simply 'au bleu', swimming in their court bouillon with melted butter on the side. Or they may be left in their cooking liquid to set to a parsley-flecked 'truite en gelée', similar to the famous Alsatian 'carpe à la juive' that can also be made with herbs or almonds and raisins; Strasbourg has had a sizeable Jewish community for centuries. Sweet-sour combinations of meat baked with fruit are an Alsatian taste remarked on by Montaigne in the 16th century.

The spine of Alsace and Lorraine is the Vosges mountains – forested, wild, and still the home of boar and deer although the last bear disappeared 200 years ago. Local connoisseurs like their game cooked in classic fashion: marinated a day or two in red wine flavoured with juniper, then roasted or braised and served in a rich sauce with perhaps a touch of cream and red currant jelly. Providentially the finest red currant jelly comes from Bar-le-Duc, in Lorraine. Other local specialities such as red cabbage and chestnuts seem designed to complete the feast, no less than the wild mushrooms of the Vosges.

Lorraine, although twice the size of Alsace, tends to be overshadowed by its neighbour, perhaps because the culture of Alsace is more unusual. Gastronomically, sauerkraut and spaetzli are instantly recognizable, whereas the potée of Lorraine could come from almost anywhere. Even quiche, the most famous regional dish, can be disguised as plain onion or cheese tart. But the cooking of Lorraine is not to be ignored. The area specializes in egg dishes like the delicious 'omelette lorraine' made with bacon, cheese, herbs and cream, and 'ramequin', an egg and cheese puff baked in moulds of the same name. While Alsatians prefer their suckling pig hot, their Lorraine cousins tend to braise it and serve it chilled in a clear jelly flavoured with white wine.

Lorraine also makes a contribution with its cakes, which are quite different from the yeast breads of Alsace. Madeleines, the little shell-shaped cakes rendered immortal by Marcel Proust, come from Commercy, and Nancy, the capital of Lorraine, is famous for its macaroons. While out on an Alsatian weekend, we would often stop in the graceful Place Stanislas built by Stanislas Leczinski, father-in-law of Louis XV. Strategically placed in one corner is a pastry shop, where we would pick up madeleines and a remarkably good almond 'pain de Gênes' cake well wrapped in foil to keep it moist and fresh.

I have always found the German yeast breads of Alsace rather heavy, though a slice of kugelhopf makes an agreeable change at breakfast. They resemble, though

by no means duplicate, recipes from the neighbouring Black Forest, and all bear dialect names – 'lierwecke' (raisin rolls) and 'kaffeekrautz' (raisin bread baked in a characteristic hour-glass shape). 'Birewecka' is a rich cake filled with dried pears, prunes, figs and dates, as well as the usual raisins, which is traditionally served at the Christmas 'réveillon' after midnight mass. Pretzels are also common in Alsace; some writers claim the knot has a religious significance, and engaged couples are supposed to share a pretzel on Good Friday as a pledge of eternal love.

Eastern France is renowned not just for food, but for its drink. To the average Frenchman, Alsace means beer or, on festive occasions, one of the white alcohols or liqueurs distilled from fruits – cherry, purple plum, pear, raspberry, greengage – that are designed to brace the digestion after a heavy meal. But to me Alsace means white wine. In tourist style, I have spent more than one Sunday traversing the 'route des vins' south of Strasbourg, stopping at one of the wine villages for lunch. One day in the medieval cobbled streets of Riquewihr we were entertained by a German glee club, complete with choirmaster and tuning fork, who had copious draughts of wine and beer on tap to quench their thirst as fast as it was generated by their boisterous song.

The scene epitomized eating in Alsace, where food and drink are taken seriously, and in public, whereas in Lorraine most good eating is done at home. One of the most respected French hotel schools is found in Strasbourg and Alsace has long been a traditional source of trained chefs, 'serious men', says one of their colleagues, 'upright, just and obstinate.' Obstinate they may be, but they have spread the cooking of Alsace throughout France, from steamy station to the grandest temples of gastronomy.

POTAGE AUX NOQUES
Dumpling soup

Dumpling soup depends for its excellence on good meat broth and fluffy dumplings; be sure not to overwork the dumpling mixture or it will become elastic.

Serves 6

	SOUP	
1·5 L	well-flavoured broth	1½ qt
60 g	butter	4 Tbsp
55 g	flour	6 Tbsp
	salt and pepper	
	pinch of grated nutmeg	
	bouquet garni	
	2 egg yolks	
185 ml	heavy cream or crème fraîche*	¾ cup
	1 Tbsp chopped herbs: parsley, chives, chervil	
	DUMPLINGS	
65 g	flour	½ cup
45 g	butter, softened	3 Tbsp
	1 egg	
	1 egg yolk	
18 g	fresh breadcrumbs	2 Tbsp
	salt and pepper	
	pinch of grated nutmeg	
	1 egg white	

For the soup: bring the broth to a boil in a pot. In a saucepan melt the butter, add the flour and stir over a low fire until the mixture begins to brown. Immediately pour in the hot broth, whisking constantly. Add salt, pepper, nutmeg and the bouquet garni. Continue stirring until the soup boils; then cover and simmer for 15–20 minutes.

While the soup is cooking, make the dumpling mixture: gently mix together the flour, butter, egg, egg yolk, breadcrumbs, salt, pepper and nutmeg to form a paste. Beat the egg white until stiff; then thoroughly fold it into the paste.

Bring a large shallow pot of salted water almost to a boil. Using two teaspoons dipped in the hot water, shape an oval of dumpling mixture and drop it into the simmering water. Continue making dumplings, being careful not to crowd the pot: it may be necessary to cook them in more than one batch. Cook dumplings for 10–15 minutes or until they are firm and no longer taste of flour. Don't let them cook too quickly; if the water boils, they will break up. Drain on paper towels and keep warm while finishing the soup.

Remove the pot of soup from the heat and discard the bouquet garni. Mix the egg yolks and cream in a bowl, then stir in a few spoonsful of hot soup. Pour this mixture back into the pot of soup, whisking rapidly. Reheat the soup gently until it thickens slightly; don't let it boil or it will curdle. Taste for seasoning. Pour the soup into a tureen and add the dumplings; they will float. Sprinkle with the freshly chopped herbs and serve hot.

RAMEQUIN
Cheese puffs

The name 'ramequin' refers both to miniature soufflé dishes and to the mixture baked inside them. Originally ramequins were made of meat, onions and cheese baked on a piece of bread; then the meat was left out and eggs were added. Today's ramequin is a cheese puff that resembles Burgundian 'gougère', a cheese mixture based on choux pastry.

Serves 4–6

30 g	flour	¼ cup
200 g	grated gruyère cheese	2 cups
	salt and pepper	
250 ml	milk	1 cup
45 g	butter	3 Tbsp
	3 eggs	

deep baking dish (1·25 L/5 cup capacity)
or 4–6 individual baking dishes

Set the oven at moderately hot (190°C/375°F). Heavily butter the baking dish. Mix together the flour, two-thirds of the cheese, the salt and pepper. Scald the milk in a saucepan, take from the heat and immediately add the flour-cheese mixture and 2 tablespoons of the butter, stirring rapidly with a wooden spoon until smooth. Return to low heat and continue stirring until the mixture no longer sticks to the sides of the pan. Take from the fire and let cool slightly. Beat the eggs into the mixture, one at a time, beating thoroughly after each addition until the dough is smooth. Taste for seasoning. Spoon the ramequin mixture into the baking dish, sprinkle with the remaining cheese and dot with the remaining tablespoon of butter. Bake in the oven for 20–25 minutes (15–20 minutes for small ramequins) or until the mixture is golden brown. The ramequin will rise, rather like a soufflé. Serve immediately, from the dish.

RAMEQUIN II

Follow the recipe given above, but add only the egg yolks to the flour-cheese mixture; then beat the whites until stiff and fold them into the cheese mixture.

QUICHES AND FRUIT TARTS

Alsace and Lorraine are the home of 'quiche', a term derived from the German 'kuchen' meaning cake, or in this case an open tart with savoury filling set in egg custard. Rich quiches contain cream; more economical ones use milk. Quiche can be made with ham or bacon, with or without cheese, and with vegetables like asparagus or pumpkin. Popular in Alsace is 'zewelwai', a quiche made with onions cooked until they are meltingly soft and sweet. Now the term is so universal that seafood quiche is found in Normandy and courgette quiche in Provence.

The equally characteristic sweet tarts of Alsace and Lorraine are deliberately made with a simple pastry so that if the juice from the fruit is absorbed the crust will not be soggy. One type of dough raised with yeast gives an even more porous crust. Plums and apricots are halved and set cut side up so their juices will evaporate quickly, while cherries are often left unpitted so the juice stays trapped inside. Bilberries, which resemble blueberries but have a sharper, more distinctive flavour, make a remarkably good Alsatian-style fruit pie, but apples which are sometimes substituted are less successful. A favourite addition to the fruit is a cream and egg-yolk custard, transforming it into a sweet version of quiche, topped by a frosty touch of sugar and perhaps a sprinkling of cinnamon.

QUICHE LORRAINE

Quiche was originally made with bread dough, but now most people use pie pastry. On May Day, quiche was traditionally served in Lorraine following a dish of sucking pig in aspic.

Serves 6–8

	FLAKY PIE PASTRY	
225 g	flour	1¾ cups
160 g	butter, softened	5 oz
5 g	salt	1 tsp
	2 Tbsp water	
	FILLING	
200 g	lean slab bacon, diced	7 oz
15 g	butter	1 Tbsp
	3 eggs	
375 ml	heavy cream or crème fraîche*	1½ cups
	salt and pepper	
	pinch of grated nutmeg	
	23–25 cm/9–10 in pie or tart pan	

Make the pie pastry: sift the flour on to a marble slab or board and lay the butter in the centre. Bring the flour over the butter, lightly squeeze them together, and rub the butter and flour between your fingers until they form particles the size of peas. Make a well in this mixture and add the salt and water to the centre. Using your fingertips, draw the butter-flour mixture into the well and mix the dough together as quickly and lightly as possible until smooth; don't knead. Wrap and chill for 30 minutes or until firm. Set the oven at moderately hot (190°C/375°F) and heat a baking sheet.

Line the pie pan* with the chilled pastry and blind bake* it on the hot baking sheet for 25 minutes. Let the pie shell cool, leaving the baking sheet in the oven.

For the filling: if the bacon is salty, blanch* it.

Sauté the bacon in the butter until brown, drain and sprinkle evenly in the base of the baked pie shell. Mix the eggs and cream together in a bowl, salt lightly, and add pepper and nutmeg. Set the pie shell in the pan on the hot baking sheet and pour the mixture into the pie shell. Bake for 30–35 minutes or until the filling is set and golden brown. Don't overcook or the filling will curdle. Serve warm or at room temperature.

QUICHE LORRAINE AU FROMAGE

Top the bacon with:

60 g	sliced gruyère cheese	2 oz

before pouring in the egg-cream filling.

QUICHE LORRAINE AUX OIGNONS

Brown 1 onion, thinly sliced, in butter; add to the bacon with some chopped fresh herbs.

ZEWELWAI

Melt:

30 g	goose fat or butter	2 Tbsp

in a frying pan. Add:

500 g	thinly sliced onions	1 lb

salt and pepper, cover and cook over a very low fire, stirring occasionally, 20–30 minutes or until very soft but not brown. Spread in the baked pie shell. For bacon zewelwai, brown:

90 g	blanched* bacon	3 oz

in:

15 g	goose fat or butter	1 Tbsp

and sprinkle on the onions in the shell. Pour over the egg-cream filling; bake as above.

ZEWELWAI PRINTANIÈRE

Early in the year this pie is good made with **spring onions**, including some of the green part as well as the white. Add ½ tsp **caraway seeds** with the salt, pepper and nutmeg, if you like.

SAUCISSON À L'AIL, POMMES À L'HUILE

Garlic sausage with potato salad

For this dish either make the Burgundian 'saucisson aux truffes et aux pistaches' (see recipe) or buy a ready-made French garlic sausage.

Serves 4–6

1-kg	whole sausage	2-lb
750 g	small or medium potatoes, unpeeled	1½ lb
	pinch of salt	
	½ small onion OR 1 shallot, very finely chopped	
	1 Tbsp vinegar, or to taste	
	2 Tbsp oil, or to taste	
	3 Tbsp chopped parsley	
	WHITE WINE VINAIGRETTE	
	2 Tbsp white wine	
	2 Tbsp vinegar	
	salt and pepper	
	1 tsp Dijon mustard (optional)	
125 ml	oil	½ cup

If the truffle sausage is already poached, remove the skin; if it is raw, poach it according to the recipe. Poach French garlic sausage, not letting the temperature of the water rise above 90°C/195°F, for 45 minutes–1 hour or until hot in the centre when tested with a skewer.

Make the vinaigrette*, adding white wine with the vinegar, and set aside.

Begin the potato salad: wash the potatoes and put them in a pot of cold salted water. Bring to a boil and simmer for 15–20 minutes or until just tender. Drain, peel while still hot and cut in thick slices. Put the potatoes in a bowl with the chopped onion. Add enough vinaigrette to moisten the potatoes well, mixing as gently as possible to prevent the potatoes from breaking up. Taste for seasoning. Leave the potato salad at room temperature for about 30 minutes, or until lukewarm.

To finish the potato salad, gently stir in vinegar, oil and 2 tablespoons of the chopped parsley, adding more vinegar, oil and seasoning to taste. Arrange the salad in the centre of a platter and sprinkle it with the remaining chopped parsley. Drain the sausage, slice it and arrange the slices around the salad. Serve immediately while the sausage is hot and the salad lukewarm.

LEWERKNEPFLES

Liver dumplings

'Lewerknepfles' are prepared in both Alsace and Germany, but Alsatians claim theirs are superior. So much so that the 18th-century King Joseph I of Bavaria summoned a cook from Alsace to make them. She was given the title of 'Faiseur de Lewerknepfles du Roi' (Royal Liver-Dumpling Maker) and the king ate happily ever after.

Serves 8–10 as a first course

15 g	butter	1 Tbsp
	1 onion, finely chopped	
250 g	calf's, pork or beef liver, ground or finely chopped	8 oz
60 g	pork fat, ground or finely chopped	2 oz
	1 clove garlic, crushed	
100 g	fresh breadcrumbs	¾ cup
	1 Tbsp chopped parsley	
65 g	flour	½ cup
	2 eggs	
	salt and pepper	
	pinch of grated nutmeg	
	FOR SERVING	
90 g	butter	6 Tbsp
20 g	fresh breadcrumbs	2 Tbsp

Heat the tablespoon of butter in a sauté pan and cook the onion, stirring occasionally, until soft and brown. In a bowl lightly stir together the liver and pork fat with the sautéed onion, the garlic, breadcrumbs, parsley, flour, eggs, salt, pepper and nutmeg. Sauté a small piece of the mixture and taste for seasoning.

Bring a large pot of salted water to a boil. Using two teaspoons dipped in the hot water, shape an oval of dumpling mixture and drop it into the simmering water. Continue making dumplings, being careful not to crowd the pot; it may be necessary to cook them in more than one batch. Poach the dumplings slowly for 8 minutes or until firm. Don't let them cook too quickly: if the water boils, they will break up. Drain them and keep hot in a serving dish. Just before serving, heat the butter and fry the breadcrumbs until brown. At once pour butter and breadcrumbs over the dumplings and serve.

LEWERKNEPFLES À L'OIGNON

A finely chopped **onion** can be browned in the melted butter before it is poured over the dumplings.

PERCHE À LA SAUVIGNY
Perch in cream sauce

Fresh perch, caught in the Meuse river and cooked with white wine and cream, have given the village of Sauvigny in Lorraine a reputation for good cooking. Other fish such as pike and carp are excellent done the same way.

Serves 6

250 g each	6 medium-sized perch	8 oz each
	1 carrot, sliced	
	1 onion, studded with 2 cloves	
	3 cloves garlic	
375 ml	dry white wine, preferably Alsatian	1½ cups
	bouquet garni	
	salt and pepper	
	pinch of grated nutmeg	
125 ml	water, more as needed	½ cup
	SAUCE	
30 g	butter	2 Tbsp
20 g	flour	2¼ Tbsp
100 ml	heavy cream or crème fraîche*	7 Tbsp
	salt and pepper	
	2 egg yolks	
	juice of 1 lemon	
	1 Tbsp chopped parsley	
	2 shallots, finely chopped	

Clean the perch, discard the fins and trim the tails to a 'V'; scale and wash them. Lay the perch in the bottom of a pot or shallow pan large enough to hold them all flat. Add the carrot, onion, garlic, wine, bouquet garni, salt, pepper and nutmeg with enough water to cover by half. Bring the liquid to a boil; then lower the heat. Poach the fish for 2–3 minutes on one side; then turn them over and poach for another 6–7 minutes or until they flake when tested with a fork. Drain and transfer to a baking dish. Boil the cooking liquid until it is reduced to about 375 ml; strain and reserve it for the sauce. Set the oven at very hot (230°C/450°F).

To prepare the sauce: melt the butter in a small pan, stir in the flour and cook until foaming; don't let it brown. Stir in the reduced cooking liquid, followed by the cream. Add salt and pepper to taste. Bring the sauce to a boil, stirring constantly, and simmer for 2 minutes. Beat the egg yolks in a bowl and stir in a few tablespoons of the warm sauce. Pour this mixture back into the rest of the sauce and stir until well blended; add lemon juice to taste. Strain the sauce over the fish and sprinkle the surface with the chopped parsley and shallots. Bake in the hot oven for 5 minutes, leaving the oven door slightly open. Serve immediately, from the dish.

CARPE À LA JUIVE
Braised carp in aspic

Traditionally the Jewish community of Strasbourg prepared carp on Friday evenings before sundown, to be served cold on the Sabbath when cooking was forbidden. One version combines raisins and almonds with the fish; this recipe is flavoured with herbs.

Serves 4

1·5-kg	1 large carp	3-lb
	2 Tbsp oil	
	2 onions, thinly sliced	
	2 cloves garlic, chopped	
	2 tsp flour	
500 ml	white wine	2 cups
500 ml	water	2 cups
	salt and pepper	
	bouquet garni	
	2 Tbsp chopped parsley	

Clean the carp, discard the fins and tail and scale the fish. Cut in 4 cm/1½ in slices and wash. Heat the oil in a large pot, add the onions and cook over a low fire, stirring often, until soft but not brown. Add the garlic and flour and cook over a low fire, stirring constantly, for 3 minutes or until lightly browned. Stir in the wine and water and add the carp with salt, pepper and the bouquet garni. Bring to a boil, stirring occasionally to prevent the flour from sticking. Simmer over a low fire for 30 minutes or until the carp flesh can be flaked with a fork. Transfer the fish to a deep serving dish.

Discard the bouquet garni. Taste the sauce and, if necessary, boil to reduce until well flavoured. Taste for seasoning. Remove from the heat, add the parsley and pour the sauce over the fish. Chill overnight; the liquid will set to a parsley-flecked aspic. Serve cold.

CARPE À LA JUIVE II

The carp can first be marinated with a little salt, pepper, parsley, thyme, bay leaf, chopped garlic and oil. Leave in the refrigerator overnight, then drain the fish and cook as above.

OIE RÔTIE À LA LORRAINE

Roast goose with apples and vegetables

Roast goose is traditional on November 11, the feast of St Martin, and this custom is still followed in many families. In this recipe, equal parts of beer and water can be used in the steaming pan in the oven.

Serves 6–8

4-kg	goose	9-lb
	salt and pepper	
1 kg	apples, peeled and cored	2 lb
125 ml	beer	$\frac{1}{2}$ cup
500 g	rutabagas	1 lb
500 g	Brussels sprouts	1 lb
30 g	butter	2 Tbsp
60 g	goose fat	$\frac{1}{4}$ cup
	(from roasting pan)	
	trussing needle and string	

Set the oven at hot (200°C/400°F). Season the inside of the goose with salt and pepper, stuff it with the whole apples and truss. Pour the beer over the goose, rubbing it well into the skin. Put the goose on a rack in an open roasting pan and set it in the hot oven. When the goose begins to brown, put a pan of water in the bottom of the oven; the water will steam and prevent the bird from drying out. Refill the pan with water whenever necessary. Roast the goose for $2\frac{1}{4}$ hours or until no pink juice runs out when the thigh is pierced with a skewer. Drain off and reserve the fat as it accumulates in the roasting pan.

Meanwhile, prepare the vegetable garnish: peel the swedes/rutabagas and cut each one into even-sized pieces. Put them in cold, salted water and boil for 20 minutes or until tender but still firm; drain them. Cook the Brussels sprouts in boiling salted water for 8–10 minutes or until just tender. Drain them, refresh with cold water, and drain thoroughly.

When the goose is cooked, spread it with the butter and turn the oven heat to very high (230°C/450°F). Put back the goose for 5–10 minutes. Heat the goose fat in a large pan, add the swedes and Brussels sprouts and a little salt and pepper; sauté briskly until light brown. When the skin of the bird has become shiny and crackling, take the goose out of the oven and transfer it to a platter, surrounded by the sautéed vegetables.

Carve the goose at the table.

FOIE GRAS

Foie gras, the enlarged liver of a force-fed goose or duck, is one of the most ancient French delicacies. The Romans are known to have force-fed geese with figs to fatten their livers to three or four times the original size; nowadays the same effect is achieved using maize. The art of making foie gras is said to have been fostered by the Jews of Alsace, who found goose fat a good alternative to lard from the forbidden pig; it is perhaps appropriate that Israel, as well as central Europe, supplies France with many of the fattened livers that go into making the 'French' canned terrines and pâtés that are exported throughout the world.

Although Alsace, like Périgord, has always been famous for its goose and duck dishes, it was only in the late 18th century that foie gras became fashionable, thanks to an Alsatian pastry cook, Jean-Pierre Clause. His way of cooking foie gras in a pie crust with a layer of chopped pork surrounding the truffle-studded liver is still occasionally followed today. Alternatively the whole foie gras is baked in brioche, or fresh foie gras is browned quickly in butter and served with noodles or sautéed apples. In Périgord, on the other hand, the livers are more often simply baked whole in a terrine with salt, pepper and slivers of fresh truffle.

Whatever the seasoning, foie gras must be prepared and treated in the same way. A perfectly fattened liver should be firm, but can vary in colour from pink to yellow ochre. It is extremely difficult to choose; even the most expert eye cannot detect certain raw livers that will dissolve into liquid fat during cooking, for which reason most foie gras enthusiasts hesitate to cook livers themselves and leave the task to professionals.

For cooking, the lobes of the fattened livers are separated and carefully trimmed of all veins and membranes, but they are never cut into pieces. When they are to be cooked in a terrine, which is almost always preferred now to the more fragile pastry case, the livers may first be marinated in port wine, salt, pepper, spices, a little brandy – but nothing too strong – and left to absorb the flavours. Finally, they may be studded with truffles, if finances permit.

Delicate seasoning and slow cooking are the keys to fine foie gras; if the cooking temperature rises even momentarily to above 90°C, the liver quite literally melts away. The best foie gras is always pink in the centre. Canned or vacuum-packed foie gras is always inferior to a freshly cooked terrine because it has to be sterilized at too high a temperature to remain pink.

Foie gras need not, of course, be baked as a pâté or terrine. To make the livers go further, they may be puréed as a mousse, which is often sold in cans. Mousse of foie gras is much less expensive than 'bloc' or 'rouleau' cans of solid liver, but it has a different texture and melts if it is heated.

In the last few years, 'foie gras de canard' has come to rival that of goose: duck foie gras is slightly less expensive and the flavour is less rich. Some connoisseurs claim it has more finesse. Whether goose or duck, the best foie gras from Alsace and from Périgord is produced only between October and April. Imported raw livers, however, are available all the year round, thanks to modern production methods which are also being adopted in France. In early December comes the climax in domestic production for the Christmas market, since no 'réveillon' is complete without foie gras.

COQ AU RIESLING
Chicken with white wine

'Coq au riesling', cooked in the aromatic white wine of Alsace, is lighter and more delicate than the better known 'coq au vin' from Burgundy. Be sure to use a white wine that is not too acidic. The chicken is good served with 'spaetzli' or home-made noodles (see recipes).

Serves 4

1·5-kg	chicken	3-lb
	salt and pepper	
	2 Tbsp oil	
60 g	butter	4 Tbsp
	4 shallots, chopped	
	1½ Tbsp cognac	
375 ml	dry white wine, preferably Alsatian riesling	1½ cups
	bouquet garni	
	pinch of grated nutmeg	
150 g	mushrooms, quartered	5 oz
	juice of ½ lemon	
80 ml	heavy cream or crème fraîche*	⅓ cup
	1 egg yolk	

Cut the chicken* into 4 pieces; season them with salt and pepper. Heat the oil and half the butter in a large pot, add the chicken pieces and brown them on all sides. Lower the heat, add the chopped shallots and continue cooking for 2 minutes. Pour in the cognac and light it; when the flame dies, stir the chicken quickly and add the wine, bouquet garni, salt, pepper and nutmeg. Bring to a boil, cover and cook over a low fire for 30–40 minutes or until nearly tender.

While the chicken is cooking, prepare the mushrooms: heat the remaining butter in a frying pan and add the mushrooms with the lemon juice. Cook slowly for 10 minutes or until the mushrooms are tender. Add the mushrooms with any liquid to the chicken and continue to simmer for 10 minutes or until the chicken is tender.

Discard the bouquet garni and transfer the chicken and mushrooms to a serving platter. Skim any fat from the cooking liquid. Mix the cream and egg yolk together in a bowl; then slowly add the cooking liquid, stirring constantly. Return the sauce to the pan and heat gently until it thickens slightly. Don't boil the sauce or it will curdle. Take it from the heat and taste for seasoning. Strain the sauce over the chicken and serve.

RÔTI DE PORC AUX QUETSCHES ET AUX CHOUX
Roast pork with plums and cabbage

Pork is the most popular meat in both Alsace and Lorraine, and as bacon, ham or sausage, it finds its way into a huge variety of dishes.

Serves 4–6

1-kg	rolled pork roast	2-lb
45 g	butter	3 Tbsp
	salt and pepper	
	a few leaves of sage	
1 kg	purple plums	2 lb
50 g	sugar	¼ cup
750 g	potatoes	1½ lb
	1 head of cabbage, cored and cut in 4–6 wedges	
45 g	lard or oil	3 Tbsp
250 ml	broth or water	1 cup

Set the oven at moderately hot (190°C/375°F). Spread the pork with the butter and sprinkle with salt, pepper and sage. Put it in a roasting pan and roast in the oven for 1½ hours or until tender and the juices run clear when the meat is pierced with a skewer; baste the meat frequently during cooking.

While the pork is roasting, prepare the fruit and vegetables. Put the plums in a pot with the sugar and enough water to cover by half; simmer for 5–10 minutes or until just tender. Remove the plums and boil the liquid for 5 minutes or until a light syrup is formed. Replace the plums in the syrup and keep them warm.

Put the potatoes in cold, salted water and boil for 15 minutes or until almost tender. Drain them. Cook the cabbage in boiling salted water for 6–8 minutes or until almost tender. Drain it, refresh with cold water and drain thoroughly. Heat the lard in a large pot and add the potatoes, cabbage, salt and pepper. Cover and cook over a low fire for 15–20 minutes until slightly brown.

When the meat is tender, carve it in thick slices, arrange on a serving platter with the potatoes and cabbage and keep warm. Discard the fat from the roasting pan, add the broth and stir to dissolve the pan juices. Boil briefly until concentrated; taste for seasoning. Strain the gravy over the roast and serve. Serve the stewed plums in syrup in a separate bowl alongside the meat.

ALSATIAN SAUSAGES

Strasbourg is the sausage capital of France. 'Saucisse de Strasbourg' itself is made of pork and beef, lightly smoked so that it resembles a plump frankfurter. It should be poached for serving and is at its best with potato purée and a touch of horseradish. Alsatian sauerkraut must contain Strasbourg sausages, and among the vegetables and smoked meats of Lorraine potée nestles a plump fresh sausage often called 'cervelas'.

Originally containing pig's brains, ('cervelle', hence their name), cervelas are stubby sausages filled with ground pork and highly seasoned with spices and garlic. Often they contain extras like pistachios, hazelnuts and even the occasional truffle, and they too are usually poached before being served.

Both cervelas and Strasbourg sausages are 'saucisses', a term which overlaps 'saucissons'. Broadly speaking, saucissons are larger, more compact and more highly seasoned than saucisses, which are often simply fresh pork sausage. However, both saucisses and saucissons can come fresh or dried, like salami, in a variety of guises. One Alsatian saucisse has the intimidating name of 'bürelewerwurscht' and is filled with calf's or, occasionally, with goose liver. Another, called in French 'saucisse à frire', turns out to be 'bratwurst'. Yet other local flights of fancy include sausages flavoured with anise, horseradish or caraway seeds, and a 'boudin' based on tongue.

FAISAN À LA VOSGIENNE

Pheasant pie with noodles and mushrooms
Pheasant 'à la vosgienne' can refer to two very different recipes: either the pheasant is cooked with sauerkraut, or it may be baked, as here, with noodles and fresh mushrooms beneath a pastry crust. The recipe is particularly good for pheasant that is too old and tough to be roasted (the end of the breastbone will be inflexible) and, if you prefer, the pastry crust can be omitted.

Serves 6

200 g	fresh noodles (see recipe)	7 oz
625-g	1 pheasant, partridge or wild duck	1¼-lb
	salt and pepper	
125 g	butter	¼ lb
250 ml	white wine, preferably riesling	1 cup
125 ml	broth	½ cup
30 g	butter, kneaded with	2 Tbsp
15 g	flour	2 Tbsp
200 g	mushrooms, sliced	7 oz
	1 egg, beaten with ½ tsp salt (for glaze)	
	PÂTÉ PASTRY	
200 g	flour	1½ cups
30 g	lard	2 Tbsp
95 g	butter	6 Tbsp
5 g	salt	1 tsp
60 ml	water, more if needed	¼ cup
1·5 L/1½ qt terrine or deep baking dish		

Prepare the noodles. Make the pie pastry* and chill it.

To cook the pheasant en cocotte: set the oven at moderately hot (190°C/375°F). Season the pheasant with salt and pepper and truss it. In a casserole heat 2 tablespoons of the butter and brown the pheasant on all sides. Add half the wine, cover and cook in the oven for 30 minutes or until very tender. Transfer the bird to a board and leave to cool; leave the oven on.

Add the remaining wine to the hot casserole and bring to a boil, scraping to dissolve the pan juices. Boil until reduced by about half. Transfer to a saucepan. Add the broth and bring to a boil. Gradually whisk small pieces of kneaded butter into the boiling sauce until it is thick enough to coat a spoon. Taste for seasoning and leave to cool.

Cut the pheasant in 6, discarding backbone and trussing strings. Cook the noodles in a large pot of boiling salted water for 2–3 minutes or until just tender. Drain, rinse with warm water and drain thoroughly. Mix with 3 tablespoons more of the butter and season to taste. Heat half the remaining butter in a frying pan, add the mushrooms and sauté over a medium fire until lightly browned and just tender.

Butter a deep baking dish and put half the noodles into it. Set the pheasant pieces and mushrooms on top and pour the sauce over them. Cover with the remaining noodles and dot them with the remaining butter.

Roll out the dough about 6 mm/¼ in thick, trimming it so it is about 2·5 cm/1 in larger than the dish. Roll out the trimmings, cut to a long strip 1·25 cm/½ in wide and press it around the edge of the dish. Brush the strip with egg glaze. Lay the pastry on top of the noodles (they should be cool) and press to stick it to the pastry rim. Brush with egg glaze and prick the top a few times. Bake in the hot oven for 30 minutes or until the pastry is firm and browned. Serve hot from the dish.

LA CHOUCROUTE MAISON

Home-made sauerkraut

An Alsatian cookbook written in 1577, while enumerating in detail all the tasks that need to be done each winter, laconically states, 'The cabbage is to be salted.' The preparation of sauerkraut required no elaboration. Until recently, professional 'cabbage cutters' would travel from village to village, knocking on doors and offering to shred the cabbage, which would be salted and turned into sauerkraut. Now, however, it is a matter of buying a giant mandoline cutter at the village hardware store.

Serves 12–15

5 kg	white cabbage	11 lb
10 g	juniper berries	2 Tbsp
	2 tsp black peppercorns (optional)	
	3 bay leaves (optional)	
45 g	coarse salt, more as needed	3 Tbsp
12 L/3 gal stoneware crock or wooden barrel;		
2·5 kg/5 kg waterproof weight or non-porous rock		

Halve the cabbages, discarding wilted leaves and the hard core; shred them or cut in very fine strips. Wash and dry thoroughly. Pack the cabbage tightly in a clean and odourless crock or barrel. Sprinkle with a few juniper berries and peppercorns, then add a bay leaf and a large pinch of coarse salt.

Continue filling the crock until all the ingredients are used, finishing with salt and spices; the container should be no more than three-quarters full. Put a clean cloth over the last layer of cabbage, then a dinner plate or a piece of wood slightly smaller than the opening of the crock. Weight the top. Store in a cool place. After 24 hours, the cabbage should have given out enough liquid to cover the plate; if not, add a little lightly salted water. The plate should always be thinly covered by liquid.

Three days later, uncover the cabbage. Skim off all the foam and as much of the water as possible. Pour fresh water over the cabbage to cover and replace the cloth, plate and weight. After a day or two a whitish film will form on the surface. If the water under the film is clear, leave it; if it is cloudy, change the water as before. A month after the cabbage was put in the crock, it will be ready for use.

Each time you take out sauerkraut for cooking, also remove a ladleful of the liquid that surrounds it. Sprinkle the surface of the remaining cabbage with a little salt and add enough cold water to keep the plate barely covered with liquid. When taking out sauerkraut, discard any pieces that are turning brown. Wash the cloth and clean the plate and weight each time you remove them from the sauerkraut.

CHOUCROUTE ALSACIENNE

Sauerkraut with pork and sausages

Among Alsatians, sauerkraut is an endless source of debate. Some cooks insist that it be cooked for a minimum time (no more than 3 hours) so that it will still be slightly crisp when served; others believe in long cooking of 5 hours or more – up to 12 in some recipes. Both methods have their merits, and either way, sauerkraut should always be cooked very slowly. If possible, use only uncooked sauerkraut bought in a good delicatessen or made at home. Pre-cooked sauerkraut will not do; canned sauerkraut may be substituted for fresh, though it will never have the same texture. Hot Dijon mustard and a glass of beer or white wine are the appropriate accompaniments to choucroute alsacienne.

Serves 6

1·5 kg	sauerkraut, uncooked	3 lb
750 g	salted or smoked shoulder or loin of pork	1½ lb
500-g	piece of bacon	1-lb
	1 bay leaf	
	2 cloves	
	8 juniper berries	
	4–5 coriander seeds	
	2 cloves garlic	
150 g	goose fat or lard	5 oz
	2 onions, sliced	
1-kg	pork shank	2-lb
	salt and pepper	
500 ml	dry white wine, more if needed, preferably Alsatian riesling	2 cups
	6 large potatoes	
500 g total	6 Strasbourg sausages or frankfurters	1 lb total
cheesecloth		

Wash the sauerkraut under cold running water and squeeze out the excess moisture; rinse and squeeze again.

Put the salted (but not the smoked) pork in a pot with the bacon, cover with water and bring to a boil. Simmer for 5 minutes and taste the water; if it is very salty, repeat the blanching process. Drain thoroughly. Cut the bacon into 6 slices. Tie the bay leaf, cloves, juniper berries, coriander and garlic in a piece of cheesecloth.

Melt all but 2 tablespoons of the goose fat in a large pot, add the onions and cook over a low fire, stirring occasionally, until they just begin to brown. Spread half of the sauerkraut over the onions; then place the salt pork, pork shank, bacon and spice bag on top. Season it very lightly. Cover the meat with the rest of the sauerkraut and enough wine to moisten the sauerkraut without covering it with liquid.

Spread the remaining goose fat over the top. Cut a piece of greaseproof waxed paper to fit inside the pot and place it directly on top of the sauerkraut. Cover and simmer on top of the stove or cook in a low oven (150°C/300°F), allowing 3 hours for crunchy sauerkraut, or 5–6 hours if you like it tender. If cooking for the longer time, remove the meat from the pan after 2–2½ hours of cooking, then replace it to reheat 30 minutes before serving. Put the potatoes in a pot of cold, salted water, bring to a boil and cook for 15–20 minutes or until tender; drain and keep them warm. Poach the sausages in water for 10–12 minutes.

To serve: discard the spice bag and taste the sauerkraut for seasoning. Carve the meat in slices. Pile the sauerkraut on a platter with the meat, sausages and potatoes on top.

CHOUCROUTE SIMPLE
Without the pork, the sauerkraut can be served as a vegetable garnish for roast meat or fowl.

CHOUCROUTE DE NAVETS À LA COLMAR
Turnip sauerkraut with pork

Turnip sauerkraut, a speciality of the town of Colmar, has never achieved the fame of true sauerkraut and it deserves to be better known. It can be prepared following the cabbage sauerkraut recipe, or by this quick method.

Serves 6

1-kg	salted pork shank or uncooked ham shank	2-lb
500 g	smoked shoulder of pork or bacon	1 lb
150 g	lard or goose fat	5 oz
	2 onions, sliced	
	2 cloves garlic, crushed	
125 ml	dry white wine, preferably Alsatian	½ cup
	water or broth	
	pepper	
TURNIP SAUERKRAUT		
3 kg	turnips, shredded	6 lb
30 g	coarse salt	2 Tbsp
	4 tsp juniper berries	
	1 tsp black peppercorns	

Prepare the turnip sauerkraut a day ahead: put a layer of turnips in an earthenware bowl, sprinkle with a little salt and a few of the juniper berries and peppercorns; press down tightly. Continue filling the bowl with layers of turnips, spices and salt until all the ingredients have been used. Cover the last layer with a clean cloth, and then with a plate or piece of wood

slightly smaller than the top of the bowl. Lay a 750 g/1½ lb weight on top. Leave the turnips overnight in a cool place.

The next day, soak the salted pork shank, if using, in cold water for half an hour. Put it in a pot with the bacon (but not with the smoked shoulder). Cover generously with water, bring to a boil and simmer 5 minutes. Taste the water; if it is very salty, repeat the blanching process. Rinse the turnip sauerkraut quickly under cold running water and drain; squeeze out the remaining moisture. Set the oven at low (150°C/300°F).

Heat the lard in a large pot, add the onions and brown them lightly. Add half the sauerkraut, spreading it evenly over the bottom of the pot. Add the pork shank, smoked shoulder and garlic. Cover the meat with the remaining sauerkraut, then add the white wine and enough water or broth to cover by two-thirds. Season with a little pepper.

Cover and cook in the oven for 2–2½ hours or until the meat and sauerkraut are tender; almost all the liquid should have evaporated, but if not, remove the lid towards the end of cooking. Taste the sauerkraut for seasoning. Pile the sauerkraut on a platter, slice the meats and arrange them around the edge. Serve very hot.

CHOUCROUTE DE NAVETS MAIGRE
Turnip sauerkraut can also be served simply as a vegetable dish. Cook as described above, omitting the meat and, if possible, using goose fat instead of lard.

POTÉE LORRAINE
Pork, bean and vegetable stew

Although different 'potée' recipes are to be found all over France, this one is among the most famous. It has the particular charm of using almost all the available garden vegetables, and furnishes a one-pot meal. 'Potée lorraine' should always be served with hot Dijon mustard. Left-over potée is excellent cold, served with vinaigrette.

Serves 6

250 g	shelled fresh white beans OR	8 oz
60 g	dried white beans	2 oz
250 g	shelled fresh peas OR	8 oz
60 g	dried split peas	2 oz
2-kg	smoked or salted piece of shoulder or shank of pork	4½-lb
250-g	slab bacon	½-lb
	1 large cabbage	
	salt and pepper	
45 g	lard or oil	3 Tbsp
350 g	carrots, quartered	¾ lb
	2–3 turnips, quartered	
	1 large onion, studded with 1 clove	
	bouquet garni, including 1 clove garlic	
500-g	1 cervelas boiling sausage	1-lb
750 g	potatoes, cut in quarters	1½ lb
250 g	green beans	½ lb
	3–4 slices toasted bread, diced	

If dried white beans and dried split peas are used, soak them overnight in water and drain.

If salt pork is used, it may need to be soaked overnight in cold water, changing the water two or three times; freshly salted or smoked pork does not need soaking. Drain and dry the pork thoroughly. Put the salt pork and bacon in a pot and add enough cold water to cover. Bring to a boil and simmer for 5 minutes. Taste the water and, if it is very salty, discard it and start again with fresh water. Remove any rind from the bacon and reserve.

Remove all wilted or damaged leaves from the cabbage and hollow out the central core. Put the cabbage in lightly salted boiling water and boil for 10 minutes; drain, refresh under cold running water, and drain thoroughly. Cut it into 6 pieces and set aside.

Melt the lard in a large pot over medium heat. Add any bacon rind, the pork, bacon, carrots, turnips, onion and bouquet garni. If using dried white beans or peas, add them now, but reserve fresh ones. Pour in enough water to cover and bring just to a boil: season with pepper, but no salt. Cover and simmer gently for 1½ hours.

Prick the skin of the sausage and add it to the pot with the cabbage, potatoes and green beans.

If using the fresh white beans and peas, add them now. Taste for seasoning. Cover and simmer for another hour or until the meat and vegetables are very tender. Taste the broth again for seasoning.

To serve: remove the meat from the pot and drain the vegetables, reserving the broth. Dice a few of the vegetables, keeping the rest warm with the meat. Reduce the broth if necessary until well flavoured; then add the chopped vegetables. Put the diced toasted bread in a soup tureen, pour the broth over it and serve as a first course.

For the second course, slice the sausage, pork and bacon and transfer them to a serving platter. Arrange the remaining vegetables around the meat and serve.

252

BAECKENOFFE
Meat and potato casserole

'Baeckenoffe' means simply 'the baker's oven'. Traditionally, Monday was laundry day in Alsace leaving no time for cooking a big midday meal. So on Sunday night the meat for the baeckenoffe would be left to marinate, and early the next morning all the ingredients would be layered into a large earthenware pot and carried to the village baker. The baker's oven would remain hot for hours, and it was in this slow oven that the baeckenoffe would cook until noon, when one of the children was sent to collect it.

Serves 6–8

750 g	boned pork loin, cut in 5 cm/2 in cubes	1½ lb
750 g	boned shoulder of lamb, cut in 5 cm/2 in cubes	1½ lb
750 g	lean stewing beef, cut in 5 cm/2 in cubes	1½ lb
30 g	lard or oil	2 Tbsp
	2 onions, thinly sliced	
2 kg	potatoes, thinly sliced	4½ lb
	salt and pepper	
500 ml	water, more if needed	2 cups
	luting paste*	
	MARINADE	
	2 carrots, thinly sliced	
	2 onions, thinly sliced	
	1 sprig of thyme	
	1 bay leaf	
	2 cloves garlic, peeled and crushed	
	1 sprig of parsley	
	3 cloves	
750 ml	dry white wine, preferably Alsatian sylvaner or riesling	3 cups
	salt and pepper	

Put the pork, lamb and beef in a large bowl (not aluminium) with the other marinade ingredients, cover and leave to marinate overnight in the refrigerator. Remove the meat from the liquid, reserving the marinade.

Heat the lard in a large casserole, add the onions and cook over a low fire, stirring occasionally, until they begin to brown; remove the pot from the heat. Put half of the sliced potatoes in a layer over the onions, then put the marinated meat on top; season lightly with salt and pepper. Cover the meat with the remaining potato slices and season again. Strain the marinade over the meat and vegetables and add enough water to cover by half. Set the oven at moderately low (165°C/325°F). Seal the gap between the casserole and lid with luting paste. Heat the casserole gently on top of the stove for 10–15 minutes; then cook in the oven for 3

hours. Don't try to open the casserole once it has been sealed; the meat should cook slowly and in an even heat. When done, break the seal and discard the luting paste. Serve the meat and vegetables directly from the casserole.

CUISSOT DE CHEVREUIL AUX POIRES
Haunch of venison with pears

Roast pears with venison are an inspired combination, popular in Germany and Switzerland as well as in Alsace. The pears can be replaced by an equal quantity of fresh or dried apples, to make 'cuissot de chevreuil aux pommes'.

Serves 6–8

250-g	piece fat pork	½-lb
2·5-kg	haunch of venison	5½-lb
2 L	milk, more if needed	2 qt
1 kg	fresh pears OR	2 lb
500 g	dried pears	1 lb
100 g	butter	7 Tbsp
	salt and pepper	
	1–2 tsp ground cinnamon	
250 ml	broth or water	1 cup
	larding needle (optional)	

Cut the fat pork into small strips and lard* the flesh of the venison. Put the meat in a large, deep dish and cover completely with milk. Cover and marinate in the refrigerator for 24–36 hours.

Soak dried pears for 2 hours, drain and set aside. Set the oven at hot (230°C/450°F).

Remove the venison from the milk and dry it with paper towels. Lay the meat in a large buttered shallow baking dish. Rub the surface with half the butter and sprinkle with salt and pepper. Roast for 30 minutes, basting the meat frequently and turning it over several times.

Meanwhile prepare the pears: peel fresh pears, leaving them whole; if using dried pears, cut them into slices. Add the pears to the dish containing the meat, sprinkle them with cinnamon and dot with the remaining butter. Cook the meat and pears for another 30 minutes, basting frequently. To test the venison insert a skewer in the thickest part for 30 seconds. If the skewer is warm to the touch when withdrawn, the meat is rare; if hot, the meat is well done.

Transfer the meat to a platter and arrange the pears around it, halving the fresh pears. Pour the broth into the roasting dish, stir to dissolve the pan juices, and strain into a small pan. Skim off the excess fat. Bring to a boil, taste for seasoning and, if necessary, reduce to concentrate the flavour. Strain a little gravy over the meat and serve the rest separately. Carve the venison at the table.

SCHNITZEN

Bacon with dried fruits and potatoes

An 18th-century Alsatian cookbook gives a vivid picture of the vegetables available. Monday was the day for schnitzen, with turnips on Tuesday, beans or peas (probably dried) on Wednesday, rice or barley on Thursday, spinach or string beans on Friday and lentils on Saturday. Sauerkraut was reserved as a Sunday treat. 'Schnitzen strasbourgeoise' has a 250 g/ ½ lb smoked Strasbourg sausage added at the same time as the potatoes.

Serves 6

150 g	dried pears	5 oz
150 g	dried apples	5 oz
300 g	bacon, thickly sliced	10 oz
65 g	sugar	⅓ cup
	2 Tbsp water	
250 ml	broth, more if needed	1 cup
750 g	potatoes, quartered	1½ lb
	salt and pepper	

Soak the pears and apples overnight in water. If the bacon is very salty, blanch* it.

Thoroughly drain the pears and apples. Make a light caramel by heating the sugar and water in a small pan until dissolved, then boiling until it begins to turn golden brown. Take from the heat and add the apples and pears, stirring to coat them with the caramel. Lay the bacon slices in a pot and spread the apples and pears on top. With the broth dissolve any caramel remaining in the pan and add it to the bacon and fruit. Cover and simmer for 35–45 minutes.

When the bacon and fruit are almost tender, add the potatoes and season with salt and pepper. Cover and cook for another 30 minutes or until the potatoes are tender. If the mixture looks dry, add more broth during cooking; when done, the potatoes and fruit should be moist but not soupy. Taste for seasoning. Either serve everything together in a dish or, if you prefer, mix the potatoes and fruit and arrange the bacon slices on top.

TOTELOTS

Hot noodle salad

'Totelots' are a type of noodle peculiar to Lorraine. They are eaten hot with a cold dressing, either as an accompaniment to a main dish or alone as a hot hors-d'oeuvre, and are traditional on Good Friday.

Serves 4

	3 hard-boiled eggs, sliced	
	NOODLE DOUGH	
260 g	flour	2 cups
	3 whole eggs, slightly beaten	
	1 egg yolk	
5 g	salt	1 tsp
	1 tsp water, more if needed	
	DRESSING	
	3 Tbsp oil	
	1 Tbsp vinegar	
	2 Tbsp sour cream, heavy cream or crème fraîche*	
	2 shallots, finely chopped	
	1 clove garlic, finely chopped	
	2 Tbsp chopped parsley	
	salt and pepper	

Make the noodle dough as for 'nouilles à l'alsacienne' (see recipe) and leave to rest for 1 hour. Roll out the dough to a thickness of about 3 mm/⅛ in and use a knife to cut it into 1·25 cm/½ in squares. Place them on a floured cloth and leave to dry for 1–1½ hours.

Meanwhile, make the dressing: in a large bowl, whisk the oil, vinegar, cream, shallots, garlic, parsley, salt and pepper until slightly thickened.

To cook the noodles, bring a large pot of salted water to a boil, add the noodles and cook for 2–3 minutes or until tender but still slightly chewy. Drain, rinse rapidly under hot water to wash away the starch, and drain thoroughly. Add the noodles to the bowl of dressing and toss to mix. Taste for seasoning. Decorate the top of the salad with slices of hard-boiled egg and serve immediately.

NOUILLES À L'ALSACIENNE
Fresh noodles with butter

Home-made noodles are a rarity in France, except in Alsace and Lorraine. They are served as an accompaniment to meat, not as a first course.

Serves 4–6

260 g	flour	2 cups
	3 eggs	
	1 egg yolk	
5 g	salt	1 tsp
	1 tsp water, more if needed	
	FOR SERVING	
60 g	butter	4 Tbsp
	salt and pepper	

Make the noodles: sift the flour on to a board and make a well in the centre. Put the whole eggs, yolk and salt in the well and work in the flour with your fingertips, adding a little water, if needed, to make a smooth dough that is soft but not sticky. Lightly flour the working surface and knead the dough energetically for at least 10 minutes or until it is very smooth. It should not stick to your hands or to the working surface; if it does, lightly flour it and continue kneading until it is very smooth and elastic and comes together in a rough ball. Cover with an inverted bowl and let stand for 1 hour to lose some of its elasticity.

If rolling the noodles by hand, divide the dough in half and roll out each half as thinly as possible on a floured board. Let rest for 30 minutes–1 hour or until fairly stiff and dry. Roll loosely, then slice each roll into 1·25 cm/½ in strips to form noodles. Spread the noodles on a floured dish towel or hang them over a chair back to dry for 1–2 hours.

If using a pasta machine, divide the dough into 3–4 balls. Run each ball through the machine three to four times on the thickest setting, or until very smooth. Continue to pass the dough through the machine, reducing the setting each time, until it is very thin. With the machine on its thinnest setting, cut the dough into noodles. Dry them on a floured dish towel or over a chair back for 1–2 hours.

To cook the noodles, bring a very large pan of salted water to a boil, add the noodles and return to a boil. Reduce the heat and simmer for 2–3 minutes or until tender but still slightly chewy. Drain, rinse rapidly under hot water to wash away the starch, and drain thoroughly.

To serve as buttered noodles, melt the butter in the pot and add the noodles. Heat, tossing constantly, and season lightly with salt and pepper. Transfer to a dish and serve immediately.

NOUILLES À LA CRÈME

Mix together:

125 ml	heavy cream or crème fraîche*	½ cup

and 2 Tbsp vinegar. Pour this sauce over the buttered noodles in the serving dish; taste for seasoning and serve at once.

NOUILLES AU LAIT

Melt in a saucepan:

90 g	butter	6 Tbsp

Stir in:

50 g	fresh breadcrumbs	⅓ cup

and brown them in the butter. Stir in:

250 ml	milk	1 cup

and bring to a boil. Pour this sauce over the buttered noodles, taste for seasoning and serve.

SPAETZLI
Noodle dumplings

'Spaetzli', slightly chewy in texture and twisted in uneven curls, are a typically Alsatian alternative to noodles. In Alsace a special type of press is sold for spaetzli; it resembles a potato masher with extra-large holes.

Serves 6

	salt and pepper	
125 g	butter, melted	¼ lb
	SOFT NOODLE DOUGH	
400 g	flour, more as needed	3 cups
	¾ tsp salt	
	2 eggs, beaten to mix	
250 ml	water, more as needed	1 cup

Make the noodle dough: sift the flour with the salt on to a board or marble slab and make a well in the centre. Add the eggs and water to the well and mix them briefly. Gradually draw in the flour to make a smooth soft dough, adding a little more flour or water if necessary. The softer the dough, the lighter the spaetzli will be, but it must not be so soft that it disintegrates during cooking. Put the dough in a bowl, cover and chill for 30 minutes–1 hour.

Bring a large pan of salted water almost to a boil. Put the dough in a colander with very large holes and push the dough through the holes so it drops into the hot water in spirals. Cook the spaetzli in 2–3 batches if necessary, as they should not be crowded. Simmer them for 4–6 minutes or until they rise to the surface and are almost tender – they should have the 'al dente' consistency of pasta. Lift out the spaetzli with a slotted spoon and add them to the melted butter; keep them warm while cooking the rest.

Season the spaetzli with pepper and a little salt, if needed. They may be served as they are, or fried in the butter until golden brown.

TARTE AUX FRUITS À L'ALSACIENNE

Fruit and custard tart

Use plums, apricots, bilberries, blueberries or cherries for this tart which has a filling resembling a quiche (see page 243).

Serves 6–8

	YEAST PIE DOUGH	
125 ml	lukewarm milk	½ cup
8 g	fresh yeast OR	½ cake
	½ pkg dry yeast	
225 g	flour, more if needed	1¾ cups
5 g	salt	1 tsp
25 g	sugar	2 Tbsp
	1 egg	
100 g	butter, softened	7 Tbsp
	FILLING	
1 kg	fresh fruit	2 lb
20 g	dry breadcrumbs	2 Tbsp
	2 eggs, beaten to mix	
60 ml	heavy cream	¼ cup
65 g	sugar	⅓ cup
	confectioners' sugar (for sprinkling)	
	30 cm/12 in pie pan	

Make the yeast pie dough: put the milk in a small bowl, crumble the yeast over it and leave for 5 minutes or until dissolved. Sift the flour on to a board or marble slab, add the salt and sugar and make a well in the centre. Add the yeast mixture and the egg and mix with your hand to obtain a dough that is soft but not sticky, adding more flour if necessary. Knead for 8–10 minutes

or until the dough is smooth and elastic; then work in the softened butter. Transfer the dough to a bowl, cover with a damp cloth and let it rise in a warm place for 1 hour or until it has doubled in bulk.

Meanwhile, prepare the fruit: halve plums or apricots, discarding the pits; wash and pick over bilberries or blueberries; cherries may be pitted or left whole, as you prefer. Set the oven at very hot (220°C/425°F). Butter the pie pan. When the dough has risen, knead it lightly to knock out any air, roll it out and line the pan.

Make the filling: sprinkle the breadcrumbs in the pie shell and arrange the fruit on top, cut side up. Bake in the heated oven for 10 minutes. Whisk together the eggs, cream and sugar and pour the mixture over the fruit. Lower the oven heat to moderate (175°C/350°F) and bake the pie for another 40–45 minutes or until the dough is browned, the fruit is tender and the cream mixture is set. Don't overbake or the custard will curdle.

Serve warm or cold, sprinkled with sugar.

TARTE AUX FRUITS À L'ALSACIENNE II

Prepare as above, but omit the breadcrumbs, eggs and cream. Arrange in the shell:

1·5 kg	prepared fruit	3 lb

Sprinkle it with the sugar and bake for about 30 minutes or until the fruit is tender. Before serving, sprinkle with sugar and **1 tsp ground cinnamon.**

BABAS AU RHUM

Rum babas

The story goes that one day the 18th-century Duke Stanislas of Lorraine improved his kugelhopf with a sprinkling of rum – the result was so delicious that he named it after his favourite character in *A Thousand and One Nights*, Ali Baba. When these stories first appeared in French they had a great influence on the taste of the day. And so was born the best yeast cake of all, rum baba. The more probable but less romantic explanation is that Stanislas brought a taste for babas with him from his native Poland, where they were made with buckwheat flour and soaked in sweet wine. ('Baba' means housewife in Polish.)

Babas are most often baked in individual moulds, but in Alsace and Lorraine giant single babas are also made. All have a characteristic bucket shape and the little ones are served tipped over on their side.

Makes 8 large or 16 small babas

	3 Tbsp lukewarm water or milk	
15 g	fresh yeast OR	1 cake
	1 pkg dry yeast	
225 g	flour	1¾ cups
5 g	salt	1 tsp
12 g	sugar	1 Tbsp
	3 eggs, beaten to mix	
95 g	dried currants	⅔ cup
	3 Tbsp rum	
	3 Tbsp hot water	
125 g	butter, softened	¼ lb
	SYRUP	
500 g	sugar	2½ cups
1 L	water	1 qt
	1 Tbsp coriander seeds	
80 ml	rum	⅓ cup
	8 large (250 ml/1 cup) or 16 small (125 ml/½ cup) baba moulds	

Put the lukewarm water in a bowl, crumble the yeast over it and let stand for 5 minutes until dissolved. Sift the flour into a warm bowl with the salt and sugar, make a well in the centre and add the yeast mixture with the eggs. Work the dough with your hand until smooth; then beat it for 5 minutes or until very smooth and elastic, lifting the dough up with your fingers and letting it fall back into the bowl with a slap. Cover the bowl with a damp cloth and let the dough rise in a warm place for 45 minutes–1 hour or until doubled in bulk. Soak the dried currants in 3 tablespoons rum and 3 tablespoons hot water.

Butter the moulds, chill them in the freezer, and butter them again. Set the oven at hot (200°C/400°F).

When the dough has risen, beat the softened butter until smooth; stir it into the dough. Drain the currants and add them to the dough. Drop spoonsful of dough into the prepared moulds to fill them by one-third. Set the moulds on a baking sheet, cover with a cloth and let the dough rise in a warm place for 15–20 minutes or until the moulds are almost full. Bake in the heated oven for 20 minutes or until the babas begin to shrink from the sides of the moulds and are golden brown. Unmould them and leave to cool on a rack. If possible, make the babas a day ahead so they are dry and absorb more syrup.

To make the syrup: in a medium saucepan, heat the sugar with the water over a low fire until dissolved; then add the coriander seeds and boil rapidly for 2–3 minutes. Take from the heat. Put the babas in the very hot syrup, a few at a time, carefully turning them over several times to make sure they absorb as much syrup as possible. The babas will swell and be very shiny. Using a large slotted spoon, carefully transfer them to a platter. Reserve the remaining syrup.

Just before serving, sprinkle the babas with the rum. Add any remaining rum to the reserved syrup and serve separately.

GRAND BABA

Prepare the dough as for individual babas but bake it in a buttered 23 cm/9 in kugelhopf mould for 25–30 minutes or until golden brown. Dip in syrup as above.

KUGELHOPF

By tradition, to achieve just the right golden crust, 'kugelhopf' should be baked in a fluted earthenware mould, though flameproof glass or metal are a good second best. The hole in the centre of the mould enables the heat to reach the centre of the kugelhopf.

Serves 8–10

45 g	sliced blanched almonds (optional)	$\frac{1}{2}$ cup
210 ml	lukewarm milk	$\frac{7}{8}$ cup
15 g	fresh yeast OR 1 pkg dry yeast	1 cake
355 g	flour	$2\frac{3}{4}$ cups
50 g	sugar	$\frac{1}{4}$ cup
	pinch of salt	
	3 eggs, beaten to mix	
125 g	butter, melted	$\frac{1}{4}$ lb
70 g	currants	$\frac{1}{2}$ cup
45 g	raisins	$\frac{1}{3}$ cup
	confectioners' sugar (for sprinkling)	
23–25 cm/9–10 in diameter kugelhopf mould		

Thoroughly butter the mould and press the almonds around the sides and base.

Put a third of the milk in a bowl, crumble the yeast over it and let stand for 5 minutes until dissolved. Stir in enough of the flour to make a sticky dough, cover and leave in a warm place for 30 minutes or until doubled in bulk.

Sift the remaining flour into a warm bowl and make a well in the centre. Add the yeast mixture, the remaining milk, the sugar, salt and eggs. Work the dough with your hand until smooth; then knead the dough by slapping it vigorously against the side of the bowl for 5 minutes or until very elastic. Gently work in the butter, then the currants and raisins. Transfer the dough to the mould; it should half fill it. Cover with a damp cloth and let rise in a warm place for 30–40 minutes or until the dough has risen to about 2 cm/$\frac{3}{4}$ in from the top of the pan. Set the oven at hot (200°C/400°F).

When the dough has risen, set the mould on a baking sheet and bake in the heated oven for 40–50 minutes or until the kugelhopf is well browned and a skewer inserted in the centre comes out clean. If the top browns too quickly during baking, cover the kugelhopf with a sheet of foil and lower the oven heat to moderate (175°C/350°F).

Let the kugelhopf stand for a few moments; then turn it out on to a wire rack to cool completely. Sprinkle with the sugar before serving.

MADELEINES

To the French, madeleines are forever linked with Commercy, the town in Lorraine that bakes huge quantities for distribution all over France.

Makes 25–30 medium madeleines

120 g	flour	$\frac{3}{4}$ cup + 3 Tbsp
	1 tsp baking powder	
135 g	sugar	$\frac{2}{3}$ cup
	4 eggs	
	1 tsp orange flower water OR the grated rind of 1 orange or 1 lemon	
125 g	butter, melted	$\frac{1}{4}$ lb
25–30 medium madeleine moulds		

Sift the flour with the baking powder. Whisk the sugar and eggs together in a bowl until thick and light; then beat in the orange flower water. Fold in the flour, sifting it over the egg mixture in three batches. When the last batch is almost mixed, sprinkle the melted butter over it and fold together as lightly as possible; the batter quickly loses volume after the butter is added. Chill the batter for 20–30 minutes or until the butter hardens slightly and the dough is stiffer. Set the oven at very hot (230°C/450°F). Thoroughly butter and flour the moulds.

Using a large spoon, pour the mixture into the moulds, filling them by two-thirds. Bake the madeleines in the heated oven for 5 minutes; then reduce the oven temperature to hot (200°C/400°F). Bake for a further 5–7 minutes or until golden brown; a peak in the centre of these cakes is characteristic. Transfer to a rack to cool.

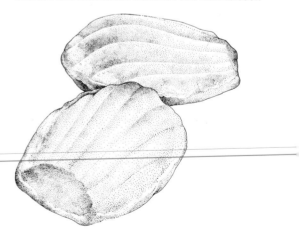

EAUX-DE-VIE AND FRUIT LIQUEURS

Fruit orchards are everywhere in Alsace and Lorraine. They spread out over the plains and nestle in the folds of the hills, supplying the raw materials for one of the region's most valuable products: fruit brandies ('eaux-de-vie') and fruit liqueurs.

Eaux-de-vie are obtained by distillation. Because they are aged in crockery, rather than in wooden casks like brandy or armagnac, they remain colourless, hence their name 'alcools blancs'. Kirsch, distilled from cherries and their stones, is the most common of these white alcohols, but beware of imitations called 'kirsch fantaisie'. The 'poire William' of Alsace is a local favourite, the most expensive variety containing a full-size pear grown inside the bottle which is attached to the tree. 'Mirabelle', made from yellow plums, and 'quetsche', from purple plums, are favourites in Lorraine. Rarest of all plum spirits is 'reine-claude' (greengage) with its powerful bouquet. 'Fraise' (strawberry) eau-de-vie can be made from both wild and cultivated strawberries and the splendid 'framboise' (raspberry) from the upper valleys of the Vosges takes nearly 30 kilos of fruit to make a single bottle. Its flavour is surpassed only by that of 'framboise sauvage', made from seed-laden wild raspberries.

Fruit liqueurs are not distilled, but are made by macerating almost any fruit – strawberry, plum, bilberry, raspberry, William pear, black currant, cherry – in alcohol. Unlike the white eaux-de-vie, they are richly coloured from the juices of the fruit and often quite sweet. Both alcohols and liqueurs are drunk as a 'digestif' after meals and some are said to have medicinal properties like 'myrtille' (bilberry) which not only heals intestinal afflictions but also 'gives those who drink it the eyes of a cat'.

MACARONS

Macaroons were once the speciality of a convent in Nancy, capital of Lorraine. At the time of the Revolution, the nuns were forced out into the world and two of the sisters set up a bakery, found to this day in the rue des Soeurs Macarons.

Makes about 12 medium macaroons

150 g	almonds, blanched and peeled	1 cup
	1½ egg whites, more if needed	
150 g	sugar	¾ cup
	½ tsp vanilla extract	
	2 Tbsp confectioners' sugar (for sprinkling)	

Use greaseproof/parchment paper to line a heavy baking sheet and grease the paper. Set the oven at hot (200°C/400°F).

Grate the almonds with a cheese grater or in a food processor. Using a mortar and pestle, pound the almonds, gradually adding half an egg white. Keep pounding until the almond paste is smooth and very fine. Add half the sugar and work it into the mixture, using the pestle. In the same way add the rest of the sugar, then another half egg white. Beat in the vanilla. The dough should be soft but not runny. If necessary add a little more egg white. Alternatively grind the almonds and the sugar in a food processor until very fine; add the egg whites gradually, with the blades turning, until the mixture just holds together. Don't overwork or the oil will be drawn out of the almonds.

Shape the mixture into balls the size of walnuts. Arrange them on the prepared baking sheets and flatten them slightly. Brush each ball with a little water and sprinkle with the sugar. Put the baking sheet in the top third of the heated oven and bake for 18–20 minutes, or until the macaroons are lightly browned. Lift one end of the paper and immediately pour a glass of water under it. The water on the hot baking sheet will form steam, loosening the macaroons. Leave the macaroons for a few minutes; then remove them from the paper and transfer to a rack to cool. They should be crisp on the outside and soft in the centre.

GÂTEAU AU CHOCOLAT DE METZ
Light chocolate cake

Metz chocolate cake is rich, yet has an unusually light texture given by potato starch.

Serves 8–10

250 g	semi-sweet chocolate, coarsely chopped	8 oz
80 ml	milk	⅓ cup
	½ tsp vanilla extract	
135 g	sugar	⅔ cup
100 g	potato starch	¾ cup
65 g	blanched almonds, finely ground	½ cup
	6 eggs, separated	
	25–28 cm/10–11 in diameter cake pan	

Set the oven at moderate (175°C/350°F). Butter the cake pan.

Put the chocolate and milk in a medium, heavy-based saucepan and heat gently, stirring constantly, until the chocolate is melted and smooth. Remove from the heat and beat in the vanilla, half the sugar and the potato starch. In a small bowl, mix the almonds with the egg yolks; then stir them into the chocolate mixture. Beat the egg whites until stiff, add the remaining sugar and beat for another 30 seconds until glossy. Stir a quarter of the egg whites into the chocolate mixture; then lightly fold this mixture back into the remaining egg whites. Pour into the buttered cake pan, filling it almost three-quarters full. Bake in the heated oven for 45 minutes; the centre of the cake should still be slightly soft. Because it is creamy in the centre, let the cake cool thoroughly before unmoulding. Serve cold.

CHEESES

The principal cheese of Alsace and Lorraine, 'munster', is notorious in and beyond France for its stunning smell, due to the bouquet of the milk of the Vosges cattle. The smell develops in the maturing process when the cheese is scrubbed with salt water. According to popular legend, the monks who came from Ireland in the 7th century to convert Alsace to christianity were the first to make the cheese. The name 'Munster', which means monastery, was given to the town that grew up around it, to the valley that enclosed it and to the cheese that was made there. Authentic munster cheese must come from this valley. The most prestigious type, still produced on farms, is called 'munster fermier' and comes as an unwrapped red disc instead of in a box. The similar 'gérômé' and 'gérardmer' cheeses are made in the neighbouring region of Gérardmer, to the west in Lorraine.

Even in Alsace, digestions quail before the onslaught of an aged munster, and the cheese is often eaten before it is fully ripe, accompanied by whole wheat, rye or country bread and a glass of fruity gewürtztraminer wine. Another traditional way of enjoying munster is to spread it on slices of boiled potato. During the autumn, munster is enjoyed with walnuts and 'bernache', wine that is still fermenting – a combination that apparently pleased emissaries of the 15th-century King Louis XI. Nowadays, munster is sometimes studded with caraway or anise seeds, and in the Vosges a fresh variety is served with cream and sugar. In Lorraine, fresh cheese may be mixed with salt and fennel, then allowed to mellow in a crock for six weeks to make 'fromage en pot'.

A milder fresh cheese from Alsace is 'bibbeleskäs', usually made only for home use. It can be plain or mixed with herbs and horse-radish and is often served as a main course with boiled or baked potatoes, or spread on toast and sprinkled with chives for a snack.

OTHER SPECIALITIES OF THE REGION
TRADITIONAL DISHES

Soupe aux cerises
Cherry soup

Soupe à la bière
Beer soup

Fiouse Lorraine
Fresh cheese tart

Oeufs Lorraine
Baked eggs with cheese and bacon

Matelote à l'alsacienne
Fish stew in white wine and cream sauce

Truite au bleu
Poached trout in court bouillon

Truites au vin blanc en gelée
Trout in white wine aspic

Tourte aux grenouilles
Frogs' legs, mushroom and garlic feuilleté

Poulet farci strasbourgeoise
Chicken stuffed with sausagemeat and foie gras

Faisan à la choucroute
Pheasant with sauerkraut

Cailles au genièvre
Quail with juniper berries

Foie gras en brioche
Foie gras in brioche

Cochon de lait à la gelée
Sucking pig in aspic

Porc rôti aux mirabelles
Roast pork with mirabelle plums

Cervelles à l'aigre-doux
Brains in sweet-sour sauce

Boeuf au raifort
Braised beef with horse-radish

Sanglier aux champignons et myrtilles
Braised wild boar with mushrooms and bilberries

Sauce au raifort
Horse-radish sauce

Pflutten
Potato noodle squares

Nouilles fraîches au foie gras
Fresh noodles with foie gras

CHARCUTERIE

Pâté lorrain
Small pork pâtés in feuilleté

Saucisson de jambon
Ham sausage

Gendarmes
Dry sausages

Saucisson de foie
Liver sausage

Kassler
Rolled and smoked pork fillet

Schiffala
Smoked pork shoulder

PÂTISSERIE AND CONFISERIE

Chaleth
Jewish apple charlotte

Gâteau lorrain, nids d'abeilles
Yeast cake filled with pastry cream

Croix
A brioche cross sprinkled with sugar

Rouyat
Apple dumpling

Jungfrauekiechlas
Ash Wednesday fritters

Visitandines de Nancy
Small almond cakes

Biscuits à la cannelle
Cinnamon biscuits

Anesbredlas
Anise macaroons

Dragées de Verdun
Sugared almonds

Bergamottes
Hard candies flavoured with bergamot

Franche-Comté and the Alps

So much of the Alps looks like a romantic painting, complete with rustic chalets, soaring peaks and ice-blue, tumbling streams that I often feel I am stepping back to the 1800s. But the population of the foothills which make up the Franche-Comté, running down through Savoy to the Dauphiné, is very much planted in the present. Hydro-electric power feeds industry, while in the ski resorts higher up tourism takes over, with visitors in the season outnumbering the locals by ten to one. In the valleys fruit growing is mechanized, and even the centuries-old dairy industry, organized long ago into 'fruitières' (cooperatives that make use of the 'fruit' of the mountains), has now marshalled itself into sparkling modernity.

Dairy country above all, the Franche-Comté and the alpine foothills demand hard labour in pocket-sized fields where the surrounding forests encroach all too quickly on to untended ground. In summer, herds are driven up to high pastures, leaving the lower land free for the hay crop which supports the cattle all winter. I once glimpsed a spring procession leaving the village, bells atinkle, the first cow decked with flowers. (Bells are no superfluous decoration, but a necessary precaution, making it easier to locate straying animals.) Perseverance is rewarded by some of the finest cheese in France, symbolized by the name of Savoy's most common breed, the 'vache d'abondance', a gentle brown and white cow which can give 3000 litres of milk a year.

The principal alpine cheese, gruyère, is a household word, with emmental, tomme de Savoie and reblochon from the Dauphiné not far behind. A well-aged, nutty gruyère is an excellent table cheese (I happen to be addicted to it) but its cheese-board reputation is far eclipsed by its importance in the kitchen. Dishes like 'fondue savoyarde' (cheese fondue), 'croûte jurassienne' (cheese toast flavoured with bacon), 'poulet au comté' (baked chicken in cheese sauce) and even cheese soufflé would hardly exist without gruyère, not to mention the soups, omelettes and gratins in which it plays an important part as flavouring or topping. My own particular cheese dream stems from a day's skiing in the mountains which ended with a big bowl of onion soup, generously coated with gruyère half chewy, half crisply brown.

Given good cows, prime veal might be expected though dairy breeds do not, in general, yield good beef. 'Escalope de veau belle comtoise' is a version of veal cordon bleu, with the cheese and ham as a coating instead of as a stuffing for the veal, and Aix-les-Bains is known for roast veal with celery, carrots and chestnuts. However, the expense of veal makes it a luxury, and the staple meat of the mountains has long been pork. The crisp air is ideal for drying hams, a speciality of Chamonix, as well as for maturing sausages like the plump 'Jésus de Morteau' (Morteau is a village in the Jura), which is first smoked over pinewood and juniper. The local equivalent of the Swiss dried beef of the Grisons is 'brési', salted fillet that is sliced wafer-thin to serve with country bread and butter.

The cooking of the plains running along the Rhône and Isère valleys is a good deal more varied than that of the hills to the east. Leaving aside the sophistication of their multi-starred restaurants, the ancient towns of Valence and Vienne as well as the modern department capital, Romans, all have distinctive specialities. 'Pognes' is a brioche bread, often topped with crushed pink pralines and sliced to spread with honey. Hot sausages at Vienne may be truffled like those of Lyon, and around Romans they are dark with spinach and herbs. Some dishes such as the anchovy-flavoured beef 'grillade marinière' of Valence look towards Provence, and others such as 'ravioles', the baby ravioli of Romans, to Italy.

Throughout Savoy and the Dauphiné the Italian influence is strong. After all, until the 1860s Savoy was not a part of France, but of the confederation of Italian states. It was the Romans who, some two thousand years ago, planted the vines and fruit trees that still spell wealth in the Dauphiné. A clear climatic line delineates the warmer terrain of Provence from the Dauphiné where most places are too prone to frost for olive trees to survive. Walnuts are a better bet, providing oil as well as nuts, and the increasingly popular use of walnut oil in salads – combined with the mechanization of walnut-picking – has led to the planting of orchards devoted to walnut trees. The Isère valley is packed with the graceful, fine-leaved trees.

Dauphiné wines belong to the full-bodied reds of the Rhône, at their best in vintages such as châteauneuf-du-pape and hermitage. Up in the Franche-Comté wines are more varied if less distinguished. They include the flinty Arbois rosé and the splendid 'vin jaune', aged in oak to give it a flavour of sherry.

> Le vin d'Arbois
> Plus on en boit
> Plus on va droit

The more Arbois wine you drink, the straighter you go, runs a local ditty.

Vin jaune is the ideal accompaniment to one of the great specialities of the region, 'poulet aux morilles', a dish which units the local chickens rivalling those of Bresse next door, with the rare perfumed morels of the region. At one leisurely lunch in Arbois, I put the combination to the test, and even the morbid gaze of stags' heads on the wall could not detract from its perfection. Morels are the most esteemed of a dozen kinds of edible mushroom that grow throughout the alpine foothills, their gathering a matter of intense rivalry. Prices are higher in France than in Italy, and near the border pickers cross at night, so as to cull the Italian crops at first light, causing blows and even shots to be exchanged.

Long famous for fish, the Alps are one of the few regions where river and lake trout are still plentiful. It is easy to see why. Away from the larger valley, communications are minimal, with many villages isolated from their neighbours a few kilometres away over the mountain peaks. So streams and lakes have remained relatively unpolluted, their fish the target of only a few determined amateur anglers. 'Omble chevalier' or Arctic char, reputed to be the finest river fish in Europe, is found mainly in Lake Annecy, but trout, pike, tench, carp and perch are common enough. Pike, with its redoubtable number of bones, is at its best in quenelles where the flesh is pounded to make dumplings, and at Nantua they meet their match with the local crayfish. An undistinguished town lying on the main route from France to Savoy, Nantua offered travellers quenelles with an incomparable crayfish sauce. Sitting not so long ago beside the chill, grey lake, pine-clad mountains looming above, I appreciated exactly why the quenelles of Nantua, in their cheerful pink sauce, have always tasted so delicious.

Heart-warming dishes seem to be a feature of the Alps. The traveller's standby of fondue is ancient, described nearly two hundred years ago by Brillat-Savarin, as being 'nothing more nor less than eggs

scrambled with cheese.' Brillat-Savarin, born at Belley in the Jura, was the first of a peculiarly French breed, the food propagandist. It was he who coined the aphorism 'Tell me what you eat and I will tell you what you are.'

Regional soups range from soupe savoyarde, a milk-based mixture of root celery, leek, turnips and potato, to cheese soup and even a tart cherry soup from the Franche-Comté, which is served sizzling hot over butter croûtons. Soup made from frogs' legs is a feature of the Doubs, a lake-strewn area north of Besançon. The chief city of the Franche-Comté, it is also known for its 'gaudes', a cornmeal pudding that is served with milk. Equally sturdy are the thick 'matefaim' pancakes of Savoy, whose name means literally 'hunger beater'.

Savoy and the Dauphiné use their milk and cheese in gratins: gratin of crayfish, gratin of sweetbreads, gratin savoyard of potatoes cooked in broth and topped with cheese. There are at least half a dozen recipes for gratin dauphinois, the sliced potato and milk mixture that is the most famous of all, some with cream, some topped with cheese, some flavoured with garlic or layered with wild mushrooms. Deceptively simple, the perfect gratin dauphinois is meltingly soft with just the right balance of seasoning: a challenge even to the best of cooks.

SOUPE SAVOYARDE

Winter vegetable soup

'A mouthful of soup, a mouthful of cheese,' goes a Savoyard saying, and here the cheese is set on croûtes of bread. Also called 'soupe montagnarde', this is a fitting end to a day's work in the mountains.

Serves 6

30 g	butter	2 Tbsp
	1 large onion, chopped	
500 g	leeks, trimmed, split and sliced	1 lb
	1 small turnip, quartered and sliced	
about 300 g	1 small celery root, quartered and sliced	about 10 oz
	2 large potatoes, quartered	
500 ml	lukewarm water	2 cups
	salt and pepper	
625 ml	milk	2½ cups
	12 small, round croûtes*, fried in butter	
150 g	tomme or gruyère, cut in thin slices	5 oz

Heat the butter in a pot, add the onion and cook over a low fire until soft but not browned. Stir in the leeks, turnip and celeriac/celery root, cover tightly and cook over a low fire, stirring occasionally, for 20 minutes or until softened.

Add the potatoes to the pot with the water, salt and pepper. Simmer for 15 minutes or until the potatoes are nearly tender. Bring the milk to a boil, add it to the soup, cover and simmer for 15 minutes or until the vegetables are very tender. Taste for seasoning.

Put the croûtes in a soup tureen and top them with the slices of cheese. Pour the soup over them and serve immediately so that the croûtes remain crisp.

TARTE AUX ASPERGES

Asparagus tart

Open tarts, with a filling sometimes of cream sauce, sometimes of egg custard, have spread into Franche-Comté from Lorraine, the home of the quiche.

Serves 6

	PIE PASTRY	
200 g	flour	1½ cups
95 g	butter	6 Tbsp
	1 egg yolk	
	½ tsp salt	
	4–5 Tbsp cold water	
	FILLING	
1 kg	white or green asparagus	2 lb
	salt and pepper	
500 ml	milk	2 cups
60 g	butter	4 Tbsp
30 g	flour	¼ cup
	pinch of grated nutmeg	
50 g	grated comté or gruyère cheese	½ cup
	2 eggs, beaten	
	3 Tbsp heavy cream or crème fraîche*	
	23–25 cm/9–10 in pie or tart pan	

Make the pie pastry* and chill for 30 minutes or until firm.

Peel the asparagus and trim off the bottom halves of the stalks; these can be saved for soup. Cook the asparagus tips in boiling salted water for 8–10 minutes (for white asparagus) or 4–5 minutes (for green asparagus) or until just tender. Drain, rinse with cold water and drain thoroughly.

While the asparagus is cooking, prepare a medium white sauce* from the milk, butter and flour. Season it lightly with salt, pepper and nutmeg. Let cool. Stir in the grated cheese followed by the beaten eggs; taste for seasoning. Set aside 250 ml of the mixture.

Set the oven at moderately hot (190°C/375°F) and put a baking sheet in the oven to heat.

Line the pie pan* with the pastry and spoon in the larger amount of the cheese mixture. Bake the tart on the hot baking sheet for 20 minutes or until the edges of the pastry are brown. Raise the heat to very hot (220°C/425°F).

Split the asparagus tips lengthwise if they are large and arrange them pointing outwards in a ring on the partly-baked tart. Add the cream to the reserved cheese mixture and spoon it over the base of the tips. Bake the tart in the hot oven for 10 more minutes or until golden brown. Serve hot.

SALADE DE GRUYÈRE

Gruyère salad

Gruyère salad is also popular in Alsace as a first course before sauerkraut.

Serves 4–6

300 g	gruyère cheese	10 oz
	VINAIGRETTE	
	2 Tbsp wine vinegar	
	salt and pepper	
	6 Tbsp oil	
	1 large onion, finely chopped	
	1–2 Tbsp chopped herbs:	
	parsley, chervil or tarragon	

Make the vinaigrette*, adding the onion and herbs and taste for seasoning.

Cut the cheese into thin matchsticks about 2·5 cm/1 in long and put them in a serving bowl. Pour the vinaigrette over the cheese and mix well. Leave in a cool place for at least half an hour so the flavours blend. Taste for seasoning and serve at room temperature.

CROÛTES JURASSIENNES

Cheese and bacon toasts

Fried toasts like these can also be topped with mushrooms in a cream sauce – a good way of using stale bread.

Serves 4

	4 slices white bread	
	cut 2 cm/$\frac{3}{4}$ in thick	
90 g	butter	6 Tbsp
120 g	bacon, cut in lardons	4 oz
	1 onion, finely chopped	
30 g	flour	$\frac{1}{4}$ cup
375 ml	milk	$1\frac{1}{2}$ cups
	salt and pepper	
	pinch of grated nutmeg	
100 g	grated comté or gruyère cheese	1 cup
60 g	comté or gruyère cheese, cut in strips	2 oz

Cut the crusts from the bread and slightly hollow the centre of each slice to form a case. Heat two-thirds of the butter in a frying pan, add the bread cases and brown them on both sides; drain on paper towels. If the bacon is salty, blanch* it.

Heat the remaining butter in a small saucepan, add the onion and cook over a low fire, stirring until soft but not brown. Stir in the bacon and cook for 2 minutes. Sprinkle with the flour and continue to cook over a low fire, stirring constantly, until bubbling. Add the milk and bring to a boil, stirring. Simmer for 2–3 minutes and remove from the heat. Season the mixture with pepper and nutmeg. Let cool slightly; then stir in the grated cheese and taste again. Leave to cool.

Set the oven at very hot (230°C/450°F) or heat the grill/broiler. Set the bread cases on a baking sheet. Spoon the bacon and cheese mixture into them and put a few strips of cheese on each. Brown in the very hot oven or under the grill/broiler and serve immediately.

FONDUE SAVOYARDE

Cheese fondue

Fondue can be made with a combination of cheeses, or simply with gruyère, as here. It is usually prepared in a shallow earthenware saucepan, a 'caquelon'. The mixture must be heated gently but steadily, and stirred in a figure of eight (say the superstitious) so that the cheese melts in the wine without cooking into strings. If a man drops his piece of bread into the fondue, he must buy the party a bottle of wine; the penalty for women is a kiss all round.

Serves 4

	$\frac{1}{2}$ clove garlic	
250 ml	dry white wine	1 cup
500 g	gruyère or comté cheese, cut in thin strips	1 lb
	salt and pepper	
	3 Tbsp kirsch	
	1 loaf French or country bread, broken in small chunks (for serving)	
	caquelon (optional); 4 fondue forks	

Rub the inside of a caquelon or a heavy-based saucepan with the cut side of the garlic; then butter the pan. Add the wine and bring it to a boil. Stir in the cheese and heat it gently, stirring constantly with a wooden spoon – in a figure-of-eight motion – until the cheese is completely melted.

Just before serving, add salt, if needed, pepper and kirsch. Set the pan over a table burner in the middle of the table and let the guests help themselves, spearing pieces of bread on special long fondue forks and dipping them in the fondue.

FONDUE FRANCHE-COMTOISE

Beat 4 eggs and:

60 g	butter	4 Tbsp

into the prepared fondue and heat briefly, stirring constantly, until thickened. Serve as above.

OEUFS BROUILLÉS AUX CHAMPIGNONS SAUVAGES

Scrambled eggs with wild mushrooms

In Périgord they replace the morels in this Savoyard recipe with truffles (see variation below).

Serves 4

250 g	fresh morels OR	½ lb
25 g	dried girolles or morels	1 oz
125 g	butter	¼ lb
	1 Tbsp chopped parsley	
	salt and pepper	
	8–10 eggs	
	toast (optional)	

Prepare fresh or dried mushrooms*. Quarter them if large. Heat half the butter in a frying pan, add the mushrooms and sauté over a high fire, stirring often, until their excess liquid has evaporated. Remove from the heat. Add the parsley with salt and pepper to taste.

Beat the eggs with a little salt and pepper. Melt the remaining butter in a heavy saucepan, add the eggs and cook over a low fire, stirring constantly, until they begin to thicken – this should take at least 5 minutes. Don't cook the eggs too long or they will be dry. Stir in the mushrooms and taste for seasoning. Serve immediately. The eggs can also be served on toast.

OEUFS BROUILLÉS AUX POINTES D'ASPERGES

Use **12 asparagus spears** instead of the mushrooms. Peel them and simmer for 12–15 minutes (for white asparagus) or 8–10 minutes (for green asparagus) in a shallow pan of boiling salted water or until just tender. Drain, rinse with cold water and drain well. Cut the tips so they are about 4 cm/1½ in long. Dice the stalks, add them to the beaten eggs and scramble as above. Meanwhile, gently heat the tips in:

30 g	butter	2 Tbsp

without letting them brown. Spoon the eggs into a serving dish and decorate with the asparagus tips. Serve immediately.

OEUFS BROUILLÉS AUX TRUFFES

Use 1 small can of **truffle pieces** instead of the mushrooms and parsley. Beat the eggs with the truffles and leave for about 2 hours so that the truffle flavour permeates the eggs. Just before cooking the eggs, add salt and pepper. Melt:

60 g	butter	4 Tbsp

in a heavy saucepan and cook the eggs as above.

TRUITES AUX NOISETTES

Trout with hazelnuts

Legend has it that Hannibal enjoyed the local trout from the mountain streams when he crossed the Dauphiné with his elephants.

Serves 4

	2 lemons	
250 g each	4 trout	8 oz each
	salt and pepper	
30 g	flour	¼ cup
125 g	butter	¼ lb
65 g	peeled hazelnuts, halved	½ cup
	2 Tbsp chopped parsley	

Peel one lemon, removing the white pith as well as the rind, and cut the flesh in slices. Halve the other unpeeled lemon lengthwise; cut it in thin semi-circles.

Discard the fins from the trout and trim the tails to a 'V'. If the fish are not already cleaned, clean them through the gills without slitting the stomach. Rinse the trout under cold running water and pat dry. Sprinkle them with salt and pepper. Coat them with flour, patting to discard the excess.

Heat the butter in a large frying pan. Add the fish and brown them on both sides over a medium-high fire. Continue to cook over a low fire for 5 minutes on each side or until the flesh is no longer transparent. (Make a small cut near the head of one of the fish to check.) Transfer the trout to a platter, cover and keep warm.

Add the hazelnuts to the frying pan and sauté over a medium fire for 3–4 minutes or until lightly browned, stirring constantly. Pour the nuts with the butter over the trout. Decorate the platter with halved sliced lemons. Decorate each fish with whole slices of lemon and chopped parsley. Serve immediately.

QUENELLES NANTUA
Fish dumplings with crayfish sauce

The quenelles served in their home town of Nantua bear little resemblance to the ethereal puffs found in smart French restaurants. Local quenelles are akin to a home-made dumpling, a substantial complement to the all-important Nantua crayfish sauce. If freshwater crayfish are not available, use large prawns or shrimps and simmer them for 4 minutes.

Serves 6–8 as a first course or 4 as a main course

15 g	1 small can truffle pieces or whole truffles (optional)	½ oz
	QUENELLE MIXTURE	
1 kg	pike, whiting, haddock or other firm fish, including heads	2 lb
125 ml	water	½ cup
	salt and pepper	
60 g	butter	4 Tbsp
65 g	flour	½ cup
	2 large eggs	
	3–4 egg whites	
250 ml	heavy cream or crème fraîche*	1 cup
	pinch of grated nutmeg	
	NANTUA SAUCE	
500 ml	fish stock*, more if needed	2 cups
125 g	butter	¼ lb
	½ onion, finely chopped	
	½ carrot, finely chopped	
	12–16 crayfish	
	2–3 Tbsp cognac	
60 ml	white wine	¼ cup
	bouquet garni	
	salt and pepper	
25 g	flour	3 Tbsp
250 ml	heavy cream or crème fraîche*	1 cup
	½ tsp tomato paste (optional)	
	pinch of cayenne pepper	

Discard the fins, scale the fish and clean it. Fillet and skin the fish; you should have 500 g/1 lb fillets. Use the heads, tails and bones to make fish stock. Wash the fillets and pat dry.

For the quenelle mixture, make the choux pastry* from the water, salt, butter, flour and eggs, using less egg than usual to get a stiff mixture. Rub with butter to prevent a skin from forming, and let cool.

Continue making the quenelle mixture: finely chop the fish fillets, pass them twice through the fine plate of a mincer/grinder or purée them in a food processor. For the best texture, also work the fish through a fine sieve. Refrigerate the fish purée in a bowl for about 30 minutes or until well chilled. Set the bowl in a pan of ice and water. Lightly beat 3 of the egg whites and

gradually work them into the fish purée, beating vigorously with a wooden spoon. Beat in the choux pastry, a little at a time; then gradually beat in the cream followed by salt, pepper and nutmeg to taste. If the quenelle mixture is soft, salt will stiffen it slightly. Refrigerate if not using immediately.

To poach the quenelles: in a large shallow pan heat 6–7 cm/3 in of salted water until simmering. Using two tablespoons dipped in the pan of hot water, shape an oval of quenelle mixture and drop it into the pan of simmering water; if it starts to break up, add another lightly beaten egg white to the mixture and beat for another few minutes over ice. Shape the remaining mixture into ovals and drop them into the simmering water. Poach them for 10–15 minutes, depending on size, or until firm. Lift them out with a slotted spoon and drain on paper towels.

Meanwhile, begin the Nantua sauce: melt a third of the butter in a shallow pan and lightly sauté the chopped onion and carrot. Add the crayfish and sauté over a high fire until they turn red. Add 2 tablespoons cognac and flame it. Add the white wine, enough fish stock barely to cover, bouquet garni, salt and pepper. Simmer for 8–10 minutes, depending on the size of the crayfish. Remove the crayfish from the liquid and shell them, discarding the intestinal vein; reserve the tails. Pound the shells in a mortar with a pestle or in a bowl with the end of a rolling pin. Return them to the cooking liquid, simmer for 10 minutes and strain, pressing hard on the shells and vegetables. Reserve the liquid.

Melt half the remaining butter in a saucepan, whisk in the flour and cook for 1–2 minutes until foaming but not browned. Let cool slightly; then gradually whisk in the crayfish liquid. Bring the sauce to a boil, whisking constantly. Add a little salt and pepper and simmer for 10–15 minutes or until the sauce coats a spoon. Add the cream and bring back just to a boil. Tomato paste may be added to give the sauce a richer colour. If using truffle pieces, add them with their liquid. Check for seasoning, adding cayenne pepper and more cognac to taste. Off the heat, stir the remaining butter into the hot sauce. Set the oven at moderately hot (190°C/375°F).

Arrange the quenelles in individual heat-proof dishes, or in one large buttered baking dish; scatter the crayfish tails over them. Coat the quenelles and crayfish generously with the sauce. If using whole truffles, slice them and top each quenelle with a slice of truffle. Bake the quenelles in the oven for 10–15 minutes or until browned and slightly puffed. Serve very hot, from the baking dish.

WILD MUSHROOMS

For all but the richest of the rich in France, fresh wild mushrooms have taken the place of truffles as a gastronomic splurge. 'Morilles' (morels), 'cèpes' (boletus), 'girolles', 'mousserons', 'pleurotes' – together their season spans four or five months of the year and at their peak they can be relatively cheap. What is more, they can all be substituted for one another (with the possible exception of morels), leading to all sorts of cooking fun and games.

By far the finest of this half-dozen is the brown, pitted morel, the only fungus to approach the truffle in intensity of bouquet. Its season is relatively short, lasting only for the fresh, dewy weeks of late April and May. (In his final hours, Louis XIII, who died in May 1643, is said to have been stringing fresh morels to be dried.) Almost all come from remote elm, ash and fir forest clearings, and morel grounds are the jealously guarded secret of a few privileged gatherers who return year after year to retrieve their black gold. Morels must always be cooked – when raw they are toxic.

Less recherché, and about half the price, are cèpes, also known as 'bolets'. Big and fleshy, with a spongy underside, ceps grow in oak, chestnut and beech forests. Several varieties have camouflage tints of green and gold and the best of all is the brown *boletus edulis*. Equally recognizable, and just as good to eat, are the egg-yolk coloured, trumpet-shaped girolles or chanterelles, *cantharellus cibarius*.

Other wild mushrooms sold commercially – of some 80 edible varieties which grow in France – include the grey-black 'cornes d'abondance' *craterellus cornucopioides*, also known as 'trompettes de la mort' (trumpets of death). Far from being lethal, they taste good, and are sometimes used as a visual substitute for truffles when making pâtés. Their curling trumpet shape and dark colour are easy to

Oyster mushroom

spot in the mossy woods where they grow. Harder to find in shops are 'oronges' *amanita caesarea*, sometimes called Caesar's mushroom or royal agaric. Reddish, with yellow gills, they make excellent eating. 'Mousserons' or fairy ring mushrooms *marasmius oreades*, being pale, spindly and fragile, do not travel well, though they are excellent eaten on the spot. Tougher altogether are the robust 'pied de mouton' *hydnum repandum*, the rubber brush or pig's trotter, and the pleurote or oyster mushroom *pleurotus ostreatus*, which is sometimes named 'weeper' from the amount of liquid it produces in the pan. With the exception of pleurotes, these mushrooms defy cultivation, many of them growing in woodland humus which is impossible to reproduce artificially.

Fresh wild mushrooms are a seasonal treat, but luckily they dry well and in many speciality grocery shops morèls, girolles and cèpes can be found all year round, though they are not cheap. Wild mushrooms can also be frozen, and retain their aroma and taste very well. Canned wild mushrooms may be a disappointment, however, since they tend to acquire a glutinous texture.

Wild mushrooms suit strong flavours like game or beef and make a refreshing change from cultivated ones in soups and sauces (as an economy, use half and half).

But perhaps wild mushrooms are at their best plainly sautéed in butter with garlic and herbs or combined with creamy scrambled eggs. 'Food of the Gods', said the ancient Greeks – yes, indeed!

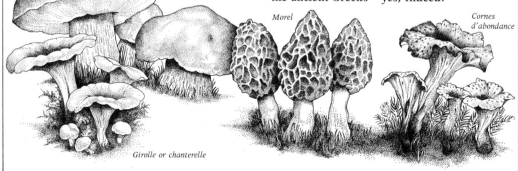
Cèpe

Morel

Cornes d'abondance

Girolle or chanterelle

POULET AUX MORILLES

Chicken with morels and cream

In the Jura the 'vin jaune' of Arbois is preferred for making this dish.

Serves 4

250 g	fresh morels OR	$\frac{1}{2}$ lb
25 g	dried morels	1 oz
1·5-kg	chicken	3-lb
80 g	butter	5 Tbsp
	salt and pepper	
250 ml	dry white wine	1 cup
185 ml	heavy cream or crème fraîche*	$\frac{3}{4}$ cup
	juice of $\frac{1}{2}$ lemon, or to taste	

Prepare fresh or dried morels*. Cut the chicken* in 8 pieces. Heat half the butter in a heavy casserole, add the chicken pieces and brown them on all sides over a medium fire. Sprinkle with salt and pepper and remove. Add the remaining butter and the morels to the casserole and cook over a high fire for 5 minutes. Stir in the wine and bring to a boil, stirring to dissolve the pan juices. Return the chicken pieces to the casserole, cover and cook over a low fire for another 30–40 minutes or until the chicken is tender. Remove the chicken pieces and keep them warm while finishing the sauce. Skim the excess fat from the cooking liquid.

Add the cream to the morels and liquid and simmer for 5 minutes. Taste for seasoning, adding lemon juice, salt and pepper. Return the chicken pieces to the sauce and reheat briefly. Serve from the casserole.

POULET AU COMTÉ

Chicken with cheese sauce

Some of the finest gruyère, called comté, is made in Franche-Comté.

Serves 4

1·5-kg	chicken	3-lb
	salt and pepper	
30 g	flour	$\frac{1}{4}$ cup
60 g	butter	4 Tbsp
375 ml	dry white wine	$1\frac{1}{2}$ cups
250 ml	broth or water	1 cup
	pinch of cayenne pepper	
	pinch of grated nutmeg	
65 g	grated comté or gruyère cheese (for sprinkling)	$\frac{2}{3}$ cup
	SAUCE	
45 g	butter	3 Tbsp
25 g	flour	3 Tbsp
	2 egg yolks	
125 ml	heavy cream or crème fraîche*	$\frac{1}{2}$ cup
35 g	grated comté or gruyère cheese	6 Tbsp
	1·5 L/1$\frac{1}{2}$ qt shallow baking dish	

Set the oven at hot (200°C/400°F). Cut the chicken* in 4 pieces. Season the pieces with salt and pepper and coat them with flour, patting off the excess. Heat the butter in a sauté pan, add the chicken pieces and brown them on all sides over a medium fire. Stir in the white wine and bring to a boil; then stir in the broth with a pinch of nutmeg and cayenne pepper and return to a boil. Bake uncovered in the oven for 30–40 minutes or until the chicken is just tender. Transfer the pieces to the buttered baking dish, reserving the cooking liquid. Raise the oven temperature to very hot (220°C/425°F).

Prepare the sauce: skim any fat from the cooking liquid. Melt the butter in a saucepan, whisk in the flour and cook over a low fire until just bubbling. Strain in the reserved cooking liquid and bring to a boil, whisking. Simmer over a low fire, whisking often, for 5–10 minutes or until the sauce is well flavoured and of coating consistency. Taste for seasoning, adding more nutmeg and cayenne if necessary.

Just before serving, beat the egg yolks with the cream. Whisk a little of the warm sauce into the yolk mixture; then return this mixture to the remaining sauce. Heat briefly, whisking until slightly thickened; don't boil or the sauce will curdle. Remove from the heat and stir in the cheese. Taste for seasoning.

Pour the sauce over the chicken pieces and sprinkle with the remaining cheese. Bake in the very hot oven for 5 minutes or until golden brown; then serve from the baking dish.

PERDREAUX AUX FIDÉS

Baked partridge with noodles and cheese

Italian influence has made pasta common in the French Alps, leading Stendhal to insist on eating pasta whenever he visited Grenoble. 'Fidés' resemble vermicelli, but unlike larger noodles they are cooked 'à la fide', first sautéed in butter before being simmered in broth. Pheasant or chicken are excellent cooked in the same way as the partridge here.

Serves 4

250 g each	2 partridges	8 oz each
	salt and pepper	
125 g	butter	$\frac{1}{4}$ lb
250 ml	dry white wine	1 cup
100 g	bacon, cut in lardons	$3\frac{1}{2}$ oz
100 g	vermicelli noodles	$3\frac{1}{2}$ oz
	1 onion, chopped	
100 g	gruyère cheese, cut in thin strips	$3\frac{1}{2}$ oz
250 ml	broth	1 cup
	trussing needle and string	

Truss the partridges and sprinkle them lightly with salt and pepper. Heat half the butter in a small heavy casserole, add the partridges and brown them on all sides. Pour in the wine, cover and simmer over a low fire for 20–25 minutes or until the birds are almost tender. Remove the partridges and cut them in half, discarding the trussing strings and the backbone. Set the oven at very hot (220°C/425°F). If the bacon is salty, blanch* it.

Heat the remaining butter in a sauté pan and add the dry noodles, onion and bacon. Cook over a medium fire, stirring constantly, until the noodles are light brown.

Transfer the noodle mixture to a buttered shallow baking dish and arrange the halved partridges on top. Season very lightly with salt and pepper. Scatter the strips of cheese over the partridges and pour the wine from cooking the birds and the broth into the dish. Bake in the hot oven for 10–15 minutes or until the liquid has been absorbed by the noodles and the cheese has browned. Serve hot from the dish.

NOIX DE VEAU À L'AIXOISE

Braised veal with vegetables and chestnuts

Veal dries out easily during roasting, so it is best cooked with a little broth or wine to keep it moist, as in this recipe from Aix-les-Bains. 'Noix' is a roast of veal consisting of the long tapering muscle from the centre leg, but any compact cut will do.

Serves 6

360 g	fresh chestnuts	12 oz
1 kg	veal leg, centre roast	2 lb
75 g	butter	5 Tbsp
	3 celery hearts, halved	
	12 baby onions	
	12 baby carrots OR	
	4 large carrots, quartered	
	12 baby turnips OR	
	4 medium turnips, quartered	
250 ml	broth	1 cup
	salt and pepper	
	pinch of thyme	
	1 bay leaf	
	trussing string	

Peel fresh chestnuts*.

Tie the veal roast in a neat, compact shape. Heat the butter in a heavy casserole, add the veal and brown it well on all sides over a medium-high fire. Remove the meat, add all the vegetables and brown them lightly also. Return the roast to the casserole, moving the vegetables so they are around, not under, the veal. Add the broth, salt, pepper, thyme and bay leaf. Cover and simmer over a very low fire, turning the veal over occasionally, for $1\frac{1}{2}$ hours or until the meat is tender.

When the veal is tender, remove it and discard the strings. Cut the meat in medium slices and transfer them to a platter. With a slotted spoon transfer the vegetables to the platter around the meat; cover and keep warm.

Skim any fat from the gravy. Taste and, if necessary, boil to reduce until well-flavoured. Discard the bay leaf and taste for seasoning. Moisten the pieces of veal with a little gravy and serve the rest separately.

BLANQUETTE DE VEAU
White veal stew

Traditionally, a good blanquette uses whole veal breast, the bones for flavour and cartilage for richness. Shoulder may be included for lean meat, but country cooks rarely bother. Above all, nothing should brown during cooking to mar the blanquette's whiteness.

Serves 6

1 kg	veal breast, including bones, cut in chunks	2 lb
500 g	boneless veal shoulder, cut in 5 cm/2 in pieces, OR	1 lb
1 kg	more veal breast	2 lb
1·5 L	water	$1\frac{1}{2}$ qt
	1 onion, quartered, studded with 1 clove	
	1 carrot, quartered	
	1 clove garlic	
	bouquet garni	
	salt and pepper	
	24–30 baby onions	
250 g	mushrooms, quartered if large (optional)	$\frac{1}{2}$ lb
45 g	butter	3 Tbsp
25 g	flour	3 Tbsp
	2 egg yolks	
125 ml	heavy cream or crème fraîche*	$\frac{1}{2}$ cup

Put the veal in a large pot and add enough water to cover. Bring slowly to a boil, skimming often. Add the onion, carrot, garlic, bouquet garni, salt and pepper. Cover and simmer over a low fire, skimming occasionally, for $1-1\frac{1}{4}$ hours or until the veal is nearly tender. Remove the onion, carrot, garlic and bouquet garni; taste the liquid for seasoning. Add the baby onions and mushrooms and simmer, covered, for another 15 minutes or until the veal, mushrooms and onions are tender. Transfer them to a bowl and keep warm. Reserve the cooking liquid.

Melt the butter in a saucepan, add the flour and cook over a low fire, whisking, until foaming but not browned. Whisk in the reserved cooking liquid and bring to a boil, whisking constantly. Simmer for 15 minutes or until the sauce is well flavoured and of coating consistency. Just before serving, beat the egg yolks with the cream. Whisk a little of the hot sauce into the yolk mixture; then whisk this mixture back into the sauce. Cook over a low fire, whisking constantly, for one minute or until the sauce thickens slightly; don't boil or the sauce will curdle. Add the meat and vegetables and taste for seasoning. Keep the blanquette warm for 5–10 minutes so the flavours blend; then transfer to a bowl and serve.

ESCALOPE DE VEAU BELLE COMTOISE
Veal escalope with ham and cheese

Local cooks like to make this dish with aged comté cheese and with smoked ham from the town of Luxeuil in northern Franche-Comté.

Serves 6

	3 eggs	
80 ml	oil	$\frac{1}{3}$ cup
	salt and pepper	
30 g	flour	$\frac{1}{4}$ cup
140 g	fresh breadcrumbs	1 cup
120 g each	6 veal escalopes	4 oz each
	6 thin slices comté or gruyère cheese	
	6 thin slices smoked ham	
185 g	butter	6 oz

In a large shallow dish, beat the eggs with the oil and a pinch of salt and pepper. Put the flour in another dish and the breadcrumbs in a third. Pound the veal escalopes between two sheets of moistened greaseproof/parchment paper until very thin. Cut the cheese and ham slices in the same shape as the escalopes. Dip each escalope in flour and pat off the excess; then dip it in the egg mixture and lastly in the breadcrumbs. Press a slice of cheese on to each escalope. Dip each slice of ham in the flour, egg and breadcrumbs and set it on the cheese. Press with the broad part of a large knife to make the ham and cheese adhere. Set the oven at moderate (175°C/350°F).

Heat one-third of the butter in a very large, ovenproof frying pan and add the escalopes, veal side down. Cook over a low fire for 3 minutes or until lightly browned. Turn the escalopes over, transfer the pan to the oven and bake for 10 minutes or until the veal is tender and the cheese is melted.

Meanwhile, heat the remaining butter in a saucepan until nut-brown. Transfer the veal to a platter and serve, passing the brown butter separately.

CÔTELETTES DE MOUTON COMTOISE
Mutton chops with creamed onions
These mutton chops should be slightly charred to contrast with the creamy onions.

Serves 6

1 kg	large onions, thinly sliced	2 lb
	salt and pepper	
80 g	butter	5 Tbsp
	6 mutton or lamb chops, about 1 cm/⅜ in thick	
125 ml	heavy cream or crème fraîche*	½ cup

Put the onions in a pot of boiling salted water and boil for 5 minutes or until softened; drain thoroughly. Melt the butter in a sauté pan, add the onions, salt and pepper and cook over medium heat, stirring often, until lightly browned.

Heat the grill/broiler and cook the chops for 3–4 minutes on each side or until well browned but still pink inside; when pressed with a finger, they should spring back slightly without being too firm. Sprinkle with salt and pepper.

Stir the cream into the onions, heat thoroughly and taste for seasoning. Spoon the onions on to a deep platter and set the chops on top. Serve immediately.

TOURNEDOS DAUPHINOISE
Tournedos with wild mushrooms
In the Dauphiné frail, spindly 'mousserons' are a favourite for this recipe, but they travel poorly and lose their flavour when dried. Any fresh or dried wild mushrooms may be substituted , for example, cèpes, girolles or morels.

Serves 4

250 g	fresh OR	½ lb
25 g	dried wild mushrooms	1 oz
60 g	butter	4 Tbsp
	1 Tbsp flour	
185 ml	heavy cream or crème fraîche*	¾ cup
	salt and pepper	
	4 tournedos steaks 4 cm/1½ in thick	
185 ml	dry white wine	¾ cup
	4 croûtes* cut the same diameter as the steaks, sautéed in butter	

Prepare fresh or dried mushrooms*. Heat half the butter in a frying pan, add the mushrooms and sauté over a high fire until most of their liquid has evaporated. Sprinkle them with the flour and cook over a low fire, stirring, for about 1 minute. Stir in the cream and a little salt and pepper and simmer for 2–3 minutes. Remove from the heat and keep warm.

Heat the remaining butter in a frying pan, add the tournedos steaks and sauté over a high fire, allowing about 3 minutes on each side for rare steak. Season the tournedos after turning. Transfer them to a dish and keep warm.

Add the wine to the frying pan and bring to a boil, stirring to dissolve the pan juices. Boil until reduced by about half; add the wine to the mushroom mixture and taste for seasoning.

To serve, set each tournedos on a croûte. Spoon the creamed mushrooms over them and serve immediately.

GRILLADE MARINIÈRE DE VALENCE
Sailor's steak with anchovies
In the centuries preceding the railway, barges were pulled by draught-horses up the Rhône to Valence. Superfluous for the journey downstream, these horses were often killed by the sailors ('marins'), who made them into a good steak dish flavoured with Provençal anchovies, onions and white wine. Nowadays a beef cut such as round or rump steak in Britain, and chuck or round in the USA, would be more fashionable.

Serves 4

625 g	beef stewing steak, cut 2·5 cm/1 in thick	1¼ lb
	salt and pepper	
60 ml	olive oil	¼ cup
350 g	onions, thinly sliced	¾ lb
80 g	butter	5 Tbsp
8 g	flour	1 Tbsp
	1 Tbsp vinegar	
	6 anchovy fillets, chopped	
	2 cloves garlic, chopped	
	2 Tbsp chopped parsley	

Cut the steak in 4 pieces and sprinkle them very lightly with salt and pepper; don't use too much salt since anchovies will be added later. Spread about 2 teaspoons of the oil in a heavy casserole and add a layer of half the onions. Lay the steaks on top and cover with the remaining onions. Soften the butter and work in the flour to make a smooth paste; put it in pieces on the onions. Cover and cook over a low fire for 30 minutes.

Mix the remaining oil with the vinegar, anchovies, garlic, parsley and a small pinch of salt and pepper. Pour the mixture over the meat and stir well to distribute the flour-butter mixture. Cover and simmer over a very low fire for another 1½ hours or until the meat is very tender. Serve hot, from the casserole.

GAME

The French and their rulers have long been ardent hunters; it was the sporting King Louis XI (he later became a saint) who in the 15th century laid down the first laws limiting the chase. Such rules proved more than necessary. In August 1789, Arthur Young was 'pestered with all the mob of the country shooting: one would think that every rusty gun in Provence is at work, killing all sorts of birds: the shot has fallen five or six times in my chaise and about my ears.' The same phenomenon can still be experienced in early autumn, when the hunting season opens in rural France. Every field of roots and patch of woodland is lined with hunters equipped to the teeth for the sport.

The higher, less accessible parts of Savoy and the Jura still harbour a good many deer, though 'chamois' (a goat-like antelope) and 'moufflon' (wild sheep) are protected by law. Meat from deer can vary considerably, the more so because 'chevreuil' (venison) can come from roe, fallow or red deer. Roe deer is the finest, but to tackle the commoner red deer says one authority, requires 'the appetite of a wolf'. Not so with 'sanglier' (mature wild boar) while baby boar or 'marcassin' is a delicacy. The strongest-tasting game animal of all is hare, whose nearest North American equivalent is jack rabbit or arctic rabbit. Often sold with its blood to thicken the sauce for a 'civet de lièvre', hare calls for a strong stomach and a full-bodied red wine as accompaniment.

Most pheasant, partridge, quail and pigeon which appear in markets have been raised like domestic fowl. At best they may be released for a few brief weeks of liberty, to fall victim to the gun of the well-to-do hunter who can afford to stock his coverts with hand-raised birds. In the kitchen, partridge and pheasant are generally interchangeable, though partridge are half the size of pheasant and have a more delicate flavour. With wild duck, as with deer, cookbooks rarely distinguish the types; they vary from region to region and in recipes they are all treated alike.

Hanging game to age it, so that the meat is tender and the flavour ripe, has never been the custom in France, as in England. The French regard a few days for a bird or a deer as ample. The best way to cook game, on the other hand, is a matter for constant debate: to marinate or not to marinate. One school of thought, led by the chefs of 'nouvelle cuisine', maintains that marinating obscures the taste. Traditionalists who like their game tender and the flavour mellow continue, however, to immerse venison and boar in red wine and appropriate herbs for two or three days. This is enough, for after several days in a strong marinade, the original flavour of any meat disappears entirely. Lamb can be taken for venison and beef for boar, a fact appreciated by dishonest restaurateurs who ignore the legitimate names of the dishes – 'gigot en chevreuil' and 'tournedos en sanglier'.

RAGOÛT DE LA VALLÉE DE LA BIRSE

Venison stew with juniper and cream

This ragoût can be made with wild boar or with hare as an alternative to venison.

Serves 6

1·5 kg	boned loin or haunch of venison, cut in 5 cm/2 in cubes	3 lb
30 g	butter	2 Tbsp
30 g	lard	2 Tbsp
15 g	flour	2 Tbsp
	salt and pepper	
250 ml	heavy cream or crème fraîche*	1 cup
	MARINADE	
750 ml	red wine	3 cups
	2 onions, quartered	
	4 shallots, halved	
	3 cloves garlic	
	1 leek, trimmed, split and sliced	
	2 carrots, sliced	
	1 Tbsp juniper berries	
	2 Tbsp oil	

Put the meat in a deep bowl with the marinade ingredients, adding the oil last. Marinate in the refrigerator for 2–3 days, stirring occasionally.

Drain the meat, reserving the marinade, and pat the meat dry with paper towels. Heat the butter and lard in a large heavy casserole, add the meat and sauté over a high fire until the meat is lightly browned on all sides. Add the onions and shallots from the marinade and continue to sauté until the onions and shallots are lightly browned. Sprinkle with the flour and stir over a low fire until the flour is lightly browned. Stir in the marinade, add salt and pepper and bring to a boil. Cover and simmer, stirring occasionally, for 1½–2 hours or until the meat is tender.

Transfer the meat to a serving dish and keep it warm. Skim any fat from the sauce. Boil the sauce, stirring often, for 5–10 minutes or until it is well flavoured and thick enough to lightly coat a spoon; then add the cream and bring back to a boil. Taste for seasoning and strain the sauce over the meat. Serve hot.

POIREAUX À LA SAVOYARDE

Leeks with cheese and breadcrumbs

Another version of a Savoyard gratin, this recipe can also be made with vegetables such as courgettes/zucchini, cabbage, celeriac/celery root, with celery itself and even with onions.

Serves 4

1·5 kg	leeks	3 lb
	salt and pepper	
	$\frac{1}{2}$ clove garlic	
45 g	butter	3 Tbsp
25 g	dried breadcrumbs	$\frac{1}{4}$ cup
100 g	grated gruyère cheese	1 cup
	pinch of grated nutmeg	

Split the leeks down to the white and clean them thoroughly under running water. Use only the white and the most tender part of the green leaves (the remaining dark green part can be used for soup). Put the leeks in a large pot of boiling salted water and cook over a high fire for 15 minutes or until tender; drain thoroughly. Set the oven at very hot (220°C/425°F).

Rub a baking dish with the cut side of the garlic and then spread the butter in the dish. Put in half the leeks and sprinkle them with half the breadcrumbs and cheese. Season with salt, pepper and nutmeg. Arrange the remaining leeks on top and sprinkle them with the rest of the breadcrumbs, and with grated cheese, salt, pepper and nutmeg.

Bake in the oven for 10–15 minutes or until golden brown. Serve from the baking dish.

GRATIN SAVOYARD

Potato and cheese gratin

Beaufort, a type of gruyère made near the Swiss frontier, is the favourite cheese for this dish.

Serves 6

1 kg	potatoes	2 lb
	salt and pepper	
	pinch of grated nutmeg	
175 g	grated beaufort or gruyère cheese	1¾ cups
250 ml	broth, more if needed	1 cup
60 g	butter	4 Tbsp
	1·5 L/1½ qt shallow baking dish	

Set the oven at hot (200°C/400°F). Cut the potatoes in very thin slices, using a mandoline cutter if possible. Don't soak them in water as this removes some of the starch needed to bind the gratin. Spread a layer of potato slices in the buttered baking dish and sprinkle them lightly but evenly with salt, pepper, nutmeg and some of the grated cheese. Continue making layers until all the potatoes and cheese are used,

finishing with a layer of cheese. Arrange the top layer of potatoes in a pattern. Pour enough broth down the side of the dish to come almost up to the top layer of potatoes. Dot with butter.

Bake in the hot oven for 10 minutes; then lower the heat to moderate (175°C/350°F) and continue baking another 50 minutes or until the potatoes are golden brown and tender when pricked with a fork. Add more broth during cooking if the potatoes are dry. At the end they should be moist but not soupy. Serve hot from the baking dish.

GRATIN DAUPHINOIS

Potato gratin with cheese and cream

If cooked too fast or for too long, the milk in gratin dauphinois has a tendency to curdle (potatoes have an unexpectedly high acid content). So, in this splendidly rich recipe, the potatoes are first blanched in milk to remove the acid, then simmered in cream.

Serves 6

	$\frac{1}{2}$ clove garlic	
750 g	potatoes	1½ lb
	salt and pepper	
	pinch of grated nutmeg	
500 ml	milk	2 cups
310 ml	heavy cream or crème fraîche*	1¼ cups
50 g	grated gruyère cheese (optional)	$\frac{1}{2}$ cup
30 g	butter	2 Tbsp
	shallow baking dish (about 1·25 L/1¼ qt capacity)	

Rub the baking dish with the cut side of the garlic; then butter the dish.

Peel the potatoes and cut them in thin slices, preferably on a mandoline cutter. Don't soak them in water as this removes some of the starch needed to give the gratin a creamy consistency. Season the slices with salt, pepper and nutmeg.

Bring the milk to a boil in a large saucepan, whisking occasionally to prevent it from burning. Add the potatoes to the boiling milk and simmer for 10–15 minutes or until slightly tender. Drain the potatoes and discard the milk or save it for soup. Set the oven at very hot (220°C/425°F).

Return the potatoes to the saucepan and add the cream. Bring to a boil and simmer, stirring occasionally, for another 10–15 minutes or until the potatoes are tender but not falling apart. Taste for seasoning.

Spoon the potatoes and cream into the buttered baking dish, sprinkle with cheese and dot with butter. Bake for 10–15 minutes or until golden brown. Serve hot from the dish.

MONT BLANC

Meringue with chestnuts and cream

Chestnut trees are common in the mountains and with imagination this combination of chestnut purée, meringue and whipped cream can be held to resemble its lofty namesake. Mont Blanc can also be made as individual gâteaux.

Serves 6

	MERINGUE	
	2 egg whites	
100 g	sugar	$\frac{1}{2}$ cup
	CHESTNUT PURÉE	
1 kg	fresh or canned	2 lb
	unsweetened chestnuts	
	1 vanilla bean OR	
	1 tsp vanilla extract	
250 ml	water	1 cup
135 g	sugar	$\frac{2}{3}$ cup
	TOPPING	
375 ml	heavy cream	$1\frac{1}{2}$ cups
50 g	sugar	$\frac{1}{4}$ cup
	1 tsp vanilla extract	
	1 egg white	
15 g	semi-sweet chocolate	$\frac{1}{2}$ oz

pastry bag, 1·25 cm/$\frac{1}{2}$ in and 3 mm/$\frac{1}{8}$ in plain tips

Thoroughly butter a baking sheet, sprinkle it with flour and mark a 23 cm/9 in circle. Set the oven at low (140°C/285°F).

Make the meringue: whip the egg whites, preferably in a copper bowl, until they hold stiff peaks. Add 2 tablespoons of the sugar and whisk for 30 seconds or until the mixture is glossy. Gently fold in the remaining sugar. Using the pastry bag and the larger tip, pipe the meringue in a spiral within the marked circle on the prepared baking sheet. Bake for 1 hour or until the meringue is firm; if it starts to brown, lower the oven temperature. Transfer to a rack to cool, loosening the meringue with a spatula.

Prepare the chestnuts: peel fresh chestnuts* and put them in a saucepan with the vanilla bean and enough water to cover. (If using vanilla extract, don't add it yet.) Bring to a boil, cover and simmer for 25–30 minutes or until the nuts are very tender. Canned chestnuts do not need to be cooked. Drain and work the fresh or canned chestnuts in a hand food mill or electric food processor to a fine powder.

In a small saucepan heat 250 ml water and the sugar until dissolved; bring just to a boil and leave to cool. Gradually beat enough of this syrup into the chestnut powder until it is thin enough to make a purée, yet thick enough to hold a shape. If a vanilla bean was not used, add the vanilla essence/extract. With the pastry bag and smaller tip, pipe several layers of the chestnut purée in a rough zigzag pattern around the edge of the meringue base; the layered curlicues of purée should resemble a bird's nest.

Make the topping: in a chilled bowl beat the cream until it starts to thicken. Add 1 tablespoon of the sugar and the vanilla and continue beating until the cream is stiff enough to stick to the whisk. Whip the egg white until stiff, add the remaining sugar and whip until very stiff. Fold the egg white into the cream and spoon this mixture into the centre of the nest, shaping it in a peak. Grate the chocolate over the peak of whipped cream, leaving the lower slopes uncovered. Chill until ready to serve.

TARTE DES ALPES

Latticed plum tart

Tarte or 'tourte' des Alpes was originally a winter dish, made with fruits – plums, apricots, strawberries, raspberries – that had been dried in the sun; Savoy is the great raspberry producer of France. The fruit should be simmered with sugar to a pulp, then covered with a pastry lattice. Today's tarts all too often contain jam.

Serves 6–8

	PIE PASTRY	
200 g	flour	$1\frac{1}{2}$ cups
95 g	butter, softened	6 Tbsp
	$\frac{1}{2}$ tsp salt	
80 ml	milk, more as needed	$\frac{1}{3}$ cup
	1 egg, beaten with $\frac{1}{2}$ tsp salt	
	(for glaze)	
	PLUM FILLING	
500 g	plums, pitted	1 lb
200 g	sugar	1 cup
60 ml	water	$\frac{1}{4}$ cup

Make the pie pastry*. Wrap and chill for 30 minutes or until firm.

For the filling: put the plums in a heavy pot with the sugar and water. Bring to a boil and simmer uncovered over a low fire, stirring often, for 50–60 minutes or until very thick and most of the liquid has evaporated. Leave to cool completely. Set the oven at hot (200°C/400°F).

Roll three-quarters of the dough to a 27 cm/11 in round; put on a baking sheet. Spread the filling on top to within 5 cm/2 in of the edge. Roll out the remaining dough and cut in thin strips. Twist them a few times and arrange in a lattice over the filling, pressing them on to the border of dough. Turn in the edges over the ends of the strips; glaze border and strips lightly. Chill 15 minutes.

Bake the tart in the hot oven for 30–40 minutes or until the pastry is golden brown; if the pastry browns too quickly reduce the heat to medium (175°C/350°F). Cool on a rack.

CHARLOTTE COMTOISE AUX POMMES

Apple charlotte with wine

The key to making a successful apple charlotte is to reduce the apple purée thoroughly so that the charlotte does not collapse when unmoulded.

Serves 4–6

2 kg	dessert apples	4½ lb
185 g	butter	6 oz
125 ml	dry white wine, preferably Jura 'vin jaune'	½ cup
	pinch of ground cinnamon	
150 g	sugar, or to taste	¾ cup
	10–12 slices firm white bread, crusts removed	
	1 L/1 qt charlotte mould	

Peel, core and thinly slice the apples. Melt half the butter in a heavy-based pan and add the apples, wine and cinnamon. Cover and cook over a low fire, stirring occasionally, for 20-25 minutes or until the apples are very soft. Uncover, add the sugar and cook over a medium fire, stirring constantly, until the purée is so thick that it falls heavily from the spoon. If the purée is too soft, the charlotte will collapse when it is unmoulded. Taste and add more sugar if necessary. Set the oven at hot (200°C/400°F). Line the base of the mould with a round of buttered greaseproof/parchment paper.

Meanwhile, clarify* all but a tablespoon of the remaining butter. Cut 7–8 slices of bread in half to form fingers to line the sides of the mould. Cut 2 more slices in triangles to line the base. Dip each finger of bread quickly in the clarified butter and arrange them overlapping on the sides of the mould. Dip the triangles and arrange them in a pattern on the base. Fill in any holes with small pieces of bread dipped in butter.

Fill the mould with the apple mixture and mound the centre slightly (it will sink during cooking). Cover with 3–4 fingers cut from the rest of the bread and dot with the remaining tablespoon of butter. Bake in the hot oven for 15 minutes or until the bread begins to brown. Lower the heat to moderate (175°C/350°F) and bake for 35–40 minutes longer or until the charlotte is firm and the sides are golden brown.

If serving hot, let the charlotte stand 10-15 minutes before unmoulding it on to a hot platter. If serving cold, chill the charlotte and unmould it just before serving.

BISCUIT DE SAVOIE

Light sponge cake

'Biscuit de Savoie' is said to have been created in the 14th century by the pastry cook of Count Amédée VI of Savoy. During a visit the Holy Roman Emperor was so impressed by the immense gâteau presented to him in the shape of a map of Savoy, that he promptly named Amédée 'Vicaire Générale' of the Empire.

Today's less grandiose biscuit de Savoie is distinguished by its lightness since it always contains some potato starch or some cornflour/cornstarch instead of all flour; arrowroot can also be used. For a cake with an attractive fluted shape, the batter can be baked in a large brioche mould.

Serves 4–6

60 g	flour	7 Tbsp
60 g	potato starch	7 Tbsp
	tiny pinch of salt	
30 g	butter	2 Tbsp
	4 eggs, separated	
135 g	granulated sugar	⅔ cup
	½ tsp vanilla extract, grated rind of 1 lemon, 1 tsp orange flower water OR 2–3 drops anise oil (for flavouring)	
	4 Tbsp sliced almonds	
	confectioners' sugar (for sprinkling)	
	20 cm/8 in springform pan	

Brush the cake pan with melted butter, line the base with a circle of greaseproof/parchment or waxed paper and butter it also. Sprinkle the pan with granulated sugar, discarding the excess. Set the oven at moderate (175°C/350°F).

Sift the flour and potato starch with the salt two or three times. Melt the butter for the cake batter and leave to cool.

Beat the egg yolks with half the sugar and the flavouring until thick and light and the mixture leaves a thick ribbon trail when the whisk is lifted. Whip the egg whites until stiff, if possible using a copper bowl; then add the remaining sugar and beat another 20 seconds or until this meringue is very stiff and glossy. As lightly as possible, fold the flour mixture and meringue alternately into the egg yolk mixture in two or three batches, adding the melted butter with the last batch of egg whites.

Pour the batter into the prepared cake pan. Sprinkle with sliced almonds; then sprinkle generously with the sugar. Bake in the heated oven for 40–45 minutes or until the cake shrinks slightly from the sides of the pan and the top springs back when lightly pressed with a fingertip. Run a knife around the sides of the cake to loosen it and turn out on to a rack to cool. The cake is best if served the day it is baked.

GÂTEAU GRENOBLOIS
Walnut cake

To the French taste this is an unusually rich and moist cake. It needs only a light caramel topping or can be served plain, in contrast to many drier French cakes that are balanced by rich fillings.

Serves 6–8

	2 slices white bread	
150 g	butter	5 oz
135 g	sugar	⅔ cup
	4 eggs, separated	
	grated rind of 1 lemon	
160 g	walnuts, ground	1⅓ cups
	TOPPING	
100 g	sugar	½ cup
60 ml	water	¼ cup
	8 walnut halves	

23–25 cm/9–10 in round cake pan or springform pan

Set the oven at moderately low (160°C/325°F). Toast the bread in the oven until very dry. Let it cool; then either grind it to a fine powder in a food processor or crush it with a rolling pin. Butter the cake pan and line it with a round of buttered greaseproof/parchment paper.

Cream the butter in a bowl, add two-thirds of the sugar and beat until very light. Add the egg yolks, one at a time, beating after each addition until smooth. Stir in the lemon rind followed by the breadcrumbs and the ground walnuts.

In a large bowl, beat the egg whites until stiff. Add the remaining sugar and continue beating for 30 seconds or until glossy. Gently fold one-quarter of the egg whites into the nut batter; then fold this mixture back into the remaining whites as lightly as possible. Spoon the mixture into the cake pan and bake for 1–1¼ hours or until a skewer inserted into the cake comes out dry; if the cake browns too quickly, cover it with a sheet of foil. Unmould the cake on to a rack and leave to cool.

Meanwhile, make the topping: in a heavy saucepan, heat the sugar in the water over low heat until dissolved, stirring occasionally. Raise the heat and boil until the sugar becomes a golden brown caramel. Immediately pour the hot caramel over the cake, and, using a metal spatula, spread it quickly to a thin layer. Take care because hot caramel can cause bad burns. Decorate at once with the walnut halves so they stick to the caramel. Leave to cool so the caramel becomes crisp.

TARTELETTES AUX NOIX
Walnut tartlets

In France these tartlets with their caramel and walnut filling would be served with tea or coffee in the afternoon.

Makes 8 tartlets

	SWEET PIE PASTRY	
130 g	flour	1 cup
	3 egg yolks	
	pinch of salt	
65 g	sugar	⅓ cup
	¾ tsp vanilla extract	
80 g	butter	5 Tbsp
	NUT FILLING	
	1 Tbsp honey	
160 ml	heavy cream	⅔ cup
300 g	sugar	1½ cups
	pinch of cream of tartar	
125 ml	water	½ cup
180 g	walnut halves, broken in half	1½ cups

8 small tartlet pans (about 7·5 cm/3 in diameter)

Make the sweet pie pastry* and chill for at least 30 minutes or until firm. Line* the tartlet moulds, being especially careful to give them a high edge. Blind bake* and leave to cool.

Meanwhile, prepare the filling: mix together the honey and cream. Put the sugar, cream of tartar and water in a deep, heavy-based saucepan and heat until dissolved. Raise the heat and boil to a light brown caramel. Stir in the cream mixture, standing back because it will splutter. Boil without stirring until the mixture reaches the soft ball stage (115°C/240°F on a sugar thermometer). Take care as the hot mixture of cream and caramel can cause severe burns. Turn down the heat to low; then immediately stir in the walnuts and remove from the heat. Spoon the filling into the cool tartlet shells. Serve at room temperature.

WALNUTS

Throughout the mountains, particularly in the Dauphiné, walnut trees dot the landscape, in much the same way as apple trees occupy any empty space in Normandy. Southwest France, too, is scattered with walnut trees, which line the river valleys and thrive even in the thin soil of the uplands. The department of the Dordogne produces the most walnuts in France – 10,000 tonnes a year – but they have not earned an 'appellation d'origine' guarantee of high quality like the walnuts of Grenoble.

Traditionally walnuts are a subsidiary crop, the ground beneath them being planted with vines, maize or vegetables, so that the nuts are a welcome extra at the end of the season. Recently, however, walnuts have come into vogue, their kernels added to breads, salads and sauces as well as to pastries, and their oil used to dress salads in smart restaurants – though because of its price, walnut oil is rarely used for cooking.

At harvest in the autumn, the ground beneath the trees is ploughed to clear it of rocks which might crack the falling nuts.

A woman, a dog and a walnut-tree
The more you beat 'em the better
they be . . .

and the trees take kindly to the rough battering which brings down a hail of velvety green nuts. These are then dried in racks open to the breeze until the green skin splits, revealing the familiar, craggy shell. Some walnuts are also picked green before the shell has hardened. They can be pickled whole, or they may be ground to make jam or macerated to make 'liqueur de noix' a speciality of both the Dauphiné and the southwest.

PETS DE NONNE
Fritters

The mountains once sheltered many convents and monasteries. One of the most exclusive, at Baume-les-Dames in Franche-Comté, demanded that a postulant be of noble lineage dating back to the time of her great-great grandparents. This particular convent was also known both for its excellent biscuits and wafers, and for its fritters known as 'pets de nonne'. The name has no polite translation; they are, quite simply, nun's farts.

Serves 6–8

185 ml	water	¾ cup
	½ tsp salt	
80 g	butter	5 Tbsp
95 g	flour	¾ cup
	3–4 eggs	
	grated rind of 1 lemon (optional)	
	1 tsp orange flower water (optional)	
	fat for deep frying	
	confectioners' sugar (for sprinkling)	
	HOT JAM SAUCE (optional)	
150 g	apricot, raspberry or strawberry jam	½ cup
250 ml	water	1 cup
	juice of ½ lemon	
	1 Tbsp rum or kirsch (optional)	

Make choux pastry* dough from the water, salt, butter, flour and eggs, adding only enough of the last egg to give a dough that falls easily from the spoon. If you like, flavour the dough with lemon rind and/or orange flower water.

Make the jam sauce: heat the jam with the water and lemon juice until the jam melts. Strain, pressing hard to extract all the fruit pulp. Just before frying the puffs, reheat the sauce and add the rum or kirsch. Remove the sauce from the heat and keep it warm.

Heat the deep fat to 175°C/350°F on a fat thermometer. Dip a teaspoon in the hot fat, scoop up a teaspoon of dough and push it into the hot fat, using another teaspoon. Don't add more than 5–6 fritters to the fat or they will crowd the pan as they swell. Increase the heat to 190°C/375°F so the fritters puff in a rising heat. They will turn over by themselves during cooking. If the fat is too hot, the fritters will be sealed before they puff and they will burst; if the fat is too cool, they will be soggy. Fry the fritters for a total of 3–4 minutes or until golden brown. Drain them on paper towels and keep hot in a moderate oven (175°C/350°F) with the door slightly open while frying the remaining fritters. Sprinkle them with sugar and serve at once. Pass jam sauce separately.

BUGNES
Pastry fritters

This old family dessert used to be prepared for Mardi-Gras. Originally from Provence, it later appeared in Franche-Comté and Lyon. The 'ganses' of Nice are similar, but are often flavoured with orange flower water and sometimes fried in olive oil.

Makes 14 bugnes

260 g	flour	2 cups
	1½ tsp baking powder	
45 g	butter	3 Tbsp
	3 eggs	
	½ tsp salt	
35 g	sugar	3 Tbsp
	1 Tbsp rum	
	grated rind of 1 orange or 1 lemon	
	deep fat for frying	
	confectioners' sugar or vanilla sugar (for sprinkling)	

Sift the flour and the baking powder into a bowl and make a well in the centre. Pound the butter to soften it. Put it in the well with the eggs, salt, sugar, rum and grated rind and mix these ingredients thoroughly. Stir in the flour and knead by slapping the mixture against the sides of the bowl until it is very smooth. If the mixture is very sticky, add more flour. Turn it out on to a work surface and continue kneading until very smooth, adding a little flour if it sticks; the dough should still be quite soft and a little sticky. Form it into a smooth ball, wrap and chill for 30 minutes or until firm.

Heat the deep fat to about 180°C/360°F on a fat thermometer. Roll out the dough as thin as possible to a rectangle and cut it lengthwise into strips about 6 cm/2½ in wide. Cut each strip into diamonds with about 7·5 cm/3 in sides, and cut a lengthwise slit in the centre of each but not all the way to the edges. Pull each of the longer corners through the slit. Set the bugnes on a floured tray until ready to fry them. Roll out the scraps and cut more diamond shapes.

Fry the bugnes in the fat; the fat should be hot enough for them to rise instantly to the surface. After 2 minutes or when brown on one side, turn them over and fry for 2 more minutes or until brown on the other side. Drain on paper towels. While they are still hot, sprinkle with plenty of sugar. Keep in a low oven with the door open while frying the rest. Serve warm.

LIQUEURS AND APERITIFS

The long association of liqueurs with the mountains, particularly in the Dauphiné, dates back to the early Middle Ages and the foundation of the great monastic orders. Following the example of alchemists like Arnaud de Villeneuve, French monks brewed elixirs and strong waters intended not as alcoholic stimulants but as potions to ensure long life: eaux-de-vie. The strongest and most efficacious elixirs were made with ingredients which could be distilled, like bilberry, raspberry, aniseed, fennel, mint, juniper, orange, lavender and thyme; wormwood has given its name to that most popular of all aperitifs, vermouth.

Two famous 'medicines' are still called after their religious foundations: Bénédictine and Chartreuse, the first made at Fécamp, in Normandy, and the second by Carthusians at La Grande Chartreuse, their famous mother house in a remote Dauphiné valley. As with most liqueurs, the formula for Chartreuse is a close secret, and only a single manuscript copy of it survived the dissolution of the monastery during the Revolution.

It was at this time that the Basques seized the opportunity to copy both yellow and green chartreuse (the latter the more highly valued 'chartreuse de santé')

in their version 'Izarra'. Modern analysis has proved the concoction to be a predictable combination of medicinal herbs, saffron, stick cinnamon and mace.

There are many more French aperitifs and liqueurs that vary from light to dark and from bitter to sweet, mostly known by their brand names like Dubonnet, Lillet, Ambassadeur and Amer Picon. 'La Vieille Cure', made at Cenons near Bordeaux, contains several kinds of brandy mixed with herbs, as does the green 'Verveine du Velay' from central France, which is based on verbena. There is also a whole family of aperitifs distilled from the yard-long roots of the mountain gentian plant. Called 'génépi' in Savoy and 'enzian' to the west in Auvergne, these 'gentiane' aperitifs, which taste like cough mixture to the uninitiated, are most familiar as 'Suze'.

Even more widespread are the anise and pastis (licorice) drinks, which, like their outlawed precursor, absinthe, turn beguilingly cloudy when diluted with water. Similar to the Greek 'ouzo' and the Arab 'arak', the bright yellow French varieties (best known under brand names like Pernod and Ricard) are found in all bars and are even used in cooking by those who like licorice and pretty flames.

CERISES À L'EAU-DE-VIE
Brandied cherries

In fruit-growing areas like the Alps and the Vosges, preserving with eau-de-vie is standard practice. Firm fruits like cherries, apricots and peaches do best and they are always packed in a glass jar as their appearance is half their appeal. If a mixture of fruits is used, added as they ripen, the jar is known as the 'Fruits du Vieux Garçon' – the fruits of the confirmed bachelor. In general these brandied fruits act as a 'digestif' at the end of dinner, with one or two fruits served in each little glass of brandy. Fruits in eau-de-vie are also excellent, if less traditional, spooned over vanilla ice-cream.

Serves 10

1 kg	slightly tart cherries	2 lb
250 g	sugar	1¼ cups
1 L	eau-de-vie or plain brandy	1 qt
	three 1 L/1 qt jars, with tight-fitting covers	

Wash the cherries and cut off half of each stem. Pat them dry and put into sterilized jars. Put the sugar in a large bowl, add the eau-de-vie and leave 10–15 minutes until the sugar has dissolved, stirring occasionally. Pour enough of the solution over the cherries to cover them. Seal

tightly and store the cherries for 2 months or more before eating them.

NOIX À L'EAU-DE-VIE

Substitute an equal weight of **unshelled walnuts** for the cherries. Shell the walnuts and then continue as in the recipe above.

CHEESES

The mountainous regions of France bordering Switzerland and Italy are one of the great cheese districts of the world. The variety of alpine cheeses is enormous – great wheels of aged hard cheese of the emmental and gruyère families, the creamy 'tommes', 'vacherin' and 'reblochon', a gamut of blue cheese and the piquant little 'St-Marcellin', a goat or cow cheese which is a favourite in Burgundy. The scale of production varies enormously from industrial factories to individual farms, with the 'fruitières' cooperatives in between.

Strictly speaking, gruyère comes from the district of La Gruyère in Switzerland, directly behind Montreux. But in France, the term 'gruyère' is used generically to mean the hard cheeses 'comté' 'beaufort' and 'emmental', which in the old days were all taxed by roving collectors called 'agents de gruyères'. Since they taxed these cheeses by number not by weight, producers made them as large as possible and gruyères are still sold in huge wheels. Emmentals weigh up to 100 kg/220 lb and can be 65 cm/26 in across.

Comté, with its pea-sized holes, has been made in the Franche-Comté since the 13th century, but beaufort of Savoy is even older, dating from Roman times. For the table, beaufort is regarded as the finest of the French gruyère family (it has earned an official label of origin) though a well-aged, nutty comté runs it a close second. Both beaufort and comté are ripened slowly, kept in curing rooms a minimum of six months (for beaufort) and three to six months (for comté). This is one reason for the cheeses' high price.

French emmental, made in the Savoy, Franche-Comté and Burgundy, is relatively new, an off-shoot of Swiss immigration in the 19th century. But the spongy texture of French emmental does not compare with beaufort or comté, and it is used mainly in cooking. French emmental is easily recognizable as the cheese with the largest holes in it, although if the holes are too closely set, it is a sign of rushed production and low quality. Similarly with comté, the smaller and fewer the holes the better the cheese. As a rule, mountain comté has fewer and sparser holes than lowland comté, while beaufort should have no holes at all.

The two dozen main varieties of 'tomme' cheeses of the region come in many shapes and sizes and yet are clearly identifiable as a group by their mild flavour and soft, almost waxy texture. Most tommes measure about 20 cm/8 in across and 5–12 cm/2–4¾ in deep.

Tommes may be made of cow's or goat's milk, having a bluish rind, as in 'tomme de Vercors' or, more commonly, a crusty grey rind, like the well-known 'tomme de Savoie'. The distinctive 'tomme au marc' is brownish-black, the outside covered in grape pips, left over from the marc in which the cheese is aged.

Morbier is the largest and thickest of the tommes, measuring about 40 cm/16 in across and 8–10 cm/3–4 in deep. It is actually two thinner cheeses, rubbed with charcoal at the interface before they are compressed into one, and Morbier is easily identifiable by this line of charcoal running through the centre like the filling in a cake. Despite its bluish centre, since Morbier is not coloured by mould, its taste and texture are quite unlike those of the other blues of the region, such as 'bleu de Gex', 'bleu de Sassenage' and 'bleu de Septmoncel'. All these blues resemble each other, but being based on cow's rather than sheep's milk, (although Septmoncel has goat's milk added), they are milder than the more famous roquefort from Languedoc.

Another mountain cheese, possibly a predecessor of the gruyères, is 'vacherin', a large, whitish soft cheese made both in Switzerland and France. Mild when young, vacherin may be aged by repeated washings in white wine and seasoning to a rich, runny cream, when it is much appreciated by lovers of strong cheese. Depending on its origin, vacherin can be cured for two to four months, but it is sometimes left to mature for only six weeks.

Better known in France is 'reblochon' from Savoy – a firmer cheese than vacherin, and smaller in size. A reblochon weighs around 500 g/1 lb, whereas a vacherin can run up to 3–4 kg/6½–9 lb. The word 'reblocher' is the local expression for squeezing the last and richest dregs from a cow's udder. Apparently, local herdsmen got into the habit of surreptitiously leaving more than a few drops in the cow at milking time, and then using their cache to make rounds of

reblochon strictly for themselves. Resembling reblochon is 'beamont', a thicker cheese with a yellow rind and mild flavour.

St-Marcellin is first recorded in the 15th century in the account books of the future Louis XI, who was cornered by a bear in the Dauphiné. Louis prayed to the Virgin but deliverance came in the more mundane form of two woodcutters who routed the bear and regaled the heir apparent with their home-made cheese. King Louis's St-Marcellin must have been made of goat's milk (large numbers of goats used to be kept for their milk, especially in the summer, when the cows were up in the mountains), but nowadays both cow and goat cheeses are available.

Both these St-Marcellins are white and slightly crumbly when fresh, but harden to become quite dry and sharp.

Odd man out in this list of cheeses is 'cancoillotte', made with fresh curds, drained of their whey then melted with butter, white wine and garlic to make a type of fondue eaten on toast or spooned over potatoes. Once prepared, cancoillotte must be eaten on the spot, but it is the exception among alpine cheeses. Their fame rests as much on their ability to travel as on their consistent quality.

Ironically, better known than all these great names is probably 'La vache qui rit', a little foil-wrapped cube with a cow on the label that is part of every French childhood.

OTHER SPECIALITIES OF THE REGION
TRADITIONAL DISHES

Soupe aux grenouilles
Soup of frogs' legs

Estouffade de marcassin
Wild boar with red wine, bacon and mushrooms

Soupe au fromage
Gruyère cheese soup

Côtelettes de chevreuil aux morilles
Venison cutlets with morels

Écrevisses en chaussons
Crayfish turnovers

Épinards à la mode de Morez
Creamed spinach with fried ham and sausages

Coq au vin jaune aux morilles
Chicken with Jura yellow wine and morels

Mousserons à la crème
Creamed wild mushrooms

Quenelles de veau
Veal quenelles

Farcement savoyard
Potato cake with bacon, prunes and raisins

Fricassée de caion
Pork stew with red wine and blood sauce

Cardons à la moelle
Cardoons with beef marrow

Rissoles du Bugey
Fried puff pastry turnovers stuffed with roast turkey, onions and currants

Poires à la crème
Pears baked in cream

CHARCUTERIE

Diots au vin blanc
Small sausages in white wine

Saucisses de Morteau et Montbéliard
Cumin-flavoured smoked sausages

Saucisses de chou
Pork and cabbage sausages

Pâté de cervelle en croûte
Brains in pastry

PÂTISSERIE AND CONFISERIE

Brioche de St Genis, pognes de Romans
Brioche with pralines

Papette
Round yeast cake covered with vanilla pastry cream

Tarte aux myrtilles
Bilberry tart

Rissoles, rizoles
Pear jam turnovers

Galette de Pérouges, gâteau de fête
Yeast cake dotted with butter and sprinkled with sugar

Gâteau de cerises au kirsch
Cherry and kirsch cake

Galette de goumeau
Brioche cake topped with orange flower water custard

Les sèches
Dry biscuits sprinkled with coarse sugar

Provence

As an English girl brought up in the placid half-tones of a northern landscape, my first visit to Provence came as a revelation. At the end of a long night in the limbo of the overnight train from Paris, I lifted the blind and there it was: sharp black cypress trees, terracotta soil, jagged, rock-encrusted hills, all outlined by the harsh glare of a sun that was hotter, even at that hour in the morning, than anything I could have imagined. Like so many Anglo-Saxons, I had been struck by the Provençal 'coup de foudre'.

It was a day or two before I began to realize that the cooking was at least as colourful as the countryside. My initial forays into the pleasures of sea bass flamed with fennel, and orange-flavoured daube were followed by an investigation into bouillabaisse and its 'sauce rouille', packed with garlic and hot red pepper. I revelled in the fresh fruit and tackled, not without misgiving, a barbecued meat whose tiny bones betrayed it as kid. A visit to the market revealed watermelons, slashed to grinning jaws of crimson, and mounds of peppers, glowing a symbolic red, green and pale yellow, almost like the Italian flag.

More than any other part of France, Provence looks south. South to the Mediterranean, southeast to her neighbour Italy, and away from the Alps at her back. So it is logical that several dishes should have spilled over the Italian border into the region around Nice, or 'pays niçois', notably ravioli, potato gnocchi and 'pissaladière', a yeast dough topped with onion, olive and anchovy which can hardly be distinguished from its Italian cousin, pizza. 'Pistou' sauce is none other than the Italian basil and garlic 'pesto', without pine nuts.

Fish is a staple in Provence, as in Italy, though I wonder how long that can continue. The last time I was there, much of the local catch seemed to be more expensive than that brought through Paris. In the warm Mediterranean waters, fish grow fast; with the honourable exceptions of sea bass, mullet and monkfish, most of them are woolly-textured with a lot of bones. Recipes are designed accordingly, with fish soups a favourite, allowing maximum flavour to be extracted from the bones without much work. They are invariably reinforced with seasonings like saffron, cayenne, garlic, tomato and herbs. Shellfish include mussels, clams, sea-urchins and spiny 'langoustes', which seem to command an exorbitant price and whose flavour is generally considered inferior to that of the Atlantic clawed lobster.

A better bet at a fraction of the price is fresh sardines, often cooked on a bed of spinach to balance their richness; or squid simmered slowly in a sauce of garlic, olive oil and wine; or tuna, whose dark flesh is usually baked or braised, more like meat than fish. There is also bream topped with a purée of fresh tomatoes and I still retain my juvenile taste for fish with fennel, provided the anise liqueur is used sparingly.

Away from the coast, Provençal life centres on its villages. Perched on hillsides like miniature fortresses, each crowned with a church tower, they also provide protection from the elements, as the foot-slogging tourist rapidly discovers. The close-walled winding streets give shade from the sun, while screening out the mistral, the withering wind that blows for three days out of ten. In the sheltered valley bottoms, fruit and vegetables are intensively cultivated; on higher ground up to 800 metres grow vines and olive trees, with wheat and pastureland above. Here in summer graze the sheep whose wool, the finest in France, is woven into finely patterned traditional fabrics.

More and more sheep are now being bred for lamb, which is the best meat in Provence. In the hills around Vence, the leg is cooked 'à la ficelle', dangling from a string in front of an open fire. Alphonse Daudet, who wrote with such affection about all aspects of Provençal life, in Le Petit Chose gives a succulent description of a lamb blanquette made from cutlets and served with a bean purée. Most people are less enthusiastic about 'pieds et paquets', a curious dish of sheep's feet with bundles of tripe which must be shaped with a confident twist of the fingers. Southerners also have a failing for little birds and their speciality shops are lined with corpses of thrush, lark, quail and pigeon which according to Madame de Sévigné were fed with 'thyme, marjoram and every ingredient that enters the composition of our perfume bags.' Tougher to eat, but less trying to the conscience, are domestic fowl. But they do poorly in the sun, and are best consigned to the pot for boiling or braising.

Herbs of Provence, now widely known thanks to the aromatic mix of the same name, are a constant theme in the countryside. In summer it is hard to walk far in the arid central hills without coming across a field of lavender, or brushing past the scented leaves of rosemary, thyme, sage and savory. In many areas, the scent is accompanied by the background hum of bees, for wild herbs not only figure in Provençal cooking, but also nourish the bees which provide a sizeable amount of honey. However, these are almost the only crop the hinterland of Provence does provide. Many picturesque villages have been abandoned and the truth behind the picture book image of a carefree, colourful Provence is that nature is here harsher than it appears to the casual tourist.

It may well be the ancient Romans who were responsible for the Provençal taste for pungent accompaniments which are more condiment than sauce. Thick, earthy and rich with olive oil, the sauces of Provence bear little resemblance to the classics of haute cuisine, though Escoffier was born just outside Nice and sneaked several of his native favourites into his *Guide Culinaire*. The impact of 'aïoli', the powerful garlic mayonnaise, is felt well outside Provence but the qualities of 'tapenade', made with capers, olives, anchovy and tuna, or 'anchoïade', strictly for anchovy lovers, are best appreciated on the spot.

These sauces are often served with raw vegetables, hard-boiled eggs, or simply on croûtes of bread in the manner of Italian 'crostini'. The Provençaux specialize in such first courses, spreading the table with little dishes whose contents are to be nibbled at leisure in the warm sun. The habit is very Arabic, and probably came to Provence by way of the Moorish occupation of Spain. Few sights are more tempting on a hot day than an array of cooked vegetable salads playing the permutations of tomato, aubergine, courgette, onion, mushroom, cauliflower and artichoke. Ratatouille is, of course, the most famous, but lesser known vegetable dishes include 'tian' made with a vegetable such as spinach or leeks. Tian can be flavoured with salt cod and the hill town of Apt has a potato version very like gratin dauphinois without the cream. All these vegetable dishes are best served hot or at Provençal room temperature, that is to say, tepid. They should never be chilled, a North American habit which deadens the aromatic flavour.

If vegetables are the standard opening to a Provençal meal, fruit is the finish; so much so that some local cookbooks do not even include a chapter on desserts. The western

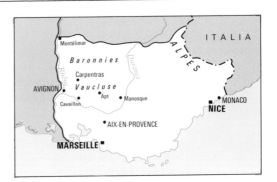

boundary of Provence, along the Rhône, is lined with orchards planted a hundred years ago to replace the vines destroyed by phylloxera blight, and nearby Vaucluse is famous for table grapes, lush muscats beloved by the French and the fresher 'gros vert' preferred in England. When they installed themselves in Avignon, the popes recorded their appreciation of the fruit jams from Apt, still a centre for preserves and crystallized fruit. The finest French figs come from Provence and the town of Cavaillon, on the Durance river, is almost synonymous with melon.

In fact, Provence is without equal as the market garden of France, if not of Europe. As early as 1764, Tobias Smollett, wintering in Nice, noticed 'green peas, asparagus, artichokes, cauliflower, beans, French beans, celery, and endive; cabbage, coleworts; radishes, turnips, carrots, beetroot, sorrel, lettuce, onions, garlic and shallot. We have potatoes from the mountains, mushrooms, champignons, and truffles.' Black truffles are still found around Carpentras but, like all truffle crops, they are sent to Paris to be sold for a small fortune. Notice the absence of tomatoes in Smollett's list. Until the 19th century they were regarded with suspicion but their final assimilation into Provençal cooking must have been a revolution, since half of today's recipes seem to contain tomatoes.

In Smollett's time, Provence was a poverty-stricken remote backwater and, indeed, remained so until the advent of the railway made it possible to carry fresh produce to the north. The railways also brought tourism. It was the 19th-century plutocrat, Lord Brougham (of carriage fame), who launched the Riviera and began the transformation of the Mediterranean littoral into the prosperous, populous area it is today. Somehow the cooking has survived the shock of all this and managed to retain its immediate sunlit appeal.

THE COOKING OF CORSICA

Corsica suffers from a centuries-old pessimism: 'Corsica, you will never be happy,' runs a proverb. Despite the benign Mediterranean climate, the land has been hard on its inhabitants, the centre being rugged and mountainous and the lower ground once prone to malaria. For centuries the population had to rely on hill produce, notably the chestnut tree, known as the 'bread tree'.

The charcuterie of Corsica shows strong Italian influence: 'prisuttu' is raw ham, 'lonzo' is pickled (and smoked) pork fillet, and 'coppa', cured pork faux-filet. Corsicans are keen on sausage too, making a pig's liver sausage flavoured with pepper and pimento called 'figatelli', and one of sheep's tripe flavoured with spinach, chard and herbs.

Cornmeal and chestnuts are a traditional foundation of breads and cakes. Cornmeal appears in 'polenta' (the Italian version of cornmeal mush) and 'panizze' which are fried cakes of cornmeal or chestnuts. In winter the chestnut crop used to be dried in drawers (leading to a Corsican expression 'to eat from the drawer'), then ground to make sweet flour for crêpes, fritters and desserts like 'tarte aux noix et châtaignes'. Only in the last hundred years has wheat been plentiful, grown on the plains on a large scale alongside olives, vines and fruit trees. In fact, Corsica now produces almost all of France's citrus crop.

The blandness of chestnut contrasts with the spice of many Corsican dishes, which befits the belligerent island character. (Like Sicily and its Mafia, many hard-core French gangsters come from Corsica and so, appropriately, do the policemen who pursue them.) Local vegetable dishes are flavoured with pimento as well as the Provençal garlic and olive oil, and fish is served in 'ziminù', a sauce with red peppers and pimento. 'Pebronata' is both a multi-purpose sauce made with peppers, garlic and tomatoes and the name given to beef, chicken or kid served with this sauce. Goat meat is, indeed, more common in Corsica than in the rest of France: another favourite way of preparing it is to stew it in red wine and serve it with a kind of chestnut-flour polenta.

Chicken was the favourite food of the most famous of Corsicans, Napoleon. His cook would prepare a roast chicken every fifteen minutes in case his master should decide on the spur of the moment to dine. When he did, he was no advertisement for Corsican gastronomy, for he prided himself on eating a complete meal in twelve minutes.

SOUPE AU PISTOU
Vegetable soup with 'pistou'

This soup, flavoured with the garlic and basil sauce, 'pistou', varies with the seasons. In summer the soup itself is based on fresh white beans and courgettes/zucchini and the pistou can be made with fresh basil. In winter, the soup has to be made with dried beans, pumpkin instead of courgette, and pistou preserved in oil. If some of the vegetables are not available, they can be omitted.

Serves 6–8

125 g	dried white beans	$\frac{1}{4}$ lb
4 L	water	4 qt
	2 carrots, diced	
	2 medium potatoes, diced	
750 g	small zucchini, cut in large cubes	$1\frac{1}{2}$ lb
	1 leek, trimmed, split and chopped	
	1 onion, chopped	
500 g	tomatoes, peeled, seeded and chopped	1 lb
125 g	green beans, cut in 2–3 pieces	$\frac{1}{4}$ lb
	bouquet garni	
	salt and pepper	
125 g	shelled green peas (optional)	$\frac{1}{2}$ cup
75 g	medium noodles	$2\frac{1}{2}$ oz
125 ml	pistou (see recipe), more as necessary	$\frac{1}{2}$ cup
	grated parmesan cheese (for serving)	

Soak the beans overnight in cold water and drain. Put them in a large pot with half the water, bring to a boil and simmer for 1 hour. Drain, discarding the liquid.

Put the carrots, potatoes, courgettes/zucchini, leek, onion, tomatoes, green beans and bouquet garni in the pot with the white beans and enough water to cover. Add salt and pepper, bring to a boil and simmer for 45 minutes or until all the vegetables are very tender.

Fifteen minutes before serving, add the peas and noodles to the soup and continue simmering for another 10–15 minutes or until they are just tender. The soup should be quite thick, but if too much of the liquid has evaporated, add a little boiling water. Discard the bouquet garni.

Take from the heat and stir in the pistou to taste; don't reheat the soup after the pistou has been added. Taste for seasoning and serve immediately. Pass grated parmesan cheese separately.

PISTOU
Basil, parmesan and garlic sauce

'Pistou' has many uses: it can be served as a sauce for spaghetti or mixed into vegetable soup to make 'soupe au pistou' (see recipe). It is an excellent dip for raw vegetables and in the Nice area pistou is also served with roast mutton.

Makes 185 ml/¾ cup of sauce

	10 basil leaves	
	3 large cloves garlic	
100 g	freshly grated parmesan cheese	1 cup
80 ml	olive oil	⅓ cup

Wash the basil leaves and dry them as thoroughly as possible. Crush the garlic in a mortar with a pestle until it becomes a paste; then add the basil and again pound to a fine paste. Transfer to a bowl. Gradually add the grated cheese, mixing and mashing with a fork. Still using a fork, gradually stir in the olive oil, drop by drop, so the sauce thickens; if the oil is added too quickly, the mixture may separate. Alternatively, make the sauce in a food processor or blender: purée the basil, garlic and cheese; then add the oil gradually, with the blades turning.

To keep pistou for use in the winter, put it in a glass jar and run a thin layer of olive oil on top to keep out the air. Cover the jar tightly and keep it in a cool dry place.

SPAGHETTI AU PISTOU
For 4 servings, cook:

250 g	spaghetti	½ lb

and drain. Toss it in a little olive oil; then add the pistou. Season with salt and pepper to taste. Serve more grated parmesan cheese separately.

POIVRONS SAUTÉS
Sautéed peppers

Try to use at least two kinds of pepper for this colourful dish, which is excellent served cold as an appetizer with sardines, salami, or vegetable salads. Hot, it is good with grilled/broiled meats.

Serves 4

	3 Tbsp olive oil	
	4–5 mixed red, green and yellow peppers, cored, seeded and cut in wide strips	
	1 clove garlic, chopped	
	pinch of thyme	
	salt and pepper	

Heat the oil in a frying pan and add the peppers, garlic, thyme, salt and pepper. Cook over a medium heat for 2–3 minutes, stirring to coat the peppers thoroughly with oil. Cover and cook over low heat for another 5–7 minutes or until tender. Taste for seasoning. Serve hot or at room temperature.

OIGNONS À LA MONÉGASQUE
Sweet and sour onion salad with raisins

From the 1880s and the time of the Ritz-Escoffier partnership, hotel restaurants in Monaco were a centre of classical and 'international' rather than regional cuisine. At home the cooking resembles that of the rest of Provence, though this sweet and sour onion salad is peculiar to Monaco.

Serves 6

500 g	baby onions	1 lb
310 ml	water	1¼ cups
60 ml	wine vinegar, more if needed	¼ cup
	3 Tbsp olive oil	
50 g	sugar, more if needed	¼ cup
	3 Tbsp tomato paste	
	bouquet garni	
	salt and pepper	
70 g	raisins	½ cup

Put all the ingredients in a pot, bring to a boil and simmer uncovered over a low fire for 45 minutes or until the onions are very tender. By the end of cooking, most of the water should have evaporated, so the mixture is moist but not liquid. Taste for seasoning; more sugar or vinegar may be added if necessary. Discard the bouquet garni and transfer the onion and raisin mixture to a serving bowl. Serve at room temperature.

RAVIOLI À LA NIÇOISE

Ravioli with meat and Swiss chard

'Ravioli à la niçoise' can have many different stuffings, the most typical being chopped left-over meat from stew such as 'boeuf en daube' (see recipe), or a vegetable like spinach. Meat gravy makes an excellent sauce.

Serves 4–6 (makes about 100 ravioli)

DOUGH		
390 g	flour	3 cups
	pinch of salt	
	4 eggs	
	3–4 Tbsp water	
FILLING		
250 g	spinach or Swiss chard leaves	½ lb
	salt and pepper	
75 g	bacon (optional)	2½ oz
150 g	raw or cooked veal, or left-over drained boeuf en daube	5 oz
	½ onion, quartered	
	2 tsp olive oil	
	1 egg	
25 g	grated parmesan cheese	¼ cup
	pinch of grated nutmeg	
FOR SERVING		
50 g	grated parmesan cheese	½ cup
500 ml	gravy from daube or tomato coulis (see recipe)	2 cups

To make the dough: sift the flour on to a work surface or into a bowl. Make a well in the centre and add the salt, eggs and 3 tablespoons water. Start to draw the flour into the centre, working the mixture together with the fingers. If necessary, add a little more water to make a smooth dough that is soft but not sticky. Knead thoroughly for 5 minutes or until very smooth and elastic. Cover with an upturned bowl and let rest for about 30 minutes.

Meanwhile, prepare the filling: discard the spinach stems, wash the leaves and cook them in a large pan of boiling salted water for 4–5 minutes or until wilted. Drain, rinse under cold running water and drain well. Squeeze out excess water, leave to cool and then chop finely with a knife. If using bacon, blanch* it if it is very salty. Mince/grind together the meat, bacon and onion. Heat the oil, add the meat mixture and cook over a low fire, stirring often, for 10 minutes if the meat is cooked and for 20 minutes if it is raw. Stir in the spinach and remove from the heat. Let cool slightly and beat in the egg and the cheese. Add pepper and nutmeg to taste; salt may not be necessary.

To assemble: cut the dough in half and roll out each piece on a lightly floured board until paper-thin. Alternatively use a pasta machine

to roll it out (see 'nouilles à l'alsacienne').

Brush one piece of dough with water and set teaspoonsful of filling at 4 cm/1½ in intervals in rows on the dough. Brush the second layer of dough with water and set it, wet side down, on the first. With a small ball of dough dipped in flour, or with a ruler, press down the top piece of dough to seal around each mound of filling. Cut in squares with a fluted pastry wheel or with a knife. If you don't want to cook the ravioli immediately, transfer them to floured greaseproof/waxed paper and leave for a few hours to dry.

To cook: add the ravioli to a large quantity of boiling salted water. Poach over a low fire for about 10 minutes. Drain, rinse under cold water and drain well.

Arrange the ravioli in a buttered baking dish in layers, sprinkling each layer with grated parmesan cheese to taste and moistening with gravy from daube or with tomato coulis. Heat in a medium oven (170°C/350°F) until very hot. Alternatively, sprinkle a generous layer of grated parmesan cheese on top and brown in a very hot oven (220°C/425°F). Serve the ravioli from the dish.

CANNELONI À LA NIÇOISE

Prepare dough as above but double the quantity of filling. Roll out the dough in as thin a layer as possible. Cut it into 10 cm/4 in squares, spread on floured greaseproof/waxed paper and leave for 2–3 hours to dry. Cook 6–8 squares at a time, in a large pan of simmering salted water for 8–10 minutes or until almost tender or 'al dente'. Stir from time to time to prevent sticking. Transfer the cooked squares to a pan of cold water and drain very well. Dry on paper towels.

Spread 1–2 tablespoons filling on each square, roll the squares up and arrange in a buttered baking dish. Moisten with gravy from daube or with tomato coulis, sprinkle with a little extra grated parmesan cheese and bake for 10–15 minutes in a hot oven (200°C/400°F) until hot and golden brown. This quantity makes about 30 canneloni.

RAVIOLES DU DAUPHINÉ

Sometimes these are smaller than regular ravioli. Drain and mash:

150 g	fresh goat cheese	5 oz

(You may use cream cheese but there is no need to drain it.) Mix with:

150 g	grated gruyère cheese	1½ cups

2 eggs, 3 Tbsp chopped parsley, salt and pepper to taste. Use to fill ravioli. Poach in broth, then drain and serve the ravioli with grated gruyère cheese.

PISSALADIÈRE

Onion and tomato yeast tart

The name 'pissaladière' comes from 'pissala', a purée of tiny fish preserved in brine, which is sometimes used instead of anchovies. This tart is the French cousin of Italian pizza.

Serves 6–8

	YEAST DOUGH	
175 g	flour, more if needed	1⅓ cups
80 ml	lukewarm water	⅓ cup
8 g	fresh yeast OR	½ cake
	½ pkg dry yeast	
	1 egg	
	¾ tsp salt	
	TOPPING	
80 ml	olive oil	⅓ cup
750 g	mild onions, thinly sliced	1½ lb
	2 tsp mixed chopped herbs: basil, thyme, rosemary	
	salt and pepper	
60 g	anchovy fillets, soaked in a little milk and drained	2 oz
1 kg	tomatoes, peeled, seeded and sliced	2 lb
50 g	Nice or Greek-style black olives, pitted	½ cup
	28–30 cm/11–12 in pie pan	

Make the yeast dough: sift the flour into a warm bowl and make a well in the centre. Pour the water into the well, crumble the yeast over it and let stand for 5 minutes or until dissolved. Add the egg and salt to the well and mix the centre ingredients with the fingers. Gradually draw in the flour to form a soft dough. Turn it out on to a floured board or marble and knead the dough for 5 minutes or until smooth and elastic, working in more flour if necessary. Transfer to an oiled bowl, turn the dough over so that the top is oiled, cover with a damp cloth and leave to rise in a warm place for 1 hour or until doubled in bulk.

Meanwhile, start the topping: heat the oil in a sauté pan and add the onions with the herbs, salt and pepper. Press a piece of foil on top, cover with the lid and cook, stirring occasionally, over a very low fire for 25–30 minutes or until the onions are very soft and almost puréed; don't let them brown. Cut the anchovy fillets in half lengthwise. Grease the pie pan and set it on a baking sheet.

When the dough has risen, knead it lightly to knock out the air. Pat the dough out into the pie pan, pushing it up the sides, and spread the onion mixture on top. Arrange the tomatoes over the onions and sprinkle with pepper (no extra salt is needed). Make a lattice of anchovy fillets, filling the spaces with olives. Leave to rise in a warm place for 10–15 minutes or until the dough is well risen. Set the oven at moderately hot (190°C/375°F).

Bake the pissaladière in the heated oven for 25–30 minutes or until browned. Serve it hot or at room temperature.

OEUFS DURS FARCIS À LA TAPENADE

Eggs stuffed with olive-caper-anchovy purée

'Tapéno' is Provençal for capers and the dull brown colour of tapenade sauce gives no clue to its lively flavour. Tapenade probably dates back to the ancient Greeks. By the 19th century it was so popular it was sold on a commercial scale. As well as being served with eggs, tapenade can be spread on bread, mixed with cooked vegetables in the same way as mayonnaise, or used as a dip for raw vegetable sticks. For a more colourful dish, serve these stuffed eggs with a tomato salad decorated with olives or anchovies.

Serves 10

	10 hard-boiled eggs	
	1 Tbsp olive oil	
	TAPENADE	
100 g	black olives, pitted	½ cup
	6 anchovy fillets, soaked in a little milk and drained	
60 g	canned tuna, drained	2 oz
60 g	capers, drained	¼ cup
	1 tsp Dijon mustard	
95 ml	olive oil	6 Tbsp
	pepper	

Make the tapenade: pound the olives, anchovy fillets, tuna and capers to a fine paste in a mortar with a pestle; then push the mixture through a drum sieve. Transfer to a bowl and whisk in the mustard. Whisk in the olive oil, drop by drop. Alternatively, purée the olives, anchovies, tuna, capers and mustard to a fine paste in a blender or food processor. With the blades still turning, gradually pour in the olive oil.

Season well with plenty of pepper, but don't add salt.

Peel the hard-boiled eggs and halve them lengthwise. Scoop out the yolks, work them through a sieve into the tapenade, and stir in the tablespoon of oil. Fill the eggs with the tapenade mixture, mounding it well in each one. Serve at room temperature.

SOUPE DE POISSONS PROVENÇALE
Puréed fish soup

This soup is made not only in Provence but also in Corsica. Like bouillabaisse, it can be flavoured with orange rind and anise liquor. A similar soup is made with mussels instead of fish and thickened with either noodles or rice cooked in the soup just before it is served. Still another variation, again with the same flavourings, is based on small Mediterranean crabs called 'favouilles'.

Serves 6

1 kg	mixed small or medium white fish, with heads	2 lb
60 ml	olive oil	$\frac{1}{4}$ cup
	2 onions, sliced	
	$\frac{1}{2}$ bulb fennel, chopped OR 2 tsp dried fennel	
500 g	tomatoes, coarsely chopped	1 lb
	2 cloves garlic, crushed	
2 L	water, more if needed	2 qt
	bouquet garni	
	2 Tbsp tomato paste	
	salt and pepper	
	1–2 pinches of saffron strands, steeped in 1–2 Tbsp boiling water	
	pinch of cayenne pepper	
	FOR SERVING	
	1 loaf French bread OR 3 long crusty rolls, sliced	
75 g	grated parmesan cheese	$\frac{3}{4}$ cup
	sauce rouille (optional, see recipe)	

Discard the fins and scale and clean the fish. Wash and dry the fish and, if medium-sized, cut in thick slices. Heat the olive oil in a large pot, add the onions and fresh fennel and sauté until soft but not brown. Stir in the tomatoes, fish and garlic and sauté over a medium fire for about 5 minutes. Add enough water to cover, then add the bouquet garni, tomato paste, salt, pepper and the saffron with its liquid; if using the dried fennel, add it now. Bring to a boil and simmer for 45 minutes or until the fish flakes very easily.

Take the fish and vegetables out of the cooking liquid, discard the large fish bones and heads and bouquet garni. Work the fish and vegetables through a food mill, coarse strainer or food processor; then strain, pressing hard. Reserve the purée. Boil the cooking liquid to reduce until well flavoured.

Meanwhile, bake the bread in a low oven (150°C/300°F) until dry and lightly browned. Whisk the fish purée back into the pot of fish liquid and bring to a boil. Taste the soup for seasoning, adding a generous pinch of cayenne pepper and, if you like, more saffron.

Serve hot. Either pass the croûtes, grated parmesan cheese and sauce rouille separately, or spread the croûtes with rouille and add some to each bowl of soup.

SOUPE DE POISSONS MARSEILLAISE

Serve the soup with noodles instead of with the croûtes. After whisking the fish purée into the liquid, add:

150 g	thin noodles	5 oz

and simmer for 12–15 minutes. Continue as above, passing the parmesan cheese and sauce separately when serving.

LOUP FLAMBÉ AU FENOUIL
Flamed sea bass with fennel

'Loup de mer' or 'sea wolf' is the southern French name for sea bass. This recipe is also good with fish like bream, hake or sea trout; use fish complete with the head if possible.

Serves 6–8

2-kg 1-kg each	large striped or sea bass OR 2 medium bass	4$\frac{1}{2}$-lb 2-lb each
	4–6 Tbsp olive oil	
	salt and pepper	
	bunch of dried fennel twigs	
	3–4 Tbsp Pernod or other anise liquor	

Cut off the fins and trim the tail of the fish to a 'V'. Scale the fish and clean it, cutting as small an incision in the stomach as possible; wash and dry thoroughly. Make 3–4 deep diagonal cuts on each side of the fish, brush it with oil, and sprinkle with salt and pepper. Insert 2–3 pieces of fennel in the stomach cavity.

Brush the grill rack with oil and lay the fish on it. Set the rack 10–12 cm/4–5 in from the heat and grill/broil, allowing 10–12 minutes on each side for a large fish or 8–10 minutes for smaller ones; occasionally brush the fish with oil.

Put the remaining fennel on a long heatproof platter, warm it in a low oven until very dry; then lay the fish on top. Heat the Pernod in a small pan, light it and pour it while flaming on to the hot platter; the fennel twigs will catch alight. Serve at once.

LOUP FLAMBÉ AU FENOUIL II

If dried fennel twigs are not available, before cooking sprinkle the cavity and top of the fish with **2–3 tsp fennel seed**. Grill/broil, and flame the fish as above.

SARDINES FARCIES AUX ÉPINARDS

Sardines stuffed with spinach

This recipe is best suited to a rich fish like herring or mackerel, though sea bass or trout can also be used. It is superb with salmon, which gives a contrast of colour as well as taste.

Serves 6

0·75–1 kg	fresh sardines	1½–2 lb
	salt and pepper	
750 g	fresh spinach	1½ lb
	3 Tbsp olive oil	
	1 onion, finely chopped	
	1 Tbsp flour	
185 ml	milk	¾ cup
	2 cloves garlic, chopped	
	pinch of grated nutmeg	
30 g	dry breadcrumbs	⅓ cup

Slit the stomach opening of each sardine slightly to clean it. Slit each sardine along each side of the backbone to free it. Continue to separate the fillet meat from the bone, until you reach the stomach. With scissors, cut through the backbone at the head and tail and pull out the bone, leaving head and tail attached, so the fish looks whole. Wipe off the scales and dry each sardine. Sprinkle the sardines with salt and pepper.

Remove the stems from the spinach and wash the leaves thoroughly. Cook the spinach in a large pot of boiling salted water for 5 minutes or until just tender. Drain, rinse under cold running water and drain thoroughly, squeezing to remove as much water as possible. Finely chop the spinach. Set the oven at very hot (220°C/425°F).

Heat half the oil in a saucepan, add the onion and cook over a low fire, stirring often, until soft but not brown. Add the spinach and cook over a medium fire, for a few minutes or until most moisture has evaporated. Sprinkle with the flour and stir over a low fire for 1–2 minutes. Add the milk, garlic, salt, pepper and nutmeg. Bring to a boil, stirring, and simmer for 3–4 minutes; taste for seasoning.

Stuff each sardine with a small spoonful of the spinach mixture. Spoon the remaining spinach mixture into a large oiled baking dish and lay the sardines on top. Sprinkle with breadcrumbs, then with the remaining oil. Bake in the oven for 10 minutes or until golden brown and just tender. Serve in the baking dish.

THON À LA MARSEILLAISE

Baked tuna with lettuce, onions and tomato

The first lettuce in France is said to have been brought from Italy by the Avignon popes (hence the name of 'romaine', Roman, lettuce). In this recipe many well-flavoured firm fish such as monkfish or swordfish can be used instead of the tuna.

Serves 6

1-kg	piece of fresh tuna	2-lb
	1 head of lettuce	
750 g	onions, thinly sliced	1½ lb
750 g	tomatoes, peeled, seeded and sliced	1½ lb
	2 cloves garlic, chopped	
	1 lemon, peeled and sliced	
	salt and pepper	
250 ml	olive oil	1 cup

Soak the tuna for ½–1 hour in water with a little vinegar; then drain it. Use a heavy knife to cut it into 6 steaks. Wash the lettuce, separating the leaves, and dry thoroughly. Coarsely shred all but 5 or 6 of the leaves. Set the oven at low (160°C/320°F).

In a well-oiled, shallow baking dish, lay half the shredded lettuce followed by half the sliced onions, then half the tomatoes, garlic and lemon slices. Sprinkle with salt and pepper. Put the tuna steaks on top and season them. Top with the remaining onions, tomatoes, garlic and lemon slices. Sprinkle with salt and pepper and pour on half the olive oil. Lay the remaining shredded lettuce on top and cover with the lettuce leaves. (The top leaves may have to be discarded at the end of the cooking time because they often scorch.) Pour the remaining oil over the lettuce and bake, basting occasionally, for 1¼–1½ hours or until the tuna is very tender and easy to flake with a fork.

Discard any burned lettuce leaves and serve the tuna from the baking dish.

BOUILLABAISSE

Like all fish stews, the greater the variety of fish used in 'bouillabaisse', the better. In theory, only Mediterranean fish should appear, but any combination of white and rich-fleshed fish can be substituted: possible white fish include scorpion fish, monkfish, John Dory, red mullet, whiting, bass, red snapper, perch, haddock, porgy and flounder, while among the rich fish are conger eel, Moray eel, mackerel, eel or striped bass. Strictly speaking, luxury shellfish like lobster and crab do not belong in a true bouillabaisse though they add a touch of class and are popular in restaurant versions of the dish.

Serves 8–10

1·5 kg	white fish, with heads	3 lb
1 kg	rich fish, with heads	2 lb
	fish stock	
	2 large Dungeness crabs OR	
	8–10 small blue crabs (optional)	
	1 large spiny lobster OR 8–10 small	
	lobster tails (optional)	
185 ml	olive oil	¾ cup
	2 medium onions, sliced	
	2 leeks, trimmed, split and sliced	
	2 stalks celery, sliced	
500 g	tomatoes, peeled, seeded	1 lb
	and chopped	
	3–4 cloves garlic, crushed	
	bouquet garni	
	thinly peeled strip of orange rind	
	2 sprigs of fresh fennel OR	
	1 tsp dried fennel	
	pinch saffron strands, steeped in	
	1–2 Tbsp boiling water	
	salt and pepper	
	1 Tbsp tomato paste	
	1 Tbsp anise liquor	
	(Pernod or Pastis)	
30 g	chopped parsley	¼ cup
	20 croûtes*, fried in oil	
	and rubbed with garlic	
	sauce rouille (optional, see recipe)	
	MARINADE	
	3 Tbsp olive oil	
	2 cloves garlic, finely chopped	
	pinch of saffron strands, steeped in	
	1–2 Tbsp boiling water	

Discard the fins and scale and clean the fish. Wash them and pat dry. Cut the fish in chunks, discarding the skin. Use the fish heads and tails to make fish stock: put them in a pan, barely cover with water, bring to a boil, cook for 15 minutes and strain. Meanwhile, marinate the fish in a bowl with the olive oil, garlic and saffron. Leave all shellfish in their shells; with a cleaver, chop large crabs and spiny lobster* into pieces, discarding the stomach and intestinal veins of the lobster and the spongy finger-like gills of the large crabs.

In a very large wide pan or flameproof casserole heat the oil, add the onions, leeks and celery and sauté lightly until soft but not brown. Add the tomatoes, garlic, bouquet garni, orange rind and fennel. Stir in the fish stock, saffron and its liquid, salt and pepper. Bring to a boil and simmer for 30–40 minutes.

Twenty minutes before serving: bring the liquid to a boil, add the rich fish and shellfish and boil uncovered as hard as possible for 7 minutes. Don't stir, but shake the pan from time to time to prevent the mixture from sticking. Put the white fish on top and boil 5–8 minutes longer or until the fish just flakes easily, adding more water, if necessary, to cover all the pieces of fish. It is important to keep the liquid boiling fast so that the oil emulsifies in the broth and does not float on the surface.

Bouillabaisse is served in two dishes, one for the pieces of fish, the other (a bowl or a soup tureen) for the broth. Take the bouillabaisse from the fire and transfer the fish into a hot deep platter, using a slotted spoon and arranging the fish so the different kinds are separated. Keep them warm.

To finish: discard the bouquet garni, piece of orange and fennel sprigs. Whisk the tomato paste and anise liquor into the hot broth, taste for seasoning and pour it into the tureen. Sprinkle broth and fish with chopped parsley and serve both at the same time. Serve the croûtes and, if you like, the sauce rouille in separate dishes.

MEDITERRANEAN FISH SOUPS

The southern coast of France is particularly rich in fish soups, partly because they suit the climate, partly because they accommodate bony local fish like 'rascasse' (scorpion fish) which defy dissection with a knife and fork. Many fish soups form a complete meal, with the broth served as a first course, followed by the fish; alternatively both can be united as one main dish. Typical is the renowned 'bouillabaisse marseillaise', which relies on saffron, tomatoes and fennel for flavour. In contrast to most fish dishes, bouillabaisse must be boiled hard during cooking so the olive oil used to enrich the soup emulsifies and thickens the broth. Extra flavour is given by garlic croûtons, fried in olive oil, and spicy 'sauce rouille'.

'Bourride', a light-coloured cousin of bouillabaisse and a favourite in both Provence and Languedoc, was declared by a local poet to be the gift of the gods who came to Marseille on one of their periodic descents from Olympus. Flavoured only with garlic, onion, herbs and fish stock, the bourride is served with toasted bread and 'aïoli' instead of the colourful rouille. East of Marseille, towards Italy, bouillabaisse competes with 'soupe de poissons', a puréed fish soup. It too is flavoured with saffron and served with croûtons and rouille, accompanied by parmesan cheese from across the border, but purists insist that parmesan should never be served with bouillabaisse.

For any fish soup, the recipe is adaptable, with fish, vegetables and seasonings being varied according to the cook's taste and the ingredients available. In Provence, a good fish soup usually includes rascasse, John Dory, monkfish, bream, red mullet, whiting, sea bass, conger eel and 'rouget grondin' (red gurnard). With the exception of rascasse and grondin, these fish are available in the USA and Britain and possible substitutes include red snapper, perch, haddock and flounder. The more fish that are thrown in the pot, the better the soup will be, but there is no need to follow the restaurant practice of dressing up fish soup by adding expensive shellfish. Nor should the dish be emasculated by filleting the fish before cooking. Fish soup is a fisherman's dish, and so it should always remain.

SAUCE ROUILLE

Red chili pepper mayonnaise

'Rouille' means rust, the colour of this powerful sauce, flavoured with garlic and red chili pepper. It is served with bouillabaisse, and sometimes with Provençal fish soup. To achieve the red colour, some chefs add tomato paste.

Makes about 125 ml/½ cup of sauce

	½ dried or fresh red chili pepper OR	
	2 tsp cayenne pepper	
	4–6 cloves garlic	
	2 egg yolks	
	salt	
125 ml	olive oil	½ cup
	4–6 tsp tomato paste (optional)	

Prepare the chili peppers*, if using, and cut them in pieces. Pound the peppers, garlic, egg yolks and a little salt in a mortar with a pestle until smooth. Work in the olive oil, drop by drop, so the sauce thickens and becomes creamy; if the oil is added too quickly, the mixture will separate. Alternatively, make the sauce in a blender or food processor: purée the pepper, garlic, egg yolks and a little salt; with the blades still turning, add the oil in a fine stream.

Add the tomato paste. Season the sauce to taste with salt and (if not using chili peppers) with plenty of cayenne pepper; the flavour should be quite hot.

LIMAÇONS À LA SUÇARELLE
Snails in meat sauce

'Limaçons' are small snails with white shells. To extract them from their shells after cooking, it is necessary to suck ('sucer') them – hence the name of this recipe. The common large snails which are specified here are less picturesque than limaçons, but easier to eat.

Serves 4

	24 large or 36 'petits gris' snails, fresh or canned	
	2 Tbsp olive oil	
	1 large onion, chopped	
200 g	ground pork, fat and lean mixed	7 oz
	2 tomatoes, peeled, seeded and chopped	
	2 Tbsp tomato paste	
	3 cloves garlic, chopped	
	3 Tbsp chopped parsley	
	salt and pepper	
	toast or French bread (for serving)	

If using fresh snails, prepare, clean and cook them (see page 224). Drain and rinse canned snails.

For the meat sauce: heat the oil in a large pot, add the onion and cook over a low fire until soft but not brown. Add the pork and cook, stirring, for 3–5 minutes or until brown. Stir in the tomatoes, tomato paste, garlic and parsley and simmer for 5 minutes, stirring occasionally.

Add the snails to the sauce and simmer over a low fire for 20–25 minutes, or until they are very tender and the sauce is well flavoured. Taste the snails for seasoning, spoon them into ramekins and serve very hot. Toast or French bread is the best accompaniment.

CANARD AUX OLIVES
Braised duck with olives

Green and ripe olives in this recipe give an attractive colour contrast. If the duck is fatty, be sure to brown it very thoroughly, so as to dissolve as much fat as possible before adding the broth.

Serves 4

2-kg	duck	4½-lb
	salt and pepper	
375 ml	broth	1½ cups
	1 tsp tomato paste	
	bouquet garni	
70 g	green olives, pitted	⅓ cup
70 g	black olives, pitted	⅓ cup
	1 Tbsp arrowroot or potato starch	
	3 Tbsp madeira	
	trussing needle and string	

Set the oven at very hot (230°C/450°F). Truss the duck, sprinkle it with salt and pepper and prick the skin all over to release fat during cooking. Put the duck in a heavy-based casserole and brown it in the oven for 20–30 minutes, or until the fat beneath the skin has thoroughly melted; turn the duck several times to ensure uniform browning. Remove the duck from the casserole and discard the excess fat. Lower the oven temperature to hot (200°C/ 400°F).

Return the duck to the casserole and add the broth, tomato paste, bouquet garni, salt and pepper. Bring to a boil, cover and cook in the oven for 45 minutes or until the duck is tender when the thigh is pricked with a skewer. Add more broth if the cooking liquid becomes too thick.

Meanwhile, blanch the olives* if they are very salty; otherwise, simply rinse them in cold water and drain. Set aside.

Transfer the duck from the casserole to a platter, cover and keep warm while making the sauce. Skim the excess fat from the sauce. Dissolve the arrowroot in the madeira. Discard the bouquet garni and bring the cooking liquid to a boil. Whisk in the dissolved arrowroot, a little at a time, to obtain a sauce just thick enough to coat a spoon. Simmer for 2 minutes, then add the olives. Bring just to a boil and taste for seasoning. Remove the trussing strings from the duck and carve it. Spoon the sauce and olives over the duck and serve. Alternatively, serve the duck whole with the sauce and olives spooned over it.

BOEUF EN DAUBE

Marinated beef with lardons and vegetables

Daube is usually thought of as being made with beef, but there are many daubes in Provence. The only criterion is that the dish is baked very slowly in a casserole known as a 'daubière' which is pot-bellied, with a small lid, so the meat keeps moist. Avignon makes a mutton daube, using leg of lamb with vegetables and white wine; hare, rabbit, goat, even boar are used if available, and there is a daube of octopus, flavoured with tomatoes and garlic. Novelist Jean Giono remembers the daubes in his area of Manosque at the beginning of this century: a huge cauldron was kept cooking from New Year's Day to St Sylvester's Feast (December 31) and never emptied. At the inn, 18 sous bought three ladlefuls of daube with any amount of bread and wine.

The classic daube of beef is cooked with salt pork, a calf's foot, tomatoes, red wine, with a strip of orange rind and olives. Some recipes include mushrooms, and many add spices like cinnamon and nutmeg. All agree that the best accompaniment to a daube is noodles or macaroni. Left-over meat should be used as filling for ravioli (see recipe), with the gravy as a sauce.

The beef for daube may be in chunks or in one piece. It must be a tough cut to hold together during long cooking until (says tradition) it is soft enough to be cut with a spoon.

Serves 6–8

2 kg	beef chuck or round roast	4½ lb
1 kg	pork rind, cut in 2 cm/¾ in squares (optional)	2 lb
375 g	lean salt pork, cut in lardons	¾ lb
	1 pig's or calf's foot, washed	
250 g	black olives, pitted (optional)	1¼ cups
1 kg	tomatoes, peeled, seeded and chopped	2 lb
500 g	carrots, quartered or sliced in thick rounds	1 lb
500 g	mushrooms, quartered	1 lb
	pepper	
750 ml	water	3 cups
	MARINADE	
1 L	red wine	1 qt
	3 onions, quartered	
	1 large bouquet garni, including a strip of orange rind (if possible, of bitter orange)	
	2 cloves garlic, crushed	
	6 black peppercorns	
	3 whole cloves	
	pinch of ground cinnamon (optional)	
	2 Tbsp olive oil	

Remove the tendons from the beef and cut it in 5 cm/2 in cubes. Put the beef in a deep bowl and add the marinade ingredients, pouring the olive oil on last. Leave to marinate in the refrigerator for about 24 hours, turning the beef occasionally.

Put the pork rind and salt pork in cold water, bring to a boil and blanch for 10 minutes. Drain, refresh under cold running water and drain thoroughly. Split the pig's foot and remove the large centre bone. If the olives* are very salty, blanch them.

Set the oven at hot (200°C/400°F). Take the beef from the marinade, strain the liquid and set aside. Remove the herbs and spices and tie them in a piece of cheesecloth; reserve the onions separately. In a heavy, deep casserole with a tight-fitting cover, arrange in layers: half the pork rind, all the salt pork, the beef cubes, pig's foot, tomatoes, carrots, mushrooms, olives and reserved onions. Add the marinade with the cheesecloth bag of herbs. Season with pepper only and add water just to cover. Top with the remaining pork rind. Cover with the lid and bring to a boil in the heated oven. Turn down the heat to low (150°C/300°F) and cook for 3½–4 hours or until the beef is very tender or, if you prefer, continue cooking until the beef can be cut with a spoon, in traditional style.

When the meat is cooked, remove the pig's foot and use a fork to pull its meat in shreds from the bones. Return the shredded meat to the daube and discard the cheesecloth bag. Skim off excess fat, taste for seasoning, and spoon the daube into a serving bowl.

STUFATU

Beef stew with macaroni

Corsicans love to eat their pasta with meat gravy. Here the gravy is made as part of a rich beef stew.

Serves 4

30 g	dried mushrooms	1 oz
1 kg	good-quality stewing beef	2 lb
125 g	Corsican ham or other raw ham, cut in thin strips	4 oz
	5–6 cloves garlic	
	salt and pepper	
45 g	lard or oil	3 Tbsp
	2 onions, sliced	
250 ml	dry white wine	1 cup
	2 Tbsp tomato coulis (see recipe)	
	pinch of ground cinnamon (optional)	
	pinch of rosemary	
	bouquet garni	
375 ml	water, more as needed	1½ cups
250 g	large macaroni	½ lb
50 g	grated parmesan cheese	½ cup
	larding needle	

Prepare the dried mushrooms*. Cut the beef into 5 cm/2 in cubes. Using a larding needle, insert a few strips of ham into each piece. Cut 2–3 cloves of the garlic in thin strips and insert them in the pieces of beef. Season lightly with salt and pepper.

Heat the lard in a heavy pot, add the beef cubes, brown them well on all sides and remove. Add the onions and cook over a medium fire, stirring often, until lightly browned. Crush the rest of the garlic and add it with the browned meat. Stir in the white wine, tomato coulis, mushrooms, salt, pepper, cinnamon, rosemary and bouquet garni and cook over a low fire, stirring often, for 30 minutes. Stir in enough water to cover the meat, cover with the lid and continue simmering over a low fire, stirring occasionally for 3 hours or until very tender. Taste for seasoning and discard the bouquet garni. Transfer the pieces of meat to a platter, cover and keep warm.

Just before serving, cook the macaroni in a large quantity of boiling salted water for 10 minutes or until just tender but still slightly chewy ('al dente'). Drain thoroughly and layer the macaroni in a serving bowl with the meat gravy and the grated cheese. Serve the meat and macaroni simultaneously in separate dishes.

RAGOÛT AUX ARTICHAUTS

Mutton and artichoke stew

Most traditional Provençal recipes call for mutton, not lamb, as the sheep were raised for wool rather than for meat. Sheep rearing is one of the most ancient Provençal occupations and in the old days the shepherd was a popular figure, carrying news from village to village as he drove his flock to and from the summer pastures, high in the foothills of the Alps. Today's twice-yearly migration is more mundane, taking place by truck.

Serves 6

2 kg	breast or shoulder of mutton or lamb	4½ lb
	2 Tbsp oil	
750 g	onions, sliced	1½ lb
	1 Tbsp flour	
185 ml	white wine	¾ cup
375 ml	broth	1½ cups
	2 cloves garlic, crushed	
	1 large tomato, quartered	
	bouquet garni	
	salt and pepper	
	12 small OR 6 medium artichokes	
	juice of ½ lemon	

Trim off the excess fat; cut breast in sections or shoulder in 5 cm/2 in chunks. Heat the oil in a heavy based casserole, add the meat and brown it well on all sides over a fairly high fire. Remove the meat, add the onions and cook over a low fire, stirring often, for 10 minutes or until soft but not brown. Sprinkle the onions with the flour and continue to cook for 2–3 minutes or until brown. Stir in the wine and the broth, return the meat to the casserole and add the garlic, tomato, bouquet garni, salt and pepper. Bring to a boil, cover and simmer for 1 hour.

While the meat is simmering, prepare the artichokes: remove the stems and break off the tough leaves. Cut tops off the other leaves to within 2·5 cm/1 in of the artichoke bottoms. Quarter the artichokes lengthwise and remove the chokes with a spoon; cut medium artichokes in eight. Drop artichokes into a bowl of water and add lemon juice.

Drain the artichokes, add them to the meat and simmer for another 30 minutes or until the meat and artichokes are tender. Skim off the excess fat and discard the bouquet garni; taste for seasoning. Serve from the casserole.

PEBRONATA

Veal stew with red wine, pepper and tomato sauce
Pebronata sauce is often served with kid in Corsica; here veal is suggested instead.

Serves 4–6

1 kg	good-quality stewing veal, cut in 5 cm/2 in cubes	2 lb
	salt and pepper	
	2 Tbsp vegetable oil or lard	
	1½ Tbsp flour	
250 ml	white or rosé wine	1 cup
250 ml	broth	1 cup
	PEBRONATA SAUCE	
60 ml	olive oil	¼ cup
	1 onion, chopped	
	4 cloves garlic, chopped	
	pinch of thyme	
	2 Tbsp chopped parsley	
1·5 kg	ripe tomatoes, peeled, seeded and coarsely chopped	3 lb
	salt and pepper	
	3 red peppers, cored, seeded and cut in thin strips	
	1 bay leaf	
	4 juniper berries, crushed	
15 g	flour	2 Tbsp
250 ml	red wine	1 cup

Set the oven at moderate (175°C/350°F). Season the meat with salt and pepper. Heat the oil in a heavy-based casserole, add the meat and brown it well on all sides over a high fire. Sprinkle with the flour, mix well and cook for a minute or two over a low fire. Stir in the wine and broth and bring to a boil. Cover and simmer in the oven, stirring occasionally, for 1½–2 hours or until the meat is very tender. Taste for seasoning.

Meanwhile, start the pebronata sauce: heat half the oil in a shallow pan, add the onion and cook over a low fire, stirring often, until softened. Add the garlic, thyme and parsley and sauté for about a minute. Stir in the tomatoes, salt and pepper and cook over a medium fire, stirring often, for 20 minutes or until very soft.

While the tomatoes are cooking, heat the remaining oil in another shallow pan and sauté the peppers with the bay leaf and juniper berries over a medium fire until softened. Add the flour and cook, stirring, for about a minute. Stir in the red wine, bring to a boil and simmer over a medium fire, stirring often, for 2 minutes. Add the tomato mixture to the peppers and simmer over a low fire until reduced to the consistency of thick cream. Discard the bay leaf.

When the veal is very tender, add the pebronata sauce and simmer for 10 minutes. Taste for seasoning and serve from the casserole.

FOIE DE VEAU MOISSONNIÈRE

Calf's liver in tomato and wine sauce
So as to keep the liver tender, it is important to reheat it in the onion and wine sauce only at the last minute.

Serves 6

75 g	lard or oil	5 Tbsp
750 g	calf's liver, cut in thick slices	1½ lb
	salt and pepper	
750 g	onions, thinly sliced	1½ lb
	bouquet garni	
	1 Tbsp flour	
250 ml	red wine	1 cup
	1 tsp wine vinegar	
	3 Tbsp tomato paste	
	1 clove garlic, chopped	
125 ml	broth or water	½ cup
	pinch of sugar (optional)	

Heat half the lard in a frying pan, add the liver and sauté over a fairly high fire for 2–3 minutes on each side, or until just tender. Sprinkle with salt and pepper. Transfer to a plate and cover.

Heat the remaining lard in the pan, add the onions and bouquet garni, and cook over a low fire, stirring often, for 20 minutes or until the onions are soft but not brown. Raise the fire to medium and continue to cook, stirring constantly, for a few more minutes or until lightly browned. Stir in the flour and cook for 2–3 minutes more. Stir in the wine, vinegar, tomato paste, garlic, broth, salt and pepper. Bring to a boil and simmer for 5–7 minutes or until thick enough to coat a spoon. Taste for seasoning; add a pinch of sugar if the sauce is too acidic.

While the sauce is simmering, cut the sautéed liver in squares or strips. Return them to the thickened sauce to reheat, but be careful not to let the liver boil or it will become tough. Discard the bouquet garni, transfer the liver and sauce to a deep serving dish, and serve immediately.

RIS DE VEAU MOISSONNIÈRE

Substitute **calf's sweetbreads** for the liver, but blanch them first: put the sweetbreads in a pot of cold water and boil for 5 minutes; then drain thoroughly and trim off all membrane. Press them between two plates with a small weight on top until cold; then cut the sweetbreads in 2 cm/¾ in diagonal slices. Coat them in seasoned flour, fry in lard, allowing 5–7 minutes' browning on each side, and continue as above.

ARTICHAUTS À LA BARIGOULE

Artichokes stuffed with mushrooms and ham
The meat stuffing makes these artichokes a substantial first course or a simple main one. The name 'barigoule' comes from 'farigoule', the Provençal word for thyme.

Serves 4

	4 large artichokes	
	$\frac{1}{2}$ lemon	
	salt and pepper	
	1 carrot, sliced	
	1 onion, sliced	
250 ml	white wine	1 cup
750 ml	broth	3 cups
	1 Tbsp arrowroot or potato starch	
	2 Tbsp water	
	PORK AND MUSHROOM STUFFING	
15 g	butter	1 Tbsp
	1 small onion, finely chopped	
250 g	mushrooms, finely chopped	$\frac{1}{2}$ lb
	1 Tbsp chopped parsley	
150 g	1 slice raw ham, finely diced	5 oz
300 g	lean pork	10 oz
100 g	fat pork	$3\frac{1}{2}$ oz
	1 small egg, lightly beaten	
	pepper	
	$\frac{1}{2}$ tsp ground allspice (optional)	
	1 tsp thyme	

For the stuffing, first make a duxelles: melt the butter in a frying pan, add the onion and cook over a low fire until soft but not brown. Add the mushrooms and cook over a high fire, stirring often, until all the moisture has evaporated. Stir in the parsley and ham and leave to cool. Mince/grind the lean and fat pork together and add to the cooled duxelles with the egg, pepper, allspice and thyme. Mix thoroughly until the mixture holds together. Sauté a small piece of the stuffing and taste for seasoning; salt may not be needed because the ham is salty. Heat the oven to moderate (175°C/350°F).

Break the stem of each artichoke and trim the base so it is flat. Cut off 1 cm/$\frac{1}{2}$ in from the top and trim the hard tips of the leaves. Rub cut surfaces with the cut lemon. Blanch the artichokes in boiling salted water for 8 minutes and drain. Remove the choke and inside leaves. Fill the resulting hollow with the stuffing and encircle the leaves of each artichoke with string.

Put the carrot and onion in a casserole deep enough to contain the artichokes. Set the artichokes on the vegetables, add the white wine and boil for 5 minutes or until the wine is reduced by two-thirds. Pour enough broth over the artichokes to cover them by half, add salt and pepper. Bring back to a boil, cover with buttered paper, and braise in the oven for 45 minutes or until tender. Transfer the artichokes to a platter and keep warm while making the sauce.

Dissolve the arrowroot in the water. Strain the cooking liquid into a small saucepan, bring to a boil and stir in enough of the dissolved arrowroot, a little at a time, to obtain a sauce the consistency of thin cream. Simmer for 2 minutes and taste for seasoning. Discard the strings from the artichokes and serve, passing the sauce separately.

AUBERGINES FARCIES AUX ANCHOIS
Eggplant stuffed with anchovies

The richness of eggplant is an excellent foil for anchovies and garlic.

Serves 4

	2 medium eggplants	
	salt and pepper	
125 ml	olive oil	$\frac{1}{2}$ cup
30 g	fresh breadcrumbs	3 Tbsp
	STUFFING	
	8 anchovy fillets	
	2 slices white bread, crusts removed	
60 ml	milk	$\frac{1}{4}$ cup
	2 cloves garlic, chopped	
	salt and pepper	

Leave the aubergines/eggplants unpeeled but discard the stems. Halve the aubergines lengthwise. Use a knife to score the flesh deeply on the cut side of each half in the centre and around the edge near the skin. Sprinkle with salt and leave for 30 minutes to draw out the bitter juices. Rinse the aubergines, drain and dry them thoroughly on paper towels.

Heat the olive oil in a frying pan. Fry the aubergines cut side down for 15 minutes or until the flesh can easily be removed. Discard all but 1 tablespoon of the oil in the pan. Set the oven at moderately hot (190°C/375°F). Using a knife and spoon, gently scoop out the aubergine flesh; be careful not to pierce the skins.

Meanwhile, prepare the stuffing: soak the anchovies in a little water. Soak the bread in the milk; then squeeze it dry. Chop the flesh with the anchovies and garlic. Beat in the soaked bread and a little pepper. Heat the reserved oil in the frying pan, add the stuffing and cook over a low fire, stirring, for 1–2 minutes. Taste for seasoning. Spoon the stuffing into the skins.

Set the stuffed vegetables in an oiled shallow baking dish. Sprinkle them with the breadcrumbs and bake for 20–30 minutes or until very tender and lightly browned. Serve hot or at room temperature.

RATATOUILLE

'Ratatouille' is among the many names that linger from the old Provençal language. Two teaspoons of the herb mixture 'herbes de Provence' may be substituted for the basil, thyme and aniseed in the recipe.

Serves 4

	1 medium eggplant, halved and cut in 1 cm/$\frac{3}{8}$ in slices	
350 g	small zucchini, cut in 1·25 cm/$\frac{1}{2}$ in slices	$\frac{3}{4}$ lb
	salt and pepper	
60 ml	olive oil	$\frac{1}{4}$ cup
	2 medium onions, thinly sliced	
500 g	tomatoes, peeled, seeded and chopped	1 lb
	2 red or green peppers, cored, seeded and sliced	
	2 cloves garlic, crushed	
	1 tsp basil	
	$\frac{1}{2}$ tsp thyme	
	$\frac{1}{2}$ tsp ground coriander	
	a pinch of crushed aniseed	
	1 Tbsp chopped parsley (for sprinkling)	

Sprinkle the aubergine/eggplant and courgette/zucchini slices with salt and let stand for 30 minutes to draw out their liquid. Drain them, rinse with cold water and dry on paper towels.

Heat half the oil in a large casserole, add the onions and cook over low heat, occasionally stirring, until soft but not brown. Layer the onions, aubergine, courgettes, tomatoes and peppers in the casserole, sprinkling the garlic, herbs, salt and pepper between the layers. Spoon the remaining oil on top. Cover and simmer for 30–40 minutes or until all of the vegetables are just tender; if overcooked, they become soft and watery. If the vegetables do produce a great deal of liquid, remove the lid for the last 15 minutes of cooking. Taste for seasoning.

Either serve the ratatouille from the casserole or transfer it to a serving dish. Sprinkle with parsley and serve hot or at room temperature.

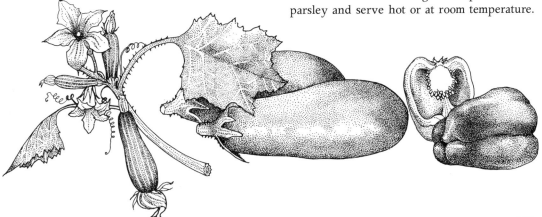

OLIVES AND OLIVE OIL

The olive tree is one of the most valuable oil-producing plants in the world. Raised from a cutting, it grows into an irregular, spreading tree that bears fruit for centuries; the ownership of olive groves is a time-honoured indication of wealth around the Mediterranean. The Assyrians first began cultivating olives in 5000 BC; from ancient times the olive branch has been a symbol of peace, and to cut down an olive tree has been a serious crime.

The bulk of the ripe olive crop is crushed for oil. Picking begins around Christmas and is done by hand or with a special rake which dislodges the fruit. At the mill the olives are first crushed and then pressed, and usually washed with a continuous flow of clear water so that the oil floats and can be skimmed off the surface. In many old villages olive mills were built beside a stream. The modern way is to extract the oil in a centrifuge. The first cold pressing yields the virgin or 'green' oil. Then heated pressings give progressively inferior grades of oil, the last runs being used for making soap, lubricants or lamp fuel.

A good test for the quality of olive oil is its colour: it should be golden or straw-yellow, and have a sweetish, nutty flavour. Bright light will make it fade, hence the green bottles often used as containers, and heat will turn it rancid. Cold makes it congeal, but this has no effect on flavour and the oil will re-emulsify on warming up. It does, however, pick up other tastes and odours and should be stored tightly covered.

Near the Mediterranean, olive oil is often used in place of butter, even on bread, and at the end of the olive harvest in Provence a festival used to be held where aïoli with salt cod and vegetables was served to all the pickers. Around the beginning of this century, the festival moved to the olive mills, where the owners offered a slice of bread which was soaked in olive oil, topped with crushed anchovies and garlic and then baked in the oven. Today both the tradition and the delicacy, the 'roustido dou moulin' seem to have vanished.

An appreciable part of the olive crop escapes the crusher to appear on the table as green (unripe), or black (ripe) olives. However, their preparation is not a simple matter of picking and serving. In spring olive trees produce small greenish flowers which develop by autumn into half-ripe straw-coloured fruits. At this stage they can be picked and cured as green olives by soaking in lye, where they ferment and acquire their astringent taste. If left on the tree, the olives darken and develop more oil until finally they turn jet-black, ready for crushing. Just before this stage, they can be picked and marinated like green olives to give plump, fleshy fruits. The wrinkled, Greek-style olives are fruit that has completely ripened on the tree, and is then simply mixed with salt and left to pickle. Even when ripe, olives are excruciatingly bitter if they are not treated. When staying in Provence three centuries ago, Racine wrote to La Fontaine that he had foolishly tried an olive straight from the tree; 'I hope to goodness I never taste anything so bitter again.'

RAITO or RAITA

Red wine sauce with herbs and olives

One of the oldest Provençal recipes, raito – like 'tapenade' – probably came from the Eastern Mediterranean. It is served hot with fried fish and, on Christmas Eve, with salt cod.

Makes 750 ml/3 cups of sauce

	2 onions	
	2 cloves	
60 ml	olive oil	$\frac{1}{4}$ cup
	1 Tbsp flour	
750 ml	red wine	3 cups
500 ml	boiling water	2 cups
500 g	tomatoes, quartered	1 lb
	3 cloves garlic	
	8 walnut halves, crushed to powder	
	1 sprig each of thyme, rosemary, fennel and parsley	
	salt and pepper	
30 g	capers, drained	2 Tbsp
50 g	black olives, pitted	$\frac{1}{4}$ cup

Stud one onion with the cloves; finely chop the other. Heat the oil in a heavy pan, add the chopped onion and cook over until soft but not brown. Raise the heat and cook, stirring, until the onion is lightly browned. Add the flour and cook over a low fire, stirring constantly, until bubbling. Stir in the wine, water, tomatoes, whole onion, garlic, walnuts and herbs. Bring to a boil, stirring, and simmer over a low fire for 1–1½ hours or until reduced by two-thirds. Discard the whole onion; then push the mixture through a fine sieve, pressing hard. Stir in the capers and olives and season to taste.

COULIS DE TOMATES

Tomato purée

This simple tomato sauce is used in Provence to accompany vegetables or pasta, to enrich sauces and soups, and even to deglaze meat juices in the roasting pan. In Provence, Anguedor and Corsica coulis is made with olive oil and basil, but in other regions vegetable oil is used and the basil omitted. Coulis is often made in large quantities as it can be kept for a week in the refrigerator. For a stronger flavour, add another chopped clove of garlic and a couple of chopped basil leaves after the coulis is cooked.

Makes 1 litre/1 quart of sauce

	3 Tbsp olive oil or vegetable oil	
	2 onions, finely chopped	
	3 cloves garlic, finely chopped	
2·5 kg	ripe tomatoes, peeled, seeded and chopped	5½ lb
	10 basil leaves, chopped (optional)	
	2 tsp sugar (optional)	
	bouquet garni	
	salt and pepper	
	pinch of cayenne pepper	

Heat the oil in a large frying pan, add the onions and cook over a low fire, stirring often, for 10 minutes or until softened. Add the garlic and cook for 1 more minute. Stir in the tomatoes, basil, sugar, bouquet garni, salt and pepper. Bring to a boil and cook over a low fire, stirring often, for 25–30 minutes or until the tomatoes have softened to a purée. Discard the bouquet garni. Add cayenne pepper and taste for seasoning.

TIAN DE COURGETTES
Zucchini gratin

'Tian' is a type of gratin dish, which also gives its name to the food cooked in it. It can be prepared with any vegetable; some favourites are spinach, leaves of Swiss chard and wild asparagus. Sometimes mixtures of vegetables are used: green peas and artichokes, spinach and pumpkin. For this recipe, the courgette/zucchini flowers are often included.

Serves 6

1 kg	zucchini	2 lb
80 ml	olive oil	$\frac{1}{3}$ cup
	salt and pepper	
50 g	rice	$\frac{1}{4}$ cup
	2 onions, thinly sliced	
	1 clove garlic, chopped	
	3 eggs, beaten	
50 g	grated parmesan cheese	$\frac{1}{2}$ cup
	2 Tbsp chopped parsley or basil	
	1·5 L/1½ qt baking dish	

Cut the unpeeled courgettes/zucchini in 6 mm/$\frac{1}{4}$ in thick slices. Heat half the oil in a frying pan, add the courgettes, salt and pepper and cook over a low fire, stirring often, for 20 minutes or until tender. Drain on paper towels; then chop them coarsely.

Cook the rice in a large pot of boiling salted water for 12 minutes or until just tender. Drain and rinse with lukewarm water. Drain thoroughly.

Heat another tablespoon of the oil in a frying pan, add the onion and garlic and cook over a low fire, stirring often, until soft but not browned. Add to the chopped courgettes. Set the oven at moderate (175°C/350°F).

Mix the vegetables with the rice. Add the eggs, cheese, parsley, salt and pepper to taste. Spoon the mixture into the oiled baking dish. Sprinkle with the remaining olive oil and bake for 15 minutes or until set. Raise the oven temperature to hot (200°C/400°F) and bake for 10 more minutes or until brown. Serve from the dish.

GNOCCHI DE POMMES DE TERRE
Potato gnocchi

Though always associated with Italy, in fact, the name 'gnocchi' comes from the Provençal 'inhocs'. Topped with cheese and melted butter, potato gnocchi can be a first course, or they can be left plain to accompany 'boeuf en daube'.

Serves 4–6 (makes about 25 gnocchi)

	3 Tbsp grated parmesan cheese	
60 g	butter, melted	4 Tbsp
	DOUGH	
500 g	large potatoes	1 lb
30 g	butter	2 Tbsp
	1 egg	
120 g	flour	1 cup
50 g	grated parmesan cheese	$\frac{1}{2}$ cup
	salt and pepper	
	pinch of grated nutmeg	

Set the oven at very hot (220°C/425°F). Bake the potatoes in the heated oven for 1 hour or until very tender. Lower the oven temperature to hot (200°C/400°F).

Halve the potatoes and immediately scoop out the pulp so that the steam evaporates. Purée the pulp with a food mill or potato masher and, while it is still very hot, beat in the butter and the egg with a wooden spoon until very smooth. The heat of the potato will cook and slightly thicken the egg. Beat in enough of the flour to give a mixture that is firm and does not stick to your fingers; then beat in the cheese. Season to taste with salt, pepper and nutmeg. Leave to cool.

On a generously floured work surface, roll a portion of the dough to a rope of about 2 cm/$\frac{3}{4}$ in diameter. With a large knife, cut the rope in 2 cm/$\frac{3}{4}$ in lengths. Flatten each piece with the back of a fork dipped in flour, working in a curve to give a shell pattern. Set the gnocchi in a single layer on a floured tray. Continue with the remaining dough.

Bring a large pan of salted water to a boil, add the gnocchi without crowding them and poach over a very low fire for 10–12 minutes or until firm and elastic; don't overcook or they will fall apart. With a slotted spoon, carefully transfer them to paper towels to drain.

Arrange the gnocchi slightly overlapping in a buttered baking dish. Sprinkle them with grated cheese, then with melted butter. Bake in the hot oven for 8–10 minutes or until golden brown. Serve hot from the baking dish.

TISANES

Camomile, mint, elderflower, lime, sage, verbena, lemon balm and wild thyme – the names of 'tisane' infusions or herb teas read like a medieval herbal. But in France these infusions are far from being a historical curiosity, the remedy of crank doctors or the solace of old maids. A cup of camomile tea stimulates the kidneys and 'verveine' (verbena) soothes the liver as well as enjoying mild reknown as an aphrodisiac. 'Tilleul' (lime) the most common of all, ensures a sound sleep and is the sovereign cure for constipation.

Most cafés offer a choice of lime or mint tea, the powdered leaves trapped in dusty little bags that, when infused in boiling water, yield only an echo of their true bouquet. A home 'infusion' made with whole dried leaves is an infinite improvement, its appeal doubled when made in the traditional 'veilleuse' – a little teapot set on a charcoal warmer or, nowadays, a nightlight candle.

Provence is a prime source of herbs for tisanes. Ninety per cent of the French lime crop comes from around the little hill town of Buis-les-Baronnies, where each July an annual market is held, the winged seeds of the limes tied in cloths like giant handkerchiefs. Most camomile comes from the Loire – 70 tonnes a year – and a good deal of mint is also produced commercially, though the French garden without its patch of spearmint spilling over the paving stones in invitation for the nightly tisane is poorly planted indeed.

Elderflower

Wild thyme

Lime

Verbena

Balm

Mint

Sage

Camomile

ORANGES GIVRÉES
Iced oranges

'Among the refreshments of these warm countries,' remarked Tobias Smollett when in Nice in 1764, 'I ought not to forget mentioning the sorbettes, which are sold in coffee-houses and places of public resort. They are iced froth, made with the juice of oranges, apricots, or peaches; very agreeable to the palate.'

Serves 8

	14 medium oranges	
	juice of $\frac{1}{2}$ lemon, more if needed	
80 ml	water	$\frac{1}{3}$ cup
	SYRUP	
150 g	sugar, more if needed	$\frac{3}{4}$ cup
125 ml	water	$\frac{1}{2}$ cup
	juice of $\frac{1}{2}$ lemon	

Make the syrup: in a heavy-based pan heat the sugar with the water and lemon juice over low heat until the sugar dissolves. Boil for 2–3 minutes or until the syrup is clear. Leave to cool.

Meanwhile, slice the top quarter off eight of the oranges to form 'hats'. Scoop out the pulp from these oranges and reserve it; chill the shells and hats in the freezer. Grate the rind of the remaining oranges into the syrup. Squeeze the juice from the oranges and from the scooped out pulp; there should be 750 ml orange juice.

Stir the orange juice, lemon juice and water into the cool syrup and taste; add more sugar or lemon juice if necessary. Freeze the mixture in a churn freezer until firm. Pack the frozen mixture into the chilled shells, mounding well, and set the hats on top. Keep in the freezer until ready to serve.

ORANGES AU GRANITÉ
If you don't have a churn freezer, proceed as follows: put the mixture in a deep metal bowl and set this bowl in a larger bowl containing coarse salt and crushed ice; there should be enough salt and ice to surround the inner bowl so the mixture chills evenly. Whisk constantly for about 20 minutes or until the mixture is too stiff to stir: it will be more granular than if made as a sorbet in a churn-freezer. Pack into the chilled shells as above.

FRUITS GLACÉS AND FRUITS CONFITS

Candied fruits from Apt were served at the papal court in Avignon in the 14th century – Pope Clement VI was especially partial to them – and the French still excel at making this sugary delicacy. There are two kinds of candied fruits: 'fruits glacés', which are preserved in sugar syrup and glazed to eat as a sweetmeat, and 'fruits confits', preserved without glaze and usually sold in pieces for flavouring cakes and pastries. Shop windows, especially at Christmas, are adorned with candied fruits, from little ones like tangerines and greengage plums to small pumpkins and whole pineapples with peel and leaves intact. Works of art it seems sacrilege to cut open.

To candy even small pieces of fruit or peel and retain the flavour takes time and is therefore expensive. Orange, lemon and citron are most commonly candied, but soft fruits such as strawberries are too juicy. The fruit is soaked in progressively more concentrated batches of hot syrup, larger fruits taking up to eight days to cook. The goal is slowly to replace the water in the fruit with sugar syrup. In the time of Clement VI, the fruits were left two to three months in syrup, a candying method that is still occasionally found in the south. Such hand-crafted confections bear little resemblance to the sickly candied fruits, sticky with syrup, that are sold ready-chopped in plastic tubs in supermarkets.

Almost more popular than the fruits themselves are their by-product 'berlingots' – little hard candies made by boiling left-over fruit syrup to a hard crack, then cooling and shaping it in twists. A candied pineapple may be a rarity, but every schoolchild is familiar with berlingots.

TOURTE DE BLETTES
Swiss chard and apple pie

This unusual pie has a biscuity crust, the Swiss chard giving sharpness to the sweet filling; spinach is an alternative to chard. The filling is even better if it is made ahead and chilled overnight before it is put in the pastry. Some serve this as dessert; others reduce the amount of sugar and serve the tourte as an appetizer.

Serves 6–8

PIE PASTRY		
390 g	flour	3 cups
250 g	butter	½ lb
	1 egg yolk	
45 g	confectioners' sugar	5 Tbsp
	5–6 Tbsp cold water	
	confectioners' sugar (for sprinkling)	
SWISS CHARD FILLING		
100 g	raisins	½ cup
80 ml	milk	⅓ cup
1·5 kg	Swiss chard OR	3 lb
400 g	fresh spinach	13 oz
400 g	apples, peeled and sliced	13 oz
75 g	pine nuts	½ cup
	2 Tbsp red currant jelly	
	10 Tbsp brown sugar	
40 g	grated mild Dutch cheese, such as gouda	6 Tbsp
	2 eggs	
	grated rind of 1 lemon	
	1 Tbsp rum	
	25 cm/10 in pie or tart pan	

Make the pie pastry*, and chill for 30 minutes or until firm. Line the pie pan* with two-thirds of the dough and chill for 15 minutes or until firm. Set the oven at moderately hot (190°C/375°F). Blind bake* the pastry and leave to cool.

For the filling: soak the raisins in the milk for 30 minutes, then simmer them in the milk for 20 minutes or until softened. Drain and discard the milk. Discard the ribs from the chard and use only the leaves. (The ribs can be used for a gratin.) Add the leaves to a large pot of boiling water and boil for 3–4 minutes. Drain and rinse under cold running water. Drain again and squeeze out all excess liquid. Chop the chard and mix it with the raisins, apples, pine nuts, jelly, sugar, cheese, eggs, lemon rind and rum.

Spoon the filling into the baked shell. Roll out the remaining dough to a thin layer and use a pan lid to cut a circle a little larger than the diameter of the top of the pie shell. Set the circle on top, pressing to stick it to the edges of the baked shell. Bake the pie for 1 hour or until the dough is golden brown. Let it cool in the pan.

Serve the pie at room temperature, sprinkled, if you like, with sugar.

TARTE AU CITRON
Lemon tart

Lemon trees are delicate and most of the French crop comes from Corsica. However, a few can be found in the sheltered corner of the Riviera near the Italian border.

Serves 6–8

SWEET PIE PASTRY		
200 g	flour	1½ cups
	4 egg yolks	
	½ tsp salt	
100 g	sugar	½ cup
	1 tsp vanilla extract	
125 g	butter	¼ lb
LEMON FILLING		
	2 eggs	
100 g	sugar	½ cup
	grated rind and juice of 1½ lemons	
125 g	butter, melted	¼ lb
60 g	whole blanched almonds, ground	⅓ cup
	27–30 cm/11–12 in pie pan	

Make the sweet pie pastry* and chill for 30 minutes or until firm. Set the oven at moderately hot (190°C/375°F).

Roll out the dough, line the pie pan and chill until firm. Bake blind* in the heated oven for 12–15 minutes or until set but not brown. Take from the oven, remove paper and beans and let the pie shell cool slightly. Put a baking sheet in the oven to heat.

Meanwhile, make the filling: beat the eggs and sugar until light and thick enough to leave a ribbon trail when the whisk is lifted. Stir in the rind and lemon juice, followed by the melted butter and ground almonds.

Set the pie shell in the pan on the hot baking sheet and pour the mixture into the shell. Bake for 25–30 minutes or until the filling is golden brown and set. Serve at room temperature.

CONFITURE D'ABRICOTS SECS
Dried-apricot jam

Most of the fresh apricots grown in France come from Provence and Languedoc. In addition, Languedoc has a large apricot canning and drying industry. When choosing dried apricots, look for fruit with a deep colour.

Makes 2–2·5 kg/5–6 lb jam

750 g	dried apricots	1½ lb
1 L	water	1 qt
750 g	sugar	3¾ cups
	juice of ½ lemon	
75 g	almonds, blanched and cut in slivers	½ cup
five or six 500-g/1-lb jars		

Soak the apricots overnight and drain. Put the apricots and the water in a large heavy pot. Bring to a boil and simmer, partly covered, for 1 hour or until very soft. Add the sugar and lemon juice and stir gently over low heat until the sugar melts. It is important that the sugar is melted before the mixture boils. Add the almonds and boil rapidly, stirring often, until the jell point is reached. Cool until tepid, and pour into sterilized jars. Cover and seal when cool.

CHEESES

Few Provençal or Corsican cheeses are well known outside the region, but an appealing Provençal contribution is the 'banon', a small cake covered in chestnut leaves and bound with rafia. Made of goat's, sheep's or cow's milk, it has a milky, almost nutty flavour. A fragrant variant, aged in sprigs of savory rather than chestnut leaves, is 'poivre d'âne' – literally donkey's pepper. The fresh goat cheese, 'brousse du Rove', from the rocky region west of Marseille, used to be made at night for sale the next morning and restaurant gourmets reserved the small supply at the beginning of their meal. Today brousse is sold in plastic packs; firm and mild, it is eaten with sugar and a sprinkling of orange flower water.

'Le cachat' is the daily cheese for Provençal farmers. It is often kneaded with pepper and a generous shot of cognac or eau-de-vie, then aged in a pot as fromage fort (strong cheese). Also called 'cachèio' (from 'cacha' meaning to crush), this cheese appears in the Var as 'broussin' and as 'brous' around the Nice region.

The cheeses of Corsica are made mainly from goat's and sheep's milk. 'Niolo' is a powerful goat cheese which is in season from October to May. A sheep cheese reminiscent of roquefort and called 'bleu de Corse' is made in Corsica; the curds may also be shipped to the Languedoc to be refined in the Roquefort caves and sold under the roquefort label.

Best known is the 'broccio' or 'brocciu' a farm cheese made of sheep's milk. Most broccio is mild, but a sharper version is aged for over six months with periodic washings in brine. Fresh broccio is the basis of the Corsican 'tarte de brocciu', a cheese tart along the lines of Italian 'torta di ricotta'. Baked in an open pastry shell, it can be flavoured with orange rind or liqueur, or made more interesting by the addition of raisins.

OTHER SPECIALITIES OF THE REGION
TRADITIONAL DISHES

Bagna caouda
Anchovy and butter sauce for raw vegetables

Moules au riz
Mussels with rice, tomatoes, garlic and parsley

Anchoïade
Anchovy spread

Scampi provençale
Sautéed scampi with garlic, tomato and parsley

Socca
Chick-pea flour crêpes

Supions frits
Deep-fried small squid

Aigo boulido
Garlic and sage soup

Cabri rôti
Corsican roast kid

Soupe de moules à la marseillaise
Mussel and tomato soup with macaroni

Boeuf avignonnaise
Sliced beef with garlic, pimento and anchovy sauce

Trouchia
Flat omelette with spinach and Swiss chard

Beignets de fleurs de courgettes
Batter-fried courgette/zucchini flowers

Omelette au brocciu
Corsican omelette with brocciu cheese

Papeton d'aubergines
Aubergine/eggplant baked with eggs and cheese

Morue aux épinards
Salt cod with spinach

Boumanio
Purée of aubergine/eggplant with cream

Porquerolles
Sea bass with herb stuffing

Barbouillade
Artichokes with broad beans

Daurade à la crème d'oursins
Sea-bream with sea-urchin sauce

Olives à la pitchoulino
Stuffed black olives with rosemary

CHARCUTERIE

Saucisson d'Arles
Dried sausage with peppercorns, pimento and garlic

Pieds et paquets à la marseillaise
Stuffed tripe

PÂTISSERIE AND CONFISERIE

Fougasse
Salty flat bread made with olive oil

Nougat de Montélimar
White nougat

Panzarotti
Corsican lemon rice fritters

Biscotins d'Aix
Little hard, dry biscuits

Campanile
Corsican yeast cake ring with hard-boiled eggs

Navettes aux oeufs
Lemon-flavoured oval cakes

Fiadone
Corsican cheesecake

Chichi-freggi
Deep-fried bread spirals, sprinkled with sugar

Glossary

This glossary provides descriptions of the principal ingredients that differ significantly between France and other countries; it also defines certain cooking terms and techniques used in the preceding pages. To avoid repetition, recipes and procedures common to many of the dishes are included; proportions vary from recipe to recipe, but the method of mixing is always that described here.

References in the text to glossary entries are marked by an asterisk (*).

A

Artichoke bottoms Choose large artichokes to make a generous cup shape. Boil a large pot of water. Add salt and juice of $\frac{1}{2}$ lemon. Add juice of another $\frac{1}{2}$ lemon to a bowl of cold water. Break stem from artichoke. With a very sharp knife held against side of artichoke, cut off all large bottom leaves, leaving a soft cone of central leaves. Trim cone level with top of artichoke base. Rub base well with another cut lemon to prevent discoloration. Cut off leaves under base and trim smooth, flattening the bottom. Rub again with cut lemon and keep artichoke in cold lemon water. Repeat with remaining artichokes. To cook: drain artichokes, put in boiling water and cover with tea-towel or heatproof plate to keep them submerged. Simmer 15–20 minutes or until tender. To serve hot, drain and scoop out hairy choke with a teaspoon. To serve cold, cool to tepid in liquid; then drain and remove choke.

B

Bacon, to blanch Cut in lardons or pieces, according to recipe. Put in pan of cold water, bring to a boil and simmer 2–3 minutes. Drain, rinse with cold water and drain thoroughly.

Béchamel sauce Proportions of flour and butter to milk vary, giving a thinner or thicker sauce as required.

Scald milk in a saucepan. Add onion, bay leaf and peppercorns. Cover and leave to infuse for 5–10 minutes. Melt butter in a heavy-based saucepan, whisk in flour and cook 1–2 minutes until foaming but not brown; let cool. Strain in hot milk and bring sauce to a boil, whisking constantly. Add a pinch of salt, pepper and nutmeg and simmer 3–5 minutes. Taste for seasoning. If not using at once smear surface of sauce with butter to prevent skin from forming.

Blind baking Pastry shells are baked blind (empty) when filling might soak the pastry, or when filling is not to be cooked in the shell.

Tarts or pies Line the chilled pastry shell with greaseproof/parchment paper, pressing it well into corners; fill with dried beans or rice. Bake in hot oven (200°C/400°F) 15 minutes or until pastry edges are set and lightly browned. Remove paper and beans and continue baking 4–5 minutes until base is just firm if tart is to be baked for filling, or 8–10 minutes if tart is not to be baked further.

Tartlets Line the chilled pastry shells with foil or greaseproof/parchment paper, or with cupcake papers, fill with dried beans or rice. Alternatively put a smaller tartlet pan inside each shell. Set pans on baking sheet and bake for 8–10 minutes. Remove paper and beans and continue baking 3–4 minutes if tartlets are to be baked with a filling, or 5–7 minutes if not to be baked further.

Bouquet garni Includes a sprig of thyme, a bay leaf and several stalks of parsley; when indicated, add celery, leek or tarragon. Tie together for easy removal.

Broth In country kitchens where pot-au-feu, poule au pot or potée (see recipes) were made regularly, left-over broth was always kept to use in other dishes. When recipes call for broth, follow this example, or use classic chicken, veal or beef stock. To make simple household broth as in a stockpot: put a few fresh chicken, veal or beef bones in a pot and cover with cold water. Simmer a few hours. Each day add left-over cooked or raw bones from meat, game or poultry. Bring broth to a boil each day and, in warm weather, refrigerate overnight. When pot is full, strain broth and start again.

Butter Most French butter is unsalted, but 'beurre demi-sel' is lightly salted and 'beurre salé' has quite a strong flavour. Use lightly salted butter for these recipes except where unsalted butter is specified, e.g. puff pastry.

Clarified butter Melt butter over low fire, skim froth from surface and let cool to tepid. Pour butter into bowl, leaving milky sediment at bottom of pan.

Kneaded butter Soften butter on a plate with a fork, add an equal amount of flour and mash mixture to a smooth paste. Whisk small pieces of paste into boiling liquid, adding only enough to give required consistency.

C

Chestnuts Peel using one of three methods: 1 Cut all shell and skin from nuts with a sharp knife (this avoids cooking the nut). 2 Pierce nuts once with a pointed knife, then grill/broil until the shells split, and peel them. 3 (the most popular method) Bring nuts to a boil in water. Drain a few at a time and peel while still hot. When they cool and become hard to peel, reheat them.

Weight for weight, canned chestnuts are the equivalent of fresh, unpeeled nuts; for the dried or frozen equivalent, a kilo of fresh medium-sized nuts contains about 50 nuts. Soak dried chestnuts and thaw frozen ones, then treat like fresh peeled chestnuts. Canned chestnuts are already fairly soft, so need little further cooking and must be reheated with care.

Chicken or duck To cut in pieces: with heavy knife, trim legs, leaving drumstick knuckle attached to leg bone. Cut off wingtips. Cut between leg and body, following outline of thigh, until leg joint is visible. Locate oyster meat lying against backbone, and cut around it so it remains attached to thigh. Twist leg sharply outwards to break thigh joint. Cut each leg from body, including oyster meat. With a knife or poultry shears, cut away backbone and cut along breastbone to halve carcass. The bird is now in 4 pieces. To cut into 6 pieces, divide each breast in half, cutting diagonally through meat, then through breast and rib bones so a portion of breast meat is cut off with wing. Trim rib bones. To cut into 8 pieces, cut legs in half through joint, using white line of fat on underside as guide. Cook backbone and wingtips with other pieces to help flavour sauce. Before serving, trim drumstick knuckles and any protruding bones with poultry shears.

Chili peppers To prepare: fresh chili peppers burn the skin so touch only with a cloth, wear rubber gloves or wash hands, knife and chopping board immediately after handling. If using dried, soak in cold water 20 minutes or until soft enough to remove seeds. For both fresh and dried peppers: discard stems, cores and seeds, then cut in pieces or chop.

Choux pastry Used to make sweet and savoury puffs. Add cheese, lemon rind or other flavourings after eggs.

In a small saucepan gently heat water, salt and butter until butter melts. Meanwhile sift flour on to a piece of paper. Bring butter mixture just to a boil (prolonged boiling evaporates water and changes proportions of dough). Take from heat and immediately add flour. Beat vigorously with wooden spatula a few moments until mixture is smooth and pulls away from pan to form a ball. Beat $\frac{1}{2}$–1 minute over low fire to dry dough. Beat one egg until mixed; set aside. With wooden spatula beat remaining eggs into dough one at a time, beating thoroughly after each addition. Beat in enough of reserved egg so dough is shiny and just falls from spoon. If too much egg is added, dough cannot be shaped.

Clams *see* Mussels

Cream cheese In France cream cheese is soft and moist and has a distinctive flavour: in England substitute 'fromage frais' or curd cheese, worked through a sieve. In the USA use Philadelphia-style cream cheese, softened with a few spoons of cream.

Crème fraîche, to make Crème fraîche tastes best if made with buttermilk, next best with sour cream; it is least good made with yoghurt, but keeps longest. Double/heavy cream is an alternative, particularly in desserts.

In a saucepan, stir together 500 ml double/heavy cream and 250 ml buttermilk, sour cream or yoghurt. Heat gently until just below body temperature, 25°C/75°F. Pour into a container and partly cover. Keep at this temperature 6–8 hours or until cream has thickened and tastes slightly acid. Cream may thicken faster on a hot day than on a cold day. Stir cream, cover and refrigerate; it will keep up to 2 weeks. When making a new batch, an equal quantity of made crème fraîche may be substituted for the buttermilk.

Croûtes Allow 1 slice white bread or 2–3 slices of a long French loaf per person. Discard crusts of white bread and cut into desired shapes; cut French bread in thin diagonal slices, including crust. Heat enough oil, butter or a mixture of the two in a frying pan so base is generously coated. When fat is very hot, add a layer of croûtes, brown them on both sides over a medium-high fire and drain on paper towels. Rub fried croûtes with garlic, if liked. For some dishes, especially salads, croûtes can be toasted instead of fried.

Croûtons Smaller than croûtes, and made from firm white bread or, occasionally, from rye bread. Allow about ½ slice per person. Trim and discard crusts and cut bread into small cubes. Heat enough oil, butter or mixture of the two in a frying pan so base is generously coated. When fat is very hot, add bread cubes, which should all touch pan base, and fry briskly, stirring constantly, until evenly browned. Drain thoroughly.

D

Duck *see* Chicken

F

Fish stock Usually made from bones of fish used in the particular recipe. Break 750 g fish bones into pieces and rinse under cold running water. Melt 1 Tbsp butter in a pot, add 1 sliced onion and cook over low fire until soft but not brown. Add fish bones, 1 L water, bouquet garni, 10 peppercorns and 250 ml dry white wine (optional). Bring to a boil, skimming occasionally, and simmer uncovered 20 minutes. Strain and cool. Makes about 1 L stock.

Flour French flour is made from soft wheat and is similar to British plain flour. US all-purpose flour is made from harder wheat, but almost always can be substituted directly for French flour, using different proportions; in the few recipes where there are problems use a mixture of all-purpose and cake flour.

G

Glaze For white, green or yellow fruit tarts: over low heat melt 360 g apricot jam with juice of ½ lemon and 2–3 Tbsp water, then strain into pan; for red fruit tarts: melt red currant jelly. If necessary, boil to consistency of thick syrup. Use while hot and melted.

H

Herbs Quantities given in the recipes are for fresh herbs: strength of dried herbs varies, but in general they are two to three times as strong as fresh ones.

L

Larding meat Use firm pork fat or mild bacon. Cut into 'lardons' – strips thin enough to fit easily into a larding needle. Sew each lardon lengthwise into meat, holding lardon in place with a finger and twisting to remove needle. Space lardons evenly so each slice has a pattern when meat is carved. If a needle is not available, pierce meat with a small knife and insert a lardon in each cut.

Lobster To kill instantaneously: lay lobster flat on a board, hard shell up, head facing right; cover tail with a cloth. Hold lobster firmly behind head with the left hand and, with point of a sharp, heavy knife, pierce down to board through cross mark at centre of head. To cut in pieces: continue splitting body lengthwise as far as tail; then cut tail from body in one piece. Save liquid that runs from lobster. Scoop out soft green meat (tomalley) and any black coral from body; reserve them. Discard head sac. Cut lobster tail, including shell, into thick slices, discarding intestinal tract. Crack claws.

Luting paste Put about 100 g flour in a bowl and stir in about 60 ml water to make a soft paste. Don't beat or paste will become elastic and shrink during cooking.

M

Mushrooms *see* Wild mushrooms

Mussels and clams Quantities given in recipes are for mussels or clams in their shells. To clean: wash under cold running water, scraping shells clean with a knife and removing any weed. Discard any shells which do not close when tapped as mussel or clam may be dead.

O

Olives Green or black olives should be tasted for saltiness before being added to cooked dishes. If mild, rinse in cold water and drain. If salty, blanch by putting olives in cold water and bringing to a boil. Simmer 2 minutes, drain, rinse in cold water and drain thoroughly.

P

Pastry cream Scald all but a few tablespoons of milk with salt. If using vanilla bean, add it, cover and leave to infuse 10–15 minutes. Whisk egg yolks with sugar until thick and light. Stir in flour and reserved milk to make a smooth paste. Remove vanilla bean; whisk boiling milk into yolk mixture. Return mixture to pan and whisk over low fire until boiling. If lumps form, take pan at once from fire and whisk cream until smooth. Cook cream over a low fire, whisking constantly, for 2 minutes or until it thins slightly, showing flour is completely cooked. Transfer to a bowl and rub surface with butter to prevent a skin forming. Whisk in any other flavouring when cream is cool.

Pâté pastry Substitute lard for part or all butter in pie pastry, adding fat with a little oil to well in flour.

Pie pastry (pâte brisée) The French pâte brisée is used for savoury or sweet pies and tartlets.

Sift flour on to work surface and make a large well. Pound butter with rolling pin to soften it. Put butter, egg yolks, salt and most of the water in the well with flavourings such as sugar or brandy. Work together with fingertips of one hand until partly mixed. Gradually draw in flour, pulling dough into large crumbs using fingertips of both hands. If crumbs are dry, sprinkle with another tablespoon of water. Press dough together; it should be soft but not sticky. Work small portions of dough, pushing away from you on the work surface, then gathering it up with a spatula; continue until dough is smooth and pliable. Press dough into a ball, wrap and chill 30 minutes or until firm.

Pie pastry (sweet) Ground almonds or hazelnuts can be substituted for part of flour; other flavourings may replace vanilla. Sift flour on to work surface and make a large well. Put egg yolks, salt, sugar and vanilla in well and mix with fingertips until sugar dissolves. Pound butter with rolling pin to soften, add it to the well and quickly work with other ingredients until partly mixed. Draw in flour, work dough and chill as when making pâte brisée above.

Praline Used to flavour desserts or as decoration. In a heavy-based pan put almonds and sugar; heat gently to melt sugar. Cook over low heat, stirring, while sugar caramelizes to dark brown and almonds begin to pop, showing that they are toasted. Pour mixture into generously oiled baking sheet to cool. When cold and crisp, grind praline a little at a time in a blender or food processor, or with a rotary cheese grater, until very fine.

Puff pastry In a hot kitchen, chill work surface with trays of ice when starting to make dough and again between rollings.

Melt a walnut-sized piece of butter, keeping rest cold. Sift flour on to cold surface, make a well and add salt, lemon juice, smaller amount of water and melted butter. Work central ingredients quickly with fingertips until mixed. Gradually draw in flour, pulling dough into large crumbs using fingertips of both hands. If crumbs are dry, add enough water to make a soft, almost sticky dough – the amount depends on dryness of the flour. Cut dough several times with a dough scraper so ingredients are evenly blended but don't knead or it will be elastic. Press dough to form a ball; wrap and chill 20 minutes or until firm enough to roll.

Lightly flour butter, flatten with a rolling pin to a square and fold sides inward. Continue pounding and folding until pliable but not sticky; butter should be same consistency as flour dough. Shape butter into a 15 cm/6 in square. Roll dough on floured surface to a 30 cm/12 in circle, thicker in centre than at edge. Set butter in centre and fold dough around it like an envelope. Pound seams lightly to seal.

Place package of dough, seams down, on floured work surface and tap 3 or 4 times with rolling pin to flatten slightly. Roll to a rectangle about 20 cm/8 in wide and 50 cm/20 in long. Fold rectangle in 3, one end inside, like a business letter, aligning layers neatly. This rolling

313

Glossary

and folding is called a 'turn'. Seal edges with rolling pin and rotate dough 90°, bringing fold to the left so dough opens like a book. Roll out again and fold in 3 for the second turn. Keep track of turns by marking dough lightly with appropriate number of fingerprints. Wrap dough and chill 30 minutes. Repeat 2 turns, working always closed seam to the left. Chill, then repeat, making a total of 6 turns. Before using dough, wrap and chill at least 1 hour or until firm.

R

Rabbit To cut in pieces: trim and discard flaps of skin, tips of forelegs and any excess bone. Using a heavy knife or cleaver, divide rabbit crosswise into three sections: back legs, back, and forelegs including rib cage. Cut between back legs to separate them; trim end of backbone. Chop front of rabbit in 2 to separate forelegs. Cut back crosswise into 2 or 3 pieces, depending on size, giving 6 or 7 pieces. Leave kidneys attached to ribs. For 8 or 9 pieces, cut each leg in two crosswise.

S

Scallops Allow 2–3 scallops per person. To prepare: simply rinse and dry shelled scallops. If using scallops in shells, put shell on chopping board, hinge downwards and flat half of shell to the right. Insert a sturdy knife between shells and prise open slightly. Carefully cut scallop meat away from flat shell, keeping knife parallel to shell. Wedging shell open with a finger, continue cutting downwards until shells fall apart. Discard flat shell. With knife, scrape scallop meat and beard from rounded shell. With fingers peel off membrane and beard surrounding scallop meat, leaving only round white 'nut' and crescent-shaped orange coral. Wash meat thoroughly and dry. Use rounded shells, washed, as containers.

Sorrel As with spinach, tear off stems and wash leaves thoroughly, using several changes of water. Allow 250 ml well-drained canned sorrel for every 500 g fresh sorrel.

Sugar 'Sugar' refers to UK castor sugar, US granulated sugar. If another type is needed, such as UK icing sugar or US confectioners' sugar, this is stated in the recipe.

T

Tarts, pies and tartlets, to line pans Either fluted or plain pans are suitable; tart pans with removable bottoms are easiest to use. Plain pie pastry should be rolled to medium thickness (6 mm/¼ in), sweet pie pastry a little thicker and puff pastry thinner.

Tarts or pies Lightly butter pan. Roll dough about 5 cm/2 in larger than pan. Lift dough around rolling pin and unroll over pan, being careful not to stretch it. Gently lift edges and press dough well into corners of pan, using small ball of dough dipped in flour. Roll pin across top of pan to cut off excess dough. With fingers press dough evenly up edge of pan to increase height of shell. Prick with fork and chill until firm.

Tartlets Set lightly buttered tartlet pans close together. Roll dough about 5 cm/2 in larger than pans. Lift dough around rolling pin; unroll over all pans at once. Ease dough down into individual pans, then proceed as above.

Tomatoes In cooked dishes, canned Italian-style tomatoes often have more flavour than fresh tomatoes not ripened on the vine. For 1 kg fresh tomatoes, allow 750 g canned tomatoes, draining thoroughly before using.

V

Vinaigrette dressing Use neutral salad oil, olive or walnut oil, as preferred. In France, wine vinegar is usual, but sometimes lemon juice is substituted. Chopped onion, shallot, garlic or fresh herbs such as parsley, tarragon, or chives should be added to dressing just before using.

Whisk 1 Tbsp vinegar with a little salt, pepper and mustard. Gradually whisk in 3 Tbsp oil so the vinaigrette thickens slightly. Taste for seasoning.

W

White sauce *see* Béchamel sauce, but omit onion, bay leaf and peppercorns.

Wild mushrooms All fresh wild mushrooms need the same preparation. Pick over to remove twigs and grass, then lightly trim stems. Shake and gently brush to remove any earth; morels are the most gritty, so brush each one well, splitting stem to remove any soil inside. Rinse with cold water, but never soak fresh mushrooms or they quickly soften to a pulp. Soak dried mushrooms in warm water 1–2 hours until fairly soft. Morels may need rinsing again, but liquid from other mushrooms adds flavour to soup or sauce. A kilo of fresh mushrooms is the equivalent of 100 g dried ones, but the flavour of both fresh and dried mushrooms varies very much in strength.

Y

Yeast If using dried yeast, allow half the weight of fresh. Sprinkle dried yeast over liquid and leave to dissolve; crumble fresh yeast into liquid, then stir to dissolve it.

WEIGHTS AND MEASURES

These summary tables show the equivalent measurements on which the recipes in the book were based: the exact equivalents have been rounded up or down for convenience.

When using the recipes, follow either one set of measurements or the other to keep the proportions correct and obtain accurate results.

WEIGHTS

Metric	UK/US	
15 g		½ oz
30 g		1 oz
45 g		1½ oz
60 g		2 oz
75 g		2½ oz
90 g		3 oz
100 g		3½ oz
125 g	¼ lb	4 oz
150 g	⅓ lb	5 oz
180 g		6 oz
200 g		7 oz
250 g	½ lb	8 oz
300 g		10 oz
350 g	¾ lb	12 oz
500 g	1 lb	16 oz
600 g	1¼ lb	
750 g	1½ lb	
1 kg	2 lb	
1·25 kg	2½ lb	
1·5 kg	3 lb	
2 kg	4½ lb	
2·25 kg	5 lb	

LIQUIDS

Metric	UK	
60 ml	2 fl oz	
80 ml	3 fl oz	
100 ml	4 fl oz	
125 ml	4½ fl oz	
150 ml	5 fl oz	¼ pt
185 ml	6 fl oz	
200 ml	7 fl oz	⅓ pt
225 ml	8 fl oz	
300 ml	10 fl oz	½ pt
400 ml	15 fl oz	¾ pt
500 ml	18 fl oz	
(568 ml	20 fl oz	1 pt)
700 ml		1¼ pt
750 ml		1⅓ pt
800 ml		1½ pt
1 L		1¾ pt
1·25 L		2 pt
1·3 L		2¼ pt
1·4 L		2½ pt
1·5 L		2⅔ pt
1·8 L		3¼ pt
2 L		3½ pt

Metric	US	
60 ml	¼ cup	
80 ml	⅓ cup	5 Tbsp
95 ml		6 Tbsp
125 ml	½ cup	
160 ml	⅔ cup	
185 ml	¾ cup	
250 ml	1 cup	
310 ml	1¼ cups	
330 ml	1⅓ cups	
375 ml	1½ cups	
410 ml	1⅔ cups	
435 ml	1¾ cups	
500 ml	2 cups	
560 ml	2¼ cups	
625 ml	2½ cups	
685 ml	2¾ cups	
750 ml	3 cups	
1 L	1 qt	

COMPARATIVE OVEN TEMPERATURES

°C	°F	gas
140	275	1
150	300	2
160	325	3
175	350	4
190	375	5
200	400	6
220	425	7
230	450	8
240	475	9

Index

Bibliography

Most of the books on regional cooking published in France deal with a particular area, occasionally as part of a country-wide series. Some are distributed only locally and rapidly fall out of print. Although they are rich in anecdote, their recipes are often repetitive, and the following selection covers most distinctive regional dishes. The ideal library would contain some prewar classics, notably by de Croze (now reprinted), as well as a number of cookbooks written in English, especially those by Elizabeth David.

All books are published in Paris unless otherwise indicated

CHANOT-BULLIER, C.: *Vieilles recettes de cuisine provençale*. Editions Tacussel, Marseille, 1972
COURTINE, Robert J.: *Grand Livre de la France à Table*. Bordas, 1979
CROZE, Austin de: *Les plats régionnaux de France*, 1928; facsimile by Daniel Morcrette, BP 25, 95270 Luzarches
ÉDITIONS HACHETTE: *Les desserts de nos provinces*, 1974
ÉDITIONS SOLAR: Occasional paperback series (*La Cuisine Alsacienne*, etc) by various authors, 1974 onwards
GUINANDEAU-FRANC, Zette: *Les secrets des fermes en Périgord Noir*. Éditions Serg, 1978
LALLEMAND, Roger: *La vraie cuisine* series: planned as a 25-volume compendium, published 1967 onwards, of French regional cooking. Quartier Latin, La Rochelle and Éditions Lanore, Paris
LA MAZILLE: *La bonne cuisine de Périgord*. Flammarion, 1929 (reprinted)
LIBRAIRIE ISTRA, Strasbourg (various authors): *Les recettes de la table alsacienne*, 1969; *Les recettes de la table niçoise*, 1972; *Les recettes de la table franc-comtoise*, 1974; *Les recettes de la table occitane*, 1977; *Les recettes de la table bourguignonne*, 1977
MARTY, Albin: *Fourmiguetto – souvenirs, contes et recettes de Languedoc*. Éditions CREER, Nonette, 1978
MORAND, Simone: *Gastronomie Bretonne d'hier et d'aujhourd'hui*, Flammarion, 1965; *Gastronomie Normande*, Flammarion, 1970; *Cuisine et gastronomie du Maine, de la Touraine et de l'Anjou*, Ouest France, Rennes, 1977
PALAY, Simin: *La Cuisine du Pays*: Armagnac, Pays Basque, Béarn, Bigorre, Landes. Éditions Marrimpouey Jeune, Pau 1936 (reprinted)
ROBAGLIA, Suzanne: *Margaridou – Journal et recettes d'une cuisinière au pays d'Auvergne*. Éditions CREER, Nonette, 1970
VENCE, Céline: *Encyclopédie Hachette de la cuisine régionale*. Hachette, 1979
VIELFAURE, Nicole et BEAUVIALA, A. Christine: *Fêtes, coutumes et gâteaux*. Éditions Bonneton, Le Puy (no date, about 1978)
VOEGELING, François: *La Gastronomie Alsacienne*. Librairie Istra, Strasbourg, 1978

The following books have provided essential background on food topics and on rural France, past and present, and are the primary or secondary source of most of the quotations in this book.

ANDROUET, Pierre: *The Complete Encyclopedia of French Cheese*. Harper's, New York, 1973
CASTELOT, André: *L'Histoire à Table*. Plon, 1972
CURNONSKY (Maurice Sailland, Prince des Gastronomes): Various works, notably *Recettes des Provinces de France*. Les Productions de Paris, 1962
EDITIONS DU SEUIL: *Histoire de la France Rurale*. 4 volumes, 1975–77
GAULT, Henri et MILLAU, Christian: *Guide gourmand de la France*. Hachette, 1970
GOLDEN PRESS, New York: *La Belle France*, 1964
KLATZMANN, Joseph: *Géographie Agricole de la France*. Presses Universitaires de France, 1972
LIBRAIRIE LAROUSSE: *Larousse Gastronomique*, 1935 (revised and reprinted); *Collection Découvrir la France*. 6 volumes, 1972–74
MICHELIN ET CIE: *Green Guides*. 19 volumes, various dates
READER'S DIGEST: *Les mille visages de la campagne française*, 1976; *La France des routes tranquilles*, 1977
ROOT, Waverley: *The Food of France*. Knopf, New York, 1958 (reprinted)
SMOLLETT, Tobias: *Travels through France and Italy*, 1766
TENDRET, Lucien: *La Table au Pays du Brillat-Savarin*, 1892 (reprinted)
YOUNG, Arthur: *Travels in France during the years 1787 to 1789* (reprinted)

A bookshop specializing in the French regions is *La Tuile à Loup*, 35 rue Daubenton, 75005 Paris

CREDITS